PRESIDENTIAL ELECTIONS
Strategies and Structures of American Politics

TWELFTH EDITION

Nelson W. Polsby | Aaron Wildavsky
with David A. Hopkins

ROWMAN & LITTLEFIELD PUBLISHERS, INC.
Lanham • Boulder • New York • Toronto • Plymouth, UK

ROWMAN & LITTLEFIELD PUBLISHERS, INC.

Published in the United States of America
by Rowman & Littlefield Publishers, Inc.
A wholly owned subsidiary of The Rowman & Littlefield Publishing Group, Inc.
4501 Forbes Boulevard, Suite 200, Lanham, Maryland 20706
www.rowmanlittlefield.com

Estover Road
Plymouth PL6 7PY
United Kingdom

British Library Cataloguing in Publication Information Available

Library of Congress Cataloguing-in-Publication Data

Polsby, Nelson W.
    Presidential elections : strategies and structures of American politics / Nelson W. Polsby,
Aaron Wildavsky, with David A. Hopkins.—12th ed.
        p. cm.
    Includes index.
    ISBN-13: 978-0-7425-5414-6 (cloth : alk. paper)
    ISBN-10: 0-7425-5414-7 (cloth : alk. paper)
    ISBN-13: 978-0-7425-5415-3 (pbk. : alk. paper)
    ISBN-10: 0-7425-5415-5 (pbk. : alk. paper)
    1. Presidents—United States—Election.   I. Wildavsky, Aaron B.   II. Hopkins, David A.   III. Title.
JK528.P63 2007
    324.973—dc22

2007001218

Printed in the United States of America

∞™ The paper used in this publication meets the minimum requirements of American National
Standard for Information Sciences—Permanence of Paper for Printed Library Materials,
ANSI/NISO Z39.48–1992.

To our grandchildren

Benjamin Polsby Stern

Eva Miriam Wildavsky

Aaron Alexander Wildavsky

Edward Polsby Stern

Saul Abraham Wildavsky

CONTENTS

TABLES, FIGURES, AND BOXES

TABLES

FIGURES

BOXES

FOREWORD

residential Elections has been available since 1964 as "one-stop shopping" for consumers of the politics of selecting a national leader. The quadrennial spectacle draws us political junkies, as well as the merely curious among students, practitioners, journalists, and the citizenry at large. The first eight editions of this staple on our shelves were the result of a collaboration between two nationally and internationally prominent scholars at the University of California–Berkeley: Nelson W. Polsby and Aaron Wildavsky. Friends from their graduate days at Yale, Polsby and Wildavsky virtually came to be one word in thinking about literature on presidential elections. A conversation at a political science convention:

"What are you using this fall?"
"Why, Polsby and Wildavsky, of course."

Wildavsky died much too soon in 1993 and so it was left to Polsby to manage future editions—updating and analyzing contemporary developments. The basic structure of the book was solid as it worked through the sequences and processes of narrowing the field, confirming candidates, campaigning through the fall, voting, and absorbing the outcome. But how all of this happened was different each time. Money was a constant, but ever so much more with different regulations. A revolution in communication occurred to shape the how, what, and who of campaigning. Candidates varied—incumbents seeking reelection, vice presidents trying to move up, takeover presidents wishing to win on their own, some candidates from in town, others from way out of town. And the issues differed dramatically from wars to scandals to (most often) "the economy, stupid." Same channel, new tributaries.

Thus it was that somewhat more than fine-tuning was involved every four years, even as the theoretical foundations remained steady. It required the constant attention of the two collaborators, then Polsby alone (and with the assistance of David A. Hopkins in the eleventh and twelfth editions), to incorporate these many changes into a descriptive account of our most vital process for choosing leadership. The task has become ever more demanding in recent elections with the lengthening, cost, complexity, and intense partisanship of campaigning.

This twelfth edition of *Presidential Elections* is a tribute to the perseverance of Nelson W. Polsby. I am reminded of a story told by former Senator Howard H. Baker Jr. (Tennessee) about his father-in-law, the memorable Senator Everett M. Dirksen (Illinois). Senator Dirksen was ailing and was asked in an interview how he carried on. His response was something like: "Most of the world's work is done by people who don't feel very well." Nelson did not "feel very well" as he completed his final edition of *Presidential Elections*. In fact, he was failing and died at home on February 6, 2007.

Readers of this volume will wonder how those who are gone can seem to be so alive in these pages. The answer is the same as for any other classic work. Done right, art outlives the artist, music the composer, and, in my world, teaching the teacher. The great contribution of the gifted is in their legacies. There will not be a thirteenth edition of *Presidential Elections* by Nelson W. Polsby. But he and his partner, Aaron Wildavsky, have shown us how to think about the subject and, if we have the wit, how to fill in the blanks.

Charles O. Jones
Hawkins Professor Emeritus of Political Science,
University of Wisconsin—Madison

PREFACE

It is now more than a dozen years since Aaron Wildavsky died, on September 4, 1993. I hope his vitality, his imagination, and his commitment to fair and accurate political science are still as visible to readers of these pages as they are to me as I write this new edition, even though the march of events and the progress of scholarship have unearthed many new matters to which we never gave much attention during the eight times we wrote this book together.

This edition—as well as the previous one—owes a great deal to the thoughtful collaboration of David A. Hopkins, a gifted student of politics who made producing a new version of this book a pleasure. As time goes by, the surviving author becomes more keenly aware of his reliance on students and colleagues in keeping this text abreast of the changes that affect strategies and structures of presidential elections. Dave Hopkins's appearance on the title page signifies an extraordinary level of enthusiastic participation and astute political judgment in getting things both readable and right for this new edition. For the ninth and tenth editions, the first two editions written on my own, I relied especially on Jonathan Bernstein, now professing politics at the University of Texas, San Antonio, and on the statistical acumen of Professor Ben Highton, now of the University of California, Davis.

We also had the assistance this time of John Hanley and Mark Oleszek, especially in updating tables, and much constructive kibitzing by the regular crew of political junkies who sustain our morale every day at the University of California's Institute of Governmental Studies. We also thank our devoted IGS librarians under the leadership of Nick Robinson.

Nelson W. Polsby
Berkeley, California

INTRODUCTION

DURING THE THANKSGIVING HOLIDAY OF 1960, AARON
Wildavsky and I had a long conversation in which we hatched the idea for
this book. We had noticed that a significant body of knowledge was accumulating in the
discipline of political science about the behavior of American voters, knowledge that was
bound to have an impact on the ways in which political parties and candidates would
conduct themselves in their pursuit of the presidency. That insight became the germ of
Presidential Elections, the first edition of which appeared in 1964, over forty years ago.

Presidential elections, because they take place in the United States, attract worldwide
attention—and not a little apprehension. No public official anywhere in the world is
selected by a process more visible or more complex than the president of the United
States, and we thought it was worth a book-length effort to describe how the process
unfolds. Every four years since the first edition of this book, we have reexamined our
treatment of the process, adding to the historical record the experience of each successive
election.

We have learned a great deal about how our presidential elections work in forty years,
and have been able to record all sorts of changes in the conduct of presidential elections
as they have come along. There have been a lot of changes. Here are a few examples: the
rise in professional management of political campaigns; the increase in the use of polls by
candidates and observers; the decline of national party conventions; the increase in the
number and significance of primary elections; the encroachment by legal regulation on
the raising and disbursement of money; the rise in the importance of television and the
news media; the rise of the Internet in setting political agendas and in fundraising; the
decline in the importance of state parties and their leaders in battles over nominations;
and changes in strategic imperatives that apply to presidential candidates, who once had
to build coalitions among state party leaders and now must mobilize factions of voters
in early primary elections.

It has been a challenge to keep up with the evolution of the presidential election
process, and integrate innovations in common practice into an ongoing story, a story that
shows how historical experience and persisting rules of the game also affect the ways in

which candidates and parties and interested observers behave. Each new election brings to the surface its own set of concerns. The election of 2004 was surely no exception.

In spite of all the changes that events have brought to presidential elections, this book adheres to its original theoretical foundation, which has helped to organize each edition since 1964. The substance of this theoretical foundation can be summarized as follows: A lot of what goes on in a presidential election can be understood if we think of these activities as strategic choices by actors who operate in a world that is partially manipulable—that is where strategies come in—and partially structured by elements that are more or less given. The main structural influences on actors' strategic choices are (1) the rules and regulations governing nominations and elections and (2) principles of behavior governing how voters acquire political attitudes and preferences and involve themselves in the process. Thus we draw attention to politicians' choices in the light of evolving structures of politics—political parties, primary elections, national conventions, campaigns and their organizations—and the emerging study of the behavior of masses of voters.

This edition sticks to the theme and explains the strategic choices of actors differently situated—Democrats, Republicans, incumbents, challengers, journalists, delegates, and voters—by seeking to understand the ways in which their world is organized and their choices are framed by incentives and prohibitions, habits, customs, regulations, and opportunities.

The aim, as always, is to help readers understand what presidential elections are all about, not to make predictions or advise people how to vote. In the spirit of previous editions, this edition of *Presidential Elections* seeks to be useful to readers no matter what their political preferences. While Aaron and I did not always agree about party politics, I hope in this edition to continue to uphold his life-long commitment to political enlightenment as a necessary attribute of a self-governing society. It will serve our purposes very well if our readers take knowledge from this book that will help them understand their political world a little better, and perhaps even find encouragement to participate in it with greater confidence and skill.

I
THE STRATEGIC ENVIRONMENT

The strategies of all the participants in presidential elections are to a certain extent constrained, and to a certain extent driven, by the ways in which actors are situated with respect to conditions that are for them given and hard to manipulate. Here are some examples: the rules governing how votes are counted; the sequence in which primary elections occur; the accepted practices of campaign journalism; whether candidates are incumbents or challengers; and the habits of voters. All these conditions need to be taken account of by participants and need to be understood by observers.

ONE

VOTERS

I N 2004 MORE THAN 122 MILLION AMERICANS VOTED IN THE presidential election. Millions more who were old enough to vote—nearly 100 million in 2004—did not. Parties and candidates depend on voter turnout. And so it is important for them to know why some people show up at the polls and why others do not. In two respects, Americans are different from citizens of other democracies. A smaller proportion of Americans will vote in any given election than citizens of other democracies, but Americans collectively vote much more often, and on more matters, than anyone else.[1] Voting behavior is one of the most carefully studied political activities. Who votes? Who doesn't vote? Who votes for which party and why? All these questions are the subjects of extensive study.

WHY PEOPLE DON'T VOTE

A lot of elections, not just presidential elections but congressional, state, and local elections, take place in the United States. Americans are noted for their lukewarm levels of participation as compared with voters in most Western European democracies. Table 1.1 compares the voting turnout rate of Americans in presidential elections, when U.S. turnout is highest, to typical turnout figures in parliamentary elections in other democratic countries. Why don't Americans vote more, or at least more like Europeans? In some respects, to be sure, the elections being compared are not exactly the same. Parliamentary elections in many places—for example, the United Kingdom—require voters to do only one thing: place a single X on a ballot to fill an office more or less like that of a U.S. representative in Congress. Who ends up running the government in these countries depends on how many parliamentarians of each political party are elected (from over 600 constituencies in the United Kingdom), and so most voters cast party-line votes and do not much care about the identity of individuals on the ballot.[2] Ballots in U.S.

TABLE 1.1 Ranking of Countries by Turnout

Country	Turnout
1. Greece	89.0 %
2. Iceland	86.2
3. Italy	84.9
4. Israel	84.4
5. Belgium	83.2
6. Denmark	83.1
7. Australia	81.7
8. Sweden	77.7
9. Finland	76.8
10. New Zealand	76.1
11. Germany	75.3
12. Spain	73.8
13. Norway	73.0
14. Austria	72.6
15. France	72.3
16. Netherlands	70.1
17. Portugal	69.3
18. Ireland	66.7
19. Japan	59.0
20. United Kingdom	57.6
21. Luxembourg	56.9
22. Canada	54.6
23. United States	**54.2**
24. European Parliament	49.4
25. Switzerland	34.9

Source: U.S. data from Harold W. Stanley and Richard G. Niemi, *Vital Statistics on American Politics, 2005–2006* (Washington, D.C.: CQ Press, 2005), p. 13. International data from International Institute for Democracy and Electoral Assistance, http://www.idea.int/vt/. European Parliament data from European Parliament UK Office, http://www.europarl.org.uk/guide/textonly/Gelecttx.htm.

Note: The percentage listed for each country is the proportion of the voting-age population casting ballots in the most recent national election as of 2001.

presidential elections are longer and more complex: they require voting for president and vice president, members of the House of Representatives, senators (two-thirds of the time), various state and local offices, ballot propositions, and so on. American ballots therefore demand quite a lot of knowledge from voters. In general, Americans do not invest their time and energy in becoming knowledgeable about all the choices they are required to make.[3]

TABLE 1.2 Voter Turnout in Presidential and Midterm Elections, 1952–2006

Year	Presidential Elections	Year	Midterm Elections
1952	62.3	1954	43.5
1956	60.2	1958	45.0
1960	63.8	1962	47.7
1964	62.8	1966	48.7
1968	62.5	1970	47.3
1972	56.2	1974	39.1
1976	54.8	1978	39.0
1980	54.2	1982	42.0
1984	55.2	1986	38.1
1988	52.8	1990	38.4
1992	58.1	1994	41.1
1996	51.7	1998	38.1
2000	54.2	2002	39.4
2004	60.3	2006	40.2

Source: Harold W. Stanley and Richard G. Niemi, *Vital Statistics on American Politics, 2005–2006* (Washington, D.C.: CQ Press, 2005), pp. 12–13; Michael McDonald, "2006 Voting-Age and Voting-Eligible Population Estimates," available at http://elections.gmu.edu/Voter_Turnout_2006.htm.

Note: Figures represent the proportion of the eligible voting-age population turning out in each election.

But voters do turn out for presidential elections more conscientiously than for elections in years when there is no presidential contest, so the complexity of presidential elections is pretty clearly not a deterrent to voting (see table 1.2). To the contrary, the added publicity of a presidential campaign obviously helps turnout, as do the greater sums of money spent by candidates and the increased level of campaign activity by political activists and interest groups in presidential elections.[4]

An often-heard explanation of low turnout in the United States (low by the standards of other Western democracies) is that Americans are unusually disaffected from politics and that abstention from voting is their method of showing their disapproval of, or alienation from, the political system. Scholars have been deeply interested in the subject of political alienation, but they have shown that this explanation of low turnout is improbable or at best incomplete.

There are several elements to their demonstration. First, scholars note that the constellation of sentiments associated with alienation—disaffection, loss of trust in government, and so on— are stronger, on the whole, in many countries where turnout is relatively high. Americans do not express especially negative feelings toward government. On more measures than not, Americans are actually more positive about government than citizens of other democratic nations (see table 1.3).

Americans are also comparatively high in other forms of political participation such as expressing interest in politics, discussing politics with others, trying to persuade others during

TABLE 1.3 Comparative Alienation: United States and Europe

Country	Political Interest Index	Political Activity Index	Political Efficacy	Trust Government
United States	48 (1)	24 (1)	59 (2)	34 (9)
West Germany	41 (2)	15 (6)	33 (7)	52 (5)
Netherlands	36 (3)	17 (2)	37 (6)	46 (7)
Austria	32 (4)	12 (7)	N.A.	55 (4)
United Kingdom	32 (4)	11 (8)	42 (4)	40 (8)
Finland	29 (6)	17 (2)	N.A.	50 (6)
Switzerland	29 (6)	16 (5)	N.A.	76 (1)
Italy	18 (8)	17 (2)	39 (5)	14 (12)
Greece	N.A.	N.A.	N.A.	62 (2)
Denmark	N.A.	N.A.	N.A.	56 (3)
France	N.A.	N.A.	N.A.	33 (10)
Belgium	N.A.	N.A.	N.A.	20 (11)

Source: Samuel H. Barnes and Max Kaase et al., "Political Action: An Eight-Nation Study, 1973–1976," Inter-University Consortium for Political and Social Research Codebook, cited in Raymond E. Wolfinger, David P. Glass, and Peverill Squire, "Predictions of Electoral Turnout: An International Comparison," *Policy Studies Review* 9 (Spring 1990): 551–74, at 557; Commission of the European Communities, *Euro-Barometre*, no. 17 (June 1982): 25; and 1980 *National Election Study Codebook* 1:614, variable 1030, cited in Wolfinger, Glass, and Squire, "Predictors of Electoral Turnout."

Note: Numbers in parentheses indicate country rank. N.A. = data not available.

Political Interest Index scores are the mean of the percentage of respondents who said they (1) were very or somewhat interested in politics, (2) often read about politics in the newspapers, and (3) often discussed politics with others.

Political Activity Index scores are the mean of the percentage of respondents who said they (1) often worked with others in their community to solve a local problem, (2) often or sometimes attended a political meeting or rally, (3) often or sometimes contacted public officials, and (4) often or sometimes worked on behalf of a party or candidate.

Political Efficacy scores for the Europeans are the percentage of respondents who agreed that "people like yourself can bring about a change," and for the Americans, the percentage who disagreed with the statement, "People like me don't have any say about what the government does."

Trust Government scores are the percentage of respondents who agreed that they could trust their government all or most of the time.

elections, and working for candidates or parties of their choice. Within the United States, people who don't like or don't trust government vote about as frequently as people who do (see table 1.4).[5]

A better explanation for what really divides Americans who vote from those who don't is registration: people registered to vote tend to vote roughly at Western European rates of participation. But people not registered cannot vote legally, and so it is important to know that registration to vote is more difficult in most parts of the United States than in the democracies with which the United States is compared. In America, permanent registration does not come automatically as an attribute of citizenship, as it does in most countries. Instead, prospective voters are required to take positive steps to sign up on a voting roll maintained in the locality

TABLE 1.4 Alienation and U.S. Voter Turnout

	Turnout Rate
How much money do the people in government waste?	
None or some	59 %
A lot	61
How much of the time can you trust the government to do what's right?	
Always or most of the time	59
Some or none of the time	61
Is the government run by a few big interests or for the benefit of all?	
For the benefit of all	61
For the benefit of a few big interests	61
Are most of those running the government smart, or do many not know what they are doing?	
Are smart	61
Don't know what they are doing	60
Are the people running the government crooked?	
Hardly any or not many are crooked	64
Quite a few are crooked	57
The federal government in Washington is doing a:	
Good job	60
Fair job	64
Poor job	66
How much attention does the government pay to what people think?	
A good deal or some	67
Not much	58
How much does having elections make the government pay attention to what the people think?	
A good deal	65
Some	65
Not much	53

Source: Chart adapted from Raymond E. Wolfinger, David P. Glass, and Peverill Squire, "Predictors of Electoral Turnout: An International Comparison," *Policy Studies Review* 9 (Spring 1990): 551–74, at 555, based on vote validated data from the 1980 National Election Studies.

where they wish to vote. Normally, you vote where you live, and because Americans change where they live quite a lot—about one-third of Americans change their local address every two years—a lot of reregistering is required.[6]

The fact that there are so many local jurisdictions and variations in registration requirements from state to state is a result of the size and diversity of the United States and of its federal heritage—the governments of the original states predated, and in fact established, the national government. Under the Constitution, eligibility to vote in national elections is determined by state laws governing eligibility to vote for the most numerous house of the state legislature.[7]

Voting itself takes place not on a national holiday, as in some countries, or over a weekend, but on a regular weekday—for presidential elections, the first Tuesday after the first Monday in November.[8] Presidential primaries (electoral events that play a major role in nominating presidential candidates) take place, state by state, on a series of dates, usually but not always on Tuesday, stretching from January or February to June of a presidential election year. These primary dates can be, and often are, changed every four years and may or may not be combined with a state's primary elections for other offices. History, geography, and custom thus play a significant part in determining contemporary patterns of turnout.

There is no convincing evidence that the basic human nature of Americans differs from that of citizens of other democratic lands. But the United States has organized itself differently—state by state rather than as a unitary nation—to do political business. The right to vote is administered in a more decentralized fashion than in most democracies, and its exercise requires more work on the part of the prospective voter (in the form of registration before the election at each new residential address). That seems better than any other explanation to account for much of the difference in turnout between American presidential elections and parliamentary elections in other comparable nations.

WHY PEOPLE DO VOTE: A THEORY OF SOCIAL CONNECTEDNESS

This still leaves open why the millions of Americans who vote in presidential elections bother to do so. This is a matter of some interest to candidates and their advisers. Even though in recent years some congressional elections have turned on a handful of votes, and the outcome of the 2000 presidential election was determined by a disputed 537-vote margin in the state of Florida, it cannot possibly be that millions of voters have convinced themselves to turn out in presidential elections because each of them believes that he or she will likely cast the deciding vote in the election. Oddly enough, the more votes being aggregated in an election and the more voters expected at the polls, the larger is the proportion of those eligible who actually show up, so that presidential elections regularly inspire higher turnout than midterm elections for Congress. But as the late, great psychologist Paul Meehl once figured the odds, the chances that a particular voter could personally affect the outcome of a presidential election are pretty slim. That voter would be far more likely to be struck by lightning going to or from the polling place.[9]

Why people vote is, after years of investigation, still a bit of a mystery. Scholars who try to understand human motivations have put forward the argument that voting must in some way or other make people feel good (or better, at least, than if they did not vote), perhaps because they see the act of voting as a civic duty or as an opportunity for personal political expression. Some political scientists argue that voters calculate that the benefits of turning out—which may be psychological rather than instrumental—exceed the costs.[10] We believe that the act of voting is on the whole probably not rationally calculated, but is instead a more or less standing decision or habit that citizens fall into as they adopt other forms of public participation in the course of becoming integrated into the ordinary social life of their communities.[11]

Essentially, voting seems to make sense mostly as an act of social participation or civic involvement. There are by now a great many studies of voting and nonvoting, and in general voters are people connected in various ways to the larger society or to their local community, and nonvoters are not. Thus people who are settled in one place vote more than people who move around. Married adults vote more frequently than the unmarried. People who belong to civic organizations or interest groups vote more than nonjoiners. Voting participation generally increases with age until late in life when social participation of all sorts drops away—frequently as the result of the loss of a spouse. The young, many of whom are unsettled and unmarried, vote much less than their elders, but as they settle down, they begin to vote. The better educated vote more than the less well educated. And people who identify with one or another political party vote more than those who claim no party affiliation or loyalty.[12]

Residence, family ties, education, civic participation in general, and party identification all create ties to the larger world, and these ties evidently create social habits that include turning out to vote. Families of government workers—a special sort of interest group—also participate at extremely high levels.[13] Perhaps these voters are voting because they perceive a monetary incentive to do so. Typically, however, their votes have little or no direct impact on their salaries. But they may feel keenly the centrality of civic involvement in their lives.

If voting were in general a rationally calculated activity, we conjecture that large numbers of the most well-educated and sophisticated citizens would become free-riding nonvoters, since showing up at the polls on Election Day is hardly worth the effort given the next-to-zero probability that any single vote will decide the outcome of an election. Yet it is precisely those citizens best equipped to see the logic of the free ride—the well-educated—who vote the most conscientiously.

This reasoning also gives a basis for the view that political life is significantly organized according to the social identities of voters. Foremost among the group affiliations that matter to voters are the political parties, organizations that specialize in political activity. Two such organizations, the Democratic Party and the Republican Party, more or less monopolize the loyalties of American voters. Either the Democratic or the Republican nominee has won every presidential election since 1852, and only twice during this time (1860 and 1912) has the candidate of the other party not finished second in the electoral college. Over the long term, the two major parties are evenly matched. Each has won ten of the past twenty presidential elections (see table 1.5).

IN THE MINDS OF VOTERS: PARTY

Most Americans vote according to their habitual party affiliation.[14] In other words, because they consider themselves Democrats or Republicans, many people will have made up their minds how to vote in 2008 before the candidates are even chosen.[15] These party identifiers are likely to be more interested and active in politics and have more political knowledge than people who call themselves political "independents."[16] Party regulars rarely change their minds. They tend to listen mostly to their own side of political arguments and to agree with the policies espoused by their party. They even go so far as to ignore information that they perceive to be unfavorable to the party of their choice.[17]

Thus party identification is important in giving a structure to voters' pictures of reality and in helping them choose their preferred presidential candidate. But where do people get their party affiliations? There seems to be no simple answer. Every individual is born into a social context and consequently inherits a social identity that may contain a political component.

TABLE 1.5 Presidential Election Results, 1928–2004

Year	Winning Candidate	Elect. Votes	Pop. Vote Pct	Losing Candidate	Elect. Votes	Pop. Vote Pct
1928	Herbert Hoover (R)	444	58.2	Al Smith (D)	87	40.8
1932	Franklin D. Roosevelt (D)	472	57.4	Herbert Hoover (R)*	59	39.6
1936	Franklin D. Roosevelt (D)*	523	60.8	Alf Landon (R)	8	36.5
1940	Franklin D. Roosevelt (D)*	449	54.7	Wendell Willkie (R)	82	44.8
1944	Franklin D. Roosevelt (D)*	432	53.4	Thomas E. Dewey (R)	99	45.9
1948	Harry Truman (D)*	303	49.5	Thomas E. Dewey (R)	189	45.1
1952	Dwight D. Eisenhower (R)	442	54.9	Adlai Stevenson (D)	89	44.4
1956	Dwight D. Eisenhower (R)*	457	57.4	Adlai Stevenson (D)	73	42.0
1960	John F. Kennedy (D)	303	49.7	Richard Nixon (R)	219	49.5
1964	Lyndon Johnson (D)*	486	61.1	Barry Goldwater (R)	52	38.5
1968	Richard Nixon (R)	301	43.4	Hubert Humphrey (D)	191	42.7
1972	Richard Nixon (R)*	520	60.7	George McGovern (D)	17	37.5
1976	Jimmy Carter (D)	297	50.1	Gerald Ford (R)*	240	48.0
1980	Ronald Reagan (R)	489	50.7	Jimmy Carter (D)*	49	41.0
1984	Ronald Reagan (R)*	525	58.8	Walter Mondale (D)	13	40.6
1988	George H. W. Bush (R)	426	53.4	Michael Dukakis (D)	111	45.6
1992	Bill Clinton (D)	370	43.0	George H. W. Bush (R)*	168	37.4
1996	Bill Clinton (D)*	379	49.2	Bob Dole (R)	159	40.7
2000	George W. Bush (R)	271	47.9	Al Gore (D)	266	48.4
2004	George W. Bush (R)*	286	50.7	John Kerry (D)	251	48.3

Source: Harold W. Stanley and Richard G. Niemi, *Vital Statistics on American Politics, 2005–2006* (Washington, D.C.: CQ Press, 2005), pp. 27–29.

Note: Asterisk denotes incumbent.

People are Democrats or Republicans, in part, because their families and the other people with whom they interact are Democrats or Republicans.[18] Most individuals come into close contact predominantly with members of only one party.[19] And just as people tend to share characteristics with their friends and families, such as income and educational level, religious affiliation, and area of residence, they also tend to share party loyalties with them.[20]

Of course, we all know of instances where this is not so, where people do not share some of these status-giving characteristics with their parents and at least some of their friends. In these circumstances, we would expect political differences to turn up when there are other kinds of differences. But by and large, voters retain the party loyalties of the primary groups—people they interact with directly—of which they are a part.

PARTIES AS AGGREGATES OF LOYAL VOTERS

As a result of this tendency, each of the major political parties maintains a reservoir of voting strength among the public that it can count on from election to election (see table 1.6). Since the

TABLE 1.6 Party Identification by Social Group, 2004

	Democrat	Independent	Republican
Nationwide	32 %	39 %	29 %
Men	27	43	30
Women	37	35	28
18–34 years	32	45	23
35–44 years	28	42	31
45–54 years	29	40	31
55–64 years	34	31	35
65 years and older	39	34	28
White	25	38	36
Black	62	37	2
Latino	40	43	17
No college education	34	43	23
Some college	28	40	32
College graduate	28	33	38
Postgraduate degree	38	29	33
Income under $20,000	36	44	20
Income $20,000–$39,999	38	37	25
Income $40,000–$59,999	31	39	30
Income $60,000–$89,000	27	35	38
Income $90,000 and over	22	38	41
Northeast	26	50	24
Midwest	29	37	34
South	35	34	31
West	30	39	31

Source: All adult respondents, National Election Study, 2004.

Note: Party "leaners" are treated as independents.

1850s, when the Republican Party was organized, Republicans traditionally have done well in the small towns and rural areas of New England, the Middle Atlantic states, and the Midwest. Over the last fifty years, the GOP has also found increasing electoral success in the South. Republican candidates draw their support from people who are more prosperous than Democratic supporters, occupy managerial or professional positions or run small businesses, live in or move into well-to-do suburban areas, and are predominantly Protestant (evangelical Protestants in particular tend to be strong Republican supporters). Democratic candidates traditionally draw substantial numbers of votes from large urban areas outside the South—Boston, New York, Philadelphia, Chicago, Los Angeles. Wage earners, union members, Catholics, African Americans and Latinos, and many of the descendants of the great waves of immigrants entering this country in the latter half of the nineteenth century—Jews, Irish, Poles—all contribute disproportionately to the Democratic vote.[21]

But why did these particular social groups come to have these particular loyalties? We must turn to history to find answers to this question. Enough is known about a few groups to make it possible to speculate about what kinds of historical events tend to align groups with a political party.

Here are a few examples. From the Civil War until the era of George Wallace and Barry Goldwater—about a century (1864–1964)—the historically "Solid South" was overwhelmingly Democratic in its presidential voting. For all those years, resentment against the harsh Reconstruction period (1865–1877), when the former confederate states were governed under the leadership of the national Republican Party, was reflected in the election returns. Less well known is the fact that the South was not unanimous in its enthusiasm for the Civil War in the first place or in its resentment of Reconstruction. In many states of the Old South—largely rural territory—there were two kinds of farms: plantations on the flat land, which grew cash crops, used slaves, and, in general, prospered before the Civil War; and subsistence farms in the uplands, which had a few or no slaves and, in general, were run by poorer white people who had little or no stake in the Confederacy and opposed secession. This latter group formed the historical core of mountain areas that year after year, well into the latter half of the twentieth century, voted Republican in presidential elections. These areas were located in western Virginia and North Carolina, eastern Tennessee and Kentucky, and southeastern West Virginia.[22] Since the 1960s, through a combination of white Republicans migrating in, black Democrats migrating out, and conversion from Democratic to Republican of conservative white southerners, the once solidly Democratic South has become a lot less Democratic and a lot more Republican.[23]

The voting habits of African American citizens, where they have voted, have been shaped by several large events. The Civil War freed them and made them Lincoln Republicans. The southern reaction to Reconstruction disenfranchised them, because most blacks at the time lived in the rural South well within the reach of Jim Crow laws preventing them from voting.[24] But the growth of American industry brought many African Americans north in the first half of the twentieth century.[25] This took them away from the most severe legal impediments to political participation but did not always lift their burden of economic destitution or relieve them of racial discrimination. The effects of the Great Depression of the 1930s on African American voters in the North brought them into Franklin D. Roosevelt's New Deal coalition, and the northern African American voter has remained overwhelmingly Democratic ever since.[26] In the South, especially after the Voting Rights Act of 1965 was enacted by bipartisan congressional majorities during the Democratic presidency of Lyndon Johnson, newly enfranchised African Americans also voted Democratic. As these voters have observed Democratic politicians (in increasing numbers themselves black)[27] espousing causes in which they believe, they have maintained their high levels of support.

If the historical events of the Civil War in the 1860s and the Great Depression of the 1930s shaped the political heritage of some people, for others the critical forces seem less dramatic and more diffuse. It is possible to see why the poor become Democrats, for the Democratic Party since the 1930s has been in favor of social welfare programs; but why do the rich lean toward the Republicans? Undoubtedly, in part, this is a negative reaction to the redistributive aspirations of some New Deal initiatives and the inclination of Democratic presidents to expand the role of government in the economy. But in all probability it is also a positive response to the record of the congressional wing of the Republican Party, which so thoroughly dominated the post–Civil

War era of industrial expansion in the 1890s and on, until the election of 1932. In this era, Republican policies vigorously encouraged, and to a degree underwrote, risk taking by private businesses, granted them federal aid in a variety of forms (notably tariffs), and withheld federal regulation from private enterprise.[28] Recent Republican presidents and members of Congress have upheld the party's traditional advocacy of policies which disproportionately appeal to affluent voters, such as income tax cuts for high earners, reduction or repeal of the federal estate tax, and the relaxation of government regulations of private corporations.

Sometimes party affiliation coincides with ethnic identification because of the political and social circumstances surrounding the entry of ethnic groups into the country. A dramatic example is the rapid influx since the 1960s of Cuban refugees—many of them well-to-do and solidly middle class or above—from the communist regime of Fidel Castro into southern Florida. For these Cuban émigrés and their families opposition to communism is extremely salient, and they favor the Republican Party. By contrast, the descendants of the Cuban cigar makers who settled many decades ago in the Tampa area, on Florida's west coast, vote more according to their pocketbooks and their union loyalties and are predominantly Democratic.[29] The vast majority of Latinos in the southwestern states of California, Arizona, and Texas are of Mexican descent, while Puerto Ricans are more numerous in New York, New Jersey, and the rest of the northeastern United States. Members of both of these nationalities have long voted overwhelmingly for Democrats, who are the traditional party of immigrants and lower-income voters.[30]

In the cities of the Northeast, politics was dominated by the Republican Party and by "Yankees" (Protestants of British ancestry) of substance and high status during the decades following the Civil War. During these decades, thousands of Irish people—many of them fleeing the potato famine of the mid-nineteenth century and rule in Ireland by the English and Scots-Irish cousins of Yankee Americans—streamed into this area. The Democratic Party welcomed them; the Republicans did not. In due course the Democratic percentage of the two-party vote began to increase, and Irish politicians, who uniquely among newer immigrants already knew the English language, took over the Democratic Party nearly everywhere they settled.[31] In the Midwest, events such as American involvement in two world wars against Germany under Democratic auspices in many cases shaped the political preferences of Americans of German descent toward the more isolationist Republicans.[32] These are a few examples of the ways in which group membership and historical circumstances have given voters special ties with particular parties.

Once voters have such ties, a great deal follows. Merely to list the functions that party identification performs for voters—reducing their costs of acquiring political information, telling them what side they are on, organizing their political knowledge by ordering their preferences, letting them know what is of prime importance—is to suggest the profound significance of parties for voting behavior. Politics is complex; there are many possible issues, relevant political personalities, and decisions to be made on Election Day. Voters who follow their party identification can simplify their choices and reduce to manageable proportions the time and effort they spend on public affairs simply by voting for their party's candidate. Voters with strong party identifications need not puzzle over each and every issue. They can, instead, listen to the pronouncements of their party leaders, who inform them what issues are important, what information is most relevant to those issues, and what positions they ought to take. Of course, citizens with greater interest in public affairs may investigate matters for themselves. Even so, their party identification provides them with important guidance in learning about the issues that interest them as well as the many matters on which they cannot possibly be well informed. All of us, including full-time participants in politics such as the president and other leading politicians, have to find ways to cut information costs on some issues.[33] For most of the millions who vote, identification with one of the two major political parties performs that indispensable function most of the time.

IN THE MINDS OF VOTERS: IDEOLOGIES, CANDIDATES, AND ISSUES

Another method of reducing the costs of information may be for voters to have or acquire a more or less comprehensive set of internally consistent beliefs, sometimes known as an *ideology*. How do ideologies structure political beliefs? Voters or party activists may be conscious of having an ideology and thus adopt views consistent with their position; they can use ideological labels as a shortcut in making decisions, or at least they can think of one issue as related to another. There is some evidence that only small numbers of voters are fully consistent in their ideological thinking; a larger minority makes use of various forms of group references when expressing preferences for a particular candidate, and a still larger group makes use of ideological labels.[34] Labels such as left and right and liberal and conservative, while commonly used in political discourse, sometimes work and sometimes do not in structuring attitudes. If we talk about social welfare or economically redistributive issues, these labels serve reasonably well in sorting people out: left for, right against. But some issues are harder to fathom. What would be the "conservative" position on abortion, for example, when conservative libertarians are pro-choice and other conservatives pro-life?[35]

Specific candidates with special attractiveness or unattractiveness may under certain circumstances sway voters to desert their habitual party in a presidential vote. The extraordinary elections of President Dwight D. Eisenhower (1952 and 1956) are examples of this. Though a Republican, Eisenhower's appeal to Democrats was quite amazing. This was possible partially because many Democrats did not perceive Eisenhower as a partisan figure, but rather as a national military hero of the recently concluded World War II (1941–1945). It is not surprising, then, that Eisenhower's personal popularity did not greatly aid Republican candidates for other offices who ran with him, or the Republican Party itself once he no longer headed the ticket. The unpopular candidacy of George McGovern in 1972 had the opposite effect; it prompted many Democrats to desert their party's nominee in favor of Republican opponent Richard Nixon.[36]

Scholars have pointed out that in recent presidential elections even successful candidates carry a burden of negative evaluations. This negativity may be a consequence of the rise to prominence in the nomination process since 1968 of primary elections—a strenuous gauntlet in which prospective candidates of the same party must run against one another in different states for many weeks during the early months of a presidential election year. These elections produce a lot of bad-mouthing. As a result, the eventual nominees usually have no significant "coattails" in the general election helping candidates of their party for other offices farther down on the ballot. High negative ratings for all surviving candidates also mean that they will be unable to lure voters for positive reasons away from the expression of their habitual party loyalties in the general election. But negative ratings may push voters to desert their party because they have heard so much bad publicity.[37]

Particular issues have much the same occasional effect as candidates on voters' loyalties.[38] This is true because for an issue to change a voter's habitual party preference, it has to reach a high degree of salience for the voter. Voters must know about the issue, they must care about it at least a little, and they must be able to distinguish the positions of the parties and their candidates on the issue. Data from public opinion polls tell us that most people are not well informed about the details of issues most of the time.[39] All but major public issues are thus eliminated for most people as important in influencing their vote. And even these major issues may enter the consciousness of most people in only the most rudimentary way.

Once voters have some grasp of the content of a public policy and learn to prefer one outcome over another, they must also find a public leader to espouse their point of view. Discerning differences on policy issues between parties is not always easy. Party statements on policy may be vague because leaders have not decided what to do. Leaders may deliberately obfuscate an issue for fear of alienating interested publics. They may try to hold divergent factions in their parties together by glossing over disagreements on many specific issues. Even when real party differences on policy exist, many voters may not be aware of them. The subject may be highly technical, or the time required to master the subject may be more than most people are willing to spend. By the time we get down to those who know and care about and can discriminate between party positions on issues, we usually have a small proportion of the electorate. The proportion of ideologically sophisticated voters appears to be no larger than 30 percent.[40]

What can we say about these people? Their most obvious characteristic is interest in and concern about issues and party positions. These are precisely the same people who are most likely to be strong party identifiers. Party loyalty thus works against the possibility that voters will shift allegiance just because of a disagreement on one or two issues.[41] Voters who pay only a moderate amount of attention to politics are most likely to be affected by new information on issues. This is because the most attentive are generally committed to a party and that party's position, whereas the least attentive are unavailable to persuasion: since they don't take in political information, they cannot be influenced by it. This leaves the middle group as most open to persuasion. Not being intensely partisan, they are not previously committed, but they learn enough so that it is possible for them to be swayed by new information about issues and by campaigns.[42] The number of issue-oriented "independents"—voters who care about public issues but have no consistent party preference—is very small. Knowledgeable citizens are more likely to have strong opinions about politics, and therefore almost always consider themselves either Democrats or Republicans. Most people who call themselves independents actually lean toward one or another of the two major parties.[43] So purely issue-oriented voters are not numerous and may be distributed on both sides of major policy questions in such a way that gains and losses balance out and the total number of votes gained or lost by the impact of any specific issue is minute. This is even true of such issues as the Vietnam War, which from 1968 to 1972 was of tremendous salience to many Americans.[44]

Even these changes may not amount to much if other issues are also highly salient to voters and work the other way. For if voters were willing to change their votes on one particular issue, why should they not switch their support back because of another? There usually are many issues in a campaign; only if all or most of the issues pointed voters in the same direction would they be likely to switch their votes. What is the likelihood that candidates will arrange their policies along a broad ideological front, forcing large numbers of weak party identifiers or "independent" voters from or into the fold? It is low, but not nonexistent. In 1964 the Republicans, led by extreme conservative Barry Goldwater, did so. And in 1972 the Democratic candidate, George McGovern, "was perceived as so far left on the issues that his Republican opponent, Richard Nixon, was generally closer to the electorate's average issue position on 11 out of 14 separate issues."[45] Supporters of the Goldwater and McGovern campaigns argued that enthusiasm for their candidates' more ideologically extreme positions would inspire a massive increase in turnout among disaffected citizens who previously declined to participate in politics (a claim known as the "hidden vote" theory). Instead, Goldwater and McGovern merely alienated large numbers of Americans who already vote regularly, including many members of their own party, resulting in landslide victories for the opposition.

Issues that arouse deep feelings can alter longer-term voting patterns, but this usually occurs when one party gets very far out of step with the preferences of voters. In the 1930s and 1940s this happened to the Republicans on the issue of social welfare programs.[46] When voters perceive a vast chasm separating them from one of the candidates, as they did with Goldwater and again with McGovern, the importance of issues relative to party is bound to grow. The research group at the Michigan Center for Political Studies estimated that in 1972, party identification and issue differences each accounted for approximately one-third of the total vote. In this election Richard Nixon received almost all Republican votes (94 percent), two-thirds of independent votes (66 percent), and nearly half the votes of people calling themselves Democrats (42 percent). This was a better showing among Democrats than Dwight D. Eisenhower managed in his landslide year of 1956, when he garnered 28 percent of the Democratic vote. Why did this happen? Because Nixon's 1972 opponent, George McGovern, "was seen as quite distant from the population's policy preferences." The Michigan group concluded that "a candidate such as McGovern who may represent only one segment of the national policy preference spectrum may capture control of a political party that shares his policy preferences but cannot go on to win an electoral victory under contemporary conditions of polarization."[47] In short, when voters disagree with a candidate and know that they disagree, they are likely to vote against him or her. Candidates and their campaigns therefore work hard to inform voters about potentially unpopular positions taken by their opponents. This strategy leads to a lot of negative campaigning, much of which works uphill against party habits and the disinclination of voters to pay much attention to the content of campaigns.

When voters wish to reject the current presidential administration, yet they are not sure that the other party's policies are better, they may nevertheless decide to take a chance on the challenging candidate. Stung by "stagflation," a politically deadly combination of high inflation and high unemployment, and dismayed over what they perceived to be President Jimmy Carter's lack of leadership, voters in 1980 chose Republican nominee Ronald Reagan despite uneasiness about Reagan's conservative issue positions. They may have thought that under then-current conditions of uncertainty about the economy, a new administration would do better. When unemployment rose in 1981 and 1982, President Reagan's popularity dropped, and Republican congressional candidates suffered. Economic recovery brought Reagan renewed support and a resounding victory in 1984. Figure 1.1 shows how closely the vote for the president's party tracks the performance of the economy.[48]

News of an economic turnaround came too late to save George H. W. Bush in 1992. He lost his bid for reelection despite his tremendous popularity two years earlier at the time of the Desert Storm operation (January 1991) when he orchestrated the defense of Kuwait against

FIGURE 1.1 Impact of Change in Disposable Income on Voting

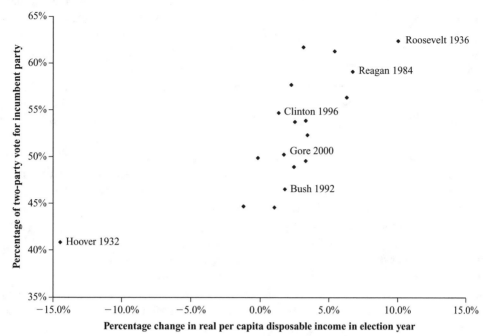

Sources: Economic data: 1932–1968, Historical Statistics of the United States; Colonial Times to 1970 (Washington, D.C.: Bureau of the Census, 1975); 1972–2000, Statistical Abstract of the United States (Washington, D.C.: Bureau of the Census, various years). Electoral data: America Votes: A Handbook of Contemporary American Election Statistics, Richard Scammon and Alice McGillivray, editors (Washington, D.C.: Congressional Quarterly, various years).

Iraqi aggression. By the fall of 1992, however, Americans were more concerned with the state of the national economy than with the nation's military successes. Bush fell victim to negative retrospective evaluations of his performance on domestic matters and to popular feelings that he demonstrated insufficient concern about an economic recession occurring on his watch, receiving only 38 percent of the vote in a three-way race. Even so, Bush won 73 percent of the votes of Republicans, as usual benefiting from the strong party loyalty of Republican voters.[49]

So while candidates matter sometimes, and issues matter sometimes, and both are capable of affecting who wins, for most voters party matters almost all the time. Activating party loyalties is the most important electoral strategy at the disposal of candidates.

CHANGES IN PARTY IDENTIFICATION: SOCIAL HABIT VERSUS CONTEMPORARY EVALUATION

Thus far we have considered factors that cause voters to deviate in voting from their underlying party allegiance. Under what conditions do they actually change their party identification?

The prevailing model of party identification holds that it is a strong social habit. It begins early in life, is remarkably stable, resists short-run political forces, and changes only through reaction to long-lasting and powerful political events, such as the Great Depression of the 1930s. This view was authoritatively propounded in 1960 by the authors of *The American Voter*. At its core is the idea that party identification constitutes a strong emotional bond and is therefore "firm but not immovable."[50] This leaves at least a little room for candidate and issue-related changes and for a more active evaluative role on the part of voters. One classic study shows that those who change party from one election to the next generally are sympathetic to some key policies of their new party. "Standpatters," in contrast, are in general sympathy with major policies of their party.[51]

Whether citizens seek a party in accordance with their independently arrived-at beliefs or are taught what to believe by party allegiance cannot be determined from evidence now available. Almost certainly, both processes are having an impact on the electorate. One synthesis that combines long-term habit with more contemporaneous evaluations concludes that "there is substantial continuity in partisanship from one point in time to the next" and that party identification "can be interpreted as the individual's accumulated evaluation of the parties."[52]

In addition to extremely rare tidal waves that change the party preferences of large groups of voters, there are also more common squalls that affect the life experiences of smaller numbers of individuals and from time to time lead a relatively few voters to alter their party identifications. Since these eddies in the larger flow of events lack a common origin, they usually cancel one another out in their net effects. Thus the big picture of relatively stable aggregate partisanship in the overall electorate can be reconciled with a more complicated picture of occasional individual change.[53] Both the thinking and feeling individuals who change parties once in a while and the large masses of people who are caught up in infrequent movements away from or toward certain parties are galvanized by their reactions to shared experiences.[54] Thus people whose partisanship was not firmly fixed early in life, perhaps because politics was seldom discussed in the home, may develop party identifications in their twenties or thirties. They adjust their party loyalties to their policy preferences or to the views of the groups with which they associate. But they do not make these adjustments often. As Charles Franklin tells us, "citizens remain open to change throughout life, though as experience with the parties accumulates, it is accorded greater weight."[55]

Is party identification a durable standing decision to vote a certain way, as the authors of *The American Voter* put it, or, as Morris Fiorina argues, a "running tally of retrospective evaluations of party promises and performance" which is subject to significant change based on unfolding political events?[56] Scholars find that citizen assessment of party performance on major dimensions of public policy—war and peace, employment, inflation, race relations—do matter.[57] Nevertheless, most changes of party identification involve switching in and out of the independent category rather than between the parties.[58] Donald Kinder sums up:

> So party identification is *not* immovable; it is influenced by the performance of government, by policy disagreements, and by the emergence of new candidates. The loyalty citizens feel for party is at least partially a function of what governments and parties do, and what they fail to do.... I do not mean to press this too hard, however. Although party identification does respond to political events, it does so sluggishly. It is one thing for Republicans to feel less enthusiastic toward their party after a period of sustained national difficulty presided

TABLE 1.7 Party Identification, 1952–2004

| Year | Democrats | | | Pure | Republicans | | |
	Strong	Weak	Independent	Independent	Independent	Weak	Strong
1952	22 %	25 %	10 %	6 %	7 %	14 %	14 %
1962	23	23	7	8	6	16	12
1972	15	26	11	13	10	13	10
1982	20	24	11	11	8	14	10
1992	18	18	14	12	12	14	11
2002	16	17	15	8	13	16	14
2004	16	16	17	10	12	12	16

Source: Harold W. Stanley and Richard G. Niemi, *Vital Statistics on American Politics, 2005–2006* (Washington, D.C.: CQ Press, 2006), p. 116; data from the National Election Studies.

over by a Republican administration; it is quite another to embrace the opposition. The latter seldom happens.[59]

Has there been an overall decline in party identification in the United States? From 1952 to 1964, the level of party identification among voters remained stable. From 1964 onward, many more Americans identified themselves as independents. Indeed, as of 1974, self-styled independents outnumbered Republicans five to three and came near to the number of Democrats. By the late 1990s, more Americans classified themselves as independents than identified with each of the two major parties. These trends have prompted some observers to claim that parties do not affect the behavior of voters nearly as much as they once did.[60] However, more than two-thirds of nominal independents admit that they "lean" toward either the Democratic or Republican Party.[61] These partisan independents are far more knowledgeable and participate much more actively in politics than "pure," nonleaning independents; they also show a far greater tendency to vote, and they nearly always vote for the party toward which they lean. In short, independents who lean toward a party behave almost the same as strong partisans and not at all like truly independent voters. By separating party identification into seven categories rather than three, table 1.7 shows that the number of pure independents is as low as 10 percent, not the 35 percent often cited.[62]

People are a lot more stable in their party identifications than in the policy preferences that are sometimes held to underlie party allegiances.[63] In the past, however, there have often been significant defections of partisan identifiers to the other party's candidate in presidential elections. From 1952 to 1968, Democrats defected about twice as often as Republicans (19 percent to 10 percent). After 1972, Republican defection rates stayed about the same, but Democratic defections increased, averaging 25 percent from 1976 to 1988. Even Jimmy Carter's successful candidacy in 1976 received just 77 percent of the Democratic vote, while 90 percent of the smaller but more loyal Republican electorate backed its party's candidate, Gerald Ford.[64]

Recent elections, however, have been different. Bill Clinton, after losing about a quarter of Democratic voters in 1992 to Republican George H. W. Bush and independent candidate Ross Perot, received 85 percent of the Democratic vote in 1996. For the first time in many years, Republicans were slightly less loyal than Democrats, with defections totaling 27 percent in 1992 and 20 percent in 1996. In the closely-fought 2000 and 2004 elections, both major candidates received overwhelming support from their parties' identifiers, reflecting the highly polarized nature of contemporary electoral politics. In 2000, 91 percent of Republicans voted for George W. Bush, while 86 percent of Democrats backed Al Gore. Four years later, Bush received 93 percent of the Republican vote, while 89 percent of Democrats supported their party's nominee, John Kerry—the highest total level of party loyalty in the American electorate since the advent of modern survey research over fifty years ago.[65]

So party as an orientation point is still very important. Most people, especially most voters (since those without any party preference are much less likely to vote), identify with or lean toward one party or the other. There are always defections, however, and the parties cannot automatically count on all their identifiers to give them unqualified support in every election. Party identification does not translate automatically into party-line voting. Voters may tend to be loyal, but they can also be driven away.

A CENTRAL STRATEGIC PROBLEM: THE ATTENTIVENESS OF VOTERS

A remarkably consistent picture emerges from the study of American voters over the past several decades:

1. Most voters (about 70 percent, or more than 90 percent if independent "leaners" are included) have a party allegiance, which determines their vote most of the time. The strategic implication for presidential candidates is that there is such a thing as a party base. Major-party candidates must mobilize this party base so that the party faithful turn out, and they must strive to minimize defections; the overwhelming evidence is that efforts in this direction will be rewarded.

2. In any election, the number of voters making a judgment to desert their customary party of preference will ordinarily be small. If there is a tide of such evaluations in a single direction, this can be decisive for the outcome. Mostly, these tides are expressed as decisions to move from partisan loyalty to weaker loyalty, from weak loyalty to neutrality or to a weakened resolution to vote at all.

3. Most citizens do not pay much attention to politics or keep well informed about the substantive details of current events. The world inhabited by politicians, a world full of public policy and of contention over complex issues, is only dimly perceived by ordinary voters. A strategic implication is that politicians must expend resources and work very hard to give meaning to the choices that voters ordinarily make according to party habit. For a candidate to become visible as an individual to voters is a difficult task. Much of the activity in an election year is understandable in the light of the fact that voters are not attentive to the specifics of public affairs, ideologically consistent in their views, or spontaneously eager to change their habitual orientations to politics. Politicians must therefore strive to capture their attention.

4. Voters participate in politics mostly in accordance with their social loyalties and involvements. They retain and sometimes exercise their capacity to make contemporary judgments on issues. Either way, their behavior is importantly influenced by the ways in which they are organized into social groups, especially political parties.

BOX 1.1 REGISTRATION AND VOTING

The American system of voter registration is at least partially responsible for comparatively low rates of voting in the United States. In most other Western democracies, all eligible citizens are registered to vote automatically by the government, while all but one American state requires potential voters to take the initiative to register—in most cases at least thirty days before the election, when political interest among the public has yet to peak.[1] This difference accounts, in part, for the significant gap between turnout rates in the United States and other world democracies. The turnout of *registered* voters in the United States is comparable to that of other nations (see table 1).[2]

While the United States now lags behind the performance of most Western democracies in overall levels of voter participation, there was once a time—in an era when the impact of the federal government was remote, mass communication absent, and electronic voting equipment unheard of—when more than 70 percent of potential (not just registered) voters participated in presidential elections: the late nineteenth century, or "Gilded Age," when partisan mobilization in the United States reached extremely high levels. In the election of 1876, for example, 82 percent of the eligible electorate (men only, of course) turned out in the nation as a whole. Soon thereafter, however, harsh registration restrictions were introduced in nearly every state, cloaked in rhetoric about reducing fraud and corruption but aimed at keeping down the vote of "undesirable elements" (code words for immigrants and blacks). As Stanley Kelley and his collaborators observed, turnout "may have declined and then risen again, not because of changes in the interest of voters in elections, but because of changes in the interest demanded of them.... [Not only are] electorates...much more the product of political forces than many have appreciated. But also...to a considerable extent, they can be political artifacts. Within limits, they can be constructed to a size and composition deemed desirable by those in power."[3]

Until relatively recently, the ease of voter registration in a particular jurisdiction could be manipulated by local political figures in an attempt to give an advantage to their electoral supporters.[4] The most extreme examples of this, of course, were the measures taken in the South by white segregationists to prevent black participation, including poll taxes and literacy requirements, which were outlawed by the Twenty-fourth Amendment to the Constitution in 1964 and the Voting Rights Act of 1965. But even after the civil rights era, state laws varied considerably on such details as the length of residence necessary before one could vote in a particular area, and registration might well require a trip to the county courthouse several months before the election. In a nation noted for the geographic mobility of its population, a majority of states required, as recently as 1972, a residence of at least one year within the state, three months within the county, and thrity days within the precinct in order to vote in any election, including for president. That year, the Supreme Court ruled that thirty days was an ample period of time for the state of Tennessee to register its voters and declared its existing six-month state residency requirement an unconstitutional denial of equal protection. In two subsequent *per curiam*

TABLE 1 Comparative Turnout of Registered Voters

Country	Turnout	Compulsory Voting	Eligible Required to Register
Australia	93.8 %	Yes	Yes
Belgium	93.4	Yes	Automatic
Austria	90.5	No	Automatic
Italy	90.5	Yes	Automatic
Iceland	90.1	N.A.	N.A.
Luxembourg	87.3	N.A.	N.A.
New Zealand	87.2	No	Yes
United States	**86.8**	**No**	**Yes**
Sweden	86.0	No	Automatic
Netherlands	85.8	No	Automatic
Denmark	85.7	No	Automatic
Greece	84.5	Yes	Automatic
Germany	84.3	No	Automatic
Norway	84.0	No	Automatic
Israel	79.7	No	Automatic
Finland	77.6	No	Automatic
Canada	75.5	No	Yes
United Kingdom	75.4	No	Automatic
Portugal	72.6	N.A.	N.A.
Japan	71.4	No	Automatic
Spain	70.6	No	Automatic
Ireland	68.5	No	Automatic
France	66.2	No	No
Switzerland	46.1	No	Automatic

Source: Thomas T. Mackie and Richard Rose, *The International Almanac of Electoral History*, 3rd ed. (Washington, DC: CQ Press, 1991). Compulsory voting information from G. Bingham Powell Jr., "American Voter Turnout in Comparative Perspective," *American Political Science Review* 80 (March 1986): 17–43, at 38, and Raymond E. Wolfinger, David P. Glass, and Peverill Squire, "Predictors of Electoral Turnout: An International Comparison," *Policy Studies Review* 9 (Spring 1990): 551–574, at 561.

Note: The percentage listed for each country is the proportion of the registered voting-age population casting ballots in the most recent national election as of 1989.

decisions, the court held that an extension to fifty days was permissible under certain conditions, but that this time period represented the absolute limit.[5]

In 1993, Congress enacted the National Voter Registration Act, commonly known as the "motor voter" law. This legislation required voter registration forms to be available at the Department of Motor Vehicles and other government offices in every state, allowed registration by mail-in form, and compelled states to allow citizens to register up to thirty days before an election. The "motor voter" law was widely expected to benefit Democrats, whose popular constituencies (especially low-income and minority citizens) tended to be underrepresented on the voting rolls; in fact, Republican President George H. W. Bush had vetoed an earlier version of the legislation in 1992. In practice, however, though the law appeared to have a minor impact on the rate of voting turnout, it produced no significant effect on the partisan affiliation of the American electorate.[6]

Several states have taken additional measures to encourage voter turnout. Minnesota, Wisconsin, and a few other states allow same-day voter registration, under which an unregistered citizen may go to a polling place on Election Day, register to vote, and immediately cast a ballot. The turnout rate in these states is noticeably higher (see table 2).[7] Other states have loosened eligibility requirements for absentee ballots, which were once reserved for those unable to vote in person due to travel or illness. For example, California now allows any voter to register as a "permanent absentee" and automatically receive a ballot by mail before each election; 33 percent of the state's vote in 2004 was cast by absentee ballot.[8] Oregon has dispensed with the traditional polling place altogether, conducting its elections entirely by mail. And a number of states, including Arizona, Colorado, Nevada, Tennessee, and Texas, offer early voting, allowing voters to cast ballots in person at designated places in the weeks before Election Day.

TABLE 2 **Turnout in States with Same-Day Voter Registration, 2004**

State	Turnout of Voting-Age Population
Minnesota	76.7 %
Wisconsin	73.0
Maine	72.0
North Dakota	70.8
New Hampshire	68.9
Idaho	66.3
Wyoming	59.7
United States Total	58.3

Source: U.S. Census Bureau, "Voting and Registration in the Election of November 2004," available at http://www.census.gov/population/www/socdemo/voting/cps2004.html.

Note: North Dakota does not require voter registration.

Still, many potential voters are kept out of the electorate. Noncitizens are not allowed to vote, whether legal or illegal aliens. Most states strip convicted felons of their voting rights; in ten states, this disenfranchisement stands for life.[9] These groups are not insignificant in size. Michael P. McDonald has estimated the number of ineligible voting-age residents as roughly 20 million people as of 2004, or nearly one-tenth of the adult population of the United States.[10]

[1] North Dakota does not require voter registration. Presumably, in a small, rural state in which nearly all potential voters are known to election officials in any given jurisdiction, the possibility of voter fraud is remote.

[2] The general outline of this argument has been known for over seventy-five years. For example, Harold Gosnell wrote in 1930 that "[i]n the European countries studied, a citizen who is entitled to vote does not, as a rule, have to make any effort to see that his name is on the list of eligible voters. The inconvenience of registering for voting in this country has caused many citizens to become non-voters." Harold G. Gosnell, *Why Europe Votes* (Chicago: University of Chicago Press, 1930), p. 185. See also Raymond E. Wolfinger and Steven J. Rosenstone, *Who Votes?* (New Haven, CT: Yale University Press, 1980); and G. Bingham Powell Jr., "American Voter Turnout in Comparative Perspective," *American Political Science Review* 80 (March 1986): 17–43.

[3] Stanley Kelley, Jr., Richard E. Ayres, and William G. Bowen, "Registration and Voting: Putting First Things First," *American Political Science Review* 61 (June 1967): 359–379, at 374–375.

[4] In Richard E. Ayres, "Registration 1960: Key to a Democratic Victory?" (unpublished senior thesis, Princeton University, 1964), cited in Kelley, Ayres, and Bowen, "Registration and Voting," p. 375, the author notes the correlation between convenience of registration and percent of the vote for the Democratic Party as proof of the Chicago Daley machine's awareness of this phenomenon.

[5] *Dunn v. Blumstein*, 405 U.S. 330 (1972); *Burn v. Forston*, 410 U.S. 686 (1972); and *Marston v. Lewis*, 410 U.S. 759 (1973).

[6] Benjamin Highton and Raymond E. Wolfinger, "Estimating the Effects of the National Voter Registration Act of 1993," *Political Behavior* 20 (June 1998): 79–104; see also Raymond E. Wolfinger and Jonathan Hoffman, "Registering and Voting with Motor Voter," *PS: Political Science and Politics* 34 (March 2001): 85–92.

[7] Stephen Knack and James White, "Election-Day Registration and Turnout Inequality," *Political Behavior* 22 (March 2000): 29–44. Not all of this difference can be explained by registration laws, however; see Benjamin Highton, "Easy Registration and Voter Turnout," *Journal of Politics* 59 (May 1997): 565–575.

[8] California Secretary of State, "Statement of Vote: 2004 Presidential General Election," http://www.ss.ca.gov/elections/sov/2004_general/contents.htm.

[9] Christopher Uggen and Jeff Manza, "Democratic Contraction? Political Consequences of Felon Disenfranchisement in the United States," *American Sociological Review* 67 (December 2002): 777–803.

[10] McDonald's statistics are available at http://elections.gmu.edu/Voter_Turnout_2004.htm. See also Michael P. McDonald and Samuel L. Popkin, "The Myth of the Vanishing Voter," *American Political Science Review* 95 (December 2001): 963–974, in which the authors argue that the much-lamented decline in electoral turnout rates since the 1970s is largely due to the growth of the ineligible population.

TWO

GROUPS

THE PRESIDENTIAL VOTE AS AN AGGREGATION OF INTEREST GROUPS

In each election, members of the various social groups that make up the American voting population turn out to vote, dividing their loyalties in varying ways between the major parties. Turnout varies enormously among different groups in the population, rising with income, occupational status, education, and age (for the details, see table B in the appendix). Since Republicans are disproportionately located in the high-turnout groups and Democrats in the low, this tends to give Republicans electoral advantages that in some measure, varying from election to election, make up for the slight overall preponderance of Democrats in the total adult population.

The two major parties are somewhat differently constituted as voting blocs of interest groups. Democrats appeal especially to identifiable segments of society—notably, disadvantaged minorities—that have specific programmatic interests. That is the Democratic base, and Democrats win presidential elections by activating these interest groups and persuading them to turn out. This is not always easy, since among the groups that characteristically do not turn out—the poor, the less well-educated, recent immigrants (such as many Latinos), the less well socially integrated—many tend to favor the Democratic Party when they do vote.

Republicans win presidential elections by doing slightly better than Democrats and better than usual for Republicans among the big battalions: aggregates of voters not necessarily organized as self-conscious groups, such as white voters (79 percent of the electorate in 2004), voters in their middle years, those with at least some college education, and Protestants. In years when Republicans do slightly less well among these very large segments of the population, Democrats win (see table 2.1).

TABLE 2.1 Republicans Win by Doing Well with Large Groups

	Percentage of	Percentage of Group Voting Republican							
Groups	2004 Electorate	1976	1980	1984	1988	1992	1996	2000	2004
Whites	79	52	56	64	59	40	46	54	58
White Protestants	41	58	63	72	66	47	53	63	67
Married	63	–	–	62	57	41	46	53	57
Suburbanites	45	–	55	61	57	39	42	49	52
All Voters	100	48	51	59	53	38	41	48	51

Source: Marjorie Connelly, "How Americans Voted: A Political Portrait," *New York Times*, November 7, 2004, sec. 4, p. 4.

Democrats maintain a strong electoral base among groups that for one reason or another can be considered less well off or out of the mainstream: black voters, union members, gay voters. Even in years when Democrats lose the presidency, they tend to do well with these groups (see table 2.2). Note, for example, the strong Democratic vote of blacks and union members even in 1984, when Republican Ronald Reagan won a landslide victory. On the whole, no large interest groups vote as overwhelmingly Republican as African Americans vote Democratic. And several other groups vote nearly as lopsidedly for Democrats.

The differences in the ways the two major parties are constituted as voting coalitions give a clue as to differences in the ways they approach public policymaking. Democrats are more overtly distributive in their concerns, Republicans more concerned with overall principles that

TABLE 2.2 The Democratic Party Base: Smaller, Loyal Groups

	Percentage of	Percentage of Group Voting Democratic							
Groups	2004 Electorate	1976	1980	1984	1988	1992	1996	2000	2004
Blacks	12	83	85	90	86	83	84	90	88
Latinos	6	76	59	62	69	61	72	67	56
Jews	3	64	45	67	64	80	78	79	74
Union Household	24	59	49	53	57	55	59	59	59
Family Income Under $15,000	8	58	49	55	62	58	59	57	63
Big City Residents	13	–	–	–	62	58	68	71	60
Gays, Lesbians, Bisexuals	4	–	–	–	–	72	66	71	77
All Voters	100	50	41	40	45	43	49	48	48

Source: Marjorie Connelly, "How Americans Voted: A Political Portrait," *New York Times*, November 7, 2004, sec. 4, p. 4; "Exit Polls," MSNBC, available at http://www.msnbc.msn.com/id/5297138/.

apply in a blanket way to the entire population.[1] Republicans figure, rightly, that policies that yield evenhanded opportunities for all will not greatly disadvantage their well-situated clientele; Democrats figure, rightly, that their relatively disadvantaged constituencies will be less well served by blanket policies that take no special account of them.

The comparatively particular and group-specific orientation of the Democratic Party is reflected in much folklore and research proclaiming the relative fragmentation of the Democrats. Republicans are far more united by ideological agreement and are better able to sustain a united front in most arenas than their Democratic counterparts. Republicans occupy a narrower range of the ideological spectrum than Democrats. This relatively strong signal over a narrower band has had a payoff, historically, in the greater loyalty of Republican voters, that is, in their disinclination to defect to the other side in presidential elections. But for most of the past half-century they were not the majority party; the Democrats, who stood for a greater variety of things, were the larger of the two major parties and remained so even in periods when the Republicans, because they were far more effective in mobilizing their voters, won presidential elections with some regularity.[2]

Since the 1970s and 1980s, the loyalty of Democratic voters to their party's presidential candidates has increased, with defection rates falling to become nearly comparable with those of Republicans. Unfortunately for the Democratic Party, this trend has occurred at the same time as an erosion in the formerly significant Democratic advantage in party identification. Whereas Democratic identifiers outnumbered Republicans in the potential electorate by 47 percent to 28 percent in 1952, by 2004 this advantage had narrowed to just five percentage points (33 percent to 28 percent), according to data from the National Election Studies. Since Republicans are usually more likely to vote than Democrats, this margin has narrowed even further among actual voters. The national exit poll sponsored by the *New York Times* and several television networks reported that the 2004 electorate was evenly split between Democrats and Republicans, with 37 percent identifying with each major party. Although John Kerry received 89 percent of his fellow Democrats' votes, almost as high as George W. Bush's 93 percent support among Republicans, he lost narrowly in the national popular vote despite outpolling Bush among self-identified independents by 49 to 48 percent.[3]

To determine the contribution that a particular social group makes to the electoral coalitions of the parties, it is necessary to know three things: how big the group is, how many of its members actually vote, and how devoted its members are to one party or another. For example, consider the voting preferences of poor people—defined as those whose household incomes are in the bottom one-sixth of the total population. As table 2.3 shows, the proportion of the total Democratic vote supplied by poor voters has ranged from 12 to 19 percent in presidential elections over the past five decades.[4] At the same time, about 90 percent of the Republican vote comes from the nonpoor—voters whose incomes place them in the top five-sixths of the population. Poor voters therefore regularly constitute a higher proportion of the Democratic electoral coalition (about 15 percent, on average) than the Republican coalition (about 10 percent).

Most people have overlapping characteristics. Thus a single individual can be white, female, Catholic, and a union member all at the same time. It would be useful to try to identify the contribution of each attribute alone. By separating subjective identification with the working class from being a union member, scholars have shown that belonging to a union creates a strong push toward Democratic allegiance. Being Jewish, being black or Latino, and being female propel

TABLE 2.3 The Parties as Coalitions of Social Groups, 1952–2004

| | Democratic Coalition | | | | | | Republican Coalition | | | | | |
Year	P	NW	U	CJO	F	C	NP	W	NU	Pro	M	SR
1952	15	8	37	40	50	39	86	99	79	76	48	71
1956	12	6	37	38	48	28	88	98	78	75	46	77
1960	12	8	33	46	49	28	87	97	81	90	45	82
1964	17	13	32	36	56	31	88	100	87	79	48	76
1968	13	20	29	41	58	33	89	98	80	80	44	79
1972	19	25	31	41	60	35	87	96	77	72	47	81
1976	13	20	31	39	56	30	93	96	82	73	44	76
1980	19	29	33	35	59	39	90	96	79	68	48	82
1984	15	29	31	46	61	32	94	92	83	66	47	84
1988	15	34	26	42	59	32	91	92	84	70	48	83
1992	15	31	21	46	59	33	92	90	86	69	48	81
1996	15	33	27	46	60	31	94	92	87	66	55	79
2000	12	31	19	48	60	36	94	89	87	59	49	83
2004	13	38	27	48	55	–	90	86	85	59	51	–

Source: National Election Studies. Measures adapted in part from Robert Axelrod, "Presidential Election Coalitions in 1984," *American Political Science Review* 80 (March 1986): 281–284.

P/NP	Poor (household income in lowest sixth of national population)/Nonpoor
NW/W	Nonwhite (Black, Latino, Asian, Native American)/White
U/NU	Union member in household/Nonunion
CJO/Pro	Catholic, Jewish, Other, or No Religion/Protestant
F/M	Female/Male
C/SR	City/Suburb or Rural Area

people toward the Democrats. So too does being Catholic or working class. The pro-Democratic tilt of these two latter groups, however, has declined since the 1950s.[5]

Black voters and other racial minorities have established themselves as a substantial component of the Democratic coalition over the past forty years. Blacks have remained throughout a relatively constant 12 to 13 percent of the total population. African American voters' vastly increased contribution to the Democratic vote since the 1960s has been the result of a near doubling of their turnout throughout the nation (thanks largely to the Voting Rights Act of 1965, which allowed many southern blacks to vote for the first time), of their high loyalty to the Democratic Party (85 to 90 percent of black voters consistently support Democratic candidates), and of fluctuations in Democratic voting by white voters. The growing Latino population, less heavily Democratic than African Americans but still significantly more so than whites, has also contributed an increasing number of votes to the Democratic coalition in recent elections. Voters of Asian descent, while less numerous, have voted Democratic at a slightly higher rate than whites in the last several elections, while the Native American population, also small nationwide but electorally important in a few western states, tends to be heavily Democratic as well. By 2004, nearly 40 percent of the votes for the Democratic presidential candidate came from nonwhite voters, while the Republican coalition remained overwhelmingly white (see table 2.3).

Members of labor unions and their families are also important to the Democratic Party because they represent between one quarter and one fifth of all adults, their turnout is reasonably high, and they vote more Democratic than other people. Even in the 1984 election, a Republican landslide in which Ronald Reagan won nearly 60 percent of the total vote, members of union households still cast most of their votes for Democratic nominee Walter Mondale (see table 2.2). But as the proportion of American workers affiliated with a union has declined since the 1950s, the labor vote has become a somewhat smaller component of the Democratic electoral coalition. Whereas union households contributed four times as many votes as African Americans and other minorities to the Democratic Party in 1960 (33 percent of the total), by the 1990s Democratic candidates had begun to receive more total votes from nonwhites than from union members and their families (see table 2.3).

Historically, Roman Catholic voters provided an important electoral base for the Democratic Party. Even in 1952, when Republican Dwight D. Eisenhower defeated Democrat Adlai Stevenson by 55 to 44 percent nationwide, Stevenson won 56 percent of the Catholic vote. In 1960, when the Democrats nominated Senator John F. Kennedy of Massachusetts, a Catholic, for president, they captured 78 percent of the vote among Catholics.[6] But as anti-Catholic prejudice in society has declined and Catholics have become less socioeconomically distinct from other Americans, they have started to vote more like the rest of the nation. Though white Catholics remain a significantly more Democratic group than white Protestants, the once enormous gap between them has narrowed, and Democratic candidates can no longer count on automatic Catholic support. For the first time since 1960, the Democrats nominated a Catholic politician for president in 2004, but unlike Kennedy, John Kerry did not benefit from strong loyalty among his coreligionists. In fact, he lost the Catholic vote to George W. Bush by 52 to 47 percent.[7] At the same time, the smaller populations of Jews, members of other religions, and those with no religion have either maintained or increased their high levels of support for Democratic candidates since the 1970s and 1980s. In 2004, Kerry received nearly half his votes from non-Protestants, while about six in ten Bush voters were Protestant (see table 2.3).

An even more dramatic change in partisan preferences has occurred among southern whites. In 1952 and 1956, southerners voted about ten percentage points more Democratic than the rest of the country. Republicans began to make inroads among this group in the 1960s and 1970s, though southern voters moved back to the Democrats in 1976 and 1980, when former Governor Jimmy Carter of Georgia headed the Democratic ticket. They gave a quarter of their votes to the third-party segregationist candidacy of George Wallace in 1968. African American southerners stayed with the Democrats in that year, but white southerners split their presidential vote among all three candidates. Since 1984, the Republicans have received very strong support from southern whites; according to the National Election Studies, George W. Bush defeated John Kerry among this voting bloc by a margin of roughly two-to-one in 2004.

What about the voting habits of young people, those under thirty years of age? Until 1972, they were not consistently a significant component of either party's coalition and their comparatively low turnout reduced any impact that their 18 percent share of the voting-age population might have given them. After the voting age was lowered in 1971 from twenty-one (in most states) to eighteen nationwide, and because of the baby boom after World War II, the proportion of the voting-age population under the age of thirty increased to 28 percent, and in the 1970s there was much talk of young people as a separate, presumably more liberal, voting bloc. Since then, as the baby boomers have aged, young people have decreased as a proportion of

TABLE 2.4 Vote for Democratic Presidential Candidate by Age Group, 1964–2004

Age	1964	1968	1972	1976	1980	1984	1988	1992	1996	2000	2004
18–29	72	38	47	51	44	40	47	43	53	48	54
30–44	69	47	34	49	36	42	45	41	48	48	46
45–59	70	37	31	47	39	40	42	41	48	48	48
60+	59	40	29	47	41	39	49	50	48	51	46

Source: For 1964–1972, National Election Studies; for 1976–2004, Marjorie Connelly, "How Americans Voted: A Political Portrait," *New York Times*, November 7, 2004, sec. 4, p. 4.

all voters, representing 17 percent of the total electorate in 2004. Are they now making a big difference?

"Whatever else young voters are," Raymond Wolfinger tells us in a well-advised note of caution, "they are not harbingers of future outcomes."[8] The reason is that most of the time people under thirty do not divide their vote much differently from the rest of the population. The belief that the youth vote was pro-Democratic began in 1972, when it was close to being true, but it has not been consistently true since 1976. A similar tale, only in the opposite, Republican direction, has been told of the allegedly big youth vote for Ronald Reagan in 1984. Actually, as table 2.4 shows, the youth vote did not differ from other age groups in that year, while in 1988 and 1992 Democrats Michael Dukakis and Bill Clinton both received their strongest support from both the youngest and the oldest groups of voters. Since 1992, the young have demonstrated a modest pro-Democratic tilt. In 1996 Clinton did slightly better among the youngest voters than he did with any other age cohort. In 2000, Al Gore edged George W. Bush 48 percent to 46 percent among voters aged eighteen to twenty-nine, with Green Party nominee Ralph Nader receiving 5 percent. Similarly, John Kerry won the under-thirty vote in 2004, by a 54 to 45 percent margin over Bush.

So the Democratic electoral coalition includes voters with low incomes, nonwhites, union members and their families, and, disproportionately, non-Protestants. What is the Republican coalition? White people, who constitute about 75 percent of the U.S. population, vote anywhere from 5 to 7 percent more Republican than the total electorate. Historically, the overwhelming majority of Republican votes came from whites: 98 percent, on average, between 1952 and 1980. Since the 1980s, nonwhites have become a slightly larger component of the Republican vote, but whites still constituted 86 percent of George W. Bush's electoral coalition in 2004. If one can conceive of nonunion families and Protestants as "social groups" in the usual sense, they make up about 75 percent and 55 percent of the population, respectively, and vote 5 to 10 percent more Republican than the nation as a whole.

The Republican Party gets its vote, then, predominantly from white people, middle- and upper-income earners, nonunion members, and Protestants, especially evangelical Protestants, outside large cities. Although Republicans received majorities of 60 percent or better from all these groups in their landslide victories of 1972 and 1984, they were able to attract at most 53 percent from any of them in 1976, when Democrat Jimmy Carter won narrowly over Republican Gerald Ford. In 1992 and 1996, defections to Democrat Bill Clinton and independent candidate Ross

Perot held Republicans to under 50 percent of the vote in most of these groups, making victory impossible. George W. Bush improved his party's standing among these voters in 2000 and 2004, winning 54 and 58 percent of the white vote, respectively, including about two out of every three votes among southern whites and white Protestants.[9]

VARIATIONS AMONG INTEREST GROUPS

Interest groups are collections of people who are similarly situated with respect to one or more policies of government and who organize to do something about it. The interest groups most significant for elections in our society are those having one or more of the following characteristics:

1. They have a mass base, that is, they are composed of many members.
2. They are concentrated geographically, rather than dispersed thinly over the entire map.
3. They represent major resource investments of members—such as bicycle producers, whose entire livelihoods may be tied up in the industry involved, as against the consumers of bicycles, for whom investment in a bicycle is not anywhere near as important.
4. They involve characteristics that give people status in society, such as race or ethnicity.
5. They evoke feelings about a single issue that are so intense as to eclipse the concerns of their members about other issues.
6. They are composed of people who are able to participate actively in politics; that is, people who have time or money to spare.

Interest groups having these characteristics matter most in presidential elections because these characteristics are most likely to claim the loyalties of large numbers of voters and form the basis for the mobilization of their preferences and their votes. Moreover, they reflect the fact that America is organized into geographic entities—states, congressional districts—as the basis of political representation.

Interest groups may be more or less organized and more or less vigilant and alert on policy matters that concern, or ought to concern, them. They are not necessarily organized in ways that make them politically effective; very often, the paid lobbyists of interest groups spend more time trying to alert their own members to the implications of government policies than they spend lobbying politicians.[10]

In American politics, interest group activity is lively and can be found nearly everywhere, even when it is not particularly effective or meaningful for policy outcomes. Three characteristics of interest groups are especially important for presidential elections. First, membership in these groups may give voters a sense of affiliation and political location. In this respect, interest groups act much the way parties do, helping to fill in the voter's map of the world with preferences, priorities, and facts. Interest groups act as intermediary agencies that help voters identify their political preferences quickly by actively soliciting their members' interest in behalf of specific candidates and parties and, more important, by providing still another anchor to voters' identities. This helps voters fix their own position quickly and economically in what otherwise would be a confusing and contradictory political environment. Second, interest groups frequently undertake partisan political activities; they may actively recruit supporters for candidates and aid materially in campaigns.

Third, interest groups may influence party policy by making demands of candidates with respect to issues in return for their own mobilized support. The extent to which interest groups can "deliver" members' votes, however, is always a problem; to a great degree interest group leaders are the prisoners of past alliances their group has made. This means that they may not be able to prevent their followers from voting for their traditional allies even when group leaders fall out with politicians. In 1993, labor union leaders vowed revenge on Democratic members of Congress who voted for the North American Free Trade Agreement (NAFTA),[11] but in the 1994 election, 63 percent of union families still voted Democratic in elections for the House of Representatives, as they had in 1980, 1986, and 1988. This was only one point worse than in 1984 when Walter Mondale, a conspicuous friend of labor, headed the Democratic ticket.[12]

Various ethnic and religious votes, the farm vote, the labor vote, the youth vote, the consumer vote, and many other "votes" are sometimes discussed as though they were political commodities that could be manipulated easily in behalf of one or another candidate. This is not as easy as it sounds. When the analysis of election statistics and opinion polls was an esoteric discipline, forty or fifty years ago, most politicians could only evaluate intuitively claims to guarantee group support or threats to withdraw it, and no one could tell with any certainty whether interest group leaders maintained sufficient influence among their constituents to deliver on their promises. The development of the craft of public opinion analysis now makes it easier to assess these political claims.

The usual argument is that if one or another candidate captures the allegiance of a particular bloc, that bloc's pivotal position or large population in a state will enable the fortunate candidate to capture all of the state's electoral votes and thus win the election. A classic example of this style of argument was a memorandum by Ted Sorensen in 1960 aimed at big-city political leaders, which claimed that John F. Kennedy's Catholicism would be a distinct electoral asset, rather than the mild liability it actually turned out to be (since the increased Democratic support among Catholics inspired by the Kennedy candidacy was outweighed by significant defections of anti-Catholic voters to Kennedy's opponent Richard Nixon).[13] Of course no one combination of states totaling more than a majority of electoral votes is more critical, valuable, or pivotal than any other such combination. In a fairly close election the shifting of any number of combinations of voting blocs or states to one side or the other could spell the difference between victory and defeat.

There is little doubt that under certain conditions and at particular times some social characteristics of voters and candidates may have relevance to the election results. Finding the actual conditions under which specified social characteristics become relevant to voter choice is difficult. We know that in a competitive political system various participants (parties, political leaders) back candidates with the hope of capturing the allegiance of various social groups. It is rarely wise to appeal to one group alone; in a very large electorate, the support of only one group will not be enough to win. Many different groups exist, with all sorts of policy preferences, and each individual voter has many social characteristics that are potentially relevant to his or her voting decision. While some people may be so single-minded that they have only one interest that is important in determining their vote—their race, religion, ethnic background, income, feelings about gun control or abortion or the State of Israel or the environment—most of us have multiple interests. Sometimes these interests conflict. Environmental organizations, for example, may have less success in mobilizing voters in areas where environmental regulation is believed to reduce employment opportunities than in areas where the two do not compete. The worse the economic conditions, the sharper the perceived conflict. Concern about increasing unemployment may influence how some voters feel about governmental support of the unemployed. Much depends on the tides of events, which may bring one or another issue to the forefront of the voters' consciousness and incline them toward the candidate they believe best represents their preferences on that particular matter.[14]

One of the largest social groups of all, women, provides an example of a group membership whose political importance has changed significantly since the 1980s. At one time gender could not be shown to have a strong partisan effect; what weak tendency existed at the time of *The American Voter* (1960) showed women to be slightly more Republican than men.[15] In 1980, however, women were substantially less pro-Reagan than were men and thus made up a much larger part of the Democratic than of the Republican coalition (see tables 2.3 and 2.5).[16] Throughout 1981, differences between men and women appeared in public opinion polls that asked about party identification, and it became commonplace to refer to President Reagan's "gender gap."[17] Yet the *New York Times* midterm 1982 election-day surveys showed only small differences between men and women voters.[18] In 1984, women voted 6 to 9 percent less for Reagan, depending on which exit poll you believe. Women cast a majority of their votes for Reagan, but Reagan's margin among women was smaller than it was among men, so women

TABLE 2.5 The Gender Gap: Votes in Presidential Elections by Sex, 1960–2004

Year	Men			Women		
	Democrat	Republican	Independent	Democrat	Republican	Independent
1960	52	48		49	51	
1964	60	40		62	38	
1968	41	43	16	45	43	12
1972	37	63		38	62	
1976	50	48		50	48	
1980	36	55	7	45	47	7
1984	37	62		44	56	
1988	41	57		49	50	
1992	41	38	21	45	37	17
1996	43	44	10	54	38	7
2000	42	53	3	54	43	2
2004	44	55		51	48	

Source: For 1960–1972, Harold W. Stanley and Richard G. Niemi, *Vital Statistics on American Politics, 2005–2006* (Washington, DC: CQ Press, 2001), p. 122; for 1976–2004, Marjorie Connelly, "How Americans Voted: A Political Portrait," *New York Times*, November 7, 2004, sec. 4, p. 4.

Note: Independent candidates were George Wallace in 1968, John Anderson in 1980, Ross Perot in 1992 and 1996, and Ralph Nader in 2000.

kept a distinctive orientation, which appears to favor liberal Democrats more than conservative Republicans. In 1988, the gender gap was only four points according to the Gallup poll, six or seven points according to the National Election Survey, CBS/*New York Times*, and NBC/*Wall Street Journal*, or ten points according to CNN/*Los Angeles Times* figures.[19] In 1992, 58 percent of Bill Clinton's vote came from women, but only 52 percent of Bush voters were women. In 1996 the gender gap widened. Among women, Clinton won a sixteen-point landslide, but Bob Dole actually maintained a slim plurality among men. The 2000 election produced a record gender gap: Al Gore carried the women's vote by eleven percentage points, but lost among men to George W. Bush by the same margin. In 2004, however, the difference between the sexes appeared to narrow a bit, with exit polls showing only a seven-point gap in the presidential vote between men and women.[20]

The case of the "women's vote" should alert us to some of the complexities of group interest. Not all women are the same: richer women are more Republican and poorer women more Democratic, just like men. In addition, single women, whether never married, divorced, or widowed, are more Democratic than married women.[21] Group memberships do not necessarily organize voters along a single dimension. The "interests" of a given group may be of greatest interest to only a subset of members. Thus the failed Equal Rights Amendment, a "women's issue" in the 1970s, was of greatest importance to highly educated women. A difference between men and women may also reflect not failure in appealing to one but success at appealing to the other. Thus there can be "women's" issues such as abortion and "men's" issues such as gun control for hunters, and what can be read as a defection of women from the Republicans may equally mean a defection of men from the Democrats.[22] Moreover, a difference in one election may or may not prefigure a permanent difference in basic coalitions.

Democratic candidates have a problem attracting white men and Republicans have a problem attracting women in general. There is no doubt about the numbers, only about the explanation. It is possible that the egalitarian bent of the Democratic Party has appealed to women and repelled men. The argument for this view would be that Democrats include women among the deprived minorities for whom affirmative discrimination is in order, leaving white males above the poverty line as the residual category who must help all the rest. The Republican Party's emphasis on opportunity rather than on more equal outcomes, by contrast, leaves the existing status or privileges of white and more affluent men untouched. In a corresponding manner, white women of low income may see the Democratic Party as providing them with concrete benefits, while middle- and upper-middle-income women, many of them influenced by the feminist movement, may see Republicans as opposed to their views on social issues, such as affirmative action and abortion.[23] As Ethel Klein says, "surveys indicate that women tend to be more liberal than men on a variety of issues, including defense, environmental protection, social services, women's rights, and economic security."[24] Women are more concerned with egalitarian issues—fairness to the poor, unemployment—and less likely than men to support defense spending.[25] If defense spending is seen as taking away from social welfare, the contrast increases.

"SPECIAL" INTERESTS AND PUBLIC INTEREST GROUPS

Is there any difference between interest groups, as we have described them here, and the "special" interests that attract so much criticism? Not as far as we can tell. Americans have always organized themselves into interest groups. Groups may have interests that are broad or narrow, but it is hard to see why interests that are narrow, and therefore presumably more "special," are any less legitimate than broad interests, which presumably require more common resources to satisfy. The language of political competition in American elections frequently requires political actors to disparage the claims of others by labeling them "special" interests and therefore some-how not worthy of consideration. "We" are presumably "the people" and "they" are "special interests." But of course the "people" have interests too. In a democracy, leaders are supposed to inform themselves about and sympathize with the policies that people want. Paying attention to these concerns of the people looks to us very much like attending to the needs of special interests.

The rise of rhetoric stigmatizing interests as "special" interests is in part the result of the rise of vocal and deeply concerned groups claiming to represent the "public" interest rather than the private or pecuniary interests of their members. Although interest groups in the past have differed over policy, they have not (at least since the acceptance of industrial unions in the 1930s and African American organizations in the 1960s) denied the rights of opponents to advocate their policy preferences. But, in one significant respect, that is no longer true. "Public interest" lobbies have attacked the legitimacy of "private interest" groups. Political parties, labor unions, trade associations, and religious groups are examples of such private interest groups, intermediary organizations that link citizens and their government. Many are indeed "special interest" groups—groups, that is, with special interests in public policy. Part of the program of public interest groups such as Common Cause or Ralph Nader's various organizations is to reduce the power of private, special interests and substitute their own services as intermediary organizations. Typically, public interest groups have fewer—sometimes vastly fewer—members than private interest groups.[26] They rely on journalists, newsletters, and the Internet to carry their messages to the population at large, and their success is an indication of the extent to which American voters now rely on mass media rather than group membership to obtain their political orientations and opinions.

A remarkable example of the ways in which the mass media have, to a certain extent, trans-formed the interest-group environment of elections is the rise of radio talk shows as instruments for the crystallization of political opinions. Radio talk show hosts with compelling personalities—the conservative Rush Limbaugh seems to have been the most popular recent example—can over a relatively short period of time mobilize strong expressions of opinion by many listeners and callers, in effect creating interest groups out of thin air by giving voice mainly to exasperated antigovernment and other negative sentiments. Limbaugh has an estimated 20 million listeners each week. His books have sold millions of copies.[27] Political leaders and opinion leaders who write for the news media are increasingly persuaded that he and others like him have touched a chord of real feeling in the American populace.

Laws have been passed and constitutional amendments proposed by public interest groups that restrict the amounts of money unions and corporations can contribute to political campaigns and use in lobbying. On the whole, however, these laws have been unsuccessful in curbing interest-group activity. What has happened is that interest groups have found new ways within the law to advance their interests. One such device is the political action committee (PAC), an organization devoted to the disbursement of campaign money from interest groups to candidates. From 1974 to 1982 the number of political action committees organized by business and unions more than

TABLE 2.6 The Rise of Political Action Committees (PACS), 1974–2004

Year	Corporate	Labor	Professional Groups	Cooperatives	Corporation Without Stock	Nonconnected	Total
1974	89	201	318	–	–	–	608
1975	139	226	357	–	–	–	722
1976	433	224	489	–	–	–	1,146
1977	550	234	438	8	20	110	1,360
1978	785	217	453	12	24	162	1,653
1979	950	240	514	17	32	247	2,000
1980	1,206	297	576	42	56	374	2,551
1981	1,329	318	614	41	68	531	2,901
1982	1,469	380	649	47	103	723	3,371
1983	1,538	378	643	51	122	793	3,525
1984	1,682	394	698	52	130	1,053	4,009
1985	1,710	388	695	54	142	1,003	3,992
1986	1,744	384	745	56	151	1,077	4,157
1987	1,775	364	865	59	145	957	4,165
1988	1,816	354	786	59	138	1,115	4,268
1989	1,796	349	777	59	137	1,060	4,178
1990	1,795	346	774	59	136	1,062	4,172
1991	1,738	338	742	57	136	1,083	4,094
1992	1,735	347	770	56	142	1,145	4,195
1993	1,789	337	761	56	146	1,121	4,210
1994	1,660	333	792	53	136	980	3,954
1995	1,674	334	815	44	129	1,020	4,016
1996	1,642	332	838	41	123	1,103	4,079
1997	1,597	332	825	42	117	931	3,844
1998	1,567	321	821	39	115	935	3,798
1999	1,548	318	844	38	115	972	3,835
2000	1,545	317	860	41	118	1,026	3,907
2001	1,508	316	891	41	116	1,019	3,891
2002	1,528	320	975	39	110	1,055	4,027
2003	1,538	310	884	35	102	999	3,868
2004	1,622	306	900	34	99	1,223	4,184

Source: Harold W. Stanley and Richard G. Niemi, *Vital Statistics on American Politics, 2005–2006* (Washington, DC: CQ Press, 2005), p. 101.

Note: Nonconnected PACs do not have a sponsoring organization.

quadrupled, increasing from 608 to 2,601; in the next six years, PACs of all types (including those unconnected to business and unions) rose to a total of 4,268 in 1988. (See table 2.6.) The number of PACs has dropped slightly since then, to 4,184 in 2004. The bulk of the original increase was accounted for by the rise in corporate PACs from only 89 in 1974 to 1,816 in 1988, but the number of these corporate PACs has slightly declined in the last twenty years, reaching a total of 1,622 in 2004.[28]

PACs are created to collect and disburse political contributions. They must contribute to more than one candidate, and the amount they may give to any one candidate is limited. In 1976, amendments to the Federal Election Campaign Act enabled individual companies or labor unions to establish multiple PACs, thus multiplying the amount of money they could funnel to any single candidate. Surprisingly, corporate PACs did not originally favor Republican campaigns as much as might be expected. Corporate PACs usually support incumbents over challengers, and for much of the 1970s and 1980s, Democratic officeholders outnumbered Republicans at both the federal and state levels. Accordingly, they reaped contributions from corporate PACs.[29] Since the Republican gains of the 1990s, corporate PAC contributions have favored the GOP.[30]

While an individual citizen is prohibited from contributing more than about $100,000 to federal candidates during any two-year election cycle, the Supreme Court decision in *Buckley v. Valeo* (1976) removed any such restrictions from PACs. Thus, "a corporate or union political action committee can collect donations and contribute an unlimited sum of money to unspecified numbers of candidates or committees so long as no single contribution exceeds $5,000."[31] In addition, once a PAC "contributes to five or more federal candidates, [it] can make unlimited independent expenditures on behalf of candidates or parties" (e.g., advertising on behalf of a candidate independent of that candidate's campaign in print or electronic media).[32] Not surprisingly, prospective presidential candidates themselves now organize PACs as a way of developing political alliances.

The rise of PACs to prominence is an ironic result of misplaced idealism. In the 1950s, reformers thought that it would be a good idea if local parties, which were held together mostly through jobs and sociability, were employed for more idealistic uses. It was thought that the replacement of a politics of patronage with a politics of issues would lead to a form of responsible party government in which informed activists could hold public officials accountable for their policy positions.[33] As government grew, however, two things happened: Business corporations, concerned about what government was doing to them, founded or reinvigorated their own interest groups, and other citizens formed and joined new groups to press their particular concerns. Instead of the integration and strengthening of parties that result in party government, parties were weakened. The weakening of parties facilitated fragmentation into a system dominated by what are called "single-issue special interest groups," groups such as those concerned to support or oppose issues like gun control or abortion. The emphasis on issues has led to fragmentation, manifested in the explosive growth of political action committees.

A second irony is that the PACs, now a leading source of political finance, were created in response to congressional efforts to restrict the role of money in elections. In 1943, Congress, following up an earlier law against corporate spending, forbade direct spending on elections by labor unions. Soon thereafter, the more militant of the union federations, the Congress of Industrial Organizations (CIO), formed a political action committee financed by a separate fund collected from its membership, as well as a National Citizen's Action Committee to solicit contributions from the community at large. When the labor federations merged in 1955, the new AFL-CIO created its own Committee on Political Education (COPE) to collect and inject money into campaigns. COPE is commonly regarded as the model of the modern PAC.[34]

But that was only the beginning. Government intervened again in 1971, 1974, and 1976 with the passage of the Federal Election Campaign Act (FECA) and subsequent amendments. By limiting the amount of money any individual or company could contribute, FECA reduced the role of large contributors and at the same time gave incentives for the formation of groups of small contributors. Once the courts decided that money raised and spent in politics was protected under the First Amendment as a necessary means to facilitate political speech and expression, the way was open for committees to proliferate, all concentrating on the issues and candidates of their choice.[35] PACs became a rival to political parties in support of candidates but without any obligations to govern or to appeal broadly to electorates. The Bipartisan Campaign Reform Act (BCRA) of 2002, popularly known as the McCain-Feingold law, placed strict limitations on parties' ability to spend on behalf of candidates, further increasing the comparative influence of PACs in American elections.

Public interest lobbies, which represent not direct material interests as corporations and unions do but "issue" interests such as tort reform[36] and reform of voting laws, have also sought to weaken the power of party leaders and strong party identifiers and to strengthen citizens who are weakly identified with parties and who emerge briefly during a particular election campaign or in response to a current issue. The stress on ease of entry into internal party affairs—more primaries, more conferences, more frequent and more open elections to party bodies—given the fact that party membership occurs in the first place by self-activation, leads to the domination of parties by activists who have time and education and are able to take the trouble to go to meetings. What kinds of people have these characteristics? Among others, they are the middle- and upper-middle-class professionals who predominate in supporting Common Cause, Nader's Raiders, and other public interest lobbies. Thus, among interest groups, if money matters less as a resource, business matters less; if time and talk and education matter more, ordinary workers matter less. As leaders of labor, business, and the parties lose power, organizers of public interest lobbies gain. These public interest lobbies are not necessarily all on one side of the ideological spectrum. People who defend corporate capitalism as well as those who attack it can organize in the public interest. And they do.

Two advantages have helped public interest groups expand their influence. One is a product of modern technology and the other has been generated by government. The use of computerized mailing lists and communication via the Internet has permitted these groups to tap contributions from large numbers of people who do not otherwise participate directly in group activities but receive mail and e-mail and thus become privileged spectators to group leaders' battles over public policy. This opportunity for vicarious participation not only generates ready cash but also simplifies somewhat the tasks of leadership. Instead of having to satisfy an active membership that might make diverse or contradictory demands, only the top leadership of public interest groups need be consulted. Leaders of public interest groups are frequently poorly paid, accepting low income as a sacrifice for their cause, but they exercise strong influence on the groups they lead.

The second advantage is that people who contribute to public interest groups are entitled to count these monies as tax-deductible. When the group wishes to undertake activities incompatible with eligibility for deduction, it often establishes a separate educational or litigating arm that can receive non-tax-deductible contributions. Without tax deductibility, the survival of some of these groups would be in doubt. The tradeoff is that they are required to engage in educational activities rather than overt lobbying, even though this may be a distinction without a difference. In addition, some of these groups achieve a status as legally authorized interveners before regulatory commissions, a role that entitles them to payment for their activity. In this sense, public interest groups are sometimes partially subsidized by government.

POLITICAL PARTIES AS ORGANIZATIONS

A third aspect of the social framework, along with voters and interest groups, that will help us account for the strategies of participants in presidential elections is the nature of political parties in this country. Here we discuss parties as organizations rather than as symbols for voters.

Party organizations are composed of three basic groups. First, professional employees of the party at the national and state levels staff the party offices and perform tasks on behalf of the party. Second, candidates and elected officials affiliated with the party carry the party label when they run for public office. Third, party activists are involved in party activities such as candidate recruitment, fundraising, and getting out the vote, but are not themselves candidates or full-time employees of the party. Each group plays a different role in party activities, and sometimes their interests conflict.

The primary goal of party professionals is to run an organization that will maintain or increase the power of the party. We define power in this situation as the ability to influence decisions made by government. Parties obtain this power by helping to elect individuals affiliated with their organization and through control of the appointive jobs (patronage) elected officials ordinarily bestow on members of their own party.[37] For party representatives—candidates and elected officials—and party activists, however, increasing the power of the party as an organization is often a secondary goal; other interests may be more important.

Candidates and elected officials are managing their own careers; their primary goal is most often personal success, both in the campaign and in governing. It used to be true that elected officials depended heavily on parties for the achievement of both these goals, but this dependency has decreased in recent years. This can be observed in such matters as the decline in the effect of "presidential coattails," whereby popular presidential candidates bring supporters out to vote who also vote for other candidates of their party. Voters are now more willing to "split tickets"— vote for representatives of different parties for different offices—and they are also more likely to view candidates as individuals than simply as representatives of a given party. Candidates for Congress, for example, usually build up their own political bases separate from support for the party and rely on these personal constituencies when running for reelection.[38]

On the national level, the rise of the primary system as a means for selecting presidential nominees (see table 2.7) has meant a corresponding decline in the candidates' reliance on traditional—especially state—party organizations. In order to win a party's nomination at the national convention, presidential hopefuls used to court the leaders of state party delegations, forging relationships with these party professionals to secure the votes of the state's delegates. In modern campaigns, state party bosses do not decide how their delegations will vote; instead, state delegates are pledged to candidates according to the results of the primary election's popular vote in their state. Aspiring presidential nominees thus spend time in states courting primary voters, not party officials, and their success is more closely tied to their personal popularity than to the support of the local party leadership. To be sure, candidates still covet the support of party

TABLE 2.7 The Growth of Presidential Primaries

	Democrats		Republicans	
Year	Number of Primaries	Percentage of Delegates Selected in Primaries	Number of Primaries	Percentage of Delegates Selected in Primaries
1960	16	38.3	15	38.6
1964	16	45.7	16	45.6
1968	15	40.2	15	38.1
1972	21	65.3	20	56.8
1976	27	76.0	26	71.0
1980	34	71.8	34	76.0
1984	29	52.4	25	71.0
1988	36	66.6	36	76.9
1992	39	66.9	38	83.9
1996	35	65.3	42	84.6
2000	40	64.6	43	83.8
2004	38	83.2	27	56.9

Source: Harold W. Stanley and Richard G. Niemi, *Vital Statistics on American Politics, 2005–2006* (Washington, DC: CQ Press, 2005), p. 66.

Note: Many states cancelled their Republican presidential primaries in 2004 because George W. Bush was unopposed for the party's nomination.

officials and other notables, but now those endorsements are valuable indirectly as tools to raise money (which is used to advertise to primary electorates) and to impress reporters (in order to obtain favorable coverage, and therefore win votes in primaries).[39]

Thus, party professionals cannot always count on their party's candidates to share the goals of the central organization. What might be the most effective strategy for a candidate to adopt in a given campaign or legislative situation may not fit with the party's overall plan or policy platform. Conflicts are certain to arise. Aware of this, party organizations have developed strategies aimed at keeping candidates and elected officials loyal to their goals.

Most significant is the fundraising that national party organizations perform in order to spend money on behalf of the party's candidates for the presidency and other federal offices. The Republican National Committee (RNC), under Chairman William Brock, began in the late 1970s to raise large sums of money from a broad network of individual donors to provide aid to state parties and to help candidates and state parties professionalize their operations.[40] The Democratic National Committee (DNC), more haltingly and less successfully, began to follow suit. This process was accelerated when the Supreme Court ruled in the case of *Colorado Republican Campaign Committee v. Federal Election Commission* in June 1996 that the First Amendment protected the right of political parties to campaign on behalf of their candidates and policy positions. In 2002, Congress raised the limit on individual contributions to national party committees from $20,000 to $25,000 per year, and indexed it to increases over time in the national cost of living (so that the limit on individual contributions to parties is $26,700 in

TABLE 2.8 The Rise of National Party Fundraising

Presidential Election Cycle	Democratic Party Funds Raised (in millions of dollars)	Republican Party Funds Raised (in millions of dollars)	Total
1983–1984	84.4	289.0	373.4
1987–1988	116.1	257.5	373.6
1991–1992	163.3	264.9	428.2
1995–1996	221.6	416.5	638.1
1999–2000	275.2	465.8	741.0
2003–2004	678.8	782.4	1,461.2

Source: Harold W. Stanley and Richard G. Niemi, *Vital Statistics on American Politics, 2001–2002* (Washington DC: CQ Press, 2001), p. 97; Stanley and Niemi, *Vital Statistics on American Politics, 2005–2006* (Washington, DC: CQ Press, 2005), p. 98.

2006). As table 2.8 makes clear, the growth in fundraising by the national party committees (the DNC, RNC, and House and Senate campaign committees on both sides) has increased exponentially over the past few presidential election cycles, nearly doubling between 2000 and 2004 alone.

Conflicts can also occur between party professionals and party activists—those individuals who make up the volunteer force of the party and a portion of the delegates to the national conventions. Party activists are often primarily concerned with questions of policy; these individuals we refer to as "purists." Purists wish their views to be put forth by the parties without much equivocation or compromise, and although they otherwise seek to win elections, they do not care to do this at the expense of self-expression.[41] In the purist conception of things, a party convention, rather than being a place where a party meets to choose candidates who can win elections by pleasing voters, becomes a site for passing resolutions and for finding a candidate who will embody the message delegates seek to express. In short, purists support parties of advocacy.

Party professionals are not indifferent to questions of policy, but, as noted earlier, their primary concern is usually getting their candidates into office and keeping them there. Party leaders are less concerned with policies in the abstract than as a means to the end of officeholding. If new policies help win elections, they are for them; if they help lose elections, they are against them. If officeholders are popular, party leaders have to accept them; if they are unpopular, threatening to bring the party into disrepute, party leaders will turn against them.

This attitude shapes the way in which parties behave. On the one hand, they must satisfy their activists and interest-group supporters by committing, or appearing to commit, to policies of concern to them. On the other hand, they are trying to lure enough people uncommitted on these policies in order to win the election. In a close election, the ability of a party to increase its support within one critical electoral group from, say, 20 to 30 percent may be crucial, even though that group still votes overwhelmingly for the opposition. The strategic implications of these remarks color all of national campaign politics: when they are trying to win, the parties try to do things that will please the groups consistently allied to them without unduly alienating other voters.

The temptation for political parties to avoid specific policy commitments in many areas, therefore, is very great. The American population is so extraordinarily varied—crisscrossed by numerous economic, religious, ethnic, racial, sectional, and occupational ties—that it is exceedingly difficult to guess at the total distribution of policy preferences in the population at any one time. Even where issues like Social Security and unemployment compensation appear to be settled, many questions remain. Should benefits be taxed or the rules of eligibility altered? Should Social Security be partially converted to private accounts?

It is even more difficult to predict how these aggregations of actual and potential interest groups might react to shifts in party policy positions, and still more hazardous to prophesy what different policy commitments might do to the margin of votes required for victory. This pervasive problem of uncertainty makes the calculations of gain from changes in policies both difficult and risky and suggests that the interests of parties and candidates frequently are best served by vague, ambiguous, or contradictory policy statements that will be unlikely to offend anyone. The advantages of vagueness about policy are strengthened by the facts that most citizens are not interested in policy or are narrowly focused on a small number of issues and that only a few groups demand many specific policy commitments from their parties and candidates.

Yet, despite all this, political leaders and parties do, at times, make policy commitments that are surprisingly precise, specific, and logically consistent. Thus we must go beyond our consideration of why the parties sometimes blur issues and avoid commitments to ask why they often commit themselves to policies more readily than their interest in acquiring or retaining office would seem to require.

Part of the answer may arise from the fact that the parties depend on their party activists and that many of these activists, especially the purists among them, demand specific policy commitments from the party. The activists are the heart of any party organization; they are the volunteers for campaigns, the people who stimulate participation in their communities, and most likely they are the party's strongest supporters and most dependable voters. Unlike most voters, who are otherwise largely disengaged from politics, activists are likely to have elaborate political opinions and preferences and to act on them even when an election is not imminent. Their desires to make these preferences internally consistent and consistent with the preferences of their party certainly lead to demands on the party leadership for policy positions that are reasonably clear and forthright.[42]

Furthermore, the interest groups most closely allied with each party make policy demands that parties must to some extent meet. Even more than voters, who are generally interested at most in only a few specific policies, interest-group leaders and their full-time bureaucracies are manifestly concerned citizens and often party activists as well. If they feel that the interests they represent are being harmed, they may so inform their members or even attempt to withdraw support from the party at a particular election. Should voters find that groups with which they identify are opposed to the party with which they identify, they may temporarily support the opposition party, or, more likely, they may withdraw from participation and not vote at all. Consequently, the party finds that it risks losing elections by ignoring the demands of interest groups, especially those that are part of the party base. The demands of many of these groups conflict, however. If unions object to party or candidate advocacy of antipollution devices on automobiles because they increase costs and decrease car sales, for example, labor and environmental groups cannot both be equally satisfied. If the costs of increasing worker safety compete with the costs of welfare payments, both cannot be obtained at the same level. Therefore, the parties may attempt to mediate among interest groups, hoping to strike compromises that, though they give no one group everything, give something to as many groups as they can. The increasing number of single-issue groups makes mediation more difficult. Many Democratic candidates have attempted to court Catholic bishops on the basis of their shared commitment to social welfare programs, only to endure sharp criticism for the politicians' opposition to the prohibition of abortion. Several bishops announced in 2004 that they would deny Democratic candidate John Kerry, a practicing Catholic, the rite of communion in their dioceses owing to his pro-choice stance.[43]

The contradictory pulls of vagueness and specificity are well exemplified in Jimmy Carter's successful 1976 campaign. He slid by such potentially divisive issues as amnesty for draft evaders or resisters—"a classic example of how to say something and not piss off people," as his press adviser Jody Powell put it—by saying he favored pardons, which implied wrong had been done but had been forgiven. On the proposed B-1 bomber, Carter said the decision should be made by the next president, leaving listeners to guess what he might do. On abortion, he was personally opposed but fudged on whether he believed government should outlaw the practice. This led a Carter speechwriter to quit with a public blast, declaring, "I am not sure what you believe in other than yourself." Yet, time after time, as in his proposal for a more progressive income tax or for a ten-cent-a-gallon duty on imported oil, candidate Carter was attacked when he became specific. His pollster, Pat Caddell, attempted to resolve the dilemma during the campaign:

> We have passed the point when we can simply avoid at least the semblance of substance. This does not mean the need to outline minute, exact details. We all agree that such a course could be disastrous. However, the appearance of substance does not require this. It requires a few broad, specific examples that support a point.[44]

In addition to the distinctions between professionals, candidates, and activists, party organizations are further divided between state organizations and national organizations, and this division provides additional occasions for conflict and disunity. The national organization concerns itself primarily with national elections, and thus is interested above all in promoting unity and support for national party candidates. State organizations devote themselves primarily to state elections, pursuing state party interests, and, to a decreasing extent, building a state base for national party activities.

On most matters, the national party organizations have difficulty producing uniformity among the states because parties are regulated primarily by state, not federal, law and respond to more localized sentiments. Furthermore, state organizations follow no single organizational pattern. Sometimes elected state chief executives run them; sometimes they are run by coalitions of party chieftains representing the local organizations of several large cities or counties. Sometimes party officials and elected officials work cooperatively; sometimes they work at cross-purposes. Sometimes the state may have little party organization or significant activity at all in one party, sometimes in both. The best evidence suggests the number of states with permanent headquarters with professional staff who recruit candidates, raise money, and help campaigns is growing.[45] State party chairs now have seats on the national committees. They mediate between national rules and state practices. They are conduits for the growing services—recruitment, polling, fundraising, issue development, vote mobilization—provided by the national parties.

What at the national level used to be a loose federation of state parties is slowly being converted, by changes in party rules and by judicial decisions, into a somewhat more centralized structure. Thus our national parties combine elements of both decentralization and centralization. The most obvious indicator of continuing decentralization is that national parties are organized on a geographical basis with the state units as the constituent elements. The party organizations from different states meet formally by sending delegates to national committee meetings, and most important, by coming together every four years at national conventions to nominate a president.

The strongest indicators of nationalization are the guidelines set out at the national level, which, especially for Democrats, are becoming increasingly important in determining who these delegates will be.[46] Still, it is the states that choose their representatives to national party bodies; the national committees and conventions do not choose officers of state parties. On the Democratic side, until the 1980s, the permanent national party organization was not in a position to help the state parties, having neither the funds nor the personnel nor the contacts to contribute substantially to the nomination or election of candidates for Congress or local offices, who must run within state boundaries. After the Republican victories in the 1980 election, the Democratic National Committee and the Democratic Congressional Campaign Committee and Senatorial Campaign Committee began to follow the lead of the GOP and provide campaign services. Both parties' national organizations now have sizable staffs who recommend effective campaign managers, consultants, pollsters, and accountants, going so far as to buy blocks of services that can then be allocated to close races. In addition, they assist state parties and candidate campaigns with fundraising contacts, political strategy, and media relations.[47] National party committees may also spend unlimited amounts of money on behalf of candidates for the presidency and other offices, as long as the expenditures are formally uncoordinated with the candidates' own campaigns.

On the other hand, when and where they are strong enough, state parties have substantial powers enabling them to claim a share in making national policy and to be influential in the nomination and election of members of Congress. The states have their own sources of patronage, as well as a share in federal patronage through their congressional representatives and senators (when they are of the president's party). The very fact that the states are each separate constitutional entities engenders a drive for autonomy as those who hold places of importance in the state governments and parties seek to protect their jurisdictions, much as the framers of the Constitution hoped they would. This is an example of federalism and it is much more than a legal fact. The states have great vitality because there exist distinct, numerous, and vigorous ethnic, religious, racial, and economic groups that demand separate recognition and that are disproportionately located in specific geographic areas. State organizations, therefore, become infused with the purposes of groups that use their state parties for the recognition and enhancement of their separate identities and needs. Italian Americans in Rhode Island, Jews and African Americans in New York, dairy farmers in Wisconsin, labor unions in Michigan, wheat growers in Kansas, gay rights advocates in California, and many others form the building blocks of unique political cultures state by state and make the idea of a decentralized party system a reality.[48]

Each of the state parties is composed of people with somewhat different interests to protect and demands to make. Control over state parties must be exercised from within each state, since the various states do not control one another and the national party exercises only partial control.

This is the essence of what is meant by a decentralized party system in which power is dispersed among many independent state bodies.

THIRD PARTIES

The unusual success of independent candidate Ross Perot in attracting support in the 1992 presidential election (he received nearly 20 million votes) added a dimension to the calculations of candidates of the two major parties because each had to figure out whom the third candidate hurt the most. It is somewhat misleading to refer to candidates such as Perot in 1992 as constituting third parties, since the organizational basis of his candidacy was a membership organization devoted only to him. This differs from a proper political party, which also runs candidates for lesser offices.[49]

In 1992 Perot used his enormous personal financial resources to support only one candidacy, his own, supplemented by a last-minute choice of retired Admiral James Stockdale as a vice-presidential running mate. There was no contest among alternatives or any decision-making process that might have led to the selection of somebody other than Perot as the candidate of his front group, United We Stand America. So he was not the founder of a third party so much as a self-promoter. This seems, more often than not, to be the case with third-party candidates; 74 percent of presidential "third parties" have persisted long enough to contest only two elections and over half contest only one, suggesting that they are built around the easily exhausted presidential aspirations of individuals, rather than longer-term party-building activities.[50]

Presidential candidates from minor parties appear on the ballot in many states, although it is rare for voters to vote for them. In New York what was once a bona fide third party, the Liberal Party, intimately connected with New York City's garment trade unions, ran candidates for local political office beginning in 1944. Many voters in the city voted on the Liberal ballot line, usually for the Democratic presidential candidate, who customarily received the endorsement of Liberal Party leaders.[51] Third party candidates have a long record of occasional success in other races; the most prominent recent example, Reform Party candidate Jesse Ventura, was elected governor of Minnesota in 1998.[52] In recent years, however, such successes have reflected individual efforts, without long-term consequences in those states.

The Perot candidacy in 1992 was kept afloat initially by the novelty value of his appearance on the scene. Journalists were impressed by his willingness to spend large amounts of his seemingly unlimited personal fortune on his own behalf, purchasing the services of such established campaign managers as Hamilton Jordan, Jimmy Carter's former chief of staff, and veteran Republican consultant Ed Rollins. So Perot was taken "seriously" by the news media, and this, as well as his television advertisements, kept his candidacy afloat for a while. In the end, he attracted a substantial number of votes, and so it is worthwhile to consider what unusual factors might have set his candidacy apart from other recent third-party candidates.

Unlike southern candidates George Wallace in 1968 and Strom Thurmond in 1948, Perot's candidacy had no particular regional base. This precluded the possibility of his winning votes in the electoral college, which requires candidates to finish first in a state. A Texan, Perot was thought to be just barely plausible as a winner there in a three-way race. This would not have been a negligible achievement, given the size of the Texas electoral vote, but at a maximum it would have spoiled the result for one or the other of the major parties rather than contribute

FIGURE 2.1   Debates Diminish Support for Anderson, 1980, and Boost Perot, 1992

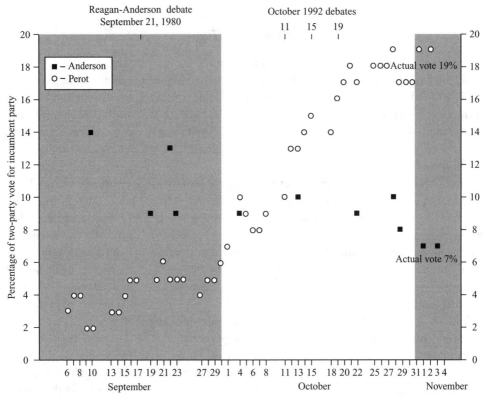

Sources: Perot data: Peter Goldman, Thomas M. DeFrank, Mark Miller, Andrew Murr, and Tom Mathews, *Quest for the Presidency, 1992* (College Station: Texas A&M University Press, 1994), 733–34; Anderson data: Roper Center, "Public Opinion On-Line," various issues.

to a likely winning coalition for Perot. It was assumed that the main loser would be Republican George H. W. Bush, whom Perot gave signs of personally disliking.[53]

Thus it was something of a puzzle that the Bush campaign calculated that Perot was hurting Democratic nominee Bill Clinton more and took steps behind the scenes to assure that Perot would be treated as a serious contender by being included in the televised series of debates organized by the bipartisan Commission on Presidential Debates. Until this eccentric decision, Perot's public opinion ratings had more or less tracked those of independent candidate John Anderson in 1980 (see figure 2.1), who, after a favorable spurt of early publicity, faded when President Carter refused to accord him parity in the debates of that year.[54] As John Zaller shows, press coverage of Perot became quite negative after he was in the race for a while, and so the decision in the Bush camp to refuse to participate in the debates without Perot was a major factor in keeping Perot's candidacy alive.[55]

Perot ended up with an extraordinary 19 percent of the popular vote in 1992, drawn from disgruntled voters from many segments of the population, and about equally from both Bush and Clinton.[56] His vote was not widely interpreted as approval of Perot so much as a conveniently visible place to park the negative feelings that the campaign had generated about both major candidates. Perot ran again in 1996 as the standard-bearer of the Reform Party and received only 9 percent of the vote; again, his candidacy did not appear to affect the outcome of the election.

It is frequently asserted, and frequently denied, that voters who vote for third parties are throwing away their vote. What is presumably meant is that voting for a third party means not voting for a potential winner of the election. But third party voters generally understand that they are not backing a winner but rather withholding their vote from a winner. They may hope that this sends a message of overall dissatisfaction with the main alternatives on offer, and hence this would not necessarily be regarded by the voter as a wasted vote.

Another way of determining whether an individual's vote is wasted is to ask who the voter's first choice is among the major party candidates, or who is the voter's second choice overall. If a third party vote contributes to the loss of that voter's second choice, and the victory of his or her third choice, then the vote has been thrown away. Thus in the 2000 election, Florida voters for Green Party nominee Ralph Nader who preferred Republican George W. Bush to Democrat Al Gore did not throw away their vote; Nader voters who preferred Gore to Bush did throw away their vote.

Most observers believe that Nader voters nationwide would have preferred Gore to Bush. So a Nader vote in any state carried by Gore would therefore not have been thrown away. But in a state like Florida, carried by Bush by 537 votes out of nearly 6 million cast, and where Nader received 97,488 votes, it is plausible to assume that the Nader vote was instrumental in defeating Gore and electing Bush. This reasoning lies behind the ironic suggestion that when Nader ran again in 2004 as an independent candidate he should have adopted the slogan "Four more years."[57]

Third-party candidacies can be seen to have a significant role in presidential elections. They can act as spoilers if they draw votes disproportionately from one major side or the other. They can focus discontent. They can raise issues.[58] But because of the rules for counting votes in the electoral college, the electoral system is stacked strongly against third-party candidates actually winning the presidency.[59]

THREE

RULES AND RESOURCES

RULES: THE ELECTORAL COLLEGE

American presidential elections are not decided directly by national popular vote. Instead, popular votes are collected within each state, and each state casts all of its electoral votes for the candidate receiving the most individual votes within the state. This "winner take all, loser take nothing" approach is called a "unit rule."[1] Later in this book we consider whether votes ought to be counted in this manner. For the moment, however, we concentrate on how the electoral college works, and why it matters.

Each state is allowed as many electoral votes as it has senators and representatives in Congress. Thus all states, no matter how small, have at least three electoral votes. This means that sparsely populated states are overrepresented in the electoral college. In 2004, 243,428 voters in Wyoming influenced the disposition of the state's three electoral votes, a ratio of one electoral vote for every 81,143 voters. In Wisconsin, on the other hand, 2,997,007 voters went to the polls and voted for ten electors, a ratio of one electoral vote for every 299,701 voters. In Florida, 7,609,810 voters for twenty-seven electors produced a ratio of one electoral vote for every 281,845 voters. One might conclude, therefore, that each voter in Wyoming had more than three times as much influence on the outcome of the 2004 election as each voter in Florida. But this is not entirely valid.

Why not? Because of the unit rule, which provides that the candidate having the most votes in a state receives the entire electoral vote of the state. This means that each Wyoming voter was influencing the disposition of all three of Wyoming's electoral votes, and each Florida voter was helping to decide the fate of all twenty-seven of Florida's votes. Ask any politician whether he or she would rather have three votes or twenty-seven—the answer is immediately apparent. Thus, unless the outcome in Florida is expected to be hopelessly one-sided, the Floridians get more attention from the campaigns, which means the candidates may promise more to Florida voters in aggregate even though each one of them does not matter so much. In fact, the present method of electing the president tends to give greater power to the large, populous states, not the small or empty states, because the big states can deliver to the winner large blocs of the votes needed to win.

Although it was true in the past that presidential nominees tended to come from populous, competitive states, this is no longer the case. The reason is that politicians, specifically the leaders of state parties, no longer control the nomination process. When they did, the size of the electoral vote in a candidate's home state mattered in their calculations. Ordinarily, candidates could be expected to carry their home states and therefore the bigger the state, the better. Since the reforms of the 1970s, however, candidates are selected by a series of primary elections in which whatever it is that sways primary election voters matters most of all: favorable publicity, not too much competition from others running in the same race, and ideological agreement with large groups of voters. These are some but probably not all the factors that may influence the outcome of presidential primaries. The adoption of the primary system has depressed the influence at the nomination stage of electoral college vote-counting rules. How votes are counted by the electoral college matters less to the political calculations of participants in the nomination process because, on the whole, it is more important for candidates to be popular in states that pick their delegates early in the election year than for them to be popular even in the largest states. This is a significant example of the way in which changing the rules of the game changes the chances for success of each and every player.

Once the party nominations are made, however, the varying strength of states in the electoral college matters a great deal for the strategies of presidential nominees seeking a majority of 270 electoral votes. They concentrate their campaigns in the big population centers, and, as politicians know, they stand or fall on the big-state votes.[2] In the weeks before the 2004 election, the Bush and Kerry campaigns identified the same set of states as highly competitive: Florida, Iowa, Michigan, Minnesota, Ohio, Pennsylvania, and Wisconsin. All except Iowa cast at least ten electoral votes. Campaign strategists targeted television advertisements and personal appearances by the candidates and their running mates to voters in these key "battleground" states while ignoring residents of states not considered competitive.[3] In previous elections, other campaigns have identified different states as potentially winnable. But the reason the electoral battleground is concentrated in the big states that might go either way is the unit rule of the electoral college.

THINKING ABOUT RESOURCES

In thinking about resources and their importance, it is necessary to distinguish between conditions that exist for the official candidates of the two major parties after they are nominated and the situation of prospective candidates—people who want the nomination of their party—during the prenomination period. Individual candidates before the nomination are pretty much on their own, and the way they look at resources is quite different from the way eventual successful party nominees do.

There are many resources that, at any given time, may be disproportionately available to Democrats and Republicans, or to different candidates. Possession of the presidential office, skill in organization, knowledge of substantive policies, a reputation for integrity, facility in speechmaking, ability to devise appealing campaign issues, personal wealth, stamina—all can be drawn on to good advantage in a presidential campaign. More resources are available to parties and candidates than any one book could deal with exhaustively. But some resources are obviously going to be more important than others, and the importance of different resources varies from occasion to occasion. It would be sensible to regard as especially important those resources that one side monopolizes—such as the presidency—and those resources that can easily be converted into other resources, or directly into public office—such as money, which can be used to buy competent staff, television time, and so on.

Although political resources are distributed unequally between the parties, in a competitive two-party system such as ours the inequalities rarely run all in the same direction. Sometimes Republican candidates reap the benefits; sometimes Democrats do. One result of these inequalities in access to different resources is that different strategies are more advantageous to each of the two parties, as we see when we examine the effects on election strategies of three resources commonly held to be extremely important: money, control over information, and the presidential office.

RESOURCES: MONEY

Presidential campaigns are terribly expensive. Radio and television advertising, travel for the candidate and campaign staff, mailings of campaign material, the salaries of consultants and advisers, office space and equipment, lawn signs and bumper stickers, taking polls, registering and mobilizing voters, and raising money itself—all cost a great deal of money.[4] In 2004, Republican George W. Bush's successful reelection campaign cost over $350 million. His Democratic rival, John Kerry, spent about $320 million, and other candidates for the Democratic nomination spent over $160 million in total.[5] Candidates for the Senate and House of Representatives collectively spent about $1.2 billion. In addition, the two major parties spent over $1.4 billion in 2004 in support of candidates at all levels of government.[6] The total amount of federal campaign spending exceeded $3.4 billion in 2004, not including additional independent expenditures made by outside groups (see table 3.1).[7] How do candidates for the presidency manage to raise such large sums in their quest for office?

In answering this question, we draw a sharp distinction between the prenomination period, when hopeful candidates are on their own and when finding money may prove to be a severe problem for some of them, contrasted with after party nominations take place, when large amounts of public financing, party spending, independent expenditures, and other factors come into the picture, shrinking the problem of the availability of money to manageable size for major-party nominees.

The Beverly Hills Primary

The primary source of money for a candidate seeking a party's nomination for president is the individual contributor. Party committees, an important source of income for candidates in the general election, do not give money to candidates for their presidential nomination, except, as Frank Sorauf points out, afterward, to help the party's nominee pay off debts incurred during the nomination campaign.[8] In addition, most political action committees (PACs) prefer to avoid prenomination campaigns and the high-risk politics associated with them.[9] The result is that

TABLE 3.1 Federal Campaign Spending, 1972–2004

Election	Spending by Presidential Candidates (Millions of Dollars)	Spending by Congressional Candidates (Millions of Dollars)	Spending by Parties (Millions of Dollars)	Total Federal Election Spending (Millions of Dollars)
1972	127	77	13	217
1976	118	115	46	279
1980	188	239	216	643
1984	194	374	420	988
1988	316	458	424	1,198
1992	323	680	488	1,491
1996	405	765	894	2,064
2000	520	1,006	1,190	2,716
2004	844	1,157	1,408	3,409

Source: Presidential candidate spending data from Herbert E. Alexander, *Financing the 1972 Election* (Lexington, MA: Lexington Books, 1976), pp. 85–87; Herbert E. Alexander, *Financing the 1976 Election* (Washington, DC: CQ Press, 1979), pp. 171–175; Herbert E. Alexander, *Financing the 1980 Election* (Lexington, MA: Lexington Books, 1983), pp. 113–116; Herbert E. Alexander and Brian A. Haggerty, *Financing the 1984 Election* (Lexington, MA: Lexington Books, 1987), pp. 85–87; Herbert E. Alexander and Monica Bauer, *Financing the 1988 Election* (Boulder, CO: Westview Press, 1991), p. 12; Herbert E. Alexander and Anthony Corrado, *Financing the 1992 Election* (Armonk, NY: M. E. Sharpe, 1995), p. 20; Federal Election Commission, "2004 Presidential Campaign Finance Activity Summarized," press release, February 3, 2005, available at http://www.fec.gov/press/press2005/20050203pressum/20050203pressum.html. Congressional candidate spending data from Herbert E. Alexander, "Spending in the 1996 Elections," in John C. Green, ed., *Financing the 1996 Election* (Armonk, NY: M. E. Sharpe, 1999), pp. 11–36, at 23; Federal Election Commission, "Congressional Candidates Spend $1.16 Billion During 2003–2004," press release, June 9, 2005, available at http://www.fec.gov/press/press2005/20050609candidate/20050609candidate.html. Party spending data from Alexander, *Financing the 1972 Election*, pp. 88–90; Alexander, *Financing the 1976 Election*, pp. 176–177, 360, 403; Alexander, *Financing the 1980 Election*, pp. 305, 311; Alexander and Haggerty, *Financing the 1984 Election*, p. 331; Alexander and Bauer, *Financing the 1988 Election*, p. 41; Federal Election Commission, "FEC Reports Major Increase in Party Activity for 1995-96," press release, March 19, 1997, available at http://www.fec.gov/press/press1997/ptyye1.htm; Federal Election Commission, "FEC Reports Increase in Party Fundraising for 2000," press release, May 15, 2001, available at http://www.fec.gov/press/press2001/051501partyfund/051501partyfund.html; Federal Election Commission, "Party Financial Activity Summarized for the 2004 Election Cycle," press release, March 2, 2005, available at http://www.fec.gov/press/press2005/20050302party/Party2004final.html.

Note: Figures correspond to the two-year federal election cycle ending in the year displayed above. Totals do not include convention costs or independent expenditures by organizations formally unaffiliated with the candidates and parties. Party spending includes expenditures by the national party and congressional campaign committees and federally regulated spending by state and local parties. It also includes "soft money" for the 1980–2000 period.

PAC contributions to candidates for presidential nominations are negligible—about $3 million in total in 2004, less than one half of one percent of the $674 million spent in the 2004 primary season.[10]

To fund their campaigns, candidates must go where the money is, organizing fundraising events in areas where large numbers of supporters will attend with checkbooks in hand. For Republicans, this means to Texas for oil money, to New York for corporate and Wall Street money, and to California. Democrats follow much the same track. The top five zip codes in the nation for political contributions of $200 or more during the 2004 election cycle were all located in Manhattan. Each of the top thirteen zip codes (and nineteen of the top twenty-three) came from the New York, Washington, or Los Angeles metropolitan areas.[11]

One especially well-documented path leads Democrats to southern California, home of the traditionally liberal entertainment industry. Beverly Hills's famous 90210 zip code ranked ninth in generosity to Democratic candidates in 2004, with the nearby Brentwood neighborhood of Los Angeles ranking twelfth. Former Governor Jimmy Carter of Georgia took this path in 1976 when he emerged as the Democrats' surprise nominee. Actor Warren Beatty organized a fundraising reception for Carter and invited fellow actors Sidney Poitier, Faye Dunaway, and Cybill Shepherd, director Robert Altman, musicians Paul Simon and Diana Ross, and *Playboy* founder Hugh Hefner.[12] In 1991, most of the Democratic candidates visited Hollywood early in the campaign. Arkansas Governor Bill Clinton came in October and November for events hosted by television producers Linda and Harry Thomason, Sony Pictures Entertainment chair Peter Guber, and former Columbia Pictures president Dawn Steel. Senator Bob Kerrey of Nebraska arrived in November, for a fundraiser organized by Fox chairman Barry Diller, a contact he had made through his highly publicized romantic relationship with actress Debra Winger. Senator Tom Harkin of Iowa benefited from events organized on his behalf by television personalities Roseanne Barr and Tom Arnold (who were married at the time), Ed Asner, and Steve Allen. Even former California Governor Jerry Brown, despite his self-imposed $100 contribution limit, held an event in Hollywood with actress Talia Shire and actor Martin Sheen present. The event, raising $40,000, was the Brown campaign's most lucrative.[13]

In 2004, the field of Democratic candidates seeking their party's presidential nomination relied on celebrity endorsements for both campaign funds and free publicity. Former Governor Howard Dean of Vermont received well-publicized support from actor and director Rob Reiner, who cochaired the Dean campaign in California; musicians David Crosby, Bonnie Raitt, and Phoebe Snow also organized a benefit concert on Dean's behalf.[14] Singer Tony Bennett performed at fundraisers for Representative Richard Gephardt of Missouri, while musicians Willie Nelson and Ani DiFranco campaigned for Representative Dennis Kucinich of Ohio.[15] Pop star Madonna invited retired General Wesley Clark to her home for a private interview, allowing his campaign to report proudly to the news media afterwards that she had been "very impressed" with the candidate.[16]

Candidates may also enjoy access to various natural constituencies. For example, then-Governor Clinton used his connections in Arkansas to raise over $2.5 million in 1992, a remarkable harvest from a state with a population of only 2.3 million. One event in Little Rock in late 1991 raised almost $1 million. Many local businesses helped organize Clinton fundraising events, no doubt mindful of the governor's control over the state's bond market, pension funds, and other regulated businesses. The Worthen National Bank of Arkansas established a credit line worth $3.5 million for the Clinton campaign. This helped tide the campaign over when allegations arose about Clinton's marital infidelity and avoidance of military service.[17]

These constituencies don't always deliver as expected. Former Massachusetts Senator Paul Tsongas found in 1992 that despite his strong connections to the Greek American fundraising network built by Massachusetts Governor Michael Dukakis during the 1988 election, the perception after Dukakis's loss to George H. W. Bush was that a Greek American could not be elected president. They were "traumatized," said Tsongas, and "for every dollar that Michael got, I get 10 cents." Tsongas's estimate was accurate: by September 1991, he had raised only $800,000, compared to the $8.1 million raised by Dukakis at the same point in the previous election cycle.[18]

Many candidates have resorted to campaign techniques designed to reach large numbers of individuals outside the traditional mechanism of fundraising events. The use of direct-mail campaigns has been particularly important. Traditionally the preserve of congressional candidates within their districts, the process of direct-mail solicitation was modernized by William Brock, chairman of the Republican National Committee in the 1970s. Brock used computers to generate lists of proven and potential contributors to the Republican national party organization. By the late 1970s, direct mail was bringing in 75 percent of the RNC's receipts, and it did not take the Democrats long to catch on.[19] Although direct-mail solicitation seemed to have declined as a source of money for the national parties by the late 1980s, it had nonetheless taken off as a means of fundraising for candidates in the prenomination phase of the presidential campaign. Massachusetts Governor Michael Dukakis raised $2.4 million in direct-mail contributions in 1988, and although one-third of this amount went toward paying for setting up his mail campaign, public matching funds brought net receipts up to $3.4 million.[20] Conservative commentator Pat Buchanan ran an extremely successful direct-mail campaign during his bid for the 1992 Republican nomination, with initial response rates of almost 14 percent for an average contribution of nearly $62, compared to more typical success rates of 3 percent and contributions of $20. Overall, Buchanan raised more than $4 million from direct mail, 85 percent of which was eligible for federal matching funds.[21]

Other creative campaign techniques besides direct-mail solicitation were used in 1992. Paul Tsongas, for example, ran a full back-page advertisement in the *Boston Globe* the week after his victory in the Democratic primary in New Hampshire, asking for contributions to his campaign. The ad cost $18,000 and raised $108,000.[22] Jerry Brown established a toll-free telephone number for people to make financial pledges to his campaign and used unconventional means to promote this device: an appearance on Howard Stern's syndicated radio show, for example, was particularly successful in yielding calls to the phone banks. Brown raised nearly $5.2 million by telephone, stimulating additional matching funds of $4.2 million. Despite its success, Brown's telephone campaign also illustrates one of the major difficulties inherent in attempts to raise money directly from the mass public—namely, overhead expense. A Brown adviser estimated that the campaign lost roughly one in every two potential contributors because of overcrowded telephone lines. At its peak, the Brown campaign could afford only eighty people staffing the phone banks, compared to the average of three thousand operators used for the telemarketing of consumer goods.[23]

More recently, primary candidates have discovered the value of the Internet in raising money from individuals across the country. Former Vermont Governor Howard Dean, in particular, benefited from an active online contingent of supporters during his bid for the 2004 Democratic nomination. At the peak of his candidacy, Dean's Web site generated about $150,000 per day in contributions, with few overhead expenses.[24] Taking a cue from Dean, Democratic nominee John Kerry also used the Internet to his advantage in 2004, raising about $82 million via his campaign web site—more than a third of his overall fundraising total. Kerry's success in attracting donations via the Web enabled him to compete financially with George W. Bush, who only took in about $16 million online out of the $270 million he raised in total from private contributions.[25]

The accumulation of money interacts with the events of the nomination process. As a candidate's defeats in state after state add up, credibility slips, and fundraising falls even as expenses mount. Tactical considerations become more and more important as dwindling resources limit the number of states that can be contested. For example, by March 3, 1992, the date of several state primaries, Nebraska Senator Bob Kerrey was forced by financial desperation to ignore the Maryland primary, to limit expenditures in Colorado to one thirty-second advertisement, to rely on personal appearances in Georgia to generate enough free press coverage to make up for his lack of any paid airtime, and to hope that $6,600 spent on radio ads in Idaho might influence the outcome in the state's low-turnout Democratic caucus. Not surprisingly, none of these tactics paid off, and Kerrey withdrew from the race for the Democratic nomination two days later.[26]

Kerrey's dilemma points to another tactical choice that the candidates must address: the extent to which they will allocate campaign funds to television and radio advertisements, or whether they prefer to spend their money on building a "ground" organization devoted to contacting and mobilizing potential voters in person or on the telephone, and making sure they turn out for primaries and caucuses. Obviously, candidates would like to be able to establish both types of campaigns in a state if possible, but funding limitations often require them to set priorities. Consider the position of former Massachusetts Senator Paul Tsongas in 1992. Having expended most of his available resources on his victory in the New Hampshire primary, he lacked the money to develop organizations in the states holding primaries two weeks later on March 3. He decided, therefore, to concentrate on Maryland, combining television ads with personal appearances and winning there with 40 percent of the vote. A television presence alone, however, was not enough to prevent solid defeats at the hands of Bill Clinton in Georgia and both Clinton and Jerry Brown in Colorado.[27] In 1996, on the Republican side, only Bob Dole was able to raise enough money to withstand setbacks without ending his campaign. By contrast, former Tennessee Governor Lamar Alexander's fundraising efforts were helped when he was perceived to have done well in the Iowa caucuses, but he could not raise money quickly enough to compete in the states after the New Hampshire primary; he had spent all of his resources in those two early contests.[28]

While presidential challengers cope with financial shortages and strategic dilemmas, incumbents, who are always well-funded and frequently unopposed for renomination, can use the primary period to stockpile campaign money until a nominee emerges in the other party. George H. W. Bush, for example, was able to attract to his 1992 reelection campaign some of the most prominent Republican fundraisers, such as Peter Terpeluk, a Washington lobbyist, Donald Bren, a Southern California developer, Lodwrick Cook, chairman of ARCO, and Henry Kravis, a Wall Street investment banker. Confident that President Bush would be renominated, they organized fundraising events in late 1991 that raised more than $1 million each. In the early stages of the 1992 campaign, the Bush organization already had thirty-eight national finance vice chairs.[29]

As a challenger in 1992, Bill Clinton was critical of such practices. As an incumbent in 1996, Clinton was, if anything, even more adept and innovative at turning the presidency into a fundraising tool. As Alison Mitchell reported in the *New York Times*:

> Mr. Clinton and Mr. Gore presided over unpublicized, small gatherings aimed at rewarding the largest donors with access to the highest echelons of power. Donors who gave roughly $50,000 or $100,000 to the Democratic Party could have dinner with the President in small groups of 10 or 20 in luxurious Washington hotels near the White House: the Jefferson, the Hay-Adams, and the Carlton.... Others were escorted in small groups to the Map Room in the White House residence for an hour long coffee with Mr. Clinton. Democrats say the President was host at an average of two White House coffees a week this [election] year for a mix of political activists and large donors.... Mr. Clinton occasionally played golf with a potential donor while other large givers were taken on overseas trips or invited to State Dinners. Some stayed overnight in the Lincoln Bedroom.[30]

Public Financing in the Prenomination Period

To assist presidential candidates seeking their party's nomination, the Federal Election Campaign Act (FECA) amendments of 1974 created a system of partial public financing in which a candidate who has established eligibility (by raising at least $5,000 in contributions of $250 or less from individuals in each of twenty states—$100,000 total) can receive public funds matching all individual contributions up to $250 from a pool created by a voluntary check-off on federal income tax returns. This provision thus doubles the value of individuals' contributions up to $250, encouraging candidates who participate in the matching funds program to seek financial support from large numbers of individual contributors. PAC contributions are not eligible for matching, nor do they help a candidate qualify for eligibility for matching funds. This makes PAC contributions less attractive to the candidates than those coming from private citizens.

In exchange for receiving matching funds from the federal government, however, candidates must abide by two key requirements. The first is a restriction on the amount of money a candidate may spend out of his or her own pocket. Candidates accepting matching funds cannot contribute more than $50,000 to their campaigns from their own assets or from those of their immediate families. Historically, this requirement effectively limited the influence of personal wealth in primary elections, since nearly all candidates preferred to observe the limit on self-financing in order to receive matching funds. In 1996 and 2000, however, multimillionaire publisher Steve Forbes declined public financing in order to spend freely ($37 million in 1996, $42 million in 2000) from his personal fortune on behalf of his ultimately unsuccessful candidacies for the Republican presidential nomination.

Candidates accepting matching funds from the federal government must also observe limits on the money spent by their campaigns in the prenomination period. FECA established an overall spending limit of $10 million in 1974, which is adjusted every four years for increases in the cost of living. For the 2004 election, the nationwide spending limit required for participation in the matching funds program stood at roughly $37 million, not including various fundraising and compliance costs that are not counted against the total. In addition, candidates must abide by spending limits in each state based on the size of the state's voting-age population.[31]

From 1976 to 1996, nearly all major presidential candidates—and all eventual nominees—accepted federal matching funds in the primaries. But the requirements have proven increasingly unattractive to candidates. As Anthony Corrado notes, the costs of basic campaign essentials, such as air travel, direct mail, and television airtime, have grown at a rate far beyond the inflation of the consumer price index since 1974.[32] The pressure of a spending limit also interacts with peculiarities in the timing of the nomination process: early primary or caucus victories are important beyond the number of voters involved. Thus in the early races candidates typically spend whatever it takes to stay visible. Gerald Ford and Ronald Reagan in 1976, Reagan again in 1980, Walter Mondale in 1984, and George H. W. Bush in 1988 all had to scale back significantly on staff and other expenditures late in their nomination campaigns because of overspending in the earlier parts of the campaign.[33] In 1996, Senator Bob Dole of Kansas secured the Republican nomination early but used practically all of his allowable spending to do so. Dole had only $1.2 million to spend between May and August, an amount that could hardly cover office rent and salaries for his staff, let alone such tangible products as polls or campaign ads. Bill Clinton, the incumbent president unopposed for the Democratic nomination that year, was nevertheless legally able to spend up to the prenomination limit as he saw fit—and, unlike Dole, he did not need to use the money in the early delegate selection contests. Instead, Clinton spent his money in the spring and early summer, while the Dole campaign was silent.[34]

Research indicates that FECA state-by-state limits on spending have not been important overall—the number of states in which candidates spend even 75 percent of the state limit remains in single figures even in highly competitive nomination campaigns.[35] The two earliest events, in Iowa and New Hampshire, take place in states so small that very low spending limits are applicable. In 2004, for example, the New Hampshire limit was $746,200, the lowest possible, matching the limit for the insignificant caucus in Guam and only 5 percent of the later and therefore less important California primary.[36] As a result, candidates observing spending limits seek loopholes, such as, when contesting the New Hampshire primary, renting cars in Massachusetts or buying television time in Boston (whose stations reach four-fifths of the New Hampshire population), and charging these expenditures against the much larger Massachusetts spending limit.[37]

Another loophole, used to circumvent both national and state spending limits, is the pre-candidacy political action committee. This is a PAC sponsored by the candidate, which, unlike a candidate's campaign committee, may receive contributions and incur expenditures without respect to FECA limits. This is because under the law as it has been implemented by the Federal Election Commission's rulings, establishment of such a PAC does not imply a declaration of candidacy for the presidency, whereas establishment of a campaign committee does.[38] This method of getting around spending limits was hit upon accidentally when Ronald Reagan's campaign committee reconstituted itself as a PAC in order to spend the $1 million surplus left over from his unsuccessful bid for the 1976 Republican nomination.

By 1988, nine of the major-party candidates were sponsors of such a PAC.[39] The number of precandidacy PACs fell in the 1992 campaign. Alexander and Corrado identify unusual circumstances that led to the dip in candidate PACs, namely President George H. W. Bush's high popularity in the year before the election, which depressed all prenomination activity.[40] No such circumstance applied in 2000 and 2004, and candidates were quick to exploit the potential of precandidacy PACs prior to the election year.[41] More than two years before the 2008 primary season, most potential candidates in both parties maintained active PACs that allowed them to raise money both for their own travel to Iowa, New Hampshire, and other key primary and caucus states, and for disbursal to candidates for other offices, who might be expected to return the favor with endorsements or fundraising efforts later on in the nomination process.[42]

While candidates have long attempted to exploit loopholes in the federal matching funds program in order to reduce the burden of its requirements, several have chosen in recent elections to bypass the system entirely. After declaring his candidacy for the 2000 Republican presidential nomination, Texas Governor George W. Bush calculated that he could raise more money for his campaign by declining federal matching funds (and the restrictions that come with them) than by participating. Bush, an extremely proficient fundraiser, collected over $95 million in individual contributions, by far a record amount at the time for a primary campaign and about three times the spending limit required of candidates, such as his chief rival Senator John McCain of Arizona, who accepted public financing.[43]

In 2004, Bush, as the incumbent president, once again chose not to accept matching funds, raising $270 million for his "primary" campaign even though he faced no opposition for the Republican nomination.[44] He was able to amass this sum in part by taking advantage of a provision of the Bipartisan Campaign Reform Act (BCRA) of 2002, known as the McCain-Feingold law, which doubled the limit on individual contributions to a federal campaign from $1,000 to $2,000 and indexed it to the cost of living for future elections. Since federal election law considers the primary period to extend until a candidate is formally nominated at a national convention, the Republican National Committee's decision to delay Bush's nomination until the beginning of September allowed him to spend his prenomination campaign war chest long after the 2004 primary elections had concluded.[45]

For the first time in 2004, two Democratic candidates also concluded that they would be better off declining public funds in the primaries than operating under the accompanying restrictions on spending. Former Vermont Governor Howard Dean, citing Bush's imposing financial advantage and his own fundraising success, announced in November 2003 that he would not seek matching funds; he was followed a few days later by Massachusetts Senator John Kerry.[46] This was a wise decision. Kerry raised a total of $235 million for his primary campaign, though most of it came after he became the presumptive Democratic nominee in early March 2004 and turned his sights on Bush, his opponent in the general election.[47] Had Kerry accepted matching funds, his campaign, subject to a spending limit of under $40 million, would have been nearly bankrupt from March through July while Bush raised and spent money freely.

The public financing system is dependent on the voluntary participation of American citizens, who must agree that $3 of their federal taxes every year will be placed in a dedicated account upon which the campaigns draw. As the number of taxpayers who check the requisite box on their income tax returns has declined—from 29 percent in 1980 to 11 percent by 2002—the pool of available money has shrunk even as campaigns have become significantly more expensive each year.[48] The Treasury Department has ruled that candidates raising the earliest contributions would receive first access to these funds if there were not enough to go around; this decision inspired George H. W. Bush's campaign to schedule a $25 million fundraising blitz in 1991, even though his advisers did not expect serious primary opposition.[49]

Unless Congress amends FECA to provide greater incentives for participation, it appears that the system of partial public financing for primary elections is on the decline. Long-shot candidates unable to raise large sums of money on their own may still be willing to abide by the accompanying restrictions in order to receive matching funds. But those in serious contention for their party's nomination in future elections will likely wish to remain free of spending limits, especially since these limits apply, even after a de facto nominee has emerged, until the nomination is made official at the party's national convention.

Raising and Spending Money in the General Election

After candidates are formally nominated by the two major parties in the late summer before a presidential election, full public funding is available to them, under FECA, if they want it—and no eligible nominee has declined public funding in the general election since the program was established in 1974.[50] Each campaign is given $20 million in 1974 dollars—$74.6 million in 2004—from the pool created by the federal income tax check-off introduced by FECA. In return for accepting these funds, candidates must limit their campaign expenditures to this amount, and cannot receive additional contributions from individuals or PACs except to pay the compliance costs incurred in following the law. (In 2004, compliance costs came to $12.2 million for Bush and $8.9 million for Kerry.) FECA permits the national party committees to raise a certain amount to be spent in coordination with their candidates' campaigns ($16.25 million for each party in 2004); the parties may collect additional funds from private individuals that must be spent independently of the candidates. The public financing program also gives each of the major parties a grant to help finance the party's national convention ($14.6 million apiece in 2004).[51]

By limiting the amount of money that the major-party nominees may spend on their own campaigns to that provided them by the public subsidy, the campaign finance system established by FECA encourages the parties to raise additional funds during the general election to spend on behalf of their presidential candidates. Under the law, most of this party money cannot be spent in formal coordination with the candidate's own campaign, but the strategies and messages emphasized by the candidates are hardly secrets, and voters may be unable to distinguish advertising funded by the candidate from that produced "independently" by the candidate's party.

Under current law, donations to parties are regulated much the same as those to individual candidates. Corporations and labor unions are not allowed to contribute, and donations by an individual citizen to a party committee may not exceed $25,000 in 2002 dollars. In the recent past, however, parties were permitted to raise funds outside these restrictions—a phenomenon known as "soft money."

Soft money was raised by the national party committees and then transferred to state and local parties. Although originally not permitted under FECA's 1974 amendments, soft money was allowed by further amendments in 1979 in order to restore to state and local parties the campaign role that the 1974 amendments had denied them.[52] The parties argued that the 1974 reforms had the unfortunate consequence of threatening traditional, grassroots styles of campaigning: for example, voter registration drives or neighborhood leafleting.

At first, soft money was chiefly used to fund local party mobilization efforts. In 1996, however, the Clinton campaign discovered a new loophole in the law that made soft money even more crucial. Under the law, parties were allowed to use this money to fund political advertising. The only requirements were that activities funded with soft money, such as advertising, could not be coordinated with the candidate's campaign, and that ads could not specifically urge anyone to vote for or against a candidate.[53] Typically, the ads discussed the strengths of the party's candidate or the deficiencies of an opposing candidate, but avoided referring to any upcoming election. Both parties used this tactic, but in 1996 the Democrats had a crucial advantage: they knew who their nominee would be long before the conventions met or even before anyone had voted in the presidential primaries, and could construct a campaign around the themes he was using as president. The Democrats spent some $34 million on such ads in the year before their convention, mainly in twelve states expected to be crucial to a Clinton victory. The Republicans waited until May of 1996 to begin their issue ads in support of the Dole candidacy.[54]

BOX 3.1 PARTY SPENDING IN GENERAL ELECTIONS

In the days before the public funding and contribution limits were established by FECA in 1974, Republican presidential candidates invariably outspent their Democratic opponents, with the exception of the unusually well-funded Kennedy campaign in 1960.[1] The creation of the public subsidy for the general election in 1974 placed both major candidates on an even financial footing, at least after their respective parties nominated them at the national party conventions. But parties may also spend unlimited funds on behalf of their presidential nominees, as long as these expenditures are not formally coordinated with the candidates' own campaigns. Candidates who choose to receive public funding for the general election may not collect private campaign contributions as well. This has worked to the advantage of the party committees, which are free to accept such donations (up to a prescribed limit for each donor). Thus, party committees benefit from the mobilization of potential donors provided by a presidential election. For most of the past century, Republicans have maintained a consistent, often overwhelming, advantage over Democrats in party fundraising. However, having the biggest bank account has not always guaranteed victory in presidential elections (see table 1).

TABLE 1 Party Spending and Electoral Results, 1972–2004

Year	Democratic Percentage of Two-Party Presidential Vote	Democratic Percentage of Two-Party Expenditures
1972	38	36
1976	51	29
1980	45	18
1984	41	25
1988	46	34
1992	53	39
1996	54	38
2000	50	43
2004	49	47

Source: See table 3.1.

Note: Spending by party committees only; does not include expenditures by candidates or by outside groups.

The narrowing of the Republican financial advantage in the 1990s was in part due to more aggressive fundraising by President Bill Clinton, the Democratic National Committee, and the party's congressional campaign committees. Democrats were particularly successful in raising soft money—that is, money not subject to federal regulation—and were much more dependent on this source of funds than Republicans. In 2000, the Democratic Party raised and spent $245 million in soft money, nearly as much as the $252 million in soft money raised and spent by the GOP. The Republican Party held a much larger edge in "hard money" donations—money subject to federal regulations—spending $427 million in 2000 compared to just $266 million for the Democrats.[2]

Although the availability of soft money disproportionately favored their own party, liberals were much more troubled by the rise of unregulated soft money than were conservatives. The Bipartisan Campaign Reform Act of 2002 (also known as the McCain-Feingold legislation) was, despite its name, supported by most Democrats in Congress and opposed by most Republicans, even though many observers predicted that the law's eradication of soft money would particularly hurt the Democratic Party. Writing before the bill's passage, Candice J. Nelson observed: "It is ironic that there is considerably more support for McCain-Feingold among Democrats in Congress than among Republicans, because if McCain-Feingold were to be enacted, Democratic fund-raising efforts would probably be hurt much more severely than Republican fund-raising."[3]

Democratic fears—and Republican hopes—that a ban on soft money would work to the GOP's advantage have yet to be realized. In the election of 2004, the first presidential contest conducted after the enactment of BCRA, the Democratic National Committee spent $390 million, compared to the $122 million in hard money (and $135 million in soft money) that it spent during the 2000 election (see table 2). The various Democratic national, state, and local party committees spent $656 million in federally regulated funds in 2003–2004. This increase in party fundraising between 2000 and 2004 was partially due to a provision in BCRA raising the amount of hard money an individual could donate to a party committee from $20,000 to $25,000 per federal election year. BCRA also indexed this limit to inflation for future elections.

While Republican committees spent a total of $753 million during the same period, maintaining their traditional financial advantage, the Democratic fundraising hardship predicted by some in the wake of BCRA did not emerge in 2004. In fact, as table 1 shows, campaign spending by the parties was the most evenly matched in decades. Future elections will reveal whether this development is a temporary phenomenon or whether it represents an increasing long-term financial competitiveness between the parties.

Many wealthy former Democratic soft-money donors instead gave large sums in 2004 to nominally independent but Democratic-leaning 527 organizations such as MoveOn and America Coming Together, which mobilized on behalf of John Kerry and other party candidates.[4] The rise of these outside groups is another consequence of BCRA's ban on the use of soft money by political parties. Like most attempts to reform the campaign finance system, BCRA appears to have succeeded more in redistributing funds among candidates, parties, and interest groups than in reducing the role of money in American elections.

TABLE 2 Party Committee Spending, 2000–2004 (in Millions of Dollars)

	2000 (Hard money)	2000 (Soft money)	2004 (Hard money)
Democratic National Committee	122.0	135.3	389.9
Democratic Senatorial Campaign Committee	41.5	63.3	88.3
Democratic Congressional Campaign Committee	49.3	58.0	92.4
State and local committees	140.0		153.7
Democratic Total	265.8	244.8	655.6
Republican National Committee	187.4	163.5	382.6
National Republican Senatorial Committee	50.7	44.6	78.7
National Republican Congressional Committee	95.4	52.9	184.8
State and local committees	165.9		164.2
Republican Total	427.0	252.8	752.6
Grand Total	692.8	497.6	1,408.2

Source: Federal Election Commission, "FEC Reports Increase in Party Fundraising for 2000," press release, May 15, 2001, available at http://www.fec.gov/press/press2001/051501partyfund/051501partyfund.html; "Party Financial Activity Summarized for the 2004 Election Cycle," press release, March 2, 2005, available at http://www.fec.gov/press/press2005/20050302party/Party2004final.html.

Note: Total expenditures for each party may not correspond precisely with the sum of party committee expenditures because of fund transfers among party committees.

[1] Herbert E. Alexander, *Financing the 1980 Election* (Lexington, MA: Lexington Books, 1983), p. 109.
[2] Federal Election Commission, "FEC Reports Increase in Party Fundraising for 2000," press release, May 15, 2001, available at http://www.fec.gov/press/press2001/051501partyfund/051501partyfund.html.
[3] Candice J. Nelson, "Spending in the 2000 Elections," in David B. Magleby, ed., *Financing the 2000 Election* (Washington, DC: Brookings Institution, 2002), p. 44.
[4] See Chris Suellentrop, "Follow the Money," *Boston Globe*, June 26, 2005, p. D1.

Until the passage of the Bipartisan Campaign Reform Act (BCRA) in 2002, neither the expenditure nor the raising of soft money was subject to the federal regulations that restrict the amount of money an individual can give to a campaign or party, and which prohibit corporations and labor unions from making direct contributions. National party committees were free to channel soft money they raised to the state and local parties, and to coordinate state and local expenditures with their own spending of "hard" money subject to federal restrictions. In the last four presidential elections in which it could be used, soft money was raised in increasingly visible and competitive ways. In 1992 the Republicans claimed 198 and the Democrats 375 individuals who gave or raised soft money totals of at least $100,000, collectively raising a total of $86 million in soft money. Although Clinton placed a limit of $100,000 on contributions from individuals and refused to accept soft money from PACs, corporations, or labor unions, these sources had already contributed large amounts to the Democratic National Committee, mainly for the purpose of financing the national party convention. George H. W. Bush placed no limits and did not back away from accepting corporate money if offered.[55] In 1996, each party raised over $120 million in soft money. About half of that was transferred directly to the state and local parties; the rest was spent in joint activities with the state and local parties, donated to state and local candidates, or spent on party-building activities not directly affecting the 1996 elections. Both sides received large donations. The large tobacco company Phillip Morris donated $1.6 million to the Republicans (and $400,000 to the tobacco-bashing Democrats), while the Association of Trial Lawyers gave $361,000 to the Democrats (and $157,000 to the trial-lawyer-bashing Republicans).[56] In 2000, both sides raised and spent record amounts of soft money: $250 million by the Republicans and $245 million by the Democrats. In fact, the Democratic Party raised nearly as much in soft money as it did in traditional "hard" contributions.[57]

The rise of soft money shows how difficult it is to regulate money in elections. On the one hand, it constituted a loophole, allowing parties to work around the contribution limits which applied to traditional party funds and raising anew the question of the motives of contributors prepared to give large sums of money to politicians. Soft money also undermined the campaign cost-limiting rationale of the FECA by allowing parties to spend huge amounts above the limit placed on the nominees' own campaigns. In 2000, each major-party candidate's campaign spent the allowable $67.6 million in the general election, while the parties "independently" spent an additional $1.2 billion, including about $500 million in unregulated soft money, mostly on behalf of the presidential candidates. The rise of soft money also created a gray area within which the application of campaign finance law became uncertain: for example, should a presidential candidate be allowed to speak at a soft-money fundraising event? This would appear to be exactly the sort of private fundraising activity that, by accepting public funding, a candidate had agreed not to engage in.

But soft money also addressed a real problem: how to energize voluntary "party-building" activities and create an incentive for the parties to encourage citizen participation. In order to qualify as a soft-money expenditure, any campaigning by the national committees or the candidates' personal committees had to be undertaken in conjunction with volunteer-based state and local party organizations. This was an incentive that would not, and did not, arise without soft money. Almost all hard-money expenditures go directly to advertising, travel, and other direct campaign costs associated with the candidate personally.[58]

Soft money became such an important part of presidential campaign financing that it fundamentally changed the basic rules instituted in 1974. From that point through about the 1984 election, campaigns were basically waged using public money. After that, public money served as a floor, not a ceiling. Thus, while both major party candidates were guaranteed a sizeable nest egg, any candidate who chose to run a campaign using only public money was at a severe disadvantage.

BCRA (or the McCain-Feingold law), enacted in 2002, contained a provision banning soft money in federal elections. This prohibition faced immediate legal challenge by Senator Mitch McConnell and a coalition of state party organizations on free speech grounds, but the Supreme

Court upheld the law in 2003.[59] While the parties could no longer receive unlimited funds from individuals, unions, and corporations to be used on issue advertising, outside organizations nominally independent of the candidates and parties could still accept such money. In response to the soft-money ban imposed by BCRA, a number of these organizations—commonly referred to as "527" committees after the section in the federal tax code under which they fall—emerged during the 2004 campaign. While officially unconnected with the Kerry and Bush campaigns and the Democratic and Republican parties (any coordination with either entity would violate federal campaign finance law), 527s made their loyalties clear, working to elect one or the other of the major candidates. The liberal group MoveOn sponsored a series of television advertising campaigns in key states that strongly criticized George W. Bush's record in office, while an organization calling itself Swift Boat Veterans for Truth attacked Kerry for his actions as a navy officer in the Vietnam War.[60] All in all, 527 organizations spent at least $350 million during the 2004 campaign, mostly on the Democratic side, prompting reform advocates to call for new laws restricting their activity.[61]

Does Money Buy Elections?

The billions of dollars spent on American elections inevitably raise serious questions about the relationship between wealth and decisions in a democracy. Are presidential nominating and electoral contests determined by those who have the most money? Do those who make large contributions exercise substantial or undue influence as a result? Is the victorious candidate under obligation to "pay off" major financial contributors? Do those who pay the piper call the tune?[62]

This was certainly the reasoning that inspired the post-Watergate political reforms of the mid-1970s, which attempted to remove the influence of money from presidential elections.[63] Before these elaborate limitations were established, however, the evidence was slight that presidential elections were unduly influenced, never mind "bought," by monied interests. Republicans did spend more than Democrats in most general elections, but the difference was not as overwhelming as some would suppose. The percentage of postnomination expenditures spent by the Democratic nominee from 1932 to 1980 varied from a low of 33 percent in 1972 (when McGovern lost) to a high of 51 percent in 1960 (when Kennedy won); the average was about 41 percent.[64] Although the Johnson forces spent more money in 1964 than Kennedy's had in 1960, Goldwater's losing campaign spent $17.2 million, significantly more than Johnson's $12 million expenditure.[65] Total spending by both parties was high in absolute terms, but outlays per voter per party were quite modest, running in the 1972 election to about $1.31 for each of the 76.02 million voters.[66]

The most obvious and most important conclusion in our view is that even in the era when the parties were free to spend whatever they could raise and were not subject to the restrictions and regulations established by FECA in 1974, money did not buy election victories. The candidate and party with the most money did not always win. Otherwise, Republicans would have won every election but one since 1932, but in fact Democrats won seven of the nine presidential elections from 1932 to 1964 and three more contests since then. Nor does there seem to be a correlation between the amount of money spent and the size of electoral victory in national elections.[67] In 1968, for example, the Republicans outspent the Democrats by more than two to one, yet they won the election by a mere 500,000 out of the 72 million votes cast. One would expect that money would flow into the coffers of the party believed to have the best chance of victory. Yet with the possible exceptions of 1968 and 2000, there does not seem to have been a single presidential election in the past century that any competent observer believes would have turned out differently if the losing candidate had spent more money.

No one doubts that money is important; parties and candidates, not to speak of ordinary mortals, can hardly function without it. If a candidate could not raise any money, or only a pitifully small amount, he or she would be dreadfully handicapped and might not be able to run at all. But this situation has never arisen (although Hubert Humphrey in 1968 came close) after the national convention has made its choice. The first part of our explanation, therefore, is that the differences in spending ordinarily have not been so great as to give any major-party nominee an overwhelming advantage. As long as the poorer candidates could raise the minimum amount necessary to mount a campaign, that is, to hire staff, distribute literature, advertise on television, travel around the country, and so on, they could do most of what they had to do. Thus, even before the 1974 law provided the nominees of both parties with equal grants of public money, spending more than the minimum amount necessary to run a campaign did not confer significant advantages. Like other goods, money is subject to diminishing returns. People may get tired of being bombarded with literature and harangued by advertisements. The candidates sometimes worry about overexposure lest they go the way of certain television celebrities who were seen once too often. Accusations of "trying to buy the election" may arise if too much time is taken on television. With the proliferation of television channels, political broadcasts are easier, nowadays, to avoid. We know that many voters are relatively impervious to advertising by the opposition, and all the leaflets in the world will not make them change. The actual result of an extensive assault by the richer party may be to give those who oppose that party additional reasons to intensify their opposition.

Given the necessary minimum amount of money, candidates in the general election can also count on a good deal of free publicity. Presidential campaigns are deemed newsworthy by the news media and are extensively reported. While Democrats may get somewhat less space than Republicans in the shrinking number of newspapers that openly display their partisanship in their news columns, they still get some, and they do better in the magazines and on the air. To some extent the candidates can make news. John F. Kennedy's grappling with the religious issue, Walter Mondale's choice of a woman as his running mate, Dwight D. Eisenhower's dramatic promise to go to Korea, Jimmy Carter's efforts to rescue the hostages in Iran or to negotiate them out, and George H. W. Bush's pledge "Read my lips, no new taxes" all made headlines at little or no financial expense. The televised debates first organized in 1960 and held in every election since 1976 are publicized without significant costs to the participating candidates. They attract millions of viewers, numbers far in excess of the political broadcasts for which fees must be paid.

Money makes a greater difference at the prenomination stage than later on. Having money early to aid in making a good showing in the first events helps to raise additional funds to sustain candidates throughout the primary season. Dwight D. Eisenhower and Robert Taft each spent about $2.5 million on their nominating campaigns in 1952.[68] George McGovern spent $12 million in 1972 on the way to his nomination.[69] Jimmy Carter spent $12.4 million in 1976 and, as an incumbent president, $19.6 million in 1980.[70] In 1984, Walter Mondale spent $26.2 million, while Ronald Reagan, despite his lack of serious opposition for the Republican nomination, spent $25.9 million.[71] In 1988, both the winning nominees had more money to work with than their rivals; Bush and Dukakis both spent $28 million, the maximum allowed at the time for candidates participating in the matching funds program.[72] By January 1, 1988, the Dukakis campaign had raised more than twice as much as any other Democratic candidate, an advantage difficult to overcome in the front-loaded primary system.[73]

As of the end of February 2004, the field of Democrats seeking their party's presidential nomination had spent a combined $190 million on their campaigns. Former Governor Howard Dean of Vermont led the pack with expenditures of $48 million, followed by Senator John Kerry of Massachusetts at $38 million, Senator John Edwards of North Carolina at $26 million, retired General Wesley Clark at $24 million, Representative Richard Gephardt of Missouri at $20 million, and Senator Joseph Lieberman of Connecticut at $18 million.[74] A well-financed campaign is necessary both to boost a candidate's name recognition among intermittently attentive primary voters and to signal to the press corps that the candidate should be taken seriously as a contender for the nomination.

Money, however, is only one factor. As Dean discovered in 2004, a large war chest manifestly does not guarantee victory in primaries. In 1984 there was a negative relationship between Colorado Senator Gary Hart's spending and his share of the vote. Hart was most successful in those states in which he was outspent by former Vice President Walter Mondale. In contrast, Hart lost four of the five major states in which he outspent Mondale by two to one or more.[75] Michael Robinson notes that "Hart had little money to spend when he was winning; he had plenty of money to spend as he lost. Spending and winning are unrelated; it is the 'drunken sailor' syndrome in presidential politics, spending what you have, regardless."[76] One can always argue with the benefit of hindsight that a small sum at a critical moment might have been decisive. "If I'd only known then what I know today," Representative Morris Udall of Arizona, a perpetual runner-up in the 1976 Democratic primaries, lamented to an interviewer, referring to his decision to stop advertising during the week before the Wisconsin primary, which he lost by 5,000 out of 670,000 votes.[77] Since Udall came in second in six states, losing three times to Jimmy Carter by a tiny margin, any number of "it might have beens" (including an entry by Senator Henry [Scoop] Jackson of Washington in the New Hampshire primary, which could have prevented Carter from getting started) might well have made the difference. Thus it cannot successfully be argued that a candidate who ran so long and so often in so many primaries lost only because he or she lacked money for a week.

Skill and strategy in using resources matters as much as having them. Witness a memorandum written to Udall by his campaign manager: "We've got a reputation, frankly, as the sloppiest campaign in memory. No one knows who is in charge."[78] In 1976, Indiana Senator Birch Bayh's indecision about entering primaries, Henry Jackson's taking a win in Pennsylvania for granted, former Vice President Hubert Humphrey's decision not to enter the race until the California primary, when it was too late, Jimmy Carter's failing to see Maryland was not for him and getting involved in a pointless scrap with Governor Jerry Brown of California, all this and more mattered. It also mattered that Carter's strategy of running early and everywhere was a good strategy that paid off. Carter not only was able to run because he could raise money, but he was able to raise money on the strength of his early victories.

Similarly, money did not seem to be the decisive factor in the 2004 Democratic presidential nomination contest. Though Howard Dean boasted the biggest bank account of all the candidates, he did not spend his ample funds wisely. In the weeks before the Iowa caucuses, Dean's campaign bused 3,500 young volunteers into the state from elsewhere at great expense to knock on doors in support of his candidacy, renting vans, cell phones, and lodging for them to use during their stay. "I had never seen a campaign spend like this one," Dean's Iowa spokeswoman later remarked. Despite the high cost, this mobilization effort did not persuade most Iowans to vote for Dean. One nineteen-year-old volunteer who traveled from Vermont to Iowa for the caucuses admitted with hindsight that "many voters . . . may have been insulted by out-of-staters rushing in to tell them how to vote." John Kerry's campaign, in contrast, focused more on courting support from veteran Iowa political organizers who cultivated ongoing personal networks within the state; these efforts paid off when Kerry placed first in the Iowa caucuses, setting him on a path to the nomination.[79] Wesley Clark was also a proficient fundraiser in the weeks before the primary season began, but his decision not to compete in Iowa cost him valuable publicity, and his campaign never recovered despite the money he spent in New Hampshire and subsequent primary states.[80] For Dean, Kerry, and Clark, strategy seemed to weigh more heavily than money in determining their electoral fortunes in 2004.

It is exceedingly difficult to get reliable information on an event that involves a decision not to act, such as a political candidate's decision not to run because he or she could not raise the money. There is only a little literature on this subject, mostly news stories announcing early decisions not to run. But undoubtedly there have been some prospective candidates whose inability to raise cash has proved fatal to their chances of being considered for the nomination. In 1995 Dick Cheney, Jack Kemp, Bill Bennett, Dan Quayle, and conceivably others might have run for the Republican nomination if more money had been available to them.[81] Whether their failure represents an inability to satisfy the monied classes or to convince enough people that their candidacies were serious and worthy is difficult to say in the abstract. A more important question concerns whether there has been a systematic bias in favor of or against certain candidates that consistently alters the outcomes of presidential nominations. We can immediately dismiss the notion that the richest person automatically comes out on top. If that were the case, Nelson Rockefeller would have triumphed over Barry Goldwater in 1964 and Richard Nixon in 1968, and Robert Taft would have beaten Dwight D. Eisenhower in 1952. In 1976, Ronald Reagan's personal wealth eclipsed Gerald Ford's, as, in 1980, Edward Kennedy's did Jimmy Carter's. Nevertheless, in both these instances, the incumbent president beat the challenger. Indeed, for candidates who accept public funds, the maximum personal contribution allowed is now $50,000. In 1988 only three candidates came close to this limit, and three others made loans of a similar size to their campaign organizations. Representative Richard Gephardt's $50,000 personal contribution must be compared with the $7 million or so that his campaign consumed. Of the $28 million spent by George H. W. Bush to win the 1988 Republican nomination, only $2,000 came out of his own bank account.[82]

Perhaps the best test of the proposition that the richest candidate will win was found in the Republican nomination contest in 1996. Rather than relying on a mixture of small contributions and matching public funds, as every major candidate for the nomination had done since the 1974 FECA regime came into effect, multimillionaire publisher Steve Forbes decided to spend his own money in an effort to secure the Republican nomination. Under the Supreme Court decision in *Buckley v. Valeo* (1976), candidates may spend as much as they want from personal funds in self-promotion. Many wealthy state-level candidates have taken advantage of that ruling, but Forbes was the first candidate for a major party presidential nomination to do so.[83] Certainly, self-financing helped Forbes. Other than money, the only obvious resource he brought to the campaign was a mild case of name recognition, since his family's name is also the title of his national business magazine. It was his ability and willingness to spend vast sums of money— $37 million, almost as much as eventual nominee Bob Dole and far more than any other candidate for the nomination—that convinced the press to treat Forbes as a serious candidate, despite his late entry, lack of organization in Iowa or New Hampshire, and absence of normal qualifications for the presidency such as previous elected office or substantial public service. His money was not, however, capable of buying Forbes the nomination. In the critical states of Iowa and New Hampshire, he failed to finish among the top three candidates. While he did win two primaries (one, in Delaware, by default since he was the only candidate to campaign there), he never really threatened to win the nomination.[84] After reinventing himself as a social conservative, Forbes ran again for president in 2000. He spent even more (over $42 million) the second time around, but fared no better among the voters, withdrawing from the race on February 10 after receiving just 13 percent of the vote in New Hampshire and finishing third in the Delaware primary.[85]

What does the case of Steve Forbes tell us about the political efficacy of personal wealth? Money could not buy him the nomination. Moreover, even the money he did spend was radically insufficient to do the job. As William G. Mayer put it, for Forbes to be even somewhat competitive, "he had to spend *enormous* amounts of money. Dropping a few million bucks here and there over a large state like New York just would not do it. Forbes absolutely needed to blanket the airwaves with his commercials, as he did in Iowa, New Hampshire, Delaware, and Arizona."[86] If this is correct, then to compete in the delegate-rich large states, Forbes would have had to spend hundreds of millions of dollars. And even then, his saturation spending only succeeded when the competition did not devote their own resources to the state, an unlikely possibility in large states.

This is not to say self-financing cannot have an effect on nomination politics. Forbes was certainly able to buy attention, if not approval, for his main campaign proposal, the flat tax. His negative ads in 1996 may well have hurt Bob Dole in both Iowa and New Hampshire. In addition, Forbes may have simply been the wrong billionaire; a different self-financed candidate with additional assets, such as experience in elective office, might do better in the future. But that underscores the point that money itself is only one of the resources important to electoral politics.

The ability to raise money is a matter not only of personal wealth but also of being able to attract funds from others. Does this mean that only candidates attractive to the wealthy can run? The question is not so much whether it helps to be rich but whether candidates who favor the causes of the rich have the advantage over those who favor the poor. There is little evidence to support such a view. Given the nature of the American electorate, no candidate would openly admit to being the candidate only of the rich. Candidates holding a variety of views on economic issues, most of which are highly technical, manage to run for the nominations of both parties. In 1995, Republicans from all parts of the political spectrum launched presidential bids, from moderates Arlen Specter and Lamar Alexander to arch conservatives Pat Buchanan and Bob Dornan. At the same time, Steve Forbes's first-choice candidate, Jack Kemp, declined to run.[87] If candidates are generally chosen from among people who differ only a little on most substantive issues, the reason is not that the rich are withholding their money from the more radical candidates. Rather, it is that the distribution of opinions in the electorate renders the radicals' cause hopeless. Our conclusion is that it is nice to be rich; some candidates who lack funds are disadvantaged in the early going. From the standpoint of the total political system, however, the need for money does not appear to bar candidates of modest means who are otherwise acceptable to the electorate.

Campaign Finance Reform

Four broad issues are raised by the ways in which money is acquired and spent in presidential elections. The least troublesome is the issue of public disclosure of campaign financing. In federal campaigns, all contributions in excess of $200 and expenditures by candidates and committees in excess of $1,000 must be publicly reported under the Federal Election Campaign Act of 1971. The availability of this information led Common Cause in 1972, and others since, to compile and publish lists of contributors to congressional campaigns.[88] These compilations document the unsurprising news that some senators and representatives attract donations from contributors having business before the committees on which they sit, and that some Senate and House races attract money from sources far away from the state or district concerned. As well they might; a few hundred thousand dollars invested in Delaware or South Dakota could help elect a sympathetic member of Congress making decisions affecting the whole nation as readily as several million dollars invested in New York or California.[89]

When these contributions are matters of public record, voters can decide for themselves whether or not their representatives are still able to represent them adequately. Against this clear public gain must be weighed the possible chilling effects of publicity on the financial angels of small, unpopular parties. Safeguards against this difficulty are not at present in the law, and so far First Amendment protections of free speech have not been successfully invoked against disclosure on the grounds that disclosure inhibits political expression by chilling support for unpopular parties.[90]

A second feature of FECA is the provision for public financing of presidential election campaigns. Among the policy issues raised by public financing are: How much should minor parties get? Should not some method be found so that people rather than legislatures allocate public funds to the parties of their choice? In view of the nearly $100 million spent by the major-party candidates in the 1972 general election, the last presidential year before public financing went into effect, was not $90 million twenty years later too little to provide adequate political communication in a nation as large and diverse as the United States? A comparative study by Howard Penniman suggests that, contrary to popular opinion, American elections actually cost less per voter than those of other democracies.[91] While the cost of federal elections increased by a factor of ten between 1972 and 1996, a substantial fraction of that increase simply reflects the growth of inflation (see table 3.2).

Related to this last question, of course, is the issue of whether private expenditures should be prohibited where public expenditures are used. Any limitation on campaign expenditures limits political communication, a class of speech that one would think would be especially protected

TABLE 3.2 Federal Campaign Spending, 1972–2004 (Adjusted for Inflation)

Year	Actual Spending (Millions of Dollars)	Consumer Price Index (1972 Base)	Adjusted Spending (Millions of 1972 Dollars)
1972	217	100.0	217
1976	279	136.1	201
1980	643	197.1	326
1984	988	248.6	397
1988	1,198	283.0	423
1992	1,491	335.7	444
1996	2,064	375.4	550
2000	2,716	412.0	659
2004	3,409	451.9	754

Source: See table 3.1. CPI data from Bureau of Labor Statistics, http://data.bls.gov/cgi-bin/cpicalc.pl.

by the First Amendment. In practical terms, limits on campaign spending often work to the advantage of incumbent officeholders, since challengers require a great deal of publicity simply to make their names known. When expenditures are limited, political competition is inhibited. At present, however, the courts have held that Congress can set expenditure limits as a condition of accepting public subsidy but not if candidates have declined matching funds or are spending their own personal money, which it is their unlimited right to do.[92]

The final issue raised by recent legislation is the issue of limitations on contributions. Here, once again, a First Amendment problem is encountered, since voluntary political contributions of their own money by citizens as a means of political advocacy can readily be construed as an exercise of free speech. Against this must be weighed a general public interest in preventing politicians from being unduly influenced by people who have large financial interests. May it not be that those who contribute or raise money in large amounts thereby gain influence not available to others? Aware that the answer to this question is not a simple one and certainly does not dispose of the First Amendment problem, we would say, "Yes, but not overly much." As one fundraiser said of Washington: "This town works on personal relationships. Any time there's an opportunity to develop those relationships, it's a plus. The most anybody figures they can get in this business is access. You can't buy a vote. What you can do is say, 'Listen, I've helped you.'"[93]

What contributors or fundraisers (the financial middlemen) get to begin with is access to centers of decision making. That is why a lot of PAC money goes to incumbent legislators. Control over money certainly makes it easier to get in the door and present one's case. Persons of wealth, however, are likely to have substantial interests that would provide them with good access whether or not they made contributions. If no significant interest feels disadvantaged by what these contributors want, the contributors may well be given the benefit of the doubt. But in matters of great moment, where the varied interests in our society are in contention, it is doubtful whether control over money goes very far with a sitting president. There are many reasons for this.

In the first place, there are issues on which a candidate is likely already to be publicly committed. Suggestions that he or she change a position during the campaign are likely to be met with little favor. If the matter is important enough to be mentioned, it has to be considered in relation to its vote-getting potential. Forced to make a choice, nominees are far more likely to prefer votes to dollars. And even if a miscalculation is made in public, candidates generally prefer not to reverse their field and appear vacillating and inconsistent. Money may be given in the expectation of future favors. To spell this out in detail would amount to bribery, however, and is likely to be rejected outright as illegal.[94] The common sense of the candidates would most likely forbid such a thing. If not, their advisers would no doubt argue that the consequences of discovery are much worse than any possible benefits. Thus, any strings attached to a gift are likely to be vague and cloudy, subject to all sorts of interpretations. When they are not, the risks of exposure are so great that the costs of corruption are as likely to be as high for the contributors as for the public.

Once a president assumes office, he or she is in a much stronger bargaining position. The president can do more to affect contributors' fortunes than contributors can do to affect the president's. A president may at that point refuse to acknowledge any alleged agreement on policy concessions in return for contributions. Wealthy contributors frequently give to both parties and, in any event, are often found on opposite sides of public issues. For candidates to give in to one of them may simply incur the wrath of others.

A decline in contributions from one source may be made up by funds from another. The president's need to gain or maintain support from voters, the limits placed on the president's powers of decision by what Congress, bureaucrats, and interest groups will accept, and his or her own preferences all place drastic constraints on benefits contributors get from campaign contributions. In brief, money becomes much less important to the things a president needs to do once in office. Contributors may be heard to complain in the hurt tones of the early twentieth century steel magnate Henry C. Frick, who, after visiting Theodore Roosevelt at the White House, said, "We bought the son of a bitch and then he did not stay bought."[95] The foregoing analysis should help to explain why presidential politicians do not necessarily "stay bought," at least on large matters of public policy, whatever their debt to their financial supporters.

It would be amazing if the exponential growth in the governmental regulation of private industry did not lead the business community to seek less visible advantages or selective forms of relief. The fact is that what government does—an airline route or a television license here, a tax ruling or an import quota there—can have an enormous impact on the fortunes of private people. Business people, as we learned from investigations of the fundraising practices of Richard Nixon's Committee to Reelect the President in 1972, feel they must act defensively. They may give to a campaign fund not so much to steal a march on their competitors as to make sure they are not left behind. Thus, for example, airlines may give to protect their routes.[96] Because government power is so pervasive, business people, not knowing when or where they may need a friend, frequently give to the campaigns of both parties. Deregulation makes this less necessary. So does public financing of elections.

There is plenty of evidence that money from private citizens finds its way into the campaigns of public officials and candidates; not infrequently these days, the money in is large quantities. The question is, what relationships are we observing when we track this money? There are at least three possibilities, crudely: bribery, extortion, or the formation of an alliance. Bribery, which is illegal, occurs when a public official is induced by monetary considerations to do something or refrain from something that he or she would not otherwise do. Extortion, which is illegal, occurs when public officials either tacitly or explicitly threaten adverse consequences to private donors unless they contribute. The third possibility, alliances, which are legal, occurs when the relationship is freely entered into on both sides in recognition of mutual agreement or parallel interests.

Unfortunately, the third possibility may readily create what is frequently referred to as "the appearance of wrongdoing." This appearance is easy to invoke, but in our opinion ought to be tested far more rigorously than it commonly is. Citizens are certainly entitled to know what the nature is of alliances between contributors and officials, and to know whether these associations in fact reveal relationships that can be classified as bribery or extortion, or, as inquiry may reveal, something else.

RESOURCES: CONTROL OVER INFORMATION

Political information is so easy to acquire during a presidential election campaign that it is hard to identify anybody in control of its spread. There are, however, features of the overall system by which information is manufactured and distributed in the United States that materially affect the fortunes of candidates and the ways in which they are perceived by electorates.

Campaign professionals generally divide sources of information into free media and paid media. Free media (sometimes called "earned media") consist of publicity that candidates do not have to pay for, as the result of news coverage. Patterns of news coverage matter enormously to candidates, and they spend great effort conforming their campaigns to the professional practices of the news media, both print and television.

News organizations customarily assign experienced journalists to campaigns they judge to be "serious" and so in the first instance aspiring candidates must attempt to be taken seriously; those deemed to have no plausible chance at winning their party's presidential nomination will be largely ignored by the press. Usually, to be judged a "serious" candidate requires being a well-known public figure and hiring a staff of campaign professionals recognized by journalists as capable. Thus, even receiving free coverage usually requires money, and sometimes quite a lot of money, since journalists often judge the relative standing of presidential candidates by the size of their campaign war chests. Television ordinarily covers prenomination debates among candidates. Appearing in debates is one good way for candidates to get publicity while keeping costs down, and being included in debates is a mark of credibility for candidates, a sign that they must be taken seriously.

Paid media refers mostly to television and radio advertisements, which candidates must produce and place on the air more or less as though they were commercial advertising. Advertising is a form of information that uninvolved observers, such as a normal American electorate, frequently find credible. Especially during the presidential primary season, when multiple candidates compete within each major party for the party's nomination, candidates must purchase advertising in order to boost their name recognition and favorability among potential voters.

What constitutes information varies with the various stages of the process, as we discuss in chapter 4. Traditional topics include horse-race information, estimating which candidates are ahead and which are behind, thereby keeping a running tally on the viability and hence the seriousness of different candidacies. The news media also cover what they call "the issues," which may be, variously, public policy proposals brought up or emphasized by one or more candidates, social and political questions of the day, or other topics—which can be less high-minded—such as the past voting record or personal behavior of a candidate.

In all these matters, the news media generally maintain a rather close consensus about who is serious, who is ahead, and which issues are important. This consensus arises from the sharply competitive conditions under which individual news organizations operate, from the shared perspective that arises because journalists from different organizations hang around together as they cover the travels of campaigning candidates, and because they keep close track of one another's product. Because television producers watch the other networks and read the newspapers, and print media keep an eye on what's on television and the Internet, there is a tendency for their stories to converge.

Sometimes this herd mentality leads the news media astray. Most political journalists, for example, believed that Howard Dean had the 2004 Democratic nomination virtually wrapped up even before the first primary events, based in part on Dean's fundraising advantage and his campaign's confident claims of organizational superiority in key states. Dean's disappointing third-place finish in the Iowa caucuses forced an immediate widespread reappraisal of the race. While the "conventional wisdom" is not dependably accurate, it nonetheless exists as a powerful force shaping campaign coverage, due in large part to the workways of professional journalists and commentators.

Newspapers

Though the onset of the electronic media age has drastically reduced the readership and circulation of most daily newspapers, driving many out of business entirely, print journalism remains a major source of political information for many Americans. Newspaper coverage of current events has maintained its importance even in the Internet era; the Web sites operated by the *New York Times*, *Washington Post*, and *USA Today* rank among the most popular online sources for information, while the news stories displayed on CNN.com and the Internet portal Yahoo! are composed chiefly of newspaper wire services such as Reuters and the Associated Press. Candidates realize the influence of newspaper coverage of their activities and pay close attention to the treatment they receive from print journalists.

Most studies of political reporters confirm that they are a liberal-leaning group.[97] A recent survey of national journalists by the Pew Research Center found that 34 percent described themselves as liberals and just 7 percent as conservatives, with the balance considering themselves ideological moderates.[98] But standards of professional journalistic practice discourage slanted political coverage. As Michael Robinson has shown, while reporters may lean to the left, it is hard to find this bias in their copy.[99] Hard, but not impossible. Overt expressions of partisan bias are regarded as unprofessional in news columns and may even be veiled in articles labeled "analysis." In at least two ways, however, attitudes shared by many journalists influence political coverage in newspapers in ways that may, in practice, systematically advantage some candidates over others, despite their formal neutrality.

In the first place, it is permissible under standard journalistic norms to entertain a general prounderdog bias. Journalists pride themselves in their calling to "comfort the afflicted and afflict the comfortable." Comforting any sizable body of afflicted persons may be well beyond the capacities of the news media.[100] It is far easier to afflict the comfortable, since this merely entails maintaining a pro forma skepticism about the presumably self-interested pronouncements of incumbents of high office. Incumbents escape this presumption only rarely. In the early stages of a foreign crisis, when there is a rally-round-the-flag effect, incumbents are permitted the luxury of being described as speaking on behalf of all the people. As George H. W. Bush discovered in the early stages of the American invasion of Kuwait in 1991, and his son similarly found after the terrorist attacks of September 11, 2001, this does wonders for their public opinion ratings. Ordinarily, however, Americans are instructed by the media to take their leaders' statements with a grain of salt.[101]

Perhaps for this reason, journalists often submit front-running candidates to stricter scrutiny than also-rans. This is particularly true in the presidential primary season, when the candidates are not widely known, making the tone of coverage more influential in shaping voters' opinions—and when reporters have an interest in prolonging the horse race excitement as long as possible. Thus candidates may emerge from nowhere to pull into contention on the basis of initially positive media coverage, as former Governor Howard Dean of Vermont did in the summer of 2003, only to face an increasingly skeptical press corps once they are anointed as "front-runners." (It didn't help Dean that he had a famously prickly relationship with the correspondents covering his campaign.)

Second, and more fundamentally, illustrating Bernard Cohen's observation that the news media tell their consumers what to think *about*, there is the issue of "framing." How issues are framed matters over the long run because frames determine the terms within which alternative solutions are debated, and indeed they frequently serve to define the very nature of the problem.[102] Thus, whether unemployment, inflation, health care reform, education funding, global warming, international famine, or other societal ills are seen as serious problems requiring political solutions at any given time is not entirely dependent on objective measurement of the phenomenon in question.[103] In part, their status as important issues of the day is determined by whether people feel that they are important, for whatever reason, and these feelings are in turn partially determined by how, or to what extent, the news media cover them. Thus the very problems our leaders are called on to solve may differ from era to era according to ebbs and flows of public attention to them.[104] Politicians work hard to seize control of this public agenda and have a considerable impact on its contents.[105] So, too, do the decisions of journalists, who give and withhold credibility to leaders according to their own collective judgments about issues and the seriousness with which politicians are addressing them.

Some candidates become personally popular or unpopular with the reporters who cover them—understandable during a long election season in which members of the press corps travel across the country with the campaigns for weeks at a stretch. Bias based on such evaluations sometimes seeps into the copy sent back home by correspondents on the road. John F. Kennedy's warm relationships with many reporters in 1960 may have given him an advantage over his opponent, Richard Nixon, who repeatedly complained about his own coverage in the newspapers.[106] (At a 1962 press conference announcing his retirement from politics—prematurely, as it turned out—Nixon told the assembled journalists that they "wouldn't have Dick Nixon to kick around anymore.") Nixon, who long had a tense relationship with the press, compensated in his 1972 reelection campaign by largely ignoring national correspondents who might pepper him with hostile questions, benefiting from the norm that anything the incumbent president does constitutes "news."[107] Ronald Reagan, with his affable personality and long experience in show business, cultivated good relations with the news media during his successful 1980 and 1984 campaigns, while Bill Clinton's charm and communication skills similarly earned him generally if not uniformly positive coverage during the 1992 and 1996 elections.[108] George W. Bush's folksy demeanor, on display in the documentary film *Journeys With George,* appears to have largely won over the traveling press corps during his successful 2000 and 2004 campaigns, especially when compared to his earnest, less outgoing opponents Al Gore and John Kerry.

So while different forms of bias may arise in the press coverage of political campaigns, it is rarely based on the partisanship or ideology of the journalists themselves. And though beat reporters as a group might lean to the left in their own personal political views, the owners and publishers of newspapers likewise tend to be conservative. The general pro-Republican orientation of newspaper management is visible particularly in the editorial endorsement process. According to the quadrennial poll conducted by *Editor and Publisher* magazine, the Democratic presidential candidate has received more newspaper endorsements than the Republican nominee in only three elections since 1932 (1964, 1992, and 2004).[109]

Just as norms of proper journalistic practice in most cases prevent overt bias from coloring campaign coverage, other considerations discourage the conservative ideology of management that may be visible on the editorial page from slanting straight news stories elsewhere in the paper. In a time of declining circulation and mounting costs for the newspaper industry, owners can ill afford to offend half their potential readership. Budget constraints have also led to consolidation among newspapers and have forced the reduction of resources devoted to the coverage of current affairs. Today, most newspapers do not maintain their own news bureaus in Washington or generate a great deal of original coverage of national politics. They increasingly rely on stories composed by wire services such as the Associated Press and Reuters, or purchase content from the news services maintained by larger newspapers such as the *New York Times, Washington Post,* and *Los Angeles Times.* These news gathering agencies serve a wide clientele with a broad spectrum of opinion, and therefore endeavor to prepare stories that appear objective and impartial.[110] While every story will not be completely fair to all sides, the final product is much closer to the canons of neutrality than would be the case if each paper prepared stories in accordance with its own editorial positions.

For these reasons, newspaper coverage of campaigns is, on the whole, not consistently slanted in favor of a particular political viewpoint. A recent meta-analysis of fifty-nine separate studies over the past fifty years concluded that "across all newspapers and all reporters, there is only negligible, if any, net bias in the coverage of presidential campaigns. To the extent that there are newspapers whose coverage is biased in favor of Democrats, they are offset by newspapers whose coverage is biased in favor of Republicans."[111]

The potential effect of journalistic bias, ideological or otherwise, has decreased still further over time, simply because the volume of political coverage in newspapers is itself on the decline. The era of crusading editors who used their papers primarily as a vehicle for advancing political causes has given way to a modern industry dominated by corporations devoted primarily to maximizing shareholder profit.[112] Extensive attention to the world of politics attracts fewer subscribers than does coverage of crime, sports, human-interest stories, and the high jinks of celebrities; especially outside the major metropolitan areas, political news, though it does have a place, is given secondary consideration simply because most newspaper readers are not terribly interested.[113]

Even if a particular news source or coverage in a particular election is biased, are ordinary citizens actually influenced in their opinions and voting choices by the newspapers that enter their homes? The fact that a newspaper arrives on the doorstep is no guarantee that its political news and editorials will be read. Most people pay little enough attention to politics; they often read nothing or just scan the headlines without carrying away much of an impression. Even if the content is perused with some care, a reader's perception of what has been written may differ markedly from the writer's intentions. An editorial may not be clear in intent, particularly if it is hedged by qualifications or watered down to minimize offense, as it often is. Readers with existing opinions on the subject may well conclude that the item supports their views, whether it was meant to or not.

Opinion studies have demonstrated the remarkable capacity of people to filter out what they do not wish to hear and come away with quite a different impression than an objective analysis of an editorial or article would warrant. Indeed, the reader may interpret the story to mean precisely the opposite of what it intends. A criticism of Harry Truman for being vituperative, for example, could be taken—as it now generally is, with the hindsight of history—as a commendation of his fighting spirit. A condemnation of Jimmy Carter for being obstinate could emerge as praise for his high principles.[114] Ronald Reagan's "detachment" could be seen by some observers as incompetence, by others as floating benignly above politics. Conservative criticism of Bill Clinton for being "slick" and "calculating" simply mirrored his supporters' regard for his charm and political skills, while George W. Bush's frequent malapropisms and lack of interest in the details of public policy simultaneously inspire contempt in liberals and admiration in conservatives, who see him as plain-spoken and a strong leader.

News stories or editorials may be interpreted correctly and still rejected as invalid. There is a great deal of suspicion of the press in the United States.[115] Party identification is so powerful that for many readers it would overwhelm almost anything a paper says. Obviously millions of citizens have no difficulty voting Democratic while reading Republican newspapers. Many people derive their political opinions from sources other than the news media; the influence of family members, friends, coworkers, ethnic and religious organizations, and other social forces can ordinarily be expected to far outweigh anything written in a newspaper.[116]

One newspaper that may have had some historical impact is the *Union Leader* of Manchester, New Hampshire. This paper has neither the resources nor the circulation of national papers such as the *New York Times* or the *Wall Street Journal*. But its location—the site of the nation's first presidential primary—and its unabashed right-wing partisanship have made the *Union Leader* a force to be reckoned with in presidential nominations. The paper's attacks on front-runner Senator Edmund Muskie (and his wife) helped derail Muskie's 1972 campaign for the Democratic nomination. In 1980, after an upset victory by George H. W. Bush in the Iowa caucuses, Ronald Reagan's candidacy appeared to be in serious trouble. David Moore argues convincingly that the *Union Leader* played a key role in Reagan's recovery and his victory in the New Hampshire primary. Moore finds that readers of the *Union Leader* were much more favorably disposed toward Reagan, by a margin of 35 to 40 points, than nonreaders. This pattern held true regardless of the voter's ideological predisposition. But it is not surprising given the stories the Bush-bashing *Union Leader* was running.[117] This illustrates a difference between primary and general elections. In primaries, when party loyalty is no help in sorting out the choices, cues from the news media matter more to voters. In general elections, where choices are better structured and candidates represent different parties, the news media are less influential.

Whatever role the press plays in influencing presidential elections varies enormously with circumstances. Against popular incumbents with publicity resources of their own (such as Franklin D. Roosevelt in 1936 or Ronald Reagan in 1984), the impact of the media may be negligible. Less well-known candidates, such as many challengers, may be more dependent on positive (or at least not dismissive) press coverage in order to make their case to voters, especially in presidential primaries. The sheer number of different issues that may become relevant during a presidential campaign may either neutralize or intensify the influence of the press, depending on whether they are "pocketbook" issues that are grasped with relative ease by voters or "style" issues that owe their existence as issues to the attention paid them by the mass media.

Television

Since the 1960s, television has eclipsed newspapers as the most important and influential news medium in the United States. A 2004 survey by the Pew Research Center for the People and the Press found that 68 percent of respondents named television as their primary source for news about political campaigns, compared to 15 percent for newspapers, 7 percent for radio, and 6 percent for the Internet.[118] The influence of television on presidential elections extends well beyond the coverage of campaigns by journalists. Expenditures for television advertising dependably constitute the largest single budget item of any serious presidential campaign.

Many observers consider the "television age" in politics to have begun in 1960, when presidential candidates John F. Kennedy and Richard Nixon participated in a series of televised debates—inaugurating what has now become a quadrennial tradition. Almost uniformly, accounts of the 1960 campaign treat the debates as a decisive event that gave Kennedy a crucial advantage in what turned out to be a very close election. The handsome, poised Kennedy came across very well on television, especially in comparison to Nixon's shifty eyes and five-o'clock shadow. In fact, the belief that Americans who listened to the debates on the radio (and thus judged the candidates purely on the basis of their words, not their looks) considered Nixon the winner, while television viewers favored Kennedy, has become a staple of American campaign lore, although little evidence actually exists to substantiate it.[119]

To candidates, strategists, pundits, and media critics alike, the lesson of the 1960 debates is clear: television coverage can significantly influence the outcome of elections, and the medium tends to reward superficiality over substance. The truth is probably more complex. Television's moving pictures and sound give it an immediacy that print journalism lacks. The medium is also better suited to covering politics as a battle of personalities than of ideas; in-depth discussions of policy tend to lack the necessary visual images to make compelling television. At the same time, the same factors that limit the influence of newspapers on the course of electoral campaigns often similarly constrain the effects of electronic media as well. Television coverage of politics is often intentionally bland in order to minimize controversy, many viewers adhere to their preexisting political beliefs and evaluations even in the face of the contradictory opinions of TV talking heads, and most Americans won't receive even strong, compelling political messages in the first place. Ratings for current affairs programming routinely pale in comparison to those for prime time entertainment, talk shows, sporting events, and other staples of the medium; even "news" broadcasts are devoting more and more attention to human interest stories, celebrity gossip, and other, more popular, topics at the expense of political issues or events.

As with newspapers, the influence of television appears to peak during the presidential primary season. Contestants for party nominations are usually much less well known to the national electorate than incumbent presidents or major-party nominees, allowing media coverage to color the public's perceptions of the candidates. Since primary elections are contested by multiple candidates within the same party, substantive differences among them on major public policy issues tend to be relatively minor, further encouraging television coverage to focus on the differing personal lives, styles, personalities, and strategies of the candidates. And the idiosyncrasies of the primary process itself—beginning with the Iowa caucuses and New Hampshire primary in January of a presidential election year and continuing through months of sequential primary elections and caucuses in all fifty states—allow for television coverage to exert significant influence on the outcome, as news media interpretations of the results in the early states have proven to have an immense effect on the behavior of voters in subsequent primaries.

For one thing, candidates for the nomination do not automatically receive equal attention from reporters. Candidates must be "taken seriously" by the media in order to earn sufficient, respectful coverage. In 2004, for example, ten Democratic candidates sought their party's nomination for the presidency. Three of them—Representative Dennis Kucinich of Ohio, former Senator Carol Moseley-Braun of Illinois, and the Reverend Al Sharpton—were, by media consensus, relegated to a second tier of candidates presumed to have no plausible chance to win the nomination. While they campaigned actively, making personal appearances, raising money, and participating in candidate debates, they were largely ignored by the news media, reducing their slim electoral chances still further.

In 2004, former Governor Howard Dean of Vermont was initially considered a secondary contender as well; though he was taken more seriously than Kucinich, Moseley-Braun, and Sharpton, he was a decided underdog in comparison to Senator John Kerry of Massachusetts, Senator John Edwards of North Carolina, Senator Joseph Lieberman of Connecticut, and Representative Richard Gephardt of Missouri. Dean compensated by attacking his rivals by name for their support of the U.S. invasion of Iraq in early 2003. Since journalists love to cover personal conflict between candidates, Dean's criticisms generated a great deal of publicity for his campaign. While Dean portrayed himself as motivated by principle, he was not reluctant to comment on the political advantages to be had in adopting such an approach. "It's made me into a candidate who's not a long shot anymore," he told reporters. "It's put me into a position where there are now five significant candidates, not four."[120]

But Dean ultimately suffered as much as he benefited from the workways of modern television journalism. Reporters and pundits obsessed primarily with the state of the "horse race" anointed Dean not only the front-runner but, in many accounts, the presumptive Democratic nominee by early 2004—even though a single primary vote had yet to be cast. Media expectations for Dean's performance in the first-in-the-nation Iowa caucuses were therefore extraordinarily high. When he placed a distant third on caucus night, behind Kerry and Edwards, journalists and pundits on the lookout for surprising results that presumably make a good story gleefully piled on.

Dean's energetic concession speech in Iowa included an improvised exhortation to his followers to take their fight to subsequent primaries and caucuses. After naming a number of states, seemingly at random, Dean raised his fist with an enthusiastic shriek. Footage of the "Dean scream" was replayed endlessly on television over the following days, as political analysts who had just weeks before been soberly predicting a certain Dean nomination now eagerly branded him a loser and perhaps something of a nut. For many Americans who had not been following the race closely until the Iowa caucuses, their first televised exposure to Dean was therefore decidedly negative. Unsurprisingly, Dean was never able to work his way back into serious contention, withdrawing from the race several weeks later without winning a single state primary.

The rise and fall of the 2004 Howard Dean presidential campaign reveals much about the role of media coverage, particularly television coverage, in shaping the outcome of presidential nominations. Television tends to emphasize candidate personalities and the "horse race" over qualifications or policy prescriptions. It treats politics as entertainment, hoping that keeping the level of excitement high will keep viewers tuning in. So, according to the study by C. Anthony Broh, reporters do what they can to hype up the contest. They

> (1) avoid predictions if they are definitive; (2) avoid reporting percentages if they are not close; (3) report the attitudes and preferences of subgroups that cast doubt on the outcome; (4) compare polls to a time period that can demonstrate a narrowing or constantly close gap between the candidates; (5) report voter reaction to spectacles of the campaign; (6) distort results that do not generate excitement; and (7) question the validity of polls that show a wide gap. Furthermore, they interpret methodological ambiguities involving undecided voters and sampling error in ways that maximize shifts in campaign support.[121]

The influence of media coverage on primaries is illustrated by the 1984 Democratic presidential nomination contest. In the Iowa caucuses on February 25, attended by around 85,000 people, former Vice President Walter Mondale received 49 percent to Colorado Senator Gary Hart's 16 percent, former South Dakota Senator George McGovern's 10 percent, 9 percent to uncommitted delegates, California Senator Alan Cranston's 7 percent, and Ohio Senator John Glenn's 4 percent. Despite Mondale's huge victory and the relatively small number of people who voted—Hart got just 12,600 votes—the media made the nominating contest into a two-man race. Glenn suffered a near-knockout blow. Hart's media coverage, with hardly a negative voice, rose dramatically, while Mondale's shrank. After Hart's victory in the next event, the New Hampshire primary, where he got most of the votes of Democrats who made up their minds after the Iowa caucuses, Hart briefly became the front-runner. At once, as Gary R. Orren reports, "in a daily series of biting critiques . . . all three networks attacked Hart's credibility." On March 13, "Super Tuesday," with four state caucuses and five primaries, amid generally mixed results, Hart received 35 percent and Mondale 31 percent of the popular vote. Yet "the media message was that this was a Mondale victory, or at least a split decision." Apparently, Mondale was helped by no longer being considered the front-runner.[122] Voting results were less important than the media interpretation of these results.

Candidate choices continuously interact with media interpretations. R. W. Apple's *New York Times* story on the 1976 Iowa caucuses was widely credited with making Carter a front-runner. Interpretations of the 1984 Iowa caucuses, as we have seen, were equally important.[123] For all we know, had there not been numerous network and newspaper polls before the 1976 Republican convention showing Ford ahead, Reagan might have been able to maneuver better against a background of uncertainty. Initially positive media coverage of Howard Dean turned intensely critical after he lost the 2004 Iowa caucuses, severely hampering his ability to get back in the race. Knowing that dramaturgical stereotypes (who the good guys are, who the leaders are, who's out in left field, and so on) tend to persist and that the front-runner of today may be carried along only by early exposure, journalists may seek to resist the obvious.[124] This, however, is hard to do, because it must be done within certain rules of the news gathering business. Newspapers and television news programs require headlines and leads. Ignoring an act can be as dangerous as attending to it, since candidate under- and overexposure may be evident only in retrospect. Since they need news, the media are swept along by the tide of events to which they contribute and in which they swim, very much like the rest of us.

For the first thirty years or so of the television age, political coverage was mainly limited to the nightly evening news broadcasts of the three major broadcast networks (NBC, CBS, and ABC), along with various public affairs programs like *Meet the Press.* The rise of all-news cable channels, beginning with CNN in the 1980s, has greatly increased the volume of coverage available. CNN, which once stood alone as a news-only network, has spun off several sister channels such as Headline News, and now faces competition from Fox News Channel and MSNBC. Media consultants now speak of a "24-hour news cycle," in which the demand for fresh content for news stories is a round-the-clock constant. Campaigns are faced with a news media perpetually desperate for new things to talk about; as a result, small developments often inspire at least temporary media frenzies. Candidates must be "on" at all times; remarks meant to be private can be picked up by open microphones—such as George W. Bush's vulgar description of a *New York Times* reporter in 2000 or John Kerry's characterization of his Republican opponents in 2004 as "the most crooked, lying group I've ever seen"—and replayed ad infinitum on cable news.[125] These episodes tend to pass without major long-term effects, but candidates concerned about their portrayal in the news media seek to avoid them whenever possible.

Of course, much of the programming aired on cable news channels does not constitute "news" at all. These media outlets often devote less time to original political reporting than to analysis and opinion. Political analysts tend to be primarily interested in describing and elaborating campaign strategy, announcing the results of public opinion polls and other measures of the candidate horse race, and making predictions about the outcome of elections and other major political events (such as the selection of running mates). Commentators often represent a particular ideological perspective that largely determines their interpretation of the candidates and campaigns. Political junkies may tune in to satisfy their particular interest in the details of the campaign or to hear reinforcement of their political views, but most Americans tend to be less interested, limiting the potential influence of such pronouncements on public opinion or voting behavior in the mass electorate.

The Internet

A growing number of Americans get significant amounts of news about candidates and campaigns from the Internet. Young people, in particular, are especially likely to look online for political information. This trend will only continue to increase over time, making political content on the World Wide Web an important segment of news media coverage in future elections.

The most widely visited Web sites for information about current affairs are operated by established news organizations such as CNN and the *New York Times*.[126] The content on these sites generally mirrors that of the organizations' print or television coverage, although special Web-only features are becoming more common. While the increasing popularity of the Internet as a source for news has further reinforced the growing demand for political content originally prompted by the rise of cable television's 24-hour news cycle, placing a great deal of pressure on organizations to be the first to report breaking news in order to scoop the competition, most Web users rely on the sites of prestigious newspapers and television channels to supply them with information about political developments. Heavily trafficked portal sites such as Yahoo!, MSN, and America Online also feature top news stories on their front pages, mostly courtesy of wire services such as the Associated Press and Reuters that supply stories to newspapers. For many people, therefore, the Internet serves as a convenient vehicle for information transmission, but the content that they consume online is not unique to the Web; it largely mimics the coverage available elsewhere in newspapers or on television.

Since the late 1990s, however, Web sites without print or television counterparts have played an increasingly prominent role in American politics. The online-only Drudge Report gained a great deal of attention during the period leading up to the impeachment of President Bill Clinton in 1998 for being the first to break several stories about independent counsel Kenneth Starr's investigation of Clinton—reports that were later confirmed by mainstream media outlets. The online magazine Salon first reported a story about past personal indiscretions by House Judiciary Chairman Henry Hyde during his committee's deliberation of impeachment articles against Clinton for lying under oath about his own relationship with White House intern Monica Lewinsky. While many Web sites traffic in rumors and speculation that often turn out to be unfounded or flat-out false, some have been proven right often enough that even reporters for traditional news organizations, despite their stated disdain for those who fail to observe conventional standards of journalistic practice, occasionally admit to checking them regularly for any hints of an explosive new story.

More recently, the Internet has witnessed an explosion of weblogs, or blogs, devoted to politics and current events. Blogs are Web sites that feature regular journal-style entries, called "posts," by one or more proprietors. Most political blogs contain a mix of original commentary and hypertext links to other sources, including news stories, documents, video and audio clips, and posts on other blogs; most also provide for reader responses to each post. Some of the most popular political blogs are maintained by journalists (such as Mickey Kaus, Andrew Sullivan, and Joshua Micah Marshall), opinion columnists (such as Michelle Malkin and Eric Alterman), academics (such as law professor Glenn Reynolds and political scientist Daniel Drezner), and other notable figures (including Arianna Huffington, a former conservative who became a left-wing author in the 1990s and ran for governor of California as an independent in 2003). But many other top blogs are operated by people whose authority is not based on their preexisting status as "experts." Markos Moulitsas, a nonpracticing attorney and Internet consultant, founded Daily Kos in 2002, which quickly became one of the Web's most popular liberal political blogs, due in part to an innovative technical design allowing readers to submit their own original content.

Blogs serve as something of a complement to traditional media outlets. While some blogs are sufficiently popular to provide their owners a full-time income from advertising revenue, none currently enjoys the resources to function as a serious news gathering organization. Occasionally, blogs will break an original story. In 2004, several conservative blogs successfully challenged a claim by Dan Rather of CBS News that records of George W. Bush's military service had been improperly altered in Bush's favor by demonstrating that the documents substantiating Rather's story had been forged. After an investigation confirmed the blogs' findings, three CBS News producers were forced to resign and one was fired by the network.[127]

Most of the time, blogs serve as filters for the immense quantity of information available on the Internet, drawing their readers' attention to existing stories that may otherwise pass without much notice. Occasionally, blogs are successful at placing an issue on the national political agenda. In December 2002, Senate Minority Leader Trent Lott of Mississippi delivered remarks at a one-hundredth birthday party for retiring Senator Strom Thurmond of South Carolina that appeared to endorse the racial segregationist platform of Thurmond's 1948 third-party presidential candidacy. Though reporters from traditional media outlets attended the event, none made much of Lott's speech until several liberal blogs posted the video footage. Within days, the remarks stirred up enough controversy to force Lott to make a series of public pronouncements in his defense, including an appearance on Black Entertainment Television in which he announced his support for affirmative action programs. Within two weeks, the affair had cost Lott his leadership position in the Senate.[128]

The Lott controversy sends a clear message to political candidates that they must comport themselves on all occasions as if the entire world is watching if they expect to survive in the Internet age. Campaigns now routinely send workers called "trackers" to follow opposing candidates at all public events with a video camera in tow, hoping to capture hard evidence of any misstatement or gaffe. In August 2006, Republican Senator George Allen of Virginia, campaigning for a second term at an event in the town of Breaks, directly addressed an American-born college student of South Asian descent sent by the campaign of his opponent James Webb to film Allen's public appearances. "This fellow here, over here with the yellow shirt, Macaca, or whatever his name is. He's with my opponent. He's following us around everywhere. . . . Let's give a warm welcome to Macaca, here. Welcome to America and the real world of Virginia," Allen said, pointing at the tracker to laughter and applause from the assembled audience.[129] The Webb campaign quickly leaked the footage onto the Internet, where it became one of the most-watched items on YouTube, a popular video hosting site. Contradicting Allen's subsequent claim that he had made up the word "macaca" to refer to the Webb staffer, Democratic bloggers discovered that the term is an ethnic slur in certain European and North African cultures, and noted that Allen's mother was raised in French Tunisia. Within days, the incident became a top story in newspapers and on television broadcasts around the state, spawning additional news reports over subsequent weeks of racially insensitive comments that Allen had allegedly made in the 1970s. Originally considered both a heavy favorite for a second term in the Senate and a possible contender for the Republican presidential nomination in 2008, the "macaca" controversy seriously damaged Allen's once-formidable political standing in his home state.[130] He ultimately lost his reelection bid to Webb by a narrow margin.

These examples demonstrate the potential power of the Internet, and blogs in particular, to change the agenda and, therefore, the course of political events. As with other forms of media, however, its influence is not unlimited. Only those who follow politics closely or have strong ideological beliefs—a small minority of the total American population—are likely readers of political Web sites. These people have relatively firm opinions that are particularly unlikely to change after exposure to new arguments or information. And such exposure is minimal if they only read Web sites promoting an ideological or partisan viewpoint with which they already largely agree. Political blogs therefore work primarily to reinforce existing beliefs and loyalties among their readers, not to persuade them to change their positions on issues.

Like newspapers and television, Internet media outlets appear to have more influence during the prenomination period, when multiple candidates within the same party vie for the party's presidential nomination. Howard Dean received a great deal of online support in the 2004 Democratic primaries from bloggers and blog readers attracted by his antiwar, outsider candidacy. Dean's popular Web site served as a means of organizing campaign activity and stimulating financial contributions.[131] While Dean was remarkably successful in assembling a corps of online devotees who vaulted him into contention for the presidency, his inability to inspire a similar depth of support among the Democratic primary electorate at large ultimately doomed his candidacy. Dean's failure to capture the Democratic nomination demonstrates the limits of Internet media in determining electoral outcomes even in primary elections.

INCUMBENCY AS A RESOURCE: THE PRESIDENCY

The presidency is one resource that, in any given election year, must of necessity be monopolized by one party or the other. A president seeking reelection enjoys many special advantages by virtue of incumbency. To begin with, a president is much better known than any challenger can hope to be. Everything the president does is news and is widely reported in all the media. The issues to which presidents devote attention are likely to constitute the national agenda because of a president's unique visibility and capacity to center public attention on matters he or she deems important. To this extent, presidents are in a position to focus public debate on issues they think are most advantageous. Presidents can act and thereby gain credit. If they cannot act, they can accuse Congress of inaction, as Truman did in 1948 and Ford did in 1976. Since Truman won and Ford lost, this strategy, like all strategies in an uncertain world, evidently has mixed effects.

Faced with a crisis in foreign affairs, and there are many, a president can gain politically by handling it well or by calling on the patriotism of the citizenry to support its chief executive when the nation is in danger. But if the problem lingers, the continuing crisis soon becomes a nagging liability. A significant example of a foreign crisis took place during the 1980 campaign, when Iranian "students" seized the American embassy in Teheran on November 4, 1979, taking American diplomats hostage just as Senator Edward Kennedy of Massachusetts announced that he would run for the Democratic nomination against the incumbent president, Jimmy Carter. Before the hostage crisis began, Kennedy was outdistancing Carter in a poll of potential Democratic primary voters by 54 percent to 31 percent (with 15 percent undecided). When the crisis occurred, voters, including Democrats, rallied around the flag, and Carter's support shot up to 48 percent, with 40 percent for Kennedy and 12 percent undecided. Carter announced that he would suspend active campaigning, and he used his crisis responsibilities as a reason to refuse to meet his rival in debates. He continued to campaign from the White House rose garden, however, and with great success.[132] Unfortunately, the crisis dragged on too long, and after he had disposed of the Kennedy primary challenge, President Carter's popularity suffered a serious decline, reverting to its pre-crisis level and resulting in his defeat in the general election.

As Carter discovered in 1980, incumbent presidents benefit from international crises on their watch only as long as the American people have confidence in their ability to handle the problem. A successful resolution of the issue may be rewarded with an impressive surge in popularity, but high approval ratings fade over time as the electorate turns its attention to other issues. George H. W. Bush lost his bid for reelection in 1992 despite reaching a job approval rating of 90 percent after the United States successfully drove the Iraqi Army out of the adjacent nation of Kuwait the year before. By the time of the election, Americans' gratitude for Bush's handling of the Persian Gulf crisis had been superseded by widespread disapproval of the performance of the national economy during his tenure in office.

And if the crisis remains unresolved, impatience sets in. American invasions of Korea in the 1950s, Vietnam in the 1960s, and Iraq in 2003 all initially received broad support from the mass public, but as military operations dragged on for several years without clear evidence of progress or troop withdrawals, Americans increasingly voiced their disapproval of the wars—and of the presidents who started them. Harry Truman (1952) and Lyndon Johnson (1968) both chose not to seek reelection due to their severely weakened public standing as a result of the events in Korea and Vietnam, respectively, while the Democratic takeover of both houses of Congress in the 2006 midterm elections reflected voters' growing frustration with the performance of George W. Bush in managing the war in Iraq more than three years after U.S. forces first occupied the country.

As the symbol of the nation, presidents can travel and make "nonpolitical" speeches to advance their candidacy subtly while appearing to remain above the partisan fray, in contrast to challengers who can be accused of exploiting troubled times for their own political advantage. Should opponents claim that they can do a better job, the president can respond by citing four years of experience in an office for which there exists no completely appropriate prior training. Moreover, as Nixon did in 1972, presidents can campaign by doing their jobs, while challengers, as George McGovern discovered, have to manufacture positions that may dissolve on close scrutiny or criticism.

The life of the incumbent is not necessarily one of undiluted joy. If the national economy worsens, if a natural disaster strikes, or if another nation is lost to hostile forces, the incumbent president is likely, at least over the long run, to be blamed. Whether actually responsible or not, presidents are held accountable for bad times and have to take the consequences.[133] Herbert Hoover deeply felt the sting of this phenomenon when the people punished him as incumbent president for the Great Depression, turning him out of office in the landslide election of 1932.[134] The defeat of incumbent presidents Gerald Ford (1976), Jimmy Carter (1980), and George H. W. Bush (1992) were also primarily due to perceptions of weak national economic performance. Incumbents Ronald Reagan and Bill Clinton were also blamed for hard economic times in the first two years of their administrations; voters expressed their disapproval with the status quo in the 1982 and 1994 midterm elections by voting out large numbers of the president's partisan allies in Congress. Fortunately for both Reagan and Clinton, the national economy in each case soon began to recover. By the time each incumbent stood for reelection two years later, voters had become much more positive about the direction of the country, and responded by awarding both presidents second terms by large margins.

Incumbents have a record; they have or have not done things, and they may be held accountable for their sins of omission or commission. Not so the candidates out of office, who can criticize freely without always presenting realistic alternatives or necessarily taking their own advice once elected. John F. Kennedy's 1960 campaign accused the incumbent Eisenhower administration of allowing a "missile gap" with the Soviet Union which turned out to be something of a chimera after he got into the White House, and he never found it possible to act much differently about the situation concerning Quemoy and Matsu islands near mainland China than did Eisenhower, despite their overpublicized "differences" about this question during the campaign. Richard Nixon could complain about the problem of "law and order" in 1968 without promising anything more concrete than a different attorney general, which any new president would have appointed anyway.

In 1980, Ronald Reagan told Americans to "ask yourself if you are as well off today as you were four years ago" and voters, for the most part erroneously, responded as Reagan hoped, in the negative.[135] Candidate Reagan was able to blame "stagflation," the unwelcome combination of high inflation and unemployment, on President Carter. The considerable Republican losses in the 1982 congressional elections, combined with the ability of Democrats to blame the Republican president for unemployment, placed Reagan in the same difficult defensive position his predecessor had been in a few years earlier. Reagan's popularity returned with economic recovery but, as the Iran-contra scandal showed, even an alleged "Teflon" president has difficulty escaping blame when things go wrong on his watch. The incumbent is naturally cast as the defender of the current administration and the challenger as the attacker who promises better things to come. We cannot expect to hear the person in office say that the opposition could probably perform as well or to hear the challenger declare that he or she really could not do any better than the incumbent, although in a political system that encourages moderation and has enormous built-in inertia, such as the American system, both statements may be close to the truth.

While opponents can to some extent permit themselves to be irresponsible or carried away by exuberance, presidents cannot detach themselves from office while campaigning, and they must recognize that other nations are listening when they make statements. The president's very superiority of information may turn out to be a handicap, if he or she cannot make certain statements or reveal sources for statements without committing a breach of security. Opponents can attack the incumbent's record, but the incumbent may have difficulty finding a comparable record to assail on the other side—unless, of course, the challenger succeeds at making his or her own proposals the issue. Both Barry Goldwater in 1964 and George McGovern in 1972 managed to do this, more or less across the board, on many issues. Walter Mondale's promise of higher taxes provided ammunition for President Reagan's 1984 reelection campaign.

Barring catastrophic events—depression, war, scandal—the president's power is most certainly strong enough to assure renomination by his or her own party within the limits imposed by the Twenty-second Amendment to the Constitution, which restricts presidents to two terms. This is not merely because the presidency is the greatest, most visible office in the land, with claims on the loyalty of many, if not all, potential rivals. The president's party can hardly hope to win by repudiating the president. To refuse the incumbent the nomination would, most politicians feel, be tantamount to confessing political bankruptcy or ineptitude. The fact that primary voters, not politicians, now make the relevant decisions lends a note of uncertainty to what used to be a sure thing.

This rule was bent but not broken in 1980 by Senator Edward Kennedy's prenomination opposition to Jimmy Carter and in 1976 by former Governor Ronald Reagan's challenge to Ford. Nor was it broken in 1968. The challenges of Eugene McCarthy and Robert Kennedy to Lyndon Johnson in that year demonstrated that the costs of party insurgency are high: not only do insurgents rarely win their party's nomination, but when party insurgency is strong, their party usually loses the general election. It was not only the fact that Edward Kennedy sought to take the Democratic nomination away from Carter in 1980, but also that he persisted right up through the convention, refusing to give Carter his wholehearted endorsement, that hurt the Democrats. Consequently candidate Carter was unable to focus on his Republican opponent as early as he would have liked. No subsequent president has faced a primary challenger with a serious chance of winning the nomination; Ronald Reagan (1984), Bill Clinton (1996), and George W. Bush (2004) all ran unopposed for renomination, while George H. W. Bush (1992) faced a protest candidate in challenger Pat Buchanan who ran an initially energetic campaign but never seriously threatened to defeat Bush in the Republican primaries.

The decline of the influence of state parties in national conventions and the rise of primary elections makes presidents less influential in nomination politics than they once were. Presidents have a harder time controlling primaries than influencing party leaders, and this affects presidential power over conventions. Overt attempts to designate a successor make less sense for an outgoing president in a system dominated by primaries, for the risks of failure are high.

INCUMBENCY AS A LIABILITY: THE VICE PRESIDENCY

The incumbent president does have some advantages; it is the incumbent vice president seeking to succeed a president of the same party who suffers the most, as Richard Nixon discovered in 1960, Hubert Humphrey in 1968, and Al Gore in 2000. A vice president suffers from the disadvantages of having to defend an existing record and of being a new face. He or she cannot attack the administration in office without alienating the president and selling their party short. At the same time, a vice president cannot claim experience in the presidential office. Even voters who approve of the performance of the incumbent administration may not give the vice president any credit for it. This is the most difficult strategic problem of all for candidates.[136]

George H. W. Bush in 1988 was the first sitting vice president to be elected in succession to a retiring president since Martin Van Buren succeeded Andrew Jackson in 1836. Why, despite the historical rarity of the event, did Bush win? He obtained the nomination of his party largely, it appears, because primary voters in the Republican Party considered him the logical successor to Ronald Reagan, and Reagan was extremely popular at the end of his second term. This may help also to explain why Bush won the election. At least three theories—all of them meritorious—have been invoked to explain his success.[137] They refer, respectively, to peace and prosperity, to the conduct of the campaign, and to structural properties of the parties and the nominating process. The first theory is refreshingly straightforward. It says, simply, that if nothing is badly disturbing the electorate, then incumbents will do well. George H. W. Bush was of course not an incumbent president, but as the sitting vice president he was as close to an incumbent president as it is possible to be without actually being one. In the 1988 election, most incumbents, whether they were Democrats or Republicans, did extraordinarily well for all offices, as they usually do in conditions of peace and prosperity. And most, unlike Bush, were Democrats. Scholars who use sophisticated models to attempt to forecast presidential elections have, on the whole, employed assumptions stressing such variables as the condition of the economy somewhat in advance of the election, and they all produced numbers suggesting a Bush victory.[138] Indeed, some of them did so even during the spring and summer months when Democratic nominee Michael Dukakis was leading Bush by a wide margin in the public opinion polls.

The second theory also seems to us entirely plausible. It points out that Vice President Bush ran an effective campaign and Governor Dukakis did not. Jerry Roberts of the *San Francisco Chronicle* gave an excellent summary of professional opinion on this subject, noting the following features of the Dukakis campaign:

A fatal reluctance to respond to Bush's bare-knuckle attacks. The Republican hit Dukakis as weak on defense and soft on crime, attacking him over the Pledge of Allegiance, prison furloughs and the death penalty. By the time Dukakis fired back in late fall, it was too late. Many voters by then believed the attacks because they had gone unanswered.

A failure to find a consistent campaign theme. Running against peace and prosperity, Dukakis tried campaigning on competence, the middle class squeeze and the unfairness of Bush's attacks before settling on traditional Democratic economic populism in the closing weeks of the race.

A disastrous media campaign. Matched against Bush's state-of-the-art television commercials—which meshed precisely with the message he was delivering on the campaign trail—Dukakis' shifting set of ads had little impact. They were produced by a series of media specialists and drafted by committee, and were criticized as confusing, obscure and without much content.

"We absolutely should have won this race," said California Democratic Party Chairman Peter Kelly. "What happened was George Bush defined Mike Dukakis before Dukakis defined himself."[139]

It is possible to dwell too long on particulars of the 1988 campaign. There is unusually strong agreement among campaign professionals that Dukakis campaigned badly in the general election. This overlooks the fact that he did well enough in the primary season, winning the Democratic nomination in a crowded field of candidates, in handling the demands of rival candidate Jesse Jackson thereafter, and in his vice presidential pick of the magisterial Senator Lloyd Bentsen of Texas. There is, likewise, strong agreement that the Bush campaign was well tailored to make the best of the vice president's chances, conveniently overlooking Bush's ill-advised selection of Senator Dan Quayle of Indiana as his running mate. So if we accept the professional assessment of the effects of the campaign—as on the whole we do—we must do so in the face of the fact that every winning campaign looks better in retrospect and every losing campaign looks worse than it probably was.

Of the third theory we are especially fond because it helps understand not only the election of 1988 but also the great and persistent anomaly in the American political system in which, from the 1950s through the 1990s, Republicans frequently succeeded in presidential elections while Democrats dominated overall, as measured by success in congressional elections, control of state governments, and party identification among the electorate. Republican gains in the 1990s put them on an even footing, but were nowhere near the large Democratic advantages that survived even the Nixon landslide in 1972 and the Reagan landslide in 1984.

Essentially, the argument is that since the drastic reforms of the presidential nominating process that took place in the wake of the chaotic 1968 Democratic National Convention, the system changed radically from a coalition-building regime to a factional-mobilization regime. Over the long run this development harms Democrats and helps Republicans in the general election because the Democrats, although historically the larger of the two parties, are also far more factionally fragmented and therefore greatly disadvantaged in a long nomination process in which there are no incentives or occasions for coalition formation. Because the Republicans are much more easily mobilized and coordinated through their basic ideological similarities, the lack of coalition-building incentives harms them less.[140]

George H. W. Bush also had to contend with the disadvantages of the vice presidency, and so did Al Gore during the 2000 election. Gore faced the strategic difficulty of claiming credit for the Clinton-Gore administration's popular economic policies while simultaneously distancing himself personally from Clinton. Thomas Riley Marshall, the genial Hoosier who was Woodrow Wilson's vice president, once observed that the office he had in the Capitol was so little protected from tourists that they used to come by and stare at him like a monkey in the zoo. "Only," he complained, "they never offer me any peanuts." This is the way vice presidents have viewed their constitutional office, not just its physical setting, for a long time. "Not worth a pitcher of warm spit" was the bowdlerized version of John Nance Garner's rueful conclusion in the mid-1930s. "A mere mechanical tool to wind up the clock" was the way the first vice president, John Adams, described himself. "My country has in its wisdom contrived for me the most insignificant office that was the invention of man."

The main constitutional function of the vice president is to wait. As the fictional publican of Archey Road, Chicago, and all-around pundit Mr. Dooley once said, "Every morning it is his business to call at the White House and inquire after the President's health. When told that the President was never better, he gives three cheers and departs with a heavy heart."[141] Clearly this is not much of a job for a major political figure who is used to active leadership. Yet suppose a sudden tragedy should befall the president. Can we afford in the inevitable days of uncertainty that follow such an event to replace the president with anything less than an experienced leader who can step into the breach immediately, do the president's job, and do it well? This is the first and fundamental dilemma of the vice presidency and, as the quotation from John Adams amply testifies, it has been with us since the founding of the Republic. From this dilemma flow the problems characteristic of the modern vice presidency.

We can date the modern vice presidency from April 12, 1945, the day Franklin D. Roosevelt died in office. The next day his successor, Harry Truman, remarked to some newspaper reporters: "Boys, if you ever pray, pray for me now. I don't know whether you fellows ever had a load of hay fall on you, but when they told me yesterday what had happened, I felt like the moon, the stars, and all the planets had fallen on me." Truman had been a respected but not a leading senator before he assumed the vice presidency. In his three months in that office, Vice President Truman saw President Roosevelt only a few short times. As vice president he had not been told of the Manhattan Project to build the atomic bomb. Sticking closely to the negligible duties of the office prescribed under the Constitution, Truman had spent most of his time on Capitol Hill, presiding over the Senate. His knowledge of the affairs of the executive branch and of foreign and military operations was the knowledge of an experienced legislator and not the inside information routinely available to top policymakers in the Roosevelt administration. Truman wrote later, "it is a mighty leap from the vice presidency to the presidency when one is forced to make it without warning."[142]

Since Harry Truman made that leap in the waning days of World War II, the world has grown more complicated, and so has the presidency. Efforts have accordingly been made to update the vice presidency to meet modern conditions. The vice president now sits on the National Security Council as a matter of right; under President Eisenhower, the vice president attended all meetings of the cabinet at the president's invitation and presided in the president's absence. In addition to his Capitol Hill quarters, Vice President Johnson had a suite of offices in the Executive Office Building adjacent to the White House. For a while, President Nixon moved Spiro Agnew to an office down the hall from his own. Nelson Rockefeller was not only made head of the Domestic Council by President Ford, but also was allowed to bring in his own people as top staff assistants in this presidential agency. Vice President Mondale, with an office in the White House only a few doors away from the Oval Office, was given an unprecedented full, though junior, partnership by President Carter. Vice President Bush's relations with President Reagan were complicated by worries among the Reagan staff about Bush's future ambitions, a common enough difficulty between presidents and vice presidents, somewhat exacerbated in this case by their differences in age and in political outlook. But Bush kept the White House office, and he played a part in foreign policy. Vice President Al Gore's role constituted a return to the modern trend. By all accounts, he was more active, influential, and trusted even than Mondale was.[143] The experienced Dick Cheney, a former White House chief of staff, secretary of defense, and House Republican Whip, without presidential ambitions of his own because of his history as a cardiac patient, similarly occupies a leading role in the administration of George W. Bush.

In return for continuous exposure to the entire range of problems confronting the government, vastly improved access to the president, and a closer view of the burdens of the presidency, the modern vice president must also carry some of these burdens. Which burdens are carried, how many, and how far are up to the president. Withholding cooperation would impair the vice president's relationship with the president. This would be bound to affect his or her capacity to fulfill the constitutional obligation of the vice presidency, which is to be genuinely prepared in case of dire need.

Most recent vice presidents—Mondale, Gore, and Cheney—come closer than earlier vice presidents to being second in command in a president's administration. More often, over the years, the vice president has been entirely removed from any chain of command in the government. This guaranteed the independence of the vice president in the days of Aaron Burr, John C. Calhoun, Charles Dawes, and other free spirits who have occupied the office. Today, the situation is quite different: it is much easier for other high members of a president's administration to maintain independence from the presidency. Top administrative officials can constitute a loyal opposition on government policy within the executive branch because their obligations run in at least three directions: upward to the president, downward to the agencies whose programs they supervise within the administration, and outward to the clientele their agencies serve. Political executives serve the president best who serve their clients with devotion and promote the interests of their agencies with vigor. Executives know, moreover, that if in the process they conflict too much with presidential plans or priorities, the president can always fire them. If the president fails them in some serious way, they can resign, as Attorney General Elliot Richardson did when President Nixon ordered him to remove Special Prosecutor Archibald Cox during the memorable "Saturday Night Massacre" of October 1973, or as Secretary of State Cyrus Vance did from the Carter administration in 1979 over the aborted rescue mission to Iran.

Vice presidents can hardly fulfill their constitutional responsibilities by resigning, nor, in midterm, can they be dismissed. They have no anchor in the bureaucracy, no interest-group constituency. Thus, uniquely in the executive branch, modern vice presidents must discipline themselves to loyalty to the president. This sometimes has painful consequences for vice presidents, especially when they attempt to emerge from the shadow of the president and run for the presidency on their own. The worst modern case was probably Vice President Hubert Humphrey's difficulty in 1968 in persuading opponents of the Vietnam War that he had deeply disagreed with President Johnson's policies, as he had privately done, while publicly defending them. Even after four years out of office, Walter Mondale found himself criticized for President Carter's perceived failures during the 1984 campaign. In 1988, Vice President George H. W. Bush was alternatively attacked as servile and insufficiently loyal.[144] Like Humphrey and Nixon before him, Bush found it difficult to run independently on his own record. Al Gore in 2000 found the legacy of Bill Clinton's personal behavior in office so burdensome that he was unable to capitalize as he should have on the Clinton-Gore public record of peace and extraordinary prosperity.

There seems to be no way for vice presidents to avoid the dilemmas built into the office. Unless scrupulously loyal, they cannot get the access to the president that they need to discharge their constitutional function; when loyal to the president, they are saddled, at least in the short run, with whatever characteristics of the president or the administration's program that the president's enemies or their own care to fasten on them. A vice president sits there in the limelight, visible, vulnerable, and for the most part, powerless.

From 1836 until 1960, when Richard Nixon was nominated, no incumbent vice president was put forward for the presidency. Since 1960, most vice presidents—Johnson, Humphrey, Ford, Mondale, Bush, Quayle, Gore—have run for president in subsequent elections; all but Quayle succeeded in capturing their party's nomination. It may be that the name recognition of vice presidents or, as Howard Reiter suggests, the decline of the ability of party leaders to select their own candidate, has made vice presidents leading candidates for the presidency.[145] Johnson and Ford became presidents before seeking election as their party's presidential nominee, but the others did it on their own. Now even defeated vice presidential candidates, from Lodge to Muskie to Shriver to Dole to Lieberman to Edwards, launch their own presidential campaigns four years later.

As long as vice presidents have some chance eventually to run for the presidency, as they do at present, and are not arbitrarily excluded from further consideration as independent political leaders in their own right, there will be plenty of takers for the vice presidential nomination. This contributes to the strength of political parties. Vice presidential nominees can balance tickets, help to unite a warring party, and campaign effectively with party workers and before the public—as, for example, Senator Lyndon Johnson of Texas did with conspicuous success in the election of 1960, and both George H. W. Bush and Walter Mondale did in 1980, and Lloyd Bentsen and Al Gore did in 1988 and 1992. Thus, vice presidential nominees can help elect a president. It is after the campaign is over that the vice president's problems begin.

CONVERTIBILITY OF RESOURCES

Clearly, the social framework within which presidential election strategies must be pursued distributes advantages and disadvantages rather importantly between candidates and parties. We have attempted to explain why the unequal distribution of key resources such as money and control over information do not necessarily or automatically lead to election victories for the parties and candidates who possess and use most of these resources. Might there not, however, be a cumulative effect that would greatly assist those who possessed both more money and more control over information? This effect may exist, but it could not be of overwhelming importance, since the Democrats, who are usually disadvantaged in both respects, have won slightly more than half the elections since 1932. We can suggest a few reasons for Democratic strength despite these disadvantages. First, the Democrats were able to convert other resources into money and control over information, thereby narrowing the gap during campaigns. Second, the Democrats have had superior access to other important resources, which may counter the Republican superiority in money and control over the media of information.

Once the Democratic Party captured the presidency in 1932 and held it for twenty consecutive years, it was able to use the resource of official position to collect campaign funds because contributors wanted access to the winner. The Democratic candidate could also get greater news coverage because the incumbent president's activities are newsworthy no matter what his or her party. The alliance of the Democrats with the large industrial unions has, at times, meant that the party has received contributions in the form of personal electioneering, for which the Republicans had to lay out cash or do without. The superiority (perhaps the mere existence) of Democratic organizations in cities of large population with strategic impact on the electoral college has sometimes led to the availability of election workers who did not have to be paid in cash—at least not in cash the presidential candidate had to raise during the campaign. Public funding has brought expenditures in the general election campaign to a fairly even level. When Democrats maintain a lead over Republicans in party identification, as they have for most of the history of public opinion polling, this is the most effective resource in the Democratic arsenal.

These Democratic assets are still important, but in each case the Democratic advantage has declined. The Republicans have controlled the White House (and the benefits that entails) for thirty-six of the last fifty-six years. Unions and urban political organizations are less important and smaller than they once were and are facing difficult times. The assistance they can offer the Democrats is not unlimited. Finally, the Democratic edge in party identification has shrunk in recent years. The Democrats' ability to counter Republican assets has eroded.

II

SEQUENCES

The next two chapters follow the chronology of the election year, first dealing with processes leading up to the nominations of major candidates, then discussing the course of the campaign leading up to election night. Many of the moves that actors execute take on meaning when they are viewed in the light of their activities at different stages of the nomination and election process.

FOUR

THE NOMINATION PROCESS

O NCE UPON A TIME, PRESIDENTIAL NOMINATIONS WERE won by candidates who courted the support of party leaders from the several states. These leaders appeared at the national convention as representatives of their state parties. That system is history. Now, nominations are won by accumulating pledged delegates in a state-by-state march through primary elections and delegate-selection caucuses—a time-consuming, complicated, and costly process.[1]

For a party with an incumbent president running for reelection, the rules for the selection of a nominee are not terribly important. Ordinarily, challenges to a sitting president from within the president's party are doomed to failure. The ground rules governing nominations are, however, extremely important in shaping the behavior of candidates and activists from any party with no incumbent. In 2004, this meant the Democrats, and for 2008, this will apply to both parties.

Some of these rules have been put in place as the result of national campaign finance laws. Others were enacted by the Democrats to govern their own procedures. Since these rules required changes in state laws governing the selection process, on the whole they affect both parties.

1. All Democratic and Republican convention delegates must be selected within a roughly four-month period from early February to early June of a presidential election year (except for the earlier events in Iowa and New Hampshire).[2] In both parties, the vast majority of delegates are selected either in state primaries, in which party voters cast a ballot at a traditional polling place for their favored candidate, or in caucuses, which consist of a number of simultaneous meetings around the state in which party members discuss and measure support for each of the candidates. Candidates must contest primaries and caucuses because convention

delegates, who choose the eventual nominee of the party, are selected in those elections. Primaries are no longer "beauty contests" functioning merely as signals to party leaders about which candidates have the support of voters, as they mostly were before 1972.[3]

2. During the prenomination primaries, candidates who demonstrate sufficiently broad appeal by raising $5,000 in contributions of up to $250 in each of twenty states ($100,000 total) are eligible to receive federal funds matching all individual campaign contributions up to $250, as long as they abide by limits on the amount their campaigns can spend in total and in each state (see chapter 3).

3. In the Democratic Party, any candidate in a statewide primary or caucus who receives more than 15 percent of the vote in any congressional district within the state receives a proportionate share of the delegates chosen in that district.

4. The Republican Party has no such nationally mandated minimum threshold. States may choose proportional representation, winner-take-all (under which the candidate finishing first in the state receives all the delegates from that state), or some combination for their primary elections or caucuses. Republican delegates are apportioned to each state by a formula that gives added weight to states that voted Republican in the last presidential, congressional, and gubernatorial elections. Thus, Republican candidates for the nomination have an incentive to win in states that vote Republican in national and state elections, but each state has its own rules apportioning delegates to candidates. Some states, such as California, are winner-take-all for Republicans.

5. Democratic elected officials (members of Congress and governors) as well as officials of the Democratic National Committee have automatic seats as delegates and voting rights in the convention and are not required to pledge their support to any candidate as a condition of delegate status. These "superdelegates" constituted 19 percent of the Democratic delegates in 2004. Democrats also require state delegations to be evenly divided between men and women.

6. Since 1972, the position of state party leaders has been reduced to making deals to support one or another candidate at the time of the state primary or caucus—not at the national convention, which is much too late. Thus the candidate's job is to attract support from state party leaders by looking like a probable winner as early as possible.

The rules are important; they drive the strategies used by candidates. The most important imperative under the rules, as they have existed since the 1972 election, is that candidates compete in state contests—mostly primaries—under which delegates are chosen by large statewide electorates. This contrasts sharply with the procedures used in an earlier era, in which candidates focused on winning support from members of the state party hierarchies, who usually chose the delegates. The rules of delegate selection and fundraising require candidates to obtain a broad base of support both within states (for delegates) and across states (for money). Especially on the Democratic side, where delegates are allocated in proportion to the support each candidate demonstrates at the polls, candidates must compete for delegates more or less everywhere to stand a chance of reaching the 50 percent plus one at the convention necessary for nomination. Proportionate rules for counting votes encourage Democrats to enter more primaries for the simple reason that there are delegates to be had even if one does not win a majority. Primaries also generate attention. This means more people will be enticed out of the woodwork to make financial contributions.

BEFORE THE PRIMARIES

The first overall constraint on the system is that the more people you have to convince, the longer it takes. The nomination process has become very long, giving early starters an advantage. The second overall constraint is that the more restrictions placed on the expenditure of money, the harder it is for newcomers to attract public notice to get into the race. This, too, dictates an earlier start to the campaign. Anybody whose name is known ahead of time—a movie star, a sports figure, an incumbent of high office—gets a boost.

Among the axioms of conventional wisdom to bite the dust in 1972 was the notion that an early announcement of candidacy was a sign of a weak candidate and that it therefore behooved front-runners to avoid an early disclosure of their plans, with all the inconvenience and running around that an active campaign entails. This coyness destroyed the chances of the 1972 early Democratic front-runner, Senator Edmund Muskie of Maine. In 1976 this lesson was greatly reinforced when former Governor Jimmy Carter of Georgia, a virtually unknown outsider before the primaries began, parlayed early, narrow wins in Iowa, New Hampshire, and Florida into the Democratic nomination. Thus the congressional elections of 1978 were barely over before a variety of Republicans announced their candidacies for the 1980 race and began to qualify for federal support. Two Democratic candidates qualified for the 1984 federal subsidy by the end of the first week of 1983.[4] By June 1987 seven candidates were campaigning for the 1988 Republican nomination and seven for the Democratic,[5] and the Democratic front-runner, former Colorado Senator Gary Hart, had already been sidelined because of publicity surrounding charges of adultery.[6] By March 1995 there was enormous activity among Republican hopefuls for the following year's nomination. Bill Bennett, Dick Cheney, Jack Kemp, and Dan Quayle had already declared themselves out of the competition, mostly because they did not believe they could raise the $20 million in early money that was generally regarded at the time as the minimum required to run a serious campaign. Senator Phil Gramm of Texas, flush with contributions, tossed his hat in the ring, as did former Tennessee Governor Lamar Alexander, conservative commentator Pat Buchanan, and Senator Richard Lugar of Indiana. Senate Majority Leader Bob Dole of Kansas and California Governor Pete Wilson hovered on the brink of an official announcement, as did three or four others.[7]

Similarly, by March 1999 the 2000 campaign was already well underway. On the Democratic side, Vice President Al Gore and former New Jersey Senator Bill Bradley had formally organized their campaigns, while four other potential candidates (Senators Bob Kerrey of Nebraska, John Kerry of Massachusetts, and Paul Wellstone of Minnesota, and Representative Richard Gephardt of Missouri) had already publicly announced that they would not seek the nomination. On the Republican side, ten candidates were actively campaigning, including the two front-runners in early public opinion polls, Texas Governor George W. Bush and former cabinet secretary Elizabeth Dole. Others had already chosen not to make the race, including Senator John Ashcroft of Missouri and former Governor Pete Wilson of California. Two contenders, former Tennessee Governor Lamar Alexander and publisher Steve Forbes, had barely ended their unsuccessful 1996 campaigns before they began seeking the 2000 nomination. Dole, Alexander, Representative John Kasich of Ohio, and former Vice President Dan Quayle ran active campaigns only to drop out, defeated, by the end of October 1999, several months before the first votes were to be cast in Iowa and New Hampshire, due principally to their inability to compete financially with the Bush campaign.[8] Evidence that the race is already in an advanced stage long before voters become

TABLE 4.1	Early Money in the 2004 Election	
Candidate	Money Raised January 1–June 30, 2003 (in millions of dollars)
Republicans	
George W. Bush	35.1
Democrats	
John Kerry	12.9
John Edwards	11.9
Howard Dean	10.2
Richard Gephardt	9.9
Joseph Lieberman	8.2
Bob Graham	3.1
Dennis Kucinich	1.8
Carol Moseley-Braun	0.2
Al Sharpton	0.1

Source: FEC Quarterly Reports, http://www.fec.gov.

Note: General Wesley Clark entered the race for the Democratic nomination in September 2003.

directly involved can be seen in the large sums candidates for the 2004 party nominations raised in the first six months of 2003, a full year before the primaries (see table 4.1).

By March 2003, nine Democrats had thrown their hats in the ring for the 2004 presidential nomination: Senators John Kerry of Massachusetts, John Edwards of North Carolina, Joseph Lieberman of Connecticut, and Bob Graham of Florida, former Senator Carol Moseley-Braun of Illinois, Representatives Richard Gephardt of Missouri and Dennis Kucinich of Ohio, former Governor Howard Dean of Vermont, and the Reverend Al Sharpton. (A tenth contender, retired General Wesley Clark, waited to enter the race until the following fall.) Former Vice President Al Gore, who actually won the popular vote in 2000, had announced by this point that he would not seek the Democratic nomination in 2004, as had Senate Democratic Leader Tom Daschle of South Dakota and Senators Hillary Rodham Clinton of New York and Christopher Dodd of Connecticut.

In early 2006, even before the midterm congressional elections, multiple potential candidates in both parties were already laying the groundwork for a possible 2008 campaign—two full years before the first presidential primaries. At the time, the Republican field appeared to include Senators John McCain of Arizona, George Allen of Virginia, Sam Brownback of Kansas, and Bill Frist of Tennessee, as well as Massachusetts Governor Mitt Romney, while several other potential candidates, including Senator Chuck Hagel of Nebraska, former mayor of New York Rudolph Giuliani, Governors George Pataki of New York and Mike Huckabee of Arkansas, and former House Speaker Newt Gingrich, did nothing to dampen public speculation that they, too, would enter the race. On the Democratic side, Senator Hillary Rodham Clinton of New York prepared for a 2008 presidential bid, as did Senators Evan Bayh of Indiana, Joseph Biden of Delaware, and Russ Feingold of Wisconsin, former Senator John Edwards of North Carolina, and former Governor Mark Warner of Virginia; other possible contenders included Governors Bill Richardson of New Mexico and Tom Vilsack of Iowa, Senator Christopher Dodd of Connecticut, former Senate Majority Leader Tom Daschle of South Dakota, retired General Wesley Clark, and the party's previous two nominees for the presidency, Al Gore and John Kerry.

By the end of 2006, this field of potential presidential contenders had already begun to solidify, as officeholders faced increasing pressure to declare themselves in or out of the 2008 contest. Some candidates had already begun to organize their campaigns, hiring experienced consultants and fundraisers while building support among political leaders in key states. Others, after testing the waters, had already decided not to jump in this time. Allen, who unexpectedly lost his bid for a second term in the Senate, and Frist announced in the fall of 2006 that they would not enter the contest for the Republican nomination, while Feingold, Warner, and Daschle similarly chose to sit out the election on the Democratic side. At the same time, new potential contenders had surfaced in both parties: Representative Duncan Hunter of California for the GOP, and Senator Barack Obama of Illinois and Representative Dennis Kucinich of Ohio for the Democrats.

During the long preprimary phase, the candidates are not just raising money and hiring campaign staff. They also undertake a certain amount of ideological preparation, attempting to shape a message that will appeal to probable voters in their party primaries. Knowing that most of the voters in Republican primaries are right of center, Vice President George H. W. Bush, Representative Jack Kemp of New York, and Kansas Senator Bob Dole spent a lot of time in 1987 aiming their remarks (and shading their voting records) toward this part of the spectrum. Similarly, the fact that the dominant faction of the Democratic Party is left of center has not been lost among Democratic contenders. As an adviser to a rival candidate described Gary Hart's preprimary activities in 1986, "he saw how liberals and labor dominated things in 1984 and he's determined he's not going to let anyone get to his left."[9] In 1995 Senate Majority Leader Dole, the most visible of the Republican hopefuls, struggled in public with the challenge of finding the correct "conservative" stand on new issues such as the conflict in Bosnia.[10] When former Governor Howard Dean of Vermont unexpectedly gained momentum in early 2003 by criticizing his Democratic rivals for supporting the U.S invasion of Iraq ordered by George W. Bush, he sent them scrambling to emphasize the ways in which they disagreed with Bush's Iraq policies, lest they be punished by Democratic primary voters for insufficient ideological loyalty.

Part of the preprimary task of the candidate is to achieve the status of being "taken seriously" by the news media. Being taken seriously ordinarily requires that a candidate should have won some major election for public office. In addition, the news media pay attention to signs that candidates are hiring experienced, competent staff—campaign managers, strategists and consultants, fundraisers, lawyers, accountants, pollsters, media buyers, advance workers, speechwriters, policy analysts, spotters of political talent in the early states—and are establishing a beachhead in early primary states, regularly visiting Iowa and New Hampshire, and doing respectably in straw polls conducted at various party meetings around the country and in public opinion surveys of potential primary voters—polls that everyone says "don't count," although of course they do. All this activity is highly visible to the increasingly watchful news media, who in turn pronounce candidates to be "serious" or "not serious," with attendant consequences for the candidate's public visibility and credibility with potential donors of campaign funds.

The lessons of the preprimary period in the emerging nomination system have become clear: before the delegate-selection season begins, candidates must organize to achieve personal visibility. Visibility is important because in order to win it is necessary to appeal to voters in primary elections and caucuses. Organization is important because that is what it takes to turn out voters. Because a great many candidates begin the election season with presidential ambitions, the course of selection is a winnowing process in which the successive hurdles of the weeks in which primaries and caucuses are held knock off more and more hopefuls until only one survivor remains in each party. In advance of these events, the candidates' tasks are to raise money, increase visibility, and give personal attention to states that will select delegates early in the process.

Preprimary activities thus take up more and more time and absorb more and more resources in preparation for primary elections, which were held in more than thirty-five states in 2004, and party caucuses, used elsewhere to select delegates to the national conventions.

IOWA AND NEW HAMPSHIRE: THE FIRST HURDLES

The party rules that provide for all delegate selection to take place in the year of the election also prescribe that the selection processes—state caucuses and primaries—take place within a limited period of time. Two exceptions, based on accidents of history, have thus far always been granted by the Democratic Party, and the Republicans have always gone along. Iowa, which selects its delegates through a series of broadly participatory local, regional, and state caucuses and conventions, has a license to be first in the nation. And New Hampshire, the first primary, comes next—in recent years, within a week.[11]

These Iowa precinct caucuses are only the first stage of a delegate selection process that actually occurs somewhat later, at state party conventions. Although it is the caucuses, the early events, that get the publicity, frequently candidates who do not win in the caucuses end up with Iowa delegates to the national convention, as George H. W. Bush did in 1988.[12]

Given the complications in ascertaining what the outcomes in eventual delegates of the precinct caucuses will be, it is a wonder that there is so much news coverage of the Iowa caucuses. In 1984, according to an actual count of news coverage appearing on all three television networks plus in the *New York Times*, Iowa, with 2.5 percent of the U.S. population, received 12.8 percent of the total news coverage accorded the presidential race from January to June.[13]

The coverage is high because the Iowa precinct caucuses are, in effect, the gateway to a long and complex nomination process, and players and observers very much want whatever information they can glean from the results in Iowa, if only to position themselves for the next round of events. The media need to know to whom to give special attention. Financial supporters of various candidates want to know whether it is worthwhile to continue to give, or to steer, money to their first choices or whether it is time to jump to other alternatives. Voters want to know which candidacies are viable, which futile.[14] Thus the grounds for paying special attention to the Iowa caucuses are that the system as a whole is conspicuously front-loaded, and Iowa is farthest to the front. What does it mean to have a front-loaded nomination process?

The temptation to ignore history is ever present. Each quadrennial nomination sequence has plenty of elements of uniqueness, and our entire historical experience of presidential elections yields very few instances at best. Even further constraining a historical view is the fact that whatever happened before the drastic changes of the post-1968 reforms should probably be ignored on the grounds that the system overall was fundamentally altered by these reforms. It is the reforms that front-loaded the presidential nominating process.[15] Consequently, considering evidence from 1968 and before is bound to be drastically misleading as a guide to the structural constraints and strategic opportunities that shape the choices of contemporary actors. So we are left, in effect, with exactly eighteen historical data points, nine Democratic, nine Republican, representing the elections of 1972, 1976, 1980, 1984, 1988, 1992, 1996, 2000, and 2004. And these, owing to the effects of incumbency, can be reduced even further.

1972

In 1972 the Iowa caucuses were for the first time set early in the year, on January 24. This date was arrived at because the Democratic state convention was to be held on May 20, owing to the availability on that date of a suitable hall. Working backward from May 20, adequate time had to be provided to prepare for each of the earlier stages of the process, and the entire sequence had to be completed within the same calendar year as the national convention. Thus the January date.[16]

In 1972 the Republican incumbent, Richard Nixon, had only token opposition in Iowa from two representatives in Congress, Paul (Pete) McCloskey of California, ideologically on his left, and John Ashbrook of Ohio on his right. Nixon's ability to win renomination was never in doubt.

The Democratic caucuses, in contrast, were quite important. The presumed front-runner, Senator Edmund Muskie of Maine, operating under obsolete strategic premises, had failed to announce his candidacy until January 4, 1972. Neither Muskie nor Senator George McGovern of South Dakota invested much effort in Iowa. The day after the first-round caucuses, the newspapers reported unofficially, with incomplete returns, that Muskie beat McGovern in the precinct caucuses in Iowa by a margin of 35.5 percent to 22.6 percent, with 35.8 percent uncommitted. The unexpected closeness of this result pushed Muskie into overwork and an unaccustomed public display of emotional behavior in front of the building housing the offices of the *Union Leader* newspaper in Manchester, New Hampshire.[17] When the news media analysts were finished with the New Hampshire results, prior "expectations" that the U.S. senator from a neighboring state should win an overwhelming victory, over 50 percent, completely obscured the fact that Muskie had in fact won (46 percent to 37 percent). Because his win was 4 or 5 points less impressive than "expected," Muskie's support, especially financial support, began to dry up, and he withdrew from the race altogether by April 27, effectively conceding the nomination to McGovern.

The front-running Muskie presidential campaign was nibbled to death by ducks before it began. This extraordinary spectacle gave unmistakable evidence of the fact that changing the rules had changed the game. Preconvention skirmishes were no longer simply important evidence to be taken into account by party leaders in making nominations: they were the contest itself.

Iowa did not administer the coup de grace to Muskie: that happened in New Hampshire. At most, what happened in Iowa energized the participants in the New Hampshire primary and structured the alternatives for New Hampshire voters.

1976

Once again, an incumbent was running on the Republican side. This time, however, Gerald Ford was the incumbent. Ford, who succeeded to the presidency when Richard Nixon resigned, had never been a Republican presidential nominee, and he was not an eloquent defender of his presidency. He was faced by a serious challenge from former California Governor Ronald Reagan. Iowa came out a dead heat between the two; both candidates ended up with eighteen delegates to the national convention. Ford won the official straw poll the night of the precinct caucuses, but by only a small margin (45 percent to 43 percent). R. W. Apple of the *New York Times* characterized the Republican effort in Iowa by both candidates as "all but invisible, with only marginal organizational efforts by the supporters of Mr. Ford and Mr. Reagan."[18] Ford's victory in New Hampshire made him the front-runner for renomination, although Reagan rallied later in the year.[19]

On the Democratic side, the candidate who focused hardest on Iowa was former Governor Jimmy Carter of Georgia. Hamilton Jordan, Carter's campaign manager, put together a strategy that was exactly three events deep, requiring strong showings in Iowa and New Hampshire, and a careful positioning as the anti-George Wallace southerner in the Florida primary.[20] The Carter strategy dovetailed nicely with those of his main competitors. Washington Senator Henry (Scoop) Jackson's campaign was designed to start late: a token effort in Iowa (January 19) and New Hampshire (February 24) followed by an unequivocal win in Massachusetts (March 2), only a week later. After all, Massachusetts's 104 delegates greatly exceeded the Iowa–New Hampshire combination of 64. Thus Jackson's decision to play from "strength."[21]

Arizona Representative Morris Udall's campaign was strategically incoherent. First Udall made an effort in Iowa, then, in an attempt to stretch his resources to cover as many primaries as possible (there were thirty Democratic primaries in 1976), Udall's campaign slackened its Iowa effort. As news coverage focused ever more strongly on Iowa, however, Udall at the last minute recommitted resources to the race.[22] He was too late. Although he finished as high as second in seven primaries in 1976, Udall came in fifth in Iowa with 6 percent of the vote, behind "uncommitted" with 37 percent of the caucus vote and Jimmy Carter with 28 percent.

The next day, *New York Times* reporter R. W. Apple minimized the strong uncommitted sentiment and created the first major instance in which the Iowa caucuses combined importantly with mass media spin to launch a presidential candidacy. His story on the front page read:

> Former Governor Jimmy Carter of Georgia scored an impressive victory in yesterday's Iowa Democratic precinct caucuses, demonstrating strength among rural, blue-collar, black, and suburban voters.
>
> Mr. Carter defeated his closest rival, Senator Birch Bayh of Indiana, by a margin of more than 2–1, and left his other four challengers far behind. The uncommitted vote, which many Iowa politicians had forecast at more than 50 percent, amounted to only about a third of the total, slightly more than that of Mr. Carter.[23]

This article, with its strong and coherent story line, cast a long shadow. It contained many elements that in later years would worry journalists, notably the use of such a word as "impressive" (to whom?) in the lead paragraph of what ostensibly was a news story and the belittling of the uncommitted vote because of the disappointed "forecasts" or expectations of anonymous politicians. *New Yorker* political writer Elizabeth Drew's diary for the day after the Iowa caucuses said:

This morning, Carter, who managed to get to New York on time, was interviewed on the *CBS Morning News*. The *Today* show and ABC's *Good Morning America* also ran segments on Carter. On the *CBS Evening News*, Walter Cronkite said that the Iowa voters have spoken "and for the Democrats what they said was 'Jimmy Carter.'"[24]

This coverage set the stage for New Hampshire, where Carter alone ran as a centrist Democrat and received 28 percent of the vote, good enough for a first-place finish in a field of multiple contenders. Although he filed a slate of delegates, Jackson sat the primary out, and no fewer than four candidates—Udall (at 23 percent), Bayh (at 15 percent), Senator Fred Harris of Oklahoma (at 11 percent), and former Ambassador and Peace Corps Director Sargent Shriver (at 8 percent)—divided the liberal Democratic vote. Despite starting the 1976 campaign as a virtual unknown, and despite receiving less than 30 percent of the vote in both states, Carter's victories in Iowa and New Hampshire made him the instant front-runner in the race for the Democratic nomination, thanks in large part to positive coverage by the press.

1980

By 1980, it was beginning to be understood that there was no such thing as a successful presidential strategy that ignored early delegate-selection events. President Carter's managers worked hard to structure the order in which states selected delegates so as to maximize the impact of favorable publicity, seeking to move southern primaries where they expected to be strong up to the head of the line.[25] Carter, aided by a rally round the flag at the start of the Iranian hostage crisis, beat Massachusetts Senator Edward Kennedy in the January 21 Iowa caucuses by a margin of 59 percent to 31 percent. Iowa momentum helped Carter amass a majority of delegates far more quickly in 1980 than he had done in 1976.[26]

On the Republican side, Iowa nearly did in the front-runner, Ronald Reagan. Saving his energy, Reagan campaigned only eight days in the state and passed up the major all-candidate Republican debate. Caucus turnout on the Republican side jumped to 110,000 participants from a mere 22,000 in 1976. Senator Howard Baker of Tennessee, a rival candidate, remarked that the Iowa caucuses had become "the functional equivalent of a primary." Former Representative, Ambassador, and CIA Director George H. W. Bush of Texas unexpectedly edged Reagan 32 percent to 29 percent in the caucus vote—actually a straw poll reported early to the news media—with Baker receiving 15 percent and four other candidates trailing behind. As political commentators Jack Germond and Jules Witcover observed, the Iowa caucuses served in 1980 to clear "the underbrush of candidates with little future . . . establishing a definite pecking order among those who remained."[27]

Only a drastic change of strategy (including the replacement of campaign strategist John Sears) and some extraordinarily vigorous propagandizing by the *Union Leader* saved Ronald Reagan's bacon by aiding his comeback in New Hampshire.[28] Reagan campaigned energetically and ambushed Bush at a key New Hampshire debate by "spontaneously" agreeing to let also-rans onto the platform. It also helped Reagan enormously that the gap between Iowa and New Hampshire was a full month (January 21 to February 26), thus permitting *Union Leader* publicity to counteract Iowa momentum. In 1976 that gap had helped Carter, a "winner" in Iowa; in 1980 it helped Reagan, an Iowa "loser."

By the 1980 election, the strong interdependence between early delegate selection and media publicity could easily be observed. The "pecking order" of which Germond and Witcover wrote was, after all, a fabrication chiefly valuable in the construction of coherent news stories. The success of Jimmy Carter in 1976, and even more striking, the failure of Henry Jackson, suggested that it would be hard, perhaps impossible, to ascertain the preferences of primary electorates unmediated by the news—and news media evaluations—of how the various candidates were doing. And these characterizations could easily take on the coloration of self-fulfilling prophecies.

1984

Nothing doing on the Republican side; Reagan's incumbency meant no contest in Iowa. Democratic rules were rewritten, ostensibly to counteract media influence: states were required to select delegates within a three-month "window" so that many states would act on any given Tuesday, thus (it was hoped) confounding media attempts to start a single unified bandwagon. The effort was a failure, in part because both Iowa and New Hampshire received exemptions from the window and continued to act first. In Iowa, on the Democratic side, former Vice President Walter Mondale overwhelmed everybody, collecting 49 percent of the vote in a large field of contenders. Colorado Senator Gary Hart came in a distant second with 16 percent of the vote.

This was enough to identify Hart, rather than Senator John Glenn of Ohio, who finished in sixth place with 4 percent, as the strongest non-Mondale candidate. The news media constructed a horse race out of the unpromising material of the Hart candidacy, gave him extraordinary news coverage for the ensuing week, and boosted him into a surprisingly decisive win in the New Hampshire primary.[29] Hart received 41 percent of the New Hampshire vote, with Mondale placing second at 29 percent and Glenn a distant third with 13 percent.[30]

It seems clear enough why the news media need a horse race, given their extraordinary investment in delegate-selection coverage and the logic of their competition for business. Iowa caucuses help the news media sort out the story: it was the Iowa caucuses in 1984 that decreed that Gary Hart and not John Glenn should be the "unexpected" horse to make the race against Mondale, and it was the media that made the horse race.

1988

In 1988, with only one week separating the Iowa caucuses and New Hampshire primary, the two events might have been expected to interact strongly. Massachusetts Governor Michael Dukakis entered Iowa as the Democratic candidate with the most money and the best organization in the most states—but not in Iowa—and with extremely high and favorable name recognition in New Hampshire, whose Democratic voters are mostly located on the fringes of the Boston metropolitan area. This meant that Iowa was the only chance the other candidates had to neutralize the favorable impact that the New Hampshire primary was bound to have on the fortunes of the governor of Massachusetts.[31]

In the event, the Iowa Democratic result did not help the Iowa winner in New Hampshire, mainly because what happened on the Republican side in Iowa had such a strong impact on the Democratic race. The big story of Iowa in 1988—and there always has to be one big story—was that the Reverend Pat Robertson, a well-known television evangelist, came in second in the

Republican straw poll (with 25 percent of the vote) to the winner, Senator Bob Dole of Kansas (37 percent), finishing ahead of incumbent Vice President George H. W. Bush (19 percent), who had won the caucuses in 1980. And that is how the story played in the news media for the week between Iowa and New Hampshire. Obviously, that was bound to have some impact on the Republican nomination contest, but a limited impact, since Robertson was never a plausible candidate to be his party's presidential nominee. In the New Hampshire primary, Bush, by defeating Dole by a margin of 38 percent to 29 percent (with Robertson finishing a distant fifth), righted his campaign and began his eventual march to the Republican nomination.

Because the Robertson blip absorbed so much immediate media attention, however, it spoiled the chances of the Democratic victor in Iowa, Representative Richard Gephardt of Missouri, to capitalize on his win to become the focal alternative to Michael Dukakis in New Hampshire. Instead, he became entangled in bitter infighting with Senator Paul Simon of Illinois, who sponsored a series of advertisements in New Hampshire criticizing Gephardt for changing his positions on several issues.[32] While Gephardt and Simon battled for second place, Dukakis won the New Hampshire primary by a wide margin (with 36 percent of the vote, compared to 20 percent for Gephardt and 17 percent for Simon), receiving a major boost to his ultimately successful campaign for the Democratic nomination.

In 1984, Gary Hart was able to parlay a 16 percent second-place showing in Iowa into a media spin that made him the winner in New Hampshire, as figures on late-deciding Democrats showed.[33] In 1976, Jimmy Carter was able to pull out in front of the pack with 28 percent of the vote in the Iowa caucuses. In 1988, a 31 percent win was not enough for Gephardt to turn the same trick. Indeed, the *Wall Street Journal* reported that in the week between the Iowa caucuses and the New Hampshire primary, the coverage Gephardt got on the network evening news programs actually diminished from the week before, from 6:05 minutes to 4:55 minutes.[34] Thus it is not farfetched to argue that although both winners in Iowa failed to receive the nomination of their party, Iowa did in fact play an influential role in determining the 1988 outcome.

1992

A Senator from Iowa, Tom Harkin, ran for president, and the other Democratic candidates quickly declared the Iowa caucuses irrelevant due to the expectation that Harkin would win overwhelmingly in his home state—a judgment reporters accepted. As Harkin's press secretary said later, "You can't force people to cover what they perceive as a nonevent."[35] The focus of press coverage leading up to the February 18 New Hampshire primary, then, was not the events in Iowa, but instead the problems of the Democratic front-runner, Governor Bill Clinton of Arkansas. Governor and Mrs. Clinton had appeared on the CBS news program *60 Minutes* immediately following the Super Bowl in January to respond to rumors of his marital infidelity, and in early February questions regarding the governor's exemption from military service during the Vietnam War made newspaper headlines around the nation. New Hampshire voters, who knew little about Clinton other than the controversies surrounding him, began to withdraw their support. Once the leader in polls of likely primary voters, Clinton lost his advantage to former Massachusetts Senator Paul Tsongas by the week before the primary, and many observers, mindful of the adultery scandal that befell Gary Hart in 1987, began to suggest that Clinton's candidacy might be doomed.[36]

The media's death watch over the Clinton campaign was suspended when Clinton finished a strong second to Tsongas in the New Hampshire primary, receiving a better-than-expected 26 percent of the vote. Clinton delivered what was, in effect, a victory speech on the night of the primary, proclaiming himself "the comeback kid"—a clever strategy which succeeded in convincing the media of his continued viability (the *New York Times* account published the following day described Clinton's "resilient candidacy").[37] Because journalists had their own doubts about Tsongas's credibility as a national candidate, and because the rest of the Democratic field (Harkin, Senator Bob Kerrey of Nebraska, and former California Governor Jerry Brown) had failed to catch on with New Hampshire voters, Clinton was still treated seriously as a potential nominee despite his loss in the primary, and he ultimately won both the Democratic nomination and the presidency later in the year.[38]

On the Republican side, early expectations of a noncontest were jarred when former White House aide and conservative commentator Pat Buchanan received 37 percent of the New Hampshire vote against incumbent president George H. W. Bush, who was held to 53 percent.[39] Just as Minnesota Senator Eugene McCarthy's surprisingly close loss to incumbent president Lyndon Johnson persuaded the press that Johnson was unpopular in 1968, Buchanan's loss to Bush focused media attention on the nation's economic recession, rather than Bush's successes in foreign policy. Though Buchanan's showing in New Hampshire was interpreted by journalists as a sign of Bush's electoral weakness, his ability to win renomination was never in doubt; Bush won every primary and took the bulk of delegates from each caucus state.

The aftermath of the 1992 New Hampshire primary once again demonstrates the capacity of the media to affect election outcomes in the primary season by interpreting results in early contests against a backdrop of "expectations" which candidates are deemed to have exceeded or failed to meet. Had Bill Clinton continued to lead in the polls during the week of the primary, journalists would have considered his nine-point loss to Paul Tsongas a devastating defeat; campaign funds and support would then have begun to dry up, possibly forcing Clinton from the race entirely.[40] But since reporters assumed that Clinton's electoral chances were seriously damaged by the emerging allegations of draft dodging and extramarital misbehavior, they interpreted his second-place finish in the primary as something of a victory, and media observers largely adopted the campaign's proffered story line of a Clinton "comeback." Likewise, much was made in the press of Pat Buchanan's showing, even though he lost to Bush by a double-digit margin, because the willingness of more than a third of New Hampshire Republicans to vote against an incumbent president of their party supposedly demonstrated Bush's political vulnerability. As both Bush and Clinton learned in 1992, losses can become wins and wins can become losses in a political world as influenced by media expectations as presidential primary elections now are.

1996

Bill Clinton was only the second president, along with Ronald Reagan in 1984, to be renominated without challenge under the reformed nomination system in place since 1972. Two incumbents, Nixon and George H. W. Bush, faced relatively minor protest candidates; two others, Ford and Carter, had to win nomination by beating back serious challenges.

The Republican race in 1996 provided a classic example of the media's bias in favor of creating a horse race. The consensus front-runner for the nomination, Senate Majority Leader Bob Dole of Kansas, won the Iowa caucuses. Not only that, but the candidates widely considered to be his most serious rivals did poorly. Publisher Steve Forbes finished fourth despite spending freely from his personal fortune. Texas Senator Phil Gramm, the only candidate to rival Dole in fundraising, finished far behind, effectively ending his candidacy. However, instead of reporting a victory for Dole, reporters focused on the (in their view) disappointingly narrow margin separating him from the rest of the candidates. (Dole received 26 percent of the Republican straw poll vote, followed by 23 percent for Pat Buchanan, 18 percent for former Tennessee Governor Lamar Alexander, 10 percent for Forbes, and 9 percent for Gramm.) Words used by pundits on the night of the caucuses and the following day to describe Dole's win included "weak," "narrow," "shaky," "vulnerable," "wobbly," and "disappointing." Dole was the "quasi-loser" according to one, while another called it an "unimpressive showing." Fred Barnes, of the conservative *Weekly Standard*, opined on *CBS This Morning* that "another victory like this for Bob Dole and he'll join the pantheon of political losers like Edmund Muskie." The following day David Yepsen of the *Des Moines Register* said of Dole: "He didn't win anything."[41]

The media interpretation of Dole's weakness had consequences, at least in the short run. Eight days later, the candidate who finished second in Iowa, Pat Buchanan, was the immediate beneficiary of Dole's perceived failure. In tracking polls taken just before the Iowa results were known, Buchanan trailed Dole in New Hampshire by about six percentage points. Within two days, he had pulled even, and he eventually beat Dole to win the New Hampshire primary by about 2,100 votes, which worked out to one percentage point.[42]

This left the national media with a rather tricky challenge in interpreting the results. Unlike Gary Hart's in 1984, Buchanan's views were well-known; he had a well-defined public image and little plausible chance of winning the nomination. Indeed, Buchanan won a smaller percentage of the New Hampshire vote in 1996 than he had four years before. So why did Buchanan receive a media puff? Primarily because the news media could not accept that Dole was so far ahead—in name recognition, organization, and finances—that there was in truth no serious competition to report. Because the media needed a horse race, for the next few weeks it was anybody but Dole in the headlines.[43]

2000

President Bill Clinton's ineligibility for a third term meant contested nominations in both parties. On the Republican side, Texas Governor George W. Bush's extraordinary success in raising campaign funds and in winning endorsements from his fellow Republican governors, and his early leads in opinion polls (no doubt owing in part to initial voter confusion with his ex-president father of the same name) made him the widely-proclaimed front-runner going into Iowa. Bush's perceived strength prompted several rivals to fold their campaigns before the first votes were even cast. With the departures of Elizabeth Dole, Lamar Alexander, and Dan Quayle from the race by the end of 1999, publisher Steve Forbes and Senator John McCain of Arizona remained as Bush's most serious competitors for the nomination.

After the failure of his 1996 campaign, built around a flat tax proposal, Forbes repositioned himself as a social conservative in order to increase his appeal to the GOP primary electorate. He finished second to Bush in Iowa (41 percent to 30 percent), significantly better than his fourth-place showing in 1996. McCain decided to skip Iowa and focus his energy and resources on New

Hampshire, where his relative lack of organizational strength (and longstanding opposition to federal subsidies for ethanol production from Iowa corn) would matter less and his reputation as a party maverick might prove more valuable, attracting registered independents who may vote in the New Hampshire primary. Because he had already conceded the caucus and barely campaigned in the state, McCain's fifth-place finish in Iowa, behind minor candidates Alan Keyes and Gary Bauer, did not appear to damage his candidacy.

In fact, as the New Hampshire primary approached, McCain began to receive a large amount of favorable media attention. Reporters were impressed by his survival as a prisoner of war for over five years in North Vietnam, and they liked his willingness to take on most of his party in the fight for campaign finance reform (always a popular cause with the press). Perhaps most importantly, McCain, unlike most candidates who remained heavily scripted and protected by handlers, granted nearly unlimited, casual access to journalists as his campaign bus, dubbed the Straight Talk Express, cruised the highways of the Granite State.[44] This strategy paid off, as McCain pulled ahead in New Hampshire polls shortly before the February 1 primary and ultimately defeated Bush by a surprisingly wide margin, 48 percent to 30 percent. Forbes, far behind in third place with 13 percent of the vote, was effectively finished by his showing in New Hampshire and ended his campaign the following week. By structuring the Republican race as a two-man contest between Bush and McCain, the New Hampshire primary gave journalists the horse race on the Republican side that they always like to have.

The Democratic side was a two-person fight from the beginning, as Vice President Al Gore faced a single challenge for the nomination from former New Jersey Senator Bill Bradley. Gore enjoyed front-runner status as the incumbent vice president in a popular administration, and he received the vast majority of endorsements from elected officials, party leaders, and Democratic-leaning interest groups such as labor unions. Gore defeated Bradley by a roughly two-to-one margin in the Iowa caucuses, 63 percent to 35 percent. Bradley's stronger showing in New Hampshire, where he came within four points (50 percent to 46 percent) of upsetting the vice president, might have given him a bigger boost had McCain's landslide win in the Republican contest not been *the* big media story of the evening.[45] But Bradley never came close to victory again and withdrew from the race on March 9 after losing primaries in eleven states to Gore two days before.

2004

The incumbency of George W. Bush precluded a contest on the Republican side. The Democrats, however, had a lively race. It produced a definitive result in Iowa that held up all the way to the nomination.

By early 2003, many political insiders saw Senator John Kerry of Massachusetts, a decorated Vietnam War veteran, as the initial Democratic front-runner.[46] However, former Vermont Governor Howard Dean began to win significant support among Democratic voters during the summer and fall of 2003, thanks to his sharp attacks on the Bush administration and his status as an "outsider," not connected with the congressional Democrats in Washington who had, according to some liberals, failed to provide effective opposition to Bush's policies. Dean's popular campaign Web site brought in large numbers of financial donations from citizens across the country, and he began to attract serious attention from journalists, many of whom had initially dismissed him as a second-tier candidate. By mid-January 2004, Dean was leading in polls of Democratic voters in Iowa, New Hampshire, and across the country; had secured the endorsements of the Democrats' previous standard-bearer, Al Gore, Gore's 2000 rival Bill Bradley, Iowa Senator Tom Harkin, and several major labor unions; and was bringing in over $1 million a week in online campaign contributions. Kerry, meanwhile, had fired his first campaign manager in November and was forced to loan his campaign over $6 million from his own very deep pocket to keep it afloat after several months of unsuccessful fundraising. Conventional wisdom in Washington said that Dean was the man to beat.[47]

Under these circumstances, Kerry's victory in the Iowa caucuses on January 19 surprised most political observers. Two weeks earlier, Adam Nagourney of the *New York Times* had written from Iowa that "not even the biggest boosters of . . . Mr. Kerry are saying [he has] much of a chance of winning the caucuses here."[48] But Kerry finished first with 38 percent of the vote; almost as unexpectedly, Senator John Edwards of North Carolina came in a strong second with 32 percent.[49]

Meanwhile, Howard Dean, finishing third with only 18 percent, was transformed overnight in media coverage from the presumptive front-runner for the nomination to something of a figure of fun.[50] Dean's unscripted concession speech on the night of the caucuses was punctuated by an exuberant whoop that was endlessly replayed on cable television news programs and late-night talk shows over the following week (more than six hundred times, by one count) as supposed evidence of an overly emotional, unhinged persona.[51] Journalists compared the "Dean scream" to the overwrought speech that helped sink Edmund Muskie in 1972.[52] Referring to the candidate's much-touted (and unprecedented) Internet support, a wisecrack also made the rounds that the Dean campaign was the latest overhyped dot-com bust.[53]

Kerry's surprise win in Iowa had a profound effect on his fortunes in the New Hampshire primary the following week. A poll taken just before the Iowa caucuses showed him running a distant third in New Hampshire, winning just 12 percent (compared to 32 percent for Dean and 23 percent for retired General Wesley Clark).[54] But the massive media publicity generated by the events in Iowa boosted Kerry (from neighboring Massachusetts) into first place while dealing Dean (from neighboring Vermont) a painful blow. Kerry won the January 27 New Hampshire primary by capturing 39 percent of the vote, with 26 percent for Dean, 13 percent for Clark, and 12 percent for Edwards, solidifying his position as the Democrats' leading candidate. By the end of February, Kerry had all but wrapped up the nomination, while erstwhile front-runner Dean failed to win a single primary outside of his home state.

WHAT DO THESE HISTORICAL VIGNETTES TEACH?

1. Candidates ignore Iowa and New Hampshire at their peril. This does not mean that losing Iowa and New Hampshire is sufficient to lose the nomination or that doing well is sufficient to win. It does mean that the results in both states can be a tremendous help or a tremendous hindrance to each and every candidacy.

2. This is so not because of their size but because of their temporal primacy: Iowa results, plus media spin, structure the alternatives for the New Hampshire primary. These two events together, plus media spin, structure alternatives for everything that follows. In 1992, when

TABLE 4.2 Early Campaigning for the 2000 Nomination

Days Campaigning in State, March 15 through August 2, 1999

Candidate	Iowa	New Hampshire	Home State	All Others
Alexander	31	8	26	23
Bauer	20	11	–	44
Buchanan	20	6	–	55
Bush	6	4	18	26
Dole	19	10	–	39
Forbes	23	11	–	38
Hatch	5	1	4	0
Kasich	13	22	11	25
Keyes	2	4	–	8
McCain	1	14	3	31
Quayle	14	7	1	34
Smith	8	8	–	18
Bradley	18	11	2	42
Gore	14	7	7	50
Totals	194	124	72	502

Source: "White House 2000 Candidate State Visit Tallies," The Hotline, August 2, 1999.

Notes: Candidates' home states are Tennessee (Alexander), Texas (Bush), Utah (Hatch), Ohio (Kasich), Arizona (McCain), Indiana (Quayle), New Jersey (Bradley), and Tennessee (Gore). For Senator Bob Smith of New Hampshire (and for those residing in Washington, D.C.), home state is left blank.

Iowa was ignored, the results in New Hampshire alone provided a structure for the rest of the nomination contest.

3. While winning Iowa or New Hampshire does not ensure nomination, losing badly quickly ends a candidacy. No eventual nominee since the modern nomination process was put in place in 1972 has ever finished below third place in either Iowa or New Hampshire. The elections in these first states effectively winnow out anyone who cannot draw at least that level of support.[55] With few exceptions, candidates have learned these lessons and responded, by focusing on Iowa and New Hampshire in the pre-primary period to the exclusion of almost every other state (see table 4.2).

Doing well in Iowa and New Hampshire requires a well-organized campaign as well as good publicity because organizations get people to caucuses and sustain their loyalty as the public shufflings and reshufflings take place. Doing well thereafter, as the result of Iowa and New Hampshire, however, chiefly requires good publicity: spin control at least to hold down expectations, but also, if possible, to attract the good luck to be the story on which the national news media converge coming out of Iowa and as the first primary approaches. The closer the next event in time, the narrower the temporal gap between Iowa and New Hampshire, the greater the potential that both events can be interpreted together, and thus the more influential the news media response to Iowa and New Hampshire becomes in the election year.

In 2004, for example, the Iowa caucuses and New Hampshire primary were separated by just eight days. This compressed calendar worked to the benefit of John Kerry, the winner in Iowa; his victory earned him a great deal of favorable publicity that boosted him into first place in New Hampshire as well. Howard Dean, by contrast, had no chance to recover from his surprisingly poor third-place finish in Iowa before he lost a second time in a neighboring state to his own, dealing his candidacy yet another serious setback. In 1980, by contrast, the two events were separated by a full month, allowing Ronald Reagan to regroup successfully in New Hampshire after losing in Iowa to George H. W. Bush. For this reason, New Hampshire's decision in recent years to schedule its primary soon after the Iowa caucuses actually increases the effect of the outcome in Iowa on the results in New Hampshire, thereby reducing the independent influence that the Granite State would otherwise retain.

STATE PRIMARIES

Candidates in contemporary presidential elections now campaign actively for a full year before the first votes are cast. Once the events in Iowa and New Hampshire have passed, however, elections in other states follow quickly in subsequent weeks, soon winnowing the field down to a single remaining candidate in each party. Each state and U.S. territory holds either primary elections or caucuses during the late winter or spring of a presidential election year in order to select that state's delegates to the national party conventions.

As we have seen, the national parties, especially on the Democratic side, impose rules on how things proceed, specifying the number of delegates allotted to each state, the time frame within which the delegates must be selected, the formulas by which candidates may be awarded delegates pledged to support them at the convention based on their performance in the primary or caucuses, and so on. However, individual states maintain some flexibility, such as the decision whether to hold a presidential primary administered by the state government or instead hold caucuses organized by the state parties. More than two-thirds of the states, selecting the bulk of the delegates, currently hold primary elections.

A more important decision than the choice between primaries and caucuses, however, is the date on which a state's elections are held. State politicians and party officials across the nation, keen observers of the dynamics of presidential nominations, have largely concluded that states that vote early in the primary season exert more influence over the outcome than those scheduled near the end of the process. Over time, most states have moved their primaries further and further ahead in the primary calendar, hoping to have a greater say in the identity of the party nominees—a phenomenon known as "front-loading."

In 1976, Democratic presidential primaries were spread out over a relatively long period: after New Hampshire on February 24, only five states held primaries in March, and only two held primaries in April. Twelve primaries were held more than three months after the New Hampshire primary, including contests on June 8 in California, New Jersey, and Ohio.[56] This schedule certainly granted greater importance to early primaries because winning in February and March helped candidates receive attention and raise money for the later events. This meant that early and vigorous participation in primaries was already the only strategy available to serious presidential aspirants. Nevertheless, many of the actual delegates were selected late in the process.

As state leaders began to understand the importance of the early contests, more and more states moved their primaries or caucuses earlier and earlier in the spring, hoping to gain more influence in the nomination process. By mid-March of the presidential election year of 1984, both major parties had chosen around a quarter of their delegates. By 1988, this proportion had increased to one-third; twenty states held primaries within a month of the New Hampshire primary.[57] While little changed in 1992, the process accelerated again in 1996, 2000, and 2004 (see table 4.3). In 1996, the big difference was the size of the states holding early primaries. New York moved its primary from mid-April to March 7; California, which had traditionally held its primary in June, moved to March 26. In 2000, California moved up again to share an early March date with New York, New Jersey, Massachusetts, Maryland, and several smaller states. By 2000, winning the early primaries was important not to signal the viability of a candidate or to raise money for future contests but because most of the delegates were chosen early in the process. After the 2000 election, the Democratic National Committee amended its rules, allowing states (other than Iowa and New Hampshire, which now scheduled their events during the month of January) to select delegates beginning in February instead of March. As a consequence, a number of states moved their elections ahead still further in the primary season. Twelve states held primaries or caucuses in the two weeks following the 2004 New Hampshire primary, and more than half of the states in the nation had voted by March 2.[58]

Front-loading represents a response by other states envious of the key role played by the Iowa caucuses and New Hampshire primary in contemporary presidential politics. By the time that most states hold their primaries, the nominees of both parties have almost always been effectively chosen, based on the outcome of the early delegate selection events. States hope to grab some influence for themselves, at the expense of Iowa and New Hampshire, by moving their elections further and further ahead in the primary calendar.

In practice, however, front-loading has not appeared to increase the number of states that can be said to play an important part in determining the winner of recent presidential nominations. Instead, it has merely reduced the amount of time between the beginning of the primary season and the point at which a de facto nominee emerges. The "invisible primary" period before the start of actual voting, a time when candidates campaign actively in order to display their policies and capabilities to party activists, donors, and the media, has been pushed forward even farther, now beginning in earnest more than a year before the primaries themselves. Even the first delegate-selection rounds in Iowa and New Hampshire are now, in the words of Republican consultant John Sears, "more the end of the process than the beginning."[59]

Once the voting starts, pressure quickly builds for unsuccessful candidates to drop out of the race. Most presidential hopefuls only contest a handful of states before they are forced to withdraw, usually due to financial hardship and pressure from party leaders to rally around the front-runner. A front-loaded primary schedule simply accelerates the process, producing a nominee in a matter of weeks instead of months, without necessarily giving more voters or more states a voice in the outcome than before.

Consider the effects of front-loading on the 2004 primary season. Ten candidates originally declared their intention to seek the 2004 Democratic presidential nomination. One, Senator Bob Graham of Florida, finding immediate difficulties in raising money and earning support, dropped

TABLE 4.3 Primary and Caucus Calendar, 1996–2004

	1996	2000	2004
January			
19			Iowa
24		Iowa	
27			New Hampshire
29	Alaska (R)		
31	Hawaii (R)		
February			
1		New Hampshire	
3			Arizona (D)
			Delaware (D)
			Missouri
			New Mexico (D)
			North Dakota
			Oklahoma
			South Carolina (D)
			Virginia (R)
6	Louisiana (R)		
7			Michigan (D)
			Washington (D)
8		Delaware (R)	Maine (D)
10			District of Columbia (R)
			Tennessee
			Virginia (D)
12	Iowa		
14			District of Columbia (D)
			Nevada (D)
17			Wisconsin
19		South Carolina (R)	
20	New Hampshire		
21			Guam (R)
22		Arizona (R)	
		Michigan (R)	
24	Delaware		Hawaii (D)
			Idaho (D)
			Utah (D)
26		American Samoa (R)	
		Guam (R)	
		Virgin Islands (R)	
27	Arizona (R)	Puerto Rico (R)	
	North Dakota (R)		
	South Dakota (R)		

(Continued)

TABLE 4.3 *(Continued)*

	1996	2000	2004
28			American Samoa (R)
			Virgin Islands (R)
29		North Dakota (R)	Puerto Rico (R)
		Virginia (R)	
March			
2	South Carolina (R)		California
	Wyoming (R)		Connecticut
			Georgia
			Maryland
			Massachusetts
			Minnesota
			New York
			Ohio
			Rhode Island
			Vermont
3	Puerto Rico (R)		
5	American Samoa		
	Colorado		
	Connecticut		
	Georgia		
	Idaho (D)		
	Maine		
	Maryland		
	Massachusetts		
	Minnesota		
	Rhode Island		
	South Carolina (D)		
	Vermont		
	Washington		
7	Missouri (D)	American Samoa (D)	
	New York	California	
		Connecticut	
		Georgia	
		Hawaii (D)	
		Idaho (D)	
		Maine	
		Maryland	
		Massachusetts	
		Minnesota (R)	
		Missouri	

(Continued)

TABLE 4.3 *(Continued)*

	1996	2000	2004
		New York	
		North Dakota (D)	
		Ohio	
		Rhode Island	
		Vermont	
		Washington	
8			American Samoa (D)
9	Alaska (D)	South Carolina (D)	Florida
			Louisiana
	Arizona (D)		Mississippi
	Missouri (R)		Texas
	South Dakota (D)		Washington (R)
10	Nevada (D)	Colorado	
	Puerto Rico (D)	Utah	
		Wyoming (R)	
11		Arizona (D)	
		Michigan (D)	
12	Florida	Minnesota (D)	
	Hawaii (D)		
	Louisiana (D)		
	Mississippi		
	Oklahoma		
	Oregon		
	Tennessee		
	Texas		
13			Kansas (D)
14		Florida	
		Louisiana	
		Mississippi	
		Oklahoma	
		Tennessee	
		Texas	
16	Michigan (D)		Illinois
18		Guam (D)	
19	Illinois		
	Michigan (R)		
	Ohio		
	Wisconsin		
20			Alaska (D)
			Guam (D)
			Wyoming (D)

(Continued)

TABLE 4.3 *(Continued)*

	1996	*2000*	*2004*
21		Illinois	
23	Wyoming (D)		
25	Utah	Wyoming (D)	
26	California		
	Nevada (R)		
27		Delaware (D)	South Carolina (R)
30	Virgin Islands		
31	North Dakota (D)		
April			
1		Virgin Islands (D)	
2	Kansas	Puerto Rico (D)	
4		Pennsylvania	
		Wisconsin	
13			Colorado
15	Virginia (D)		
17		Virginia (D)	North Carolina (D)
			Virgin Islands (D)
22		Kansas (D)	
23	Pennsylvania		
24			Kansas (R)
27			Pennsylvania
May			
1			Nevada (R)
2		District of Columbia	
		Indiana	
		North Carolina	
4	Guam		Indiana
6		Wyoming (R)	
7	District of Columbia		
	Indiana		
	North Carolina		
8			Arizona (R)
			Utah (R)
			Wyoming (R)
9		Nebraska	
		West Virginia	
11			Nebraska
			West Virginia
14	Nebraska		
	West Virginia		

(Continued)

TABLE 4.3 *(Continued)*

	1996	2000	2004
15			Delaware (R)
			Maine (R)
16		Oregon	
18			Arkansas
			Kentucky
			Oregon
19		Hawaii (R)	
20		Alaska (D)	
21	Arkansas	Nevada (D)	
22			Alaska (R)
			Michigan (R)
23		Arkansas	North Carolina (R)
		Idaho (R)	
		Kentucky	
25		Kansas (R)	Idaho (R)
		Nevada (R)	
28	Idaho (R)		
	Kentucky		
June			
1	Virginia (R)		Alabama
			New Mexico (R)
			South Dakota
4	Alabama		
	Montana		
	New Jersey		
	New Mexico		
5			Virginia (R)
6		Alabama	Hawaii (R)
		Montana	Puerto Rico (D)
		New Jersey	
		New Mexico	
		South Dakota	
8			Montana
			New Jersey

Source: For 1996, "Primary and Caucus Dates," CNN/Allpolitics Web site, http://www.cnn.com/ALLPOLITICS/1996/candidates/calendar/primaries.html; for 2000, Federal Election Commission, "2000 Presidential Primary Dates," available at http://www.fec.gov/pages/2kdates.htm; for 2004, Federal Election Commission, "2004 Presidential Primary Dates," available at http://www.fec.gov/pubrec/fe2004/2004pdates.pdf.

out of the race in October 2003—more than three months before the first primaries. A second, former Senator Carol Moseley-Braun of Illinois, ended her candidacy on January 15, 2004, just a few days before the Iowa caucuses. Next, Representative Richard Gephardt of Missouri folded his campaign after a fourth-place finish in Iowa on January 19. Senator Joseph Lieberman of Connecticut dropped out on February 3, after placing fifth in New Hampshire and winning just 11 percent of the vote in the Delaware primary. Retired General Wesley Clark was the next to abandon his campaign, in response to disappointing third-place finishes in the Tennessee and Virginia primaries on February 10. Former Governor Howard Dean of Vermont, at one time the media-anointed front-runner for the nomination, left the presidential race the following week after a loss in the Wisconsin primary. North Carolina Senator John Edwards was the next candidate to drop out after losing multiple state primaries on March 2. At this point, only six weeks after the Iowa caucuses, and with three more months remaining in the primary season, presumptive nominee John Kerry was left facing just two minor candidates, Representative Dennis Kucinich of Ohio and the Reverend Al Sharpton, who were running primarily for symbolic reasons and had never stood a legitimate chance of winning the nomination. (Sharpton, too, ended his campaign several weeks later.)

Gephardt withdrew after contesting caucuses in a single state. Lieberman's campaign folded after nine state primaries and caucuses (although he did not compete in Iowa). Clark lasted for fourteen state events, Dean for seventeen, and Edwards for thirty. Why did these candidates campaign actively for a year before the primaries, only to drop out of the race so soon after the voting began?

An explanation lies in the common interpretation of electoral outcomes in early states by political elites, journalists, and voters. Richard Gephardt, for example, remained as the sole midwesterner in the 2004 Democratic race after the departure of Moseley-Braun; in fact, his home state is a neighbor to Iowa. Gephardt had also won the Iowa caucuses in his first campaign for president in 1988. If Gephardt could not place first in Iowa, most observers concluded, he probably could not win anywhere outside of Missouri. His Iowa fourth-place finish represented a fatal blow to his candidacy; even if Gephardt himself wished to soldier on, hoping for better luck in other states, what remained of his popular support and financial backing would surely dry up, and the news media would cease to treat him as a plausible contender for the nomination. Likewise, northeasterner Lieberman's weak showings in New Hampshire and Delaware were quite sufficient to demonstrate, for many, his general lack of appeal as a candidate. When Wesley Clark, a military man from the South, proved unable to defeat Massachusetts liberal John Kerry in both Tennessee and Virginia, he had little justification for continuing his effort to win the nomination by contesting subsequent state primaries.

If 2004 is any guide to future nominations, continued front-loading of the primary calendar may only serve to increase the influence of Iowa and New Hampshire, the opposite effect from what is intended. Victorious candidates—or those who exceeded media expectations for their performance—in the first events can ride their "momentum" to further success in states holding primaries in the following weeks, as Kerry did in 2004. At the same time, candidates who stumble early on, as Dean did, will have little opportunity to right their campaigns in time to prevent additional defeats that will only compound their problems.

The central limitation facing the advocates of front-loading is the dependable tendency of party leaders, journalists, and voters to interpret the very first events of the primary season as important evidence of the relative standing of the candidates. As long as political elites consider the results in Iowa and New Hampshire worthy of extensive attention, hyping winners and disparaging losers, the outcomes in those states will exert a strong effect on the results of subsequent elections. As long as voters, confronted with a field of multiple contenders within the same party who are mostly unknown to them, look to the decisions of their counterparts in previous primaries for guidance about which candidate to support, the states voting first will retain the greatest influence over the nomination process.

Some advocates of nomination reform have argued in favor of revoking the special dispensation given to Iowa and New Hampshire under party rules to hold the first caucuses and first primary in every presidential election. This issue has emerged regularly in recent years. Several states have attempted to press the issue by moving their own events up in the schedule to rival Iowa and New Hampshire, even if doing so requires them to give up some of their convention delegates for violating party policy. In 1996, Delaware Republicans positioned their primary just four days after the New Hampshire primary, infringing on the traditional weeklong buffer period between New Hampshire and subsequent states. Louisiana Republicans went even farther, holding their first-round caucuses a few days before Iowa.

In the end, this strategy was not particularly successful. Iowa and New Hampshire officials, who jealously guard their first-in the-nation status, asked candidates to boycott Delaware and Louisiana, threatening retribution by their own states' voters if they failed to comply. Most agreed. Only Steve Forbes risked the anger of the New Hampshire electorate by actively campaigning in Delaware. He did win there—but he finished fourth in New Hampshire, and his candidacy never recovered. Delaware continued this challenge in 2000, and Iowa and New Hampshire responded once again by urging candidates to ignore the state.[60]

Within the Democratic Party, representatives of labor unions and racial minorities, two key components of the party's electoral coalition, have often complained that their constituents are significantly underrepresented in the electorates of Iowa and New Hampshire, and therefore exert less influence on the outcome of presidential nominations than they believe that they deserve based on their share of the national population. After the 2004 election, the Democratic National Committee appointed an internal commission, cochaired by former Secretary of Labor Alexis Herman and Representative David Price of North Carolina, to study the issue. The Herman-Price commission recommended that the party continue to recognize the traditional right of Iowa to hold the first presidential caucuses and New Hampshire the first primary, but that it should also allow two additional states to hold early events before the bulk of other primaries and caucuses take place. The party voted to authorize Nevada, a state with a significant union presence and Latino population, to hold caucuses in 2008 after Iowa but before the New Hampshire primary. South Carolina, a state in which a large proportion of the Democratic electorate is African-American, received approval to hold the second primary of 2008, within one week after New Hampshire.[61]

These changes to the primary calendar may increase the influence of those two states on the 2008 nomination. Alternatively, they could merely further enhance the effect of the Iowa caucuses, if the victorious candidate in Iowa simply rides media-driven momentum to sweep the events that immediately follow. Given the awkward tendency of reforms to work in ways not originally envisioned by their proponents, only experience can tell us whether they will have the intended effect—or any effect at all—on the outcome of presidential nominations within the Democratic Party.

Over the years, states have attempted to gain influence over presidential nominations in ways other than front-loading. One common strategy employed to attract candidate and press attention is the organization of regional primaries. Perhaps if several contiguous states with presumably similar interests coordinate their delegate selection events on a single date, candidates will be forced to show interest in whatever issues are peculiar to that region. The most famous of these attempted regional primaries was organized in 1988, when eleven southern or border states held a "Super Tuesday" on March 8. In 1996, North and South Dakota held primaries on the same day; a week later, five of the six New England states (all but New Hampshire) held their primaries, and four midwestern states (Illinois, Michigan, Ohio, and Wisconsin) coordinated their primaries later in the process. In 2000, the five New England states again held primaries together on March 7, although their influence was severely diluted since other, larger states (including California, Georgia, Missouri, New York, and Ohio) scheduled primaries for the same day.

Such primaries have not, for the most part, been particularly successful. For one thing, states are unable to monopolize a date. Should other states share the day, then candidates may choose to campaign only in the largest states within the region (say, Massachusetts in a New England regional primary) and ignore the smaller states. Even worse, some candidates might skip the region altogether and concentrate on the other states.

The case of Super Tuesday in 1988 is instructive in demonstrating how these reforms often fail to work as intended. The idea (at least on the Democratic side) behind the creation of the Super Tuesday primaries was twofold: (1) to give the South a larger voice in presidential nominating politics; and (2) by switching from caucuses to primaries, and by holding primaries relatively early in the campaign (that is, before it was all decided), southern politicians hoped that some more moderate or conservative Democratic politicians would be in the race, thereby attracting voters into the primaries. But it was not to be. Turnout in Super Tuesday primaries in 1988 was only 25.5 percent as compared to 33.8 percent for the other primaries.[62]

The results of the southern Super Tuesday of 1988 also did not achieve its creators' goal of helping moderate or conservative candidates win the Democratic nomination. Though it kept the southern moderate candidate, Senator Al Gore of Tennessee, in the race temporarily, it also helped the Reverend Jesse Jackson, who won primaries in several southern states on the basis of strong support from black voters and some liberal whites.[63] It ended the candidacy of Representative Richard Gephardt of Missouri. This harmed the front-runner, Governor Dukakis, by helping Jackson, who with his small but devoted following and his thirst for publicity was determined to persist until he could appear on television at the national convention. But Dukakis, a liberal candidate from the Northeast, was still probably the biggest winner, owing to his victories in the two largest southern states, Florida and Texas. He also won primaries that day in Maryland, Rhode Island, and his home state of Massachusetts.

Possibly in reaction to the questionable success of regional primaries, some states have opted for a contrasting strategy, separating themselves from others in their region. In 1988, South Carolina Republicans held a primary on the Saturday before the southern Super Tuesday; in 1992, the Georgia primary was held a week before six other southern states. In each case, a southern candidate (George H. W. Bush of Texas in 1988, Bill Clinton of Arkansas in 1992) won the early state and then swept the rest of the region. The same result was repeated in 1996. Bob Dole's solid victory on March 2 in South Carolina foreshadowed his sweep in eight mostly southern states on March 5. By separating themselves from their region, these states gamble that candidates will spend more time on them than on any other individual state in a regional primary.

At least one other strategy is common. States that are home to a prospective candidate may manipulate the delegate selection process in order to help the "favorite son." If the candidate is expected to win the state, the victory presumably provides extra publicity. If the candidate is worried about losing the state or failing to meet "expectations," however, he or she may not benefit from an early home-state primary. Even hinting at this may generate negative publicity. This happened to Arizona Senator John McCain in 1999. Arizona Republicans had moved their primary to mid-February in 1996, following New Hampshire by only a week. McCain was reported to be in favor of moving the primary back in the schedule, after the delegate-rich California and New York primaries, presumably in order to avoid the possibility of an embarrassing loss—or narrow win—in his home state affecting results elsewhere. In this case, however, Arizona Republicans failed to respect McCain's wishes and left the date of the primary early, on February 22, 2000. McCain's fears in the event went unrealized; he won the state easily.[64]

Selecting a date is not the only way states can affect what candidates do. The varying rules of the major parties for counting primary votes make a difference to candidate strategies. Under Republican rules, state primaries and caucuses may follow plurality "winner-take-all" procedures, and most do. This gives Republican candidates a strategic opportunity not available to Democrats. A Republican late bloomer, by winning later "mop-up" primaries, conceivably could hope to overcome a front-runner's early lead. Ronald Reagan in 1976, for instance, though he won no primaries until late March, almost took the nomination away from Gerald Ford by getting all the delegates from such large states as California and Texas. In contrast, Democratic rules requiring proportional representation make it difficult for lagging Democratic candidates to catch up. Even if front-runners falter, proportional representation slows their momentum only a little in the later primaries.

What helps a candidate overcome an early poor showing? "One of the problems of being a dark horse," notes Hart's 1984 poll taker, Dotty Lynch, "is that you need some true believers with you. Without an issue like George McGovern had in 1972 or a [devoted, ethnically based] constituency like Jesse Jackson has, a lot of people give up on you and you may give up on yourself."[65] Raising enough money up front to outlast disappointing showings is also important. The two factors—a loyal activist following and the capacity to raise money early—may be but do not have to be connected.

The existence of candidates with narrow but intense followings leads us to ask how such candidates might be affected by a Super Tuesday or a similar regional primary. If moderate or more broadly based candidates are numerous and divide the great middle among themselves, it is quite possible for a candidate with a narrow, intense following to do extremely well. Under Republican "winner-take-all" rules, such candidates are less likely to prevail because a substantial majority of party identifiers oppose them. The Reverend Pat Robertson in 1988 was a good test of this proposition. Following proportional representation, Democrats presumably would be more likely to reward with delegates candidates who have narrowly focused but intense followings. The Reverend Jesse Jackson was a good test of this deduction. And in 1988 Jackson lasted longer in the presidential campaign than Robertson did.

Thus the design of the presidential primary process continues to be an ongoing saga of trial and error. A good summary of the way in which the various forces are aligned is Rhodes Cook's: "Regardless of the different nominating rules, . . . there is a dynamic affecting both parties that makes early defeats devastating. No candidate in either party in recent years has mounted a successful comeback during the mop-up period."[66]

Because primaries are the battlegrounds of the nomination process, the role of the news media is central to how nominees are chosen. Since primary voters lack the guidance that party endorsements provide during general elections, and since primary events are often full of uncertainty, media reporting about who is ahead or behind or how seriously candidates should be taken assumes considerable importance. Were officials of political parties able to select their own candidates, the media would matter much less. But with primaries largely replacing state caucuses and conventions, candidates have to care much more about how they do on television than whether they please leaders of their party.

Therefore, a significant part of the nomination process includes trying to manipulate what the mass media say about primary elections both before and after they take place. This is known as "spin control."[67] The contestant who loses but does better than expected may reap greater advantage from a primary than the one who wins but falls below expectations. It is therefore manifestly to the advantage of a candidate to hold his preelection claims down to a minimum. John F. Kennedy tried in 1960 to follow this strategy in Wisconsin, but the press, radio, and television took note of his extensive organization and of favorable polls and in advance pinned the winner-by-a-landslide label on the senator from Massachusetts.[68] Early predictions in the 1968 New Hampshire primary were that Eugene McCarthy would receive somewhere around 10 percent of the vote. When he eventually polled 42 percent—against Lyndon Johnson's 48 percent write-in vote—it was widely interpreted as a victory, in part because it was so unexpected.[69] George McGovern benefited from a similar process in 1972.

A good example of spin control was the effort of Bill Clinton's 1992 campaign to declare a victory in New Hampshire as the "comeback kid," even though he had lost the primary to Paul Tsongas.[70] The press accepted the idea of a resurgent Clinton, ignored the other candidates, and gave Tsongas little of the positive coverage a front-runner might ordinarily receive.[71] In contrast, Bob Kerrey's decisive victory (with 40 percent of the vote) in South Dakota one week later netted him much less favorable publicity than Clinton's second-place showing in New Hampshire. Kerrey succeeded with the voters, but failed in the crucial job of spin control.

Is the selection of presidential nominees best carried out by party leaders bargaining in conventions (old system) or by the mass electorate voting in primaries (new system)? In order to discuss this question, we need to know something about the information possessed by those who do the selecting. Do primaries convey enough information to voters about a candidate's character, competence, issue positions, electability, and capacity to govern? What the media do best is to provide information on the viability of candidates, their standing in the nomination race. Primary voters soak up this information. Substantial evidence exists that voters absorb opinion poll results and gather other impressions of viability, and these exert considerable influence over voting decisions. But information on policies, character, and leadership ability is comparatively scarce and is assimilated slowly.[72] "It appears safe to conclude," John G. Geer writes, "that most primary voters do not compare the issue positions of candidates when voting."[73] One reason that primary voters do not perceive much issue distance between the candidates, is, perhaps, because,

TABLE 4.4	Reasons for Supporting a Candidate for Nomination (in Percentages)

	N	Personality	Issues	Ideology	Group	Campaign	Other	Don't Know
Erie Dems	264	70.1	10.2	0.8	9.5	8.7	0.4	0.4
Erie Reps	101	79.2	15.8	2.0	0.0	2.0	1.0	0.0
L.A. Dems	270	68.9	15.9	5.2	1.9	7.8	0.4	0.0
L.A. Reps	161	73.9	19.9	3.0	0.0	1.2	1.9	0.0

Source: John G. Geer, *Nominating Presidents: An Assessment of Voters in Presidential Primaries* (New York: Greenwood, 1989), p. 77.

being members of the same party, there is in fact not that much difference. Another reason may be that candidates are purposely unclear. Since it may well be advantageous for candidates to appeal differently to various audiences, they may, like Bill Clinton or George H. W. Bush, appear moderate to some people, liberal to others, and conservative to still others.

There are bandwagon effects in primaries. Gary Hart rose from 2 percent of national support early in February 1984 to 33 percent in three weeks. Jimmy Carter went from near obscurity, 1 percent in January 1976, to 29 percent by mid-March. John Kerry was the favored candidate of 9 percent of Democrats nationwide in a *Time*/CNN poll conducted in mid-January 2004, before the Iowa caucuses. After his victories in Iowa and New Hampshire, Kerry surged to 43 percent in the same poll by February 6.[74] As Collat, Kelley, and Rogowski define the term, "a bandwagon effect may be said to exist if a given decision-maker supports, from among some set of contenders, not the contender he most prefers, but the contender who seems most likely to win."[75]

If voters can be swept along by the sheer momentum of events, the strength of their issue preferences or of their assessments of leadership ability must be very low. On what basis, then, do citizens choose? As the nominating campaign moves along, voters do develop feelings about the personalities of the candidates. In a study of primary voters in Los Angeles, California, and Erie, Pennsylvania, John Geer demonstrates that comments centered on the candidates' personalities predominate in the reasons given for voting in primaries (see table 4.4).[76]

Since much of the debate in the primary is about who among members of the same party can provide the best leadership, Geer thinks voter concentration on candidates' personal qualities is reasonable. Others disagree. Henry E. Brady and Michael G. Hagen argue that "primaries seem to be seriously flawed by forcing voters to commit to candidates before they can learn about . . . policy positions, electability and leadership ability of those standing for the nomination. . . . American primaries force people to choose before they are ready."[77]

The political parties have written their rules in a way that makes it impossible to avoid primaries. Now that the national party conventions ratify rather than choose candidates, the function of reducing uncertainty about which candidates are ahead and behind is transferred from successive convention ballots to the sequence of primary elections.

It could be said that primaries are more important than general elections because primaries do more to limit the choices available to voters. Since the effects of primaries are cumulative, it is especially important to study how earlier events affect later ones. Larry Bartels argues that the nomination victories of Republican Gerald Ford and Democrat Jimmy Carter in 1976 were due to the accumulation of momentum, with over half of Carter's support in primaries coming from his early successes.[78] Perhaps the most interesting finding comes from a study by Richard Brody and Larry Rothenberg showing that voter turnout declines toward the end of the primary season.[79] This makes sense; if the early primaries dominate the process, and sharply constrain alternatives available later on, then it would follow that people would see less purpose in turning out for later ones.

Since primaries have become so important—indeed, indispensable—for presidential nominations, it increases our interest in such questions as: Which candidates, and which interests represented by them, are advantaged or disadvantaged by primaries? Do radicals, conservatives, or moderates perform better or worse owing to the current extensive use of primaries? Are citizens' preferences more or less likely to be reflected in the results? If not citizens', then whose preferences are expressed? How do the rules for counting votes affect the results? We begin with this last important question because it turns out that the way votes are counted in large measure determines whose preferences count the most.

No one pretends that primaries are perfect representations of the electorate that either identifies with a particular political party or is likely to vote for the party's leading vote-getter. For one thing, voters are not allowed to rank their preferences, so a candidate's popularity with voters who gave their first-choice votes to others is unknown. It is quite possible for a candidate to be the first choice of the largest clump of voters but to be only the fourth or fifth choice of all voters taken together. In 1972, for example, the candidates of the Democratic Party's ideological right and left wings—George Wallace and George McGovern, respectively—won pluralities in more states than any other candidates, yet they also attracted widespread opposition. This opposition was ineffectively expressed in the primary process. Voter turnout in primaries is usually much lower than in the general election and is likely to contain a larger proportion of dyed-in-the-wool party supporters than would be true in a general election. Austin Ranney has shown that average turnout in primaries is approximately 27 percent of all people of voting age, compared with roughly double that in the presidential election.[80] It is not so much low turnout, however, as the combination of low turnout with plurality elections that biases the results. In 1972, McGovern won a plurality in six states. In those states his total primary vote compared with the total vote cast in the general election ranged from 4 to 22 percent. Clearly, his primary voters could not have been fully representative of those who actually voted in November.[81]

Nevertheless, it may appear that McGovern was entitled to most of the primary delegates because he won more often than any other candidate. This would depend, however, on how the votes were counted. There are three basic ways of counting votes. One is winner take all: whichever candidate gets a plurality of votes in the entire state gets all the delegates. Another is proportional: all candidates who pass a certain threshold, say, 15 percent, divide the delegates among themselves in accordance with their percentage of the vote. A third is congressionally districted: after delegates are allotted (by population or past party vote or both) to districts, the candidate who wins a plurality in each area gains all of its delegates.

Rumination about the three rules reveals the kinds of constituencies (and hence interests) they are likely to favor. Winner take all gives more power to populous and competitive states, which have a large number of delegates. These are, Texas and Florida excepted, the states of the Northeast and California, known for their large concentration of urban voters, ethnic minorities, and labor union members. The proportional rule favors noncompetitive areas because in these places a high degree of support for a single candidate pays off. That is why George Wallace did so well in 1972 wherever the proportional rule was in force. The congressional district rule would fragment the large states, where many candidates could get some support, but not the smaller, less competitive states that have a few homogeneous districts. It should be evident, as James Lengle and Byron Shafer conclude, that

> the widespread adoption of Districted primaries after 1968, or the prohibition of Winner-Take-All primaries after 1972 [by Democrats], were not, then, just inconsequential decisions to hand out delegates via a certain mechanism. They were far-reaching, if almost accidental, choices about the type of candidates who would bear the party's standard, the type of voters who would have the power to choose those standard bearers, and the type of issues with which both groups would try to shape history. They were, in short, a decision on how to (re)construct the Democratic Party.[82]

The purpose of the McGovern-Fraser Commission, which rewrote Democratic delegation selection rules between the 1968 and 1972 elections, was to take control of the presidential nomination away from state and local party officials, as well as from national officeholders, and give it over to party activists attached to candidates and elected through primaries with safeguards to assure representation of those deemed insufficiently represented: women, youth, racial minorities. After each of the elections from 1972 through 1984, the Democrats sought to refine the version of representativeness enacted by the McGovern–Fraser Commission. Should proportional representation always be the rule, or was winner take all an acceptable system in some form? What was the proper threshold for representation in a proportional system? Should special rules ensure a place for party leaders and elected officials at the convention, even if they chose not to endorse any candidate early in the process?

The compromise system established by the Hunt Commission in the wake of the crushing defeat of the Democrats in 1980 was to insist on strict proportional representation and to add about 15 percent of the slots for delegates to be reserved for uncommitted party and public officials, now commonly called "superdelegates." In each state, positions were reserved for the party chair and vice chair, as well as members of the state's Senate and House delegations. The remainder of the unpledged delegates were turned over to state parties with the suggestion they be given to governors and mayors of large cities. Finally, 305 delegates were allotted to pledged elected and party officials.[83]

So far, we have the results of the 1984, 1988, 1992, 1996, 2000, and 2004 Democratic nominating processes to gauge the effects of these rules changes. In five of these six elections (all but 1984), close nomination battles did not develop, so superdelegate behavior was not important. In 1984, the uncommitted delegates overwhelmingly supported Walter Mondale, and did so not late in the convention but relatively early in the primary season. Whether Mondale could have won without them, or, as is more likely, they helped sustain his strength during his bid, the superdelegates did matter.

How did the rules for counting votes in primaries affect the outcome in 1984? Where Jesse Jackson's highly concentrated 18 percent of the vote got him just 10 percent of the delegates, and Hart came out even with 36 percent of the vote and the delegates, Mondale won 49 percent of the delegates with 39 percent of the vote. Jackson was hurt by the concentration of his support in largely black areas. Hart's results were proportional because he happened to win mostly in states following proportional rules. Mondale was helped because he won in big states with bonus "winner-take-more" systems, which the Democrats outlawed again after the 1988 contest.[84]

Did the Hunt Commission reforms enacted before the 1984 election enhance the prospects of moderates with close ties to party officials, as they were intended to do? Walter Mondale fit this description and, as we have seen, the rules in 1984 worked to his advantage. Still, reserving 15 to 20 percent of convention seats for party officials is unlikely to be enough to reverse the trends we discussed earlier. The declining role of state parties, the greater emphasis on primaries, and the logic of primary election choice all favor candidates with intense factional followings over moderate insiders.

In any event, for party officials to play a moderating role, they must be moderate. Recent trends toward party polarization make this somewhat less likely. As conservatives, mostly southerners, have left the Democrats and moved into the Republican Party, conflict between the parties increasingly substitutes for conflict within them. Certainly, the prospects of a conservative Democratic or a liberal Republican presidential candidate have diminished. To the extent this is so, party officeholders may no longer be the bastions of moderation they once were. To test this hypothesis, we would need to know whether the views of politician delegates are closer to or further from those of Democratic voters than are activist delegates chosen through primaries or caucuses. We do know that politician delegates are more loyal to their party, 85 percent saying they support its candidates every year compared to two-thirds of the other delegates. Tom Mann argues that some politicians at the 1984 convention tried to push the Democratic Party platform farther to the left. Similarly, some Republican delegates from the House of Representatives pushed hard to the right.[85] In 1988 the House Republicans put public pressure on George H. W. Bush to select a vice-presidential candidate from the right wing of the party.[86]

Where once it was useful to be the second choice of 90 percent of all delegates, today first choices, even of as few as 30 percent, are far preferable. This is a good measure of the change over the past three decades in the nomination process. Whether the country will do better with presidents who are the strong preference of party minorities rather than the weak preference of party majorities remains to be seen. One key test for presidents selected by modern processes will be what happens when they attempt to gather the support they need to govern or, even more significantly, what happens to them and to their governments if they neglect to make the attempt. The warning words of a British observer, Anthony Teasdale, merit careful consideration:

> One irony of the primaries may . . . be that in the name of greater democratic participation, nominations more often go to those less representative of party opinion. A second irony seems to be that in pursuit of more authoritative and legitimate government, primaries often favour candidates with less governmental experience, reduce the usefulness of party, increase popular expectations of politicians, and generally make America more difficult to govern. . . .
>
> Above all, by establishing direct personal contact between candidates and the mass electorate, primaries erode the importance of party as an intermediary between the elected and the elector in the United States. Candidates establish their own national organization, with their own mobile campaigners now imported into states as necessary. In government, this weakens the attachment of party loyalty which might give the President additional leverage to secure action on his proposals in Congress and the states.[87]

STATE CAUCUSES

As we have mentioned, the vast majority of delegates to the national party conventions are selected through the state primary process. In 2004, for example, 67 percent of the delegates to the Democratic convention were chosen in primaries, 19 percent were unelected superdelegates, and state caucuses or conventions chose the other 14 percent. How do candidates go about securing delegates through the state caucus system?

In the past, attempts by candidates to influence delegates chosen outside of primaries were usually made after these delegates were selected by state parties. The first strategic requirement for the candidate seeking to influence these delegates was an intelligence service, a network of informants who could report on which delegates were firmly committed, which were wavering, and which might be persuaded to provide second- or third-choice support. Advance reports on the opportunities offered by internal division in the state parties, the type of appeal likely to be effective in each state, and the kinds of bargains to which leaders were most susceptible were also helpful. The costs of this information were high in time, money, and effort, but it was worthwhile to the serious candidate, who needed to know how to move to increase support and block opponents.

These days, no one wants to wait for delegates to be chosen before trying to influence them. The idea is for candidates to get their supporters selected as delegates. By the time they are selected, delegates are likely to be committed to a particular candidate or point of view. In any event, they cannot be selected before the year of the election. The same forces that persuade candidates to begin their drive for the nomination ever earlier impel them to begin the hunt for delegates ahead of time. Since fundraising must go on across the country in order to collect enough money to run an adequate campaign, it can be combined with the identification of local allies, who eventually will be designated delegates if the candidate does well in the state selection process.

The major change between past and present stems from the rules adopted by the Democrats after 1968. Delegates, even where there is no primary, are almost always pledged from the moment they are chosen. In the past, delegates were chosen to represent the state parties, and the preferences of delegates could not easily be influenced by the candidates. Now, delegates are chosen to reflect the presidential preferences of some set of voters, whether those voters are a primary electorate, party activists, or party officials. Therefore, even in strong party states, the delegates are representatives not of the party but of the candidates who attracted support within the party. The only role remaining for party leaders is influencing the electorate. Even if the party should choose this role, it is one of advocacy rather than the traditional party role of intermediation.

When and where there were strong state party organizations in the past, aspiring candidates had to deal with them. Candidate decisions on whether to enter a primary or influence delegate selection were mediated through party leaders. If party leaders thought a contest in a state would be divisive, candidates would have to worry about incurring their enmity. The decline of state parties in the nomination process has removed these obstacles. Relatively small numbers of activists without a continuing connection to the party may mobilize around a candidate and, by appealing to caucus attendees and primary electorates, overwhelm the party regulars. If the test is numbers of followers who will come to a particular meeting, rather than present party position or past service, an activist surge can carry the day, as McGovern (1972) and Goldwater (1964) demonstrated so well.

Aspirants for nomination vary greatly in the degree to which they know other politicians throughout the country. Candidates like Bob Dole, Richard Nixon, Hubert Humphrey, and Barry Goldwater, who traveled extensively and gave assistance to members of their parties, simply needed to keep their files up to date in order to have a nationwide list of contacts. When the time came, they knew from whom they could request assistance in gathering information, persuading delegates, and generally furthering their cause. Candidates who lacked this advantage had to take special steps in order to build up their political apparatus.

Nowadays every candidate seeks to sway voters, not party leaders, and contacts of a different sort are more valuable. The sort of organization that candidates need today includes pollsters, fundraisers, and media experts—paid consultants who aim their message at voters. Indeed, it may not be too much to say that a key question for candidates today is which pollsters or consultants to attract to their campaigns, rather than which party leaders.[88] Before the 2004 nomination process began, the media devoted a great deal of attention to the efforts of several Democratic candidates to persuade veteran political strategist Bob Shrum to join their campaigns. Shrum decided to work for John Kerry, who was proclaimed the winner of the "Shrum primary."[89] Now everybody believes, and with good reason, that candidates increase their chances of winning the nomination by organizing their campaigns as early and as visibly as possible. Candidates need more publicity than they once did, and the nomination campaign begins at an earlier point with each succeeding election.

This could be seen in the way George H. W. Bush in 1988 and Bill Clinton in 1992 sought their nominations. Bush and Clinton had extensive contacts with party leaders across the nation, cultivated over many years of preparation for eventual White House bids. Bush, of course, was also the sitting vice president. Yet each of them campaigned for the nomination in exactly the same way political unknown Jimmy Carter had in 1976, appealing directly to voters through small events in Iowa and New Hampshire, and via television ads and large public rallies in the larger states. Political networks nowadays may help candidates raise money or survive scandal (if their allies are willing to go on television to support them), but the nomination is fought and won among mass electorates.

Modern caucuses are in principle open to any voter who identifies with the party; some state parties allow independents to take part as well. In practice, caucus participation rates are quite low, since the sacrifice in time and energy required exceeds that of a simple primary election. This generalization does not apply to Iowa, site of the first and most prominent caucuses, where turnout rates tend to resemble those of presidential primaries due to the extraordinary amount of candidate activity and media coverage that descends on the state every four years, attention that stimulates unusually high levels of voter participation.

Caucuses tend to reward candidates that have extensive campaign organizations in the state able to mobilize voters to attend the caucus meetings. Candidates with particularly devoted followings also do better in caucuses than in primaries, since their supporters are more willing to make the required effort to participate. In 2004, for example, Representative Dennis Kucinich of Ohio, running as an outspoken left-wing candidate for the Democratic presidential nomination, consistently performed much better in caucuses than in primaries. Of the nine states in which Kucinich received at least 10 percent of the vote, seven held party caucuses. His strongest showing was in the February 24 caucuses in Hawaii, where he took 31 percent of the vote, placing second to John Kerry. Kucinich's appeal was quite limited even within the Democratic electorate, but the low-turnout caucus system allowed his small faction of fervent supporters to cast a greater share of the vote than they did in primaries dominated by more casual, more moderate voters.

THE NATIONAL PARTY CONVENTIONS

While the selection of a site for the national party convention has often been interpreted as one of the preballot indicators of various candidates' strength, in the past it usually was the rather routine outcome of the weighing of one major and several very minor factors. The major factor was the size of the convention city's proffered contribution to the national party committee. This contribution, in cash or in services, came partly from the city government but mostly from various business groups—local organizations of hotels and restaurants—that stood to profit from a week-long visit of 6,500 delegates and alternates, their families and friends, and thousands of media representatives, dignitaries, and convention personnel. The cloud over the offer of several hundred thousand dollars by the Sheraton hotel chain as part of San Diego's bid to host the 1972 Republican convention, as well as the reaction to Watergate, inspired some changes. The federal government now makes available a sum, $14.6 million in 2004, to each of the national parties to help finance their nominating conventions, thereby lessening the pressure to acquire cash contributions or contributions in kind.[90] But while the pressure has lifted, the temptation has not; in 1992, the Republicans selected Houston over front-runner San Diego in part because the Texas city donated $10.6 million in cash to the party coffers, as well as providing free security and bus services.[91]

A variety of other factors may tip the balance between competing cities. Political consider-ations are often important. San Francisco was chosen by Democrats in 1984 partly because the party was having trouble competing in the West and partly because the city had a popular female Democratic mayor.[92] In 1988, both parties wanted to bolster their strength in the South, Republi-cans because they were gaining and Democrats because they were declining, and so the Democrats selected Atlanta and the Republicans New Orleans.[93] Cities in large states, especially those ex-pected to be competitive in the fall, are logical choices. Thus the Democrats selected Los Angeles and the Republicans chose Philadelphia for their conventions in 2000. Of course, there is no ev-idence that the site of national conventions makes the least bit of difference to the average voter, but party officials take these factors into account when deciding where to meet every four years.

Other considerations include the quality of the facilities, the suitability of the convention hall to television coverage, sufficient hotel and entertainment accommodations, and (for Democrats) the presence of places to meet and stay with acceptable records on the treatment of labor unions.[94] For example, Philadelphia's James Tate headed as large and as loyal a Democratic organization in 1968 as Chicago's Richard Daley, and his city was closer geographically to Lyndon Johnson in Washington, but Philadelphia simply could not provide 20,000 first-class hotel rooms.[95] San Diego's proposal in 1992 to split the Republican proceedings between the convention center and an outdoor stadium was considered too complicated and inconvenient.

The parties prefer to bring their publicity and their business to cities and states where the mayor and the governor are friendly members of the party, since this may give added access to (and control of) public facilities. The aloof attitude of California's Governor Jerry Brown toward the site-selection committee of his party evidently tipped the decision of the Democrats toward New York in 1976 and away from Los Angeles.[96] In 1984, the fact that the party chairman, Charles Manatt, was a Californian may have tipped the balance back to San Francisco for the Democrats. The desire to maintain the autonomy of the convention from demonstrators, who were involved in the Democratic debacle in Chicago in 1968, led to a choice in 1972 of Miami Beach, where a causeway facilitated crowd control.

In 1992, Democratic National Committee Chairman (and native New Yorker) Ron Brown's close relationship with New York City Mayor David Dinkins was considered a significant factor in that city's selection for the Democratic convention. In 2004, the Republicans also selected New York, thanks in part to the presence of a Republican mayor, Michael Bloomberg, and governor, George Pataki. Bush campaign officials also wished to use the convention to emphasize the president's record on fighting terrorism by holding it in the same city as the World Trade Center attacks of September 11, 2001. Democrats, meanwhile, chose Boston as the site of their 2004 convention, which turned out to be the hometown of their nominee that year, John Kerry.

The time of a convention varies between mid-July and early September. The "out" party normally holds its convention before the "in" party, on the theory that its candidate will need a publicity boost earlier in the campaign. In 1972, 1976, 1984, 1988, 1992, and 2004, this put Democrats before Republicans; in 1964, 1968, 1980, 1996, and 2000 it was the other way around. In 2004, the Democrats, the "out" party, met July 26–29, while the Republicans waited until August 30–September 2. The Democratic National Committee has announced that the 2008 Democratic convention will be held August 25–28, after the conclusion of the Summer Olympics; the Republican convention will occur the following week, September 1–4.[97] An incumbent president will schedule the convention to fit the presidential timetable. At its most momentous, the convention may coincide with an international peace offensive; in 1968, the date of the Democratic convention seems to have been set with nothing more momentous in mind than President Johnson's birthday.

Once assembled, the national convention is a mass meeting in which the participants necessarily play widely varying and unequal roles. The candidates and their chief supporters are presumably busy, perfecting their organizations and trying to maintain communication with as many of their delegates as they can. In the old days, "pledged" delegations actively supported their candidate, while "bossed" delegates negotiated for the disposal of their votes. The leaders of these delegations were the people who conducted negotiations among the delegations when an impasse developed. There were also factional leaders and independent delegates within state delegations who played an important part in determining what their delegation or a part of their delegation would do. They bargained within their delegation, rather than among the various state delegations. Now the roles of both these relatively autonomous types of politicians have sharply diminished, since most delegates come to the convention pledged to one or another presidential candidate. This means that candidate organizations, not state party leaders, have to do the bargaining (e.g., over the party platform) if there is any bargaining to do. But it will be difficult for the candidates' representatives to bargain if they cannot transfer the votes of their supporters; it will be even harder if the nomination has already been decided as it normally is in caucuses and primaries.

CANDIDATE ORGANIZATIONS AT THE CONVENTIONS

At the national convention, before the balloting for the presidential nomination starts, one or more days are consumed in a variety of party rituals: listening to welcoming speeches, qualifying and seating delegates, presenting the platform, and so on. During that time, delegates and their leaders mill about, exchanging greetings and gossip. This set of circumstances challenges the tracking capacities of even the most efficient candidate organization.

There is a wide divergence among candidate organizations. They range from the comprehensive, integrated, and superbly effective to the fragmented, uncoordinated, and virtually nonexistent. We can only suggest the range of organizational alternatives through some general comments and a few historical examples.

The first modern candidate organization at a national convention, tied together with sophisticated communication equipment, was the expensively mounted organization of Senator John F. Kennedy in 1960. His communication network provided him with a continuing and accurate stream of vital information.[98] He wanted detailed personal knowledge about as many delegates as possible in order to know how they were likely to vote and how they might best be persuaded to stay in line or change their minds. This was all quite necessary in the days, now gone by, when conventions made significant decisions rather than merely ratifying the results of decisions previously made elsewhere. More than a year before the convention, the Kennedy-for-President organization—still in the pre-computer age—started a card file containing information on people throughout the nation who might be delegates and who might influence delegates. Included on each card were the prospective delegate's name, occupation, religion, party position, relation (if any) to the Kennedy family or its leading supporters, ambitions, policy preferences if strongly held, and likely vote. This was brought up to date before convention time, and entries were made in a central register as new information developed. Thus, when it appeared that a delegate needed to be reinforced or might not vote for Kennedy, his card was pulled and the information was used in order to determine the best way to convince him.

In order to keep an up-to-date and, when necessary, an hour-by-hour watch on developments within the state delegations, the Kennedy organization assigned an individual coordinator to each state. This person might be a delegate or an observer, such as a senator or a member of the candidate's staff. When it was deemed inadvisable to choose a delegate for fear that any choice would alienate one faction or another, a person outside the state was chosen. These coordinators kept tabs on individual delegates and maintained a running record of the likely distribution of votes. When necessary, the coordinators sent messages to the candidate's headquarters, and reinforcements were called in. At the Kennedy headquarters the seriousness of the report would be judged and a decision made on how to deal with it. Senator Kennedy himself might call the wavering delegate, one of his brothers might be dispatched, a state party leader might intervene, or some other such remedy might be applied.

In the hurly-burly, crush, and confusion of convention activity, it cannot be assumed that messages sent are received or that decisions are communicated to those who must carry them out. The Kennedy organization took great care to establish a communication center that would receive messages and locate the intended recipients and that could send out instructions and receive feedback on the results. In this prebeeper, precell phone era, each key staff person was required to phone his whereabouts periodically to a central switchboard. This made it possible for the Kennedy forces at the convention to deploy and reassign their people on a minute-by-minute basis as developments required.

A system set up only to deal with emergencies would have limited usefulness to a candidate who wanted regular reports that could be appraised in a consistent way. Every morning, the coordinators assigned to the Kennedy headquarters attended a staff meeting at which they deposited with the secretary a report on their activities for the previous day. These reports were sent to what was called the "secret room," and the information was transferred to state briefing files. From these files, a daily secret report on delegate strength was written and given to the candidate and his top advisers.

At the morning staff meetings, Robert Kennedy, who acted as campaign manager for his brother, would ask each coordinator for his estimate of the number of Kennedy votes. Keenly aware of the dangers of seeming to want high estimates, Robert Kennedy challenged the coordinators if he felt that their estimates were too high, but not if they appeared too low. On occasion he would reprimand a coordinator for including a delegate as a certain Kennedy supporter when other information indicated that this was not true. The success of this procedure was indicated by the fact that when the alphabetical balloting reached Wyoming on the first (and last) ballot, the Kennedy organization's estimate of its delegate strength was proved correct within a one-vote margin.[99]

The danger of confusion and mishap is multiplied during the balloting because the convention floor is filled, and it is difficult to move about freely. To deal with this, the Kennedy organization arranged for telephones on the convention floor. Six were set up beneath the seats of chairmen of friendly delegations who were seated around the gigantic convention hall. These phones were connected to the Kennedy headquarters outside the hall. Inside the headquarters, staff members sat near the telephone and simultaneously scanned several television sets to look for possible defections. Had the pretested telephones failed to work, walkie-talkie radios were available to take their place.[100]

By comparison with the Kennedy efforts, most of the organizations that have successfully nominated presidential candidates in American history have been uncoordinated, diffuse affairs. For example, in 1952 none of the various factions in the Democratic Party that favored the nomination of Adlai Stevenson had the wholehearted cooperation of their candidate; information gathering was casual and tactical maneuvers were in some cases hit upon accidentally or as afterthoughts. The factions working for the Stevenson nomination did not cooperate to a significant degree and squabbled on occasion. Yet Stevenson was nominated; his success came about because he was the second choice of an overwhelming number of delegates who could not agree on any of their first choices and the first choice of a significant number of leaders in spite of his disinclination to pursue the nomination in an organized fashion.[101]

We have devoted so much space to the Kennedy organization because, unlike the Stevenson example, it became a harbinger of the future. Candidate organizations since then are like Kennedy's, only more so—more telephones, more communication apparatus, and computer networks have replaced the old-fashioned file cards. No nomination since 1976 has been in real doubt when the convention opened, but worries about defections as the result of floor fights on the platform or rules require candidates to prepare for the worst.

An interesting test of the importance of convention organizations took place in 1976 at the closely contested Republican convention. Following the evolving practice, the President Ford

Committee installed an effective communication apparatus. Rather than rely entirely on the geographic leaders of their earlier delegate monitoring operation, the President Ford Committee divided the convention floor into zones, whose floor leaders wore red hats. They were tied by telephone to the Ford trailer outside the convention hall and to subleaders responsible for each state. By contrast, Ronald Reagan, in his unsuccessful first bid for the nomination, relied on style and ideology, rather than hierarchy and division of labor. As a convention leader said, "Our conservatives don't like to be told what to do, and they don't need to be. The Ford people need all that hardware because they can't count on their delegates to vote with them consistently." F. Christopher Arterton, who observed the convention, believes that at crucial moments, such as when the Mississippi delegation caucused on the floor before a crucial vote, Reagan "was handicapped by key coordinators having to fight their way through jammed aisles."[102]

The closest thing to a contested convention since then was the 1984 Democratic convention, when Walter Mondale had the nomination sewed up in advance but both Gary Hart and Jesse Jackson had won large numbers of delegates. The Mondale nerve center composed of 14 delegate trackers in a trailer, 35 cluster organizers (clusters were groups of states) covering 300 to 350 delegates each, 60 state whips, and 390 line whips, all responsible for seeing to it that delegates fulfilled their pledges. Thus, by the 1980s, all serious candidates brought to the convention as part of their normal equipment a full complement of electronic communication gear. All had trailers parked near the convention hall in which they could monitor trends on the floor and entertain friends and allies. What was extraordinary about the Kennedy effort in 1960 has, with the passage of time and the progress of technology, become commonplace.

PARTY DELEGATES AT THE CONVENTIONS

Through improved use of technology, modern strategy, and teamwork, candidate organizations have clearly increased their control over delegates. It is still important, however, to know something of the delegates themselves. Who are they? What do they believe? How loyal to their parties are they? Excellent studies of convention delegates allow us a perspective on the changing nature of party activists. In recent conventions, delegates, pledged to particular candidates and chosen in state primaries and caucuses, have had little influence in the choice of the party's nominee. Still, they play a role in platform debates and in establishing the image the party projects on television. If we should ever have a deadlocked convention, in which delegates are released from their pledges, delegate attitudes and behavior will take on importance.

Each of the major parties has its own distinctive style and norms. "Republicans," Jo Freeman observes, "perceive themselves as insiders even when they are out of power, and Democrats perceive themselves as outsiders even when they are in power."[103] This difference can be elaborated: Republicans in convention are relatively unified, while Democrats think of themselves as members of subgroups. As the more hierarchical party, Republicans stress loyalty to the chosen leader and the organization. The more varied and egalitarian Democratic Party, in Freeman's words, "has multiple power centers that compete for membership support in order to make demands on, as well as determine, the leaders."[104] For Democratic delegates, therefore, subgroup caucuses are significant reference groups. The component parts of the Republican Party, states and geographic regions and ideological factions, do not maintain robust lives outside the party structure,

TABLE 4.5 Income of Delegates and Party Identifiers (in Percentages)

Democrats' Income			
Identifiers, 2004		Delegates, 2004	
Less than $50,000	57	Less than $50,000	18
$50,000 to $75,000	19	$50,000 to $75,000	21
$75,000 to $100,000	12	$75,000 to $100,000	19
Over $100,000	9	Over $100,000	42
Republicans' Income			
Identifiers, 2004		Delegates, 2004	
Less than $50,000	37	Less than $50,000	8
$50,000 to $75,000	20	$50,000 to $75,000	26
$75,000 to $100,000	14	$75,000 to $100,000	16
Over $100,000	20	Over $100,000	42

Source: "Convention Delegates: Who They Are . . . ," New York Times, August 29, 2004, sec. 15, p. 1.

as do the Democratic caucuses of African Americans, union members, gays, or environmental activists, nor on the Republican side do they make decisions and proposals as much as serve as conduits of information downward to delegates. At national conventions Democrats go to caucuses, as Freeman says, while Republicans go to receptions. Republicans "network" with the candidate organizations, while Democrats make demands. Democrats expect their nominee to pay attention to their problems, while Republicans are more likely to think that the winner ought to get his or her way until the next time.[105]

The Democratic rules governing delegate selection have succeeded in increasing the proportion of African Americans and women at the past nine Democratic conventions. But even if delegates differ somewhat by income and education, political activists are still a rather elite group. Table 4.5 reveals the differences in income between delegates and party identifiers for both parties in 2004.

Educational differences between delegates and party rank and file were even more striking. About seven in ten delegates from both parties had college degrees, compared to one in five among rank-and-file Democrats and one in three of rank-and-file Republican identifiers. Little had changed from 1975, when Jeane Kirkpatrick concluded, "the delegates to both conventions were an overwhelmingly middle to upper class group."[106] Table 4.6, prepared by Barbara G. Farah, on the composition of delegates from 1944 to 1984 reveals that the big change over that time is the four-and-a-half-fold increase in the participation of women. Much smaller changes involve decreases in delegates with little formal education, lawyers, and public officials. The categories of executive and teacher, where there have been considerable changes, deserve further examination.[107]

From 1972 to 1976, half of female Democratic delegates were employed in the public sector, either in government itself or in public education. This was also true of a little over a third of

TABLE 4.6 Delegate Surveys Forty Years Apart (1944–1984) (in Percentages)

	1944 Dem.	1944 Rep.	1968 Dem.	1968 Rep.	1976 Dem.	1976 Rep.	1984 Dem.	1984 Rep.
By sex								
Men	89	91	87	83	67	69	49	54
Women	11	9	13	17	33	31	51	46
By education								
High school or less	24	23	N.A.	N.A.	N.A.	N.A.	11	12
Some college	18	18	N.A.	N.A.	N.A.	N.A.	18	25
College graduate	12	16	10	–	21	27	20	28
More than college degree	46	41	44	34	43	38	51	35
By age								
Average age (in years)	52	54	49	49	43	48	44	51
By occupation								
Lawyer	38	37	28	22	16	15	17	14
Union leader	2	–	4	–	6	–	6	–
Executive	9	10	27	40	17	30	14	26
Other professional/teacher	24	35	8	2	26	12	36	27
Public official	11	6	13	13	12	9	9	6
Homemaker	6	5	*	*	7	15	4	13
Convention attendance								
Never attended convention before	63	63	67	66	80	78	74	69
By ideology								
Liberal	–	–	–	–	40	3	50	1
Moderate	–	–	–	–	47	45	42	35
Conservative	–	–	–	–	8	48	5	60

Source: Barbara G. Farah, "Delegate Polls: 1944 to 1984," *Public Opinion* (August/September 1984): 44. Reprinted with permission of American Enterprise Institute for Public Policy Research.

Notes: 1984 figures are a combination of the CBS News poll, the *New York Times* poll, and the *Los Angeles Times* poll; the 1968 and 1976 figures come from the CBS News poll. The occupation categories are not exactly the same for the 1944 study and the later polls. That will explain the disparity between values for "executive" in the early year and the later ones.

Democratic male delegates. Among Republicans, somewhat more than a third of female and just under a fifth of male delegates were government employees. Over a quarter of all delegates were union members, most of them from teachers' and other public-sector unions. For women in particular, then, M. Kent Jennings concludes, "public employment is a key route to the avenues of party power."[108]

As the party traditionally favoring government, it is to be expected that Democratic delegates would come more frequently from the public sector. This may also explain why they seek higher spending on domestic programs. But there is nothing inherent in public-sector employment that would necessarily lead to a preference for lower spending on defense or against military intervention in the Middle East or for liberal positions on social issues. For that we must look to an ideological explanation. Jo Freeman conjectures that

> [T]he 1984 conventions solidified the direction in which both parties had been moving for the previous ten years. The Democrats adopted the feminist perspective on all public issues directly affecting women and made it clear that women, under feminist leadership, were an important part of the Democratic coalition. The Republican Party adopted antifeminist positions on almost every issue. Its public script was written by [conservative activist] Phyllis Schlafly. But it didn't repudiate women; instead it affirmed their importance by showcasing them extensively and devoting more real resources to help women, as individuals, get elected, than the Democratic Party has done.[109]

What happens when party and ideology conflict? A "requirement of participating in the mainstream of the party," Freeman says, "is that one not become an electoral liability. NOW (National Organization for Women) demonstrated its awareness of this rule by endorsing Democratic men running against Republican feminist women, arguing that anyone who supports [President Ronald] Reagan's economic program, and . . . doesn't support [a] pro-choice [position on the abortion issue], is not really a feminist."[110]

Both parties run one risk. Delegates are more likely to represent the ideological extremes, while the bulk of the voters out in the country remain firmly in or near the center. This pattern has occasionally resulted in the nomination of a presidential candidate who is also ideologically extreme. The classic examples were the 1964 Republicans and the 1972 Democrats. The former selected the very conservative Senator Barry Goldwater of Arizona, while the latter chose the very liberal Senator George McGovern of South Dakota. In each case, studies found that convention delegates held issue positions not shared by ordinary party identifiers. In each case, the nominee lost badly in November partially because of defections from his own party. In the McGovern convention, his supporters shared the same political attitudes whether they were male or female, white or black, young or old. Perhaps what happened is that activists in both parties, enjoying high social and economic status but without professional commitment to party unity or party organization, grew at once farther apart from one another and from the voters. The participant sectors of the parties were far more polarized in 1972 than they had been in the 1940s and 1950s in two directions—one party from the other at the elite level, and elites in both parties from their followers.[111]

Evidence from representative governments throughout the world demonstrates that voters have more ideologically moderate views than elected officials, who in turn are more moderate than party activists.[112] While the general public prefers smaller government and restrictions on abortion far more than Democratic elites do, it also likes environmental regulation and deficit reduction a lot more than Republican elites do. Tables 4.7 and 4.8 compare the views of delegates to the Democratic and Republican national conventions in 2004 to the positions of Democratic and Republican identifiers, and to all voters. On nearly every issue, convention delegates are significantly more extreme than the rank-and-file members of their own party, and are far more so than the generally centrist American electorate.

We conclude that when political elites talk about the great issues that divide the nation, they are referring less to the public at large than to themselves. With the increase of ideological consistency among activists in the major parties has come a decline in their loyalty to the

| TABLE 4.7 | Democratic Delegates to the Left of Rank-and-File Party Members and Public, 2004 (Percentages in Agreement with Statements) |

	All Voters	Democratic Voters	Democratic Delegates
Government is doing too many things best left to businesses and individuals	52	45	12
The U.S. was right to invade Iraq in 2003	46	21	7
Abortion should be permitted in all cases	26	37	64
Gay couples should be allowed to marry	26	36	44
The federal government should do more to regulate the environmental and safety practices of business	59	71	85
Reducing the federal budget deficit will help the economy more than cutting taxes	58	72	87
Government should do more to promote traditional values	40	26	15

Source: *New York Times* poll, 2004, available at http://www.nytimes.com/packages/html/politics /20040724poll/20040724_delegates_poll_results.pdf.

party itself as an organization. While Republican delegates have consistently seen themselves as stronger party supporters than have Democrats, delegates from both parties (with the exception of moderate Carter delegates at the 1976 and 1980 conventions) show a steady decline in strong party support.[113]

Asked to say who they represented at the convention—the party organizations, a candidate support group, an interest group, or voters—Democrats from 1972 to 1984 overwhelmingly chose their favorite candidates. Their support for party never went above 25 percent. Their adherence to special groups has grown in recent years to 22 percent, double that of Republicans.[114]

In summary, trends in the ideological dispositions of party activists in the two parties are reflected in changes in the composition of the two delegate populations over time. Notably, Republican delegates include more women and more ex-Dixiecrats; Democratic delegates include more women and fewer conservative southerners. Democratic delegates are becoming somewhat more liberal, and Republicans more mixed and less cohesive. Similar trends can be observed in the Democratic caucus of the House of Representatives, where the subtraction of a large number of Dixiecrat seats over the past thirty years led to the emergence of liberal mainstream sentiment strongly expressed through caucus action.[115]

Now we can guess why in the midst of a considerable change in policy preferences, wholesale party realignment fails to appear: the major parties have realigned themselves internally. This

TABLE 4.8 Republican Delegates to the Right of Rank-and-File Party Members and Public, 2004 (Percentages in Agreement with Statements)

	All Voters	Republican Voters	Republican Delegates
Government is doing too many things best left to businesses and individuals	52	58	85
The U.S. was right to invade Iraq in 2003	46	78	96
Abortion should be permitted in all cases	26	13	8
Gay couples should be allowed to marry	26	11	3
The federal government should do more to regulate the environmental and safety practices of business	59	45	15
Reducing the federal budget deficit will help the economy more than cutting taxes	58	38	14
Government should do more to promote traditional values	40	61	55

Source: *New York Times* poll, 2004, available at http://www.nytimes.com/packages/html/politics/20040829_gop_poll/2004_gop_results.pdf.

is most evident in the South as white newcomers and young voters have become increasingly Republican.[116] The view that the major parties were essentially alike, which was never true, is even less true today.

The consequences of ideological polarization, which is what we have been describing, are well known: heightened conflict and the risk of political instability. According to the venerable theory of crosscutting cleavages, when people agree on some issues and disagree on others, the need to call on each other for support sometimes moderates the severity of conflict at other times. Polarization, recently on the increase, by putting the same people in opposition on issue after issue, increases antagonism.

THE CONVENTION AS ADVERTISING

Party conventions were probably always seen, in part, as a means of advertisement. At the least, listening to convention speeches and talking to peers might furnish delegates with rhetoric to use in local campaigns. But until the age of television, conventions were primarily concerned with nominating candidates and conducting other party business.

Television arrived at the conventions in 1952 and changed all that, with the help of party reforms that ended the old business of conventions. Now, conventions are for launching campaigns.[117] Conventions are planned in order to sell the nominees and the party to a national audience. The actual business of conventions, such as putting the names of candidates before the assembled delegates and approving the platform, is scheduled for afternoon or early evening sessions before the broadcast networks' news coverage goes on the air. Prime time is filled with speeches meant to appeal to voters, along with documentary films prepared beforehand to keep the audience interested.[118] Indeed, conventions are now judged by pundits on how well they are organized as advertisements. Any intrusion of party business (such as platform disagreements) into the convention is considered a breach of unity and therefore a sign of weakness in the party. More serious still is poor entertainment. Woe to any convention such as Jimmy Carter's renomination convention in 1980 in which the mechanism for releasing the brightly colored balloons malfunctioned, thus providing commentators with a handy metaphor for Carter's stalled reelection bid.[119]

The advertising content of the conventions is influenced by the decisions of network news teams; the parties try to provide programs they believe the network will allow people to see, now that the parties cannot count on full, gavel-to-gavel coverage. Currently, the broadcast networks cover the conventions through their nightly news broadcasts, their morning shows, and one- or two-hour live wrap-up shows from the conventions during prime time.[120] Examples of the old gavel-to-gavel coverage can be found only on cable; in 1992 ABC, for example, "did not go live to the podium even once" on the second day of the Democratic convention.[121]

By using the convention as advertising, the parties hope to receive a "bounce" in the approval their candidates get from the polls. Over the past forty years, only Lyndon Johnson in 1964 (who was high in voter approval to begin with) and George McGovern in 1972 (who had a disastrous convention) failed to improve in voter surveys taken immediately after their conventions. One might think that this effect would dissipate as broadcast networks reduced the amount of convention coverage and as viewers had more options than network television. But the public appeared as ready to be influenced by the conventions in 1992 as ever: Bill Clinton's bounce in the polls after his convention, which was everywhere reported to be a success, was as large as any on record.[122] In 1996, both Clinton and Bob Dole had healthy bounces of several percentage points in the polls, as did George W. Bush and (especially) Al Gore in 2000.[123] The nominees in 2004, Bush and John Kerry, each received a more modest convention bounce, pegged at 4 percentage points apiece by the *Washington Post*/ABC News poll.[124]

How do the parties turn what once was a business meeting into advertising?

1. The layout of the convention hall itself is designed with television, not the comfort of the delegates, as the first priority. As the late Bob Squier, a leading Democratic media consultant in the 1980s, said, "To be blunt, the room is designed to be a television set." Another high-profile Democratic media expert, Frank Greer, said in praise of the 1988 convention: "It has become clear that, as it should be, this is a convention designed and presented for TV viewers more so than for delegates on the floor. It's a chance to talk to people in their living rooms and not the delegates on the floor."[125]

2. Not just the appearance of the hall is designed for television. The delegates, far from having an important role in deciding party business, have been reduced to serving primarily as extras. "Homemade" handwritten signs are actually constructed by the party to reinforce campaign themes; neither party allows delegates to bring in their own banners. Not even

crowd noises are left to chance: the GOP in Houston in 1992 "arranged that, at key moments, troops of rehearsed young people flooded onto the floor and filled the first fifty feet in front of the podium and in the aisles. They knew what to chant when, and they were standing in front of most of the delegates so they couldn't be missed by the cameras."[126]

3. Both parties try to script all the words spoken at the convention, whether that means carefully orchestrating the words and images delivered from the podium or faxing suggested responses to likely interview targets. The Republicans in 1992 required each of the more than one hundred podium speakers to submit their speeches to a small team of speechwriters charged with keeping the talk from the podium tuned to the "theme of the day." The speechwriters' job ranged from fine-tuning some speeches to drafting others from scratch.[127] Speeches are eventually fed into teleprompters and timed so that signs and chants from the floor can be properly coordinated with them. Convention organizers try to present an appealing public image by attempting to contradict stereotypes about the kinds of people who belong to their party. Observers at the 2004 Republican convention noted that there was a far higher proportion of members of minority groups at the speaker's podium, or providing the musical entertainment, than in the hall as delegates.[128] Similarly, the Democrats that year emphasized the Navy service of their nominee, John Kerry, in order to counter perceptions that the party was anti-military. Kerry began his acceptance speech by giving a salute to the assembled delegates and telling them that he was "reporting for duty."[129]

Very little is left to chance: the parties coordinate their schedules with network broadcast plans. As Tom Rosenstiel reported in 1992:

> The parties and the networks worked together for months planning and organizing these affairs in tandem, setting camera angles for mutual benefit, coordinating logistics, all of it off the record.
>
> The coordination was sometimes secret, sometimes not. And sometimes the network news was even temporarily allied with the party to gain leverage inside their own network. Once the Republicans decided they would have Patrick Buchanan speak on the Monday of their Houston convention in prime time and sent ABC a schedule with Buchanan going on shortly after 10 p.m., ABC vice-president Jeff Gralnick would quietly call Republican convention chairman Craig Fuller.
>
> Put Buchanan on at 9:50, Gralnick would tell the party official, not 10:05. Then I can convince my network to let me go on at 9:30, not 10:00 and we can both get thirty minutes more airtime....
>
> Lane Vernardos, Gralnick's counterpart at CBS, would put in a similar call to Republican organizers.
>
> Fuller would quickly agree.[130]

The parties, then, treat their conventions as four-day-long commercials for the presidential ticket and for the party as a whole.[131] This is not necessarily a bad thing: many pundits have urged the networks to make available free airtime for the parties to present their messages directly to the voters during the fall campaign, not realizing that the conventions already serve that purpose (though broadcast networks have devoted progressively less time to convention coverage over the last several elections). The presidential campaign is limited to the extent that some of the delegates may belong to losing candidates. Thus Bush and Clinton were required in 1992 to negotiate with losing candidates Buchanan, Brown, and Tsongas to ensure that their delegates would act like fully cooperating extras for the cameras, and each losing candidate received what he wanted—an opportunity to address the convention. Better still were the positions of the 1996 nominees. Clinton was unopposed for nomination and therefore could select all the delegates, and Bob Dole had dominated the Republican primaries enough that almost all the delegates were loyal to him. In 2000 and 2004, the two party nominees enjoyed the active support of a large majority of convention delegates, and cooperation was not a problem.

First and foremost, the candidate wants a united party.[132] Party leaders who are in a position to disrupt unity may extort small advantages from the nominee, a significant strategic resource for Jesse Jackson's candidacies in the 1980s. As Jackson approached the Democratic convention of 1988, he made speeches demanding a greater role in the party, threatening to stage a floor fight over the party platform, "and renewed his threat to challenge [Lloyd] Bentsen's [vice presidential] nomination."[133] Michael Dukakis's backers voted down Jackson's platform proposals. These would have raised taxes to much higher levels, frozen military spending, tilted to the Palestinian side in their Middle East conflict with Israel, and pledged the United States not to be the first to use nuclear weapons. Instead, Jackson temporarily won changes in Democratic Party rules, cutting the number of superdelegates nearly in half and requiring that all delegates be awarded to candidates on a proportional rather than a winner-take-all basis. All along, Jackson's complaint had been that it was undemocratic for him to have fewer delegates as a proportion of the whole convention than votes in the primary elections.[134] In order to preserve the peace, Dukakis gave in on the procedural issues, just as Hubert Humphrey gave in to Eugene McCarthy delegates in 1968 and granted them the formation of what became the McGovern–Fraser Commission.[135]

THE VICE-PRESIDENTIAL NOMINEE

When the convention finally nominates a presidential candidate, it turns to the anticlimactic task of ratifying the nominee's choice of running mate. The vice-presidential nominee is chosen to help the party achieve the presidency. Party nominees for president and vice president always appear on the ballot together and are elected together. Since 1804 a vote for one has always been a vote for the other.

The vice president's post in the legislative branch of the government is mostly honorific, and his or her powers and activities in the executive branch are determined by the president.[136] The electoral interdependence of the two offices gives politicians opportunities to gather votes for the presidency. Therefore, the prescription for the "ideal" vice-presidential nominee is the same as for presidential nominees, with two additions: the vice-presidential nominee must possess some desirable qualities the presidential nominee lacks and must be acceptable to the presidential nominee, who does the actual picking.

The vice presidency is the position from which presidents of the United States are most frequently drawn. One third of our forty-three presidents, and four of the last eight, were once vice presidents. Five were later elected to the presidency in their own right; eight first took office on the death of a president; and Gerald Ford succeeded because of President Nixon's resignation. American history has given us fourteen good reasons—one for each vice president who succeeded to the presidency—for inquiring into the qualifications of vice presidents and for examining the criteria by which they are chosen.

A presidential candidate who has firm control over the nomination is in a position to use the vice-presidential slot to help win the election. This is what Abraham Lincoln did in 1864 when he chose a "War Democrat," Andrew Johnson, whom he hoped would add strength to the ticket.[137] In 1960, John F. Kennedy chose Senate Majority Leader Lyndon Johnson to help gather southern votes, especially in Texas, and Richard Nixon chose Senator Henry Cabot Lodge of Massachusetts to help offset the Democratic Party's advantage in the Northeast. In 1964, President Johnson chose an outstanding liberal, Senator Hubert Humphrey of Minnesota. Johnson's own credentials as a liberal Democrat down through the years had weakened from his early days as a New Deal Congressman; when Kennedy picked him as vice president, he had been opposed on these grounds by labor leaders and by party officials from several of the most important urban Democratic strongholds.

Recent vice-presidential candidates sometimes have been distinguished politicians who had a great deal to recommend them as holders of high office. But the help they could offer their parties in winning the election was undoubtedly an important consideration. In choosing Senator Humphrey, President Johnson adhered to the familiar strategy of ticket balancing, as Kennedy had done in choosing him. President Ford, with his midwestern and congressional background, may have had the same thing in mind when he chose a more liberal, eastern establishment figure, Governor Nelson Rockefeller of New York, to be his vice president on his elevation to the presidency. Later, threats from the right wing of the Republican Party to his own nomination chances caused him to dump Rockefeller and replace him for the 1976 election with Senator Bob Dole of Kansas. Reagan, more securely tied to the Republican right wing than Ford, leaned toward the moderate side of his own party in picking George H. W. Bush. Bush, in turn, looked to the right when selecting a running mate, settling on Senator Dan Quayle of Indiana, who not only offered solid conservative credentials but also, Bush hoped, would appeal to young people and women, two groups of voters the Republicans were targeting.[138] One measure of how the Republican Party had changed in twenty years was that Bob Dole, once chosen to please party conservatives, turned to former Representative Jack Kemp of New York in 1996 in part to placate those in the party not convinced of Dole's zeal for cutting taxes.[139]

Another way of balancing the ticket is to focus on experience. Jimmy Carter, who had never served in Washington, chose a popular senator, Walter Mondale, in part to make up for his own lack of "insider" qualifications. Similar considerations drove three other state governors without federal experience to choose prominent Washingtonians as their running mates—Michael Dukakis's selection of Texas Senator Lloyd Bentsen in 1988, Bill Clinton's choice of Tennessee Senator Al Gore in 1992, and George W. Bush's selection in 2000 of former House Republican Whip, presidential chief of staff, and Secretary of Defense Dick Cheney all fit this model.

Walter Mondale's choice of Representative Geraldine Ferraro of New York in 1984 did not fit either of these patterns of ticket balancing; her views were quite similar to his own, and Mondale had served longer than Ferraro in federal office. Instead, Mondale hoped that the historic choice of a woman on a major-party ticket could help exploit the "gender gap" that had emerged in 1980. Far behind in the polls, Mondale may also have been gambling that a bold move would invigorate his campaign. Richard Brookhiser argues that "the best justification for Mondale's audacity, though, was that it was audacious.... Prudent losers remain losers. The first woman on a major party ticket might shake things up."[140]

Sometimes a presidential candidate will try to help heal a breach in the party by offering the vice-presidential nomination to a leader of a defeated party faction. Or the presidential candidate may try to improve his relationship with Congress by finding a running mate who has friends there. Humphrey balanced his ticket in 1968 by choosing Senator Edmund Muskie, a quietly eloquent moderate man, and a member of an ethnic group (Polish Americans) concentrated in the cities of the eastern seaboard, to balance his own midwestern populist background and fast-talking style. In the 2000 election, both presidential candidates had problems that they sought to address with their vice presidential pick. Al Gore picked the upright and conspicuously pious Connecticut Senator Joseph Lieberman to offset the charge that Democrats were morally lax; George W. Bush picked the capable Dick Cheney of Wyoming to offset the perception that he was incapable of governing. John Kerry, a liberal senator from Massachusetts with a reputation for aloofness, chose Senator John Edwards of North Carolina as his running mate in 2004 in order to benefit from Edwards's southern roots and telegenic style.

A Republican presidential candidate from the East will try to pick a vice president from the Midwest or Far West. It has been thought desirable, as in the case of Ronald Reagan (California) and George H. W. Bush (Texas) in 1980, for both to reside in large, two-party "swing" states. In 1996, Bob Dole, from Kansas, managed to find a running mate, Jack Kemp, who claimed both New York and California as home states. With the mode of delegate selection among Democrats biased in favor of one-party states (owing to the abolition of the unit rule and the winner-take-all primary), however, this tendency may no longer prevail. None of the Democratic presidential nominees since the post-1968 rules changes has been from a large state. But a liberal Democrat running for president will frequently try to find a more moderate running mate. If it is impossible to find one person who combines within his or her heritage, personality, and experience all the virtues allegedly cherished by American voters, the parties console themselves by attempting to confect out of two running mates a composite image of forward-looking, conservative, rural-urban, energetic-wise leadership that evokes hometown, ethnic, and party loyalties among a maximum number of voters. That, at least, is the theory behind the balanced ticket.

Especially able politicians may become vice president more because of good luck or coincidence than because their potential performance in office outweighs the political advantages that they bring to the campaign trail in the mind of the presidential nominee. If good results require noble intentions, then the criteria for choosing vice presidents leave much to be desired. Why should the parties, we might ask, not set out deliberately to choose the vice presidential candidate best able to act as president in case of need, ignoring all political calculations? Should ticket balancing and similar considerations be condemned as political chicanery? Former Vice President Henry Wallace once declared: "The greatest danger is that the man just nominated for President will try desperately to heal the wounds and placate the dissidents in his party.... My battle cry would be—no more deals—no more balancing of the ticket." In 1964, the Republican Party evidently also endorsed this view. The selection of the 1964 Republican vice-presidential nominee, Representative William Miller of upstate New York, was intended to violate criteria used in the past for balancing the ticket. Although he came from a region different from presidential nominee Barry Goldwater and, unlike Goldwater, was a Catholic, Miller was chosen primarily because of his ideological affinity with the presidential candidate. The special style of Goldwater and his supporters required that consistency of views, opposition to the other party on as many issues as possible, and refusal to bargain prevail over the traditional political demands for compromise, flexibility, and popularity.[141] This was also apparently the sentiment of many Republicans in 1976. Yet the candidate of the conservatives that year, Ronald Reagan, said he would choose as his running mate a liberal easterner, Senator Richard Schweiker of Pennsylvania. This was his last-ditch attempt to win the nomination away from Gerald Ford, and it was a gamble Reagan lost. But it was consistent with Reagan's view four years later, when he said: "There are some people who think that you should, on principle, jump off the cliff with the flag flying if you can't have everything you want . . . . If I found when I was governor that I could not get 100 percent of what I asked for, I took 80 percent."[142]

From the standpoint of the electoral success of candidates, balancing the ticket seems only prudent. But there are other reasons for ordinary citizens to prefer that candidates make an effort in this direction. One of the chief assets of the American party system in the past has been its ability, with the exception of the Civil War period, to reduce conflict by enforcing compromise within the major factions of each party. A refusal to heal the wounds and placate dissidents is easily interpreted as a declaration of internal war. It can only lead to increased conflict within the party. Willingness to bargain and make concessions to opponents is part of the price for maintaining unity in a party sufficiently large and varied to be able to appeal successfully to a nationwide population divided on economic, sectional, racial, religious, ethnic, and perhaps also ideological grounds. To refuse entirely to balance the ticket would be to risk changing our large, heterogeneous parties into a multiplicity of small sects of true believers who care more about maintaining their internal purity than about winning public office by pleasing the people.

There is obvious good sense in providing for a basic continuity in policy in case a president should die or be disabled. But this need not mean that the president and vice president should be identical in every respect, even if that were possible. Within the broad outlines of agreement on the basic principles of the nation's foreign policy and of the government's role in the economy, for example, a president would have no great difficulty in finding a variety of running mates who appealed to somewhat different groups or who differed in other salient ways. To go this far to promote party unity, factional conciliation, and popular preference should not discomfort anyone who understands the costs of failing to balance the ticket.

Actually, there is little evidence that running mates add greatly to or detract severely from the popularity of presidential candidates with the voters. By helping unite the party, however, and by giving diverse party leaders another focus of identification with the ticket, a vice-presidential nominee with the right characteristics can help assure greater effort by party workers, and this may bring results at election time. Even if balancing the ticket does not aid the party at the polls, it may indirectly help the people. Our political parties may maintain unity within diversity and thereby perform their historic function of bringing our varied population closer together.

One of the destructive effects of the newer norms of media coverage of politicians might be to make such balancing somewhat less likely in the future. Candidates, of course, have access to sophisticated polling, and are aware that they are unlikely to win election merely by finding the perfect running mate. However, intense negative publicity can turn the advertising potential of the convention into a highly-publicized embarrassment. No presidential candidate has the resources fully to research every aspect of a potential vice president's background. Instead, nominees have increasingly in recent years turned to the one pool of people who not only have been fully investigated but also have extensive experience dealing with the national media: former presidential candidates. John Edwards in 2004, Jack Kemp in 1996, Al Gore in 1992, Lloyd Bentsen in 1988, and George H. W. Bush in 1980 had all been tested in previous presidential primaries. None of them encountered scandal or significant bad press during the fall campaigns. Two vice presidential nominees over that period who had not been previously exposed to the national media, Geraldine Ferraro in 1984 and Dan Quayle in 1988, had far more than their share of turmoil during their campaigns, as did George McGovern's original running mate in 1972, Senator Tom Eagleton of Missouri, who left the ticket during the campaign after it was revealed that he had been treated medically for depression. If future presidential nominees want to play it safe, they will give special attention to this small group of pre-screened possibilities.

THE FUTURE OF NATIONAL CONVENTIONS

If conventions are really only for advertisement, why are the delegates still important? A comparison with the electoral college is instructive. Ever since the early days of the republic, electors virtually always vote as they have been instructed by their states. The majority wins. Should no candidate receive a majority, electors still have no say in the outcome, because under the Constitution the selection is made by Congress.[143]

Delegates to nominating conventions, even under the current rules, are in a somewhat different position. While their votes on the nomination are (in normal years) simply a matter of registering the choices of the voters who chose them, even then they have to vote on platforms and rules. These votes may be important, and the delegates are free to make their own decisions. Even hand-picked delegates have the option of opposing their candidate, should they so choose.

Far more important, however, is that in the event of deadlock—if no single candidate controlled a majority of delegates going into the convention—the delegates would have the responsibility of selecting the nominee. If the contest is merely close, we would expect few delegate defections, since they have been in most cases selected by candidates mainly on grounds of potential loyalty. A good test of that was the Democratic convention in 1980, when Senator Edward Kennedy hoped to use favorable preconvention publicity to sway the convention. The hope turned out to be unrealistic. In the key test vote, Carter delegates stayed loyal.

However, should no candidate enter the convention with a majority, loyalty to the candidate might no longer matter. These scenarios are mainstays of pundit thinking every four years early on in the primaries, when no candidate has yet built a sizeable majority in the delegate count. But as we have seen, an "open" or "brokered" convention is not particularly likely. Such a result would almost certainly require not two, but at least three candidates to reach the convention with large numbers of delegates; if only two candidates have delegates, one or the other will have a majority, no matter how slender. Since the normal operations of primaries and caucuses, along with the media interpretations of victory and defeat, quickly winnow out most candidates in a typical year, a deadlocked convention with three or more candidates is an improbable result.

TABLE 4.9 Number of Presidential Ballots in National Party Conventions, 1928–2004 (Nominations Won by Incumbents are in Parentheses)

Year	Democrats	Republicans
1928	1	1
1932	4	(1)
1936	(1)	1
1940	(1)	8
1944	(1)	1
1948	(1)	3
1952	3	1
1956	1	(1)
1960	1	1
1964	(1)	1
1968	1	1
1972	1	(1)
1976	1	(1)
1980	(1)	1
1984	1	(1)
1988	1	1
1992	1	(1)
1996	(1)	1
2000	1	1
2004	1	(1)
First Ballot Total	18/20	18/20
	(7 incumbents)	(7 incumbents)

Combined (Democratic and Republican) first-ballot nominations:
Nonincumbents   22/26
Incumbents   14/14

This is particularly true on the Republican side, where numerous winner-take-all primaries reduce the capacity of spoiler candidates to accumulate delegates. The last convention requiring more than one delegate roll call vote to choose a presidential nominee occurred in 1952, well before the modern system of delegate selection was established (see table 4.9). Still, deadlock is theoretically possible, and if it happens, it will be the delegates who will have to choose the party nominee.

How would a modern, postreform convention handle such a decision? The same rules that have made conventions rubber stamps for voters in primaries also would make bargaining difficult once there. In order to reach the convention, candidates would need intense factional support; delegates selected for those traits would, presumably, be ill-equipped to negotiate away their vote for the candidate to whom they were loyal. The candidates themselves, then, might be the only ones able to negotiate—and candidates fresh off the campaign trail, having endured negative ads and other attacks from each other, might not be eager to cut a deal, or even able to bring along their supporters if they did make a deal.

If the candidates did not resolve their differences, how else would the delegates reach a decision? Some, no doubt, would turn to factional leaders. State delegations might work together, even across candidate lines. Still others might remain unconnected, waiting until someone found a resolution. Given the enormous size of modern conventions (the Democrats in 2004 seated over 4,300 delegates, compared to the 1,100 delegates who nominated Franklin D. Roosevelt in 1932), it would be impossible for serious, one-on-one deliberation to take place without some sort of organization emerging. If not, we might expect the media to dominate the proceedings, with delegates swayed by the latest reported rumors and speculations.

We remain convinced that a mixed system, including both primaries and deliberative state conventions, is a good method for our parties to select their nominees. We doubt that national conventions as presently constituted are properly equipped to handle that job. Chief among the needs of a deliberative convention would be a manageable size and delegates who represent someone other than the candidates to which they are pledged. In part this problem may have been mitigated by the 1982 decision of the Democrats to admit public officeholders to the convention as unpledged superdelegates. About 19 percent of the 2004 convention was constituted in this fashion. So far, it has made no difference.

A healthy political party requires activists as well as voters. As long as the policy preferences and group identifications of these two populations are reasonably compatible, their differing interests can be reconciled by bargaining. Once they grow far apart, however, the tension between them may become unbearable until one or another leaves their ancestral party. In Europe, this tension frequently takes the form of a clash between militant party activists and more moderate parliamentarians interested in winning elections. Where members elect party leaders in Parliament, including the prime minister, they have real resources with which to combat militants. The separate elections of senators and representatives in Congress and the federal system in the United States, however, take the presidential nomination outside of normal politics. Congressional and gubernatorial candidates, who want to win elections, rarely run on as radical or conservative a basis as the rhetoric of their activist supporters might suggest, and they participate less than they used to in picking the presidential nominee. Thus these elected officials have much less of a stake in the presidency. On the Democratic side, the party leaders who used to guard that stake have been so weak or absent during the conventions after 1968 that further reforms in the 1980s and 1990s were required to ensure that all Democratic members of Congress, governors, and national committee members maintained the right to attend the convention and vote as unpledged superdelegates.

What is remarkable, when one thinks of it, is that special arrangements were necessary to bring party officeholders back into the conventions or to allow the people who probably know most about the candidates to support whomever they think best. Leaving politicians—who have to appeal to electorates—out of the presidential selection process, we think, was a poor way to choose candidates for the highest national office.

Bringing into the convention a bloc of uncommitted superdelegates composed of office-holders and public officials might appear on the surface to reflect a desire to give the convention greater discretion in choosing a candidate. It has not worked out that way. The chair of the

Democratic National Committee and other party leaders attempt to assure a consensus behind a single candidate well before the convention meets. In the 1980s, the party chairman raised a concern that the nominating decision not "be taken away from the millions who do participate in our primaries and caucuses and be given to a few in the 'back rooms' of a brokered convention."[144]

In 1984 the superdelegates went early and massively for Walter Mondale. Jesse Jackson and Gary Hart supporters, as part of their price for uniting behind Mondale, got agreement that the Democratic National Committee would appoint superdelegates later in the 1988 process, after the caucuses and primaries were over.[145] Would inserting politicians into the national conventions in this fashion lead to different convention choices? There would have to be differences in candidate preference between these politicians and the other delegates. And the other delegates, pledged to various aspiring candidates, would themselves have to be split because, if they were united, they would have more than enough for a majority.

Just as the news media have interacted with political forces to produce the ratifying rather than the deciding convention, so the two have combined to give the conventions their electoral meaning. Deprived of their decision-making role, the conventions become an opportunity for campaign publicity with the party united behind a single candidate. Not having to worry about winning the nomination at the convention, candidates can more carefully consider how they want to manage the presentation of their party for advertising purposes. Thus national conventions have changed from being the big guns of the nominating process to the first shots of the general election campaign.

The candidates may want their delegates to look presentable to television viewers, but they are not in a position to do much about it. They can, as we have seen, assure the presence of delegates pledged to them, making sure the delegates do their duty by voting for them. From the candidate's point of view: so far, so good. While the delegates have mostly pledged their votes, however, they have not hocked their souls. As Jimmy Carter discovered in 1980, platform issues were all the more important to delegates by virtue of the fact that they had no other decisions to make. What is more, delegates who have come to the convention to express support for their varied lifestyles can do that simply by being who they are and showing up on television. Republican or Democrat, liberal or conservative, black or white, male or female, straight or gay, delegates can make a statement about what they stand for simply by being there.

To appear before the public, of course, delegates must get on television. What gets across to the voter is what television journalists choose to show. Aside from the few obligatory famous names, the usual principles apply: controversy and deviance make better copy than uncomplicated gestures of support. Whatever the delegates appear to be, television accentuates that pattern at its edges, stressing differences rather than similarities with the past. Should voters look in and say to themselves and friends and neighbors that these delegates are not "my kind of people," candidates may find that their ability to project a certain image is overwhelmed by contrary notions that voters have gathered for themselves.

FIVE
THE CAMPAIGN

AFTER THE END OF THE NATIONAL CONVENTIONS, IT WAS ONCE A tradition for the two presidential candidates to "relax" for a few weeks until Labor Day, when they were supposed to begin their official campaigning. Nowadays, the general election campaign begins once both parties have in effect chosen their nominees, usually well in advance of the national conventions in the spring prior to the November election. Once the conventions ratify their selection, the two candidates confront the voters directly, each carrying the banner of a major political party. How do the candidates behave? Why do they act the way they do? What kind of impact do their activities have on the electorate?

For the small minority of people who are party workers, campaigns serve as a signal to get to work. How hard they work depends in part on whether the candidates' political opinions, slogans, personalities, and visits spark their enthusiasm. The workers may sit on their hands, or they may pursue their generally unrewarding jobs—checking voting lists, mailing campaign flyers, ringing doorbells—with something approaching fervor.

For the majority of the population, most of whom keep their distance from politics, campaigns call attention to the advent of an election. Some excitement may be generated and some diversion (as well as annoyance) provided for those who turn on the television to find that their favorite program has been preempted by political talk or who answer the phone only to hear a prerecorded message exhorting them to vote. The campaign is a great spectacle. Conversation about politics increases, and some citizens may even become intensely involved as they get caught up by campaign advertising and mobilization.

For the vast majority of citizens in America, campaigns do not function so much to change minds as to activate or reinforce previous convictions. As the campaign wears on, the underlying party identification of most people rises ever more powerfully to the surface. Republican and Democratic identifiers are split further apart—polarized—as their increased awareness of party competition emphasizes the things that divide them.[1]

The substance of election campaigns depends on the political context. The swiftly changing nature of events makes it unwise for candidates to lay down all-embracing rules for campaigning that cannot meet special situations as they arise. Candidates may prepare for battle on one front and discover that the movement of events forces them to fight on another. Yet a political strategist has to rely on some sort of theory about the probable behavior of large groups of voters under a few likely conditions. There are too many millions of voters and too many thousands of possible events to deal with each as a separate category. The candidates must simplify their pictures of the political world or its full complexity will paralyze them; the only question is whether or not their theories, both explicit and implicit, will prove helpful to them.

What kind of organization should they use or construct? Where should they campaign? How much time should they allocate to the various regions and states? What kinds of appeals should they make to what voting groups? How specific should they be in their policy proposals? What kind of personal impression should they seek to create or reinforce? How far should they go in attacking the opposition? These are the kinds of strategic questions for which presidential candidates need answers—answers that vary depending on their party affiliations, their personal attributes, whether they are in or out of office, and on targets of opportunity that come up in the course of current events.

THE WELL-TRAVELED CANDIDATES

The candidate's main responsibilities are to get the campaign's message out to the voters and to energize activists. This requires showing up at events all over the country and talking to the crowds assembled there, thus making "news."

Long ago, when publicly campaigning on one's own behalf was considered undignified, presidential nominees faced the serious choice of whether to conduct a "front porch" campaign or to get out and meet the people. The first president to make a campaign speech, William Henry Harrison at Columbus, Ohio, in June 1840, was scolded for his pains: "When," the *Cleveland Adviser* asked, "was there ever before such a spectacle as a candidate for the Presidency, travers-ing the country advocating his own claims for that high and responsible station?"[2] Now, each candidate rents an airplane and hires speechwriters, maps out an itinerary, and flies off in all directions. Patrick Anderson, who wrote speeches for Jimmy Carter in 1976, describes how it feels:

> We were so isolated on the plane. Our world extended from Peanut One [the name of Carter's campaign plane] to the motorcade to the rally to the hotel, and was populated by the candidate, four or five staff people, and a dozen or so reporters. Everything beyond that was a blur. There are few experiences more exhilarating than to see tens of thousands of people cheering your candidate, to feel the tide running your way, to think your man will win and you helped this miracle come to pass. The cities flew by: Erie, Cleveland, Gary, Toledo.[3]

There is method in this. In deciding where to campaign, the candidates are aided by distinc-tive features of the national political landscape that go a long way toward giving them guidance.

They know that it is not popular votes as such that matter but electoral votes, which are counted on a state-by-state basis. The candidate who places first in a state, even if by a small margin or with less than a majority, gains all of that state's electoral votes. The candidates realize that a lopsided victory in a state with a handful of electoral votes will not do them nearly as much good as a slim plurality in a populous state with a large number of electoral votes, such as California or Texas. So the first guideline is: campaign in states with large numbers of electoral votes.

But candidates do not waste their effort in states where they know they are bound to win or to lose. Thus, states that almost always go for a particular party receive less attention. In recent presidential elections, most of the South (except for Florida) and the interior West have voted heavily Republican. Most of the Northeast—New England, New York, New Jersey, Maryland—and the Pacific Coast constitute a similarly reliable geographic base for Democrats. Candidates of both parties largely ignore these parts of the country, preferring to devote their time and campaign resources to states expected to be highly competitive. In September and October 2004, neither presidential candidate or running mate made a public appearance in Alabama, Alaska, Georgia, Indiana, Kansas, Kentucky, Louisiana, Mississippi, Montana, Nebraska, North Dakota, Oklahoma, South Dakota, Tennessee, Utah, and Virginia (all considered safe for Republican George W. Bush), or California, Connecticut, Delaware, Illinois, Massachusetts, New York, Rhode Island, Vermont, and Washington (all safe states for Democrat John Kerry).[4]

So the original guideline may be modified to read: campaign in states with large numbers of electoral votes that are doubtful. In practice, a "swing" or "battleground" state is one that either party has a decent chance to capture. Politicians usually gauge this chance by the extent to which the state has delivered victories to both parties within recent memory, and according to the results of public opinion polls conducted within the state during the campaign. Candidates of both parties thus spend more time in swing states such as Pennsylvania, Ohio, Florida, Michigan, Wisconsin, and Iowa than they do elsewhere.[5] On August 4, 2004, George W. Bush and John Kerry found themselves campaigning for votes at the same time within a half-mile of each other in Davenport, Iowa.[6] Their campaigns' focus on the state as a key electoral battleground was vindicated by the results of the 2004 election in Iowa, won by Bush with a margin of only about 10,000 votes out of more than 1.5 million cast.

As the campaign wears on, the candidates take soundings from opinion polls and are likely to redouble their efforts in states where they believe repeated personal visits might turn the tide. In 1976, Jimmy Carter's campaign manager Hamilton Jordan had these matters worked out to a mathematical formula—awarding points to states based on size and winability and then allocating campaign days to each of them for Carter, the vice-presidential candidate Walter Mondale, and members of the Carter family.[7]

The actual itinerary is made by a campaign scheduling team—a phalanx of up to 250 employees, approximately 30 to 40 to plot the schedule and the rest to handle the press and advance work. Schedulers start the process rolling as they determine where the candidate will appear. They adopt two rules for this task: "Go where the polls say an appearance by the candidate can make a difference. Make it look good on television."[8] Peter Hart, a Democratic pollster, broke the scheduler's job down into units: the 1988 presidential campaign was made up of approximately 80 working days with an average of four events a day, which gave the scheduler a total of 320 "units" to work with.[9] The scheduler's task is to manage these units so the candidate gets the most value from his or her appearances. Thus schedulers arrange more candidate appearances in big competitive states such as Ohio or Pennsylvania than in smaller, more secure states.

Schedulers try to make plans in advance if possible, but arrangements can change as the poll numbers suggest increasing margins of safety in a given state or reveal new states in need of targeting. In 1976, scheduler Eliot Cutler was convinced that Jimmy Carter would win or lose the entire election based on what happened in Ohio. He suggested that the campaign bombard the state and schedule 65 percent of running mate Walter Mondale's time there during the last two weeks. Overcoming resistance by threatening to quit, Cutler had Mondale skipping across Ohio, sometimes visiting the same city twice in one week. It turned out to be a good idea. Carter and Mondale eventually won Ohio by 11,000 votes, a critical victory in a very close election.[10]

BOX 5.1　A DAY IN THE LIFE OF THE CANDIDATE

The Schedule of Bill Clinton on October 3, 1992 in St. Louis, Missouri, and Washington, D.C.

9:00 A.M.	Departs Adams Mark Downtown Hotel en route to Soulard Farmer's Market, St. Louis, Mo.
9:15 A.M.	Arrives Soulard Farmer's Market, 730 Carroll Street.
9:20 A.M.	Tours Soulard Farmer's Market.
9:40 A.M.	Addresses the people of St. Louis, Soulard Farmer's Market.
10:30 A.M.	Departs Soulard Farmer's Market en route to airport.
10:55 A.M.	Arrives Lambert-St. Louis International Airport and proceeds to private time.
NOON	Departs St. Louis, Mo., en route to Washington, D.C.
2:40 P.M.	Arrives Washington National Airport, Washington, D.C.
3:15 P.M.	Departs airport en route to Washington Hilton Hotel.
3:30 P.M.	Arrives Washington Hilton Hotel, 1919 Connecticut Avenue, NW.
4:00 P.M.	Announces formation of Italian American Leadership Council, Washington Hilton Hotel. Press coverage arrangements TBA.
9:00 P.M.	Attends National Italian-American Foundation's Jeno Paolucci Dinner, International Ballroom, Washington Hilton Hotel.

Remains overnight in Washington, D.C.

Source: The Reuters Daybook of Presidential Campaigns, Reuters Washington Report, October 3, 1992.

The Schedule of George H. W. Bush on October 3, 1992 in Clearwater, Homestead, Fort Lauderdale, Orlando, Florida, and Washington, D.C.

8:25 A.M.	Boards motorcade and departs Holiday Inn, Clearwater, Fla., en route to On Top of the World Retirement Community.
8:42 A.M.	Arrives on Top of the World Retirement Community.
9:05–9:50 A.M.	Gives remarks at retirement community. Open press coverage.
9:55 A.M.	Boards motorcade and departs on Top of the World Retirement Community en route to St. Petersburg/Clearwater International Airport.
10:15 A.M.	Arrives St. Petersburg/Clearwater International Airport and boards Air Force One.
10:20 A.M.	Departs Clearwater, Fla., en route to Homestead, Fla.
11:15 A.M.	Arrives Homestead Air Force Base, Homestead, Fla., to view hurricane relief efforts. Pool coverage.
1:45 P.M.	Departs Homestead, Fla., en route to Fort Lauderdale, Fla.
2:10 P.M.	Arrives Hollywood International Airport, Fort Lauderdale, Fla., for Fort Lauderdale welcome.
2:15 P.M.	Gives remarks. Open press.
2:50 P.M.	Boards motorcade and departs AMR COMBS Hangar en route to Naval Warfare Center Detachment.
2:55 P.M.	Arrives Naval Warfare Center Detachment for Historical Association Ceremony. Travel pool coverage.
3:25 P.M.	Boards motorcade and departs Naval Warfare Center Detachment en route to AMR COMBS Hangar.
3:30 P.M.	Arrives at AMR COMBS Hangar for private time.
4:10 P.M.	Departs Fort Lauderdale, Fla., en route to Orlando, Fla.
5:15 P.M.	Arrives Orlando International Airport, Orlando, Fla.
5:20 P.M.	Boards motorcade and departs Orlando International Airport en route to Church Street Market.
5:50 P.M.	Arrives Church Street Market for Church Street Market Rally.
6:00 P.M.	Gives remarks at rally. Open press coverage.
6:35 P.M.	Attends private reception. Closed press.
7:05 P.M.	Boards motorcade and departs Church Street Market en route to Orlando International Airport.
7:35 P.M.	Arrives Orlando International Airport and boards Air Force One.
7:40 P.M.	Departs Orlando, Fla. en route to Andrews Air Force Base.
9:25 P.M.	Arrives Andrews Air Force Base.
9:35 P.M.	Boards Marine One and departs Andrews Air Force Base en route to the White House.
9:45 P.M.	Arrives White House.

Source: The Reuters Daybook of Presidential Campaigns, Reuters Washington Report, October 3, 1992.

Schedulers also decide on the type of event to put into the candidate's itinerary. Early on in a campaign, a candidate will attend many fundraisers, some large dinners, some intimate gatherings of significant contributors. As the campaign gains momentum, fundraising is increasingly transferred to a full-time staff and the candidate's time is geared to large rallies, usually with a theme to attract media attention and television news coverage. For example, in 1992 George H. W. Bush visited a Waffle House restaurant in South Carolina to make a symbolic reference to his criticism of Bill Clinton for waffling on his draft record. That same day, Bush spoke to a rally of Republican supporters in Thomasville, North Carolina, home of The Largest Chair in the World, rode a train through southern towns, waving at crowds from the back of the caboose, spoke again in Burlington, North Carolina, and joined Senator Jesse Helms and stockcar racing hero Richard Petty for a public appearance in Raleigh—all potential media events. In 2004, John Kerry's campaign organized a number of large outdoor rallies that often included appearances from musicians and other celebrities supporting Kerry. A late October appearance by Kerry in Madison, Wisconsin, featuring a performance by rock star Bruce Springsteen was claimed to be the largest political event in the history of the state, with attendance possibly reaching 80,000.[11]

Once the schedulers have booked an appearance for the candidate, the press and advance team move in. Their responsibility is to ensure that the event happens without a hitch and that the candidate's message is presented to an adequately prepared press corps, ready to include the day's sound bite in their story or on the evening news. The advance team's responsibilities include ensuring security for the candidates, arranging transportation (candidates can change vehicles a dozen times or more in one day) and housing, overseeing site setup, and providing campaign signs, buttons, and banners for the crowd. They must make sure that the press has audio and visual access to the candidate, that equipment feeds are working, and that the promotional materials on the spot evoke the campaign's theme. Late in the 1992 campaign, the Bush advance team provided local events with banners stating that the community "trusts George Bush." Trust was the principal theme in the later Bush campaign.[12]

It is beside the point that no one knows whether this frenetic campaign activity does much good. Richard Nixon learned from his enervating experience in 1960, when he pledged to visit all fifty states and then had to follow through on his promise despite a severe illness. In 1968, Nixon ran a different kind of campaign, taking account of the fact that radio and television made it possible to reach millions without leaving the big metropolitan areas. Nixon did a small amount of traditional campaigning, which was faithfully chronicled by the press corps that followed him around the country. But more basic to his strategy was the technique of fixing upon regional centers and making major appearances and speeches in these places, followed by elaborate, regionally oriented television commercials that reached the voters directly—"over the heads," so to speak, of the news media that were covering and interpreting only the part of the campaign they could see, which did not include Nixon's television programs.[13] Nowadays, most candidates follow a regional strategy geared to earning coverage on local news broadcasts in key competitive states, but they benefit from the existence of national news media as well. No matter where the candidates are, the network news shows are likely to report on their activities, extending the reach of a candidate's message beyond his or her immediate audience.[14]

It is the candidate's job, in this environment, to stay "on message"—that is, if the campaign theme is trust, to emphasize words such as "honesty" or "reliable" in prepared speeches and to work themes of trust into impromptu remarks to audiences and to the press. It is also the candidate's job to deliver a speech with great enthusiasm, no matter how many times he or she has had to reuse the same lines; to avoid doing or saying anything that could be considered embarrassing; and, generally, to be "on" at all times. Presidential candidates must expect to appear before audiences live and on television throughout the campaign, knowing that a small mistake can have devastating consequences.

Sheer physical endurance is required. Bob Dole, running behind in the polls in the final stages of the 1996 contest, embarked on a "96 Hours to Victory Tour," the idea being that he would not stop campaigning (except for quick naps) during the four days before the election:

> Dole caught a cold, and by Monday he could barely speak. But he was buoyant and cheerful, drinking a tea called Throat Coat and gaining strength from surprisingly large and lively crowds that showed up at diners and bowling alleys, high-school gyms and airport hangars, in small towns across the country.... Dole's plane got a flat tire on Monday afternoon, so Dole moved into [the press plane], where he dozed up front while his aides tried to hush the serenades by reporters.[15]

The press, not the public, is the immediate audience for much of what candidates do while running for the presidency. John Buckley, press secretary to Representative Jack Kemp of New York in 1988, estimated that "if you discount travel time, I'd say that the media take a third of a candidate's entire day. It's not just the news conferences, but one-on-one interviews, hotel room press briefings, radio and television shows, editorial board discussions, back-of-the-car interviews and conversations."[16] "In a sense," media consultant Bob Squier said, "presidential candidates are their own spot-makers as they get their messages across on the stump before the television cameras."[17]

It appeared at one time as if the nationalization of mass media and improvements in technology, such as satellite communication, might actually reduce the necessity for campaign travel. The 1992 independent candidacy of Ross Perot served as a model for this type of campaign. Perot made few public appearances and did not meet with interest groups, preferring to spend time in the television studio, taping his infomercials.[18] Most candidates since Perot, however, have concluded that voters expect a great deal of in-person campaigning, even though public events and speeches are deemed important primarily for the coverage they receive on television. With these considerations in mind, candidates often organize highly publicized travel events. In July 1992, Bill Clinton and his running mate Al Gore embarked on a week-long bus tour with their wives and families though eight key midwestern states. The bus tour generated a great deal of positive press coverage, especially in smaller cities and towns unused to visits from presidential candidates, but also in the national news media.[19] As the Democratic nominee in 2000, Gore took a four-day boat trip down the Mississippi River, stopping in several strategically important states along the way, while John Kerry and running mate John Edwards organized several whistle-stop campaigns by train in 2004.

The effect of all this planning and the demands on the candidates' time mean that candidates can seem to be puppets with the schedulers and advance team pulling the strings, ushering the candidates from performance to performance. Indeed, candidates often complain of stress, fatigue, and sometimes confusion as they are whirled from place to place. But this view underestimates the importance of the candidate, who is ultimately responsible for communicating his or her vision to the voters and, if victorious, is responsible for implementing it.

GETTING GOOD PRESS

Although we have seen that it is highly questionable whether media coverage, on television or in newspapers, markedly influences voter opinion when the strong cue of party is present, it is still considered important for a candidate to get the most favorable treatment possible from journalists. At least, the candidates and their organizations behave as though it is important; they can and do assiduously court the newspaper, periodical, and television reporters assigned to the campaign.[20] Not only do candidates and their staff coddle the journalists who travel with them, but they follow their press coverage and complain about it if dissatisfied.[21]

The space candidates get in the newspaper, their time on television, and the slant of the story may depend to some extent on how the reporters regard them. If journalists find it difficult to get material, if they find the candidate uncommunicative or unlikable, these impressions may affect the tone of campaign coverage. ABC's then-White House correspondent Brit Hume speculated that this was part of George H. W. Bush's press problems in 1992. He told White House press secretary Marlin Fitzwater that reporters were uncomfortable with the president's responses to challenges—he appeared uncertain, rather than confident, and reporters didn't like it.[22]

Getting good press, like the rest of the campaign, has become professionalized, with press and communication assistants who know how to make the candidate look good on television and in the newspapers. Little things, such as phasing news to meet the requirements of both morning newspapers and the evening network news shows, or supplying reporters with human-interest material, can be helpful to candidates. The personality of the candidates, their ability to command the respect of the sometimes rather jaded men and women assigned to cover them, may count heavily. Democratic candidates probably have to work a little harder at cultivating good relations in order to help counteract the editorial slant of most newspapers. But Republicans have to work harder to win the sympathies of reporters of liberal tendency who dominate the national press corps.[23] Candidates also must make the most of their opportunities in public speeches or appearances on radio and television. If what they say and do "makes news," and their press secretaries are effective in promoting the stories, they may get space through the desire of the media to attract customers.

Thus far, we have spoken of the news media as if they were a monolithic entity. But there are all sorts of news outlets with differing biases, needs, and audiences. A great deal of a candidate's attention is devoted to generating coverage in local newspapers and television in key battleground states. Local reporters, who are not used to covering presidents and other national political figures, may ask fewer tough questions and produce more positive stories than the more skeptical and campaign-weary journalists from national publications and broadcast networks, and their coverage may have more of an influence on the impressions of voters in strategically important states. Likewise, the circulations of racial, religious, and ethnic interest-group publications may not be huge, but candidates court them as well, assuming that their readers are concerned with topics of special interest to smaller and more attentive constituencies. A story on religion in politics in a religious journal may do more to convince people than much broader coverage in the daily press.

Web-published writers may have different audiences than print or television reporters, as well as different news cycles and norms, as Matt Drudge, who operates online, demonstrated when he broke the news of scandal during the Clinton administration.[24] In recent years, campaigns have reached out to sympathetic bloggers, hoping to gain positive online coverage. Both parties gave press credentials to representatives of popular blogs to attend their national conventions in 2004.

Finally, there is the overwhelming importance of staging the daily bit of news for the nightly network television programs. Candidates know that they will be on these programs every night; but doing and saying what? In order to seize control of the situation, they stage little dramas: an announcement in front of the Statue of Liberty or in the midst of a picturesque slum; visits to a series of ethnic shops, delicatessens, farms, factories, and shopping centers. If the backdrop is right, the candidate thinks, the coverage may be too. Sometimes it is.

In the 1988 campaign, there was a great contrast between the two campaigns' abilities to control the news agenda. Republican George H. W. Bush's media advisers planned the vice president's appearances in camera-ready settings that provided excellent videotape for the newscasts. In front of a defense plant in St. Louis, he talked up America's need to remain strong. Democrat Michael Dukakis made speech after speech in front of a drab blue curtain, behind a wooden podium.

Another Bush success was the ability to deliver manufactured "sound bites"—one-liners that he knew would be broadcast on television. "Dukakis gives me the impression that he is opposed to every new weapon since the slingshot," said Bush. NBC used the line immediately, and the other networks followed suit when he repeated the line a few days later. "I wouldn't be surprised," Bush said in another sound bite, "if [Dukakis] thought that a naval exercise was something you find in Jane Fonda's workout book."[25] Consultants and speechwriters, aware that only a few seconds of a speech will likely appear in network news broadcasts, craft short, memorable statements reinforcing the campaign's message of the day.

A new use of television emerged during the 1992 campaign: the appearance of a candidate on television talk shows such as *Larry King Live* and *Good Morning America*. Bill Clinton was the first to make use of this tactic in the weeks before the New Hampshire primary. His campaign staged several "Ask Bill" television shows in which candidate Clinton took questions from the audience. Clinton, a gifted extemporaneous speaker, did extremely well in this format, and from early on in the campaign, media consultant Mandy Grunwald was pushing him to do more such appearances. In an April 27 memorandum entitled "Free Media Scheduling," Grunwald told the candidate:

> We have spoken generally about the need to do pop-culture shows like [the *Tonight Show* with] Johnny Carson, but we have yet to lay out a plan to do this sort of thing, or to incorporate local radio talk shows into our schedule in any concerted way. What are we waiting for? We know from research that Bill Clinton's life story has a big impact on people. We know that learning about the fights he's taken on (education reform, welfare reform, dead-beat dads, etc.) tells people a lot about his personal convictions. We know that moments of passion, personal reflection and humor do more for us than any six-second sound bite on the network news or for that matter any thirty-second television spot.[26]

Overcoming concerns that such appearances made Clinton seem insufficiently serious and presidential, the campaign took Grunwald's advice and placed the candidate on a number of television programs that did not ordinarily host political figures. On Phil Donahue's daytime talk show, Clinton stood up for his right not to have the privacy of his marriage dissected by the press, and the audience applauded him.[27] He took questions on *Larry King Live* several times, as well as on *Good Morning America* and *Today*. Clinton attempted to use television appearances to reach young voters whom his campaign was especially targeting as potential supporters. On the *Arsenio Hall Show*, a late-night talk show popular at the time with under-thirty viewers, Clinton played the saxophone and talked about welfare reform. He also conducted a televised question-and-answer session organized by MTV's *Rock the Vote* campaign.

Clinton performed consistently well in this format; his handlers felt that it brought out the personal side in him and allowed voters to get to know and connect with the candidate. Another candidate who succeeded on this circuit, albeit with some significantly bad moments, was independent Ross Perot. Perot actually announced his willingness to run for president on a talk show: Larry King on *Larry King Live* was, with persistent prodding, able to get a "reluctant" Perot to agree to run if volunteers placed his name on all fifty ballots before the deadline.[28] With that single interview, King launched a candidate and achieved the status of the premier political interviewer of the 1992 campaign season.

Perot appeared on King's program several more times and made a number of appearances on other talk shows. In the beginning, the talk shows, like all the media, were easy on him and generally gave him a forum for promoting his glib slogans and folksy ideas. After a while, however, the media became more probing and Perot became less folksy. In one famous confrontation, Katie Couric of the *Today* show persisted in asking Perot to provide the details of his plans. Perot, unwilling to discuss specifics in this appearance as in others, resisted and finally blew up at Couric. He later criticized Couric in front of reporters as trying too hard to "prove her manhood."[29]

Perot was perhaps more effective in the talk shows he produced himself—the "infomercials" that consisted of Perot pointing at a large array of graphs, numbers, and, his favorite, pie charts. The Perot broadcasts during which he explained the problems of the economy and deplored the federal budget deficit were actually very popular with American television viewers. An estimated 16 million viewers tuned in to his first program.[30]

Since Clinton and Perot popularized the practice in 1992, presidential candidates now routinely make appearances on national talk shows, hoping to reach a wider audience of potential supporters. Often, the appearances are staged, sometimes awkwardly, to showcase a candidate's personal charm, sense of humor, or status as a "regular guy." In 2000, both George W. Bush and Al Gore appeared several times on *The Late Show with David Letterman*, sitting for interviews with the host and participating in the nightly "Top Ten List" comedy routine. Bush and Gore also appeared—separately—to poke fun at themselves on an NBC prime-time special broadcast of *Saturday Night Live* sketch comedy material that aired several days before the election.[31] In 2004, John Kerry sought to shed his stiff public image by riding his Harley-Davidson motorcycle onto the set of the *Tonight Show* clad in a leather jacket.[32] Kerry also appeared on the *Daily Show with Jon Stewart*, a satirical news program on the Comedy Central cable network that is especially popular among young viewers.

The overall value of these appearances is unclear. Some political commentators have criticized the strategy, arguing that the hosts of these programs are pushovers for the candidates and do not ask tough questions or follow up on answers the way "serious" journalists do. Instead, these commentators argue, candidates should spend more time on the Sunday morning political shows such as *This Week* and *Meet the Press*, where confrontational interviewers will make sure the candidates meet a certain standard.

Of course, even "entertainment" shows carry risks for candidates. George W. Bush appeared once on David Letterman's program via satellite during the 2000 campaign; the resulting transmission delays between Letterman in the studio and Bush at his remote location made the candidate come across as slow on the uptake. The satirical *Daily Show* spinoff *The Colbert Report* found it difficult to book members of Congress for appearances after a congressman cosponsoring legislation that would require a display of the Ten Commandments in the U.S. Capitol building could only name three of the commandments when questioned on-camera.[33]

Others argue that pop-culture shows are good for the political system because they allow the candidates to reach viewers who do not regularly watch news programs and give them a chance to display a more informal, personal side of themselves to the public. Whatever the contribution these shows make to American political life, positive or negative, there is no doubt that candidates will continue to make appearances as long as show hosts will invite them. The free media and direct access to voters are valuable properties, especially for candidates, like Bill Clinton, who shine in such situations.[34]

ISSUES

Advising the Candidate

Everyone has advice for the would-be president. In the old days most of the policy advice came after the general election as the victor prepared to assume office. Nowadays the advising process has been incorporated into the process of campaigning. The function of the policy adviser is no longer simply to help the future president govern but to help the candidate define and publicize the campaign's position on the issues. There is still some reluctance on the part of candidates to publish official lists of advisers, but all campaigns develop extensive contacts with academics and policy analysts who draw up position papers on specialized issues of foreign and domestic policy and help set the general ideological tone of the campaign.[35] The experts do this at least in part to position themselves to have influence on national policy if their candidate wins.

The lengthy duration of presidential campaigns means that candidates have to develop issue positions at least two years in advance of the election. It is at this initial period, long before a candidacy is officially announced, that decisions on national policy issues will be made. "If you're . . . in the policy-advising business," explains Pat Choate, an economist and policy analyst who was Ross Perot's running mate in 1996, "you must move on that time schedule."[36] Introducing a novel idea later on in the game, during the heat of the campaign, is risky, first because the candidate may gain a reputation as an opportunist or a waffler, and second because there will be no opportunity to test the new idea for technical or political feasibility, to get its rough edges smoothed out.

Since in the course of the campaign the candidate is expected to offer judgments on world events as they break into the news, every campaign will typically rely on a "little black book" with the telephone numbers of advisers in different policy areas who can be contacted during emergencies. News of a crisis in international finance surfaced in 1980 as the Reagan campaign was in flight, remembers Martin Anderson, Reagan's policy research coordinator. By the time the plane had touched down at the next location the campaign had contacted famous economists Milton Friedman and Arthur Burns, formulated a response, and issued a press release.[37]

Campaign policy experts come in three flavors, according to Janne E. Nolan, Gary Hart's foreign policy and defense adviser in the 1984 campaign: those who believe in the issues they are pushing, those adrenaline junkies attracted by the chance to participate in the events of a presidential campaign, and those who have attached their ambitions to a particular candidate in the hopes of achieving a position in a new administration.[38]

Policy advisers, even of the third type, are a very different breed from pollsters and media consultants. With the possible exception of the candidate's most senior policy coordinators, they are usually not paid. Their ties to the day-to-day campaign may be tenuous, and they all have nonpolitical careers to return to. Well-known academics may offer advice in an informal capacity to several campaigns in the same election.

Not surprisingly, there is a certain degree of tension between the "flack masters and [the] idea mongers," as Richard Allen (of the latter camp) puts it. "People in flackery don't know ideas and wouldn't know if one hit them at a great rate of speed," continues Allen, who headed the foreign policy issues team on the Republican side for the Reagan elections.[39]

There may be some justification for this, in view of the demands of the presidential campaign. "There's a big difference," explains political philosophy professor William A. Galston, Mondale's issues director in 1984, "between having a position paper and having a politically salable commodity."[40] "If an idea can't be communicated to the public, then it won't be part of the campaign," concludes John Holum, Gary Hart's issues man in 1984 and 1988. Someone, in other words, must administer the "test of political marketability."[41]

Economic Issues

On the broad range of economic affairs and "pocketbook" issues, the Democrats, since the New Deal, are usually favored as the party most voters believe will best meet their needs. Statements like "The Democrats are best for the working man" and "We have better times under the Democrats" abounded when people were asked to state their feelings about the Democratic Party. The Republicans, in contrast, were often viewed as the party of depression under whose administration jobs were scarce and times were bad.

These attitudes have had considerable staying power through the years. In 1987 and again in 1990 the *Times Mirror* asked samples of American adults, "What does it mean to be a Democrat? What does it mean to be a Republican?" and got the spontaneous replies shown in table 5.1. A campaign in which the salient issues are economic, therefore, is more likely to aid the Democrats than the Republicans (see table 5.2).[42] Of course, if the incumbent president is Democratic and the economy is faltering, emphasizing economic issues may not do much good. After the advent of "stagflation" under the Democrats in the late 1970s, the Republican Party was for some time deemed the party of prosperity. Recession during the first Bush presidency reversed those gains. The party that is in office when the economy is suffering does badly.

The Democratic Party's modern tendency has been to be "liberal" in several senses of that word. It promises something for everyone. Democrats support extensions of social welfare programs financed by the federal government, an increased minimum wage for the underpaid,

TABLE 5.1 What Does It Mean to Be a Republican? (Unprompted Replies, in Percentages)

Top Mentions	1987	1990
Conservative	21	22
Rich, powerful, monied interests	18	21
Business oriented	13	10
Not for the people	5	4
Against government spending	5	6

What Does It Mean to Be a Democrat? (Unprompted Replies, in Percentages)

Top Mentions	1987	1990
For working people	21	18
Liberal	18	18
Too much government spending	7	3
Cares for poor, disadvantaged	7	7
For social programs	7	9

Sources: *The Polling Report* (October 1, 1990) and Times Mirror Center for the People and the Press press release (undated).

health care coverage for the uninsured, job training for the unemployed, better prices for the farmer, additional federal funding for education, programs to protect the environment, and so on. No one is left out, not even business people, who are promised prosperity and given tax benefits, although they tend to remain opposed to the additional government regulation

TABLE 5.2 Which Party Is Better for Prosperity? (in Percentages)

	Republican	Democratic	No Opinion
1952 January	31	35	34
1956 October	39	39	22
1960 October	31	46	23
1964 October	21	53	26
1968 October	34	37	29
1972 September	38	35	27
1976 August	23	47	30
1980 September	35	36	29
1984 August	48	36	24
1988 September*	52	34	14
1990 October	37	35	28
1992 October*	36	45	19
1996 July	41	42	17

Source: Data from *Gallup Poll Monthly*, August 1996, p. 5.
*Based on registered voters.

of private industry supported by most Democratic candidates. Although voters say they are in favor of these programs, they do not like the spending totals that emerge from them—hence Democratic vulnerability to being tagged as serving the "special interests," especially labor unions. When voters become concerned that excessive government spending has led to inflation, large budget deficits, or high taxes, Democrats are at a disadvantage. This remains more or less true even though recent Republican presidents Ronald Reagan and George W. Bush have overseen unprecedentedly large budget deficits associated with enormous tax cuts, coupled with huge increases in military spending.

Republicans were once clearly on the defensive in the realm of economic policy, a situation stemming from the fact that they were in office when the Great Depression began in 1929 and during three sizable but shorter recessions more recently (1970–1971, 1982–1983, 1991–1992). They try to play down economic issues when their president is in office during a depression and play them up when the Democrats are in office and the economy is weak or their party is in power during good times. The "misery index," a combination of inflation and unemployment, taken together with which party is in office, is a nearly infallible guide to how economic policy is used, and by whom, in the campaign. Republicans attack the Democrats as the party that likes to tax and spend. The Republican candidate is thus well placed to benefit if voters become concerned about high taxes or excessive spending. As most specific large federal spending programs, such as Social Security and Medicare, are quite popular, candidates are well advised to be vague concerning the exact types of excessive spending that they oppose. Ronald Reagan in 1980, for example, directed his attacks mainly against "inefficiency" and "waste" and ran on a platform promising tax cuts that would (he claimed) actually raise tax revenues by stimulating economic growth, while George W. Bush assured his audiences during the 2000 campaign that, due to the federal budget surplus which existed at the time, his ambitious tax cut would not require reductions in spending on popular entitlement programs. Republican candidates are understandably upset at Democratic insinuations that they and their party have not become fully reconciled to Social Security. Indeed, when Walter Mondale challenged him on the issue during a 1984 debate, President Reagan promised not to cut Social Security then or the next year or ever.

Foreign Issues

The fact that the Democrats occupied the presidency during World Wars I and II, the Korean War, and the initial stages of heavy American involvement in Vietnam once convinced most voters that Democrats tend to lead the country into war. Republicans were then known as the party of peace, a position underscored by Senator Bob Dole (a decorated hero of World War II) in the 1976 vice-presidential debate when he said: "I figured up the other day, if we added up the killed and wounded in Democrat wars in this century, it would be about 1.6 million Americans, enough to fill the city of Detroit."[43] Republicans once tended to be the party of isolationism, arguing that the U.S. should refrain from joining international organizations or alliances, while Democrats often favored heavier engagement in world affairs.

After 1964, when Senator Barry Goldwater of Arizona, the Republican nominee, convinced people that he would use the American military to intervene in a great many places around the world, the Democrats became the party of peace, a feeling reinforced by George McGovern's anti–Vietnam War candidacy in 1972, by President Jimmy Carter's concern with international

TABLE 5.3 Democrats Versus Republicans on Foreign Policy (in Percentages)

	Republican	Democratic	No Opinion
1952 January	36	15	49
1956 October	46	16	38
1960 October	40	25	35
1964 October	22	45	33
1968 October	37	24	39
1972 September	32	28	40
1976 August	29	32	39
1980 September	25	42	33
1984 August	30	42	28
1988 September*	43	33	24
1990 October	34	36	30
1992 February*	39	39	22

Source: "Party Best for Peace," *Gallup Poll Monthly*, February 1992.
1992 question: "Which party is the best for peace?" Prior to 1992: "Which party will keep the country out of World War III?"
*Based on registered voters.

human rights and peace agreements, by President Ronald Reagan's belligerent rhetoric against the Soviet Union and other American enemies in the 1980s, and the two wars against Iraq fought by Presidents Bush senior and junior in the 1990s and 2000s. Thus, in recent years, the Democrats have enjoyed the advantage of being considered the peaceful party. While neither party remains "isolationist" in the historical sense, Republicans tend to be more protective of American sovereignty in international affairs, and are therefore more skeptical of the United Nations and other international organizations, as well as American ratification of multilateral treaties.

The Republicans hold other advantages in the realm of foreign policy. They are generally considered better able to handle military affairs, or to manage a war should the need arise.[44] George W. Bush won reelection in 2004 in part because most Americans believed that he would better lead the "war on terrorism" than Democratic nominee John Kerry.[45]

The distinction between domestic and foreign policy has always been a bit artificial. It has been maintained because of the ability of the United States to insulate its domestic economy

TABLE 5.4 Party Images After Impeachment (Percentage Believing the Following Apply to the Republican Party/Democratic Party)

	Republican Party	Democratic Party
Out of touch with the American people	60	41
Too extreme	55	39
Has a good program for the country	53	64

Source: CNN/Gallup Poll, February 4–8, 1999, reported in *Polling Report*, March 1, 1999, p. 2.

from international forces. Today, in the age of globalization, that ability is diminishing. The Reagan, George H. W. Bush, and Clinton administrations wanted to reduce international trade barriers to serve their foreign policy and business allies, but each had a hard time beating back protectionist forces worried about domestic unemployment. Policies such as the North American Free Trade Agreement, a Republican presidential initiative adopted by Clinton once he took office, were supported or attacked for their effects on international relations and on the domestic economy. During the Cold War, it was possible to see American relationships with European or Asian nations mainly in the context of containing the Soviet Union; since then, it has become increasingly clear that American workers and consumers have foreign policy interests.

Whereas the major parties once enjoyed long-term advantages in foreign or domestic policy, these have lately become more sensitive to evaluations of performance. For example, the fact that Jimmy Carter was in office when national income declined during an election year gave the Democrats a turn at being blamed for a recession. Nor can we say with any certainty that foreign and domestic economic policies are the only issue areas that over the long run will matter to voters.

Social Issues

What about the third great cluster of problems, the "social issues"—variously labeled (and understood) as crime, race relations, gay rights, abortion, school prayer, and gun control—that involve lifestyles as well as distributions of benefits?[46] As Richard Scammon and Ben Wattenberg pointed out, the first two grew enormously in salience to voters during the 1960s and thereafter: "Suddenly, some time in the 1960s, 'crime' and 'race' and 'lawlessness' and 'civil rights' became the most important domestic issues in America."[47] Although it is difficult to tell whether this entire cluster of issues works consistently for or against a particular political party, some believe that the increasing political importance of these issues benefits the more culturally conservative Republicans.[48]

Social issues affect the parties in different ways. The Republican Party may be thought of as a coalition of social conservatives and free-market libertarians. As long as the party concentrates on economic issues, both factions can usually agree on limited government. But on social issues the libertarians favor individual choice and are against government intervention even to protect traditional values. Social conservatives, however, oppose abortion and support school prayer, both of which entail a more intrusive government.

Democratic activists, as we have seen, despite their social diversity, are more united than previously on some issues. As the larger of the two major parties, spanning the entire country, the Democrats have in the past experienced difficulty in uniting on any programmatic principles. One consequence of the migration of conservative southerners into the Republican Party since the 1950s has been to facilitate the emergence of a more ideologically coherent Democratic mainstream, but as recently as the *Times Mirror* survey of political attitudes in 1987 (reported in *The People, Press and Politics*), the Democrats at the grassroots level divided into four separate and distinct blocs of voters, whereas the Republicans were split into only two groups on issues.[49]

In the National Election Studies, respondents have been asked to indicate their positions on policy issues by placing themselves on a series of seven-point scales; and to indicate how favorably they view a variety of politically active groups by rating each group on a one-hundred-point

TABLE 5.5 Party Unity

	Democrats' Standard Deviation	Republicans' Standard Deviation	Difference (Democrats – Republicans)
1994 Seven-Point Scale			
Aid to blacks	1.78	1.44	0.34
Ideology	1.30	1.10	0.20
Defense spending	1.51	1.31	0.20
Guaranteed jobs	1.76	1.61	0.15
Health insurance	1.89	1.82	0.07
Role of women	1.76	1.71	0.05
Services vs. spending	1.50	1.51	−0.01
1988 Feeling Thermometers			
Gays and lesbians	30.80	26.35	4.45
Big business	22.80	18.61	4.19
Christian fundamentalists	28.70	24.87	3.83
Wealthy people	21.21	18.12	3.09
Illegal immigrants	26.95	23.94	3.01
People on welfare	23.46	22.32	1.14
Conservatives	20.24	19.41	0.83
Labor unions	22.23	23.49	−1.26
Liberals	19.44	22.16	−2.72
Environmentalists	20.59	23.60	−3.01
Women's movement	21.04	25.48	−4.44

Source: Nelson W. Polsby and William G. Mayer, "Ideological Cohesion in the American Two-Party System," in Nelson W. Polsby and Raymond E. Wolfinger, eds., *On Parties: Essays Honoring Austin Ranney* (Berkeley, CA: Institute of Governmental Studies Press, 1999), pp. 219–254, at 232.

"feeling thermometer." In table 5.5, we have tried to assess how united or divided each party is by calculating the standard deviation—a measure of central tendency, hence of agreement—among party identifiers' responses to these questions. As the table clearly shows, Democratic respondents are more divided on the vast majority of issues and in their feelings toward important political groups. This pattern holds for all the years in which results are reported. On some issues, the difference between the two parties is not large; in other cases, however, the spread of Democratic opinion shows the Democrats' standard deviation more than 50 percent larger than the Republicans'.[50]

The existence of greater policy disagreement within the Democratic Party has inspired consistent efforts by Republican candidates over the years to emphasize issues that divide the Democrats substantially more than the Republicans, with the hope that Democratic voters who disagree with their party's nominee will defect to the GOP in presidential elections. These "wedge issues" are often social issues such as crime and affirmative action (prominent campaign topics in the 1970s and 1980s) and, more recently, gun control, gay marriage, and partial-birth abortion.

Democratic candidates often feel as if they are on the defensive when these issues emerge during a campaign; they usually prefer to discuss economic questions on which their party holds an advantage. Although social issues now receive a great deal of attention from the media, most academic studies conclude that economic preferences still weigh more heavily in determining the party identification and candidate choice of American voters.[51]

CAMPAIGN PROFESSIONALS

Presidential candidates have never lacked for willing accomplices in their quest for office. In the first partisan election battle in American history, the election of 1800, the crucial New York campaign was led by Alexander Hamilton (for the Federalists) and Aaron Burr (for the Democratic-Republicans). With the resumption of party competition in the 1830s, campaign managers assumed primary responsibility for the conduct of the battle, a pattern that has continued to the present.

Contemporary campaigns—since, let us say, 1952—have evolved into something qualitatively different from the pattern of the previous century. It is not the professionalization of the campaign that is new, for the old-time party managers were extremely interested in monetary rewards for their services, but the fact that consultants in modern times are business professionals, not party professionals. The individuals who directed the first century and a half of presidential elections were closely tied to one or another of the political parties and were often part of the party structure. Moreover, the communications technologies and strategies at the disposal of modern consultants that can help them sell their candidates have transformed the entire process of running for the nation's highest office.

In the nineteenth century, campaigns were often carried out by the party organizations. Nowadays, candidates must form their own campaign organizations. These are typically comprised of: paid staff, including a campaign manager; paid consultants and pollsters; volunteers; close advisers, often known as a "kitchen cabinet"; and a formal organization, typically consisting of a campaign committee and a finance committee. The first two categories, paid staff and consultants, are campaign professionals.[52]

What is the nature of campaign professionals? In some ways, they are very different from the party professionals of earlier eras. The people who ran campaigns through the first half of the twentieth century generally were compensated by the spoils system: winning candidates hired or appointed their supporters to a variety of government jobs. Those who run campaigns now are mostly compensated in salaries and fees for services, although some may receive positions in the White House if their candidate wins the election. Earlier generations of party professionals were mainly generalists. Now, the business of electioneering requires specialization and therefore diversity.[53] There are still old-style generalists who coordinate campaigns from top to bottom, but increasingly the business of the campaign is subcontracted to firms that specialize in a particular aspect of the process. *Campaigns and Elections*, the trade magazine of political consultancy, lists the following categories of consultants (among forty-five subcategories) in its "Annual Directory of Political Consultants, Products and Services": attorneys, database/file management, direct mail (strategy and creative), fax services, field operations and organization, fundraising consultants, media buying, media and speech training, online information services, printing and promotional groups, website managers, research (opposition), research (issues, voters, and legislative), satellite services, targeting, video duplication.[54]

The professionalization of political campaigns has advanced, by all accounts, considerably further in the United States, with its long drawn-out nomination and election processes, than anywhere else among the world's democracies. What is the cumulative effect of the introduction of modern polls, media campaigns, fundraising efforts, and the people who run these operations on the conduct of the presidential campaign? Does the new agenda-setting mechanism of the opinion poll change the character and conduct of presidential campaigns? Have the campaign professionals altered the substantive content of politics? Are they in it for the money, or do they have their own ideological axes to grind?

We can get a grasp on the relationship between candidates and paid professionals by looking closely at its initial phases. Although candidates are more typically to be found in the role of the suitor, it is not at all unusual for consultants to go prospecting for a candidate if they are short on contracts in a particular election cycle.[55] Once the initial contact has been made, the two sides bargain over a contract that, if signed, will formalize responsibility, set payment agreements, and establish general ground rules that will guide their interactions over the course of the campaign. Key resources, for both parties, are money and a winning reputation. Candidates are looking for the most successful consultant their money can buy, which generally means a firm with a strong recent win-loss record on their side of the ideological spectrum. Consultants likewise prefer winners over probable losers (so they can protect their record) and fat cats over lean. And neither side wants to end up with a partner who is ideologically or personally incompatible.[56]

Not surprisingly, top-flight consulting firms are besieged with offers from candidates and would-be candidates. Direct-mail wizard Richard Viguerie claimed (with possible exaggeration) to have turned down 98 percent of the campaigns in 1978 that requested his help.[57] Democratic strategist Bob Shrum received offers from several presidential contenders in 2004, ultimately deciding to sign on with John Kerry's campaign. Big-name presidential hopefuls are similarly able to pick and choose, while no-name candidates must often wait patiently until relatively late in the game and settle for whoever is left. Sometimes a prominent consultant will take on a long-shot candidate to advance a political agenda or because of a personal friendship. Even if the campaign is not generously bankrolled, the publicity attached to running a presidential campaign may lead to future business opportunities for the firm.

Has the increasingly sophisticated technological component of presidential campaigns altered the essential character of the enterprise of seeking office? No longer limited to the analysis of poll data, computers have colonized every level of the campaign process. In 1988, according to one survey, computers and electronic machines were used "for tracking convention delegates, writing fundraising letters and thank-you notes, processing donations, drafting news releases, maintaining electronic news libraries, . . . communicating between field and headquarters," and automatic telephoning. "Asking a political professional in 1988 how he uses a computer is a little bit like asking a reporter how he uses his telephone," declared Pamela Lowry, director of computer operations for Democratic candidate Michael Dukakis.[58] In the ensuing years, as computers have become even more powerful, their role in campaigns has grown accordingly.

The results of this electronic revolution are a higher rate of computer literacy among campaign managers, a small reduction in envelope stuffing and stamp licking on the part of campaign volunteers, and the greatly enhanced ability of the campaign to raise small amounts of money and get its message across to specially targeted segments of the electorate. But unless there exists a "computer gap" among competing candidates, the partisan effect of the new technologies is marginal.

How powerful are the campaign professionals within the campaign organization? The candidate-client relationship varies considerably from case to case, depending on the experience and stature of each party and the terms of the original contract. It is the candidate, all agree, who has the last word in approving the general strategy of the campaign.[59] Having done this, however, many candidates apparently prefer to absent themselves from the nitty-gritty choices that follow. One survey found that 44 percent of a population of consultants agreed that candidates generally backed off from making decisions on the priority of different campaign issues. Most "were neither very involved nor influential in the day-to-day tactical operation of the campaign."[60]

Consultants (not a shy and self-effacing group of people) will gladly tell you all about the power they enjoy—and should enjoy—as campaign strategists. The late Bob Squier, for instance, who worked for Democrats, said: "It is very possible to go through an entire campaign with a candidate, and when it is all over, they have no idea what went on. It is not to our advantage to explain to them. It is to our advantage to get them to do what we want—what's best for them—with the least amount of fuss."[61]

In recent years, some political consultants have become minor celebrities in their own right, often as a result of news media coverage that portrays them as the brains behind victorious campaigns—a view that most consultants are happy to encourage. James Carville, a plainspoken Louisiana native who served as Bill Clinton's chief campaign strategist in 1992, parlayed his candidate's success in winning the presidency into a lucrative second career as a writer, speaker, and television personality, becoming sufficiently well known that he appeared in cameo roles in several major Hollywood movies. Karl Rove, chief political adviser to George W. Bush, has become even more prominent a public figure than Carville, widely celebrated (and vilified) as the intellectual force behind Bush's two successful campaigns for the White House. Rove is the subject of two major biographies,[62] a *Frontline* special on PBS television, and even a documentary film titled *Bush's Brain*.

Explanations for the rise of consultants can be found in several related developments. The increasingly advanced technology involved in the campaign process means a candidate must hire technocrats to do most of the work. Volunteers, family and friends, and party leaders will tend to be sidelined to one degree or another because they lack technical experience in law, accounting, media production, media buying, advertising, and the like. The significance and sophistication of modern opinion research boosts pollsters into the role of oracles. Similar developments in media marketing produce parallel results for these manufacturers of public opinion.

The average campaign organization has a brief life. Even in the age of the so-called permanent campaign, a campaign organization lasts only a year or two. This means that the candidate needs in addition to expertise a base of institutional experience to draw on. Instead of having to build a national organization from scratch, it is now possible—and often desirable—to buy one ready-made. "All-service" consultants will cover everything that needs to be done, from general strategy to licking stamps.[63]

Have consultants made presidential campaigns more ideological? Probably not. With the exception of a few ideologically motivated firms, consultants tend to be party loyalists but not issue advocates. There are exceptions. Fundraising and direct-mail firms (an overlapping set of categories) can afford to be more purist than other sorts of consultants because they are holding the purse strings and they generally target a narrow range of like-minded, politically motivated donors.[64] Possessed of precious lists of the names of cobelievers, they are more likely to administer an ideological litmus test before entering into a relationship with a candidate, and more likely to call the candidate on the carpet afterward if his or her behavior does not reflect true belief.

Nevertheless, as Larry Sabato says, "for most consultants ideology is a surprisingly minor criterion in the selection of clients."[65] The business logic of consultancy militates against an approach that would too severely limit a firm's clientele, and the game-playing logic of the campaign itself encourages the use of any strategy that will win, regardless of its ideological fit.

Do campaign professionals help candidates obfuscate and blur the issues? With candidates from both parties being coached to court the swing vote in the middle, perhaps consultants contribute to a "Tweedledum-Tweedledee" effect in presidential elections. Mitchell E. Daniels, Jr., who became President George W. Bush's first Budget Director and later the governor of Indiana, sums up the consultant effect this way: "You tend not to make major gaffes, because somebody will spot them. On the other hand, you may not take very many bold actions, because someone will be very nervous."[66]

Has the professionalization of campaigns lowered standards of conduct in presidential elections? Even though the candidate is ultimately responsible for all campaign decisions, the use of paid staff and consultants may change the range of campaign options available and the types of strategies ultimately chosen. Consider the use of negative campaigning. "I love to do negatives," declared media consultant Bob Squier. "It is one of those opportunities in a campaign where you can take the truth and use it just like a knife to slice right through the opponent. I hate the kind of commercials that are just music and pretty pictures."[67] This bit of refreshing candor raises the possibility that the average campaign professional may in fact be different from the average politician. One study found that "most media consultants admitted often having considerable difficulty in convincing their clients to go negative."[68]

Candidates are aware, of course, of most of what goes on in their name, but it is easier to sign on the dotted line and have someone else take care of your dirty business for you than to have to haul the bodies away yourself.[69] Other commentators point out that there are limits to what campaigns can say on television, limits that did not apply to old-fashioned campaigns run by thousands of semi-independent and localized party bosses, newspapers, and partisans. In the Internet age, any effort by a campaign to engage in underhanded tactics or smear the opposition can be publicized instantly across the nation. On the other hand, current campaign finance regulations encourage the growth of nominally independent 527 organizations and other groups that can spread misleading information for the benefit of their favored candidate while allowing the candidate's own campaign to deny any responsibility.

Do campaign professionals undermine partisanship? There is no doubt that consultants have replaced party leaders as major actors in the campaign process. But the decline of traditional party leaders was not caused by the rise of consultants; it was caused by changes in the rules governing the party nomination and election system, which demand that candidates form their own organizations so that they can appeal to large primary electorates in order to win nomination. Those who are hired by those organizations, with rare exceptions, have strong partisan affiliations and do not work both sides of the street. In fact, many have worked for party organizations, and parties provide training in electioneering skills in order to have reliably partisan professionals.[70] "Party affiliation," according to one study, "is by far the most important factor considered by consultants in selecting their clients, outweighing a candidate's electability, ideology, or financial standing."[71] A good example of the way this works can be seen by looking at Republican nominee Bob Dole's campaign manager from 1996, Scott Reed. Reed was a deputy regional campaign director for the Reagan campaign in 1984. In 1988 he was the Iowa coordinator for the presidential campaign of then-Representative Jack Kemp of New York. When Kemp became Secretary of Housing and Urban Development, Reed was his chief of staff. In 1993 Reed became executive director of the Republican National Committee. Only in 1995 did he first meet Bob Dole when he was hired to run the Dole campaign.[72]

Polling

Multimillion-dollar polling is the norm in today's presidential elections. Public opinion polls have been used in politics, in varying ways, since the 1930s,[73] but they have not always been as important in shaping campaigns as they are today. As recently as the 1950s, most candidates still viewed polls with considerable skepticism. Some, like Harry Truman, were downright hostile. "I wonder," he said, "how far Moses would have gone if he'd taken a poll in Egypt? What would Jesus Christ have preached if he'd taken a poll in Israel? Where would the reformation have gone if Martin Luther had taken a poll? It isn't polls or public opinion of the moment that counts. It is right and wrong leadership—men with fortitude, honesty and a belief in the right—that makes epochs in the history of the world."[74] Winston Churchill, inhabiting the same political universe, said: "Nothing is more dangerous than a Gallup poll, always taking one's pulse and taking one's political temperature."[75] Like all long-lived politicians in democracies, these exemplary figures undoubtedly paid attention to their intuitions about public opinion. But intuition has now been largely replaced by more accurate methods, and it is hard to ignore these more thorough soundings of the popular will.

The first significant use of polls within a campaign organization occurred in 1960, when surveys taken by Louis Harris helped guide John F. Kennedy's campaign in key primary states. Pioneers such as Harris and George Gallup were followed in succeeding decades by hundreds of polling firms throughout the country that now make up the polling industry.[76] General nationwide public opinion polls not owned or paid for by particular candidates are now regularly taken by Gallup, Harris, Zogby, the Pew Research Center, and several national media groups: *The Wall Street Journal*/NBC News, *New York Times*/CBS News, *Washington Post*/ABC News, CNN, *Newsweek*, Fox News, and the *Los Angeles Times*.

Other poll takers work for political campaigns, and among these, a few are involved in all phases of presidential campaigning.[77] The modern pollster's role goes far beyond gathering data and analyzing trends. "There's no question that our role has changed from collector of facts to interpreter and strategist," Richard Wirthlin says.[78] They ask: What should be the major campaign issues and themes, or, at least, which would be most attractive to the electorate? Should the candidate attack an opponent's record? If so, how? Which regions and states should be emphasized? What is the proper role of the vice-presidential candidate? The campaign pollster helps make these and a variety of other crucial campaign decisions, such as which states to visit and which groups within the electorate to court, all subject to the candidate's approval.

The first nationwide polls on behalf of candidates typically begin many months before the first caucuses or primaries. These initial polls, called "benchmark polls," are based on twenty- to thirty-minute interviews with large samples (600–1,000 people in a state, and up to 4,000 nationally) of potential voters.[79] The object of this poll is to determine what proportion of the population is committed to various candidates, how many are still undecided, and why people are disposed to vote (or not vote) as they indicate. A second poll of benchmark length is often done several months before the general election. There can also be "trend" polls of shorter length. Sometimes, pollsters conduct callback interviews to see if respondents' opinions have changed.[80] All such polls are used to test the political climate and try out possible campaign themes.

In June 1979, Richard Wirthlin conducted a national study on behalf of Ronald Reagan of "six scenarios for the future." Given a choice of options ranging from "less is better" to "America can do," the majority chose the "can do" theme. This theme pervaded Reagan's campaign. "Don't let anyone tell you that inflation can't be controlled," Reagan declared in a thirty-second television spot. "It can be, by making some tough decisions to cut federal spending."[81]

Campaigns monitor any number of "target voters"—blocs of the electorate considered key swing votes—to determine which themes should be stressed. The 1988 Dukakis campaign targeted two major groups: white Democrats who had defected to Ronald Reagan in previous elections (about 10 percent of the voters) and white independents (about 20 percent of the voters), but the campaign failed to win enough of these voters back from the Republicans.[82] In 1992 Clinton's team adopted a similar strategy; they hoped to target white suburban voters: the Reagan Democrats, political independents who supported "change" in politics, and women disaffected with the Republican Party. The first blow to this strategy came during the New Hampshire primary when allegations of womanizing hit Clinton, damaging his standing with some female voters. The second blow came shortly thereafter: Ross Perot's entrance into the race took Clinton's message of change away and bestowed it on the folksy billionaire who spoke strongly about cleaning out the barn.

That left the white suburban vote as the primary target for Clinton and, as it turned out, for George H. W. Bush. Although they aimed their messages at the same voters, the two campaigns adopted strikingly different strategies. Clinton focused on the economy, describing the previous twelve years as a failed experiment that had enriched the wealthy at the expense of the "forgotten middle class." He advocated such proposals as health-care reform and family medical leave to help the struggling middle class and attacked Bush for being out of touch with the needs of the American people. In his acceptance speech at the Democratic convention he showcased this message: "In the name of all those who do the work, pay the taxes, raise the kids and play by the rules, in the name of the hardworking Americans who make up our forgotten middle class, I proudly accept your nomination for president of the United States. I am a product of the middle class. And when I am president, you will be forgotten no more."[83]

Bush polls showed that voters did not trust Clinton. They either thought that he "lied" about incidents in his past or that he stretched and molded the truth so much that he could not be trusted.[84] Bush played on these results, referring to Clinton as "Slick Willie" and continually calling on Clinton to "tell the truth" and "set the record straight." Bush attacked Clinton for his changing stories about his draft experience. During one *Larry King Live* appearance, Bush challenged Clinton's patriotism, alleging that he had "demonstrated against the United States on foreign soil" (referring to antiwar demonstrations at Oxford during Clinton's time as a Rhodes

Scholar there) and hinted that a Clinton trip to Moscow as a student was for more than a vacation.[85]

The intricacies of campaign strategy often seem to fascinate the news media, if not the electorate at large. Campaign consultants may encourage this interest by attempting to convince reporters of their cleverness in identifying particular subgroups of voters deemed critical to the construction of an electoral majority and developing a campaign message aimed at these narrow segments of the population. In 1996, the Clinton reelection campaign famously targeted what its advisers called "soccer moms"—white suburban women with children—as a key constituency. Political reporters began to write endless stories about this strategy, finding actual mothers of soccer-playing children to interview in order to find out what they thought about politics.[86] Such supposed social groups as "office park dads" and "security moms" have been identified by journalists as key voting blocs in subsequent elections, although it is often unclear whether such claims are based more on unfounded assumptions or spin from campaigns than on true survey research.[87] Still, the increasing sophistication of polling methods now allows campaigns to focus their attention on undecided or persuadable voters whom they think will determine the outcome of the election.

In 2000, the dilemma facing Al Gore's presidential campaign was underscored by the results of polls indicating that while most Americans approved of President Clinton's performance in office, particularly on economic issues, they held much less positive opinions of Clinton personally after an investigation by independent counsel Kenneth Starr disclosed a relationship between Clinton and White House intern Monica Lewinsky. Gore took pains to distinguish himself from the incumbent under whom he had served for eight years, dissuading Clinton from campaigning for him, and declaring in his speech accepting the Democratic presidential nomination that "I stand before you tonight as my own man." By emphasizing his independence from Clinton, however, Gore ran the risk of failing to capitalize on his association with the popular policies of the Clinton administration.

George W. Bush's campaign strategy in 2000 was similarly inspired by the results of public opinion polls. The Bush campaign discovered that voters were tired of the constant partisan warfare in Washington that characterized the later Clinton years, particularly during the impeachment proceedings of 1998–1999 that left both the president and the Republican-controlled Congress with significant political damage. As the governor of Texas during that time, Bush could credibly claim no association with the unpopular impeachment effort. He promised to be a "uniter, not a divider," and to seek to "change the tone in Washington," noting his success as governor in working with Democrats in the Texas state legislature. To reassure Americans that he would not pursue a strongly ideological agenda—as former House Speaker Newt Gingrich had done in the mid-1990s, to the dismay of many voters—Bush described himself as a "compassionate conservative." His rhetoric was expressly designed to appeal to swing voters and political independents who generally found little fault with Clinton's policies but were more critical of Clinton's personal behavior; Bush's oft-repeated promise to "restore honor and dignity to the White House" represented an indirect but easily identifiable reference to the Lewinsky affair.

The 2004 campaign was conducted under very different circumstances; the terrorist attacks of September 11, 2001 and President Bush's declared "war on terror" placed foreign and military policy at center stage. Polls conducted by both campaigns found Bush's chief strength to lie in

Americans' support of his fight against Islamic terrorism. Thus Bush endeavored to maintain a link in voters' minds between terrorism and the American-led invasion of Iraq, while the Kerry campaign attempted to distinguish the two, noting that Saddam Hussein's regime had no proven link to the al-Qaeda organization that perpetrated the 2001 attacks. Bush's strategy of labeling his opponent a "flip-flopper" represented an attempt to convince voters that Kerry was weak and indecisive, and therefore unfit for leadership during wartime. Kerry emphasized his record as a decorated Vietnam War veteran—a record called into question by Bush surrogates during the course of the campaign—who possessed the appropriate skills and experience to face the challenges of the day.

Other issues emerged as well in 2004. Polling by the Kerry campaign revealed that Bush's economic policies were considerably less popular than his attempts to fight terrorism, prompting Kerry to criticize Bush's job creation record repeatedly on the campaign trail. While the Bush campaign courted independent voters, it also pursued a strategy of maximizing electoral turnout among his presumed "base" of self-identified Republicans and conservatives. Bush's campaign rhetoric became more explicitly ideological than it had been in 2000, and his public support for a constitutional amendment prohibiting same-sex marriage represented an attempt to inspire high levels of participation among evangelical Christians and other socially conservative segments of the population.

Polling within particular states allows campaigns to decide which states to contest fiercely and which to ignore. In 1984, when Richard Wirthlin's polls revealed Reagan's strength in the South, the campaign decided to invest its scarce resources in the less secure Northeast. They reasoned that it was a waste of time, energy, and money to campaign in states they were already assured of winning.[88]

In the 1988 campaign, pollsters realized that with the exceptions of Texas, Colorado, and possibly Montana, the Republicans were solidly ahead in the entire South and Mountain West regions. As Republican pollster Vincent Breglio noted, "approximately 125 to 135 electoral votes in eighteen or nineteen states were going to end up in the Republican column unless a major mistake was made."[89] With these 130 electoral votes out of reach, Dukakis had to win a majority of 270 votes from the remaining 408. But Bush needed only 140 of those 408 to win entrance to the White House. That is why talk among Democrats of a "fifty-state strategy," an approach emphasized at their convention in Atlanta, quickly subsided. For Dukakis to win, he would have to sweep the Northeast, the industrial belt, and the Pacific states. Both candidates spent little time in states where Dukakis was far behind; there was no point since the outcome was not likely to change. They emphasized states with many electoral votes over those with few votes.[90] Thus, over the final six weeks of the campaign, Dukakis spent nearly three-fourths of his time in only eight states—California, Illinois, Michigan, Texas, New York, Ohio, Pennsylvania, and Missouri. Bush spent more than half his time in only six—California, Illinois, Michigan, Missouri, Ohio, and New Jersey.[91]

In 1992 the situation was almost exactly reversed. Early in the campaign, Democratic National Committee strategist Paul Tully had decided that the Democrats could not afford to concede the South and the West to the Republicans. He devoted himself to designing a more sophisticated targeting strategy than the Democrats had used in the past. His first step was to analyze the 1988 campaign and identify mistakes made by the Dukakis campaign. Most significantly, Tully found that Dukakis had spent most of his money on national media buys, a waste of money because they were more expensive and less targeted than Republican advertising. Next, to identify the places where the Democrats should make media buys in 1992, Tully looked at individual media markets—generally smaller than states—and analyzed their election returns. Tully identified markets that showed some tendency to vote Democratic as "persuadable," and these markets, even if they were in the South or West, were targeted for media buys by the Clinton campaign.

Clinton's team adopted Tully's map and created a sophisticated media-targeting plan from his findings. The results were positive. By the beginning of September, Clinton was leading Bush in virtually every state, giving the Democrats the luxury of specifically targeting very close states while forcing the Republicans to spread themselves out more and thus spend more. In the last few weeks of the campaign, the Clinton team was confident of winning California, New York, Hawaii, Rhode Island, and Massachusetts, and they were ten to fifteen points ahead in Pennsylvania, New Jersey, and Illinois. There were ten states they considered closely contested—those where they led by only 1 to 10 percentage points—and these states were targeted for the most attention, both by personal appearances by Clinton and running mate Al Gore and through media buys. Of these ten states—Colorado, Michigan, Ohio, Georgia, Louisiana, North Carolina, Connecticut, New Mexico, Kentucky, and Tennessee—Clinton lost only one, North Carolina.[92]

Polling likewise determined the states targeted by candidates in the 2000 and 2004 elections. George W. Bush's 2000 campaign discovered that Bush was competitive in the traditionally Democratic state of West Virginia and that he also polled strongly in Tennessee, even though the latter was the home state of Bush's opponent, Democrat Al Gore. The Bush campaign devoted time and resources to these states, initially considered safe for Gore, and carried them both—two key victories in an extremely close election. Likewise, early assumptions that Florida would not be competitive in 2000 (the state usually voted Republican, and Bush's younger brother Jeb served as its governor) were contradicted by polling results indicating a tight race, especially after Gore's selection of a Jewish running mate, Senator Joseph Lieberman of Connecticut, won him significant support in the Jewish communities of South Florida. Both campaigns invested heavily in Florida in the final weeks before the election; on Election Day, the state was so closely divided between Bush and Gore that it took weeks of recounts and extensive litigation before a winner could be determined.

The electoral battleground map in 2004 closely resembled that from four years before. Once again, top campaign targets on both sides included Florida, Pennsylvania, Michigan, Wisconsin, Iowa, Nevada, and New Mexico. Both sides conducted continuous polling in each state in order to determine the latest developments and react accordingly. While the Gore campaign had pulled its resources from Ohio in the last weeks before the 2000 election, choosing to focus on winning Pennsylvania and Florida instead, in 2004 the state remained a hard-fought battleground up until Election Day, with multiple public appearances from Bush and Kerry and their running mates, constant television advertising and campaign mobilization efforts, and a frenzy of activity by party organizations and outside groups on both sides. Initially promising polls led the Bush campaign to invest resources in the traditional Democratic strongholds of Minnesota and Oregon, while the Kerry campaign actively contested Colorado, a state Gore had conceded to Bush in 2000. Bush's running mate Dick Cheney even took an all-night airplane trip to Hawaii for a campaign appearance a few days before the election after an opinion poll suggested (falsely, as it turned out) that the state, normally a Democratic bastion, was politically competitive.[93]

Focus Groups

Benchmark polls are the first and most basic tool of the pollster. Focus groups have been a tool of communication and advertising research for forty years, including earlier presidential campaigns. But it was not until the 1980s that they became an integral part of campaign strategy. The ideal group is about twelve to fifteen people, voters chosen from the general population to discuss the election and the candidates. A much smaller number is likely to place too much of a burden on each individual, while more than fifteen or so tends to reduce each member's participation. A moderator guides the discussion, focusing on matters of interest to the campaign. Discussions are lengthy—anywhere from one-and-a-half to three hours—so that participants have a chance to express their feelings. The 1988 George H. W. Bush campaign picked Paramus, New Jersey, for their main focus group site because to them it represented a typical American city. They conducted similar sessions in other middle-America settings across the country.

Unlike opinion polls, which depend for their validity on randomly selecting a representative cross-section of voters, focus groups are usually structured to be socially homogeneous "so that the numerous interacting demographic variables do not confuse the issues; to be most productive, all the participants must be on the same wavelength."[94] For example, Young and Rubicam Enterprises, which conducts hundreds of focus groups every year, almost never puts married, full-time housewives with children at home in the same group as unmarried, working women because the firm regards their lifestyles and goals as too different.[95] "The key to focus groups is homogeneity," Bill Clinton's sometime pollster Stanley Greenberg says. "The more homogeneity, the more revealing."[96]

The composition of the various groups depends on the needs of the campaign. In 1988, the Bush team interviewed white Catholic Reagan Democrats because these Democrats were considered a critical swing group. The idea was for Bush to pursue groups that voted for Reagan but were in danger of drifting back toward the Democrats. In 1992, both Bush and Clinton were targeting these white middle-class voters, and both campaigns featured them in their focus groups.

Focus-group interviewing violates most of the accepted canons of survey research. As William D. Wells of the University of Chicago Graduate School of Business says:

> Samples are invariably small and never selected by probability methods. Questions are not asked the same way each time. Responses are not independent. Some respondents inflict their opinions on others; some contribute little or nothing at all. Results are difficult or impossible to quantify and are not grist for the statistical mill. Conclusions depend on the analyst's interpretive skill. The investigator can easily influence the results.[97]

With so many defects, why have focus groups come to be so widely used in political campaigns? Part of the reason is that they are fast and relatively cheap—a few thousand dollars as opposed to $20,000 to $25,000 or more for sample surveys. Another reason to use focus groups is to test ideas or ads not yet released to the general public. Regular opinion polls have long been used to test campaign themes and specific ideas that campaigns may use. Typically, respondents are asked questions about a candidate, then read some new information about that candidate, and then are asked again for views of that candidate. In this way, a pollster can check whether a candidate's potential weakness would actually affect voters if it received publicity. Focus groups allow campaigns to go further. Instead of merely mentioning a piece of information about a candidate, the moderator can show the group an actual ad and ask them for a reaction. Like Hollywood movies, which can be changed if preview audiences object to something, political ads can be altered or discarded if focus groups don't like what they see.

The most important reason focus groups are employed is that they give the campaign an opportunity to probe respondents to a greater depth than in regular polls. Deeper feelings and half-formed thoughts of ordinary voters emerge, and in their own words. It is true that the group's responses cannot easily be quantified, but in the hands of a sensitive analyst, focus groups may reveal important insights. "Focus groups allow you to put flesh on the bones," Democratic pollster Mark Mellman says; they provide "a sense of texture you can't get from a poll."[98]

Using focus groups in 1988, Bob Teeter discovered that when Bush spoke of "a thousand points of light," his oft-used rhetorical theme, nobody knew what he was talking about. Bush fared best, Teeter found, when he sounded strongest, as when he depicted his opponent Michael Dukakis as overly liberal on every issue from the death penalty to taxes to prison furloughs to saluting the flag.[99]

The Dukakis campaign also used focus groups extensively and, interestingly, found many of the same sentiments in the population that the Bush people were discovering.[100] "We polled. We had extensive focus groups," said Susan Estrich, Dukakis's campaign manager. "You know, you can go wrong, but you don't go wrong for lack of trying—at least in the general election we were polling constantly. We were focus grouping their ads probably as much as they were."[101] The polls and focus groups enabled the Democrats to identify their weaknesses. "They told us that we were vulnerable on the liberal-conservative issues and on crime," said Irwin "Tubby" Harrison. "We looked at Dukakis' involvement in the prison furlough program in Massachusetts early and knew we had a problem. There was a possible vulnerability on defense, on taxes, and on capital punishment, too."[102]

But recognizing a problem and remedying it are two different things. Pollsters reign supreme at the former task, but there may be little they can do about the latter. Dukakis's closest aide, Nicholas Mitropoulos, said that the governor was uncomfortable responding to Bush's attacks. "Dukakis deep down inside is just a good guy and felt that . . . the American people were going to see that these issues were not real issues," Mitropoulos said. "He wanted to take the campaign on the high road . . . he wanted to stay positive."[103] A Bush pollster, Vincent Breglio, took a different view. "Dukakis tried to explain away the furlough program, [the pollution in] Boston harbor, his Pledge [of Allegiance] position," Breglio said. "It just didn't work."[104]

In 1992, Bill Clinton was heading into the general campaign in a weak and vulnerable position after enduring a brutal primary season. Besieged by questions of character brought on by allegations of womanizing, draft dodging, and noninhaling drug use, Clinton's popularity ratings before the Democratic convention were low.

Clinton's consultants began a search for a revival strategy, a search they privately called the "Manhattan Project." The first step they took was to convene focus groups consisting of targeted white middle-class voters. They found that the focus-group participants viewed Clinton's difficulties as part of a larger problem: that Clinton was just another "typical politician." The memorandum to Clinton summarizing the findings read as follows:

For the most part, people were reluctant to write [Clinton] off as corrupt, dishonest or immoral, but the highly publicized "shading of the truth" has reinforced an impression that he will do what is necessary to "look good." The questions about personal morality certainly matter, but their larger impact is contained in the general impression that he will say what is necessary and that he does not "talk straight."[105]

By providing the focus groups with additional information, Clinton's political consultants found that this negative perception could be turned around. Specifically, participants responded positively to information about Clinton's life, to stories about how Clinton had stood up to "special interests" in the past, and to proposals that avoided political talk and showed empathy and concern for people. Ultimately, the findings from these focus groups helped convince Clinton that he needed to tell voters about his past—his childhood as the older son of a widowed mother, his adolescent showdown with his abusive stepfather, his success at putting himself through both college and law school—and helped shape his communication with voters during the rest of the campaign. This meant more direct contact through such media as popular talk shows and the bus tours, less traditionally political events and speeches.

Clinton's polling team in 1996, Mark Penn and Doug Schoen, were less impressed with the quality of focus-group research. They believed that the setting of focus groups—people sitting around having a conversation dedicated to talking politics—was too far from the circumstances in which ordinary Americans thought about politics. Instead, they preferred polling in shopping malls. For Penn and Schoen, this gave them answers that matched, as they saw it, the way most people thought of politics, as a "momentary distraction in their lives."[106]

Instead of asking focus groups to discuss ads, some pollsters prefer a more direct response. Using hand-held, dial-equipped boxes, participants watching an ad or a candidate's performance are asked to twist a knob on a scale of zero to one hundred. Two reporters who watched a demonstration of this technology in 1988 reported that their colleagues in the press "sat transfixed as computer-generated graphics, showing the audience's second-by-second reactions, were superimposed above the television image of each candidate."[107]

Jimmy Carter's analysts used a similar instant-reaction technique to measure responses to the debate with Reagan in 1980 and determined that Carter was most liked when he promised to keep Social Security sound. Reagan peaked with his call for a strong military and with his recitation of the "misery index" (the continuation of unemployment and inflation, which, as the challenger, Reagan could blame on the incumbent).[108] Richard Wirthlin used the "pulse dials" in 1984 to study the Reagan-Mondale debates. Bob Teeter used the tool in several of his focus groups and included EKG-like etchings in his memorandum to the other workers on the Bush campaign in 1988. Many of Teeter's core findings found their way into the advertising campaign, and public feelings about Dukakis's negatives began their steady uphill climb.[109]

Dial groups were also used by Clinton's consultants in the Manhattan Project campaign-revival effort. While trying to figure a way out of Clinton's problems, pollster Stanley Greenberg convened a group of middle-aged white women at a hotel in Dayton, Ohio, and asked them to "dial" their reactions to prepared presentations of the candidate and the campaign. Greenberg found that Clinton scored poorly when he looked and sounded like a politician but did well when he answered questions directly and addressed certain popular issues, such as welfare reform. When presenting the results to the campaign, Greenberg superimposed a tracing of the dial readings on the video the subjects had watched, giving Clinton a blow-by-blow report on the "grades" the dial group had given his various responses.[110]

Both campaigns convened dial groups for the 1992 presidential debates, hoping to identify the sound bites and ideas that pleased voters and thus deserved repeating in the general campaign. During the first presidential debate, however, any information the campaigns were able to glean was greatly overshadowed by the dial groups' response to Ross Perot's performance. Everything he said—from a joke about the size of his ears to a complaint about "America's crazy aunt locked up in the basement" (Perot's characterization of the federal budget deficit)—won an immediate and strongly positive response from the observers. Both campaigns' private conclusion after the debate was that Perot had won hands down.[111]

Still, the campaigns gained some positive information from their dial groups. After the first debate, Bush's team told him that he did better when he explained why he opposed a policy, such as committing troops to Bosnia or legalizing drugs. "You were more convincing in this context than when you were explaining what you were for," his pollsters wrote. "Keep counter-punching—you do it well. However, you need to improve your presentations of what you are proposing for your second term." The memorandum also recommended that Bush back off on his criticism of Clinton for "demonstrating on foreign soil," that he not object to others' descriptions of the country being in economic trouble (it made people think he was out of touch), and that he immediately attack Clinton any time he used the word "change," because that was a powerful word for his opponents.[112]

The benchmark poll gives general strategic guidelines to the campaign, but day-to-day tactical decisions are driven by another polling technique, overnight tracking, especially in the last weeks of an election. Rarely used until the late 1970s, tracking polls have "become de rigueur in the business," says Democratic pollster Paul Maslin.[113] Shifts in sentiment among voters are "tracked" by calling approximately one hundred voters each night, asking a half dozen very specific questions, usually about perceptions of the latest ads, issues, or the candidates. With each increment of new respondents, the responses from six-day-old interviews are dropped. Thus, rolling averages can be calculated. The overnight figures facilitate fine-tuning of a campaign in the crucial last days.

In late October 1988, Dukakis made a last-minute surge, narrowing the gap between himself and Bush, who was so distressed by Dukakis's improvement that aides tried to keep the tracking numbers from him. "Bush would start each morning agreeing that they [the numbers] were bad for him," Peter Goldman and his colleagues report, "but his resolve not to ask would typically break down by, say, 8 a.m. 'What did Teeter tell you?' he would ask urgently. 'Have you heard from Teeter?'" Teeter's disconcerting tracking results kept the entire Bush team in suspense right up to Election Day.[114]

Bush's concern in 1988 might have been mitigated, however, if he had known just how imprecise tracking polls can be. Four years later, just days before Bush was defeated by Clinton, several tracking polls were reporting Bush ahead or trailing by only an insignificant two points. The general consensus among pollsters was that these results were wrong—both Bush's polling team and the Clinton pollsters were reporting gaps of six to eight points in Clinton's favor, and there was no other evidence to suggest a major shift in support during the last few days.

The pollsters agreed: there was no way that Bush could be ahead. Indeed, the small sample size of the tracking polls meant that the results were unreliable from day to day and the "snapshot" results some tracking polls were reporting were surely mistakes. To address this concern, pollsters generally average tracking results over several days to increase reliability, and they still consider tracking results good only for spotting trends, not predicting outcomes.[115]

Why are polls and pollsters so important in the campaign? Why have they replaced party bosses, cronies of the candidate (these are still in evidence, but at the top levels the campaign staff is, increasingly, a meritocracy), and the candidate himself as the key decision makers? Plenty of attention has been focused on the mistaken or misleading results of polling. Nevertheless, taken together, polls are reasonably accurate indicators of public sentiment. Thus they are a better tool for shaping campaign strategy and content than anything else now available, and this, in the uncertain universe of the presidential campaign, is all that is really necessary to make polls indispensable to the candidate.

One need only consider the information sources that used to govern campaign strategy to appreciate the significance of the advent of modern polling techniques. Nineteenth- and early-twentieth-century campaign indicators consisted of reports from precinct captains and state party leaders, crowd sizes and responses, newspaper editorials and letters to the editor, the candidate's mail, man-in-the-street interviews, and pure hunches. Most of these indicators were unreliable. Editorials may signify the views of only a few newspaper owners; letters to the editor represent a lot of writing by a rather small number of activists; crowd responses can be manipulated, or variously interpreted; party leaders may let the candidate know only what they think the candidate wishes to hear.

While polls themselves may be indispensable, their interpreters are frequently playing much larger roles in presidential politics than would seem warranted for mere keepers of statistics. George H. W. Bush, to take one example, was persuaded by Bob Teeter (with the aid of his managers Roger Ailes and Lee Atwater) to adopt the get-tough strategy of his 1988 campaign.[116] The modern-day poll taker, in the words of one practitioner, plays an instrumental role in deciding "which states to hit, where people should go, how much money should be spent where, which groups [to] target, and the kinds of money and messages [to] use."[117]

The explanation for this abdication of authority on the part of the candidates and their personal advisers lies partly in the changing nature of polling. With computer-assisted sample selection processes and polling techniques, it has been possible to increase the number of polls taken in the course of a campaign to as many as the 133 surveys from separate states that Pat Caddell took between late August and election eve for Jimmy Carter in 1980—which works out to about one every other day.[118] In addition to conducting their own polls, polling experts are responsible for gathering and interpreting whatever other public or private polls are available. Whereas the polling consultant after 1960 might have reported to the campaign on a monthly basis during the spring and fall of an election year, the present-day pollster is always around, with daily, and sometimes hourly, updates to report.

Moreover, the information obtained from polls has expanded greatly. Originally, polls were merely a device to measure candidate support; good pollsters would try to isolate which groups within the electorate were more and less likely to vote for the candidate. Nowadays, polls are constructed to address not just how social groups will vote—and the categories here have become progressively more precise—but why they will do so and what might change their behavior.

Pollsters, in other words, are now being asked to do more than simply report on the state of public opinion; they are now routinely expected to aid in influencing it.

ADVERTISING

Television

Campaigns expend considerable resources on political television commercials. Commercials serve a variety of purposes. They can be used to establish name identification or to improve a candidate's personal image. They can focus on campaign issues, targeting key subgroups in the population. They can be used to capture the attention of the press. Or they can be used to attack the candidate's opponent. This practice has come to be called negative advertising.

In 1948 less than 3 percent of the population owned a television set.[119] That year marked the debut of television advertising in presidential campaigns. President Truman filmed just a single speech encouraging citizens to vote.[120] Since that modest beginning, campaigning via television has taken on a life of its own.

The watershed presidential election year, by all accounts, was 1952. By then, 45 percent of the nation's households owned a set,[121] and presidential campaign teams felt they could ill afford to ignore the medium. Republican candidate Dwight Eisenhower's campaign engaged the services of the Ted Bates advertising agency in New York. The three central themes of his commercials—corruption, high prices, and the Korean War (all the fault of the Democrats, of course)—were chosen after consultation with pollster George Gallup.[122] Spot ads developed with Gallup's advice managed to overcome Ike's abrupt speaking style and to create the confident, avuncular figure now associated with Eisenhower.

There is no standard formula for a political ad, but there are standard time slots. When introduced in the 1950s, television advertising was generally produced to fill five-minute slots. One-minute spots predominated in the 1960s and 1970s, to be eclipsed in the late 1970s by the thirty-second ad. Finally, around 1982, the now-popular ten-second spot was introduced.[123]

After the advertisement is filmed, edited, and approved by the candidate, a schedule is prepared that is supposed to help the ad reach the right people. Every ad campaign is somewhat different and must be crafted to take account of the unique assets and deficiencies of the candidate. But amid the varying styles of each campaign, a relatively small number of tried-and-true themes have established themselves over the past several decades. These constitute the advertising consultant's tool kit, from which virtually every television campaign is built. There is the "man-in-the-street" ad, sometimes scripted and sometimes culled from actual interview footage, showing the average voter (or the average member of a targeted constituency group) endorsing the candidate's accomplishments or general integrity. The "sainthood spot" is "devoted to celebrating the candidate's life story and accomplishments." The "news-look" spot ad attempts to use the legitimacy of experts and television newscasters who relate facts about the candidate's record. The "apology" ad is used, usually out of desperation, when a liability develops that is considered so threatening to the candidate's chances of election that he or she must personally apologize to the electorate. "Cinema-verité" spots offer the audience a view into the life of the candidate as he or she is working, walking, or addressing another audience, while the older "talking head" approach (still a staple of spot ads) places the candidate directly in front of the camera so that he or she can talk personally and directly to the audience. The "issue-position" spot defines the candidate's record on an issue of high salience to the electorate or to a swing group of voters.[124]

One measure of the centrality of television advertising in the current campaign process can be found in the recently developed "back-and-forth" ad. This innovative format begins with an excerpt from an opponent's spot ad, which is then "answered" in the second sequence, an ad within an ad. This is possible because technological developments have enabled campaigns to produce television ads more quickly, cheaply, and easily. Campaigns can respond to the opposition's latest round of advertising in a matter of days. Evidence shows that technology may be closing this time lag even more. In one exceptional case, the Clinton campaign team in 1992 was able to respond to a Bush ad within forty-eight hours of its first broadcast.

The key to this quick turnaround was satellite technology. The Clinton team had hired a satellite tracking company to monitor Bush's activity and alert them whenever a new Bush commercial was broadcast in hard-fought locations. When the Bush campaign broadcast a commercial criticizing Clinton's tax record in Arkansas, claiming that Clinton's campaign proposals would require $220 billion in taxes, the Clinton campaign knew about it within five minutes. Within an hour, campaign team members had consulted with Clinton, reviewed the ad that the satellite company had beamed to campaign headquarters, and devised a plan for response. That night, Clinton's economists analyzed the Bush ad, trying to determine how the opposition had come up with its numbers. The next morning, campaign staff called reporters at major newspapers and encouraged them to write critiques of the new Bush ad. These commentaries on political advertising had become common in major newspapers and news magazines. Next, the media team headed by Mandy Grunwald put together a response ad on the "back-and-forth" model: they included some of the copy from the Bush ad and added a stamped "UNTRUE" across a frozen frame. By six in the evening after the Bush ad's first airing, Grunwald was showing the ad and the Clinton response to a focus group in Pennsylvania. She determined that the ad needed more authority, and so the campaign gathered quotes from the newspaper critiques they had set in motion that morning. By the next day—less than forty-eight hours after the Bush ad's debut—the Clinton campaign had distributed its response ad to reporters and television stations across the country.[125]

It is important to note that ad makers are not always guided by the pollster's revelations. In the 1980 general election, ads showed Jimmy Carter working long hours at the White House. "The responsibility never ends," said the voice-over. "Even at the end of a long working day, there is usually another cable addressed to the Chief of State from the other side of the world where the sun is shining and something is happening." But polls said that voters never doubted that Carter worked hard. They doubted whether all the hard work was paying off. This crucial point—Carter's effectiveness—was not addressed in the ad.[126]

Targeting

Media professionals attempt to place political commercials so as to reach a targeted viewing audience. "Dissimilar kinds of people," Larry Sabato notes, "watch and listen to different sorts of programs at various times of the day. The better educated, information-oriented, undecided voters have been found to cluster around late news shows." A media manager might go after such a group with information-packed ads or spots discussing issues. Middle-aged housewives, Sabato believes, are partial to family-oriented or charismatic image spots during afternoon soap operas.[127]

The latest frontier in targeting promises to extend this strategy by exploiting the rapidly expanding media market of cable television. More than two-thirds of the households in the country now subscribe to cable systems.[128] The audience watching any particular cable channel is often more socially and culturally homogeneous than even the smallest local television station, so messages can be tailored accordingly. Also, according to one researcher, cable audiences tend to be more politically active than regular television viewers, raising the prospect of media advertising aimed at recruiting not just voters but also volunteer campaign workers.[129] The late Richard N. Neustadt, a communications law attorney, predicted: "When we watch the narrowcasting [approach of cable] networks, we may see campaign ads and news programs showing candidates advocating bilingual education on Spanish channels, defending Social Security on channels aimed at the elderly, or playing football on sports channels."[130]

Radio and Newspapers

Like television talk shows, radio talk shows were used by the 1992 candidates to deliver their messages directly to the people. When Clinton was in trouble in the April New York primary, for example, he appeared on the Don Imus morning show. On the advice of his media consultant Mandy Grunwald, other radio guest spots were booked for Clinton across the country.[131]

Eventually the Clinton campaign went further in pursuing radio publicity. Over the summer, campaign aides set up a computerized voice mail system that allowed radio producers to call a 1-800 number, select from the digital menu, and download recorded sound bites and campaign information. The system was individualized for different markets: Latino radio stations could hear a message in Spanish, African American stations had a message aimed at their audience, and there were further choices of sound bites from Clinton, vice-presidential candidate Al Gore, and prominent Clinton supporters. The campaign also set up local substations of the system so that endorsements from local personalities could be added to the menu and made available to area radio shows. This effort was enormous. One author estimated that the system allowed the campaign to deliver its message to 2,200 stations every day, 30 percent of the national radio market.[132]

Ross Perot, too, benefited greatly from the national growth in talk radio; indeed, his 1992 candidacy might have died at birth had it not been for talk radio. In the two weeks after his announcement of candidacy on *Larry King Live*, the major newspapers ignored Perot; only the *Los Angeles Times* ran a small story, burying it on page 18 of the paper. But the day after the King show appearance, talk radio stations across the country were deluged with callers wanting to talk about the billionaire and his candidacy. Talk-show hosts were apparently taken by surprise by this indication of interest, but they caught on quickly; the traditional media were not as quick. By the time the major media outlets started paying attention to Perot, he was winning 20 percent support in the polls.[133]

Radio remains a staple in the advertising diet of presidential campaigns. The main advantage over television, of course, is its low cost. With audiences that are frequently more demographically focused than even cable television, radio outlets also offer a campaign the opportunity to pitch to narrow slices of the electorate. The 1972 George McGovern campaign, for example, was the first to take aim at the rock 'n' roll audience, which contained many of the eighteen- to twenty-one-year-olds just enfranchised by the Twenty-sixth Amendment to the Constitution.[134]

Newspapers have clearly lost out in the bid for campaign advertising dollars in the contemporary period. Consultants, according to one survey, consider the effect of a print ad to be "almost negligible." Several factors account for this revolutionary change in campaign strategy. First, people tend to view newspapers as less credible than other media as sources of information. Second, a newspaper ad can be more easily ignored than a television or radio spot. Third, the portion of the electorate that reads newspapers is more highly educated and more politically committed than the portion that attends to electronic media and therefore is less likely to be swayed by advertising of any sort. If you want to communicate to the politicians or to activists, take out a newspaper ad. If you want to communicate with the voters, use radio and television. Such is the orthodoxy among the consultants.

One continuing attraction of newspapers for the presidential campaign has nothing to do with advertising. "Some candidates," according to Democratic pollster Bill Hamilton, "particularly on the Democratic side, are forced to buy newspaper ads if they want to get the paper's endorsement."[135]

Other Media

A large majority of the electorate now owns VCRs and DVD players, a fact which has not been lost on political consultants. Walter Mondale became the first presidential candidate to produce a videocassette for mass circulation during the 1984 campaign. The purpose in this case was fundraising, but the trend is clearly to use the new medium to replace personal campaigning. Eleven of the thirteen major-party candidates in 1988 distributed videos of themselves. "Video parties" were held by the thousands in New Hampshire before that state's primary elections.

Why the sudden popularity? Frank Luntz explains:

> At a cost of from $10,000 to $40,000 . . . , home videos are relatively inexpensive to prepare, and can also save the campaign money by using video footage for their television advertising, or vice versa. These cassettes allow the candidate to appear "in person" at five or even fifty places at once, and are designed to give voters a personal sense of the candidate, not just a recitation of proposals or issues.

As John Buckley, Jack Kemp's press secretary, put it, "It's the political equivalent of cloning."[136]

In 1992 the Clinton campaign put together a video that included "The Man from Hope," the Hollywood-produced story of Clinton's life that was screened at the Democratic Convention, and a tailored message from Bill Clinton. The video was distributed to loyal Democrats for use at "Clinton House Party" fundraisers and was a successful part of the campaign's money plan.[137]

The first use of satellite broadcasting in a presidential campaign is described by Richard Armstrong:

> During one . . . impossible week in 1984, when both Florida and Georgia were preparing for their primaries, Walter Mondale took an hour out of his campaign schedule in Georgia to go to an Atlanta television studio. [Frank] Greer [the first consultant to use the new satellite technology] had arranged for an "uplink" to a satellite and had made appointments with

the news anchormen of Miami's three biggest television stations. As Mondale stared into the camera, each Florida newsman took turns asking him questions over long-distance phone lines. Mondale's replies were shot in Atlanta, relayed by microwave to an uplink dish outside the city, beamed 22,300 miles through space to a satellite over the equator, reflected back to the downlink dishes in three Miami television stations, and recorded for use on the evening news later that day.[138]

The result? Mondale captured the lead spot on all three network-affiliated stations' news shows that day in Miami. As his face appeared on the screen behind the news anchors, each repeated the questions asked earlier in the taped satellite interview. "To the viewers it appeared to be a live interview in the studio, a real coup for the local news team. But as virtually everyone in southern Florida watched Mondale live on local television, Mondale himself was busy meeting his commitments in Georgia."[139] Mondale, one technological step ahead of his opponent John Glenn, managed to appear in three places while actually being in none, and scooped up the nightly news programs in the process.

In addition to facilitating press conferences in situations where the candidate and the press audience are on different parts of the planet, satellite communications can be used to disseminate stories to local media across the country, to bring the candidate into direct contact with potential donors at several locations, and to bring many local groups of campaign workers together for one, big television conference.

An innovation of the 1992 election was the use of 1-800 numbers. Virtually every candidate in the 1992 primary and general election campaigns at one point set up a 1-800 number for supporters to call. Ross Perot's candidacy was built on a 1-800 number that supporters called to volunteer for the campaign and get in touch with the individual state Perot organizations. The surprising strength of Jerry Brown's primary campaign was attributable in part to his refusal to accept campaign donations larger than $100 and in part to his constant promotion of his 1-800 number. Calls flooded in with offers of support and money, and his insubstantial campaign was sustained for a while.[140] Clinton, Bush, and Perot all promoted 1-800 numbers during the general election campaign; in many cases, a call to the 1-800 number would get the caller a copy of the candidate's policy "plan."

From the 1996 election forward, the role of these telephone numbers was largely replaced by candidate Web sites. Supporters and interested voters can now access information provided by the candidate online, including biographical sketches, policy positions, lists of endorsements, press releases, and personal appearance schedules for the presidential candidate, running mate, and their families. Internet users can sign up for the candidate's mailing list and receive regular e-mail updates from the campaign; some candidates also use their Web sites to recruit volunteers for campaign activities like voter registration drives and phone-banking.

The explosion in popularity of political blogs between 2000 and 2004 did not go unnoticed by the campaigns. Candidate Web sites now often feature official blogs with entries at least purportedly written by the candidates, their spouses and running mates, and top campaign officials. The Kerry campaign blog in 2004 featured frequent posts from vice-presidential candidate John Edwards's wife Elizabeth, a declared blog aficionado, who regularly contributed anecdotes from the campaign trail. Such activity is designed to keep spirits high among supporters and make them feel personally connected to the campaign and the candidates.

BOX 5.2 FORECASTING THE OUTCOME

As an election draws closer, more and more interest focuses on attempts to predict the outcome. This process of forecasting elections is not at all mysterious; it depends on well-settled findings about the behavior of American electorates, many of which have already been discussed. But it may be useful for citizens to understand how the "experts" go about picking the winner.

There are several ways to do it. One way, popularized a half-century ago by journalists Joseph Alsop and Samuel Lubell, is to interview the residents of locations which in the past have voted with great stability in one pattern or another. Some neighborhoods, for example, always vote for the Republicans by a margin of 80 percent or better. Let us say that the interviewer finds that only 50 percent of the people questioned in such a neighborhood say that they are going to vote for the Republicans this time, but respondents in traditionally Democratic areas continue to support the Democratic nominee heavily. A finding such as this permits the reporter to make a forecast, even though it is based on only a very small number of interviews that may not represent the opinions of most voters.

Reporters who use this technique very rarely make firm predictions about election outcomes. Instead, they concentrate on telling stories about the clues they have picked up: what they learned in heavily black neighborhoods, what the people in Catholic areas report, what midwestern farmers think, which way people from localities that usually vote for the winning party are leaning, and so on.[1] This technique is impressive because it digs into some of the dynamic properties of what goes into voting decisions. Like a focus group out on the doorstep, it reports which issues seem to be on people's minds. It examines the ways in which members of different social groups view the candidates and the campaign. It is also a technique that can be executed at relatively low cost. But it is unsystematic, because the people interviewed are not selected randomly. Thus the results of this technique would be regarded as unreliable in a scientific sense, even though they may enhance an observer's intuitive grasp of what is going on. The results are also unreliable in the sense that two different journalists using this method may come to drastically different conclusions, perhaps because they seek out interview subjects who confirm their preexisting expectations of what they will find. There is no certain way of resolving the disagreement; nor is there any prescribed method for choosing between their conflicting interpretations.

The strength of forecasting on the basis of historical voting patterns arose out of the general stability of American voting habits from one election to the next. But the weakness of such a technique is also apparent. Sometimes significant changes in the population of an area due to migration or changes in the appeals of parties to different voting groups will throw the historical two-party vote ratios in the sample area out of joint. When a forecast made with this technique is wrong, it is usually quite difficult to tell immediately whether transitory or lasting causes are at the root of it. This limits the usefulness of the forecast greatly because, in the end, it rests on assumptions that have only partial validity in any one election, and nobody can say precisely how or where or to what extent they may be valid.

For these reasons, journalists and other observers have largely turned to public opinion polls conducted during the campaign as more reliable indicators of the standing of the candidates and the likely electoral outcome. Thanks to the fact that modern news media are constantly preoccupied with the candidate horse race, these polls are plentiful during the months before an election. Television pundits also devote attention to the results of opinion surveys, speculating in great detail about the meaning of any apparent trends in the levels of support for each candidate.

Most widely-reported polls, such as those conducted by Gallup, Harris, Zogby, and the major newspapers and television networks, consist of a national sample of roughly one thousand respondents selected by dialing telephone numbers at random. Pollsters screen respondents for their likelihood to vote, asking them if they are registered, if they are paying attention to the campaign, and if they have voted in past elections. They then ask which candidate the respondent would support if the election were held that day. Pollsters often collect other information, such as age, race, sex, and party identification, in order to draw conclusions about the standing of candidates among various social groups in the electorate.

Many people are distrustful of poll results because of the relatively small sample size of most surveys. They wonder how the opinions of the thousand or so potential voters interviewed in any particular poll can accurately represent the views of the more than 100 million Americans who vote in a presidential election. This, by and large, is a false issue. The laws of statistics confirm that a sample of this size chosen at random will almost always be broadly representative of the larger population from which it is drawn. Pollsters commonly report "margins of error" along with their results, which represent the interval within which ninety-five of every one hundred samples could be expected to fall due to chance if the population were sampled repeatedly—usually about four or five percentage points for a standard media poll. In other words, if Candidate A is "really" ahead of Candidate B by ten percentage points in the total American voting population, a poll of one thousand randomly sampled voters might easily find a seven- or twelve-point gap. But it would be extremely unlikely for the poll to report incorrectly that Candidate B is in the lead simply due to random error in the sampling of respondents.[2]

When polls turn out to be wrong, the cause is much more likely to be systematic bias in either the means by which interview subjects are sampled or in their likelihood to respond to the survey than chance error under random selection. One famous instance of a systematic response bias occurred when polling was in its most rudimentary stages. In 1936, the *Literary Digest* magazine mail survey predicted a victory for the Republican presidential nominee, Kansas Governor Alf Landon.[3] When Democratic incumbent Franklin D. Roosevelt won overwhelmingly, carrying every state except Maine and Vermont, the *Digest* became a laughingstock and soon thereafter went out of business. What had happened was simple enough. The magazine had sent out millions of postcards to people who had telephones asking them how they intended to vote. The returns showed a huge Republican triumph. Surely, the *Digest* must have thought, we cannot possibly be wrong when our total response is so large and so one-sided. But, of course, something was terribly wrong. Only 2.3 million people responded out of 10 million recipients of the cards, and these were all voluntary respondents. So the *Digest* got its returns from a group in the population more likely to vote Republican and completely missed the larger number of poorer people who were going to vote Democratic. There is a much greater tendency for people of wealth and education to return mail questionnaires, so there was a systematic bias favoring the minority of voters who supported Landon's candidacy.[4] As Peverill Squire says, "The 1936 *Literary Digest* poll failed not because of its initial sample, but because of the non-random response rate. Those who received straw vote ballots were strongly supportive of the president. But a slight majority of those who returned their ballot favored Landon."[5]

In 1948, a whole series of errors were made by pollsters attempting to forecast the outcome of the presidential election, but none of them was connected with the size of the samples used. In that year, the Gallup, Roper, and Crossley polls all predicted that the Republican nominee, New York Governor Thomas E. Dewey, would unseat President Harry Truman. Truman's victory on Election Day was so unexpected that the early edition of the *Chicago Tribune* the following morning famously featured the headline "Dewey Defeats Truman." A committee of social scientists convened after the election to determine what went wrong found the following problems with the pre-election surveys:[6]

1. The poll takers were so sure of the outcome that they stopped taking polls too early in the campaign, assuming that the large population of undecided respondents would vote, if they voted at all, in the same way as those who had already made up their minds.
2. The undecideds voted in just the reverse proportions.
3. Many instances were revealed where polling organization analysts, disbelieving pro-Truman results, arbitrarily "corrected" them in favor of Dewey. The methods of analysis employed were not traced in any systematic way, however, because they could not be reconstructed from records of the polling organizations.
4. Sampling error occurred not because of the size of the samples, but because respondents were selected by methods that gave interviewers too much leeway to introduce biases into the sample. The so-called quota-control system used widely in 1948 (which instructed interviewers, for example, out of twenty interviews to pick ten men, ten women; fifteen Protestants, four Catholics, one Jew; seventeen whites and three blacks, and so on) has since been replaced with random sampling. The old method, which in the days before near-universal telephone access relied on door-to-door surveys, allowed interviewers to select respondents who lived near them or who were conveniently accessible in some other way, introducing systematic bias into the results.[7]

Modern pollsters remain vigilant against possible sources of bias in their survey results. If nobody answers the telephone when they first call, they try again the next day if possible. (Pollsters usually prefer to conduct surveys during weekday evenings, when respondents are most likely to be home and free to answer their questions.) Researchers polling in an area with a significant Latino population will attempt to hire bilingual interviewers, lest they fail to take the preferences of Spanish-speaking voters into account in their surveys. Many people—sometimes more than half of those contacted—refuse to answer altogether, and this proportion is increasing over time. As long as Republicans and Democrats are equally reticent about sharing their political opinions with telephone interviewers, this tendency will not skew the results, although low response rates make it more difficult for pollsters to achieve their target sample size. Since most surveys sample only traditional land-line telephones, some researchers increasingly worry that they may systematically ignore the growing proportion of voters who use only cell phones. If this relatively young and prosperous population of cell phone users votes differently from the rest of the electorate, polls that exclude them will not accurately reflect the status of public opinion.[8]

Pollsters differ in their methods, occasionally producing inconsistent results. For example, most survey organizations employ a screen for likely voters, excluding from their reported results the preferences of poll respondents who they believe are unlikely to vote. These screens vary in composition and degree of strictness. Some voters will claim to be undecided between the candidates, especially well in advance of Election Day. Pollsters differ in their eagerness to push these respondents into declaring a preference. Particular surveys may or may not ask about third-party candidates, who usually perform better in pre-election polls than they do in the election itself.

While the findings of competing survey organizations often differ slightly at any given point in the election season, and while the events of the campaign—conventions, debates, advertisements, gaffes—cause candidates to rise and fall over time even in the surveys conducted by a single pollster, contemporary survey research has an impressive track record in forecasting the outcome of most recent elections. Most of the final pre-election surveys in 2004 measured a narrow lead for George W. Bush in the national popular vote of one or two percentage points over John Kerry; Bush ultimately won by 2.5 points.[9] The 2000 election, closer still, was predicted to be such by numerous opinion polls finding a virtual dead heat between Bush and Al Gore, while the more comfortable leads enjoyed by Bill Clinton in 1992 and 1996, George H. W. Bush in 1988, and Ronald Reagan in 1984 in surveys conducted during the final weeks of previous campaigns allowed observers to foresee their decisive victories with ease.

Of course, presidential elections in the United States are not decided by direct national popular vote, as demonstrated by the events of 2000. Election analysts are also therefore intensely interested in the relative standing of the candidates in key battleground states. While the number of publicly-released statewide polls has increased substantially over the last few elections, they are still less common—and, sometimes, less reliable—than the traditional national surveys. When the election is not close, state results are less important; a candidate who is ahead by five or ten percentage points in the national popular vote can be confident of a victory in the electoral college as well. In the 2000 and 2004 elections, two of the closest presidential contests in American history, the differences between the popular and electoral vote proved much more consequential.

In 2000, uncertainty over the election outcome extended far beyond the pre-election telephone surveys of potential voters to encompass the exit polls used by television networks to forecast the state-by-state results on the night of the election. Exit polls are surveys of actual voters in key precincts who are asked about their vote choice as they leave their polling place. Exit polls are not based on random samples of the entire voting population, and are subject to both sampling bias (since voters at some precincts are more likely to be sampled than others, and those who vote early or via absentee ballot will not be sampled at all) and response bias (since some voters may be more willing to respond to a news media survey at their polling place than others). But the news media find exit polls useful, both for "calling" results on election night before all the votes are actually counted, and for drawing preliminary conclusions about the demographic and ideological composition of the electorate in a given year.

Exit polls had occasionally caused problems before 2000. In 1980, NBC declared a landslide Reagan victory on the basis of decisive survey results nearly three hours before polling places closed on the West Coast. Many believed that this announcement depressed turnout, as westerners who hadn't already voted decided not to bother, and thus affected the outcome of more competitive local races in those states.[10] In 1996, several television networks incorrectly projected a Democratic victory in a U.S. Senate race in New Hampshire based on exit polls showing a five-point margin between the candidates; the declared "winner" ultimately lost by 3 percentage points.[11]

The events of election night in 2000 turned out to be utterly disastrous. Television networks pronounced Al Gore the winner in Florida on the basis of erroneous exit polls shortly after voting ended in most (though not all) of the state. Several hours later, as George W. Bush pulled ahead in the reported vote returns, the networks retracted their Florida projections. As Bush clung to a small lead in the early hours of the morning, networks then called the state—and therefore the election as a whole—for the Texas governor, though within hours Gore had drawn even on the strength of late-reporting South Florida precincts, requiring yet another retraction as it became clear that the winner could not be determined at least until all absentee votes were tallied. Thus began a weeks-long battle over the counting of punch-card ballots that ended only when the U.S. Supreme Court halted all recounts in mid-December by a five-to-four vote, effectively handing the presidency to Bush.

The embarrassing performance of the television networks in 2000 prompted some post-election soul-searching among journalists. Joan Konner, former dean of Columbia University's Graduate School of Journalism, was a member of an independent commission formed by CNN after the 2000 election debacle to determine what went wrong. She found that "among the obvious failings were an emphasis on speed over accuracy in reporting; excessive competition [among networks] and the pressure to come in first; outdated technology; human error; a flawed polling and projection system; and, finally, overconfidence in the system and in the polls themselves."[12] It is troubling in retrospect that the networks did not exercise more caution when reporting results based on exit polls with known sampling and response biases. Surely few viewers would remember afterwards which network was the first to project the outcome in any given state; the damaged credibility resulting from an incorrect prediction far outweighs any "credit" gained from the aggressive declaration of winners and losers.

The television networks' newfound election-night patience was immediately put to the test in 2004. Exit polls conducted on Election Day for a consortium of news media clients indicated an electoral college victory for John Kerry. By mid-afternoon, the poll results had leaked onto the Internet, even affecting the performance of the stock market.[13] Displaying a relative abundance of caution, however, the networks declined to make projections in close states based purely on the exit polls. As Web-savvy Democrats who had been reveling in the leaked poll numbers looked on in horror, the polls were proven wrong again as the actual vote returns came in. By the end of the evening, enough actual votes in key states had been counted to declare Bush the winner.

Predicting presidential elections is largely a matter of satisfying curiosity. It is a great game among political experts and other interested parties to guess who will win, and we look to the polls for indications of the signs of the times. But this kind of forecasting is ultimately of limited importance. After all, we get to know who has won very soon after the polls close (except in the 2000 election) with much greater detail and accuracy than surveys can supply. The bare prediction of the outcome, even if it is reasonably correct state by state, tells us little about how the result came to occur. More may be learned if it is possible to analyze survey data in order to determine what kinds of groups— ethnic, racial, economic, regional—voted to what degree for which candidates. Yet our enlightenment at this point is still not great. Suppose we know that in one election 60 percent of Catholics voted Democratic and in another election this percentage was reduced to 45. Surely this is interesting, but unless we have some good idea about why Catholics have switched their allegiance, our knowledge has hardly advanced. The polls often tell us "what" but seldom "why." The more comprehensive post-election surveys by academic researchers—such as the University of Michigan's National Election Studies, conducted for every presidential election and most midterm elections since 1948—can provide additional evidence addressing the "why" questions.[14]

The usual polling technique consists of interviewing cross-sectional samples of the American public at various points in time. The samples may each be perfectly representative of the population at large, but different individuals constitute each successive sample. This method makes it difficult to determine with any reliability why particular individuals or classes of people are changing their minds because pollsters do not interview the same people more than once. To overcome this limitation, a researcher can conduct a panel survey, in which a single sample of the voting population is interviewed at various intervals before Election Day and perhaps afterward.[15] This technique makes it possible to identify the people who make up their minds early and those who decide late. These groups can be reinterviewed and examined for other distinguishing characteristics. More important, perhaps, voters who change their minds during the campaign can be studied. If a panel of respondents can be reinterviewed over a number of years and a series of elections, it may become possible to discover directly why some people change their voting habits from election to election. Or focus groups can be used to frame survey questions more sensitively. On the other hand, the added attention given to panel respondents may completely contaminate their responses and make them wholly atypical of the general population.[16]

The attentive reader may have observed that reports of the overall distribution of party identification in the American public vary somewhat according to the source. Why don't all surveys agree? One reason for the discrepancy involves the time the poll was taken; the nearer to the election, the more likely that voters will bring their party preferences into line with their chosen candidates. A second reason is that different polls often sample somewhat different populations. Exit polls, for instance, sample only those who actually go to polling stations to vote on the day of the election, and miss absentee and early voters. Other polls report results only for registered voters or those who say they are likely to vote, which is different from sampling a cross-section of the adult population. The closer the population polled is to the actual electorate (which is far smaller than the total population eligible to vote), the more likely it is to reflect factors that influence the election.

A third way to produce discrepancies concerns wording. A question that includes a phrase such as "as of today" is more likely to tap current feelings about the parties than one that specifically asks the respondent to answer "usually" or "generally" or "regardless of how you may vote." A test of these factors by Stephen Borrelli, Brad Lockerbie, and Richard G. Niemi reveals that question wording explains most of the discrepancies among polls reporting different figures in partisan allegiance. As they say,

> [A]ll else equal, 1980 and 1984 polls that worded the partisanship question in a general way reported a Democratic-Republican gap roughly five percentage points larger than reported by polls that asked "as of today"; nonexit polls in those years reported gaps, on average, five points larger than did exit polls; polls taken more than 10 days before or after the election in 1984 reported gaps three points larger than did polls taken within 10 days of the election.[17]

Understanding what is being measured, when, and how, is indispensable in interpreting the results of polls.

[1] See, for example, Samuel Lubell, *The Future of American Politics* (New York: Harper, 1951); his "Personalities and Issues," in Sidney Kraus, ed., *The Great Debates: Kennedy versus Nixon, 1960* (Bloomington: Indiana University Press, 1977), pp. 151–162; and Joseph Alsop, "The Negro Vote and New York," *New York Herald-Tribune* (and elsewhere), August 8, 1960. Reporting of this sort became a feature of the election-year *Washington Post* coverage. See, for example, Rowland Evans and Robert Novak, "Stronghold Lost," *Washington Post*, August 4, 1980.
[2] There are several sources readers can consult about the technology and tactics of polling. Many years ago George Gallup published *A Guide to Public Opinion Polls* (Princeton: Princeton University Press, 1948). See also *Opinion Polls, Interviews* by Donald McDonald with Elmo Roper and George Gallup (Santa Barbara, CA: Center for the Study of Democratic Institutions, 1962); and Charles W. Roll Jr. and Albert H. Cantril, *Polls* (New York: Basic Books, 1972). In 1972, Representative Lucien Nedzi of Michigan held congressional hearings on the possible effects of information about polls on subsequent voting. See *Public Opinion Polls, Hearings Before the Subcommittee on Library and Memorial*, Committee on House Administration, House of Representatives, 93d Cong., 1st sess., H.R. 5503, September 19, 20, 21, and October 5, 1972. A further flap occurred in 1980 as the result of Jimmy Carter's concession of defeat and the television network predictions of a Reagan victory before voting was completed on the West Coast. See Raymond Wolfinger and Peter Linquiti, "Tuning In and Turning Out," *Public*

Opinion 4 (February/March 1981): 56–60; John E. Jackson, "Election Night Reporting and Voter Turnout," *American Journal of Political Science* 27 (November 1983): 615–635; *Election Day Practices and Election Projections, Hearings Before the Task Force on Elections of the Committee on House Administration and the Subcommittee on Telecommunications, Consumer Protection, and Finance of the Committee on Energy and Commerce,* U.S. House of Representatives, 97th Cong., 1st and 2nd sess., December 15, 1981 and September 21, 1982, and Tannenbaum and Kostrich, *Turned-On TV/Turned-Off Voters.*

[3] Robert Sherwood, *Roosevelt and Hopkins* (New York: Harper, 1948), p. 86. See also Archibald M. Crossley, "Straw Polls in 1936," *Public Opinion Quarterly* 1 (January 1937): 24–36; and a survey of the literature existing at that time, Hadley Cantril, "Technical Research," *Public Opinion Quarterly* 1 (January 1937): 97–110.

[4] Maurice C. Bryson, "The Literary Digest Poll: Making of a Statistical Myth," *The American Statistician* 30 (November 1976): 184–185. As a matter of fact, this method produced a correct prediction four years earlier, in 1932, when the *Literary Digest* said that Roosevelt would win. Sampling error is tricky; an atypical sample may still give the correct prediction by luck, but sooner or later, the law of averages is bound to catch up with it.

[5] Peverill Squire, "The 1936 Literary Digest Poll," *Public Opinion Quarterly* 52 (Spring 1988): 125–134.

[6] Frederick Mosteller et al., *The Pre-Election Polls of 1948*, Social Science Research Council Bulletin 60 (New York, 1949).

[7] For an even more detailed discussion of the problems of election forecasting, see Andrew Gelman and Gary King, "Why Are American Presidential Election Campaign Polls So Variable When Votes Are So Predictable?" *British Journal of Political Science* 23 (October 1993): 409–451.

[8] James Sterngold, "World of the Wireless Stymies Political Pollsters," *San Francisco Chronicle,* October 10, 2004, p. A4.

[9] See the Polling Report compilation of 2004 survey data at http://www.pollingreport.com /2004.htm.

[10] On the import of early projections, see Philip L. Dubois, "Election Night Projection and Turnout in the West," *American Politics Quarterly* 11 (July 1983): 349–364. Dubois argues (against a number of other studies) that the early projections did have a significant impact on turnout. For a sophisticated analysis of the policy problems involved, see Percy Tannenbaum and Leslie J. Kostrich, *Turned-On TV/Turned-Off Voters: Policy Options for Election Projections* (Beverly Hills, CA: Sage, 1983).

[11] Michael Cousineau, "Exit Poll Wrong Call in Senate Race Leaves Anger, Hurt, Red Faces," *Union Leader* (Manchester, NH), November 7, 1996, p. A1.

[12] Joan Konner, "The Case for Caution: This System Is Dangerously Flawed," *Public Opinion Quarterly* 67 (Spring 2003): 5–18 (quote on p. 7). See also Paul Biemer, Ralph Folsom, Richard Kulka, Judith Lessler, Babu Shah, and Michael Weeks, "An Evaluation of Procedures and Operations Used by the Voter News Service for the 2000 Presidential Election," *Public Opinion Quarterly* 67 (Spring 2003): 32–44.

[13] Matt Krantz, "Exit Poll Rumors Push Dow Into Loss," *USA Today,* November 3, 2004, p. 4B.

[14] See Angus Campbell, Philip E. Converse, Warren E. Miller, and Donald E. Stokes, *The American Voter* (New York: Wiley, 1960); and Warren E. Miller and J. Merrill Shanks, *The New American Voter* (Cambridge, MA: Harvard University Press, 1996).

[15] See Paul F. Lazarsfeld, "The Use of Panels in Social Research," *Proceedings of the American Philosophical Society* 92 (November 1948): 405–410.

[16] This is known as the "Hawthorne effect," named after a famous experiment in industrial psychology. See George C. Homans, *The Human Group* (New York: Harcourt, Brace, 1950), pp. 48–155.

[17] Stephen Borrelli, Brad Lockerbie, and Richard G. Niemi, "Why the Democrat-Republican Partisanship Gap Varies from Poll to Poll," *Public Opinion Quarterly* 51 (1987): 115–119; quote on pp. 117–118. See also Howard Schuman, *Questions and Answers in Attitude Surveys: Experiments on Question Form, Wording, and Context* (Thousand Oaks, CA: Sage Publications, 1996).

STRATEGIES AND TACTICS

Historically, the outstanding strategic problem for Democratic politicians is to get their adherents to turn out to vote for Democratic candidates. Democrats therefore stress appeals to the faithful. One of the major problems, as we saw in chapter 1, is that most citizens who identify as Democrats are found at the lower end of the socioeconomic scale and are less likely to turn out to vote than those with Republican leanings. So the Democrats put on mobilization drives and seek in every way to get as large a turnout as possible. If they are well organized, they scour the lower-income areas for voters, they provide babysitters, and they arrange for cars to get the elderly and infirm to the polls, or make sure they have absentee ballots.[141] Whether the neutral appeals on radio, television, and newspapers stressing the civic obligation to vote help the Democrats more than the Republicans depends on whether, in any given locality, there are more Democrats who are unregistered because they are poor and uneducated than Republicans who are unregistered because they have recently moved. Raymond Wolfinger and his colleagues, who have studied the matter closely, conclude that nationwide the partisan advantage is about a wash.[142]

For Republicans involved in presidential elections, the most important fact of life is that their party has been the long-term minority party in the United States. In presidential elections in which considerations of party are foremost, and allowing for the greater propensity of Republicans to turn out to vote, it was plausibly argued in 1960 that the Democrats could expect to win around 53 or 54 percent of the vote.[143] Nowadays it appears that the Republicans have better presidential prospects. The party's share of citizens who actually vote (40 percent in 1980) is considerably greater than its proportion of voters in the eligible general population (34 percent in 1980). The gap the Republicans have had to overcome has diminished since the 1960s, from 20 percentage points (54 percent Democratic versus 34 percent Republican) to 12 percentage points (52 percent Democratic to 40 percent Republican) by the 1980s. In 2000, 39 percent of voters identified as Democrats, 35 percent as Republicans; by 2004, the Republicans had drawn even among actual voters (37 percent each).[144] Additionally, Democratic voters have historically been somewhat more likely to vote for a Republican candidate than Republican voters have been to defect to Democrats, although Democratic party loyalty among voters has been increasing significantly over the past twenty years.[145]

Further factors in calculating party advantage are the various biases built into the electoral college. On the one hand, Republicans have an advantage because they tend to do better in sparsely populated states, and therefore benefit from the extra weight those states receive from the electoral college formula. On the other hand, Democrats receive an advantage because their votes are better distributed among the states, leading to fewer "wasted" votes. That is, Republican candidates, even in close elections, will generally win quite a few states by lopsided margins, while fewer states will return Democratic landslides. Overall, any consistent partisan advantage due to the structure of the electoral college is small, and scholars disagree about which party benefits the most.[146]

When one party is considered more likely to win, either because it has more party identifiers (as the Democrats have had since the Great Depression) or because it holds the presidency (as the Republicans have in most elections since 1972), the strategic alternatives available to the underdog party can hardly be regarded as secret. We consider these possibilities from the perspective of the Republicans, the in party in 2008. First, Republicans can attempt to deemphasize the impact of party habit as a component of electoral choice by promoting a more compelling cue to action. The nomination in 1952 and 1956 of General Dwight D. Eisenhower, the most popular hero of World War II, overrode party considerations and is a clear example of the efficacy of this strategy.[147] Another example would be exploitation of the "rally round the flag," a strategy available to incumbents in time of war, but, as George H. W. Bush discovered in 1992, subject to rapid decay once the war is over. George W. Bush, although not eligible to succeed himself under the Twenty-second Amendment, emphasized the war on terrorism as an issue in the run-up to the 2008 election in an attempt to give an advantage to his fellow Republican candidates.

Efforts to play on popular dissatisfaction in a variety of issue areas, such as economic concerns during a recession, also exemplify the strategy of deemphasizing party, but these dissatisfactions must already exist in the population and must be widespread and intense before they will produce the desired effect. When issues do come to the fore in a compelling way, the payoff to the advantaged party is sometimes enormous because these are the circumstances under which new party loyalties can be created. Or the Republican candidate can do as Ronald Reagan did in 1980 and emphasize popular themes of patriotism and national renewal, while hoping his opponent's personal unpopularity will keep enough Democratic voters at home to make a Republican victory possible. The Republican candidate also can stress the issue differences between his party and the other, as Barry Goldwater did in 1964, Reagan, less stridently, did in 1984, and George H. W. Bush did against Michael Dukakis in 1988. When Democratic policies are popular, as they were in 1964, this tactic is suicidal. But when they are unpopular, as was the case for "liberalism" and "crime" in 1988, stressing differences works very well.

Goldwater thought that conservative elements of the population were alienated from politics and were sitting in the wings, frustrated, immobilized, and without party loyalties, until someone gave them the "choice" they were looking for. In 1964 he called this a "hidden vote" theory. But it was nonsense. What evidence we have points to the probability that the dedicated conservatives sufficiently interested in politics to hold strong opinions about public policy do in fact belong to political parties and participate actively in them. These people are almost all Republicans. This is especially true in the South, where many conservatives—now strong Republican voters—used to vote Democratic.[148]

Another assumption underlying the hidden-vote theory is that in 1964 it would have been possible to attract this mythical vote in substantial numbers without losing the allegiance of large numbers of more moderate people. Not so. Goldwater aroused great antipathy among the general population. Louis Harris surveys found that sizable majorities in the general population defined themselves as opposed to positions they believed Senator Goldwater held.[149] They let him know it at the polls.

NEGATIVE CAMPAIGNING

At various points in a campaign, there may be a temptation for the candidates or parties to let loose a stream of negative advertising about the other side. This may have its greatest effect very early, before the opposition can establish its own image with the voting population. As *The New Republic* explained in response to an outbreak of negative ads in 1986:

> [T]he proliferation of negative ads is simply a result of the consultants' discovery that attacks make a more lasting impression on voters than positive commercials. More candidates are making the attacks personally, rather than working through stand-ins, because research shows that the ads work better that way. The surge in negative advertising has even given rise to the countertactic known as "inoculation": ads designed to answer potential negative ads even before the attacks air.[150]

Of course, the nominees of the two major parties will always differ quite substantially on public policy questions, or on the performance of an incumbent administration. Negative advertising that simply criticizes the other side for its issue positions or record in office is a constant part of every presidential campaign. Somewhat less common, but often effective, is a more personal attack by a candidate or campaign on an opponent—one that claims or implies that he or she is weak, unintelligent, corrupt, mentally unbalanced, dishonest, untrustworthy, morally lax, or even unpatriotic.

Negative campaigning is hardly new to American politics, or even new to television advertising. In 1964, Tony Schwartz produced the most famous political advertisement of its era, the "daisy spot" for the Lyndon Johnson campaign. It shows a little girl standing in an open field, plucking petals from a daisy as she miscounts "four, five, seven, six, six . . . " When she reaches "nine," an ominous voiceover begins a countdown of its own: "ten, nine, eight . . . " At zero, an explosion is heard and a mushroom cloud appears. President Johnson's voice is heard saying, "These are the stakes: to make a world in which all of God's children can live, or to go into the dark. We must love each other or we must die." Like many effective attack ads, the "daisy spot" capitalized on a fear that already existed. Voters saw Barry Goldwater, Johnson's Republican opponent, as a man who might start a nuclear war, and the ad, although it aired only once and never mentioned Goldwater, gained sufficient notoriety to reinforce this perception.[151]

Johnson's campaign also attacked Goldwater for his views on the United Nations, the Social Security Administration, and Medicare. Goldwater responded with his own negative ads, linking the Johnson administration to the "moral decay" of America as the screen filled with pictures of race riots, drug use, alcoholism, and crime. Another spot accused Johnson of corruption and voting fraud.[152]

In the commercial world, this is known as "comparative advertising." The campaign consultants' trade journal *Campaigns and Elections* regularly counsels candidates, in the words of one article title, to "Nail the Opposition."[153] This can be a risky strategy. Research has shown that voters prefer positive, informational advertising that appears to be fair.[154] Negative advertising is not, therefore, the consultants' panacea, but it is a tool to achieve several common campaign objectives: to stigmatize or "characterize" a relatively unknown opponent, to focus the agenda of the campaign on the weaknesses of the other side, or to call attention to an embarrassing blunder on the part of the opposition.[155]

Media consultants pay especially close attention to polling results when devising negative ads because they are risky. In the 1980 primaries, for example, Patrick Caddell's polls revealed that voters disillusioned with President Carter nevertheless liked and trusted him personally. His primary opponent, Edward Kennedy, however, was perceived as untrustworthy. Thus, Gerald Rafshoon, Carter's ad maker, invited a comparison between Carter's and Kennedy's integrity. Concluded one ad: "You may not always agree with President Carter. But you'll never wonder whether he's telling the truth. It's hard to think of a more useful quality in a president than telling the simple truth. President Carter—for the truth." In the general election, the Republicans noted the voters' respect for Carter as a person and so decided to attack his performance in office and not the man himself.[156]

In the 1988 campaign, the results of focus groups and polls were instrumental in devising the ad campaign. The result was a series of harsh negative ads. Why did George H. W. Bush's campaign go on the attack? As his political adviser Roger Ailes explains it, Bush sought to capitalize on the fact that Michael Dukakis was known to very few voters at the beginning of the campaign:

> We always knew we would have to define Dukakis . . . and whichever of us defined the other and ourselves most effectively would win. . . .
>
> You've got to understand that the media has [sic] no interest in substance. Print has a little more interest because they have to fill a lot of lines. But electronic media has no interest in substance.
>
> There are three ways to get on the air: pictures, attacks, and mistakes, so what you do is spend your time avoiding mistakes, staying on the attack and giving them pictures.[157]

In August 2004, an organization calling itself the Swift Boat Veterans for Truth funded a small advertising campaign claiming that Democratic nominee John Kerry did not deserve the Bronze Star and Purple Heart awards he received for his service as a navy lieutenant in the Vietnam War. Though the initial ads cost less than $500,000 and ran in only a few television markets, they were quickly noticed by the national political media, who publicized the unconfirmed charges more widely. While the Swift Boat organization was not officially connected to the George W. Bush campaign (which would have been illegal under campaign finance law), its attacks effectively dovetailed with Bush's own strategy of labeling Kerry a "flip-flopper" who could not be trusted, and Bush refused to condemn the ads.[158] Believing that a response would only give the charges more publicity, the Kerry campaign initially ignored them, counterattacking several weeks later only when polling showed that the allegations were hurting Kerry's standing among voters.[159]

One of the results of the Watergate scandals of the early 1970s was said to have been the advent in the populace at large of a "post-Watergate morality" in which failure to abide by rules of common decency was expected to be strongly disfavored. This did not necessarily provide much guidance to candidates, however. It may, in fact, be a gross violation of common decency, as elites understand such matters, to hurl an accusation at an opponent that forces him or her into a complex explanation that few people will understand. Yet it may be winning politics to indulge in such tactics under the incentives set up by post-Watergate morality. For example, there are frequently adequate and legitimate reasons of public policy for members of Congress to travel abroad on public funds, even if they have a good time doing it. But woe betide the member of Congress who for one reason or another is forced to defend this practice before an aroused electorate.

Many observers claim that Senator Edmund Muskie fatally injured his campaign for the 1972 Democratic nomination by showing too much emotion in response to a Republican smear that falsely branded his wife a bigot. Muskie, it is true, had in many prior campaigns managed with enormous success to show indignation at the moral lapses of opponents who attacked him,[160] but this time something went awry, and he was widely criticized for showing the wrong demeanor. Perhaps on this one occasion he should have taken a leaf from the book of Franklin D. Roosevelt, who paid no attention to most accusations about him but seized on an attack involving his dog, Fala, to rib his opponents unmercifully for impugning an animal that could not reply.[161]

Both Jimmy Carter and Gerald Ford in 1976 passed up opportunities for mudslinging. When it looked like his fortunes were in decline, Carter was urged to link Ford explicitly to Watergate through his pardon of Nixon. Carter refused, saying, "It will rip our country apart."[162] Presented with an opportunity to accuse Carter of corruption in regard to his family peanut business, Ford squelched the matter.[163]

It is ironic that President Richard Nixon and his campaign managers should have sought, in 1972, to adapt to their own uses the tactics they attributed to the far-out left. The contempt of insiders for a political system that nurtures them is a far more serious phenomenon than the antics of dissidents. Yet the Nixon campaign hired people to fake evidence tending to discredit former Democratic presidents and to harass Democratic presidential candidates by playing "dirty tricks" on them (such as ordering the delivery of huge numbers of pizzas to their campaign headquarters in their name). Presumably the passage of laws prohibiting such behavior in the future will be of some help, but the fact that the reelection campaign of a president of the United States sheltered such disgusting behavior is a shameful blot on our history.[164]

Campaign professionals maintain that there is a clear line between legitimate attacks on the record, or even the personal background, of opposing candidates, and illegitimate dirty tricks. They even argue that "comparative" ads are beneficial, because they give voters important information they otherwise might not learn. There is some justification for this view. But the line between fair and unfair is easily blurred.

One relatively new wrinkle in dirty tricks is called "push polling." As we have seen, legitimate polls sometimes test specific pieces of information by telling respondents the story and gauging reactions. In Iowa in 1996, Bob Dole's campaign called potential caucus-goers and under the guise of polling (and without identifying which campaign was making the calls), spread negative information about his Republican opponents.[165]

In the United States we seem to be in a middle position in regard to mudslinging. It is not everyday practice, but neither is it a rarity. It works best, as one might guess, when it is not answered; when it is effectively countered, it can backfire. A glance at the history of presidential campaigns suggests that vituperation is usually irrelevant to the outcomes of campaigns and that it may have the problematic effect of reducing political participation by turning off potential voters.[166] John G. Geer argues, on the other hand, that negative advertising in presidential elections actually focuses more on issues and less on personal characteristics than positive advertising does, thus providing voters with more and better information about their electoral choices.[167] Either way, we expect candidates in the future to turn to negative campaigning and mudslinging when they believe the potential benefits outweigh the risks to their own reputations for fair play and serious attention to the issues of the day.

PRESENTATION OF SELF

Another set of strategic problems concerns the personal impression made by the candidates. A candidate is helped by being thought of as trustworthy, reliable, mature, kind but firm, devoted to family and country, and in every way normal and presentable. No amount of expostulation about the irrelevance of all this ordinariness as qualification for an extraordinary office wipes out the fact that candidates must try to conform to the public stereotype of goodness, a standard that is typically far more demanding of politicians than of ordinary mortals. Gary Hart's precipitous withdrawal from the 1988 race for the Democratic nomination following charges of adultery tells a part of the story. Bill Clinton faced similar charges in 1992, but was able to overcome them, in part, we assume, because the experience of Hart had removed some of the shock factor from the revelations. Clinton also had to face attacks on his avoidance of service in Vietnam—charges Republican running mate Dan Quayle had faced in 1988—as well as investigations into his financial dealings and his well-reported noninhaling marijuana use. Because the media now feel obliged to report on such matters, their importance is bound to grow. Back in John F. Kennedy's time, reporters knew of his philandering but evidently thought it wrong to say so in public.

It would be a painful process for a candidate to remodel his or her entire personality along the indicated lines. And, to be fair, most of the people who run are not so far from the mark as to make this drastic expedient necessary. What the candidates actually try to do is to smooth off the rough edges, to counter what they believe are the most unfavorable impressions of specific aspects of their public image. Kennedy, who in 1960 was accused of being young and immature, hardly cracked a smile in his debates with Nixon, whereas the latter, who was said to be stiff and frightening, beamed with friendliness. Michael Dukakis, suspected of excessively pacific leanings, allowed himself to be driven around in an army tank.[168] George H. W. Bush was told to lower his voice so as to subdue the impression that he was a "wimp."[169] Clinton was told to "talk straight" and avoid smiling too much, for his previous persona had come across as too slick and insincere.[170] After his first 2000 debate with George W. Bush, Al Gore was urged to stop sighing, rolling his eyes, and miming impatience when Bush was speaking. Kennedy restyled his youthful shock of hair, and Nixon thinned his eyebrows to look less threatening. Jimmy Carter made intimate revelations to show he was not cold and calculating but serious and introspective. Gerald Ford was photographed a lot around the White House to show he was in command. Ronald Reagan smiled and ducked when Jimmy Carter tried to portray him as dangerous. And just as Kennedy made it possible for Roman Catholics to be considered for the presidency, Reagan (and Adlai Stevenson) broke the taboo on divorce. John Kerry was both Catholic and divorced without occasioning unfavorable comment on either count.

The little things that some people do not like may be interpreted favorably by other people. Hubert Humphrey was alleged to be a man who could not stop talking. His garrulousness, however, was just another side of his encyclopedic and detailed knowledge of the widest variety of public policies. He might have talked too much to suit some, but the fact that he knew a lot pleased others. Was Bill Clinton thoughtful and full of nuance, or just evasive? (It depends, we suppose, on what "full" means.) Was Ronald Reagan amiable and charming or was that a vacuous expression on his face?

The political folklore of previous campaigns provides candidates with homilies—helpful or not—about how to conduct themselves. Typical bits of advice include the following: always carry the attack to your opponent; the best defense is offense; separate the other candidate from his or her party; when in doubt as to the course that will produce the most votes, do what you believe is right; guard against acts that can hurt you because they are more significant than acts that can help you; avoid making personal attacks that may gain sympathy for the opposition. Unfortunately for the politicians in search of a guide, these bits of folk wisdom do not contain detailed instructions about the conditions under which they should and should not be applied, and they are not altogether internally consistent.

The experience of Adlai Stevenson, the Democratic nominee in 1952 and 1956, suggests a familiar dilemma for candidates. Shall they write (or cause to have written for them) new speeches for most occasions, or shall they rest content to hammer home a few themes, embroidering just a little here and there? No one really knows which is better. Stevenson is famous for the care he took with his speeches and the originality he sought to impart to his efforts. Had he won office, he might have established a trend. Clinton, too, was known for addressing large numbers of issues in his speeches. On the one hand, this tendency contributed to Clinton's image as a highly intelligent man who understood complex issues. On the other hand, he was criticized for being unfocused, scattered, and long-winded.

Most candidates are likely to follow Kennedy and Nixon, Johnson and Goldwater, and Carter and Ford in using just a few set speeches. Ronald Reagan's virtuoso shuffling of his well-worn index cards, with their anecdotes of questionable accuracy, seems to have served him well enough. In view of the pervasive inattention to public affairs and political talk in our society, this approach may have the advantage of driving a few key points home (as well as driving mad the news correspondents who must listen to the same thing all the time).[171] Newspaper and television journalists who cover the campaigns complain quite a lot about the repetitiousness of presidential candidates, as though the campaign should be designed mostly to amuse them. In 1996 Bob Dole frustrated his campaign staff by constantly departing from his prepared text in stump speeches. Dole, an easily bored man, was more concerned that he was boring the reporters in the back of the room by repeating the same lines night after night than he was with making sure that the partisans in the rest of the room would hear his prepared remarks. It did not work. Rather than being pleased with the variety, reporters wrote that Dole's campaign wasn't properly disciplined and organized.[172] This dilemma ranks high on the list of unsolved (and no doubt unsolvable) problems of American democracy: how to get through to the relatively inattentive American people without totally alienating the superattentive mandarins of the news media through whom a candidate ordinarily reaches the rank-and-file voter.

More important, perhaps, is the desirability of appearing comfortable in delivery. Televised speeches are the major opportunities for a candidate to be seen and evaluated by large numbers of people. Eisenhower's ability to project a radiant appearance helped him; Stevenson's obvious discomfort before the camera hurt him. On this point we have evidence that those who listened to Stevenson's delivery over radio were more favorably impressed with him than those who watched him on television.[173] Jimmy Carter's paste-on smile and rigid bearing contrasted poorly with

Ronald Reagan's easy grin and relaxed manner, though these surface indicators, like Gerald Ford's alleged clumsiness, may have nothing to do with performance in office. During his successful campaigns and first term as president, George W. Bush was widely praised for being decisive, folksy, plain-spoken, and comfortable in his own skin, in contrast to his opponents Al Gore and John Kerry, who were often characterized as awkward, insincere, and pedantic. As Bush's popularity began to decline markedly during his second term in office, however, his decisiveness came to be seen by many as stubbornness, and his folksiness as demonstrating a lack of gravity and engagement.

The major difficulty with the tactical principles we have been discussing is not that they are too theoretical but that they do not really tell the candidates what to do when they are mutually incompatible. Like proverbs, one can often find principles to justify opposing courses of action: "Look before you leap," but "He who hesitates is lost." Nixon in 1960 could not take full advantage of his superior command of international affairs without hitting so hard as to reinforce the unfavorable impression of himself as being harsh and unprincipled. Kennedy could hardly capitalize on the Rooseveltian image of the vigorous leader without attacking the foreign policy of a popular president. The result is that the candidates must take calculated risks when existing knowledge about the consequences of alternative courses of action is inadequate. Hunch, intuition, and temperament necessarily play important roles in choosing among competing alternatives.

TELEVISED DEBATES

The famous television debates of 1960 between Vice President Richard Nixon and Senator John F. Kennedy, the first of their kind in American history, provide an excellent illustration of the difficulty of choosing between competing considerations in the absence of knowledge of the most likely results. With the benefit of hindsight, many observers now suggest that Nixon was obviously foolish to engage in the debates. Let us try to look at the situation from the perspective of each of the presidential aspirants at the time.

Kennedy issued a challenge to debate on television. The possible advantages from his point of view were many. He could use a refusal to debate to accuse Nixon of running away and depriving the people of a unique opportunity to judge the candidates. Among Kennedy's greatest handicaps in the campaign were his youth (he was only forty-three years old) and the inevitable charges of inexperience. Television debates could help to overcome these difficulties by showing the audience not so much that Kennedy was superior in knowledge but the two candidates were about equally informed and of similar age and stature. Whatever administrative skills or inside information Nixon might have had as the sitting vice president would not show up on the screen as the candidates necessarily confined themselves to broad discussions of issues known to all politically literate people. Kennedy could only guess but he could not know that Nixon would not stump him in an embarrassing way in front of millions of viewers. But Kennedy understood that despite the reams of publicity he had received, he was unknown to many voters, much less known than the vice president. Here was a golden opportunity to increase his visibility in a sudden and dramatic way. Moreover, his good looks would not hurt him with those who like to judge the appearance of a man.[174]

Nixon was in a more difficult position. Refusing to debate would not have been a neutral decision; it would have subjected him to being called a man who was afraid to face his opposition. Saying yes had a number of possible advantages. One stemmed from the numerical disadvantage of the Republican Party in the electorate at the time. Normally, most people do not pay very much attention to the opposition candidate, making it difficult to win them over. Televised debates would provide a unique instance in which huge numbers of people attracted to both parties could be expected to tune in attentively. Nixon had good reason for believing that if he made a favorable impression, he would be in a position to convince more of the people he needed to convince (weak Democratic identifiers) than would Kennedy. The risk that Kennedy might use the opportunity to solidify the support of Democratic voters simply had to be taken. Another potential advantage that might have occurred to Nixon arose from his previous political life. He had been labeled by some people as "Tricky Dick," an untruthful and vindictive man. This picture could be supplanted on television by the new Nixon of smiling visage and magnanimous gesture who greatly surpassed his opponent in knowledge of public affairs. Nixon had to judge whether his handicap was serious or whether it was confined to confirmed liberals whose numbers were insignificant and who would never vote for him in any event.[175] Perhaps a record of success in debate situations going back to high school was not irrelevant in guiding Nixon to his eventual decision to go on television with his opponent.[176]

Surveys taken after the debates suggest that Nixon miscalculated—that the 1960 debates helped Kennedy.[177] But if Nixon had won the election instead of losing it by a wafer-thin margin, he would hardly have been reminded of any error on his part, and there would probably have been discussions of what a brilliant move it was for him to go on television.

Just four years later, the election of 1964 presented an entirely different set of circumstances. President Johnson, an incumbent enjoying enormous personal popularity at the head of the majority party, had nothing to gain and everything to lose by debating his rival. And so, despite strenuous efforts by Senator Goldwater and his allies to organize another series of televised debates, none was held. By 1968, observers were beginning to question whether candidates would ever again seek an epic confrontation with one another on the 1960 model. What seemed to be required before the occurrence of such a debate was two major candidates equally eager for such a battle. A candidate who is an incumbent, or who feels securely in the lead, has little incentive to jeopardize that position in a debate. Hubert Humphrey pursued Richard Nixon fiercely on this point in 1968, but Nixon prudently refrained from a debate that would needlessly have risked his chances of victory. His excuse for refusing to debate George McGovern in 1972 was that a president in office could not tell all he knew.

Because inertia had begun to work against the idea of debates, the fact that they occurred again in 1976 was somewhat surprising. Neither candidate had been elected to the presidency, but Gerald Ford, the less articulate of the two, was the incumbent president. Although the Democrats did not do especially well in the debates (which included, for the first time, a debate between the vice-presidential nominees as well), Ford's side, the Republicans, which had the most to lose by debating, undoubtedly lost ground twice. One time was when Ford left the impression that in his opinion Poland and Eastern Europe were not under domination at the time by the Soviet Union, a gaffe requiring a subsequent week's worth of "clarifications." The other was when Senator Bob Dole of Kansas, Ford's running mate, misjudged the audience entirely and bounced partisan one-liners ineffectually off the beatific brow of Senator Walter Mondale of Minnesota, thus spoiling one of the few chances the Republicans had to woo Democratic voters.[178]

The strategy of participation in presidential debates was well illustrated in the 1980 Democratic Party primaries. In the fall of 1979 President Carter's public popularity was exceedingly low, Senator Edward Kennedy's was exceedingly high, and Governor Jerry Brown of California was struggling for recognition as a serious candidate. Thus, each of the three candidates had an interest in participation: the president needed it because he was way behind; Senator Kennedy needed it because he was still a challenger; and Governor Brown needed it most of all because he considered himself a good debater and hoped to show that he could hold his own with the front-runners. Then the Iranian seizure of American hostages served almost instantly to raise the president's popularity. Senator Kennedy's popularity plummeted after he gave an embarrassingly bad television interview to Roger Mudd and had difficulty explaining the 1969 Chappaquiddick incident, an accident in which the senator drove his car off a Massachusetts bridge, drowning a young campaign staffer who was his passenger. Thus, the situation changed. President Carter no longer stood to gain a lead but to lose one, so he bowed out of the debates on the grounds that it would be inappropriate to campaign while the hostages were being held, a circumstance that might continue almost indefinitely. The senator and the governor protested in vain. Hurt worst of all, Brown lost the chance to share the limelight with the president, which, at that stage, might have given him the public prominence he needed.

In 1980, there were problems in deciding what to do about including the major independent candidate, Representative John Anderson of Illinois, in debates after the major parties picked their nominees. President Carter refused to publicize Anderson, who he believed was damaging his chances for reelection, and so in the end only one debate took place instead of a series, and it was held very late in the campaign only between Carter and his Republican challenger, Ronald Reagan. On balance it seems to have helped Reagan, who may have lost on high-school debate rules but projected a benignity that was helpfully at odds with the picture of a dangerously radical opponent that Jimmy Carter was trying to paint.[179] So Carter became another incumbent who lost ground by submitting to a televised debate.

There were two presidential debates in 1984; after the first, it looked as if the incumbent had lost ground. President Reagan's performance was followed by a series of negative news and television stories telling the public how badly the president had performed. A *Wall Street Journal* article suggested that perhaps Reagan's age was catching up with him.[180] Challenger Walter Mondale moved up slightly in the polls. Perhaps, it was thought, Mondale could come from behind to win. In the second debate, President Reagan put in a stronger showing, and the age issue was put to rest. "I will not make age an issue of this campaign," the president joked. "I am not going to exploit, for political purposes, my opponent's youth and inexperience."[181] Reagan regained the large lead he had held throughout the campaign and went on to a landslide victory.[182]

Unlike John Anderson in 1980, independent Ross Perot was allowed to participate in the three 1992 presidential debates, at the insistence of George H. W. Bush's campaign. The decision to invite him appears to have been a major strategic error. Apparently, the thinking in the Bush camp was that since Perot was disproportionately hurting their candidate, Bush needed to take him on and show, as one author put it, that Perot was "too small and too shifty to be president."[183] The tactic failed. During the first debate, the overwhelming consensus was that Perot had in fact won the contest. His folksy, quick one-liners were popular with viewers. Both major candidates' dial groups recorded more positive ratings when Perot spoke than anyone had ever seen before.[184] Bush, in contrast, did poorly. He needed to come off as strong and capable; instead, he seemed confused, mangled the one-liners he had practiced, and generally gave a weak performance.[185] Bill Clinton did better, but his performance was still second to Perot's.

The second debate in 1992 used a new format—questions from a specially selected studio audience of voters rather than from news media personalities, as was traditional. This format, known as a "town hall" debate, favored Bill Clinton, and he was indeed the winner by media consensus. Perot, being short, refused to sit on the stools provided, as his two opponents did, because his feet would not touch the floor. Instead, he stood awkwardly and his discomfort permeated his performance. Overall, Bush did fairly well, but one major gaffe marred his performance and that was all the press would discuss for days afterward. A woman from the audience asked him what effect the "deficit" had had on him personally. She probably meant to say the "recession" but misspoke, and Bush did not understand her meaning. "I'm not sure I get it," Bush said, essentially confirming the message the Clinton campaign had been putting forward throughout the year: Bush was out of touch with voters, he didn't even acknowledge that there was economic distress in the country, much less suffer from it himself.[186] There was a third debate, but it had no major impact on the race.[187]

In 1996, Bill Clinton and his Republican challenger, Bob Dole, debated twice. Dole wanted four debates, but the incumbent—with a large lead in the polls—agreed to only two. Perot, far behind in the race and without the benefit of Bush's mistaken strategy, was not invited this time. The innovation from 1992, the "town hall" format, was retained for the second debate. However, this time the debates produced few memorable moments, and appeared to change little in the race.[188]

Though Democrat Al Gore was not an incumbent president in 2000, he faced the same danger most incumbents do in presidential debates: the burden of high expectations. Gore's reputation as a disciplined, "on-message" speaker with an impressive command of facts and figures contrasted with Republican nominee George W. Bush's public persona as a man less interested in the details of public policy and prone to the occasional malapropism. As with the results of presidential primaries, journalists tend to designate winners and losers in debates based on which candidates exceed or fall short of expectations—a point grasped by the Bush campaign, which sought to influence these expectations before the first event by referring to their opponent as a "world-class debater" while suggesting that any performance by their own candidate which did not end in embarrassment would be a significant victory.[189] Indeed, Bush held his own in the first debate with no major gaffes, while Gore's aggressive style—repeatedly interrupting Bush and moderator Jim Lehrer and sighing into his microphone at many of Bush's responses—prompted critical comments from media observers. The day before the second debate, worried campaign staffers forced Gore to watch a parody of his performance on the sketch comedy program *Saturday Night Live*, in which actor Darrell Hammond portrayed the vice president as a condescending know-it-all who obsessively repeated the word "lockbox" (Gore's metaphor for his plan to protect Social Security and Medicare funding), who responded to a question asked of Bush as if it were his turn to speak, and who asked for the chance to deliver two closing statements.[190] In the collective media judgment, Gore overcompensated in the subsequent debate, at times appearing excessively deferential to Bush. In the end, though polls showed that viewers were about evenly split over which candidate won, the debates in 2000 were a disappointment to Gore campaign staff who hoped to use them to demonstrate their candidate's strengths, while the Bush side claimed victory since their man performed better than expected.[191]

The 2004 presidential debates reinforced the historical trend that debates, when they matter at all, usually help the challenging candidate. The first debate, held on the topic of foreign policy on September 30 in Coral Gables, Florida, and featuring a single moderator, was generally judged as a victory for Democrat John Kerry—or, rather, a loss for George W. Bush. Media observers focused less on the substantive content of the candidates' responses to questions than on their bearing and body language. Bush was captured several times on camera making disapproving faces while Kerry was speaking, and seemed generally ill at ease and annoyed by his opponent, fidgeting at his podium and occasionally speaking in broken sentences.[192] The second and third debates—a "town hall" debate held in St. Louis, Missouri, on October 8 and an event focusing on domestic policy in Tempe, Arizona, on October 13—proved less eventful, although Kerry caused a stir at the final debate by mentioning Vice President Dick Cheney's daughter Mary in response to a question about gay marriage.[193] Overall, the debates seemed to help Kerry slightly more than Bush. Kerry improved his standing in the polls over the period that the events were held, drawing nearly even with his Republican opponent in many surveys by the middle of October.[194]

The strategic imperatives surrounding debates seem to be emerging with some clarity. Debates can hurt incumbents. Challengers have far less to lose and may gain in stature simply by keeping their countenance and appearing on the same stage as the holder of high public office. Opinion makers and the custodians of the flame of disinterested public spiritedness seem agreed that debates are wonderful exercises in public enlightenment. This scarcely seems credible to minimally intelligent viewers of the actual debates we have had, in which candidates' facial expressions, tones of voice, and use of clever one-liners have often been judged more important to the outcome than any substantive discussion of public policy. Still, this belief in the value of debates nevertheless exists and may force candidates to participate even when they are more likely to be hurt than helped by the experience.[195]

Indeed, there is growing sentiment to institutionalize debates so that the number and format of events will no longer be a matter for the candidates to decide for themselves. In the beginning, presidential debates were run as a public service by the League of Women Voters, who represented a nonpartisan perspective in working out the arrangements. This meant that the candidates could protect their own interests in deciding whether to debate and under what conditions. Much haggling took place over ground rules, as anxieties in the camps of candidates ran high over such matters as use of the presidential seal on the podium, or bad camera angles, or which journalists would appear as moderators or to ask questions. In 1987 the Democratic and Republican national committees formed a bipartisan commission to determine the format (number, location, ground rules) and run the debates. This was designed to reduce the power of candidates to influence the conditions under which they would appear. In a joint statement explaining why they thought they should control the debates, Paul G. Kirk Jr., chairman of the Democratic National Committee, and Frank J. Fahrenkopf Jr., chairman of the Republican National Committee, stated that "we will better fulfill our party responsibilities; to inform and educate the electorate, strengthen the role of political parties in the electoral process and most important of all, we can institutionalize the debates, making them an integral and permanent part of the presidential process."[196]

Once a candidate is nominated, however, the leverage of the national committee to compel participation largely disappears. Candidates find most of the alternative formats that have been suggested to them too risky. And so the Presidential Debate Commission has had not much more power over these events than the League of Women Voters used to have. The commission certainly had no such power in 1992 when debates were held under its auspices. For months, the Bush campaign delayed agreement on the debates because it disagreed with the format and because the candidate was not enthusiastic about participating. The Clinton team seized on the situation, playing up their willingness to participate and Bush's reluctance to debate their candidate. The Democrats even took to sending a staffer dressed up like a chicken to Bush's campaign appearances.

Eventually the criticism and a drop in Bush's poll ratings made debating essential to the president's campaign. Having reached this conclusion, Bush's people tried to win back some momentum by challenging Clinton to a series of six debates, one every Sunday until Election Day. The Clinton campaign demurred, saying they preferred to stick with the format originally devised by the commission—three presidential debates and one for vice-presidential candidates. After a meeting between the campaign representatives, the Clinton team got essentially what it wanted—three debates crammed into little more than a week with two weeks to spare before the election—time to recover, they hoped, if anything went wrong.[197] This confirms the view that debates are important campaign events primarily because of the chance that a candidate might make a major mistake or gaffe, not because they provide public enlightenment or reveal the capacity of each party's nominee to govern the nation.

BLUNDERS

One hears much about campaign blunders, as if there really were objective assurance that a different course of action would have turned out better for the unfortunate candidate. An example was Republican nominee Thomas E. Dewey's decision in 1948 to mute the issues, which was said to have snatched defeat from the jaws of victory.[198] A vigorous campaign on Dewey's part, it was said, would have taken the steam out of Democrat Harry Truman's charges and would thus have brought him victory. Perhaps. What we know of the 1948 election suggests that it provoked a higher degree of voting on the basis of economic class than any of the elections that succeeded it.[199] A slashing attack by Dewey, therefore, might have polarized the voters even further. This would have increased Truman's margin, since there are many more people with low than with high incomes. Had the election gone the other way—and a handful of votes in a few states would have done it—we would have heard much less about Dewey's strategic blunder and much more about how unpopular Truman was in 1948.

A whole series of "mistakes" have been attributed to Richard Nixon in 1960, the year he lost the election to John F. Kennedy by a very small margin. Here are two, culled from Theodore H. White's bestselling book on the 1960 campaign. On the civil rights plank of the Republican platform:

> The original draft plank prepared by the Platform Committee was a moderate one. . . . This plank, as written, would almost certainly have carried the Southern states for Nixon and, it seems in retrospect, might have given him victory. . . . On Monday, July 25th, it is almost

certain, it lay in Nixon's power to reorient the Republican Party toward an axis of Northern-Southern conservatives. His alone was the choice.... Nixon insisted that the Platform Committee substitute for the moderate position in civil rights (which probably would have won him the election) the advanced Rockefeller position on civil rights.... [200]

On Nixon's failure to protest the imprisonment of Martin Luther King Jr., during the campaign:

> He had made the political decision at Chicago to court the Negro vote in the North, only now, apparently, he felt it quite possible that Texas, South Carolina, and Louisiana might all be won by him by the white vote and he did not wish to offend that vote. So he did not act—there was no whole philosophy of politics to instruct him. [201]

Hindsight is capable of converting every act of a losing candidate into a blunder. Victory can have the same effect in reverse. Consider the situation of Richard Nixon, 1968 version, as he dealt with the same southern-white/northern-black dilemma, in the same way. In the 1968 election, Nixon, again the Republican candidate, was facing Democratic nominee Hubert Humphrey as well as third-party candidate George Wallace, who was running on a platform of racial segregation. Theodore White reports:

> Nixon had laid it down, at the Mission Bay gathering, that none of his people, North or South, were to out-Wallace Wallace. He insisted, as he was to insist to the end of the campaign, that he would not divide the country; he wanted a campaign that would unify a nation so he could govern it. To compete with Wallace in the South on any civilized level was impossible.... Instead, Nixon would challenge Wallace in the peripheral states—Florida, North Carolina, Virginia, Tennessee, South Carolina.... It was only later that the trap within this strategy became evident—for, to enlarge his base in the Northern industrial states, Nixon would have to reach across the rock-solid Republican base there, across center, to the independents, the disenchanted Democrats, to the ghettos. But to do that would be to shake the peripheral strategy in the new South. And to hold to the course he had set for the peripheral strategy limited his call in the North. [202]

Nixon's strategy was aimed, in both years, at chipping off the "peripheral" southern states—then part of the solidly Democratic south—while not taking such a strong anti-civil rights position as to bring northern black voters to the polls in great numbers and to turn northern suburban whites against him.

In 1968, of course, he won; his margin over 1960 consisted of North Carolina, South Carolina, Illinois, and New Jersey. Would it have been a gain for him to "out-Wallace Wallace"? Not likely, in view of the heavy margins Wallace piled up in the states he did carry (Alabama, Arkansas, Georgia, Louisiana, and Mississippi) and his inability to do very well elsewhere. Would it have been a gain for Nixon to repudiate all possible anti-civil rights votes? Not likely, in view of the near unanimity against him of the black vote and probably of most strongly pro-civil rights white liberals. In short, did his strategy of equivocation almost win or almost lose the presidency for Richard Nixon in 1960 and/or 1968? Absent the opportunity to rerun these elections with different strategies, no one can say.

More recently, Michael Dukakis in 1988 declared that the presidential campaign would be about "competence, not ideology." But he did not campaign competently, failing to answer the barrage of charges George H. W. Bush's campaign made in its attempt to introduce Dukakis, unfavorably, to the mass of American voters who had never heard of him. The list of Dukakis's campaign errors, real and alleged, is a long one. The should-haves and should-not-haves are legion. When asked in one debate what he would do if his wife were raped and murdered—a question, one must observe, that candidates are not usually asked—Dukakis took it not as a signal to pour out his emotions, an act he viewed with distaste, but as a request for the recitation of the kind of governmental policies that might cut down on rapes and murders. This, according to the consensus media interpretation, showed that he lacked emotion and was heartless.

Dukakis's critics spoke of a "candidate possessed of little understanding of the voters or the election and, more important, of a candidate offering no compelling message or rationale for his campaign."[203] The first part of the criticism is merely a restatement of the fact that he lost, for had he won he would obviously have possessed the correct understanding. As for the second, he did offer a message, which was that he was the more competent of the two and that his party had better answers to the questions facing the American people. This was not, to be sure, the answer his critics wanted to hear, but it was his genuine answer, and it might have served him well if the electorate had felt they were in bad straits and needed a competent president.

As the *Times Mirror* National Survey reported in late September 1988, more voters were satisfied with the way things were going in America than were dissatisfied, and this represented a change in the final few months before the election.[204] Dukakis's detractors wanted him to portray himself as a populist (i.e., more liberal), claiming this would have rescued his campaign from the beginning. Not according to anything we know. The *Times Mirror* poll, in its own words, "shows that Bush has succeeded in portraying the Massachusetts governor as a liberal by focusing on such issues as Dukakis's prison furlough program, his veto of 'pledge of allegiance' legislation, and his opposition to major weapons systems." Whereas 31 percent thought Dukakis was a liberal in June, when he had a huge lead over Bush, 46 percent considered him a liberal in September, when his support had dropped precipitously. We therefore may well suspect that being perceived as liberal was not the best thing that could happen to a candidate. Indeed, the proportion of people in the electorate who considered themselves to be more conservative than Dukakis increased from 22 percent in June to 35 percent three months later.[205]

Over and over again, Dukakis told his campaign managers that he would not engage in mudslinging no matter what the provocation. Presumably this eminently desirable position was seen as a source of weakness.[206] "How many times do I have to tell you?" an aide heard him say, "That's not me."

Candidate Dukakis was also governor of Massachusetts and felt he should abide by a pledge to the citizens of that state to spend several days a week doing the job. He might have done better had he put full time into the campaign.[207] There were other faults. Dukakis failed to answer questions about national defense, which is, after all, a major presidential responsibility. He did not intervene to decide how to halt damaging internal squabbles in his campaign team. Almost from the beginning, the organization of the campaign was poor in that phones were not answered, supplies were not provided, activities were not coordinated.[208] By September 1989, Dukakis had learned how to blame himself. "I have reluctantly come to the conclusion," he told students at the University of California, "that if they throw mud at you, you've got to throw it back."[209]

The problem, in our opinion, was not the candidate but the party. By the beginning of October 1988, according to the Gallup poll, Republicans led the Democrats by wide margins on the two big issues of peace and prosperity. Another large-scale national poll, taken early in May when Dukakis was supposed to have lost his edge, shows that except for items on which Bush's long experience in national government gave him an edge, Dukakis came out very well.[210] What happened as a result of cumulative developments, including the fading of the Iran-Contra incident and the warming of relations between the United States and the Soviet Union, was that voter optimism began to rise. President Reagan's popularity went way up; confidence in the economy was rising. "Simply put," John Dillon wrote for the *Christian Science Monitor*, "Americans are feeling better about things."[211] The highest level of support for Dukakis naturally came from those citizens who felt that times were getting worse. Sixty-two percent of them voted for him. "Unfortunately for Dukakis," as Dillon commented, "there just aren't enough of those people."[212]

No election campaign is without its faults. What are we to make of Vice President Bush's explanation—that his supporters were at country clubs helping their daughters come out in society—for his relatively poor showing in the 1988 Iowa caucuses? His Freudian slips might have become legendary. But he won. In 1992 he was not so lucky, and the many mistakes Bush made caught up with him. Perhaps the first crucial mistake was to deny the existence of the economic recession of 1991–1992 and to refuse to put together a legislative proposal to address the situation. From record high approval ratings after the Gulf War, Bush's popularity plummeted as he was increasingly seen as "out of touch" with the country. A second mistake compounded the first—Bush dragged his feet in starting his campaign. Many close associates suggested that Bush himself was uncertain that he even wanted to run again until late in 1991.[213]

Although Bush did declare his candidacy for reelection and did indeed end up campaigning, his uncertainty remained and seemed to permeate his campaign. His staff tried to convince Bush to "get a plan" and stick to it, but his proposals seemed to change almost daily. When the campaign finally came up with a domestic and economic agenda for a second Bush term, its presentation was mishandled. Bush's unveiling of the new plan was scheduled for a rally in Detroit, but the expected press coverage failed to materialize owing to advance team oversights.[214] The campaign was not able even to use video images of the speech—one of Bush's best during the campaign—because the camera platforms had not been properly reinforced and the resulting film footage was shaky and unfocused.[215]

Republican candidate Bob Dole's campaign in 1996 certainly had its share of blunders. Like Dukakis in 1988, Dole hesitated in responding to attack ads. Like Bush in 1992, Dole had difficulty settling on campaign themes and strategies. All three suffered from internal dissension in their campaigns. Decisions never seemed to be made. For example, Dole was given two drafts for his convention speech, one nostalgic and one future oriented. Rather than choose one, he patched them together, delivering a two-headed speech that was reviewed as inconsistent and confused.

Dole had other difficulties. A good example was the fate of an ingenious plan his campaign hit on for the first debate. To remind voters of scandals associated with Bill Clinton, and especially to throw the incumbent off his stride, the Dole campaign arranged for Billy Dale, the former head of the White House Travel Office (and the victim, or so Republicans argued, of Clinton corruption), to have a prominent seat in the audience. With any luck, Clinton would be distracted, or possibly even lose his cool. Alas, Bill Clinton had no idea what Billy Dale looked like; the incident wound up as nothing more than another chance for the press to remark on the Dole camp's inadequacies.[216]

Clinton was reelected easily, so it is easy to dwell on Dole's campaign weaknesses. Again, this can be taken too far. A list of Clinton campaign blunders and problems in 1996 would be almost as long. Right before the Democratic convention, the campaign lost its chief strategist, Dick Morris, to a sex scandal. Gleeful reaction to Morris's downfall by many in the White House proved that the Dole campaign had no monopoly on internal dissension. Whether to classify various White House scandals as campaign blunders is a judgment call, but scandals involving how money was raised during the campaign certainly would qualify. When Bob Dole became personally involved in campaign strategy, he was seen as incapable of delegating; when Bill Clinton did the same thing, he was praised for his political instincts.[217] None of this means that campaigns are irrelevant, only that blunders in losing campaigns are the ones that are remembered. No campaign is perfect; winning campaigns only seem so in retrospect.

Consider the 2000 election, ultimately decided by a Supreme Court ruling after several weeks of recounts and lawsuits over the treatment of ballots in the State of Florida. In the view of most observers, including many bitter Democrats, Al Gore gave away the election by failing to emphasize the economic prosperity of the nation under the Clinton administration. Gore's debate performance was roundly criticized, as was his low-key, uninspiring public persona, for costing him the race. Yet Gore finished first in the national popular vote, and probably would have won the electoral vote as well if not for a flawed, confusing ballot design in one Florida county that apparently led many votes intended for Gore to be counted instead for Reform Party candidate Pat Buchanan. Had Gore prevailed in the Florida recount, he would have been credited for running an effective campaign instead of facing accusations of political incompetence.

George W. Bush, by contrast, was seen as a particularly skilled candidate. His chief strategist, Karl Rove, has often been labeled a political "genius." Yet a different outcome in Florida would have forced Bush and Rove to return to Texas as utter failures. Rove sent Bush to campaign in California during the weekend before the 2000 election, on the theory that a visit by the candidate to a state considered safe for the Democrats would inspire a flurry of news stories about how confident the Bush campaign was of victory. Late-deciding voters, Rove argued, would interpret this coverage as a sign that Bush was going to prevail in the election, and would eagerly jump on the bandwagon of a likely winner, producing a self-fulfilling prophecy. This was almost certainly a misguided strategy that would have led to endless second-guessing in Republican circles had Bush, not Gore, lost the election by a few hundred votes in Florida.

Criticism of John Kerry's campaign after his own narrow loss to Bush in 2004 seemed to combine the widely-identified mistakes of Gore in 2000 (stiff, elitist, overly programmed, unappealing candidate) with those of Dukakis in 1988 (personal weakness, failure to respond to attacks from the opposition). Yet Kerry competed effectively with the allegedly more popular Bush throughout the entire campaign, and came within a single state of winning the presidency. Bush enjoyed not only the usual advantages of incumbency, but had seen his job approval rise to near-record levels after the terrorist attacks of 2001. His strikingly risky strategy—again, primarily masterminded by Rove—of advocating strongly conservative policies in order to mobilize the party "base" ultimately alienated a majority of independent voters and nine out of every ten Democrats, leaving little electoral margin for error. Bush's slim victory left him without the ability to claim a broad popular mandate for his ambitious policy agenda. The centerpiece of his second-term domestic program, partial privatization of the Social Security system, quickly foundered in Congress, and further deterioration of the conditions in U.S.-occupied Iraq led directly to significant Democratic gains in the 2006 midterm elections, leaving Bush's legacy in question. A more centrist, conciliatory approach to governing during his first term might well have given Bush a more decisive victory in 2004, and would have better preserved his political standing in the face of subsequent adversity.

Should the candidate arrive at a coherent strategy that fits reasonably well with what is known of the political world, he or she will still find that the party organization has an inertia in favor of its accustomed ways of doing things. The party workers, on whom candidates are dependent to some extent, have their own ways of interpreting the world, and a candidate disregards this point of view at some risk. Should the candidate fail to appear in a particular locality as others have done, the party workers may feel slighted. More important, they may interpret this as a sign that the candidate has written off that area and they may slacken their own efforts.

Suppose the candidate decides to divert funds from campaign buttons and stickers to polls and television or transportation, as during the years before soft money, campaigns were more or less required to do given expenditure limitations under the federal subsidy? The candidate may be right in believing that the campaign methods he or she prefers will bring more return from the funds that are spent. But let the party faithful interpret this as a sign that the candidate is losing—where, oh where, are those familiar indications of popularity?—and their low morale may encourage a result that bears out this dire prophecy. An innovation in policy may shock the loyal followers of the party. It may seem to go against time-honored precepts that are not easily unlearned. Could a Republican convince the party that a balanced budget is not sacred? Or a Democrat that it is? Both parties adopted these views, innovative for them, in 1984. But it left each of them unhappy. The Democrats were left without the rationale for deficit spending in behalf of good causes that had kept them going since the 1930s. The Republicans, who were in office when Reagan built up deficits of unprecedented size in peacetime, had more to worry about. Any adverse economic results—a too-high or too-low dollar on world markets, inflation, lack of industrial competitiveness, unemployment, a cloud of dust keeping food from growing—would surely be attributed to the deficit.

Anthropologists tell us that everyone in the tribe knows what happens when a taboo is violated: bad things happen. If Republicans are not more frugal than Democrats, what are they good for? A selling job may have to be done on the rank and file; otherwise they may sit on their hands during the campaign. It may make better political sense (if less intellectual sense) to phrase the new in old terms and make the departure seem less extreme than it might actually be. The value of the issue in the campaign may thus be blunted. The forces of inertia and tradition may be overcome by strong and persuasive candidates; the parties are greatly dependent on their candidates and have little choice but to follow them, even if haltingly. But in the absence of a special effort, in the presence of enormous uncertainties and the inevitable insecurities, the forces of tradition may do as much to shape a campaign as the overt decisions of the candidates.

BOX 5.3 COUNTING THE VOTE

How votes are counted—how efficiently and how accurately—becomes interesting mostly when elections are close. This therefore became a significant issue in the 2000 election. On election night it appeared that the Democratic candidate, Vice President Al Gore, led the Republican candidate, Texas Governor George W. Bush, very narrowly in popular votes nationwide, and that the candidates were virtually tied in the electoral college. The outcome of the entire election depended on the popular vote in the state of Florida, a state in which—to put it mildly—there were complications in the administration and the mechanics of voting and vote counting.

Each county in the state had its own ballot type and format, and in at least one populous county the ballot was laid out in a way that caused voters to be confused about how to indicate their preferences.[1] In numerous locations, ballots were cast that could not be counted by the machinery available to produce an automatic count and issues therefore arose about whether, and how, these ballots could be counted by hand.

The settlement of these issues required an appeal to the Florida judiciary, but the Florida Supreme Court's ruling was preempted by a decision of the U.S. Supreme Court more or less along partisan lines to take jurisdiction and to halt the counting of ballots that had to be examined manually, awarding the official popular vote in the state to George W. Bush by a 537-vote margin (2,912,790 to 2,912,253). As a result, Bush received Florida's 25 electors and won the election with 271 total electoral votes, one more than a majority.[2]

The Supreme Court's decision to intervene in the vote-counting process was highly irregular, or at least highly unusual. Election administration has in general been treated as a matter to be dealt with by the states, and the very justices who stepped in to overrule the Florida courts had been in the vanguard of the judicial movement to uphold state responsibility on all sorts of issues.[3] There were, of course, important questions about the capacity of the State of Florida to count by hand the thousands of disputed ballots in a timely fashion and using impartial standards, but, according to the rules of the game until they were upended by the narrow Supreme Court majority, this headache had been squarely allocated to state- and county-level officials.[4]

The legal issues raised by the conduct of the 2000 election and the court case *Bush v. Gore* will resonate for some time, judging from the volume of commentary generated in law journals and elsewhere.[5] The relevant political issues are somewhat easier to identify. They come under the following headings:

1. The winner in the electoral college actually lost the national popular vote for the first time since 1888, but constitutional rules governing the outcome are evidently so well settled that there was no serious claim that President Bush's entitlement to hold office was in any way impaired. Indeed he not only assumed office without difficulty, but was free to interpret his mandate to govern without much concern for the narrowness of his victory. The 2000 election renewed calls from some

quarters for the reform or abolition of the electoral college, but these proposals never gained significant support among members of Congress or state legislatures.

2. The entire topic of election administration needs thorough ventilation. In fact, not much information is widely available on this subject. We know that different states administer elections differently, that there are several kinds of machinery used for recording and counting ballots, each with technical imperfections, that legal requirements for uniformity are themselves not uniform, and that ballots in different localities differ in their contents and design.[6] There may be systematic flaws that deprive different subgroups in the population of equal access to the ballot or equal treatment in the counting of their votes.[7] Ballot design and electoral administration have, as the result of the 2000 election, become matters for intensive further study.

3. There has been an assumption that on the whole votes in presidential elections are counted more or less as cast. The slovenly performance of the State of Florida in 2000 in accurately and efficiently determining the voting preferences of its citizens suggests that this assumption may be wrong, and not only in Florida. As a matter of political strategy, one presidential candidate, Governor Bush, strenuously worked to prevent Florida ballots that did not register a preference on the automatic machinery from being counted at all. Impartial studies after the fact by news organizations established that he needn't have worried; if they had been counted he would have won anyway.[8] The spectacle of a candidate for public office going to court to attempt to deprive voters of their vote is nonetheless worth contemplating.

Voters who go to the polls on Election Day currently use one of six major voting methods. The simplest is a *paper ballot*, filled out by hand (usually by marking an X next to the names of preferred candidates), and then manually counted by elections officials. This system, though at one time the most common method of tallying the votes, is now used only in small or rural jurisdictions in which the number of ballots and candidates is low and each ballot can be personally inspected.

A modern version of the paper ballot is the *optical scan ballot*, which uses a method familiar to anyone who has taken a standardized test or bought a lottery ticket: voters use a pen or pencil to fill in an oval corresponding to a candidate or connect two sections of an arrow next to the candidate's name. A machine then scans the paper, recording which candidates are chosen. Optical scan systems are now in widespread use across the United States. They are popular because ballots can be counted automatically by machine, yet a paper ballot remains that can be examined manually if the scanner malfunctions.

About 13 percent of voters in 2004 used *lever machines*, in which the voter pushes down small switches next to the names of each candidate. Before the voter leaves the machine, he or she pulls a large lever to open the curtain. This activates mechanical counters on the back of the machine that register the vote and keep a running tally for each candidate. Counting the vote merely requires election officials to inspect the vote counters on the machine after the polls have closed. Lever machines are no longer manufactured in the United States and are therefore becoming less common as a vote-counting mechanism.

A growing number of jurisdictions use *electronic systems*: the voter indicates the candidates he or she wishes to vote for via a computer touchscreen, and the results are saved on memory cards that are then processed once the polls close. While touchscreen machines became more prevalent nationwide after the 2000 election exposed the defects of punch card ballots, they have been criticized for being vulnerable to voter fraud via surreptitious reprogramming. Even if a machine simply malfunctions, a recount is impossible unless the system provides paper backup. This issue arose in the 2006 midterm election, when a large number of touchscreen machines in Sarasota County, Florida mysteriously failed to register voter preferences in a hard-fought congressional race.[9] For this reason, a growing number of states and localities are requiring electronic systems to provide a "paper trail."

Finally, there are two systems that require voters to punch bits of cardboard out of an individual cardboard ballot, which is then fed into a machine for counting. A *Datavote* machine uses a mechanical punch to register votes, while the ballots in a *Votomatic* system come with small rectangles that are perforated so that they will detach when the voter punches them with a pointed instrument. Votomatic machines have been popular in the United States because they allow for easy and inexpensive administration of elections. However, use of a Votomatic system requires individual voters to line up a book with the names of the candidates and offices to correspond with the ballot in order to register their votes in different columns. This system leads many voters to make mistakes. They may cast multiple votes in error, or they may not register votes for any candidate.

Additionally, problems arise with the perforated bits of paper, called chads, which sometimes are not completely dislodged from the ballot. When a voter casts more votes than permitted in a race, this is called an overvote and the ballot is classified as invalid. Sometimes, the Votomatic counting machine records that a voter has not cast any votes in a race when close human examination of the ballot paper shows a clear intention to vote; this is known as an undervote. In most jurisdictions, this limitation of the Votomatic system was well known before 2000, and procedures accordingly existed in most jurisdictions for manual recounts in contests where the result was very close. Even so, manual recounts do not necessarily provide a clear result; the controversy over the 2000 recount in Florida was compounded by the state's widespread use of punch card ballots. It is difficult to impose an objective standard for determining voter intent from a ballot on which the chad can be "detached," "hanging" (three of four corners detached from the ballot), "swinging" (two corners detached from the ballot), or even "pregnant" (not detached but bulging). The adoption of different standards for counting disputed ballots in different counties led to intense partisan disagreement over the validity of the outcome in Florida.

The Florida recount was further clouded by the virtual certainty that the votes of some demographic groups were lost at higher rates than others. Research has demonstrated that undervotes using punch card technology occur at disproportionately high rates in precincts with high proportions of minorities and low-education voters, though the specific mechanism for this is not fully understood. In places where punch card systems have been abandoned in favor of optical scan or electronic systems, the proportion of undervotes has declined regardless of the racial or educational profile of the voting population.[10] Electronic systems can also prevent overvotes, since the election software will not permit an individual to vote for two or more candidates for any single-member office.

The Help America Vote Act (HAVA), enacted by Congress in 2002, married Democratic concerns about uncounted votes with Republican concerns about voter fraud. In addition to providing almost $4 billion in federal funding for the purchase and implementation of new voting systems by state election administrators, HAVA required the creation of statewide voter registration lists and that persons registering to vote supply a driver's license number or social security number, set requirements for disabled access to voting equipment, and established a voter's right to cast a provisional ballot in the event that his or her name did not appear on the registration rolls. The legislation also requires that states establish uniform standards describing what constitutes a valid vote.[11]

As a result of the Florida recount and the passage of HAVA, many states and municipalities have replaced old voting equipment with newer machines. In 2000, over 20 percent of counties in the United States used punch card ballots; by the 2006 midterm election, more than three-quarters of these counties had moved to other voting technologies. Over 80 percent of voters now use either optical scan or electronic voting systems; 10 percent (mostly in New York) continue to use lever machines; another 7 percent of voters live in counties using a combination of systems, mostly optical scan and electronic.[12] A number of states have taken advantage of federal funding to replace their voting equipment; others, while not requiring a uniform system, have acted as intermediaries between vendors and counties, negotiating lower purchase prices and thus substantially reducing the within-state variation in machine type.

Facing another close presidential election in 2004, both the Republican and Democratic parties mobilized large teams of poll-watchers and lawyers to monitor election procedures in several states where the vote margins were expected to be narrow. Though the presidential contest transpired without major problems, irregularities in a state-level election in North Carolina and an extremely close and disputed result in the Washington governor's race showed that voting in the United States did not yet meet high standards for accuracy or reliability. Since 2004, electronic voting machines have been scrutinized by computer scientists and others worried about the possibility of hackers reprogramming the machines to register incorrect results. Many of those already in use give the voter no written assurance that a vote has been recorded and cannot be upgraded to provide such a "paper trail." While most advocates of vote verification in electronic systems are concerned about the possibility of intentional manipulation of vote totals, the simple malfunction of a machine is a more likely event. As Americans increasingly engage in early voting, an individual machine is sometimes used to record several thousand votes over a period of days or weeks. Erasure of these votes could throw a close contest into question.

It should be recalled that despite intense division over the 2000 presidential result, at no point did a crisis develop. Armies did not mobilize. Tanks did not rumble in the streets. There was never a moment when the politicians responsible for the flow of events could not refer to valid laws stipulating what they were supposed to do. Though the problematic punch card system primarily responsible for the Florida controversy has almost completely disappeared from American voting booths, no system can completely eliminate inaccuracy or the possibility of a disputed election. For the foreseeable future, close elections will no doubt stimulate careful attention to election procedures from experts and others with legal training, as was the case in 2004. Greater oversight of election administration and the adoption of better voting technology may reduce the likelihood that another presidential election will be decided by the courts on the basis of disputed results.

[1] The design of the ballot in Palm Beach County probably led a number of voters intending to vote for Democratic nominee Al Gore to cast ballots instead for Reform Party candidate Pat Buchanan. This alone may have cost Gore the presidency. See Henry E. Brady, Michael C. Herron, Walter R. Mebane Jr., Jasjeet Singh Sekhon, Kenneth W. Shotts, and Jonathan Wand, "Law and Data: The Butterfly Ballot Episode," *PS: Political Science and Politics* 34 (March 2001): 59–69.

[2] The U.S. Supreme Court first became involved in the Florida recount legal struggle on November 24, 2000 (*Bush v. Palm Beach County Canvassing Board*, 531 U.S. 1004). The Court granted a stay sought by Bush halting the recount of ballots ordered by the Florida Supreme Court on December 9 (*Bush v. Gore*, 531 U.S. 1046), foreshadowing its eventual five-to-four decision on the merits in Bush's favor on December 12 (*Bush v. Gore*, 531 U.S. 98). Al Gore formally conceded the election in a nationwide address the following day. All of the justices who favored Bush had been appointed by Republican presidents; two of the justices on the other side had also been Republican appointees.

[3] For example, the same five justices who ruled in Bush's favor constituted the majority striking down provisions of the federal Gun-Free School Zones Act of 1990 (*U.S. v. Lopez*, 514 U.S. 549) and the Violence Against Women Act of 1994 (*U.S. v. Morrison*, 529 U.S. 598) on federalism grounds, arguing that Congress infringed upon the constitutional rights of the states by enacting such legislation.

[4] Article II, Section 1 of the Constitution explicitly grants states the authority to determine how their presidential electors are chosen. Though all states now select their electors by popular vote (and all except Maine and Nebraska employ a winner-take-all system), this method is not constitutionally required; the legislatures in most states chose members of the electoral college until the 1830s. Though the Constitution requires popular election of the House of Representatives (and, since 1913, the Senate), the administration of elections to federal office is left to the states. See Paul S. Herrnson, "Improving Election Technology and Administration: Toward a Larger Federal Role in Elections?" *Stanford Law and Policy Review* 13 (2002): 147–159.

[5] See, for example, Howard Gillman, *The Votes That Counted: How the Court Decided the 2000 Election* (Chicago: University of Chicago Press, 2001); Cass R. Sunstein and Richard A. Epstein, eds., *The Vote: Bush, Gore and the Supreme Court* (Chicago: University of Chicago Press, 2001); and Ronald Dworkin, ed., *A Badly Flawed Election: Debating* Bush v. Gore, *the Supreme Court, and American Democracy* (New York: New Press, 2002).

[6] See Henry E. Brady, Justin Buchler, Matt Jarvis, and John McNulty, *Counting All the Votes: The Performance of Voting Technology in the United States* (Berkeley, CA: Survey Research Center and Institute of Governmental Studies, 2001), available at http://ucdata.berkeley.edu/new_web/countingallthevotes.pdf.

[7] For example, precincts in Florida using the problematic punch-card ballots were more likely to contain significant minority populations than places with other ballot types. See Josh

Barbanel and Ford Fessenden, "Racial Pattern in Demographics of Error-Prone Ballots," *New York Times*, November 29, 2000, p. A25. See also Michael Tomz and Robert P. Van Houweling, "How Does Voting Equipment Affect the Racial Gap in Voided Ballots?" *American Journal of Political Science* 47 (January 2003): 46–60. Their data are from South Carolina and Louisiana.

[8] Ford Fessenden and John M. Broder, "Study of Disputed Florida Ballots Finds Justices Did Not Cast the Deciding Vote," *New York Times*, November 12, 2001, p. A1.

[9] Peter Whoriskey, "Vote Disparity Still a Mystery in Fla. Election for Congress," *Washington Post*, November 29, 2006, p. A03.

[10] Henry E. Brady, "Detailed Analysis of Punch Card Performance in the Twenty Largest California Counties in 1996, 2000, and 2003," report, 2003, available at http://ucdata.berkeley.edu:7101/ new_web/recall/20031996.pdf.

[11] Robert Pear, "Bush Signs Legislation Intended to End Voting Disputes," *New York Times*, October 29, 2002. p. A22.

[12] Election Data Services, "69 Million Voters Will Use Optical Scan Ballots in 2006, 66 Million Voters Will Use Electronic Equipment," report, 2006, available at http://www.electiondataservices. com/EDSInc_VEStudy2006.pdf.

III
ISSUES

I n the concluding chapters we discuss issues of public policy raised by the way in which Americans conduct their presidential elections. There are always complaints about election processes, as there are about nearly every aspect of American politics. Our discussion attempts to deal with some of the more long-lasting and widely held criticisms. We attempt also to put presidential elections into the broader context of the American political system, asking whether and how these elections serve the purposes of democracy.

SIX

APPRAISALS

I N 1968 THE DEMOCRATIC PARTY ENDURED A SEASON OF TURMOIL: its incumbent president, Lyndon Johnson, withdrew his candidacy to succeed himself; a leading candidate to succeed him, Senator Robert Kennedy of New York, was assassinated; and its national convention was conducted amid extraordinary uproar. In that convention, delegates chose Vice President Hubert Humphrey, who had not entered a single primary, to be the Democratic nominee for the presidency. In the aftermath of that convention, a party commission on reform of the nomination process—the McGovern-Fraser Commission, as it was called—was constituted and a year later brought in some proposals for changing presidential nominations. These were adopted by the Democratic Party.

After every national nominating convention from 1968 through 1984, the Democrats formed such a commission. Table 6.1 gives pertinent facts about their leadership and their main effects. Even Republicans were affected by the changes sparked by those commissions, since in some cases new state laws had to be enacted to comply with changes in Democratic Party regulations. Since 1984 the Democrats have not made major changes in their national party rules, although their national committee retains the power to tinker, a reminder that within the Democratic Party centralized reform efforts are never entirely off the agenda. After 1988 the Democratic National Committee (DNC) used that authority to require strict proportional representation for allocating delegates in states using primary elections. After the 2004 election, a new Democratic commission, chaired by former Labor Secretary Alexis Herman and Representative David Price of North Carolina, addressed concerns that Iowa and New Hampshire played too large a role in candidate selection by recommending that other, more ethnically diverse states be allowed to hold early primaries and caucuses as well.[1]

Even without significant changes in the national rules, changes adopted by the states such as organizing regional primaries and moving primaries to earlier time slots have

TABLE 6.1 Reform Commissions of the Democratic Party, 1969–2005

Name	Duration	Leadership	Main Effects
McGovern-Fraser	1969–1972	Senator George McGovern (S.D.); Representative Donald M. Fraser (Minn.)	Established guidelines for the selection of delegates; outlawed two systems of delegate selection.
Mikulski	1972–1973	Barbara A. Mikulski, Baltimore city councilwoman	Banned open crossover primaries; replaced stringent quotas on blacks, women, and youths with nonmandatory affirmative action programs.
Winograd	1975–1980	Morley Winograd, former chairman of Michigan Democratic Party	Eliminated loophole primary; shortened delegate selection season; increased size of delegations to accommodate state party and elected officials; required states to set filing deadlines for candidates 30 to 90 days before the voting.
Hunt	1980–1982	Governor James B. Hunt Jr. (N.C.)	Provided uncommitted delegate spots for major party and elected officials; relaxed proportional representation; ended ban on loophole primary; shortened primary and caucus season to a 3-month window; weakened delegate binding rule.
Fowler, or "Fairness"	1985	Donald L. Fowler, former chairman of South Carolina Democratic Party	Slightly expanded superdelegate spots; allowed certain states to return to open crossover primaries; lowered from 20 percent to 15 percent the threshold of primary voters candidates must surpass to receive delegates.
DNC Rules and Bylaws Committee	1989–1990	Fowler and Anne D. Campbell (N.J.)	Slightly expanded superdelegate spots; rebanned loophole primaries.
Presidential Nomination Timing and Scheduling	2005	Former Secretary of Labor Alexis Herman, Rep. David Price (N.C.)	Proposes 1–2 additional caucuses after Iowa but before New Hampshire primary, 1–2 additional early primaries; states chosen for early contests to reflect racial, geographic, economic diversity

Source: Adapted from William Crotty, *Party Reform* (New York: Longman, 1983), pp. 40–43. Additional sources: Adam Clymer, "Democrats Adopt Nominating Rules for '80 Campaign," *New York Times*, June 10, 1978; Clymer, "Democrats Alter Delegate Rules, Giving Top Officials More Power," *New York Times*, March 27, 1982; Rhodes Cook, "Democrats' Rules Weaken Representation," *Congressional Quarterly Weekly Report*, April 3, 1982, p. 750; Austin Ranney, "Farewell to Reform—Almost," in Kay Schlozman, ed., *Elections in America* (Boston: Allan and Unwin, 1987), 106; Rhodes Cook, "Democratic Party Rules Readied for '92 Campaign," *Congressional Quarterly Weekly Report*, March 17, 1990, p. 847; "Democrats Alter Nominating Rules," *Congressional Quarterly Weekly Report*, April 14, 1990, p. 148; and Democratic Party Committee on Presidential Nomination Timing and Scheduling website, http://www.democrats .org/page/s/nominating.

Note: Loophole primaries include direct district election of delegates and therefore do not necessarily yield proportional allocation of delegates.

made important differences in the way nominees are chosen, and have sparked calls for further regulation of the process. It is fair to say that for much of the past thirty years, reform has been in the air.

Previous chapters have incorporated the results of these reforms into the description we have given so far, concentrating on features of the presidential nomination process as it exists at present and on the political consequences that flow from the system as it is now organized. Some of these features have been part of the landscape of American politics for a generation or more; others are new, and the changes they may bring about lie mostly in the future. Nevertheless, if there is one certainty about presidential elections, it is that this process is subject to continuous pressure for change.

In this chapter we appraise some of these changes and proposals for future change of the American party system and its nomination and election processes. Because of the rapid reforms of the past few years, some of the impetus behind certain suggestions for further reform has slackened, while other ideas seem likely to be pursued with renewed vigor. Few observers are satisfied with the nomination or election process as it now exists. As past solutions lead to future problems, new proposals enter the agenda and old ones depart. As times change, moreover, old concerns become outdated and new ones take their place. Under the party system of the 1950s and 1960s, for instance, with conservative Democrats and liberal Republicans limiting policy agreement within their respective parties, the cry went out for greater cohesion within the parties. Too little ideological unity within the parties was widely blamed for the lack of consistent party policy positions across a wide range of issues. How, it was then argued, could voters make a sensible choice if the parties did not offer internally consistent and externally clashing policy views? This is not so great a problem today, as evidence of ideological consistency within each party grows. Instead, we often hear concern about the negative consequences of polarization between the parties. In the same way, reforms stressing mass participation have in due course been succeeded by measures emphasizing the benefits of elite experience, such as the creation of superdelegates. Thus the preoccupations of one era give way to those of its successors.

New proposals for change stem on the whole from two camps, which for purposes of discussion we wish to treat as distinct entities. The first movement we call *policy government*; the second we refer to as *participatory democracy*. Advocates of policy government urge strengthened parties, not as the focus of organizational loyalties so much as vehicles for the promulgation of policy. Participatory democrats urge "openness" and "participation" in the political process and advocate weakening party organizations and strengthening candidates, factions, and their ideological concerns. While the two sets of reformers appear to disagree about whether they want parties to be strong or weak, this comes down to a difference in predictions about the outcome of the application of the same remedy, for both in the end prescribe the same thing: more ideology as the tie that binds voters to elected officials and less loyalty to political parties as organizations.

THE POLITICAL THEORY OF POLICY GOVERNMENT

Policy government reform had its antecedents at the turn of the twentieth century in the writings of Woodrow Wilson, James Bryce, and other passionate constitutional tinkerers who founded and breathed life into the academic study of political science. The descendants of these thinkers have through the years elaborated a series of proposals that are embodied in a coherent general political theory. This theory contains a conception of the proper function of the political party, evaluates the legitimacy and the roles of Congress and the president, and enshrines a particular definition of the public interest. Different advocates of this reform have stated the theory with greater or less elaboration; some reformers leave out certain features of it, and some are disinclined to face squarely the implications of the measures they espouse. We try here to reproduce correctly a style of argument that, though it ignores the slight differences separating these party reformers from one another, gives a coherent statement of their party reform theory and contrasts it with the political theory that critics of their position advance.[2] Over time we seem to be achieving an approximation of the party cohesion that these reformers of yesteryear wanted, and so it is worthwhile to attend to the pros and cons of the debate their proposals brought about.

This group of party reformers suggested that democratic government requires political parties that (1) make policy commitments to the electorate, (2) are willing and able to carry them out when in office, (3) develop alternatives to government policies when out of office, and (4) differ sufficiently to "provide the electorate with a proper range of choice between alternatives of action."[3] They thus come to define a political party as "an association of broadly like-minded voters seeking to carry out common objectives through their elected representatives."[4] In a word, party should be grounded in policy.

Virtually all significant party relationships are, for these reformers, mediated by policy considerations. The electorate at large—not merely political activists—is assumed to be policy motivated and officeholders conscious of mandates. Policy discussion among party members is expected to create widespread agreements upon which party discipline will then be based. Special interest groups are to be resisted and accommodated only as the overall policy commitments of party permit. The weaknesses of parties and the disabilities of governments are seen as stemming from failure to develop and support satisfactory programs of public policy. Hence we refer to this theory of party reform as a theory of policy government. This theory holds "that the choices provided by the two-party system are valuable to the American people in proportion to their definition in terms of public policy."[5] It differs from the participatory brand of party reform (which we address later) in that policy reformers believe they are revitalizing party organizations, whereas participatory democrats are likely to be indifferent to party organization.

Opponents of policy reform believe that democratic government in the United States requires that parties first and foremost undertake the minimization of conflict between contending interests and social forces.[6] We call them supporters of consensus government. For consensus government advocates, the ideal political party is a mechanism for accomplishing and reinforcing adjustment and compromise among the various interests in society to prevent severe social conflict. Whereas policy government reformers desire parties that operate "not as mere brokers between different groups and interests but as agencies of the electorate," supporters of consensus government see the party as an "agency for compromise." Opponents of party reform through policy government hold that "the general welfare is achieved by harmonizing and adjusting group interest."[7] In fact, they sometimes go so far as to suggest that "the contribution that parties make to policy is inconsequential so long as they maintain conditions for adjustment."[8] Thus, the theory of the political party upheld by critics of the policy reform position is rooted in a notion of consensus government. Advocates of policy government behave as if problems of consensus, of gaining sufficient agreement to govern, have already been solved or do not need to be solved. Believing that there is no problem of stability, they concentrate on change. Their critics downplay policy not because they think it unimportant but because they think maintaining the capacity to govern is more important than any particular policy. Fearing instability, they are less concerned with enhancing the system's impulses to change.

A basic cleavage between advocates of policy government and advocates of consensus government may be observed in their radically opposed conceptions of the public interest. For advocates of consensus government, the public interest is defined as whatever combination of measures emerges from the negotiations, adjustments, and compromises made in fair fights or bargains among conflicting interest groups. They feel the need for no external criteria by which policies can be measured in order to determine whether or not they are in the public interest. As long as the process by which decisions are made consists of intergroup bargaining, within certain specified democratic, constitutional "rules of the game," they regard the outcomes as being in the public interest.

For advocates of policy government, the public interest is a discoverable set of policies that represents "something more than the mathematical result of the claims of all the pressure groups."[9] Some overarching notion of the public interest, they argue, is necessary if we are to resist the unwarranted claims of "special interest" groups. While this suggests that there are, in principle, criteria for judging whether a policy is in the public interest, apart from the procedural test applied by supporters of consensus government, these criteria are never clearly identified. This would not present great difficulties if policy government advocates did not demand that an authoritative determination of party policy be made and that party members be held to it. But information about the policy preferences of members is supposed to flow upward, and orders establishing and enforcing final policy decisions are supposed to flow downward in a greatly strengthened pyramid of party authority. Without criteria of the public interest established in advance, however, party leaders or commentators can define the public interest in any terms they may find convenient.

If we were to have parties that resembled the ideal of this first set of party reformers, what would they be like? They would be coherent in their policies, reliable in carrying them out, accountable to the people, disciplined and hierarchical internally, sharply differentiated from and in conflict with partisan opponents. What would it take to create a party system organized by the principles of policy government?

For the parties to carry out the promises they make, the people responsible for making promises would have to be the same as or in control of the people responsible for carrying them out. This means, logically, one of two alternatives. Either the people who controlled party performance all year round would have to write the party platforms every four years at the national conventions, or the people who wrote the platforms would have to be put in charge of party performance. In the first case, the party platforms would have to be written by leaders such as the members of Congress who at present refrain from enacting laws favored by both national conventions. State and local political leaders would write their respective platforms. Under such an arrangement, which reflects the procedural complications introduced by the separation of powers and the federal structure embedded in the U.S. Constitution, very little formal, overall coordination or policy coherence seems likely to emerge. Since the main point of policy government is to create logically coherent, unified policy that makes possible rational choices by voters, we observe that this first alternative as a way to fulfill the demands of party reformers will not work.

In fact, the alternative most often recommended by advocates of policy government is that the ideas animating the platforms at the national party conventions should be in charge. These platforms must make policy that will be enforced on national, state, and local levels by means of party discipline—that is, getting rid of party officeholders who disagree. This arrangement also has a fatal defect: it ignores the power of the people who do not write the convention platforms—all those party activists not selected to represent the candidate-centered forces at the national convention. How are independently elected members of Congress to be bypassed? Will present-day local and state party leaders acquiesce in this rearrangement of power and subject themselves to discipline from a newly constituted outside source? It is hard to see what the enforcement mechanism would be. Party reform has already gone some distance toward reducing the influence of elected officials in the presidential nomination process. Will they give up their independent capacity as public officials to make policy in their own arenas—Congress, the state legislatures—as well? Generally, we assume they will not.

One reformer says: "As for the clash of personal political ambitions in the United States, they are being completely submerged by the international and domestic concerns of the American public. War and peace, inflation and depression are both personal and universal issues; tariff, taxes, foreign aid, military spending, federal reserve policies, and hosts of other national policies affect local economic activities across the land. Politicians who wish to become statesmen must be able to talk intelligently about issues that concern people in all constituencies."[10]

But the increasing importance of national issues will not necessarily lead to greater power in the hands of party leaders with national (that is to say, presidential) constituencies. There is no necessary connection between political power in the national arena and the emergence of issues having national scope. Politicians who exercise national political power such as congressional committee chairs frequently themselves come to be influential because of their local control of their own nomination and alliances with interest groups back home in their several constituencies, plus the workings of the congressional seniority system over time, subject to the lottery of the committee assignment process. National issues undoubtedly have great importance, especially among the ideologically more cohesive Republicans.[11] But delivery on national promises is frequently thwarted by the power of local interests able to influence national institutions, for example, as mentioned, the people in the congressional districts that elect influential members of the House of Representatives. So far, the increasing nationalization of policy has been most conspicuously accompanied not by the rise of nationally cohesive groups but by increases in the strength of single-issue groups.

The people who have the most to lose from policy government are the leaders of Congress. The major electoral risks facing national legislators are local. This does not mean that legislators will necessarily be parochial in their attitudes and policy commitments. But it does mean that they cannot be bound to support the president or national party leaders on issues of high local salience. In order to impose discipline successfully, the national parties must be able either to control sanctions at present important to legislators, such as nomination to office, or to impose still more severe ones upon them. At the moment, however, our system provides for control of congressional, state, and local nominations and elections by geographically localized candidates, electorates, and (to a lesser extent) party leaders. Presidents are not totally helpless in affecting the outcomes of these local decisions, but their influence, especially considering the power of incumbent members of Congress to maintain themselves in office, is in most cases quite marginal.[12]

In the light of this, one obvious electoral precondition of disciplined parties would have to be that local voters were so strongly tied to national party issues that they would reward their local representatives for supporting national policy pronouncements, even at the expense of local advantage. To a certain extent, by virtue of the influence of national news media and the rising educational level of the electorate, as well as some increase in the general propensity of the most active citizens to think ideologically, this condition can be met.[13] The issues on which the national party makes its appeal must either unify a large number of constituencies in favor of the party or appeal at least to some substantial segment of opinion everywhere. But even if this could be accomplished with regularity, it would be strategically unwise for parties to attempt to discipline members who lived in areas that were strongly against national party policy. This would mean reading the offending area out of the party and weakening the party's overall appeal in presidential elections. Therefore, reformers must show how they intend to contribute to the national character of political parties by enforcing national policies on members of Congress in those areas where local constituencies are drastically opposed to national party policy or whose constituents do not pay attention to issues but care more for the personality or the constituent services of their representatives in Congress.[14] Insofar as leeway exists, let us say, for liberal northeastern Republicans, a diminishing breed, to support liberal programs and for conservative Democrats, who are much more scarce in the South than they once were, to oppose them, the parties will, in fact, have retained their old, "undisciplined," "irresponsible" shapes. Insofar as this leeway does not exist, splinter groups of various kinds are encouraged to split off from the established parties. Party changing among officeholders, once unheard of, becomes more common.

Another way of achieving disciplined parties may be more promising. We have seen that party activists and, to a lesser but meaningful extent, legislators have become ideologically more coherent. This has not occurred by command but by evolution: northern liberal Republicans have moved into the Democratic Party and conservative southern Democrats into the Republican Party.[15] As the parties have become more ideologically distinctive across a wider range of issues—social, environmental, and defense, as well as economic—some activists who feel most uncomfortable have been changing allegiances.[16] For proponents of party cohesion, this is the good news. The bad news is that a strong party line breeds splits. Among Republicans, this means the prospect of future conflict between free-market libertarians and social conservatives. Among Democrats, factionalism has become so severe that it may be preventing them from mobilizing their historic edge in party identification for presidential elections.[17] Party leaders increasingly seek to activate "wedge issues" that divide their opponents. Democrats raise environmental and education issues, which split Republicans; Republicans talk about partial-birth abortion and gay marriage, which divide Democrats.

Conflict within and between parties may be good for them and for the nation. Conflict can invigorate discussion and enlighten the public about the bases of party differences. Much depends on the extent to which discussion quickly polarizes groups that have strong interests in definitions of the situation that are already so well formed and structured as to inhibit the search for creative solutions.

A second method for reducing the independent power over policy of independently elected congressional leaders has begun to have an effect in national politics. This method addresses not the prospects for nomination and election of congressional leaders but rather their opportunities to lead in Congress. Adherence to the conservatism of the majority of Republicans in Congress has in general always been a prerequisite of leadership within the Republican Party. What internal conflict there has been among Republicans has been based not on ideology but style. The emergence of Newt Gingrich in the 1990s as Republican leader meant not a shift to the right but the adoption of a confrontational approach to House business by Republicans. Gingrich's successors have, like him, been mainstream conservatives, as are the leaders of the Senate Republicans.[18]

Among congressional Democrats, in the past more room existed for congressional leaders—at any rate for committee chairs, who were selected by seniority—to take whatever policy positions they pleased. Since the late 1950s, sentiment grew in Congress that conservative Democratic committee chairs should be more responsive to the policy preferences of the majority of the majority party, and the Democratic caucus of the House of Representatives acted to remove committee chairs they regarded as unresponsive. This did not, however, proceed strictly along ideological lines. One of the first chairmen to be removed, Wright Patman of Texas, was as liberal as any Democrat in the House, including his replacement, Henry Reuss of Wisconsin. Another chairman, Edward Hebert of the Armed Services Committee, was replaced by a leader ideologically indistinguishable from him on matters coming before the committee.[19] So, despite the unlimbering of a new weapon—the House Democratic caucus—that could encourage party cohesion in Congress, it was not used consistently quite in this way, and concerns related to the management of Congress itself turned out to be more significant than the shaping or enforcement of party policy in the activities of the reactivated Democratic caucus when the Democrats were in the majority. The Republicans, during the Gingrich speakership (1995 to 1998), violated seniority regularly as part of an effort to centralize control of policy. The revolt that deposed Gingrich in 1998 was at least in part an effort to return greater powers to the committees. But Republican leaders still retained significant influence over committee chairs.

This series of reforms since the early 1970s has resulted in congressional parties in which a strongly ideological leadership retains a great deal of power over committee chairs and rank-and-file members. By any measure, both Republicans and Democrats are currently more internally unified and more dissimilar from each other than at any time in living memory. During the presidential administration of George W. Bush, this new model of policy government extended still further to an increased degree of authority enjoyed by the executive over the legislature. Republican party leaders in Congress acted as if their primary duty was to carry out a programmatically coherent agenda set by the president. Disputes between the White House and Capitol Hill were few (Bush did not veto a single bill during the first five years of his presidency), and independent congressional oversight of executive branch activity nearly disappeared.

We might expect advocates of policy government to be cheered by such developments. After all, Bush and the Republican majorities in Congress came closest during the 2000–2006 period to instituting their vision of a clear, ideological policy agenda implemented via strong party discipline. Voters were presented with a stark choice between the parties at election time, allowing Republican officeholders to claim that their victories represented a "mandate" in behalf of the party's principles.

But it is not at all clear whether this increasing importance of party ideology has been good for the parties, much less the nation itself. Many of the policies implemented by the Bush administration proved unpopular with voters, demonstrating that narrow election victories do not actually confer broad mandates to execute a comprehensive issue agenda. Bush's popularity ratings dropped as the U.S. war in Iraq suffered significant setbacks. In 2006, voters communicated their disapproval of his performance in office by turning control of both houses of Congress over to the opposition Democrats. Congressional Republicans suffered particularly heavy losses in liberal and moderate districts in the North, where voters registered their strong objections to the policies of the ruling GOP by defeating even centrist Republican incumbents.

Are parties that take relatively extreme positions more "responsible" or "accountable" to the generally moderate and ideologically inconsistent American electorate than parties that allow for greater flexibility on issues? Reforms that reinforce party polarization risk offering voters a clear choice—but between two equally unpalatable options. To a large extent, advocates of policy government have succeeded in implementing their goals, but the results may prove less popular—and less conducive to well-functioning government—than they foresaw.

REFORM BY MEANS OF PARTICIPATORY DEMOCRACY

The second type of reform movement we identify as participatory democracy. The efforts of those who advocate participatory democracy and who have attempted to make the Democratic Party the vehicle of this approach to government have met with considerable success over the past fifty years, as the history of presidential nomination reform attests.[20] Here we wish to contemplate the theory of politics that underlies this position. Ordinarily, participatory democrats criticize the American political system in two respects. First, they argue that elections have insufficient impact on policy outcomes of the government. These critics see too weak a link between public policy and what they believe to be the desires of electoral majorities. Second, there is the critique of the electoral process itself, which argues that policy does not represent what majorities want because undemocratic influences determine election results. These criticisms are simple-minded in one sense and cogent in another. They are simple-minded in that they ignore the immense problems that would have to be overcome if we were truly serious about transforming America or any large, diverse population into a participatory democracy. They are cogent in that responsiveness to majorities on questions of policy is a fundamental value that gives legitimacy to democratic government. The connection between such criticism and the legitimacy of government makes it important to deal at least briefly with some of the issues and problems that should be raised (and usually are not) by judgments of this fundamental nature.

The first and obvious question to ask is whether the criticisms are based on fact. Is the American system unresponsive to the policy desires of a majority of its citizens? Unfortunately, there is no unambiguous way to answer this question. If we focus our attention, for example, on the mechanics of the policy process, we find what appears to be government by minorities. In some policy areas a great number of people and interests, organized and unorganized, may have both a say in the open and some influence on the final product. But fewer individuals may be involved in areas dealing with other problems and policies, some of which will be of a specialized nature, of limited interest, and so on. Even members of Congress do not have equally great influence over every decision: committee jurisdictions, seniority, special knowledge, party, individual reputation, all combine to weigh the influence of each member on a different scale for each issue.

So we must conclude that if we adopt direct participation in and equal influence over the policy decisions of our government (the decisions that "affect our lives") as the single criterion of democracy, then our system surely fails the test. So, we might note, does every contemporary government of any size known to us, possibly excepting two or three rural Swiss cantons.

Another approach might focus on public opinion as an index of majority desires. Using this standard, a quite different picture emerges. Policy decisions made by the government mostly have the support of popular majorities. Where this is not true, the apparent lack of "responsiveness" may have several causes, not all of them curable: (1) conflicts between majority desires and intractable situations in the world (for example, a hypothetical desire for peace in the Middle East); or (2) public attitudes favoring certain sets of policies that may be mutually incompatible (such as the desire for low taxes, high benefits, and balanced budgets); or (3) clear, consistent, and feasible majority desires are ignored by the government because the desires are unconstitutional or antithetical to enduring values of the political system, to which leaders are more sensitive than popular majorities. Surveys, for example, have from time to time revealed majorities in favor of constitutionally questionable repressive measures against dissenters and the press.

Criticisms of the popular responsiveness of presidential elections are more difficult to assess. American electoral politics does respond to the application of resources such as money that are arguably nondemocratic and that cause the influence of different actors to be weighed unequally. In a truly democratic system, it could be argued, the system would respond to votes and only votes. All methods of achieving political outcomes other than registering preferences by voting would be deemed illegitimate. As we have indicated, however, money, incumbency, energy and enthusiasm, popularity, name recognition, ability, and experience are all valuable assets within the structure of American politics. Is this avoidable? Should we attempt to eradicate the influence of these resources?

Political resources and the people who possess them are important primarily because campaigns are important. Campaigns are important because the general public needs to be alerted to the fact that an election is near. Partisans must be mobilized, the uncommitted convinced, perhaps even a few minds changed. Resources other than votes are important because—and only because—numerical majorities must be mobilized.

American politics responds to diverse resources because many citizens abstain from voting and are hard to reach by campaigners. Sometimes this is described as political apathy. Why is political apathy widespread? There are several alternative explanations. Perhaps it is because the system presents the citizenry with no real alternatives from which to choose. In the election of 1964, however, there was at least a partial test of this "hidden vote" theory, and the evidence was negative. And in 1972, another year when there was an unambiguous choice, nonvoting hit a high for elections up to then. Voting participation in presidential elections seems to rise and fall without much regard for the ideological distance between candidates of the major parties.

Perhaps there is apathy because the public has been imbued with a "false consciousness" that blinds them to their "real" desires and interests. They would participate if they knew better. This explanation is traditionally seized on by the enlightened few to deny value to the preferences of the ignorant many. The people, we are told, are easily fooled; this testifies to their credulity. They do not know what is good for them; this makes them childlike. But when the people cannot trust their own feelings, when their desires are alleged to be unworthy, when their policy preferences should be ignored because they are not "genuine" or "authentic," or there are not enough of them, they are being deprived of their humanity as well. What is left for the people if they are held to have no judgment, wisdom, feeling, desire, and preference? Such an argument would offer little hope for democracy of any sort, for it introduces the most blatant form of inequality as a political "given": a structured, ascribed difference between those who know what is "good" for themselves and those who must be "told." No doubt it is true that much of the time we do not know (without the advantage of perfect foresight) what is best for us. But that is not to say that others know better, that our consciousness is false but theirs is true. Persons who make the "false consciousness" argument do not believe in democracy.

A more hopeful and less self-contradictory explanation of political apathy might note that throughout American history a substantial number of citizens have not wished to concern themselves continually with the problems and actions of government. Many citizens prefer to participate on their own terms, involving themselves when they feel like it with a particular issue area or problem. These citizens' participation is necessarily sporadic and narrower than that of the voter interested in all public problems and actively involved in general political life. Many other citizens (surely a majority) are more interested in their own personal problems than in any issue of public policy.[21] These citizens meet their public obligations by going to the polls at fairly regular intervals, making their selections on the basis of their own criteria, and then supporting the actions and policies of the winners, whether they were their choices or not. In the intervals, unless they themselves are personally affected by some policy proposal, most of these citizens may wish to be left alone. Given the complexity of issues and the uncertainty surrounding the claims of candidates, citizens may arrive at their voting decisions by asking themselves a simple, summary question: are things (the domestic economy, world affairs) better or worse than they were? This is a reasonable way to decide, but it does not offer much future policy guidance to political leaders.[22]

The literature on apathy may say more about the values of the students of the subject than about the ostensible objects of their studies. Those observers who approve of existing institutions are likely to view apathy as relatively benign; they believe people do not participate because they are satisfied and they trust institutions to do well by them. Those who disapprove of existing institutions naturally find the defect in the institutions themselves; they believe people do not participate because they are denied the opportunity or because they rightly feel ineffectual. Observers who view individuals as capable of regulating their own affairs see these individuals as deciding case by case whether it is worth the time and effort to participate. Projecting the investigator's preferences onto citizens does not seem to us a useful way of learning why this or that person chooses to participate in political life. As political scientists and citizens, we think self-government an ideal so valuable that we would not impose our own views on those who decide they have better things to do.

Studies have from time to time shown unfavorable citizen attitudes toward the political system, a phenomenon sometimes called "alienation," which appears to have increased since the 1960s. As we argued earlier in this book, these attitudes do not explain low rates of voting participation; persons who score high in these unfavorable attitudes have been shown to participate at about the same rate as the nonalienated.[23] So we surmise that a great many citizens who do not vote abstain because they are concerned with other things important to them, like earning a living or painting a picture or cultivating a garden, and not because they feel it is so difficult to influence outcomes. In short, for them, politics is peripheral. Given the peripheral importance of politics in many people's lives, making it easier to vote does increase voter turnout. But because politics is peripheral, even making voting easier does not reduce abstention from voting to zero or anything like zero.

Consider a society in which all citizens were as concerned about public matters as the most active. Such a society would not require mobilization: all who were able to would vote.[24] The hoopla and gimmickry associated with political campaigns would have little effect: this citizenry would know the record of the parties and the candidates and, presumably, would make reasoned choices on this basis. Should such an active society be the goal of those whose political philosophy is democratic? This question should not and cannot be answered without first addressing the problem of how such a society could be achieved.

Without attempting to be comprehensive, a few difficulties merit some specific comment. First and foremost, political participation, as Aristotle made clear several thousand years ago, takes a great deal of time. For this reason (among others) a large population of slaves was felt necessary to assist participatory government: it freed Athenian citizens from the cares of maintaining life and thus provided them the leisure time that made their political activity possible. But having rejected some 150 years ago this ingenious solution to the problems related to relatively large-scale participation, we must deal with the fact that most American citizens work for a living. They lack the disposable time that permits professionals and college students and other privileged people to choose their working hours. Most citizens lack the time, even if they had the temperament and training, to engage continually in politics. To the degree that representative institutions—political parties, legislatures, elected executives—are disregarded in favor of more direct modes of activity, the majority of the people will be without the means through which they can most effectively make their will felt. In short, to impose requirements of direct participation on those desiring a voice in decisions would be to ensure that the incessant few rather than the sporadic many would rule: thus the 1960s slogan "power to the people" really proposed to replace a representative few, who were elected, with an unrepresentative few, who were self-activated.

In well-known work, the philosopher Jürgen Habermas has argued that the only way to make a democracy legitimate, for it to be considered a true democracy worthy of support, is for it to approximate the conditions of what he calls "an ideal speech situation." Every person would be equally interested and active. Each would have equal rights, money, information, and all other resources necessary for effective participation.[25] What could be wrong with such an ideal? Nothing at all, we think. If it were to be realized in practice in a very diverse society, however, it might lead to surprising results. For a diverse society may lead to the expression of diverse values. Individualists, for example, adhere to the ideal of equality of opportunity so that people can be different, and some may consequently end up with more resources than others. This expresses a different equality from that postulated by Habermas. Other people, for example, Christian fundamentalists, may prefer a more patriarchal or hierarchical set of values in which different people occupy different statuses. Thus it is helpful to consider whether democracy is only about equality or whether it may be about enabling people who hold different values to live together peaceably.

Thus there are practical difficulties with a theory that requires high levels of political participation. We raise this issue not because we are opposed in principle to the idea of an active, participatory, democratic society. By persuasion and political education the majority of our citizens might indeed be convinced that the quality of our shared existence could be improved through more continuous devotion to public activity. This is quite different from arguing that the rules of the game should be changed to reduce the influence of those who at present lack the opportunity or desire to be active. Efforts to implement ideal goals when the preconditions and the means of achieving these goals do not exist are self-defeating. Actions that in the name of participatory democracy restrict the ability of most of the people to have their political say are not as democratic as advertised.

SOME SPECIFIC REFORMS

Comprehensive reform of the party system rides in on tides of strong feeling. Until such feelings exist among party activists, rational advocacy looking toward reform is wasted; once such feeling exists, rational advocacy is superfluous. So the type of analysis we undertake here is bound to be uninfluential. We attempt it only because thoughtful citizens may find it instructive to consider the consequences of the best-laid plans. Once these consequences have had an opportunity to manifest themselves, however, a new generation of reform may be in order. After all, practically everything that reformers object to now was once somebody's favorite reform.

We suspect that the achievement of many—not all—of the specific objectives of party reformers would be detrimental to their aims and to those of most thoughtful citizens. Let us consider, for example, specific reforms of governmental machinery that are commonly advocated to make the parties more responsive to popular will and more democratic. Party reformers often advocate a variety of changes in the nomination process, including changes in party convention procedures and modification or abolition of the electoral college.

The Nomination Process

In order to evaluate the nominating process, it would be helpful to suggest a set of goals that most Americans might accept as desirable and important.[26] The following seven standards appear to meet this test: any method for nominating presidents should (1) aid in preserving the two-party system, (2) help secure vigorous competition between the parties, (3) maintain some degree of cohesion and agreement within the parties, (4) produce candidates who are likely to win voter support, (5) lead to the choice of candidates who are reasonably well qualified, (6) lead to the acceptance of candidates as legitimate, and (7) result in officeholders who are capable of generating support for public policies they intend to pursue. We first look at some suggested alternatives to the current nominating system.

A national direct primary to select party candidates for the presidency has often been suggested. Many people took heart in 1968 from the way in which the piecemeal primaries around the country facilitated the expression of anti-Vietnam War sentiment, and they noted that nonprimary states were on the whole less responsive to persons whose participation in party activities was largely precipitated by strong feelings about the war. Their conclusion was that primaries were rather a good thing and that, therefore, a national primary was in order.

We believe this would have serious disadvantages. First, it would have been self-defeating as far as the professed goals of many antiwar people who advocated it were concerned. By entering primaries one at a time in 1968, Senator Eugene McCarthy of Minnesota, and later Senator Robert Kennedy of New York, were able to construct "test cases." We doubt that McCarthy, given the limitations of his resources before New Hampshire, could have even entered a national primary.

Charles O. Jones has said that in some respects we already do have a national primary, and that it is held in New Hampshire. He is entirely correct to call attention to the enormous influence that early delegate-selection processes have on the fortunes of candidates later on. But the Iowa caucuses and New Hampshire primary do differ from a national primary in one major respect: they are small, and as Everett Carll Ladd says,

> By leading off, manageable little Iowa and New Hampshire enable less well-known and well-heeled candidates to gain attention through presenting their wares to real people in real election settings. If a candidate with moderate resources, and previously lacking a national reputation, manages to impress a fair number of voters in these small states, isn't this laboratory experience of some considerable interest to the country?[27]

This merely points to a more general problem of financing national primary elections. It is quite probable that many candidates—perhaps as many as ten of them—might obtain enough signatures on nominating petitions or qualify by some other device to get on the ballot for a true, fifty-state, national primary. In a year when there is no incumbent president in the race, it is not hard to imagine a crowd of challengers in both parties hustling all over the United States campaigning in such a primary. It would take, of course, enormous amounts of money. The parties could hardly be expected to show favoritism and so could not finance these candidates. Although some government financing would no doubt be made available, this would have to depend on demonstrated ability to raise money previously in order to discourage frivolous candidates, and would in all likelihood be inadequate to fund an effective national campaign. The preprimary campaign, therefore, would assume enormous importance and would be exceedingly expensive. Nationwide challengers would have to have access to very large amounts of money. It would help if they were already well known. They would also have to be quite sturdy physically.

Ordinarily, nobody would win a clear majority in a primary with a large number of contenders. Since all contenders would be wearing the same party label, it is hard to see how voters could differentiate among candidates except by already knowing one or two of their names in favorable or unfavorable contexts, by liking or not liking their looks, by identifying or not identifying with their ethnic or racial characteristics, by attending to their treatment in the press and in television news reports, or by some other means of differentiation having nothing whatever to do with ability or inclination to do the job, or even with their policy positions. Since patents on policy positions are not available, it is reasonable to suppose that more than one candidate would adopt roughly the same set of positions. Or they might, for the purpose of the primary, falsely portray themselves as disagreeing. Thus, voters would be fortunate if the intellectual content of the campaign consisted of quibbling about who proposed what first and, more relevantly, who could deliver better.

Suppose, then, that the primary vote was divided among several candidates. Suppose, as was once the case for gubernatorial elections in some southern states, that ten or twelve aspirants divided the votes. One possibility is that the party nominee would be the candidate with the highest number of votes, say, 19 percent of those cast, a much less democratic outcome than we now have, since who knows how the other 81 percent might have distributed themselves if they had known what the rank order of the candidates was going to be? Another possibility would be for the two highest candidates to contest a fifty-state runoff after the first primary and before the general election in a campaign that would begin to remind observers who can remember that far back of a marathon jitterbug contest. The party might end up with a good candidate, of course, if there was anything left of that candidate to give to the party in the real election campaign, which would follow. Then the poor candidate, if elected, would have to find the energy to govern. By following this procedure, the United States might have to restrict its presidential candidates to wealthy athletes.

We are not ready to give up at least some of the state primaries we now have, although it is now widely believed—and we agree—that we have too many. It is eminently desirable that it be possible in a number of states, separated geographically and in time, for test cases to be put to voters and for trial heats to be run among aspirants for high office. But a national primary would be like a steady diet consisting exclusively of dessert.

National primaries would lead not only to the weakening of political parties but also to the weakening of the party system. It is not unusual for a party to remain in office for a long period of time. If state experience with primaries is any guide, a prolonged period of victory for one party would result in a movement of interested voters into the primary of the winning party, where their votes would count for more.[28] As voters deserted the losing party, it would be largely the diehards who were left. They would nominate candidates who pleased them but who could not win the election because they were unappealing to a majority in the nation. Eventually, the losing party would atrophy, seriously weakening the two-party system and the prospects of competition among the parties. The winning party would soon show signs of internal weakness as a consequence of the lack of opposition necessary to keep it unified.

A national primary might also lead to the appearance of extremist candidates and demagogues who, unrestrained by allegiance to any permanent party organization, would have little to lose by stirring up mass hatreds or making absurd promises. On the whole, the convention system of the past discouraged these extremists by placing responsibility in the hands of party leaders who had a permanent stake in maintaining the good name and integrity of their organization. This is one of the costs of the eclipse of national party conventions as serious decision-making bodies. Some insight into this problem may be had by looking at the historic situation in state elections in several southern states, where most voters voted only in the Democratic primary and where victory in that primary, even with only a small percentage of the vote, was tantamount to election. The result was a chaotic factional politics in which there were few or no permanent party leaders; the distinctions between the "ins" and "outs" became blurred; it was difficult to hold anyone responsible; and demagogues sometimes arose who made use of this situation by strident appeals.[29] The fact that under some primary systems an extreme personality can take the place of party in giving a kind of minimal structure to state politics should give pause to the advocates of a national primary.

We believe that very widespread use of direct primaries weakens the party system. It encourages prospective candidates to bypass regular party organizations in favor of campaigns stressing personal publicity, and it provides for no peer review, that is, consideration of those aspects of fitness of candidates to hold office that can best be observed by politicians who actually know the candidates, who have themselves a heavy investment of time and energy in making the government work, and who know that they may have to live at close quarters with the results of their deliberations.

It is difficult to persuade activists who participate only casually in politics, and those who tend to do so only when moved by a great issue of the day, that the intensity of their feelings does not confer a sweeping mandate. These feelings, no matter how worthy, do not make occasional participants more worthy than steady participants. They do not bestow a special moral status on latecomers to politics as compared with people who are already active. Party regulars or even party leaders cannot be excluded on grounds of their moral inferiority from decision making in the presidential nomination process.

The great virtue of state-by-state piecemeal primaries is, of course, that they provide a means—increasingly supplemented by polls—of gauging the popularity of various candidates and their effectiveness in public speaking under adverse circumstances. The virtue of conventions has been that by living at closer quarters than ordinary citizens with the results of the collective choice, party leaders can bring to the selection greater knowledge and even, sometimes, a higher sense of responsibility.

It is generally conceded that eventual nominee Adlai Stevenson would have made a better president than Senator Estes Kefauver of Tennessee, who ran and won in most of the Democratic primaries in 1952. Stevenson, for his entire career in elective office, was the product of selection by party leaders—in some cases even by "bosses"—who were knowledgeable and continuously involved in the political process, acquainted with what governing demanded and with the personal capabilities of the politicians among whom they chose. Senator Walter Mondale of Minnesota, who withdrew from the 1976 preprimary sweepstakes because of a reluctance to spend a year in various motels around the country, was not a conspicuously worse—indeed, by some standards he was a better—public servant than some of those who leaped joyfully into the fray. Mondale first served in the Senate by appointment and was picked by Jimmy Carter to be his running mate without the sanctification of an election. Yet nobody supposes Mondale was picked without regard for democratic constraints. In 1984 either Mondale decided that motels had improved or he had become more ambitious, and he ran for—and won—the Democratic presidential nomination. In any event he certainly represented the views of the mainstream of his party. While it is unlikely that any Democrat could have beaten Ronald Reagan that year, few doubted that Mondale was well qualified to be president.

Giving politicians some rights to influence political choices does not necessarily create an evil system. Unchecked by the ultimate necessity to appeal for votes, no doubt any system would degenerate. Political leaders would not dominate a system that responded easily to short-run opinions of high intensity in the electorate. Sometimes this sort of system will pick a popular candidate over a candidate in whose personal capacities the delegates have more faith. This, we think, is what delegates to the Republican convention of 1952 did when they nominated Dwight D. Eisenhower over Senator Robert A. Taft of Ohio. Even when they decide to make a popular choice rather than go with their personal favorite, party leaders can invoke criteria of judgment unavailable to mass electorates.

In short, we believe that as long as there are many things we demand of a president—intelligence as well as popularity, integrity as well as speaking ability, private virtue as well as public presentability—we ought to foster a selection process that provides a mixture of devices for screening according to different criteria. The mixed system we advocate is not perfect, of course, but it is greatly superior to the unmixed nonblessing of the national primary.

The use of primaries at the state level has produced a variety of anomalous experiences: totally unqualified candidates whose names have resembled those of famous politicians have been nominated by innocent voters; ethnic minorities concentrated in one party have defeated attempts by party leaders to offer "balanced tickets," thus dooming to defeat their entire ticket in the general election; and palpable demagogues have defeated responsible candidates. All these consequences may not persuade reformers that the increased use of direct primaries is not a good idea, but they must be faced. If we value political parties, which reformers often profess to do, then we must hesitate to cut them off from the process of selecting candidates for public office, to deprive them of incentives to organize, and to set them prematurely at the mercy of masses of people whose information at the primary stage is especially poor.[30]

Responsible political analysts and advocates must face the fact that party identification for most people provides the safe cognitive anchorage around which political preferences are organized. Set adrift from this anchorage, as they are when faced with an intraparty primary election, most voters have little or nothing to guide their choices. Chance familiarity with a famous name or stray feelings of ethnic kinship or regional ties under these circumstances seem to provide many voters with the only clues to choice.[31] Given the conditions of popular interest and participation that prevail, we question throwing the future of the party system entirely into the hands of primary electorates.

What is more, a nomination process dominated by primaries gives the media great—possibly too much—influence. Their extensive influence was illustrated in a dramatic way in the spring of 1987, when the front-running candidate for the Democratic nomination, former Senator Gary Hart of Colorado, suddenly fell victim to publicity calling attention to a close personal relationship that he evidently was pursuing with a young woman who was not his wife. This episode of intensive negative commentary caused many thoughtful journalists to express concern about the extraordinary influence of the news media in the nomination process. Some journalists felt that they and their colleagues were unable to do justice to the special circumstances of the private lives of public figures, and that even public figures have rights to privacy in those areas of life that have little to do with the performance of public duties. Others argued that the way people behave in private is bound to affect the way they do their public chores.

Not long ago, when there was something like peer review in the nomination process, other politicians who were influential in the process and who knew the candidates could make assessments about the suitability of presidential hopefuls for office. Perhaps they would be forgiving in cases of alcoholism, chronic pettiness, bad temper, manic-depressive behavior, marital infidelity, laziness, bigotry, slowness of wit, vindictiveness, duplicity, stubbornness, or any of the other infirmities and imperfections that afflict human beings. Or perhaps not. At least, it was possible for reasonably well-informed judgments to be made about the qualities of candidates by people who knew something about what these qualities were.

Today, when presidential nominations are made almost entirely by primary electorates, we must ask: What do these electorates know of the human qualities of the candidates? Typically, very little. But virtually all of what they do know comes via the news media. So journalists, through no fault of their own, have had thrust on them far greater responsibilities to tell what they know and to find out whether what they suspect is true or not.

Not all candidates receive the same treatment, however. In 1972 the history of emotional depression of Senator Tom Eagleton of Missouri, briefly the Democrats' vice-presidential candidate, weighed more heavily in the scale than did the history of receiving bribes of Spiro T. Agnew, former governor of Maryland, his Republican opponent. Journalists found out about one but not the other in time to influence an election; Eagleton was forced to withdraw from the Democratic ticket, while Agnew was reelected to the vice presidency before being indicted and resigning from office in October 1973.

So we must wonder whether attention to any candidate's possible flaws of character ought not to be compared more conscientiously against flaws that some of the others may have. Surely, if these are qualities of candidates, they will also be qualities of the presidents these candidates might become. But it is hard to predict just how these qualities will work in any given presidency. There is no foolproof method for making sensible inferences from private behavior about the conduct of public office. Can we suppose that a lazy candidate will be a lazy president? Possibly. Still, some candidates hate campaigning but love governing and may be mediocre in a stump speech but superb negotiating a legislative compromise.

What is worse, the opposite may be true, and a great campaigner may turn out to be an incompetent president. Equally serious difficulties may be in store for those who attempt to make inferences about the conduct of the presidency from knowledge of candidates' sexual irregularities (or regularities), drinking habits, relations with their children and grandchildren, and so on.

So what are ordinary citizens to do? Ignore information that might be relevant to our primary vote if we knew about it? Attend to information about candidates even though it may be irrelevant to their conduct of the presidency? If we could tell in advance the difference between relevant and irrelevant information, it would help. But mostly we cannot, nor can the journalists who must decide what to report and what not to report. As long as primary elections and, therefore, the votes of citizens matter as much as they currently do, the only hope of achieving informed choices is by means of publicly available information. Thus, it may be regrettable but it is understandable that journalists are leaning toward disclosure and away from the protection of candidates' private lives.[32]

Regional primaries, of which 1988's Super Tuesday was a harbinger, have apparent appeal as a halfway house between a single national primary and a multitude of state primaries. There are basically three "degrees" of regional primary that have been proposed thus far. The mildest form merely requires that all states holding presidential primaries schedule them for one of four sanctioned dates, spaced a month apart, and that all candidates on a list prepared by the Federal Election Commission appear on the ballot. A second proposal would group states into geographic regions. All states within a given region that choose to have a primary would be required to hold it on the same day, on the second Tuesday of a month between March and July. Further down the slippery slope is a plan to make primaries mandatory for all states.[33]

Under the regional primary system candidates would not have to campaign in as many distant places at nearly the same time; this would save them money and effort. Since each election would encompass a large geographic area, however, the need to campaign earlier, to be better known at the start, and to have more money with which to begin would be even greater than it is now. It also seems likely that regional primaries would, in effect, push all states to hold primaries, thereby increasing the total territory a candidate must cover and the consequent cost of campaigning. The major advantage of regional primaries, assuming they were spaced about one month apart, as in one plan, would be that both politicians and people could reconsider their earlier choices in the light of the latest information. Yet if delegates were pledged to candidates, their flexibility as bargainers—in the event they were needed at the national conventions—would still be diminished. In addition, the predilection of the media to simplify complex phenomena would mean that voters in states allocated later dates would have their choices severely constrained because of the results of earlier primaries. It is possible that conflicts among states may doom the entire enterprise. If not, we suspect that regional primaries, which create an opportunity to reconsider the rules of voting, will become stalking horses for a national primary. Thus all the difficulties of a national primary should be weighed as these partial alternatives are proposed. As long as the relevant choice is between a mixed system of delegate selection and a national primary, our choice lies with the mix.

The Decline of the National Convention

High on the list of practices that in the past were regarded as objectionable was the secret gathering of party leaders in the smoke-filled room to select a presidential nominee. Some likened this to a political opium den where a few irresponsible men, hidden from public view, stealthily determined the destiny of the nation.[34] Yet it is difficult to see who, other than the party's leaders, should have been entrusted with the delicate task of finding a candidate to meet the majority preference. If head-on clashes of strength on the convention floor could not resolve the question, the only alternatives were continued deadlock, anarchy among scores of leaderless delegates splitting the party into rival factions, or some process of accommodation.

National conventions no longer pick presidential nominees; they merely ratify the work of primaries and caucuses. But let us suppose that some national convention in the future has authentic work to do, and because no single candidate has the nomination sewed up, it must pick a nominee. Would we require that a smoke-free successor to the smoke-filled room be abolished and with it all behind-the-scenes negotiations? All parleys would then be held in public, before the delegates and millions of television viewers. Could the participants resist spending their time scoring points against each other in order to impress the folks back home? Bargaining would not be taking place because the participants would not really be communicating with one another. No compromises would be possible; if they were attempted, leaders would be accused by their followers of selling out to the other side. Once a stalemate existed, breaking it would be practically impossible, and the party would probably disintegrate into warring factions.

An extensive system of state primaries in which delegates are more or less compelled to vote for the candidate who wins in the state has led to the eclipse of negotiation processes without any formal action of a convention. Since delegates cannot change their positions except by direction of the candidate to whom they are pledged, there is little point in bringing party leaders together for private conferences. Sharply increasing the number of pledged delegates introduces great rigidity into the convention because under conditions of stalemate no one is in a position to switch his or her support.

This more or less resembles the situation of the two parties today. Recent rule changes have led to the following contradiction: by fragmenting delegations, they have increased the chances of a contested convention, and by giving preference to pledged delegates they have decreased the likelihood that delegates will be able to bargain with one another. These conditions have been masked by the overriding influence of primaries and television, which, by forcing earlier and earlier decisions, have spared the parties so far the consequences of a meaningful convention under conditions of extreme fragmentation. Failure to arrive at a decision to nominate a candidate acceptable to all could conceivably lead to withdrawal of the defeated factions from the party. Since the national party is unified, if at all, only by the choice of a presidential candidate, inability to bargain out an agreement invites serious party fragmentation. Therefore, if as is now unlikely, primaries do not produce a nominee who is certain to be ratified, what happens at a national convention will matter.

Even though the nominee has actually already been chosen, each party has a stake in the presentation it makes of itself to the public. Much criticism over the years has been leveled at the raucousness of demonstrations that once took place on the convention floor while candidates were being nominated.[35] Criticism of demonstrations on the grounds that they are unseemly and vulgar seems to us to be trivial. There is no evidence to substantiate a claim that the final decision would be better in some way if demonstrations were banned. Undoubtedly, the demonstrations were in the past overdone, but not in recent years owing to the requirements of television. Briefer demonstrations retain the attention of the vast television audience that both parties would like very much to influence in their favor. The dominance of primaries has actually made demonstrations into what their critics always said they were—purely stage-managed affairs with no relation to the final outcome.

The convention, as we have said, normally aids party unity in a variety of ways. It provides a forum in which initially disunited fragments of the national party can come together and find common ground as well as a common nominee. The platform helps in performing this function. In order to gain a majority of electoral votes, a party must appeal in some way to most major population groups. Since these interests do not always want the same thing, it is necessary to compromise and, sometimes, to evade issues that would lead to drastic losses of support.

Reformers' concerns with party platforms stem primarily from two assumptions: first, that there is a significant demand in the electorate for more clear-cut differences on policy; second, that elections are likely to be a significant source of guidance on individual issues to policymakers. Yet both these assumptions are either false or highly dubious. As we have seen, on a wide range of issues leaders in both parties are much further apart than are ordinary citizens, who have been separated by rather small differences.[36] When party platforms spell out clear and important differences between the parties on policy, it usually reflects a desire of party leaders to please themselves rather than demands from the electorate.

Some critics objected to the traditional convention's stress on picking a winner, rather than the "best candidate," regardless of popularity. This objection is not compatible with the democratic notion that voters should decide who is best for them and communicate this decision in an election. Only in dictatorial countries does a set of leaders arrogate unto themselves the right to determine who is best regardless of popular preferences. Unpopular candidates can hardly win free elections. Unpopular presidents can hardly secure the support they need to accomplish their goals. Popularity can be regarded as a necessary element for obtaining consent in democratic politics.

Although popularity is normally a necessary condition for nomination, it should not be the only condition. The guideline for purposes of nomination should be to nominate the best of the popular candidates. But "best" is a slippery word. A great deal of what we mean by "best" in politics is "best for us" or "best represents our policy preferences," and this can hardly be held up as an objective criterion. What is meant by "best" in this context are such personal qualities as experience, intelligence, and decisiveness. Nevertheless, it is not at all clear that an extreme conservative would prefer a highly intelligent liberal to a moderately intelligent candidate who shared his conservative policy preferences. Personal qualities clearly are subject to discount based on the compatibility of interests between voter and candidate.

For some critics, the defect of conventions lies not only in their poor performance in nominating candidates but also in their failure to become a sort of "superlegislature," enforcing the policy views of the platform on party members in the executive branch and Congress. We have previously indicated that such enforcement is most unlikely to be achieved. Let us suppose for the purposes of argument that the conventions could somehow become much more influential on matters of national policy. How could either party retain a semblance of unity if the stakes of convention deliberations were vastly increased by converting the platform into an unbreakable promise of national policy? If one believes that an increase in heated discussion necessarily improves the chances of agreement, then the problem solves itself. Experience warns us, however, that airing sharp differences, particularly when the stakes are high, is likely to decrease agreement. At the 1964 Republican convention, for example, African American delegates, bitter about the defeat of Pennsylvania Governor William Scranton's proposed amendment on civil rights to the GOP education plank, held a protest march around the arena and, when Senator Barry Goldwater of Arizona was nominated, announced that they would sit out the campaign.[37] This did not help Goldwater's chances of election. The fact that platforms are not binding permits a degree of unity necessary for the delegates to stay put long enough to agree on a nominee. By vastly increasing the number of delegates who would bitterly oppose platform decisions and possibly leave the convention, the binding platform would jeopardize the legitimacy of the convention's nominating function. Paradoxically, in such circumstances it would be difficult to resist the temptation to make the platform utterly innocuous in order to give offense to no one at all. Republican nominee Bob Dole went so far in 1996 as to say that he hadn't read the platform he was presumably running on.

Even so, platforms do have a far from negligible impact on public opinion. Platform planks are enacted as governmental policy slightly more than half the time.[38] Programs favored by the public, according to opinion polls, are twice as likely to be enacted if they also appear in party platforms.[39] When large majorities favor programs, both parties are likely to put them in their platforms; when the public is somewhat more divided and important constituencies object, the parties are capable of going against popular majorities. Thus Republican platform planks on welfare and economic issues and Democratic provisions on labor unions and affirmative action tend to run counter to majority opinion.[40] The question of whom the parties are for, special or general constituencies, is resolved by going for the majority when it is substantial and modifying that position when it conflicts with special party concerns.

Even though they no longer have a role other than as advertising, the superiority of the traditional, decision-making national conventions to presidential selection by alternative means is clear. Only the convention permits us to realize in large measure all of the seven goals—maintenance of the two-party system, party competition, some degree of internal cohesion, candidates attractive to voters, qualified candidates, acceptance of nominees as legitimate, and a connection between winning the nomination and governing later on—that we postulated earlier would commonly be accepted as desirable.

The Electoral College

For the first time in 112 years, the presidential candidate in 2000 who received the most popular votes failed to become president. But while many Democrats looked upon George W. Bush's ascension to the presidency as illegitimate, their objections were based primarily on the controversy over the counting of votes in Florida and the active role of the Supreme Court in halting recounts, not the rare discrepancy between the popular and electoral vote. A few calls for reforming or abolishing the electoral college temporarily generated some media attention, but the issue quickly receded. Like presidential primaries or the campaign finance system, the electoral college appears to be a uniquely American institution that endures even while the original logic inspiring it has faded with time.

Close presidential elections, those in which the new president has only a narrow margin in the total popular vote, always lead to renewed public discussion of the merits of the electoral college. Reform interest surges even higher when a regionally-based third party, such as the party George Wallace led in 1968, or a conspicuous independent candidate, such as Ross Perot in 1992, becomes strong enough conceivably to prevent any candidate from having an electoral vote majority. In such a situation the Constitution designates the U.S. House of Representatives as the official arbiter of the decision; under this procedure, each state delegation casts one vote regardless of size.[41]

The number of reform plans generated in the aftermath of the 1968 election and more or less in play since the 2000 election was legion. There were, however, only three basic alternatives to the present system proposed, and the rest were variations. One would abolish the electoral college outright and weigh individual votes equally everywhere in a simple popular election. The net effect of such a proposal would be to undermine slightly the current strategic advantage enjoyed by populous, competitive, urbanized states. It might also have some long-run effects on the two-party system itself, but these would depend on other changes in the social situation within the country. The second proposal would retain the apportionment of the electoral college (which gives numerical advantage to the smaller, rural states) but abolish the unit-rule electoral vote within states (which operates strongly in favor of populous states). This proposal is quite extreme in its import, which would be to confer an additional political bonus on states traditionally overrepresented in positions of congressional power. A third, quite similar, proposal also retains the apportionment of the electoral college but distributes an electoral college vote for the plurality vote winner in each congressional district and two additional electoral votes for the winner in each state. Since this system maximizes the strength of one-party states, it could work to realign the presidential coalition in fundamental ways.[42]

The Constitution provides that each state, regardless of its population, shall be represented in the Senate by an equal number of senators. This means that the ten largest states, with 52 percent of the voters in 2004, elect 20 percent of the senators. In the course of legislative proceedings, these twenty senators' votes can be canceled by the twenty votes of the senators from the ten least populous states, with 3.2 percent of the voters in the 2004 presidential election. At one point in early 1960, an average vote in Nevada was worth eighty-five times as much as an average vote in New York in elections for the Senate. The imbalance roughly corresponds to the advantage that more populous, urbanized, two-party states enjoy in the electoral college, and thus in access to the presidency.

The present electoral college system, with its votes apportioned according to the total of Senate and House seats a state has, awarded on a "winner-take-all" basis state by state, does provide a clear advantage to two groups of states. It yields a secondary advantage to the smallest states, since their overrepresentation in the Senate guarantees them overrepresentation in the electoral college; after the 2000 census, the seven states with three electoral votes each had a ratio of 301,000 or fewer citizens per electoral vote, while every state with thirteen or more electoral votes had a ratio of 536,000 or more citizens per electoral vote.

But it is primarily the larger states, through the unit-rule principle, which benefit from the electoral college. Candidates who can get a narrow majority in California alone can bag more electoral votes (55) than they could by carrying all of the fourteen smallest states plus the District of Columbia (54); they can, mathematically, carry California by one vote and not receive any votes in those fourteen states and do just as well. This fact suggests that presidential candidates should spend their energy in the larger states and tailor their programs to appeal to voters there, provided that energy expended there is likely to yield results.[43] In fact, the larger states are somewhat more likely to be close in their division of the major-party vote, while a fair number of the smaller states are more commonly "safe" for one party or the other.

The large states are also the home of many organized minorities, especially racial and ethnic minorities, and this has traditionally meant that both presidential candidates have had to pitch their appeals to attract these groups, or at least not to drive them off. Some of the critics of the current system have pointed to this advantage for the larger states, and especially their urban minorities, as a drawback of that system, to be reformed out of existence,[44] but most have concentrated their fire on the possibility of the "wrong winner" and the "undemocratic" nature of the unit rule.

Allowing a majority (or plurality) of voters to choose a president has a great deal to commend it. This is the simplest method of all; it would be most easily understood by the greatest number of people; it is the plan favored by the majority of Americans; and it comes closest to reflecting intuitive notions of direct popular sovereignty through majority rule.

Moreover, the outright abolition of the electoral college, and the substitution of the direct election of the president, would reduce the importance of the larger states. It would mean that the popular vote margin that a state could provide, not the number of electoral votes, would determine its importance. For example, under the present system a candidate who carries California by 350,000 votes (as George H. W. Bush did in 1988) has garnered one-fifth of the support needed to win, while under the direct-vote system, medium-size states such as

Massachusetts or Alabama can sometimes generate more than twice that margin. In the two-party states, in which category most of the larger states fall, voters are cross-pressured in many ways, and candidates can seldom count on defeating their opponents by a very large margin. The reason, then, that the large states lose influence is that direct election switches influence from the close states to one-party states; in some states where one party's organization is weak, it is easier for the other party to achieve a large turnout at election time, and special rewards might be forthcoming for interest groups particularly strong within states that could provide a large margin of victory for their candidate. As candidates currently look with favor on those who can bring them support in the large states, so might they be expected to look with favor on those who can bring them large popular margins in the one-party states, should that become the preferred strategy for winning. The emphasis would not be on which candidate was going to win the state, already a foregone conclusion, but by how many votes he or she was going to win.[45] The small states do not gain, however, because even when they are one-party, they are not large enough to generate big numbers of voters. Direct election thus changes the advantage from the biggest and the smallest two-party states to the medium-sized one-party states, and these, in recent elections, happen most commonly to be located in the South.[46]

This does not, of course, settle the matter, for one of the reasons that direct election is touted is that third parties cannot deadlock the process. In fact, those southern states with the largest 1968 margins—when George Wallace was a sectional candidate—were not powerful but weak, for they did not contribute to a winner but to a third-place loser.

How one feels about direct elections depends on (1) how one feels about the diminution of large-state influence and the gain by sundry other smaller states, (2) how much of a plurality one feels a newly elected president should have, and (3) how this plurality limit will affect others in the system.

Clearly, third-party votes under a direct election system are wasted if the candidate with a plurality is declared the winner, no matter how small that plurality. At best, voters could express only their feelings of frustration by voting for third-party candidates, and this would be at the cost of foregoing the chance to influence an election. We suspect, however, that most Americans would feel uncomfortable with a president who, even though winning a plurality, was elected by, say, only 35 percent of the voters. One of the virtues of the present electoral vote system is that it magnifies the margin of a presidential victory (as, for instance, in 1996, Clinton's 8 percent popular victory margin gave him 72 percent of the electoral vote), presumably conferring added legitimacy and with it acceptance of the new president's responsibility to govern in fact as well as in title. Any system of direct election would almost have to eliminate the majority principle in favor of some plurality, or it would clearly lead to much more, not less, deadlock; in three out of our last four presidential elections, the winning candidate lacked an absolute majority of the popular vote.

Reformers have generally agreed, though, that the winner must win by at least a substantial plurality; consequently, the electoral college reform amendment that passed the House in late 1969 provided for a runoff between the top two candidates if no one secured as much as 40 percent of the popular vote in the initial election.[47] The first effect of this provision would be to hand back influence to splinter parties. If a satisfactory major-party candidate is going to have a second chance to win the office anyway, there is an incentive for any sizable organized minority to contest the first election on its own. That the runoff would likely be used if it were provided for is suggested by 1992, when there was a fairly strong third-party candidate, Ross Perot, in the race. A fourth candidate would have needed only 6 or 7 percent of the national total to keep either major-party candidate from having the required 40 percent (Clinton won with 43 percent, although he had 68.8 percent of the electoral vote).[48] Once this becomes even a plausible expectation, there is an incentive for various intense minorities to put up their own candidates, and visions of an evangelical Christian party, an African American party, a labor party, a peace party, an environmentalist party, a right-to-life party, a farmers' party, and so on, appear. Whereas one of the strong points of the present system is that it enforces a compromise by penalizing all minorities that will not come to terms, the direct election system could well encourage a continental European situation, in which numerous groups contest the first election and then recombine for the second; at the least, severe changes would be worked on the present system.[49] Should such a result occur in the future, the simplicity, ease of comprehension, and inherent majoritarian rightness of the direct election solution would quickly disappear. One of the hidden effects of the electoral college is to restrict the number of parties contesting for the presidency. This helps focus the electorate on a limited menu of choices. In turn, this increases the chance that winners will have the backing of a sizable number of voters and the legitimacy to lead Congress and the nation.

The direct election plan passed by the House in 1969 received a warmer reception in the Senate than the previous time it appeared there—in 1956, it was voted down 66 to 17—but there were, not surprisingly, two major opposition groups. The first was the bloc of liberal senators from the biggest states, which had most to lose. The second was composed of some of the conservative senators from the smallest states, whom we have named as the group deriving second-greatest benefits from the current system. They argued that direct election would be a complete break with the federalism underlying our Constitution, since it would abolish the importance of state boundaries in presidential elections.[50]

Another proposal, embodied in the 1950s in the unsuccessful Lodge-Gossett Resolution, is seen by some reformers as an acceptable "compromise" between outright abolition of the electoral college and its retention.[51] In this scheme, the electoral vote in each state is split between the candidates according to their proportion of the state's popular vote. This may seem to be a procedural compromise, but it is a rather extreme reform in political terms.

Under proportional allocation of electoral votes, campaigning presidential nominees would have to give special attention to those states in which they felt a large difference in electoral votes could be attained. Once again, the proposed reform emphasizes the amount of difference within the state between the winner and the loser. In this case, however, the electoral votes of the states are divided, rather than the popular votes. This effectively cancels out the advantage of the large states entirely. The fact that the electoral college underrepresents the large states in the first place even further reduces their influence. The beneficiaries are again the one-party states, as well as the smaller states, since in any particular election West Virginia and Utah, for example, may have more to contribute to the difference in electoral votes than Illinois, New Jersey, Ohio, or Florida.

There are two versions of this plan, one that divides electoral votes to the nearest vote and one that divides them to the nearest tenth of a vote. Most proponents favor the plan to divide them to the nearest tenth, since the nearest whole vote in many cases still would understate the closeness of the vote in a large number of states, especially those with few electoral votes to divide, and "representativeness" is the primary theoretical advantage of the plan. Since preventing deadlock is supposed to be one of the goals of electoral college reform, it is interesting to note that with the majority-vote victory required by proponents of both plans, the tenth-vote system would have thrown all of the close elections beginning in 1960 into the House of Representatives, including the 1992, 1996, and 2000 elections (Kennedy and Carter would have won in 1960 and 1976 using whole votes; the 1976 result using tenth-votes would depend on whether 270 electoral votes were needed, as under the current rules, or only 269.1). Under the tenth-vote plan, elections would wind up in the House so frequently (requiring only a very close election, as in 1960, or a moderately strong third candidate, as in 1996, or both, as in 1968 or 2000) that the presidency would be primarily dependent on Congress, not on the presidential election.[52]

The reduction in influence suffered by the large states under proportional proposals might mean, in effect, that the sparsely populated and one-party states would entirely dominate the national lawmaking process, unchecked by a president obliged to cultivate urban and two-party constituencies. The same problem is present if deadlock is dealt with by letting the plurality candidate win. Even with a plurality provision, splintering is facilitated under this plan because a party need only pull a fraction of a percentage point of a major state's total vote in order to get some electoral votes. The present system at least cuts off splinter groups without a strong regional base.

A third plan, the district plan, has been proposed as still another "political compromise" between the other two major reform proposals, on the grounds that since thirty-eight states must ratify a constitutional amendment on electoral reform, the seventeen states with five or fewer electoral votes are not likely to support either of the first two proposals because each dilutes their current strength. The district plan would give a presidential candidate one electoral vote for every congressional district carried, plus two more for every state. This is how electoral votes are now distributed in the states of Maine and Nebraska. It has been pushed largely by conservative senators; it is clearly the most radical of all the reform proposals in its effect on the U.S. political system, and it is least advantageous to the big states. This system would have given Nixon victory in 1968 (290-190-58), but if it had already been in effect, he probably would not have been running, since it would have already reversed the results of the election of 1960 (Nixon 280, Kennedy 252). It would also have easily elected George W. Bush in 2000 by a greater electoral college majority than he received under the existing winner-take-all rules, even though Bush lost the national popular vote to Al Gore. It is hard to see how the district plan makes the electoral college more "democratic" than the current system.

Since the goals of electoral reform are supposedly to prevent the wrong candidate from winning, to avoid deadlock, and to do away with winner-take-all arrangements, it is hard to see what is offered by a system that (1) gives the less popular candidate victory, (2) provides no more guarantee against deadlock than the present system (Wallace in 1968 got 45 electoral votes under the actual system, but would have received 57 under the district plan), (3) uses a winner-take-all principle, and (4) has the incidental feature of ending the activist character of the American presidency and handing policy control over to one-party areas for the foreseeable future.[53]

Table 6.2 shows outcomes under the various plans for presidential elections since 1960. The election of 1988 would have come out the same way under all the plans for counting votes we have been considering. Under proportional allocation, the three presidential elections between 1992 and 2000 would have been thrown into the House of Representatives, but Bill Clinton (in 1992 and 1996) and George W. Bush (in 2000) would still have won under district representation. Plans

TABLE 6.2 Electoral Outcomes under Various Plans

Year	Present Plan		Direct Plan		Proportional Plan		District Plan	
2004	*Bush wins*		*Bush wins*		*Bush wins*		*Bush wins*	
	Bush	281	Bush	50.7 %	Bush	272.8	Bush	317
	Kerry	251	Kerry	48.3	Kerry	259.9	Kerry	221
	Others	1	Others	1.0	Others	5.4	Others	0
2000	*Bush wins*		*Gore wins*		*Winner unclear*		*Bush wins*	
	Bush	271	Bush	47.9 %	Bush	259.2	Bush	288
	Gore	266	Gore	48.4	Gore	258.3	Gore	250
	Abstention	1	Others	3.7	Others	20.5	Others	0
1996	*Clinton wins*		*Clinton wins*		*Winner unclear*		*Clinton wins*	
	Clinton	379	Clinton	49.2 %	Clinton	264.0	Clinton	345
	Dole	159	Dole	40.7	Dole	220.0	Dole	193
	Perot	0	Perot	8.4	Perot	45.4	Perot	0
1992	*Clinton wins*		*Clinton wins*		*Winner unclear*		*Clinton wins*	
	Clinton	370	Clinton	43.0 %	Clinton	230.6	Clinton	323
	Bush	168	Bush	37.4	Bush	202.6	Bush	215
	Perot	0	Perot	18.9	Perot	101.6	Perot	0
1988	*Bush wins*		*Bush wins*		*Bush wins*		*Bush wins*	
	Bush	426	Bush	53.4 %	Bush	288.0	Bush	377
	Dukakis	111	Dukakis	45.6	Dukakis	244.7	Dukakis	161
	Others	1	Others	1.0	Others	5.3	Others	0
1976	*Carter wins*		*Carter wins*		*Carter wins*		*Winner unclear*	
	Carter	297	Carter	50.1 %	Carter	269.7	Carter	269
	Ford	240	Ford	48.0	Ford	258.3	Ford	269
	Others	1	Others	1.9	Others	10.0	Others	0
1968	*Nixon wins*		*Nixon wins*		*Winner unclear*		*Nixon wins*	
	Nixon	301	Nixon	43.4 %	Nixon	231.0	Nixon	290
	Humphrey	191	Humphrey	42.7	Humphrey	225.5	Humphrey	190
	Wallace	46	Wallace	13.5	Wallace	79.4	Wallace	58
1960	*Kennedy wins*		*Kennedy wins*		*Winner unclear*		*Nixon wins*	
	Kennedy	303	Kennedy	49.7 %	Kennedy	265.6	Kennedy	252
	Nixon	219	Nixon	49.6	Nixon	264.0	Nixon	280
	Others	15	Others	0.7	Others	7.4	Others	5

Note: "Winner unclear" denotes scenarios in which no candidate receives a majority of electoral votes. The House of Representatives would then select the president from among the three candidates receiving the most electoral votes, with each state casting one vote, as specified by the Twelfth Amendment to the Constitution.

to abolish the electoral college, by damping down even large landslides, would bring stronger and more splinter parties into the electoral competition, thus changing the climate of electoral competition altogether.

Under the present electoral college system, there has been no time since 1876 when any splinter group has been able to make good on its threat to throw the election into the House. Even in 1948 Harry Truman won an electoral college majority despite sizable threats from both a third (Henry Wallace, Progressive) and a fourth (Strom Thurmond, States' Rights) party. Only once in the past century—in 2000—has the loser of the popular vote become president. On the other hand, a direct election plan that required a 40 percent plurality might well have forced a runoff in 1968 and 1992. The proportional plan would have created deadlocks in two recent elections; and the district plan would have thrown the election to the popular vote loser in at least one recent case. In view of this analysis of the effect of electoral reforms, it is curious that many reformers have supported these changes in the electoral college.

Underlying all these arguments, of course, is the premise that most structural reforms "tend" to shift influences in certain ways. There may well be situations of social polarization that electoral system alternatives by themselves cannot paper over. But while we have argued that there is no better system than the current one, from the standpoint of the professed goals of most reformers, there is one minor change that would aid them. Under the present plan the actual electors who make up the electoral college are in fact free to vote for whomever they wish. These electors are usually party faithful who are chosen in each state by party leaders. As an almost invariable rule, they vote for the winner in their state, but abuses are possible, and two within recent memory come to mind:

1. The unpledged electors chosen by citizens in Mississippi and Alabama in 1960 decided for whom they would vote only well after the election, treating the preferences of citizens as advisory, not mandatory. This clearly thwarts popular control.
2. This liberty allowed George Wallace to hope that he could run for president, create an electoral deadlock, and then bargain with one of the other candidates for policy concessions in exchange for his electors.

An amendment making the casting of electoral votes automatic would dispel both these possibilities.

A final device deserves consideration, the creation of a private commission set up by the Twentieth Century Fund (now the Century Foundation) some years ago. It came up with a proposal for a National Bonus Plan, which would award 102 electoral votes en bloc (two for each state plus the District of Columbia) to the plurality winner of the nationwide popular vote. This plan would make it highly probable that no president could be elected who did not get more votes than the nearest rival. An additional feature is that candidates would be encouraged to get as many votes as they could, even in states where they were pretty sure to lose, because these would add on to the candidate's national popular total.[54] The Bonus Plan would guard against a minority president, preserve the form and the spirit of the constitutional structure, and do all this without encouraging splinter parties.

We have argued that there is no serious reason to quarrel with the major features of the present system, since in our form of government "majority rule" does not operate in a vacuum but within a system of "checks and balances." The president, for example, holds a veto power over laws enacted by Congress. If the veto is exercised, a two-thirds vote of each house is required to override it. Treaties must be ratified by two-thirds of the Senate, and amendments to the Constitution must be proposed by two-thirds of Congress or of the state legislatures and ratified by three-fourths of the states. Presidential appointments, in most important cases, must receive senatorial approval. The Supreme Court passes upon the constitutionality of legislative and executive actions. And of course there is impeachment, a political check on the presidency available to Congress. Involved in these political arrangements is the hope that the power of one branch of government will be counterbalanced by certain "checks" from another, the result being an approximate "balance" of forces. In our view, it is not necessarily a loss to have slightly different majorities preponderant in different institutions, but it is definitely a loss to have the same majority preponderant in both political branches while other majorities are frozen out. In the past the electoral college had its place within this system. Originally designed to check popular majorities from choosing presidents unwisely, the electoral college later on provided a check on the overrepresentation of rural states in the legislative branch by giving extra weight to the big-state constituencies of the president.

PARTY PLATFORMS AND PARTY DIFFERENCES

Having reviewed some of the major changes proposed by party reformers, let us return to consider their key argument. Parties, reformers claim, are insufficiently ideological. The voters are not being offered clear choices, and the parties, once in office, are not responsibly carrying out the promises made in their platforms. We argue that American parties do indeed differ—more so now than in the recent past—and that, much of the time, they respond to changes in voter sentiment. We believe that the solutions offered by reformers are unnecessary and would lead to consequences that even they might not desire.

Party platforms written by the presidential parties should be understood not only as ends in themselves but as means to obtaining and holding public office. It would be strange indeed if a party understood that policies such as Social Security and unemployment compensation were enormously popular and yet refused to incorporate them into its platform.[55] This would have to be a party of ideologues who cared everything about their own ideas and nothing about winning elections. Nor would it profit them much because they would not get elected and would never be in a position to do something about their ideas. Sooner or later, at least in a political system like the United States, ideologues have to make the choice between pleasing themselves and winning elections.

Even when the major political parties are in the hands of moderate leaders, there are clear differences between the doctrines espoused by the two parties, and these are reflected in party platforms. Moreover, party platforms change over a period of time in a cyclical movement. The differences between the parties may be great for one or two elections, until innovations made by one party are picked up by the other.

The net change from one decade to the next is substantial. Let us begin when platforms are more or less alike. Their similarity begins to give way as it appears that certain demands in society are not being met. The minority party of the period senses an opportunity to gain votes by articulating and promising to meet these demands. The majority party, reluctant to let go of a winning combination, resists. In one or two elections the minority party makes its bid and makes the appropriate changes in its platforms. Then, in the ensuing elections, if the party that has changed its platform loses, it drops the innovation. If it wins, and wins big, the other party then seeks to take over what seem to be its most popular planks, and the platforms become more alike again.

We can see this cycle clearly in the New Deal period. The 1932 Democratic platform, though hinting at change, was much like the Republican one, especially in its emphasis on balancing the budget. A great difference in platforms could be noted in 1936 as the Democrats attempted to consolidate the New Deal and the Republicans stood pat. The spectacular Democratic triumph signaled the end of widely divergent platforms. By 1940, the Republicans had concluded that they could not continue to oppose the welfare state wholesale if they ever wished to win again. By 1952, the parties had come much closer to each other as the Republicans adopted most of the New Deal. Though the platforms of the major parties were similar to each other in both 1932 and 1952, the differences between 1932 and 1952 for either party were enormous.[56] In keeping with our finding that party leaders are, by historic standards, currently more polarized than usual, it is not surprising to find sharp differences in the party platforms for 2004 (see box 6.1).

Sometimes reformers deplore what they regard as an excessive amount of mudslinging in campaigns, but they also ask that differences among the major parties be sharp in order to give the voters a clear choice. The two ideas are incompatible. It is unreasonable to require that parties disagree more sharply about more and more subjects in an increasingly gentlemanly way. Far more likely would be an increase in vituperation as the stakes of campaigns increased, passions rose, tempers flared, and the consequences of victory for the other side appeared much more threatening than had earlier been the case.

The case for the desirability of party reform used to rest on the assumption that American political parties were identical, that this was confusing and frustrating to American voters, and that it was undesirable to have a political system where parties do not disagree sharply. Now we have a chance to find out what happens during a period of relative party polarization.

Imagine for a moment that the two parties were in total and extreme disagreement on every major point of public policy, more so than they are in the United States. One party would limit American military power to our borders, the other would intervene in every tense situation across the globe. One group would go all-out to improve productivity; the other would put environmental values first. One group would stop Social Security; the other would expand it drastically. One group would raise tariffs; the other would abolish them. Obviously one consequence of having clear-cut parties with strong policy positions would be that the costs of losing an election would skyrocket. If parties were forced to formulate coherent, full-dress programs and were forced to carry them out "responsibly," and in full, then people who did not favor these programs would have little recourse (until the next election). Clearly their confidence in a government whose policies were so little to their liking would suffer, and, indeed, they might feel strongly enough about preventing these policies from being enacted to do something drastic, like leaving the country or not complying with governmental regulations or, in an extreme case, seeking to change the political system by impeachment or by force.

The presidency of Republican Ronald Reagan may give pause to liberal reformers. Though Reagan's campaign rhetoric was too general to alarm voters, in many respects he played the part of the responsible-party president who proposed and attempted to carry out a wide-ranging program designed to modify, if not to undo completely, the efforts of his Democratic predecessors. There was no mistaking his thrust—less domestic government and more money for defense. Indeed, if any president has performed according to the "responsible government" model, it is Ronald Reagan, who tried and to some extent succeeded, at least early in his administration, to carry out his campaign promises. If the results did not meet with universal approval, citizens cannot say they were not forewarned as to the direction the candidate would take in the event he was elected.

Or consider the performance in office of George W. Bush, who promised to change the climate of partisanship in Washington and to be "a uniter, not a divider" but who in fact wielded his razor-thin majority in Congress in energetic pursuit of a right-wing presidency. Bush was installed in the presidency by a ruling of the Supreme Court that halted the counting of votes in Florida and awarded him the state's electoral votes. Later investigations indicated that had the votes all been counted, Bush would have won, very narrowly, in the electoral college, but owing to the popular votes in other states, Bush became president without winning the popular vote nationwide. The election overall yielded a popular vote that was closely split between the major parties. Yet Bush, so long as his party controlled both houses of Congress, made few concessions to the middle ground expressed in the net result.

If some citizens prefer more moderation and compromise, they should then consider whether they really want parties and candidates to carry out their programs. Is the argument for party reform that the nation needs more Reagans or more George W. Bushes, whether of the right or left? Evidently, given favorable political conditions such as existed in Lyndon Johnson's first term and Ronald Reagan's first year, coherent presidential programs enacted en masse by Congress are possible without constitutional reform or further changes, such as we have been discussing, in electoral machinery. It is necessary to have enthusiastic party activists, determined and skillful leaders, and public consent. These are not always available, but they sometimes are. When they are not, perhaps it is wise to make the achievement of large changes not too easy.[57]

BOX 6.1 SELECTIONS FROM THE REPUBLICAN AND DEMOCRATIC PLATFORMS, 2004

REPUBLICAN PLATFORM
Economic Policy

America's economy is the strongest in the world, and it is getting stronger thanks to lower taxes, fewer burdensome regulations, and a focus on encouraging investment.... In 2001, President Bush and the Republican Congress worked together to pass the most sweeping tax relief in a generation. By letting families, workers, and small businesses keep more of the money they earn, they helped bring America from recession to a steadily expanding economy.... We support legislation requiring a super-majority vote in both houses of Congress to raise taxes.... We support a cap on discretionary spending that will limit the growth of overall spending while ensuring that priorities such as our nation's security will continue to be met.

Education

We recognize that under the American Constitutional system, education is a state, local, and family responsibility, not a federal obligation. Since over 90 percent of public school funding is state and local, not federal, it is obvious that state and local governments must assume most of the responsibility to improve the schools, and the role of the federal government must be limited as we return control to parents, teachers, and local school boards.... On just his fourth day in office, President Bush presented the No Child Left Behind initiative to Congress.... Results are now measured on the basis of student achievement rather than simply dollars spent.... With this success, Republicans have transformed the debate on education.... We believe that competition between schools is an effective option to improve the educational benefits for our children. The Republican Party supports the efforts of parents who choose faith-based and other nonpublic school options for their children.

Environment

Republicans know that economic prosperity is essential to environmental progress . . . [W]e link the security of private property to our environmental agenda because environmental stewardship has been best advanced when property is privately held. After all, people who live on the land, work the land, and own the land also love the land and protect it.... Using the most sophisticated technologies, we can explore and develop oil resources here at home with minimal environmental impact. Our Party continues to support energy development of the Arctic National Wildlife Refuge (ANWR), which, according to the U.S. Geological Survey, holds as much as 16 billion barrels of oil— enough to replace oil imports from Saudi Arabia for nearly 20 years.... Republicans are committed to meeting the challenge of long-term global climate change by relying on markets and new technologies to improve energy efficiency. These efforts will help reduce emissions over time while allowing the economy to grow. Our President and our Party strongly oppose the Kyoto Protocol and similar mandatory carbon emissions controls that harm economic growth and destroy American jobs.

Affirmative Action

The Republican Party favors aggressive, proactive measures to ensure that no individual is discriminated against on the basis of race, national origin, gender, or other characteristics covered by our civil rights laws. We also favor recruitment and outreach policies that cast the widest possible net so that the best qualified individuals are encouraged to apply for jobs, contracts, and university admissions. We believe in the principle of affirmative access—taking steps to ensure that disadvantaged individuals of all colors and ethnic backgrounds have the opportunity to compete economically and that no child is left behind educationally.... Finally, because we are opposed to discrimination, we reject preferences, quotas, and set-asides based on skin color, ethnicity, or gender, which perpetuate divisions and can lead people to question the accomplishments of successful minorities and women.

Terrorism and Iraq

The world changed on September 11, 2001, and since that day, under the strong, steady, and visionary leadership of George W. Bush, Americans have helped make the world not only safer, but better.... Terrorists long ago declared war on America, and now America has declared war against terrorists. We are defending the peace by taking the fight to the enemy. We are confronting terrorists overseas so we do not have to confront them at home.... Nations that support terrorism are just as dangerous, and just as guilty, as the perpetrators of terrorism. Every nation must make a choice to support terror or to support America and our coalition to defeat terror.... Iraq, which once had the worst government in the Middle East, is now becoming an example of reform to the region. Iraqi security forces are fighting beside coalition troops to defeat the terrorists and foreign fighters who threaten their nation and the world. Today, because America and our coalition helped to end the violent regime of Saddam Hussein, and because we are helping to raise a peaceful democracy in its place, 25 million Iraqis are free and the American people are safer.... We are ever mindful that American troops remain on the ground in Iraq, working steadfastly to help the Iraqi people achieve stability and democracy. We therefore welcome declarations from responsible political leaders of both parties that our nation will persevere in our mission there, not cut and run.

DEMOCRATIC PLATFORM
Economic Policy

Under John Kerry and John Edwards, we will revive America's manufacturing sector, create new jobs and protect existing ones by ending tax breaks for companies that ship jobs overseas and cutting taxes for companies that create jobs here at home; by fighting for free, fair and balanced trade; by encouraging investment in small businesses and helping companies deal with rising health care costs; by promoting new technologies, like energy, that will lead to the companies and jobs of tomorrow; and by ensuring that people of every age learn the skills to succeed in today's economy.... With the middle class under assault like never before, we simply cannot afford the massive Bush tax cuts for the very wealthiest. We should set taxes for families making more than $200,000 a year at the same level as in the late 1990s, a period of great prosperity when the wealthiest Americans thrived without special treatment.

Education

In President George Bush's America, our government ignores the shameful truth that the quality of a child's education depends on the wealth of that child's neighborhood.... Under John Kerry and John Edwards, we will offer high quality early learning opportunities, smaller classes, more after school activities, and more individualized attention for our students, particularly students with special needs, gifts, and talents.... We need to do more to attract and retain teachers, more to encourage their excellence, and more to ensure that all teachers are offering high-quality teaching. We must raise pay for teachers, especially in the schools and subjects where great teachers are in the shortest supply.... Instead of pushing private school vouchers that funnel scarce dollars away from the public schools, we will support public school choice, including charter schools and magnet schools that meet the same high standards as other schools.

Environment

The health of our families, the strength of our economy, and the well-being of our world all depend upon a clean environment. But in President George Bush's government, where polluters actually write environmental laws and oil company profits matter more than hard science and cold facts, protecting the environment doesn't matter at all.... We reject the false choice between a healthy economy and a healthy environment.... We will use our natural resources to fuel our economy, but end Republican giveaways to special interests that exploit public lands without regard for environmental consequences.... We know that America's fight for a healthy environment cannot be waged within our borders alone. Environmental hazards from around the globe reach America through the oceans and the jet streams encircling our planet. And climate change is a major international challenge that requires global leadership from the United States, not abdication.

Affirmative Action

This year we recall two of our country's biggest steps toward equality and inclusion—fifty years ago, *Brown v. Board of Education,* and forty years ago, the Civil Rights Act of 1964. Those great achievements of the civil rights movement strengthened America immeasurably—by breaking down the legal barriers to equal citizenship for African Americans and expanding the circle of equal opportunity for all.... We support affirmative action to redress discrimination and to achieve the diversity from which all Americans benefit.

Terrorism and Iraq

We face a global terrorist movement of many groups, funded from different sources with separate agendas, but all committed to assaulting the United States and free and open societies around the globe. Despite his tough talk, President Bush's actions against terrorism have fallen far short.... His doctrine of unilateral preemption has driven away our allies and cost us the support of other nations. . . . People of good will disagree about whether America should have gone to war in Iraq, but this much is clear: this Administration badly exaggerated its case, particularly with respect to weapons of mass destruction and the connection between Saddam's government and al Qaeda. This Administration did not build a true international coalition. . . . To succeed, America must do the hard work of engaging the world's major political powers in this mission. We must build a coalition of countries, including the other permanent members of the UN Security Council, to share the political, economic, and military responsibilities of Iraq with the United States.

SEVEN

AMERICAN PARTIES AND DEMOCRACY

O VER A RELATIVELY SHORT PERIOD OF TIME (SINCE THE 1960s), a new sort of American political system has come into being. Among its features are high degrees of mass participation in formerly elite processes, such as the nomination of presidential candidates, the replacement of political parties with the news media as primary organizers of citizen action and legitimizers of public decisions, the rise in the influence of media-approved and media-sustained interest groups, and the decline of interest groups linked to party organizations. Certain sorts of decision making are easy in a system structured in this way: simple voting, for example, in which alternatives are few and clear-cut. However, complex, deliberative decision making, in which various alternatives are compared one after the other, contingencies are weighed and tested tentatively, second and third choices are probed for hidden consensuses, or special weight is given to intensity of likes and dislikes, is extremely difficult in such a system. Therefore, much influence flows into the hands of those who structure alternatives in the first place—self-starting candidates and the news media.

But the need for organizations to do the job of the parties continues even as the party organizations decline in influence. For presidential elections, we have observed the replacement of the convention with primary elections as the most significant part of the process and the rise of party activists who are more ideological and sometimes more extreme than the rest of the population.[1]

Because the American political system is moving toward a role for political parties that stresses their activities as policy advocates, it seems to us important to give some attention to the implications of this trend for democratic government. Our argument makes two main points. The first is that it is necessary for parties of advocacy in a democracy to receive mandates on public policy from popular majorities of convinced believers in their programs, but that this condition is not met in America because of the ways in which electorates actually participate in elections and conceive of public policy.

Our second point is that in view of the actual disposition of attitudes toward public policy in the electorate as compared with party elites, the fact that we are moving toward, or have actually entered into, an era of parties of advocacy poses some significant and largely unaddressed problems for American democracy. This is because it is not the policy preferences of the bulk of the electorate that are being advocated. Moreover, the implementation of policy through government requires the sort of institutional support that parties can orchestrate only if they have some permanency and are not required to give birth to themselves anew every four years to nominate a candidate, and then wither away.

ELECTIONS AND PUBLIC POLICY

Uncoerced and competitive elections aid in making the political system open and responsive to a great variety of people and groups in the population. But elections do not transmit unerringly the policy preferences of electorates to leaders or confer mandates on leaders with regard to specific policies. Consider the presidential landslide of 1972, which resulted in a Republican president but also in a Democratic Congress that was bound to disagree with him. Or consider the following complex sequence. In 1980, Ronald Reagan won comfortably, with Republicans also gaining control of the Senate, but not the House. By 1982, the Democrats had recouped. President Reagan won even more decisively in 1984, but failed to do much of consequence in Congress; two years later the Democrats made a strong comeback and regained control of the Senate. The Clinton era elections are even more difficult to interpret. Bill Clinton won presidential elections twice by decisive margins over his Republican opponents but without achieving a majority of the popular vote. In between those elections, Republicans won a landslide election that gave them control of both houses of Congress. And then, in 1998, Clinton's party bucked history to gain House seats (and broke even in the Senate). Even in a landslide, winners can sensibly claim only a temporary, equivocal mandate. And in any case elections that are clear-cut are rare. George W. Bush assumed the presidency, we recall, after the election of 2000 in which his main opponent, Al Gore, won more popular votes.

It is easy to be cynical and expect too little from elections or to be euphoric and expect too much from them. A cynical view would hold that the United States was ruled by a power elite—a small group outside the democratic process. Under these circumstances the ballot would be a sham and a delusion. What difference can it make how voting is carried on or who wins if the nation is actually governed by other means? In contrast, a euphoric view, holding that the United States is ruled as a mass democracy with equal control over decisions by all or most citizens, would enormously magnify the importance of the ballot. Through the act of casting a ballot, it could be argued, a majority of citizens would determine major national policies. What happens at the polls would not only decide who occupies public office; it also would determine the content of specific policy decisions. In a way, public office would then be a sham because the power of decision in important matters would be removed from the hands of public officials.

A third type of political system, in which numerous minorities compete for shares in policy making within broad limits provided by free elections, has more complex implications. It suggests that balloting is important but that it often does not and sometimes should not determine individual policy decisions. The ballot guides and constrains public officials, who are free to act within fairly broad limits subject to their anticipations of the responses of the voters and—this is important in a separation of powers system—to the desires of other active participants.

It is evident that the American political system is of this third type. Public officials do make major policy decisions, but elections matter in that (with very rare exceptions) they determine which of the two main competing parties holds public office. In a competitive two-party situation such as exists in American presidential politics, the lively possibility of change provides an effective incentive for political leaders to remain in touch with followers.

But voters in presidential elections do not transmit their policy preferences to elected officials with a high degree of reliability. There are few clear mandates in our political system because elections are fought on so many issues and in so many incompletely overlapping constituencies. Often the same voters elect candidates to Congress and to the presidency who disagree on public policies. Thus, even if mandates could be identified, they might well be impossible to enact because of inconsistency in the instructions issued to officials who must agree on legislation.[2]

Presidential elections are not one-issue referendums. The relationship between presidential elections and policies is a great deal more subtle than the relations between the outcomes of referendums and the policies to which they pertain. In principle, the American political system is designed to work like this: Two teams of politicians, one in office, the other seeking office, both attempt to get enough votes to win elections. In order to win, they go to various groups of voters and, by offering to pursue policies favored by these groups, or by suggesting policies they might come to favor, hope to attract their votes. If there were only one office-seeking team, its incentive to respond to the policy preferences of groups in the population would diminish; if there were many such teams, all on a more or less equal footing, the chances that any one of them could achieve a sufficient number of backers to govern would diminish. Hence a two-party system might be regarded as a kind of compromise between the goals of responsiveness and effectiveness.

The proponents of a different theory would say that elections give the winning party a mandate to carry out the policies proposed during the campaign. Only in this way, they maintain, is popular rule through the ballot meaningful. A basic assumption in this argument is that the voters (or at least a majority of them) approve of all or most of the policies advocated by the victorious candidate. No doubt this is plausible, but not in the sense intended because, as we have seen, a vote for a presidential candidate is often an expression of a party habit: particular policy directions are therefore not necessarily meant by the vote. Indeed, citizens may be voting not for a candidate but rather against his or her opponent, or against a past president, saying, in effect, no more of this but not necessarily more of the other party's policies.

Most voters in the United States are not ideologically oriented. They do not seek to create or to adopt systems of thought in which issues are related to one another in some highly consistent manner. Caring about more than one value, sometimes they prefer a strong government here and a weak one there, or want just not to decide at the present time. Thus voters can hardly be said to transmit strong preferences for a uniform stream of particular policies by electing candidates to public office.

Other basic objections may also be raised to the idea that our elections are designed to confer mandates on specific public policies. First, the issues debated in the campaign may not be the ones in which most voters are interested. Campaign issues may be ones that interest the candidates or that, for tactical reasons, they want to stress, or that interest segments of the press. There is no clear reason to believe that any particular issue is of great concern to voters just because it gets publicity. Time and again, voting studies have demonstrated that what appear to be the major issues of a campaign turn out not to be significant for most of the electorate. In 1952, for example, three great Republican themes were communism, Korea, and corruption. It turned out that the communism issue, given perhaps the most publicity, had virtually no impact. Democrats simply would not believe that their party was the party of treason, and Republicans did not need that issue to make them vote the way they usually did. Korea and corruption were noticeable issues.[3] Yet how could anyone know, in the absence of a public opinion poll (and perhaps not even then), which of the three issues was important to the voters and which therefore conferred a mandate? There were, in any event, no significant policy differences between the parties on these issues: Democrats were also against communism and corruption and wanted an end to the war in Korea. A broadly similar story can be told, as we have shown, for more recent elections, in which nobody was for welfare fraud or large budget deficits, everybody was for a strong economy, and nobody favored crime.[4]

A second reason why voting for a candidate does not necessarily signify approval of that candidate's policies is that candidates pursue many policy interests at any one time with widely varying intensity, so that they may collect support from some voters on one issue and from other voters on another. It is possible for a candidate to get 100 percent of the votes and still have every voter opposed to most of the candidate's policies, as well as having every one of those policies opposed by most of the voters.

Assume that there are four major issues in a campaign. Make the further, quite reasonable, assumption that the voting population is distributed in such a way that people who care intensely about one major issue support the victorious candidate for that reason alone, although they differ with that candidate mildly on the other three issues. Thus, voters who are deeply concerned about the problem of defense against nuclear weapons may vote for candidate Jones, who prefers a minimum deterrence position, rather than Smith, who espouses a doctrine that requires huge retaliatory forces. This particular group of voters disagrees with Jones on farm price supports, on the overall size of government, and on national health insurance, but they do not feel strongly about any of these matters. Another group, meanwhile, believes that farmers, the noble yeomanry, are the backbone of the nation, and that if they are prosperous and strong, everything else will turn out all right. So they vote for Jones, too, although they prefer a large defense budget and disagree with Jones's other policies. And so on for other groups of voters. Lucky Jones. He ends up with all the votes. Yet each of his policies is preferred by less than a majority of the electorate. Since this is possible in any political system where many issues are debated or otherwise up for grabs at election time, it is hard to argue that our presidential elections give unequivocal mandates on specific policies to the candidates who win.[5]

People vote for many reasons not directly connected with issues. They may vote on the basis of party loyalty alone. Party habits may be joined with a general feeling that Democrats are better for the common citizen or that Republicans will keep us safe, or vice versa—feelings too diffuse to tell us much about specific issues. Some people vote on the basis of a candidate's personality, or "image." Others follow a friend's recommendation. Still others may be thinking about policy issues but may be all wrong in their perception of where the candidates stand. It is ordinarily impossible to distinguish the votes of these people from those who know, care, and differentiate accurately among the candidates on the basis of issues. We do know, however, that issue-oriented persons are usually in a minority, while those who cast their ballots with other things in mind are generally more numerous. Voters, if asked, may say they want to move government in a more liberal or conservative direction, but desires of this sort are so general in character, they can be read as approving of nearly anything.

Even if there is good reason to believe that a majority of voters do approve of specific policies supported by the victorious candidate, the mandate may be difficult or impossible to carry out. A candidate may get elected for a policy he pursued or preferred in the past that has no relevance to present circumstances. Some may have voted Republican in 1956 because Dwight D. Eisenhower got rid of the rascals in the Truman administration (three years earlier), or Democratic in 1976 in response to Watergate; but this did not point to any future policy that was currently in the realm of presidential discretion. John F. Kennedy promised in 1960 to get the nation "moving." This was broad enough to cover a multitude of vague hopes and aspirations. More specifically, as president, Kennedy might have wished to make good his promise by increasing the rate of growth in the national economy, but no one was quite sure how to do this. Lyndon Johnson was able to deliver on many of his 1964 campaign promises on domestic policy, but observers after the election could not readily distinguish his subsequent Vietnam policies from those they may have wanted to reject by voting against Barry Goldwater. The 1980 and 1984 elections can be seen as referendums on the economic performance of the incumbent administrations. Clearly voters thought the economy was doing poorly under Carter and better under Reagan. More than likely, however, it was the monetary policies of the Federal Reserve under the leadership of Paul Volcker, a Republican Carter appointee, that produced the pro-Reagan electoral results. The opposite may be the case in the 1992 and 1996 elections. Then, voters approved of the economic performance of the Clinton administration but not that of the George H. W. Bush administration, presumably giving the Democrats credit for a success in no small measure designed by Federal Reserve Chairman Alan Greenspan—a Republican appointee.

Leaving aside all the difficulties about the content of a mandate, there is no accepted definition of what size electoral victory gives a president special popular sanction to pursue any particular policy. Would a 60 percent victory be sufficient? What about 51 percent or 52 percent, or cases such as 1992, 1996, and 2000 in which the winner receives less than half the votes cast? And is it right to ignore the multitudes who do not vote and whose preferences are not directly registered? We might ignore the nonvoters for the purpose of this analysis if we were sure they were divided in their preferences between candidates in nearly the same proportions as those who do vote. There is now reason to believe that this is, more or less, true.[6] But we cannot be sure this is always the case. In practice, this problem is easily solved. Whoever wins the presidential election under our current rules—which means winning in the electoral college, not necessarily the popular vote—is allowed to pursue whatever policies he or she pleases, within the very important constraints imposed by the checks and balances of the rest of the policy-making institutions (notably, Congress) in the political system. This, in the end, is all that a "mandate" is in American politics.

Opinion polls and focus groups may help the politician gauge policy preferences, but there are always lingering doubts as to their reliability. It is not certain in any event that they tell the political leader what that leader needs to know. People who really have no opinion but who care only a little may be counted equally with those who are intensely concerned. Many people giving opinions may have no intention of voting for some of the politicians who heed them, no matter what. The result may be that a politician will get no visible support from a majority that agrees with him or her, but instead will get complaints from an intense minority that disagrees. The people who agree with the politician may not vote, while those who differ may attempt retribution at the ballot box—as single-issue interest groups are reported to do. Those voters who are pleased may be the ones who would have voted for the public official in any case.

Unless the poll is carefully done, it may leave out important groups of voters, overrepresent some, underrepresent others, and otherwise give a misleading impression. The correlations that are made showing that support comes disproportionately from certain economic or social groups do not explain why some people, often a substantial minority, possessing these self-same characteristics vote the opposite way.

Let us turn the question around for a moment. Suppose a candidate loses an election. What does this signify about the policies he or she should have espoused? If one or two key issues were widely debated and universally understood, the election might tell the candidate a great deal. But this is seldom the case. More likely, there were many issues, and it was difficult to separate out those issues that did from those that did not garner support for the opponent. Perhaps the election was decided on the basis of personal images or some events in the economic cycle or a military engagement—points that were not debated in the campaign and that may not have been within anyone's control. Losing candidates may always feel that if they continue to educate the public to favor the policies they prefer, they will eventually win. Should a candidate lose a series of elections, however, the party would undoubtedly try to change something—policies, candidates, organization, maybe all three—in an effort to improve its fortunes.

How do winning candidates appraise an election? What does this event tell officeholders and their parties about the policies they should pursue when in office? Some policy positions undoubtedly were rather vague, and specific applications of them may turn out quite differently from what the campaign promised. Others may founder on the rock of practicality; they sounded fine, but they simply cannot be carried out. Conditions change and policies that seemed to make sense a few months before turn out to be irrelevant. Democrats may want to spend more on welfare and Republicans to cut taxes, but huge deficits endanger both policies. As the time for putting policies into practice draws near, the new officeholders may discover that the policies generate a lot more opposition than when they were merely campaign oratory. And those policies that are pursued to the end may have to be compromised considerably in order to get the support of other participants in the policy-making process. Nevertheless, if they have even a minimal policy orientation, newly elected candidates can try to carry out a few of their campaign proposals, seeking to maintain a general direction consonant with the approach that may—they cannot be entirely certain—have contributed to their election.

The practical impossibility in our political system of ascertaining mandates in some objective sense is one important reason why it is so difficult for parties successfully to fulfill their function as policy advocates. It is, however, entirely possible for parties claiming a mandate to adopt policies that have little or no support in the general population. It is to the exploration of this possibility that we now turn.

PARTIES OF ADVOCACY VERSUS PARTIES OF INTERMEDIATION

The presidential election process in the United States has undergone a major transformation. As late as 1952, a president of the United States could, and with good reason, dismiss a prospective victory in the New Hampshire primary by the now little-remembered Senator Estes Kefauver of Tennessee as "eye-wash." Now primaries select most convention delegates, and combined with media spin, have an overwhelming impact on the outcome of the nominating process.[7]

Behind the shift in the role of primary elections lie shifts in the roles of political activists, both candidate enthusiasts and party regulars, and changes in the powers and the significance of the news media. We believe that these changes and other changes that we have discussed— the shift to the heavy regulation of political money not only in the general election but also in primary elections, the vast increase in the number of primaries, and the new rules for converting votes into delegates—add up to a fundamental redefinition of the place of the national political parties in our public life. One way to characterize this redefinition is to say that the conception of parties as agents of consensus government has begun to fade. If we are right, then more and more we can expect candidates and party leaders to raise divisive issues and to emphasize party differences rather than paper them over, in an effort to mobilize adherents to their side of the argument (this was called gratifying the party "base" in the George W. Bush administration) rather than appeal to the masses of people in the uncommitted middle.

Activists are now favored by the rules of the game, and officeholders and party officials are comparatively disfavored. In the early days of preprimary activity, the people who become most active are apt to be those who have the most spare time, the most ideological commitment, and the most enthusiasm for one candidate above all others. Since the rules are now written to encourage activity at an earlier and earlier date, as a basis for federal subsidies during the primaries and as a necessary condition for being taken seriously by the news media, it follows that activists will have more to say about the eventual outcome of the nomination process.[8] Party officials in the various states, in contrast, who once preferred to wait until they could see a majority forming, under the new rules of the game must ally themselves with one or another active candidate early in the process or forfeit their influence. This applies even to the Democratic high officeholders who get a free ride to the convention and make up around 15 percent of the total number of delegates. By the time their peculiar skills and interests in majority building might be needed—for instance, at a convention—it is too late for them to steer the process: most of the seats will have been taken by the enthusiasts for particular candidates who won in the various primaries and state conventions.

We can therefore ask how the emerging structure of presidential election politics helps and hinders political parties in performing the tasks customarily allotted to them in the complex scheme of American democracy. In essence, we believe that the parties have been greatly strengthened in their capacities to provide advocacy and weakened in their abilities to provide intermediation or later to facilitate implementation in the political system, i.e. governing. Consensus among party activists is now achieved at the expense of increasing dissension within government. Thus party platforms become ever more internally consistent, while government finds it increasingly difficult to relate revenues to expenditures.

Advocacy is strengthened because the rules of the game offer incentives to party leaders and candidates who are able to attract personal followings on an ideological basis. What is lost, in our view, is a capacity to deliberate, weigh competing demands, and compromise so that a variety of differing interests each gain a little. This loss would not be so great if the promise of policy government—to select efficacious programs and implement them successfully—were likely to be fulfilled in performance. But, on the record so far, this is doubly doubtful.

It is doubtful because for many of the problems that form the basis of political campaign discussion—economic growth, crime, racism, terrorism—there are no known, sure-fire solutions. And second, even if we knew what to do about more of our problems, it is improbable, given the ways in which various forces in our society and responsibilities in our constitution are arranged, that presidents alone could deliver on their promises.

This last dilemma is especially poignant for candidates who speak to a very wide spectrum of issues. Were they elected, then program implementation would require support in Congress, the bureaucracies, state and city governments, and elsewhere. The ability of such policy-oriented candidates to gain the agreement of others depends on many factors that typically are neither discussed nor understood in election campaigns. Yet gaining the agreement of others is part of making policies work. Policy government might enhance the legitimacy of government if it increased the effectiveness of programs, but the insensitivity of its advocates to the needs for consensus makes that unlikely. Under these circumstances, neither policy nor consensus, advocacy nor intermediation, are likely to be served.

Two factors account for the decline in the vital function of intermediation by parties. First, candidates have far fewer incentives than heretofore to deal either with interest groups organized on traditional geographic or occupational lines or with state and local party leaders. These leaders and groups have in the past provided links between national politicians and ordinary people in all their variety and have focused the hopes and energies of countless citizens on the party organizations as meaningful entities in the nomination process. Nowadays, as we have been told by politicians as varied as Richard Nixon and Jimmy Carter, a candidate for the presidency need no longer build up a mosaic of alliances with interest groups and party leaders. Candidates such as Walter Mondale or Bob Dole who do work to secure these alliances are attacked for being beholden to "special interests." Now, through the miracle of the mass media (especially television), through mass mailings and Internet messages to appeal for money, and through federal subsidy if these appeals are successful, presidential candidates can reach every home and touch every heart and claim the allegiance of followers based on ideological affinity rather than concrete bargains.

This is the first sense in which parties have been diminished in their capacity to mediate between the desires of ordinary citizens and the policies of government: candidates no longer need parties to reach voters. In a second sense, parties are losing the capacity to mediate between leaders and followers because the formal properties of plebiscitary decision making simply by voting, such as occurs in primary elections, leave little room for a bargaining process to occur. Contingent choices are impossible to express in primary elections straightforwardly through the ballot. Thus a candidate who is acceptable to a sizable majority but is the first choice of only a few systematically loses out under the current primary-driven rules to candidates who might be unacceptable to most voters but secure in their control over a middle-sized fraction (20 to 30 percent, depending on how many candidates play the game) of first-choice votes.

In this sense we can say that "participatory" democracy, as the American party system has begun to practice it, undermines "deliberative" democracy. As more and different people have won the right to participate in the nomination process by voting in primaries, the kinds of communications they have been able to send to one another have not correspondingly been enriched. Participants can vote, but they cannot bargain. They can make and listen to speeches, but they cannot discuss or deliberate.

Let us see what happens when a free spirit like George McGovern breaks through the network of old politicians and gets nominated for president, as happened in 1972. A piece of bad luck afflicts his campaign: his vice-presidential candidate, Tom Eagleton, has concealed a medical history that may weaken the ticket. The *New York Times* writes, "Dump Eagleton." The *Washington Post* writes, "Dump Eagleton."

What does an "old" politics candidate tied to interest groups do? Presumably he or she gets on the telephone and asks around among interest-group leaders and state and local party bosses, "Can we stand the flak?" "What do the party workers think?" "What do you think?"

What do "new" politics candidates do? Well, what choice have they? To whom can they place a telephone call other than the far-flung members of their immediate families? There is no negotiating with the editorial board of the *New York Times* in or out of a smoke-filled room. There is no give-and-take with the moderator of *Meet the Press*. The moderator gives. Politicians take. This is also true in the preprimary process, where bad news can drive candidates out of contention before their candidacies are even tested by primaries or caucus activity, as happened to Gary Hart in 1987, even though he was far and away the Democratic front-runner at the time.

We have no way of knowing whether the democratic paradox of participation swallowing up deliberation has had the net effect of turning citizens away from political parties. It is, in any event, true that by a variety of measures—nonvoting, propensity of voters to decline to identify with a political party, direct expressions of disapproval of parties—political parties, like so many other institutions of American society, suffered substantial losses in public confidence after the 1960s. In our view, the most promising way for parties to regain public confidence would be to avoid factional candidates and not only to nominate and elect good candidates but also to help them govern.

What is objectionable about policy government? What could be wrong with so intuitively attractive an idea? Governments must make policies. Surely candidates should be judged, in part at least, on their policy preferences, as well as on indications of their ability to perform when in office. Has there not been, in the recent past, too much obfuscation of issues and too little candor in speaking one's mind? Obviously our society needs more, rather than less, discussion of issues, and greater, rather than less, clarification of alternatives. The problem is that the premises on which policy government is based are false. Most people do not want parties that make extreme appeals by taking issue positions far from the desires of the bulk of the citizenry.[9] Perhaps people feel safer if their parties give them a choice, but they do not want losing to be a catastrophe. This may be why they see no great difficulty in voting for a president of one party and a Congress of another.[10]

Advocates of issue expression have so far managed to control no more than one presidential nominating convention at a time; but suppose they manage in the future to face off a right-wing Republican against a left-wing Democrat? The trends now perceived as products of consensus government—alienation, nonvoting—would, we conjecture, show an alarming increase if the vast majority of citizens discovered that their preferences for moderation in politics had been totally disregarded and that they had nowhere to turn. Indeed, it may well be that the vastly increased participation of activists, by making campaigns distasteful to the majority, has led to the very decline in participation that they deplore.

It is one thing to say that policy options have been insufficiently articulated and quite another to create conflict and develop disagreements where these did not exist before. Political activists in the United States are more ideological and polarized than at any time since studies were first conducted in the 1930s, and possibly since the 1890s, or even the Civil War. Should ordinary citizens be compelled to choose from policy alternatives that appeal to these activists, or are they entitled to select from a menu closer to their tastes? The question is not whether there will be issues, for inevitably there must be, but who will set the agenda for discussion and whether this agenda will primarily reflect differences in the general population or those among elites. Thus one objection to a party of advocacy is that it imposes on the great majority of people preferences to which the majority is largely indifferent or opposed.

The rationale behind parties of advocacy leads to plebiscitary democracy. If it is not only desirable for all citizens to vote in general elections but also for them to choose candidates through preelection primaries, it must be even more desirable for them to select governmental policies directly through referendums. Instead of rule by special interests or cliques of congressmen, the public's interest would supposedly be expressed by the public.

Experience with initiatives and referendums in California and Oregon, where they are thickest on the ground, and elsewhere, however, suggests that this is not quite how things work in practice. Without measures for limiting the number of referendums voters may face at a given election, citizens are swamped by the necessity of voting on dozens of items. Elites, not the people, determine the selection and wording of referendums. And how they are worded is, of course, extremely important. Money—to arrange for the signatures on petitions to get referendums on the ballot—becomes more meaningful than ever. The public is faced with a bewildering array of proposals, all sponsored by special interests that want a way around the state legislature. To learn what is involved in a single seemingly innocuous proposal takes hours of study. To understand twenty or more per election is unduly onerous. Are citizens better off guessing or following the advice of the local newspaper instead of trying to choose a legislator or a party to represent their interests?[11]

To take a famous case, were citizens or legislators better qualified to understand that Proposition 13 in California (passed in 1978) would not only keep property taxes down, which it was advertised to do, but would also, by depriving localities of resources, centralize control at the state level over many areas of public policy, which no one wanted? Were citizens of California, where referendums abound, wise to vote at widely separated intervals for so many mandatory expenditures as to make it difficult for the state legislature to mobilize resources to meet new needs?[12]

A plebiscitary democracy, stressing the direct connection between candidates and voters, could not abide the electoral college. Only direct democracy, mass voting for candidates, would do. Abolishing the electoral college, however, as we have seen, would further decrease the need for forming diverse coalitions. Both the agents of consensus, mediating parties, and the fact of consensus, with political leaders who nurture it, would decline.

After a few decades of severe internal difficulty, when confidence in virtually all national institutions has suffered repeated blows, the need for consensus-building parties seems more clear than ever. Ideological parties might be desirable for a people homogeneous in all ways except the economic; but can a very large multiracial, multiethnic, multireligious, multiregional, multiclass nation such as the United States sustain itself when its main agents of political action—the parties—strive to exclude rather than include, to sharpen rather than dull the edge of controversy?

It is even doubtful that the rise of parties of advocacy leads to a more principled politics. If principles are precepts that must not be violated, when contrary principles are firmly embedded in the programs of opposing parties, one person's principles necessarily become another's fighting words. A few principles, such as those enshrined in the Bill of Rights, may be helpful—indeed essential—in establishing boundaries beyond which governmental action may not go. But too many principles thwart the cooperative government required by the design of the Constitution. As being a Democrat increasingly requires adherence to litmus-tested liberal positions and a Republican to litmus-tested conservative positions, cross-cutting cleavages—organizing people who support one another on some issues while opposing on others—are bound to diminish. With officeholders opposing each other on more issues, and with more issues defined as moral issues, political passions are liable to rise. And so, we suppose, will negative campaigning and popular disapproval of government and of politicians.

Compromise, of course, can also be a curse. If everything were bargainable, including basic liberties, no one would feel safe, and, indeed, no one would be. Similarly, if candidates cared everything about winning and nothing about how they win, if they were not restrained by internal norms or enforceable external expectations, elections would become outrages.

Parties without policies would be empty; parties fixated on only a narrow band of policies are dangerous. Without the desire to win elections, not at any cost but as a leading motive, there is no reason for politicians to pay attention to the people who vote. Winning requires a widespread appeal. Thus the desire to win can lead to moderation, to appeals to diverse groups in the electorate, and to efforts to bring many varied interests together. This is why we prefer parties of intermediation to parties of advocacy. Parties of advocacy do not sustain themselves well in government. They fail to assist political leaders in mobilizing consent for the policies they adopt, and this widens the gap between campaign promises and the performance of government.

Because so many of the rules of presidential election politics are changing, we cannot say with a high degree of assurance how parties, candidates, and voters will adapt to the new incentives and disabilities that are continuously enacted into law. We are confident only in asserting that the adaptations they make will be of enormous consequence in determining the ultimate capacity of the American political system to sustain the fascinating and noble experiment in self-government begun on this continent more than two hundred years ago.

APPENDIXES

Appendix A: Vote by Groups in Presidential Elections, 1952–2004

	1952		1956	
	Stevenson (D)	*Eisenhower (R)*	*Stevenson (D)*	*Eisenhower (R)*
National	45 %	55 %	42 %	58 %
Sex				
Men	47	53	45	55
Women	42	58	39	61
Race				
White	43	57	41	59
Nonwhite	79	21	61	39
Education				
Grade school	52	48	50	50
High school	45	55	42	58
College	34	66	31	69
Occupation				
Professional and business	36	64	32	68
White collar	40	60	37	63
Manual labor	55	45	50	50
Labor union household	61	39	57	43
Age				
Under 30 years	51	49	43	57
30 to 49 years	47	53	45	55
50 years and older	39	61	39	61
Religion				
Protestant	37	63	37	63
Catholic	56	44	51	49
Party Identification				
Democratic	77	23	85	15
Republican	8	92	4	96
Independent	35	65	30	70
Region				
East	45	55	40	60
Midwest	42	58	41	59
South	51	49	49	51
West	42	58	43	57

	1960		1964	
	Kennedy (D)	Nixon (R)	Johnson (D)	Goldwater (R)
National	50 %	50 %	61 %	39 %
Sex				
Men	52	48	60	40
Women	49	51	62	38
Race				
White	49	51	59	41
Nonwhite	68	32	94	6
Education				
Grade school	55	45	66	34
High school	52	48	62	38
College	39	61	52	48
Occupation				
Professional and business	42	58	54	46
White collar	48	52	57	43
Manual labor	60	40	71	29
Labor union household	65	35	73	27
Age				
Under 30 years	54	46	64	36
30 to 49 years	54	46	63	37
50 years and older	46	54	59	41
Religion				
Protestant	38	62	55	45
Catholic	78	22	76	24
Party Identification				
Democratic	84	16	87	13
Republican	5	95	20	80
Independent	43	57	56	44
Region				
East	53	47	68	32
Midwest	48	52	61	39
South	51	49	52	48
West	49	51	60	40

	1968			1972	
	Humphrey (D)	Nixon (R)	Wallace (I)	McGovern (D)	Nixon (R)
National	43 %	43 %	14 %	38 %	62 %
Sex					
Men	41	43	16	37	63
Women	45	43	12	38	62
Race					
White	38	47	15	32	68
Nonwhite	85	12	3	87	13
Education					
Grade school	52	33	15	49	51
High school	42	43	15	34	66
College	37	54	9	37	63
Occupation					
Professional and business	34	56	10	31	69
White collar	41	47	12	36	64
Manual labor	50	35	15	43	57
Labor union household	56	29	15	46	54
Age					
Under 30 years	47	38	15	48	52
30 to 49 years	44	41	15	33	67
50 years and older	41	47	12	36	64
Religion					
Protestant	35	49	16	30	70
Catholic	59	33	8	48	52
Party Identification					
Democratic	74	12	14	67	33
Republican	9	86	5	5	95
Independent	31	44	25	31	69
Region					
East	50	43	7	42	58
Midwest	44	47	9	40	60
South	31	36	33	29	71
West	44	49	7	41	59

	1976			1980		
	Carter (D)	Ford (R)	McCarthy (I)	Carter (D)	Reagan (R)	Anderson (I)
National	50 %	48 %	1 %	41 %	51 %	7 %
Sex						
Men	53	45	1	38	53	7
Women	48	51	0	44	49	6
Race						
White	46	52	1	36	56	7
Nonwhite	85	15	0	86	10	2
Education						
Grade school	58	41	1	54	42	3
High school	54	46	0	43	51	5
College	42	55	2	35	53	10
Occupation						
Professional and business	42	56	1	33	55	10
White collar	50	48	2	40	51	9
Manual labor	58	41	1	48	48	5
Labor union household	63	36	1	50	43	5
Age						
Under 30 years	53	45	1	47	41	11
30 to 49 years	48	49	2	38	52	8
50 years and older	52	48	0	41	54	4
Religion						
Protestant	46	53	0	39	54	6
Catholic	57	42	1	46	47	6
Party Identification						
Democratic	82	18	0	69	26	4
Republican	9	91	0	8	86	5
Independent	38	57	4	29	55	14
Region						
East	51	47	1	43	47	9
Midwest	48	50	1	41	51	7
South	54	45	0	44	52	3
West	46	51	1	35	54	9

	1984		1988	
	Mondale (D)	Reagan (R)	Dukakis (D)	Bush (R)
National	40 %	59 %	45 %	53 %
Sex				
Men	37	62	41	57
Women	44	56	49	50
Race				
White	35	64	40	59
Black	90	9	86	12
Latino	62	37	69	30
Education				
Not high school graduate	50	50	56	43
High school graduate only	39	60	49	50
Some college	38	61	42	57
College graduate	41	58	37	62
Postgraduate	–	–	48	50
Income				
Under $15,000	55	45	62	37
$15,000–$29,999	42	57	50	49
$30,000–$49,999	40	59	43	56
$50,000 and over	30	69	37	62
Labor union household	53	46	57	42
Age				
Under 30 years	40	59	47	52
30 to 44 years	42	57	45	54
45 to 59 years	40	60	42	57
60 years and over	39	60	49	50
Religion				
White Protestant	27	72	33	66
Catholic	45	54	47	52
Jewish	67	31	64	35
Marital status				
Married	38	62	42	57
Unmarried	47	52	53	46
Party Identification				
Democratic	74	25	82	17
Republican	7	92	8	91
Independent	36	63	43	55
Region				
East	47	53	49	50
Midwest	41	58	47	52
South	36	64	41	58
West	38	61	46	52

	1992			1996		
	Clinton (D)	Bush (R)	Perot (I)	Clinton (D)	Dole (R)	Perot (I)
National	43 %	38 %	19 %	49 %	41 %	8 %
Sex						
Men	41	38	21	43	44	10
Women	45	37	17	54	38	7
Race						
White	39	40	20	43	46	9
Black	83	10	7	84	12	4
Latino	61	25	14	72	21	8
Education						
Not high school graduate	54	28	18	59	28	11
High school graduate only	43	36	21	51	35	13
Some college	41	37	21	48	40	10
College graduate	39	41	20	44	46	8
Postgraduate	50	36	14	52	40	5
Income						
Under $15,000	58	23	19	59	28	11
$15,000–$29,999	45	35	20	53	36	9
$30,000–$49,999	41	38	21	48	40	10
$50,000 and over	39	44	17	44	48	7
Labor union household	55	24	21	59	30	9
Age						
Under 30 years	43	34	22	53	34	10
30 to 44 years	41	38	21	48	41	9
45 to 59 years	41	40	19	49	41	9
60 years and over	50	38	12	48	44	7
Religion						
White Protestant	33	47	21	36	53	10
Catholic	44	35	20	53	37	9
Jewish	80	11	9	78	16	3
Marital status						
Married	40	41	20	44	46	9
Unmarried	51	30	19	57	31	9
Party Identification						
Democratic	77	10	13	84	10	5
Republican	10	73	17	13	80	6
Independent	38	32	30	43	35	17
Region						
East	47	35	18	55	34	9
Midwest	42	37	21	48	41	10
South	41	43	16	46	46	7
West	43	34	22	48	40	8

	2000			2004	
	Gore (D)	Bush (R)	Nader (G)	Kerry (D)	Bush (R)
National	48 %	48 %	2 %	48 %	51 %
Sex					
Men	42	53	3	44	55
Women	54	43	2	51	48
Race					
White	42	54	3	41	58
Black	90	8	1	88	11
Latino	67	31	2	56	43
Education					
Not high school graduate	59	39	1	50	49
High school graduate only	48	49	1	47	52
Some college	45	51	3	46	54
College graduate	45	51	3	46	52
Postgraduate	52	44	3	55	44
Income					
Under $15,000	57	37	4	63	36
$15,000–$29,999	54	41	3	57	42
$30,000–$49,999	49	48	2	50	49
$50,000 and over	45	52	2	43	56
Labor union household	59	37	3	59	40
Age					
Under 30 years	48	46	5	54	45
30 to 44 years	48	49	2	46	53
45 to 59 years	48	49	2	48	51
60 years and over	51	47	2	46	54
Religion					
White Protestant	34	63	2	32	67
Catholic	49	47	2	47	52
Jewish	79	19	1	74	25
Marital status					
Married	44	53	2	42	57
Unmarried	57	38	4	58	40
Party Identification					
Democratic	86	11	2	89	11
Republican	8	91	1	49	48
Independent	45	47	6	6	93

	2000			2004	
	Gore (D)	Bush (R)	Nader (G)	Kerry (D)	Bush (R)
Region					
East	56	39	3	56	43
Midwest	48	49	2	48	51
South	43	55	1	42	58
West	48	46	4	50	49

Source: Data for 1952–1980 from the final pre-election Gallup survey, as summarized in *Gallup Poll Monthly* 374 (November 1996), pp. 17–20. Data for 1984–2004 from *New York Times* exit polls, as summarized in Marjorie Connelly, "How Americans Voted: A Political Portrait," *New York Times*, November 7, 2004, sec. 4, p. 4; "Exit Polls," MSNBC, available at http://www.msnbc.msn.com/id/5297138/.

Appendix B: Voter Turnout in Presidential Elections, by Population Characteristics, 1968–2004

	1968			
	Persons of Voting Age (in thousands)	Persons Reporting They Voted (in thousands)	Percent Reporting They Voted	Percent Reporting They Did Not Vote
Total	116,535	78,964	67.8	32.2
Men	54,464	38,014	69.8	30.2
Women	62,071	40.951	66.0	34.0
White	104,521	72,213	69.1	30.9
Nonwhite	12,014	6,751	56.2	43.8
18–24 years old	11,602	5,851	50.4	49.6
25–34 years old	23,198	14,501	62.5	37.5
35–44 years old	22,905	16,223	70.8	29.2
45–64 years old	40,362	30,238	74.9	25.1
65 years and older	18,468	12,150	65.8	34.2
Metropolitan	75,756	51,503	68.0	32.0
Nonmetropolitan	40,778	27,461	67.3	32.7
Nonsouth	81,594	57,970	71.0	29.0
South	34,941	20,994	60.1	39.9
Under 9 years of school	30,430	16,592	54.5	45.5
9–11 years of school	20,429	12,519	61.3	38.7
12 years	39,704	28,768	72.5	27.5
More than 12 years	25,971	21,086	81.2	18.8
Employed	70,002	49,772	71.1	28.9
Unemployed	1,875	977	52.1	47.9
Not in labor force	44,657	28,215	63.2	36.8

Source: U.S. Bureau of the Census, *Current Population Reports*, Series P-20, no. 192 (December 1969).

Note: Voting age population defined as civilian noninstitutional population (including noncitizens) aged 21 years and over except: 18 years and older in Georgia and Kentucky, 19 years and older in Alaska, and 20 years and older in Hawaii.

1972

	Persons of Voting Age (in thousands)	Persons Reporting They Voted (in thousands)	Percent Reporting They Voted	Percent Reporting They Did Not Vote
Total	136,203	85,766	63.0	37.0
Men	63,833	40,908	64.1	35.9
Women	72,370	44,858	62.0	38.0
White	121,243	78,166	64.5	35.5
Nonwhite	14,960	7,600	50.8	49.2
18–24 years old	24,612	12,214	49.6	50.4
25–34 years old	26,933	16,072	59.7	40.3
35–44 years old	22,240	14,747	66.3	33.7
45–64 years old	42,344	29,991	70.8	29.2
65 years and older	20,074	12,741	63.5	36.5
Metropolitan	99,248	63,799	64.3	35.7
Nonmetropolitan	36,955	21,967	59.4	40.6
Nonsouth	93,653	62,193	66.4	33.6
South	42,550	23,573	55.4	44.6
Under 9 years of school	28,065	13,311	47.4	52.6
9–11 years of school	22,277	11,587	52.0	48.0
12 years	50,749	33,193	65.4	34.6
More than 12 years	35,113	27,675	78.8	21.2
Employed	80,164	52,899	66.0	34.0
Unemployed	3,735	1,863	49.9	50.1
Not in labor force	52,305	31,004	59.3	40.7

Source: U.S. Bureau of the Census, *Current Population Reports*, Series P-20, no. 253 (October 1973).

Note: Voting age population defined as civilian noninstitutional population (including noncitizens) aged 18 years and over.

	Persons of Voting Age (in thousands)	Persons Reporting They Voted (in thousands)	Percent Reporting They Voted	Percent Reporting They Did Not Vote
		1976		
Total	146,548	86,698	59.2	40.8
Men	68,957	41,079	59.6	40.4
Women	77,591	45,620	58.8	41.2
White	129,316	78,808	60.9	39.1
Nonwhite	17,232	7,890	45.8	54.2
18–24 years old	26,953	11,367	42.2	57.8
25–34 years old	31,533	17,472	55.4	44.6
35–44 years old	22,769	14,411	63.3	36.7
45–64 years old	43,293	29,763	68.7	31.3
65 years and older	22,001	13,685	62.2	37.8
Metropolitan	99,590	58,943	59.2	40.8
Nonmetropolitan	46,959	27,755	59.1	40.9
Nonsouth	99,403	60,829	61.2	38.8
South	47,145	25,869	54.9	45.1
Under 9 years of school	24,947	11,010	44.1	55.9
9–11 years of school	22,216	10,481	47.2	52.8
12 years	55,665	33,058	59.4	40.6
More than 12 years	43,719	32,150	73.5	26.5
Employed	86,034	53,314	62.0	38.0
Unemployed	6,430	2,812	43.7	56.3
Not in labor force	54,085	30,573	56.5	43.5

Source: U.S. Bureau of the Census, *Current Population Reports*, Series P-20, no. 322 (March 1978).

Note: Voting age population defined as civilian noninstitutional population (including noncitizens) aged 18 years and over.

	1980			
	Persons of Voting Age (in thousands)	*Persons Reporting They Voted (in thousands)*	*Percent Reporting They Voted*	*Percent Reporting They Did Not Vote*
Total	157,085	93,066	59.2	40.8
Men	74,082	43,753	59.1	40.9
Women	83,003	49,312	59.4	40.6
White	137,676	83,855	60.9	39.1
Nonwhite	19,409	9,211	47.5	52.5
18–24 years old	28,138	11,225	39.9	60.1
25–34 years old	35,733	19,498	54.6	45.4
35–44 years old	25,552	16,460	64.4	35.6
45–64 years old	43,569	30,205	69.3	30.7
65 years and older	24,094	15,677	65.1	34.9
Metropolitan	106,627	62,703	58.8	41.2
Nonmetropolitan	50,459	30,363	60.2	39.8
Nonsouth	106,524	64,963	61.0	39.0
South	50,561	28,103	55.6	44.4
Under 9 years of school	22,656	9,643	42.6	57.4
9–11 years of school	22,477	10,246	45.6	54.4
12 years	61,165	35,998	58.9	41.1
More than 12 years	50,787	37,179	73.2	26.8
Employed	95,041	58,778	61.8	38.2
Unemployed	6,893	2,838	41.2	58.8
Not in labor force	55,151	31,449	57.0	43.0

Source: U.S. Bureau of the Census, *Current Population Reports*, Series P-20, no. 370 (April 1982).

Note: Voting age population defined as civilian noninstitutional population (including noncitizens) aged 18 years and over.

	1984			
	Persons of Voting Age (in thousands)	Persons Reporting They Voted (in thousands)	Percent Reporting They Voted	Percent Reporting They Did Not Vote
Total	169,963	101,878	59.9	40.1
Men	80,327	47,354	59.0	41.0
Women	89,636	54,524	60.8	39.2
White	146,761	90,152	61.4	38.6
Nonwhite	23,202	11,726	50.5	49.5
18–24 years old	27,976	11,407	40.8	59.2
25–34 years old	40,292	21,978	54.5	45.5
35–44 years old	30,731	19,514	63.5	36.5
45–64 years old	44,307	30,924	69.8	30.2
65 years and older	26,658	18,055	67.7	32.3
Metropolitan	NA	NA	NA	NA
Nonmetropolitan	NA	NA	NA	NA
Nonsouth	112,376	69,183	61.6	38.4
South	57,587	32,695	56.8	43.2
Under 9 years of school	20,580	8,833	42.9	57.1
9–11 years of school	22,068	9,798	44.4	55.6
12 years	67,807	39,773	58.7	41.3
More than 12 years	59,508	43,473	73.1	26.9
Employed	104,173	64,213	61.6	38.4
Unemployed	7,389	3,247	44.0	56.0
Not in labor force	58,401	34,418	58.9	41.1

Source: U.S. Bureau of the Census, Current Population Reports, Series P-20, no. 405 (March 1986).

Note: Voting age population defined as civilian noninstitutional population (including noncitizens) aged 18 years and over.

	1988			
	Persons of Voting Age (in thousands)	*Persons Reporting They Voted (in thousands)*	*Percent Reporting They Voted*	*Percent Reporting They Did Not Vote*
Total	178,098	102,224	57.4	42.6
Men	84,531	47,704	56.4	43.6
Women	93,568	54,519	58.3	41.7
White	152,848	90,357	59.1	40.9
Nonwhite	25,250	11,867	47.0	53.0
18–24 years old	25,569	9,254	36.2	63.8
25–34 years old	42,677	20,468	48.0	52.0
35–44 years old	35,186	21,550	61.3	38.7
45–64 years old	45,862	31,134	67.9	32.1
65 years and older	28,804	19,818	68.8	31.2
Metropolitan	139,134	79,505	57.1	42.9
Nonmetropolitan	38,964	22,719	58.3	41.7
Nonsouth	117,373	69,130	58.9	41.1
South	60,725	33,094	54.5	45.5
Under 9 years of school	19,145	7,025	36.7	63.3
9–11 years of school	21,052	8,698	41.3	58.7
12 years	70,033	38,328	54.7	45.3
More than 12 years	67,878	48,173	71.0	29.0
Employed	113,836	66,510	58.4	41.6
Unemployed	5,809	2,243	38.6	61.4
Not in labor force	58,453	33,471	57.3	42.7

Source: U.S. Bureau of the Census, *Current Population Reports*, Series P-20, no. 440 (October 1989)

Note: Voting age population defined as civilian noninstitutional population (including noncitizens) aged 18 years and over.

	Persons of Voting Age (in thousands)	Persons Reporting They Voted (in thousands)	Percent Reporting They Voted	Percent Reporting They Did Not Vote
	1992			
Total	185,684	113,866	61.3	38.7
Men	88,557	53,312	60.2	39.8
Women	97,126	60,554	62.3	37.7
White	157,837	100,405	63.6	36.4
Nonwhite	27,847	13,461	48.3	51.7
18–24 years old	24,371	10,442	42.8	57.2
25–34 years old	41,603	22,120	53.2	46.8
35–44 years old	39,716	25,269	63.6	36.4
45–64 years old	49,147	34,399	70.0	30.0
65 years and older	30,846	21,637	70.1	29.9
Metropolitan	144,593	88,222	61.0	39.0
Nonmetropolitan	41,091	25,644	62.4	37.6
Nonsouth	122,025	76,276	62.5	37.5
South	63,659	37,590	59.0	41.0
Under 9 years of school	15,391	5,406	35.1	64.9
9–11 years of school	20,970	8,638	41.2	58.8
12 years	65,281	37,517	57.5	42.5
More than 12 years:				
1 to 3 years of college	46,691	32,069	68.7	31.3
4 or more years of college	37,351	30,236	81.0	19.0
Employed	116,290	74,138	63.8	36.2
Unemployed	8,263	3,820	46.2	53.8
Not in labor force	61,131	35,908	58.7	41.3

Source: U.S. Bureau of the Census, *Current Population Reports*, Series P-20, no. 466 (April 1993).

Note: Voting age population defined as civilian noninstitutional population (including noncitizens) aged 18 years and over.

1996

	Persons of Voting Age (in thousands)	Persons Reporting They Voted (in thousands)	Percent Reporting They Voted	Percent Reporting They Did Not Vote
Total	193,651	105,017	54.2	45.8
Men	92,632	48,909	52.8	47.2
Women	101,020	56,108	55.5	44.5
White	162,779	91,208	56.0	44.0
Nonwhite	30,872	13,809	44.7	55.3
18–24 years old	24,650	7,996	32.4	67.6
25–34 years old	40,066	17,265	43.1	56.9
35–44 years old	43,327	23,785	54.9	45.1
45–64 years old	53,721	34,615	64.4	35.6
65 years and older	31,888	21,356	67.0	33.0
Metropolitan	155,735	83,984	53.9	46.1
Nonmetropolitan	37,916	21,033	55.5	44.5
Nonsouth	125,571	69,467	55.3	44.7
South	68,080	35,550	52.2	47.8
Under 9 years of school	13,986	4,188	29.9	70.1
9–11 years of school	21,002	7,099	33.8	66.2
12 years	65,208	32,019	49.1	50.9
More than 12 years:				
1 to 3 years of college	50,939	30,835	60.5	39.5
4 or more years of college	42,517	30,877	72.6	27.4
Employed	125,634	69,300	55.2	44.8
Unemployed	6,409	2,383	37.2	62.8
Not in labor force	61,608	33,335	54.1	45.9

Source: U.S. Bureau of the Census, *Current Population Reports*, Series P-20, no. 504 (August 1997).

Note: Voting age population defined as civilian noninstitutional population (including noncitizens) aged 18 years and over.

	2000			
	Persons of Voting Age (in thousands)	*Persons Reporting They Voted (in thousands)*	*Percent Reporting They Voted*	*Percent Reporting They Did Not Vote*
Total	202,609	110,826	54.7	45.3
Men	97,087	51,542	53.1	46.9
Women	105,523	59,284	56.2	43.8
White	168,733	95,098	56.4	43.6
Nonwhite	33,876	15,728	46.4	53.6
18–24 years old	26,712	8,635	32.3	67.7
25–34 years old	37,304	16,286	43.7	56.3
35–44 years old	44,476	24,452	55.0	45.0
45–64 years old	61,352	39,301	64.1	35.9
65 years and older	32,764	22,152	67.6	32.4
Metropolitan	NA	NA	NA	NA
Nonmetropolitan	NA	NA	NA	NA
Nonsouth	130,774	72,385	55.4	44.6
South	71,835	38,441	53.5	46.5
Under 9 years of school	12,894	3,454	26.8	73.2
9–11 years of school	20,108	6,758	33.6	66.4
12 years	66,339	32,749	49.4	50.6
More than 12 years:				
1 to 3 years of college	55,308	33,339	60.3	39.7
4 or more years of college	47,960	34,526	72.0	28.0
Employed	133,434	74,068	55.5	44.5
Unemployed	4,944	1,734	35.1	64.9
Not in labor force	64,231	35,023	54.5	45.5

Source: U.S. Bureau of the Census, *Current Population Reports*, Series P-20, no. 542 (February 2002).

Note: Voting age population defined as civilian noninstitutional population (including noncitizens) aged 18 years and over.

	2004			
	Persons of Voting Age (in thousands)	Persons Reporting They Voted (in thousands)	Percent Reporting They Voted	Percent Reporting They Did Not Vote
Total	215,694	125,736	58.3	41.7
Men	103,812	58,455	56.3	43.7
Women	111,882	67,281	60.1	39.9
White	176,618	106,588	60.3	39.7
Nonwhite	39,076	19,148	49.0	51.0
18–24 years old	27,808	11,639	41.9	58.1
25–34 years old	39,003	18,285	46.9	53.1
35–44 years old	43,130	24,560	56.9	43.1
45–64 years old	71,015	47,326	66.6	33.4
65 years and older	34,738	23,925	68.9	31.1
Metropolitan	NA	NA	NA	NA
Nonmetropolitan	NA	NA	NA	NA
Nonsouth	138,506	82,224	59.4	40.6
South	77,188	43,512	56.4	43.6
Not high school graduate	33,293	10,132	30.4	69.6
High school graduate only	68,545	35,894	52.4	47.6
Some college	58,913	38,922	66.1	33.9
College graduate	36,591	26,579	72.6	27.4
Postgraduate	18,352	14,210	77.4	22.6
Employed	138,831	83,250	60.0	40.0
Unemployed	7,251	3,362	46.4	53.6
Not in labor force	69,612	39,124	56.2	43.8

Source: U.S. Bureau of the Census, Current Population Reports, Series P-20, no. 556 (March 2006).

Note: Voting age population defined as civilian noninstitutional population (including noncitizens) aged 18 years and over.

NOTES

Chapter 1 Voters

1. Anthony King, *Running Scared: Why America's Politicians Campaign Too Much and Govern Too Little* (New York: Martin Kessler, 1997).

2. See Bruce Cain, John Ferejohn, and Morris Fiorina, *The Personal Vote: Constituency Service and Electoral Independence* (Cambridge, MA: Harvard University Press, 1987), p. 13; and Leon D. Epstein, *Political Parties in Western Democracies* (New York: Praeger, 1967), p. 43.

3. Richard Boyd's research suggests that heavy demands on U.S. voters may be depressing participation in any one election. In the Connecticut town he studied, he found that more people voted at some time during the year than voted in any given election: "a system that holds elections as frequently as we do in the United States must expect that even citizens who are attentive to politics and its obligations will not be at the polls every election. I would argue, then, that the frequency of elections in the United States is one explanation of the somewhat lower voting rate we experience in any given election compared to European countries." Richard W. Boyd, "Decline of U.S. Voter Turnout: Structural Explanations," *American Politics Quarterly* 9 (April 1981): 133–159. Switzerland, the other low-turnout democracy, also has frequent elections, and referendums; see David Butler and Austin Ranney, eds., *Referendums around the World: The Growing Use of Direct Democracy* (Washington, DC: AEI Press, 1994). In *Running Scared*, Anthony King argues that the U.S. pattern of frequent elections has important consequences for governing. Note also that turnout in recent European Union elections was substantially lower than national elections in most European countries; the 2004 EU election featured an overall turnout rate of under 50 percent. See Robert Anderson, Christopher Condon, and Stefan Wagstyl, "Apathy Rules Among Newest Member States," *Financial Times*, June 15, 2004, p. 14.

4. See Steven J. Rosenstone and John Mark Hansen, *Mobilization, Participation, and Democracy in America* (New York: Macmillan, 1993), pp. 178–179.

5. Ibid., pp. 146–150. Americans do least well on "trust in government" questions, but respond much more positively to questions about their efficacy (rejecting such statements as "people like me have no say in what the government does") and to questions asking if a political party expresses their point of view.

6. Peverill Squire, Raymond E. Wolfinger, and David P. Glass, "Residential Mobility and Voter Turnout," *American Political Science Review* 81 (March 1987): 45–84.

7. U.S. Constitution, Art. I, sec. 2, says: "The House of Representatives shall be composed of members chosen every second year by the people of the several states and the electors in each state shall have the qualifications requisite for electors of the most numerous branch of the state legislature."

8. This is presumably pegged to completion of the harvest in the colonial Northeast.

9. Paul E. Meehl, "The Selfish Voter Paradox and the Thrown-Away Vote Argument," *American Political Science Review* 71 (March 1977): 11–30.

10. The classic statement of this view is that of Anthony Downs, whose best effort is: "The advantage of voting per se is that it makes democracy possible. If no one votes, then the system collapses because no government is chosen. We assume that the citizens of a democracy subscribe to its principles and therefore derive benefits from its continuance; hence they do not want it to collapse. For this reason they attach value to the act of voting per se and receive a return from it." Downs, *An Economic Theory of Democracy* (New York: Harper, 1957), pp. 261–262. See also John A. Ferejohn and Morris P. Fiorina, "The Paradox of Not Voting: A Decision Theoretic Analysis," *American Political Science Review* 68 (June 1974): 525–546; and William H. Riker and Peter C. Ordeshook, "A Theory of the Calculus of Voting," *American Political Science Review* 62 (March 1968): 25–42. For a perspective critical of turnout explanations based on rational calculations of voters' personal utility, see Donald P. Green and Ian Shapiro, *Pathologies of Rational Choice Theory* (New Haven: Yale University Press, 1994), pp. 47–71; and Raymond E. Wolfinger, "The Rational Citizen Faces Election Day," in M. Kent Jennings and Thomas E. Mann, eds., *Elections at Home and Abroad: Essays in Honor of Warren E. Miller* (Ann Arbor: University of Michigan Press, 1994), pp. 71–91. Wolfinger quotes Gary Jacobson: "It's the California model; people vote because it makes them feel good" (p. 84).

11. See Rosenstone and Hansen, *Mobilization, Participation, and Democracy in America*, pp. 23, 156–158.

12. Still an excellent summary of the voting turnout and participation literature is Raymond E. Wolfinger and Steven J. Rosenstone, *Who Votes?* (New Haven, CT: Yale University Press, 1980). See also Kay Lehman Schlozman, Sidney Verba, and Henry E. Brady, "Participation's Not a Paradox: The View from American Activists," *British Journal of Political Science* 25 (January 1995): 1–36. This study asks American activists why they participate. The authors conclude: "In an era when surveys show Americans to be disillusioned about politics, distrustful of politicians, and impatient with the level of political debate, we might have expected that activists would either characterize their own political involvement in cynically self-interested terms or see themselves as spectators at an exciting, if sometimes foolish or dirty, sport. On the contrary, their retrospective interpretations of their activity are replete with mentions of civic motivations and a desire to influence policy. Of course, many participants also report selective material or social gratifications. Still, it is striking the extent to which references to doing one's share and making the community or nation a better place to live run as a thread through activists' reports of the concerns that animated their involvement and the number of participants who discuss nothing but civic motivations for their activity" (p. 32).

13. Wolfinger and Rosenstone, *Who Votes?* pp. 94–101.

14. This is one of the most venerable and most secure generalizations in the entire literature of voting behavior studies. See Angus Campbell, Philip E. Converse, Warren E. Miller, and Donald E. Stokes, *The American Voter* (New York: Wiley, 1960), pp. 120–134; and Warren E. Miller and J. Merrill Shanks, *The New American Voter* (Cambridge, MA: Harvard University Press, 1996), pp. 117–150. For variations on this interpretation, see Arthur S. Goldberg, "Social Determination and Rationality as a Basis of Party Identification," *American Political Science Review* 63 (March 1969): 5–25; Morris P. Fiorina, *Retrospective Voting in American National Elections* (New Haven, CT: Yale University Press, 1981), pp. 89–90; Gregory B. Markus and Philip E. Converse, "A Dynamic Simultaneous Model of Electoral Choice," *American Political Science Review* 73 (December 1979): 1055–1070; and Sven Holmberg, "Party Identification Compared Across the Atlantic," in Jennings and Mann, eds., *Elections at Home and Abroad*, pp. 93–121. Larry M. Bartels, "Partisanship and Voting Behavior, 1952–1996," *American Journal of Political Science* 44 (January 2000): 35–50, argues that "[i]n the current political environment, as much or more than at any other time in the past half-century, 'the strength and direction of party identification are facts of central importance' in accounting for the voting behavior of the American electorate" (p. 44; quotation from Campbell et al., *The American Voter*, p. 121). For more recent evidence that party identification is a stable component of social identity—akin, for example, to religious affiliation—see Donald Green, Bradley Palmquist, and Eric Schickler, *Partisan Hearts and Minds: Political Parties and the Social Identities of Voters* (New Haven, CT: Yale University Press, 2002).

15. William H. Flanigan and Nancy H. Zingale, *Political Behavior of the American Electorate*, 8th ed. (Washington, DC: CQ Press, 1994), give findings on the timing of voters' decisions: "In all recent elections

the independents and weak partisans were more likely to make up their minds during the campaign, while strong partisans characteristically made their decisions by the end of the conventions" (p. 162). A study of voters who waited until the last two weeks before the election to choose a candidate found that "late deciders . . . are less interested in the political outcome, less subject to conventional political forces, and far less predictable than other voters." J. David Gopoian and Sissie Hadjiharalambous, "Late-Deciding Voters in Presidential Elections," *Political Behavior* 16 (March 1994): 55–78, at 76.

16. Earlier research did not differentiate among the various sorts of independents and characterized the entire population of independents as comparatively uninvolved in politics, less interested, less concerned, and less knowledgeable than party identifiers. These generalizations hold better for the truly nonpartisan subset of "pure" independents, that is, people who do not "lean" toward one party or the other. See Campbell et al., *The American Voter*, p. 143; Bernard Berelson, Paul F. Lazarsfeld, and William N. McPhee, *Voting* (Chicago: University of Chicago Press, 1954), pp. 25–27; and Bruce E. Keith, David B. Magleby, Candice J. Nelson, Elizabeth Orr, Mark C. Westlye, and Raymond E. Wolfinger, *The Myth of the Independent Voter* (Berkeley: University of California Press, 1992), pp. 65–67. For a somewhat different treatment, see Robert Agger, "Independents and Party Identifiers," in Eugene Burdick and Arthur J. Brodbeck, eds., *American Voting Behavior* (Glencoe, IL: Free Press, 1959), chap. 17.

17. Berelson, Lazarsfeld, and McPhee, *Voting*, pp. 215–233; John R. Zaller, *The Nature and Origins of Mass Opinion* (New York: Cambridge University Press, 1992). George Belknap and Angus Campbell state that "for many people Democratic or Republican attitudes regarding foreign policy result from conscious or unconscious adherence to a perceived party line rather than from influences independent of party identification." Belknap and Campbell, "Political Party Identification and Attitudes toward Foreign Policy," *Public Opinion Quarterly* 15 (Winter 1951–1952): 601–623, at 623. See also Robert Huckfeldt, Paul E. Johnson, and John Sprague, "Political Environments, Political Dynamics, and the Survival of Disagreement," *Journal of Politics* 64 (February 2002): 1–21.

18. Many voting studies contain substantial discussions of this subject. See Robert E. Lane, "Fathers and Sons: Foundations of Political Belief," *American Sociological Review* 24 (August 1959): 502–511; Campbell et al., *The American Voter*, pp. 146–147; and H. H. Remmers, "Early Socialization of Attitudes," in Burdick and Brodbeck, eds., *American Voting Behavior*, pp. 55–67. V. O. Key, *Public Opinion and American Democracy* (New York: Knopf, 1961), pp. 293–314, sums up in these words: "Children acquire early in life a feeling of party identification; they have sensitive antennae and since they are imitative animals, soon take on the political color of their family" (p. 294). See also Fred I. Greenstein, *Children and Politics* (New Haven, CT: Yale University Press, 1965), chap. 4. In a later work, Paul R. Abramson presents an interesting discussion of this familial link and the forces that later play against it; see *Generational Change in American Politics* (Lexington, MA: Lexington Books, 1975), esp. chaps. 3 and 4. See also Richard G. Niemi and M. Kent Jennings, "Issues and Inheritance in the Formation of Party Identification," *American Journal of Political Science* 35 (November 1991): 970–988.

19. "People are more likely to associate with people like themselves—alike in political complexion as well as social position." Berelson, Lazarsfeld, and McPhee, *Voting*, p. 83. See also Robert D. Putnam, "Political Attitudes and the Local Community," *American Political Science Review* 60 (September 1966): 640–654; Ada W. Finifter, "The Friendship Group as a Protective Environment for Political Deviants," *American Political Science Review* 68 (June 1974): 607–626; and Robert Huckfeldt and John Sprague, "Networks in Context: The Social Flow of Political Information," *American Political Science Review* 81 (December 1987): 1197–1216.

20. Paul F. Lazarsfeld, Bernard Berelson, and Hazel Gaudet, *The People's Choice* (New York: Duell, Sloan and Pearce, 1944), pp. 16–28.

21. Ibid.; Angus Campbell and Homer C. Cooper, *Group Differences in Attitudes and Votes* (Ann Arbor: University of Michigan Press, 1956); Julian L. Woodward and Elmo Roper, "Political Activities of American Citizens," *American Political Science Review* 44 (December 1950): 872–875; Key, *Public Opinion and American Democracy*, pp. 99–120, 121–181; Berelson, Lazarsfeld, and McPhee, *Voting*, pp. 54–76; Robert Axelrod, "Where the Votes Come From: An Analysis of Electoral Coalitions, 1952–1968," *American Political Science Review* 66 (March 1972): 11–20; Axelrod, "Communication," *American Political Science Review* 68 (June 1974): 717–720; Axelrod, "Communication," *American Political Science Review* 72 (June 1978): 622–624; Axelrod, "Communication," *American Political Science Review* 76 (June 1982): 393–396;

Axelrod, "Presidential Election Coalitions in 1984," *American Political Science Review* 80 (March 1986): 281–284; Robert A. Jackson and Thomas M. Carsey, "Group Components of U.S. Presidential Voting Across the States," *Political Behavior* 21 (June 1999): 123–151; Miller and Shanks, *The New American Voter*, pp. 212–282. See also table 2.3.

22. V. O. Key Jr., *Southern Politics in State and Nation* (New York: Knopf, 1949), pp. 25, 75–81, 223–228, 280–285. Indeed, conflict over secession was at the root of the formation of the state of West Virginia, which broke away from Virginia and was admitted as a separate state in 1863.

23. See Earl Black and Merle Black, *Politics and Society in the South* (Cambridge, MA: Harvard University Press, 1987); Raymond E. Wolfinger and Michael G. Hagen, "Republican Prospects: Southern Comfort," *Public Opinion* 8 (October/November 1985): 8–13; Earl Black and Merle Black, *The Rise of Southern Republicans* (Cambridge, MA: Harvard University Press, 2002); David Lublin, *The Republican South: Democratization and Partisan Change* (Princeton: Princeton University Press, 2004); and Byron E. Shafer and Richard Johnston, *The End of Southern Exceptionalism: Class, Race, and Partisan Change in the Postwar South* (Cambridge, MA: Harvard University Press, 2006). For an account explaining how these changes made an impact on Congress, see Nelson W. Polsby, *How Congress Evolves: Social Bases of Institutional Change* (New York: Oxford University Press, 2004).

24. See C. Vann Woodward, *The Strange Career of Jim Crow* (New York: Oxford University Press, 1966); and Woodward, *Origins of the New South* (Baton Rouge: Louisiana State University Press, 1951).

25. Nicholas Lemann says: "In 1940, 77 percent of black Americans still lived in the South—49 percent in the rural South. The invention of the cotton picker was crucial to the great migration by blacks from the Southern countryside to the cities of the South, the West, and the North. Between 1910 and 1970, six and a half million black Americans moved from the South to the North; five million of them moved after 1940, during the time of the mechanization of cotton farming. . . . For blacks, the migration meant leaving what had always been their economic and social base in America and finding a new one." Lemann, *The Promised Land* (New York: Knopf, 1991), p. 6.

26. Campbell et al., *The American Voter*, p. 160. See, more generally, James Q. Wilson, *Negro Politics* (Glencoe, IL: Free Press, 1960); and Nancy Weiss, *Farewell to the Party of Lincoln* (Princeton: Princeton University Press, 1983), esp. pp. 209–235. Republican presidential nominee Barry Goldwater, who opposed the Civil Rights Act of 1964, intensified the Democratic loyalties of black voters, who voted Democratic at about a two-to-one rate from the 1930s until 1960 and at an eight-to-one rate from 1964 onward. See Edward G. Carmines and James A. Stimson, *Issue Evolution: Race and the Transformation of American Politics* (Princeton: Princeton University Press, 1989). For more recent data on the black vote, see Miller and Shanks, *The New American Voter*, pp. 256–259.

27. The 110th Congress of 2007–2008 included forty African-American members of the House of Representatives, an all-time high, and one African-American senator, Barack Obama of Illinois. All were Democrats.

28. George H. Mayer, *The Republican Party, 1854–1966*, 2nd ed. (New York: Oxford University Press, 1967), pp. 221–271.

29. Maria de los Angeles Torres says: "In the late 1800s, Cuban workers migrated to the United States in search of employment. Eventually they formed the backbone and the most radical element of the independence movement against Spain. Interestingly, Cuban tobacco workers also participated in the radical wing of the American Federation of Labor. . . .

"After 1959, Cubans migrated to the United States in great numbers. This time it was not workers, but rather the middle and upper classes.

"After the revolution, the tradition of the progressive Cuban immigrant changed radically. Since those sectors most affected by the radical programs of the revolution supplied the initial post-revolutionary immigrations from Cuba, most tended to be politically conservative." Torres, "From Exiles to Minorities: The Politics of the Cuban Community in the United States," Ph.D. dissertation, University of Michigan, Ann Arbor, 1986, pp. 7–8.

30. While political journalists have recently devoted a great deal of attention to Republican efforts to capture a larger share of the growing Latino vote in the United States, evidence indicates that Latinos remain, with the exception of the Cuban population in southern Florida, strongly Democratic. See David

L. Leal, Matt A. Barreto, Jongho Lee, and Rodolfo O. de la Garza, "The Latino Vote in the 2004 Election," *PS: Political Science and Politics* 38 (January 2005): 41–49.

31. See David Hackett Fischer, *Albion's Seed: Four British Folkways in America* (New York: Oxford University Press, 1989), p. 17; Steven Erie, *Rainbow's End: Irish-Americans and the Dilemmas of Urban Machine Politics, 1840–1985* (Berkeley: University of California Press, 1988), pp. 25–28; Duane Lockard, *New England State Politics* (Princeton: Princeton University Press, 1959); Robert A. Dahl, *Who Governs? Democracy and Power in an American City* (New Haven: Yale University Press, 1961), pp. 33–51, 216–217; Elmer E. Cornwell, "Party Absorption of Ethnic Groups: The Case of Providence, R.I.," *Social Forces* 38 (March 1960): 205–210; and J. Joseph Huthmacher, *Massachusetts People and Politics* (Cambridge, MA: Harvard University Press, 1959), pp. 118–126.

32. Samuel Lubell, *The Future of American Politics* (New York: Harper, 1951), pp. 129–157; Willi Paul Adams, *The German-Americans: An Ethnic Experience*, translated and adapted by LaVern J. Rippley and Eberhard Reichmann (New York: Max Kade German-American Center, 1993).

33. A notable study developing the implications of this notion is Downs's classic, *An Economic Theory of Democracy*.

34. Philip E. Converse, "The Nature of Belief Systems in Mass Publics," in David E. Apter, ed., *Ideology and Discontent* (New York: Free Press, 1964), pp. 206–262; William Lyons and John M. Scheb II, "Ideology and Candidate Evaluation in the 1984 and 1988 Presidential Elections," *Journal of Politics* 54 (May 1992): 573–584; M. Kent Jennings, "Ideological Thinking Among Mass Publics and Political Elites," *Public Opinion Quarterly* (Winter 1992): 419–441.

35. See Aaron Wildavsky, "Choosing Preferences by Constructing Institutions: A Cultural Theory of Preference Formation," *American Political Science Review* 81 (March 1987): 3–22; and Michael Thompson, Richard Ellis, and Aaron Wildavsky, *Cultural Theory* (Boulder, CO: Westview Press, 1990).

36. On Eisenhower, see Campbell et al., *The American Voter*, pp. 55–57, 525–528, 537; and Herbert H. Hyman and Paul B. Sheatsley, "The Political Appeal of President Eisenhower," *Public Opinion Quarterly* 17 (Winter 1953): 443–460. On McGovern, see Arthur H. Miller, Warren E. Miller, Alden S. Raine, and Thad A. Brown, "A Majority Party in Disarray: Policy Polarization in the 1972 Election," *American Political Science Review* 70 (September 1976): 753–778; and Samuel L. Popkin, John W. Gorman, Charles Phillips, and Jeffrey A. Smith, "Comment: What Have You Done for Me Lately? Toward an Investment Theory of Voting," *American Political Science Review* 70 (September 1976): 779–805.

37. Martin P. Wattenberg, *The Rise of Candidate-Centered Politics* (Cambridge, MA: Harvard University Press, 1991), pp. 45–65. See also Wattenberg, "The Reagan Polarization Phenomenon and the Continuing Downward Slide in Presidential Candidate Popularity," *American Politics Quarterly* 14 (July 1986): 219–245.

38. The portions of this analysis that deal with voters and issues are adapted from chap. 8, "Public Policy and Political Preference," in Campbell et al., *The American Voter*, pp. 168–187. See also Zaller, *The Nature and Origins of Mass Opinion.*

39. See Hazel Gaudet Erskine, "The Polls: The Informed Public," *Public Opinion Quarterly* 26 (Winter 1962): 669–677. This article summarizes questions asked from 1947 to 1960 of national samples of Americans in order to ascertain their information on current news topics. Similar data for 1935–1946 are contained in Hadley Cantril and Mildred Strunk, *Public Opinion, 1935–46* (Princeton: Princeton University Press, 1951). In light of this and later work, Philip E. Converse was able to conclude: "Surely the most familiar fact to arise from sample surveys in all countries is that popular levels of information about public affairs are, from the point of view of the informed observer, astonishingly low." Converse, "Public Opinion and Voting Behavior," in Fred I. Greenstein and Nelson W. Polsby, eds., *Handbook of Political Science* (Reading, MA: Addison-Wesley, 1975), volume 4, pp. 75–169, at 79. See also Michael X. Delli Carpini and Scott Keeter, *What Americans Know About Politics and Why It Matters* (New Haven, CT: Yale University Press, 1996); and Philip E. Converse, "Assessing the Capacity of Mass Electorates," *Annual Review of Political Science* 3 (June 2000): 331–353.

40. The data on which this conclusion is based refer to issues in rather general categories such as "economic aid to foreign countries," the "influence of big business in government," and "aid to education" (Campbell et al., *The American Voter*, p. 182). It is highly probable that the proportion of people meeting the

requirements of having an opinion and differentiating among the parties would be substantially reduced if precise and specific policies within these general issue categories formed the basis of questions in a survey. See also Converse, "Public Opinion and Voting Behavior."

41. Campbell et al., in *The American Voter*, tentatively conclude that in the Eisenhower years, covered by their study, "people who paid little attention to politics were contributing very disproportionately to partisan change" (p. 264). Zaller, *The Nature and Origins of Mass Opinion*, confirms these findings. He shows that the greater the level of political awareness, the more likely people are to possess "cueing messages" that help them filter out information contrary to their existing viewpoint on a given issue. Thus greater awareness results in an increasing ratio of ideologically consistent to inconsistent considerations governing opinion formation. This means that more aware liberals, for example, are more likely to support liberal positions (pp. 100–101). The implications for partisan change are clear: political awareness leads to stability in issue preferences and discourages change. Political inattentiveness, conversely, leads to unstable issue preferences and is therefore more likely to lead to partisan change.

42. Philip E. Converse, "Information Flow and the Stability of Partisan Attitudes," *Public Opinion Quarterly* 26 (Winter 1962): 578–599. John R. Zaller says: "When people are exposed to two competing sets of electoral information, they are generally able to choose among them on the basis of their partisanship and values even when they do not score especially well on tests of political awareness. But when individuals are exposed to a one-sided communication flow, as in low-key House and Senate elections, their capacity for critical resistance appears quite limited.

"The conclusion I draw from this is that the most important source of resistance to dominant campaigns . . . is countervalent information carried within the overall stream of political information." Zaller, *The Nature and Origins of Mass Opinion*, pp. 252–253.

43. According to the 2004 National Election Study, 39 percent of respondents considered themselves independents, but nearly three-quarters of these leaned toward either the Democratic or Republican Party. Only 10 percent of respondents were "pure," nonleaning independents, and many of them did not vote. See Keith et al., *The Myth of the Independent Voter*.

44. See Sidney Verba, Richard A. Brody, Edwin B. Parker, Norman H. Nie, Nelson W. Polsby, Paul Eckman, and Gordon S. Black, "Public Opinion and the War in Vietnam," *American Political Science Review* 61 (June 1967): 317–333; and Benjamin I. Page and Richard A. Brody, "Policy Voting and the Electoral Process: The Vietnam War Issue," *American Political Science Review* 66 (September 1972): 979–995.

45. Miller, Miller, Raine, and Brown, "A Majority Party in Disarray," p. 760. The issues studied included Vietnam withdrawal, amnesty for draft dodgers, reducing military spending, government health insurance, guaranteed standard of living, urban unrest, campus unrest, protecting the rights of those accused of crime, government aid to minorities, equal rights for women, abortion, legalization of marijuana, busing, and a "liberal-conservative philosophic position." For similar findings, see Jeane Kirkpatrick, "Representation in the American National Conventions: The Case of 1972," *British Journal of Political Science* 5 (July 1975): 265–322; and Kirkpatrick, *The New Presidential Elite* (New York: Russell Sage Foundation, 1976).

46. See David W. Brady, *Critical Elections and Congressional Policy Making* (Stanford: Stanford University Press, 1988), pp. 85–89.

47. Miller, Miller, Raine, and Brown, "A Majority Party in Disarray," pp. 761–772.

48. Gary C. Jacobson, *The Electoral Origins of Divided Government* (Boulder, CO: Westview Press, 1990), p. 125. For a detailed discussion of the relationship between presidential popularity and economic performance, see Richard A. Brody, *Assessing the President: The Media, Elite Opinion, and Popular Support* (Stanford: Stanford University Press, 1991), pp. 91–103; for a study of the effects of economic conditions on presidential vote choice, see Richard Nadeau and Michael S. Lewis-Beck, "National Economic Voting in U.S. Presidential Elections," *Journal of Politics* 63 (February 2001): 159–181.

49. Marjorie Connelly, "How Americans Voted: A Political Portrait," *New York Times*, November 7, 2004, sec. 4, p. 4.

50. Campbell et al., *The American Voter*, p. 148.

51. V. O. Key Jr., with the assistance of Milton C. Cummings Jr., *The Responsible Electorate: Rationality in Presidential Voting, 1936–1960* (Cambridge, MA: Harvard University Press, 1966). This was

the finding that led Key to his famous remark: "The perverse and unorthodox argument of this little book is that voters are not fools" (p. 7).

52. Charles H. Franklin, "Issue Preferences, Socialization and the Evaluation of Party Identification," *American Journal of Political Science* 28 (August 1984): 459–475.

53. The degree of aggregate stability in the electorate over time, and the sensitivity of the overall distribution of party identification to the performance of incumbent officeholders, is a matter of some dispute among scholars. See Donald Green, Bradley Palmquist, and Eric Schickler, "Macropartisanship: A Replication and Critique," *American Political Science Review* 92 (December 1998): 883–899; and Robert S. Erikson, Michael B. MacKuen, and James A. Stimson, "What Moves Macropartisanship? A Reply to Green, Palmquist, and Schickler," *American Political Science Review* 92 (December 1998): 901–912.

54. Janet M. Box-Steffensmeier and Renee M. Smith, "The Dynamics of Aggregate Partisanship," *American Political Science Review* 90 (September 1996): 567–580.

55. Franklin, "Issue Preferences, Socialization, and the Evaluation of Party Identification," p. 474.

56. Fiorina, *Retrospective Voting in American National Elections*, p. 84.

57. Donald R. Kinder and D. Roderick Kiewiet, "Sociotropic Politics: The American Case," *British Journal of Political Science* 11 (April 1981): 129–161; Douglas A. Hibbs Jr., with the assistance of R. Douglas Rivers and Nicholas Vasilatos, "The Dynamics of Political Support for American Presidents Among Occupational and Partisan Groups," *American Journal of Political Science* 26 (May 1982): 312–332.

58. Converse, "The Nature of Belief Systems in Mass Publics"; Philip E. Converse and Gregory B. Markus, "Plus Ça Change: The New CPS Election Study Panel," *American Political Science Review* 73 (March 1979): 18–30. In view of the resistance to change of individual voters and the fact that nevertheless in aggregate there are changes, it is worth considering the idea that change occurs through processes by which old voters are replaced by new. This is strongly suggested for Canada by Richard Johnston in "Party Alignment and Realignment in Canada, 1911–1965," Ph.D. dissertation, Stanford University, 1976. V. O. Key Jr. also supported a mobilization-of-new-voters interpretation in "A Theory of Critical Elections," *Journal of Politics* 17 (February 1955): 3–18. Arthur S. Goldberg's study of American data finds that children tend to defect from the party identification of their parents when the parents' party identification is atypical for their status and the children are relatively well educated. See Goldberg, "Social Determinism and Rationality as Bases of Party Identification," *American Political Science Review* 63 (March 1969): 5–25. Kristi Andersen, *The Creation of a Democratic Majority, 1928–1936* (Chicago: University of Chicago Press, 1979), argues that "the surge in the Democratic vote in 1932 and 1936 came primarily from newly mobilized groups" (p. 69): those who came of political age in the 1920s but did not vote until 1928, 1932, or 1936, and those who came of age between 1928 and 1936. On the other side, see the intriguing arguments for opinion change by individual voters in Robert S. Erikson and Kent L. Tedin, "The 1928–1936 Partisan Realignment: The Case for the Conversion Hypothesis," *American Political Science Review* 75 (December 1981): 951–962.

59. Donald R. Kinder, "Diversity and Complexity in American Public Opinion," in Ada W. Finifter, ed., *Political Science: The State of the Discipline* (Washington, D.C.: American Political Science Association, 1983), pp. 389–425, at 410 (including footnote; emphasis in original).

60. See Martin P. Wattenberg, *The Decline of American Political Parties, 1952–1996* (Cambridge, MA: Harvard University Press, 1998).

61. Keith et al., *The Myth of the Independent Voter*, p. 13.

62. Partisan independents—leaners—vote their party preferences less frequently than strong party identifiers but more frequently than weak party identifiers, and pure independents do not vote very much at all. Between 1952 and 1988, an average of 67 percent of Democratic-leaning independents voted Democratic in presidential elections, as compared to 63 percent of "weak" Democrats; 86 percent of Republican-leaning independents voted for Republican candidates during the same period, as compared to 85 percent of "weak" Republicans. Keith et al., *The Myth of the Independent Voter*, p. 68. Party identification was considered strong in 1952 at a time when, according to National Election Studies data, 23 percent of the adult population declared themselves to be independents: 10 percent leaning to the Democrats, 7 percent leaning to the Republicans, and 6 percent pure independents. By 1980, the proportion of self-styled independents had risen to 34 percent: 13 percent pure, 11 percent Democratic, and 10 percent Republican. It has remained more or less stable since: 39 percent in 2004 (10 percent pure, 17 percent Democratic, and

12 percent Republican). Thus, while the number of pure independents has nearly doubled, they are still not a large fraction of the potential electorate. It is easy to overstate the political impact of the decline in party identifiers, in view of the fact that the increase among independents is divided between two-thirds who are in effect hidden party supporters and one-third who are mostly nonvoters. Keith et al., *The Myth of the Independent Voter*, pp. 47–51; Harold W. Stanley and Richard G. Niemi, *Vital Statistics on American Politics, 2005–2006* (Washington, DC: CQ Press, 2005), p. 116.

63. Converse, "The Role of Belief Systems in Mass Publics"; Kinder, "Diversity and Complexity in American Public Opinion"; Green, Palmquist, and Schickler, *Partisan Hearts and Minds.*

64. Nelson W. Polsby, *Consequences of Party Reform* (New York: Oxford University Press, 1983), p. 87; Raymond E. Wolfinger, "Dealignment, Realignment, and Mandates in the 1984 Election," in Austin Ranney, ed., *The American Elections of 1984* (Durham, NC: Duke University Press, 1985), pp. 277–296, at 281; Connelly, "How Americans Voted."

65. Connelly, "How Americans Voted."

Chapter 2   Groups

1. Some years ago, David R. Mayhew noticed this pattern of difference in the congressional parties. See Mayhew, *Party Loyalty Among Congressmen: The Difference Between Democrats and Republicans, 1947–1962* (Cambridge, MA: Harvard University Press, 1966).

2. Nelson W. Polsby and William G. Mayer, "Ideological Cohesion in the American Two-Party System," in Nelson W. Polsby and Raymond E. Wolfinger, eds., *On Parties: Essays Honoring Austin Ranney* (Berkeley: Institute of Governmental Studies Press, 1999), pp. 219–254. The authors examine data from the National Election Studies conducted between 1968 and 1996, finding that Democratic respondents were more spread out than Republicans on 115 of 127 items measuring opinions on public policy issues. See table 5.5.

3. Marjorie Connelly, "How Americans Voted: A Political Portrait," *New York Times*, November 7, 2004, sec. 4, p. 4.

4. This table is an adaptation and update of Robert Axelrod's research on the electoral coalitions of the parties. See Robert Axelrod, "Where the Votes Come From: An Analysis of Electoral Coalitions, 1952–1968," *American Political Science Review* 66 (March 1972): 11–20; Axelrod, "Communication," *American Political Science Review* 68 (June 1974): 717–720; Axelrod, "Communication," *American Political Science Review* 72 (June 1978): 622–624; Axelrod, "Communication," *American Political Science Review* 76 (June 1982): 393–396; and Axelrod, "Presidential Election Coalitions in 1984," *American Political Science Review* 80 (March 1986): 281–284. David A. Hopkins and John Hanley revised and updated Axelrod's findings based on data from the National Election Studies.

5. Harold W. Stanley, William J. Bianco, and Richard G. Niemi, "Partisanship and Group Support over Time: A Multivariate Analysis," *American Political Science Review* 80 (September 1986): 969–976.

6. *Gallup Poll Monthly* 374 (November 1996): 17–20.

7. Connelly, "How Americans Voted."

8. Raymond E. Wolfinger, "Dealignment, Realignment, and Mandates in the 1984 Election," in Austin Ranney, ed., *The American Elections of 1984* (Durham, NC: Duke University Press, 1985), pp. 277–296, at 290.

9. Axelrod, "Communication," June 1982, p. 395; Axelrod, "Presidential Election Coalitions in 1984"; Connelly, "How Americans Voted."

10. See Raymond A. Bauer, Ithiel de Sola Pool, and Lewis Anthony Dexter, *American Business and Public Policy* (New York: Atherton Press, 1963), pp. 323–399, esp. p. 373. A similar argument is made in John R. Wright, "PACs, Contributions, and Roll Calls: An Organizational Perspective," *American Political Science Review* 79 (June 1985): 400–414.

11. Richard L. Berke, "Trade Vote Effect May Ebb Over Time," *New York Times*, November 23, 1993, sec. 1, p. 23; R. W. Apple Jr., "Unions Faltering in Reprisals against Trade Pact Backers," *New York Times*, February 21, 1994, p. A1.

12. Marjorie Connelly, "Portrait of the Electorate: Who Voted for Whom in the House," *New York Times*, November 13, 1994, sec. 1, p. 24.

13. Aaron B. Wildavsky, "The Intelligent Citizen's Guide to the Abuses of Statistics: The Kennedy Document and the Catholic Vote," in Nelson W. Polsby, Robert Dentler, and Paul Smith, eds., *Politics and Social Life* (Boston: Houghton Mifflin, 1963), pp. 825–844; and Philip E. Converse, Angus Campbell, Warren E. Miller, and Donald Stokes, "Stability and Change in 1960: A Reinstating Election," *American Political Science Review* 55 (June 1961): 269–280.

14. See Seymour M. Lipset, Paul F. Lazarsfeld, Allen H. Barton, and Juan Linz, "The Psychology of Voting: An Analysis of Political Behavior," in Gardner Lindzey, ed., *Handbook of Social Psychology* (Cambridge, Mass.: Addison-Wesley, 1954).

15. Angus Campbell, Philip E. Converse, Warren E. Miller, and Donald E. Stokes, *The American Voter* (New York: Wiley, 1960), pp. 483–494.

16. CBS News/*New York Times* 1980 exit polls showed men voting 54 percent Reagan to 37 percent Carter and women 46 percent Reagan to 45 percent Carter. Everett Carll Ladd, "The Brittle Mandate: Electoral Dealignment and the 1980 Presidential Election," *Political Science Quarterly* 96 (Spring 1981): 1–25, at 16.

17. See Kathleen Frankovic, "Sex and Politics: New Alignments, Old Issues," *PS: Political Science and Politics* 15 (Summer 1982): 439–448; and Frankovic, "Women and Men: Is a Realignment Under Way?" *Public Opinion* 5 (April/May 1982): 21–32.

18. Adam Clymer, "Polls Show a Married-Single Gap in Last Election," *New York Times*, January 6, 1983.

19. Paul R. Abramson, John H. Aldrich, and David W. Rohde, *Change and Continuity in the 1988 Elections* (Washington, DC: CQ Press, 1990), pp. 123–125.

20. Connelly, "How Americans Voted."

21. Herbert F. Weisberg, "The Demographics of a New Voting Gap: Marriage Differences in American Voting," *Public Opinion Quarterly* 51 (Autumn 1987): 335–343; Eric Plutzer and Michael McBurnett, "Family Life and American Politics: The 'Marriage Gap' Reconsidered," *Public Opinion Quarterly* 55 (Spring 1991): 113–127; Laura Stoker and M. Kent Jennings, "Political Similarity and Influence Between Husbands and Wives," in Alan S. Zuckerman, ed., *The Social Life of Politics* (Philadelphia: Temple University Press, 2005), pp. 51–74.

22. Frankovic, "Sex and Politics"; Karen M. Kaufmann and John R. Petrocik, "The Changing Politics of American Men: Understanding the Sources of the Gender Gap," *American Journal of Political Science* 43 (July 1999): 864–887.

23. Karen M. Kaufmann, "Culture Wars, Secular Realignment, and the Gender Gap in Party Identification," *Political Behavior* 24 (September 2002): 283–307.

24. Ethel Klein, "The Gender Gap: Different Issues, Different Answers," *Brookings Review* 3 (Winter 1985), p. 34.

25. Pamela Johnston Conover and Virginia Sapiro, "Gender, Feminist Consciousness, and War," *American Journal of Political Science* 37 (November 1993): 1079–1099; Carole Kennedy Chaney, R. Michael Alvarez, and Jonathan Nagler, "Explaining the Gender Gap in U.S. Presidential Elections, 1980–1992," *Political Research Quarterly* 51 (June 1998): 311–339.

26. Indeed, some of the most vocal groups have no membership at all and exist only as lobbying organizations. See Jeffrey M. Berry, *Lobbying for the People: The Political Behavior of Public Interest Groups* (Princeton: Princeton University Press, 1977), p. 186; and Robert D. Putnam, *Bowling Alone: The Collapse and Revival of American Community* (New York: Simon and Schuster, 2000), pp. 49–64.

27. "Why Americans Are Mad: An Interview with Rush Limbaugh," *Policy Review* 61 (Summer 1992): 47; "Behind the Bestsellers," *Publishers Weekly*, October 4, 1993, p. 14; Joyce Howard Price, "Scandal Rushes Limbaugh Back into Radio's Top Spot," *Washington Times*, September 27, 1998, p. A3; Dana Milbank, "My Bias for Mainstream News," *Washington Post*, March 20, 2005, p. B01.

28. Joseph E. Cantor, "PACs: Political Financiers of the '80s," *Congressional Research Service Review*, February 1982, pp. 14–16; Xandra Kayden and Eddie Mahe Jr., *The Party Goes On: The Persistence of the Two-Party System in the United States* (New York: Basic Books, 1985); Harold W. Stanley and

Richard G. Niemi, *Vital Statistics on American Politics, 2005–2006* (Washington, DC: CQ Press, 2005), p. 101.

29. "Corporate Political Action Committees Are Less Oriented to Republicans Than Expected," *Congressional Quarterly*, April 8, 1978, pp. 849–854; Theodore J. Eismeier and Philip H. Pollock III, *Business, Money and the Rise of Corporate PACs in American Elections* (New York: Quorum Books, 1988), pp. 79–96.

30. Thomas J. Rudolph, "Corporate and Labor PAC Contributions in House Elections: Measuring the Effects of Majority Party Status," *Journal of Politics* 61 (February 1999): 195–206; Gary C. Jacobson, *The Politics of Congressional Elections*, 6th ed. (New York: Longman, 2004), pp. 63–75.

31. Edwin M. Epstein, "Corporations and Labor Unions in Electoral Politics," *Annals of the American Academy of Political and Social Science* 425 (May 1976), p. 49. The Bipartisan Campaign Reform Act (BCRA) of 2002, sometimes known as the McCain-Feingold or Shays-Meehan law after its congressional sponsors, did not change the contribution limits applicable to PACs.

32. Ibid., p. 50. For more on PACs, see William J. Crotty and Gary C. Jacobson, *American Parties in Decline* (Boston: Little, Brown, 1980), pp. 100–155; Edwin M. Epstein, "PACs and the Modern Political Process," in Betty Bock et al., eds., *The Modern Corporation: Size and Impacts* (New York: Columbia University Press, 1984), pp. 399–496; Michael J. Malbin, ed., *Parties, Interest Groups, and Campaign Finance Laws* (Washington, DC: American Enterprise Institute, 1980); Elizabeth Drew, *Politics and Money* (New York: Macmillan, 1983); Theodore J. Eismeier and Philip H. Pollock III, "A Tale of Two Elections: PAC Money in 1980 and 1984," *Corruption and Reform* 1 (1986): 189–207; Anthony Corrado, *Creative Campaigning: PACs and the Presidential Selection Process* (Boulder, CO: Westview Press, 1992); David M. Hart, "Why Do Some Firms Give? Why Do Some Give a Lot? High-Tech PACs, 1977–1996," *Journal of Politics* 63 (November 2001): 1230–1249.

33. This is a venerable idea. For example, see American Political Science Association, "Toward a More Responsible Two-Party System," Report of the Committee on Political Parties, 1950.

34. Frank J. Sorauf, *Money in American Elections* (Glenview, IL: Scott, Foresman, 1988), pp. 72–80; Edwin M. Epstein, "Business and Labor under the Federal Election Campaign Act of 1971," in Malbin, ed., *Parties, Interest Groups, and Campaign Finance Laws*, pp. 107–151.

35. Frank J. Sorauf, "Parties and Political Action Committees in American Politics," in Kay Lawson and Peter Merkl, eds., *When Parties Fail* (Princeton: Princeton University Press, 1988), pp. 35–62.

36. This issue is also about money, mainly restricting the amount of money litigants can extract from business enterprises.

37. There are, of course, numerous ways of gaining access to public officials, but participation in their original selection is the primary avenue of access used by political parties. Our interpretation of parties is based on a rich literature: for example, Pendleton Herring, *The Politics of Democracy: American Parties in Action*, rev. ed. (New York: W. W. Norton, 1965); V. O. Key Jr., *Politics, Parties and Pressure Groups*, 5th ed. (New York: Crowell, 1964); David B. Truman, "Federalism and the Party System," in Arthur MacMahon, ed., *Federalism: Mature and Emergent* (New York: Doubleday, 1955), pp. 115–136; Anthony Downs, *An Economic Theory of Democracy* (New York: Harper, 1957); Leon D. Epstein, *Political Parties in the American Mold* (Madison: University of Wisconsin Press, 1986); and a burgeoning literature on state and local political party organizations. See especially David B. Truman, *The Governmental Process* (New York: Knopf, 1971), pp. 262–287; Malcolm E. Jewell and Sarah M. Morehouse, *Political Parties and Elections in American States*, 9th ed. (Washington, DC: CQ Press, 2001); David R. Mayhew, *Placing Parties in American Politics* (Princeton: Princeton University Press, 1986); and Larry J. Sabato and Bruce Larson, *The Party's Just Begun: Shaping Political Parties for America's Future*, 2nd ed. (New York: Longman, 2002).

38. See Jacobson, *The Politics of Congressional Elections*, 6th ed., pp. 122–146; and Bruce Cain, John Ferejohn, and Morris Fiorina, *The Personal Vote: Constituency Service and Electoral Independence* (Cambridge, MA: Harvard University Press, 1987). For evidence that parties are beginning to reassert influence over candidate nominations, see Casey B. K. Dominguez, "Before the Primary: Party Participation in Congressional Nominating Processes," Ph.D. dissertation, University of California, Berkeley, 2005.

39. For a more expansive view of endorsements, see Marty Cohen, David Karol, Hans Noel, and John Zaller, *Beating Reform: The Resurgence of Parties in Presidential Nominations* (Chicago: University of Chicago Press, forthcoming).

40. See John F. Bibby, "Party Renewal in the National Republican Party," in Gerald M. Pomper, ed., *Party Renewal in America* (New York: Praeger, 1980), pp. 102–115; and Cornelius P. Cotter and John F. Bibby, "Institutional Development of Parties and the Thesis of Party Decline," *Political Science Quarterly* 95 (Spring 1980): 1–27.

41. An acutely self-satiric evaluation of the purist mentality is contained in the following excerpt from Richard M. Koster, "Surprise Party," *Harper's*, March 1975, p. 31, on the Democratic Party conference of that year: "Alan Baron, the sharpest of the young pros, who had coached the liberals brilliantly on the Mikulski and charter commissions, decided that, whatever happened, the conference was a success: we might lose organized labor, but we'd brought in God."

42. Herbert McClosky, Paul J. Hoffman, and Rosemary O'Hara, "Issue Conflict and Consensus among Party Leaders and Followers," *American Political Science Review* 54 (June 1960): 406–427. The authors compared large samples of Democratic and Republican leaders on twenty-four major public issues and conclude that "the belief that the two American parties are identical in principle and doctrine has little foundation in fact. Examination of the opinions of Democratic and Republican leaders show them to be distinct communities of cobelievers who diverge sharply on many important issues." They add, "little support was found for the belief that deep cleavages exist among the electorate but are ignored by the leaders. One might, indeed, more accurately assert the contrary, to wit: that the natural cleavages between the leaders are largely ignored by the voters" (pp. 425–426). They found in 1956 that on most issues, the Democratic Party elite held positions not only closer to the Democratic rank and file but also closer to the Republican rank and file than those of the Republican elite. While the party elites still differed significantly from each other in 1972, the tables had turned and the "Republican elite held views that were more representative of the views and values of rank and file Democrats than were the views of Democratic delegates." Jeane Kirkpatrick, "Representation in the American National Conventions: The Case of 1972," *British Journal of Political Science* 5 (July 1975): 265–322. Differences between the party elites have increased substantially since 1972; see Warren E. Miller and M. Kent Jennings, *Parties in Transition: A Longitudinal Study of Party Elites and Party Supporters* (New York: Russell Sage Foundation, 1986); and Marc J. Hetherington, "Resurgent Mass Partisanship: The Role of Elite Polarization," *American Political Science Review* 95 (September 2001): 619–631.

43. Charlotte Allen, "For Catholic Politicians, A Hard Line," *Washington Post*, April 11, 2004, p. B01.

44. Martin Schram, *Running for President, 1976: The Carter Campaign* (New York: Stein and Day, 1977), pp. 92, 93, 114, 150.

45. John F. Bibby, Robert J. Huckshorn, James L. Gibson, and Cornelius P. Cotter, *Party Organization and American Politics* (New York: Praeger, 1984), p. 314; John F. Bibby, "State Party Organizations: Strengthened and Adapting to Candidate-Centered Politics and Nationalization," in L. Sandy Maisel, ed., *The Parties Respond: Changes in American Parties and Campaigns*, 4th ed. (Boulder, CO: Westview Press, 2002), pp. 19–46.

46. The Supreme Court gives the national convention the right to regulate standards for admission to it, even overriding enactments of state legislatures on the subject of primary elections, and in this important respect national standards can be imposed on state party organizations. See *Cousins v. Wigoda*, 419 U.S. 477 (1975) and *Democratic Party of the U.S. et al. v. LaFollette et al.*, 450 U.S. 107 (1981). See also Everett Carll Ladd Jr. with Charles D. Hadley, *Transformations of the American Party System* (New York: Norton, 1975); Austin Ranney, *Curing the Mischiefs of Faction: Party Reform in America* (Berkeley: University of California Press, 1975); William Crotty, *Party Reform* (New York: Longman, 1983); James Ceaser, *Reforming the Reforms* (Cambridge, MA: Ballinger, 1982); Gary D. Wekkin, *Democrat versus Democrat* (Columbia: University of Missouri Press, 1984); and Nelson W. Polsby, *Consequences of Party Reform* (New York: Oxford University Press, 1983).

47. Paul S. Herrnson, "National Party Organizations at the Dawn of the Twenty-First Century," in Maisel, ed., *The Parties Respond*, pp. 47–78.

48. See William S. Livingston, "A Note on the Nature of Federalism," *Political Science Quarterly* 67 (March 1952): 81–95; Mayhew, *Placing Parties in American Politics*; Michael Barone with Richard E. Cohen, *The Almanac of American Politics, 2006* (Washington, DC: National Journal Group, 2005).

49. See Ronald B. Rapoport and Walter J. Stone, *Three's a Crowd: The Dynamic of Third Parties, Ross Perot, and Republican Resurgence* (Ann Arbor: University of Michigan Press, 2005).

50. Steven J. Rosenstone, Roy L. Behr, and Edward H. Lazarus, *Third Parties in America*, 2nd ed. (Princeton: Princeton University Press, 1996), p. 19. By the time of his second presidential campaign in 1996, Perot had formed a party, the Reform Party, which ran candidates for offices other than the presidency.

51. In *Timmons v. Twin Cities Area New Party*, 520 U.S. 351 (1997), the Supreme Court allowed states to prohibit third parties from choosing major party candidates as their own nominees. See Leon D. Epstein, "The American Party Primary," in Polsby and Wolfinger, eds., *On Parties*, pp. 43–72, at 66–67. New York is one of the few states in which candidates may run on more than one party line. The Liberal Party disbanded as an official party following the 2002 gubernatorial election, in which it failed to receive enough votes to retain its status as a recognized party under New York law.

52. This surprising victory remains the Reform Party's only notable electoral success, but Ventura left the party midway through his term of office after a power struggle with Perot and subsequently decided not to seek reelection. See Dean Lacy and Quin Monson, "The Origins and Impact of Votes for Third-Party Candidates: A Case Study of the 1998 Minnesota Gubernatorial Election," *Political Research Quarterly* 55 (June 2002): 409–437.

53. At least one study suggests that Perot's candidacy hurt Bush more than Clinton; see R. Michael Alvarez and Jonathan Nagler, "Economics, Issues and the Perot Candidacy: Voter Choice in the 1992 Election," *American Journal of Political Science* 37 (August 1995): 714–744, at 737–738. Alvarez and Nagler estimate that Perot supporters would have divided about evenly between Bush and Clinton had Perot not run, while the rest of the electorate preferred Clinton to Bush 53 percent to 47 percent. In addition, Perot drew most of his support from men, who are otherwise more likely to vote Republican than are women.

54. Robert G. Meadow, "Televised Campaign Debates as Whistle-Stop Speeches," in William C. Adams, ed., *Television Coverage of the 1980 Presidential Campaign* (Norwood, NJ: Ablex, 1983), p. 91.

55. John R. Zaller and Mark Hunt, "The Rise and Fall of Candidate Perot: The Outsider vs. the System," *Political Communication* 12 (January 1995): 97–123.

56. Herbert F. Weisberg and David C. Kimball, "Attitudinal Correlates of the 1992 Presidential Vote," in Herbert F. Weisberg, ed., *Democracy's Feast: Elections in America* (Chatham, NJ: Chatham House, 1995), p. 104.

57. In 2000, as the nominee of the Green Party, Nader received 2,883,105 votes nationwide, or 2.7 percent of the total. Nader ran again in 2004 as an independent candidate and received only 463,655 votes, or about 0.4 percent. This showing fits a common general pattern in which candidates outside the two-party system reach an early peak of support and then decline in popularity as their voters return to the major parties or to nonparticipation.

58. Daniel Mazmanian has shown that third-party candidates do best in years in which there is an intensely conflictual issue on the political agenda, suggesting that focusing discontent and raising issues are, for these candidates, functions most profitably performed in unison. Mazmanian, *Third Parties in Presidential Elections* (Washington, DC: Brookings Institution, 1974), p. 28.

59. See Paul R. Abramson, John H. Aldrich, Phil Paolino, and David W. Rohde, "Third-Party and Independent Candidates: Wallace, Anderson, and Perot," *Political Science Quarterly* 110 (Fall 1995): 349–367.

Chapter 3 Rules and Resources

1. The unit rule is not prescribed in the Constitution or by federal law. Instead, it is the result of individual state action that provides, in all states except Maine and Nebraska, that electors for party nominees are grouped together and elected en bloc on a "general ticket" such that a vote for one elector is a vote for all the electors on that ticket, with a plurality vote electing all electors for the state. Missouri Senator Thomas Hart Benton said in 1824: "The general ticket system . . . was the offspring of policy. . . . It was adopted by the leading men of [ten states] to enable them to consolidate the vote of the state . . . ." Thomas Jefferson had earlier pointed out that "while ten states choose either by legislatures or by a general

ticket it is folly and worse than folly for the other states not to do it." In short, once a few states maximized their impact by using the unit rule, the others followed suit. See Motion for Leave to File Complaint, Complaint and Brief, *Delaware v. New York*, No. 28 Original, U.S. Supreme Court, October term, 1966; and Neal R. Peirce, "The Electoral College Goes to Court," *The Reporter*, October 6, 1966.

In Maine and Nebraska the electoral vote of each congressional district (two in Maine and three in Nebraska) is determined by the vote within the district, and the two electoral votes that the states have by virtue of their senators are cast according to the overall vote in the state as a whole. Here is a summary of the Maine law, taken from *Nomination and Election of the President and Vice President of the United States Including the Manner of Selecting Delegates to National Political Conventions* (Washington, DC: Government Printing Office, 1980), p. 356:

> "Electors shall vote by separate ballot for one person for President and one person for Vice President. A presidential elector is elected from each congressional district and two at large. They shall convene in the Senate chamber in Augusta on the first Monday after the second Wednesday of December at 2:00 p.m. following their election. The presidential electors at large shall cast their ballots for President and Vice President of the political party which received the largest number of votes in the State. The presidential electors of each congressional district shall cast their ballots for the candidates for President and Vice President of the political party which received the largest number of votes in each congressional district."

2. Further confirmation of this view is provided by Steven J. Brams and Morton D. Davis, "The 3/2's Rule in Presidential Campaigning," *American Political Science Review* 68 (March 1974): 113–134; Claude S. Colatoni, Terrence J. Levesque, and Peter D. Ordeshook, "Campaign Resource Allocations under the Electoral College," *American Political Science Review* 69 (March 1975): 141–152; and John A. Yunker and Lawrence D. Longley, "The Biases of the Electoral College: Who Is Really Advantaged?" in Donald R. Matthews, ed., *Perspectives on Presidential Selection* (Washington, DC: Brookings Institution, 1972), pp. 172–203.

3. Battleground states, by this definition, are the states in which the two major candidates and their running mates made at least fifteen total personal visits between September 3 and November 1, 2004; advertising campaigns were conducted in each of these states during the month of October. Candidate visit data from Democracy in Action, George Washington University, http://www.gwu.edu/~action /2004/chrnfall.html; advertising data from the Wisconsin Advertising Project, University of Wisconsin, http://www.polisci.wisc.edu/tvadvertising/.

4. Our discussion of money in elections owes a great deal to the work of Herbert Alexander who, over the years, built up an unequaled store of knowledge on this subject. Important legislation affecting money in politics includes the Federal Election Campaign Act of 1971, the Federal Election Campaign Act Amendments of 1974 (2 USC 431), and, more recently, the Bipartisan Campaign Reform Act of 2002 (Pub. L. No. 107-155, 116 Stat. 81). For a wide-ranging set of materials on election reform up to and including the 1971 Act, see U.S. Senate Select Committee on Presidential Campaign Activities, *Election Reform: Basic References* (Washington, DC: Government Printing Office, 1973). A compact summary of the state of the law as of 1975 is contained in U.S. Senate Subcommittee on Privileges and Elections of the Committee on Rules and Administration, *Federal Election Campaign Laws* (Washington, DC: Government Printing Office, 1975). For a useful discussion of the law's political implications, see the American Bar Association, *Symposium on Campaign Financing Regulation* (Chicago: American Bar Association, 1975); and Jo Freeman, "Political Party Contributions and Expenditures under the Federal Election Campaign Act: Anomalies and Unfinished Business," *Pace Law Review* 4 (Winter 1984): 267–296.

5. Federal Election Commission, "2004 Campaign Finance Activity Summarized," press release, February 3, 2005, table 1, available at http://www.fec.gov/press/press2005/20050203pressum /20050203pressum.html.

6. Federal Election Commission, "Party Financial Activity Summarized for the 2004 Election Cycle," press release, March 2, 2005, available at http://www.fec.gov/press/press2005/20050302party /Party2004final.html.

7. Federal Election Commission, "Congressional Candidates Spend $1.16 Billion During 2003–2004," press release, June 9, 2005, available at http://www.fec.gov/press/press2005/20050609candidate/20050609candidate.html.

8. Frank J. Sorauf, *Money in American Politics* (Glenview, IL: Scott, Foresman, 1988), p. 192.

9. Ibid., p. 191.

10. Federal Election Commission, "PAC Activity Increases for 2004 Elections," press release, April 13, 2005, table 1, available at http://www.fec.gov/press/press2005/20050412pac/PACFinal2004.html.

11. Center for Responsive Politics, "The Big Picture, 2004 Cycle: Top Zip Codes," available at http://www.opensecrets.org/bigpicture/topzips.asp.

12. Patrick Anderson, *Electing Jimmy Carter: The Campaign of 1976* (Baton Rouge: Louisiana State University Press, 1994), p. 89.

13. Herbert E. Alexander and Anthony Corrado, *Financing the 1992 Election* (New York: M. E. Sharpe, 1995), pp. 41–42, 62–63, 74, 80. A detailed historical account of the relationship between Hollywood and Washington is given by Ronald Brownstein, *The Power and the Glitter* (New York: Pantheon, 1990).

14. Cesar G. Soriano, "Candidates Bask in Hollywood Glamour, Greenbacks," *USA Today*, December 8, 2003, p. 1D.

15. Brian Faler, "Willie Nelson Is On the Road Again for Kucinich in Iowa," *Washington Post*, August 3, 2003, p. A04.

16. Joshua Green, "Madonna Wants Me," *The Atlantic Monthly*, March 2004, pp. 32–33.

17. Alexander and Corrado, *Financing the 1992 Election*, pp. 44–46.

18. Ibid., p. 54.

19. Sorauf, *Money in American Politics*, pp. 128–130.

20. Herbert E. Alexander and Monica Bauer, *Financing the 1988 Election* (Boulder, CO: Westview Press, 1991), p. 22.

21. Alexander and Corrado, *Financing the 1992 Election*, pp. 99–100.

22. Ibid., p. 71.

23. Ibid., pp. 81–86.

24. Francis X. Clines, "The Doctor and the Net: His Bloggers and Donors Pursue Victory Via the Mouse," *New York Times*, November 17, 2003, p. A20.

25. Glen Justice, "Kerry Kept Money Coming with Internet as His A.T.M.," *New York Times*, November 6, 2004, p. A12.

26. Alexander and Corrado, *Financing the 1992 Election*, p. 69. See also Charles T. Royer, ed., *Campaign for President: The Managers Look at '92* (Hollis, NH: Hollis Publishing Company, 1994), pp. 83–84.

27. Alexander and Corrado, *Financing the 1992 Election*, p. 57.

28. Anthony Corrado, "Financing the 1996 Elections," in Gerald M. Pomper, ed., *The Election of 1996: Reports and Interpretations* (Chatham, NJ: Chatham House, 1997), pp. 144–145.

29. For political operatives such as these, according to Robert Farmer, one of their Democratic counterparts, "the issue is simply this: Is this guy going to win?" What do they want if their guy should win? "A lot of them want to change their first name to 'Ambassador' or 'Secretary.' A lot of them want the candidate's attention. A lot of them would like to sleep in the Lincoln bedroom, or be on the board of the Kennedy Center, or go to a state dinner at the White House, or ride on Air Force One. Some of them want to be appointed to Federal positions in their state. Some of them just want to know the candidates on a first name basis." Sorauf, *Money in American Politics*, p. 195.

30. Alison Mitchell, "Building a Bulging War Chest: How Clinton Financed His Run," *New York Times*, December 27, 1996, p. A12. The joke made the rounds that in the Clinton years the Lincoln Bedroom was in the only first-class hotel where it was the guests, not the housekeeping staff, who put a mint on the pillow.

31. Federal Election Commission, "Public Funding of Presidential Elections," brochure, February 2005, available at http://www.fec.gov/pages/brochures/pubfund.shtml.

32. Anthony Corrado, *Creative Campaigning: PACs and the Presidential Selection Process* (Boulder, CO: Westview Press, 1992), p. 35. For example, while the consumer price index increased by 40 percent between 1976 and 1980, direct-mail costs increased by 50 percent, television time by 100 percent, and air fares by 300 percent over the same period.

33. Ibid., p. 35.

34. Evan Thomas and Peter Goldman, "Victory March: The Inside Story," *Newsweek*, special election issue, November 18, 1996, pp. 66–72, 80–82; Corrado, "Financing the 1996 Election," pp. 146–150.

35. Ibid., pp. 36–39. Alexander and Bauer point out that if the state limits were aggregated, the resulting total would be almost three times the national spending limit (Alexander and Bauer, *Financing the 1988 Election*, p. 18). Thus the national limit serves also to restrict the number of states in which a candidate can spend close to the state limit.

36. Federal Election Commission, "Presidential Spending Limits, 2004," available at http://www.fec .gov/pages/brochures/pubfund_limits_2004.shtml.

37. Alexander and Bauer, *Financing the 1988 Election*, p. 18. The FEC has since tried to remove some of the need for subterfuge by ruling that certain kinds of expenditures do not apply to the state limits, for example, placement fees for advertisements, salaries of staff while they are in the state, and their travel expenses. Alexander and Corrado, *Financing the 1992 Election*, p. 26.

38. For a full discussion of the regulatory history of this loophole, see Corrado, *Creative Campaigning*, pp. 43–70. FEC rulings on precandidacy PACs have upheld rather than struck down their activities, despite the fact that they seem to undermine much of the logic of the FECA.

39. Democrats Bruce Babbitt, Richard Gephardt, Joseph Biden, and Paul Simon; and Republicans George H. W. Bush, Robert Dole, Jack Kemp, Alexander Haig, and Pat Robertson. Ibid., p. 74.

40. Alexander and Corrado, *Financing the 1992 Election*, pp. 19–23.

41. Jill Abramson, "Unregulated Cash Flows Into Hands of P.A.C.s for 2000," *New York Times*, November 29, 1998, sec. 1, p. 1.

42. Susan Page and Jill Lawrence, "White House Hopefuls, Activists Are Stirring," *USA Today*, February 8, 2006, p. 5A.

43. Anthony Corrado, "Financing the 2000 Elections," in Gerald Pomper, ed., *The Election of 2000* (Chatham, NJ: Chatham House, 2001), p. 99.

44. Federal Election Commission, "2004 Presidential Campaign Activity Summarized."

45. Richard W. Stevenson and Adam Nagourney, "A Fund-Raising Sprint by Bush Will Put His Rivals Far Behind," *New York Times*, June 15, 2003, sec. 1, p. 1.

46. Diane Cardwell and Benjamin Weiser, "Kerry, Following Dean, Rejects Public Financing for Primaries," *New York Times*, November 15, 2003, p. A1.

47. Federal Election Commission, "2004 Presidential Campaign Activity Summarized."

48. Glen Justice, "Campaign Finance System May Be Facing Its Endgame," *New York Times*, November 6, 2003, p. A26.

49. Alexander and Corrado, *Financing the 1992 Election*, p. 89.

50. Though some speculated that President George W. Bush might decline public funding of his 2004 general election campaign in order to raise and spend more money than provided for by FECA, in 2003 the White House announced Bush's intention to accept public financing and abide by the accompanying spending restrictions for the general election, though not for the presidential primaries. See Jim Drinkard, "Tax-Funded Campaigning Spirals Toward Irrelevance," *USA Today*, January 30, 2003, p. 1A; and Mike Allen, "Bush Launches Drive to Raise $200 Million," *Washington Post*, June 18, 2003, p. A13. It is perhaps only a matter of time before party nominees choose to decline the general election subsidy as well, in order to raise and spend more money than the FECA restrictions currently allow.

51. Federal Election Commission, "2004 Presidential Campaign Activity Summarized."

52. Sorauf, *Money in American Politics*, p. 211.

53. This requirement, known as the "magic words" test, is in practice ineffective, as most political advertising—even that financed directly by candidates—does not use "explicit advocacy" terms such as "vote for," "elect," or "defeat" anyway. To the viewer, advertising funded by soft money from parties is therefore virtually indistinguishable from that paid for by hard money campaign donations to candidates. See David B. Magleby, "Dictum Without Data: The Myth of Issue Advocacy and Party Building," unpublished paper, Brigham Young University, 2000, available at http://csed.byu.edu/Publications/Dictum.doc; and Michael Franz and Kenneth Goldstein, "Following the (Soft) Money: Party Advertisements in American

Elections," in L. Sandy Maisel, ed., *The Parties Respond: Changes in American Parties and Campaigns*, 4th ed. (Boulder, CO: Westview Press, 2002), pp. 139–162.

54. Corrado, "Financing the 1996 Elections," pp. 145–150.

55. Alexander and Corrado, *Financing the 1992 Election*, p. 144.

56. Corrado, "Financing the 1996 Elections," pp. 151–155.

57. Federal Election Commission, "FEC Reports Increase in Party Fundraising for 2000," press release, May 15, 2001, available at http://www.fec.gov/press/051501partyfund/051501partyfund.html.

58. Corrado, "Financing the 1996 Elections," pp. 144–146. For more on the party-building effects of soft money, see Ray La Raja, "Political Parties in the Era of Soft Money," in Maisel, ed., *The Parties Respond*, pp. 163–188.

59. *McConnell vs. Federal Election Commission*, 540 U.S. 93 (2003).

60. Glen Justice and Kate Zernike, "'527' Groups Still at Work Raising Millions For Ads," *New York Times*, October 16, 2004, p. 10.

61. Glen Justice, "Even With Campaign Finance Law, Money Talks Louder Than Ever," *New York Times*, November 8, 2004, p. 16.

62. For a perspective critical of the alleged effects of campaign money on the political system, see Elizabeth Drew, *The Corruption of American Politics: What Went Wrong and Why* (Secaucus, NJ: Birch Lane Press, 1999).

63. See Edwin M. Epstein, "Corporations and Labor Unions in Electoral Politics," *Annals of the American Academy of Political and Social Science* 425 (May 1976): 33–58.

64. Herbert E. Alexander, *Financing the 1980 Election* (Lexington, MA: Lexington Books, 1983), p. 109.

65. Herbert E. Alexander and Harold B. Meyers, "The Switch in Campaign Giving," *Fortune*, November 1965, pp. 103–108.

66. Herbert E. Alexander, *Financing the 1972 Election* (Lexington, MA: Lexington Books, 1976).

67. For expenditure figures, see ibid., pp. 17–24, and for 1956 to 1976, see Herbert E. Alexander, *Financing the 1976 Election* (Washington, DC: CQ Press, 1979).

68. Herbert E. Alexander, "Financing the Parties and Campaigns," in Paul T. David, ed., *The Presidential Election and Transition, 1960–61* (Washington, DC: Brookings Institution, 1961), p. 119.

69. Alexander, *Financing the 1972 Election*, p. 98; and Alexander, *Financing the 1976 Election*, p. 169.

70. Alexander, *Financing the 1976 Election*, p. 246; Alexander, *Financing the 1980 Election; FEC Reports on Financial Activities 1979–1980*, Final Report, Presidential Pre-Nomination Campaign (Washington, DC: Government Printing Office, October 1981).

71. Herbert E. Alexander and Brian A. Haggerty, *Financing the 1984 Election* (Lexington, MA: Lexington Books, 1987), p. 149.

72. Alexander and Bauer, *Financing the 1988 Election*, pp. 37–38.

73. Ibid., p. 34; former Arizona Governor Bruce Babbitt's 1988 attempts to cope with the high-tech requirements of a modern campaign without front-runner money are described in Maxwell Glen, "Running on a Shoestring," *National Journal*, April 25, 1988, pp. 998–1002.

74. Federal Election Commission, "Disbursements, Cash, and Debts of Presidential Campaigns Through February 29, 2004," available at http://www.fec.gov/press/bkgnd/pres_cf/atm0229/presdis-bursem32004.pdf.

75. Michael J. Robinson, "Where's the Beef? Media and Media Elites in 1984," in Austin Ranney, ed., *The American Elections of 1984* (Durham, NC: Duke University Press, 1985), pp. 166–202, at 173–177.

76. Ibid., p. 175.

77. Schram, *Running for President*, p. 55.

78. Ibid., p. 16.

79. Roger Simon, "Turning Point," *U.S. News and World Report*, July 19, 2004, pp. 34–75.

80. Edward Wyatt, "Clark Ending His Campaign After Poor Showing in South," *New York Times*, February 11, 2004, p. A25.

81. Jack Kemp, for example, on declining to enter the race in 1996, said of the nomination campaign, "There are a lot of grotesqueries, not the least of which is the fundraising side of it. I have no passion for that." Similarly, Bill Bennett declared, "I sat down and looked at reality. How am I going to raise enough

money to win in the New York media market?" Richard L. Berke, "To Campaign (v): to Beg, to Borrow, to Endure," *New York Times*, February 5, 1995, sec. 4, p. 1. Texas Senator Phil Gramm, by contrast, was a candidate who seemed actually to enjoy raising money. Gramm boasted of spending two hours each day in 1995 asking for money on the telephone in support of his ultimately unsuccessful bid for the Republican presidential nomination. "I don't have trouble asking people for support," says Gramm, "I believe in what I am doing." John Harwood, "Cash Machine: Candidate Gramm Rarely Skips a Chance to Raise More Money," *Wall Street Journal*, February 17, 1995, p. 7.

82. Alexander and Bauer, *Financing the 1988 Election*, pp. 37–40.

83. Like Forbes, most self-funding candidates lose their elections, proving that wealth cannot necessarily buy votes (or at least enough votes). See Jennifer A. Steen, *Self-Financed Candidates in Congressional Elections* (Ann Arbor: University of Michigan Press, 2006).

84. For the details on the Forbes campaign, see Corrado, "Financing the 1996 Elections," pp. 143–145; and William G. Mayer, "The Presidential Nominations," in Pomper, ed., *The Elections of 1996*, pp. 36–56.

85. John C. Green and Nathan S. Bigelow, "The 2000 Presidential Nominations: The Cost of Innovation," in David B. Magleby, ed., *Financing the 2000 Election* (Washington, DC: Brookings Institution, 2002), p. 55; Howard Kurtz and Ben White, "Forbes Signals He Will Withdraw," *Washington Post*, February 10, 2000, p. A6.

86. Mayer, "The Presidential Nominations," p. 55; emphasis in original.

87. Thomas and Goldman, "Victory March: The Inside Story," p. 64.

88. This information is now continuously available to the public on various Internet sites, such as Political Money Line, http://www.fecinfo.com.

89. *1972 Congressional Campaign Finances*, 10 vols. (Washington, DC: Government Printing Office, 1973).

90. *Buckley et al. v. Valeo et al.*, 424 U.S. 1 (1976). See also Daniel D. Polsby, "*Buckley v. Valeo*: The Special Nature of Political Speech," *Supreme Court Review*, 1976, pp. 1–43.

91. Howard R. Penniman, "U.S. Elections: Really a Bargain?" *Public Opinion* 7 (June/July 1984): 51–53; see also Herbert Alexander, "Do the Presidential Candidates Need Even More Funds?" *San Diego Union*, October 9, 1988, p. C4; and Stephen Ansolabehere, John M. de Figueiredo, and James M. Snyder Jr., "Why Is There So Little Money in U.S. Politics?" *Journal of Economic Perspectives* 17 (Winter 2003): 105–130. For an analysis of media biases in reporting on PACs and campaign spending, see Frank J. Sorauf, "Campaign Money and the Press: Three Soundings," *Political Science Quarterly* 102 (Spring 1987): 25–42.

92. In a *per curiam* opinion in 1976, the Supreme Court wrote: "The ceiling on personal expenditures, like the limitations on independent expenditures . . . , imposes a substantial restraint on the ability of persons to engage in protected First Amendment expression. The candidate, no less than any other person, has a First Amendment right to engage in the discussion of public issues and vigorously and tirelessly to advocate his own election and the election of other candidates. Indeed, it is of particular importance that candidates have unfettered opportunity to make their views known so that the electorate may intelligently evaluate the candidates' personal qualities and their positions on vital public issues before choosing among them on election day. . . . Section 608(a)'s ceiling on personal expenditures by a candidate in furtherance of his own candidacy thus clearly and directly interferes with constitutionally protected freedoms." *Buckley v. Valeo*, 424 U.S. 1 (1976), p. 53.

93. Bill Keller and Irwin B. Arieff, "Special Report: Washington Fund Raisers," *Congressional Quarterly*, May 17, 1980, p. 1335.

94. In October 1968, for example, multimillionaire Stewart Mott offered to raise a million dollars for Hubert Humphrey, then in desperate need of cash. Mott "made it clear that the Presidential candidate would have to modify his views on Vietnam." Humphrey refused Mott's offer. Herbert Alexander and H. B. Meyers, "A Financial Landslide for the GOP," *Fortune*, March 1970, p. 187.

95. Quoted in Jasper B. Shannon, *Money and Politics* (New York: Random House, 1959), p. 35.

96. See Mark V. Nadel, *Corporations and Political Accountability* (Lexington, MA: Heath, 1976), pp. 27–28, 32, on American Airlines' sense of being a victim of virtual extortion by the Nixon campaign.

97. See William L. Rivers, "The Correspondents after 25 Years," *Columbia Journalism Review* 1 (Spring 1962). "In 1960," he says, "57 percent of the daily newspapers reporting to the *Editor and Publisher* poll supported Nixon, and 16 percent supported Kennedy. In contrast, there are more than three times as many Democrats as there are Republicans among the Washington newspaper correspondents; slightly more than 32 percent are Democrats, and fewer than 10 percent are Republicans" (p. 5). See also S. Robert Lichter and Stanley Rothman, "Media and Business Elites," *Public Opinion* 4 (October/November 1981): 42–46, 59–60; and S. Robert Lichter, Stanley Rothman, and Linda S. Lichter, *The Media Elite* (Bethesda, MD: Adler and Adler, 1986).

98. Pew Research Center for the People and the Press, "The State of the News Media, 2004: An Annual Report on American Journalism," report, May 23, 2004, available at http://people-press.org/reports/display.php3?ReportID=214.

99. Michael J. Robinson, "Just How Liberal Is the News? 1980 Revisited," *Public Opinion* 5 (February/March 1983): 55–60.

100. For a definitive, though fictitious, commentary, see Nathanael West, *Miss Lonelyhearts* (New York: Harcourt, Brace, 1933).

101. See Richard Brody and Catherine R. Shapiro, "A Reconsideration of the Rally Phenomenon in Public Opinion," in Samuel Long, ed., *Political Behavior Annual*, vol. 2 (Boulder, CO: Westview Press, 1989). See also John E. Mueller, "Presidential Popularity from Truman to Johnson," *American Political Science Review* 64 (March 1970): 18–34; Kenneth N. Waltz, "Electoral Punishment and Foreign Policy Crises," in James N. Rosenau, ed., *Domestic Sources of Foreign Policy* (New York: Free Press, 1967), pp. 263–293; and Richard A. Brody, *Assessing the President: The Media, Elite Opinion, and Popular Support* (Stanford: Stanford University Press, 1991).

102. Amos Tversky and Daniel Kahneman, "Rational Choice and the Framing of Decisions," *Journal of Business* 59 (1986): 251–278.

103. Aaron Wildavsky and Karl Dake, "Theories of Risk Perception: Who Fears What and Why," *Daedalus* 119 (Fall 1990): 41–60; Aaron B. Wildavsky, *But Is It True? A Citizen's Guide to Environmental Health and Safety Issues* (Cambridge, MA: Harvard University Press, 1995); Christopher J. Bosso, "Setting the Agenda: Mass Media and the Discovery of Famine in Ethiopia," in Michael Margolis and Gary A. Mauser, eds., *Manipulating Public Opinion: Essays on Public Opinion as a Dependent Variable* (Pacific Grove, CA: Brooks/Cole, 1989), pp. 153–174.

104. Joanne M. Miller and Jon A. Krosnick, "News Media Impact on the Ingredients of Presidential Evaluations: Politically Knowledgeable Citizens Are Guided by a Trusted Source," *American Journal of Political Science* 44 (April 2000): 301–315.

105. John R. Zaller, *The Nature and Origins of Mass Opinion* (New York: Cambridge University Press, 1992), pp. 6–16. Zaller's main work in this area remains unpublished: "The Role of Elites in Shaping Public Opinion," Ph.D. dissertation, University of California, Berkeley, 1984.

106. See Theodore H. White, *The Making of the President, 1960* (New York: Atheneum, 1961), pp. 333–338. Corroborative testimony is given by Benjamin C. Bradlee, *Conversations with Kennedy* (New York: Norton, 1975). On Barry Goldwater's press relations, see Charles Mohr, "Requiem for a Lightweight," *Esquire*, August 1968, pp. 67–71, 121–122.

107. Timothy Crouse, *The Boys on the Bus* (New York: Random House, 1973), pp. 189–190; Theodore H. White, *The Making of the President, 1972* (New York: Atheneum, 1973), pp. 251–268. See also Jules Witcover, *The Resurrection of Richard Nixon* (New York: Putnam, 1970); and Joe McGinniss, *The Selling of the President, 1968* (New York: Trident Press, 1969).

108. Daron R. Shaw and Brian E. Roberts, "Campaign Events, the Media and the Prospects of Victory: The 1992 and 1996 U.S. Presidential Elections," *British Journal of Political Science* 30 (April 2000): 259–289.

109. Harold W. Stanley and Richard G. Niemi, *Vital Statistics on American Politics, 2005–2006* (Washington, DC: CQ Press, 2005), pp. 198–199; George Garneau, "Clinton's the Choice," *Editor and Publisher* 125 (October 24, 1992), p. 9; Dorothy Giobbe, "Dole Wins . . . in Endorsements," *Editor and Publisher* 129 (October 26, 1996), p. 7; Greg Mitchell, "A Bird in the Hand for Bush?" *Editor and Publisher* 133 (November 6, 2000), p. 24; "Letting the Sun Shine," editorial, *Editor and Publisher* 138 (January 2005), p. 19.

Garneau says: "Since 1940, newspapers have endorsed Republicans by overwhelming margins—except when Johnson edged Goldwater [in 1964], 440 endorsements to 359. A larger proportion of newspapers than ever before—66.7%—have not endorsed a candidate [in 1992]. . . . In 1988, 62.8% of papers had not endorsed."

110. See Frank Luther Mott, *The News in America* (Cambridge, MA: Harvard University Press, 1952), p. 110; and Edwin Emery and Henry L. Smith, *The Press and America* (Englewood Cliffs, NJ: Prentice Hall, 1954), p. 541ff.

111. Dave D'Alessio and Mike Allen, "Media Bias in Presidential Elections: A Meta-Analysis," *Journal of Communication* 50 (September 2000): 133–156, at 148–149.

112. The classic formulation is by A. J. Liebling: "With the years, the quantity of news in newspaper is bound to diminish from its present low. The proprietor, as Chairman of the Board, will increasingly often say that he would like to spend 75 cents now and then on news coverage, but that he must be fair to his shareholders." Liebling, *The Press* (New York: Ballantine Books, 1961), p. 5. Occasionally, there is evidence of an improvement in the news coverage in some communities when the papers have been taken over by the more responsible chains. Cases in point include Philadelphia and San Jose, where the Knight-Ridder chain upgraded newspapers they purchased. However, these gains have recently been jeopardized everywhere by conditions of economic decline in the newspaper business. Knight-Ridder itself was sold in 2006 under pressure from stockholders who thought their shares were undervalued. See Katharine Q. Seelye and Andrew Ross Sorkin, "Newspaper Chain Agrees to a Sale for $4.5 Billion," *New York Times*, March 13, 2006, p. A1.

113. Bernard C. Cohen, *The Press and Foreign Policy* (Princeton: Princeton University Press, 1963), presents figures from a variety of sources on foreign affairs news (chap. 4). His conclusion: "The volume of coverage is low." See also Elie Abel, ed., *What's News: The Media in American Society* (San Francisco: Institute for Contemporary Studies, 1981).

114. Elmo Roper observed that "on the civil rights issue [in 1948], Mr. Dewey draws the support of voters favoring exactly opposite things, and more than that, each side thinks Dewey agrees with them." Hugh A. Bone, *American Politics and the Party System* (New York: McGraw-Hill, 1955), p. 477. In 1968, the bulk of those voting for Eugene McCarthy in the New Hampshire primary were not Vietnam "doves," as McCarthy was, but were even more belligerent about the war than Lyndon Johnson. See Philip E. Converse, "Public Opinion and Voting Behavior," in Fred I. Greenstein and Nelson W. Polsby, eds., *Handbook of Political Science* (Reading, MA: Addison-Wesley, 1975), vol. 4, pp. 75–169, at 81.

115. When asked by the Gallup poll in 1979 to gauge how much confidence they had in newspapers, among other institutions, 51 percent of the respondents said "a great deal or quite a lot," 47 percent said "some or very little," 1 percent said "none," and 1 percent had no opinion. *The Gallup Poll: Public Opinion 1979* (Wilmington, DE: Scholarly Resources, 1980), p. 159. In 1980 only 42 percent said "a great deal or quite a lot." *The Gallup Poll: Public Opinion 1980* (Wilmington, DE: Scholarly Resources, 1981), p. 247. By 1986, the number of respondents saying "a great deal or quite a lot" had shrunk to 37 percent. Since then, reported confidence has remained fairly steady, falling as low as 29 percent in 1994 and rising as high as 39 percent in 1990. It stood at 35 percent in 1997. Frank Newport, "Small Business and Military Generate Most Confidence in Americans," *The Gallup Poll Monthly* 383 (August 1997): 21–24. A CBS News/*New York Times* poll in early 2006 reported that 15 percent of respondents had "a great deal" of confidence in the news media, compared to 48 percent who had "a fair amount" of confidence and 36 percent who had little or no confidence. CBS News, "The State of the Media," press release, February 3, 2006, available at http://www.cbsnews.com/htdocs/pdf/020306POLL.pdf.

116. This paragraph summarizes the major findings of researchers on what has come to be called the "two-step flow" of information, emphasizing the influence of group membership and face-to-face interaction. See Elihu Katz and Paul F. Lazarsfeld, *Personal Influence* (Glencoe, IL: Free Press, 1955).

117. David W. Moore, "The *Manchester Union Leader* in the New Hampshire Primary," in Gary R. Orren and Nelson W. Polsby, eds., *Media and Momentum: The New Hampshire Primary and Nomination Politics* (Chatham, NJ: Chatham House, 1987), pp. 104–126.

118. Pew Research Center for the People and the Press, "Cable and Internet Loom Large in Fragmented Political News Universe," report, January 11, 2004, available at http://people-press.org/reports /display.php3?ReportID=200.

119. David L. Vancil and Sue D. Pendell, "The Myth of Viewer-Listener Disagreement in the First Kennedy-Nixon Debate," *Central States Speech Journal* 38 (1987): 16–27. See also James N. Druckman, "The Power of Television Images: The First Kennedy-Nixon Debate Revisited," *Journal of Politics* 65 (May 2003): 559–571.

120. Adam Nagourney, "Antiwar Stance Buoys Howard Dean in Iowa," *New York Times*, March 29, 2003, p. B12.

121. C. Anthony Broh, "Horse Race Journalism," *Public Opinion Quarterly* 44 (Winter 1980): 514–529.

122. Gary R. Orren, "The Nomination Process: Vicissitudes of Candidate Selection," in Michael Nelson, ed., *The Elections of 1984* (Washington, D.C.: CQ Press, 1985), pp. 27–82, at 53–54.

123. Orren, "The Nomination Process," pp. 53–54.

124. See, for example, Jules Witcover's comments about reporters' attempts to deny Gerald Ford the advantage of the White House in 1976. Witcover, *Marathon: The Pursuit of the Presidency, 1972–1976* (New York: Viking Press, 1977), pp. 528–556.

125. Charles Babington, "Kerry Says He Won't Apologize," *Washington Post*, March 12, 2004, p. A04.

126. See the list of most popular Web sites as measured by Alexa at http://www.alexa.com/site/ds /top_500.

127. Jacques Steinberg and Bill Carter, "CBS Dismisses 4 Over Broadcast on Bush Service," *New York Times*, January 11, 2005, p. A1.

128. Helen Dewar and Mike Allen, "Lott Resigns as Leader of Senate Republicans," *Washington Post*, December 22, 2002, p. A01.

129. Tim Craig and Michael D. Shear, "Allen Quip Provokes Outrage, Apology," *Washington Post*, August 15, 2006, p. A01.

130. Michael D. Shear, "'Macaca Moment' Marks a Shift in Momentum," *Washington Post*, September 3, 2006, p. C01.

131. Dean's Internet support received a great deal of press attention in 2003 and early 2004. For example, see Michael Janofsky, "Internet Helps Make Candidate a Contender," *New York Times*, July 5, 2003, p. A24; Ruth Marcus, "The People Powering Howard," *Washington Post*, July 5, 2003, p. A19; Lois Romano, "Dean, Driven by the Grass Roots," *Washington Post*, September 22, 2003, p. A01; and Samantha M. Shapiro, "The Dean Connection," *New York Times Magazine*, December 7, 2003, p. 56.

132. Nelson W. Polsby, "The Democratic Nomination," in Austin Ranney, ed., *The American Elections of 1980* (Washington, DC: American Enterprise Institute, 1981), pp. 37–60; and *The Gallup Opinion Index*, Report No. 183, December 1980, p. 51. Another example occurred during the 1964 campaign, when it was announced that U.S. vessels in the Gulf of Tonkin had been fired upon and President Johnson took to the airwaves to promise vigorous defensive measures. In late July, just before the incident, he received favorable ratings from 59 percent of the voters, to 31 percent for Goldwater; in early August, just after the incident, the president's score went up to 65 percent, and Goldwater's declined to 29 percent. American Institute of Public Opinion Survey, released October 18, 1964. For other examples, see Nelson W. Polsby, *Congress and the Presidency*, 4th ed. (Englewood Cliffs, NJ: Prentice Hall, 1986), p. 73; and Brody, *Assessing the President*.

133. Christopher Achen and Larry Bartels have demonstrated that when voters believe that conditions are worsening, they respond by punishing incumbents at the polls, even if public officials could not possibly be responsible for the causes of distress (such as a drought, or, remarkably, a series of shark attacks which ruined the vacation season for New Jersey resort towns in the summer of 1916). Christopher H. Achen and Larry M. Bartels, "Blind Retrospection: Electoral Responses to Drought, Flu, and Shark Attacks," unpublished paper, Princeton University, 2004, available at http://weber.ucsd.edu/~jlbroz /PElunch/achen_bartels_blind.pdf.

134. Howard S. Bloom and H. Douglas Price, "Voter Response to Short-Run Economic Conditions: The Asymmetric Effect of Prosperity and Recession," *American Political Science Review* 69 (December 1975): 1240–1254. For a more recent discussion of the relationship between economic performance, other events, and presidential popularity, see Brody, *Assessing the President*, pp. 91–132; and Samuel Kernell, *Going Public: New Strategies of Presidential Leadership*, 3rd ed. (Washington, DC: CQ Press, 1997).

135. A good indicator of whether or not people were better off in 1980 is real disposable income per capita, which increased by about 10 percent in constant dollars between 1976 and 1980: from $5,477 to $8,176 in current dollars ($4,158 to $4,571 in 1972 dollars), according to the U.S. Department of

Commerce, Bureau of Economic Analysis, *Survey of Current Business* 61 (March 1981), p. 10; and *Survey of Current Business* 62 (July 1982), p. 37.

136. Much of the material in this section is adapted from Nelson W. Polsby, *Political Promises: Essays and Commentary on American Politics* (New York: Oxford University Press, 1974), pp. 156–159.

137. See Nelson W. Polsby, "The American Election of 1988: Outcome, Process, and Aftermath," Ernst Fraenkel Lectures, Free University of Berlin, 1989, pp. 1–23.

138. Ray C. Fair, "Econometrics and Presidential Elections," *Journal of Economic Perspectives* 10 (Summer 1996): 89–102; Alan I. Abramowitz, "An Improved Model for Predicting Presidential Election Outcomes," *PS: Political Science and Politics* 21 (Fall 1988): 843–847. See also James E. Campbell and Thomas E. Mann, "Forecasting the Presidential Election: What Can We Learn from the Models?" *The Brookings Review* 14 (Fall 1996): 27–31; and Larry M. Bartels and John Zaller, "Presidential Vote Models: A Recount," *PS: Political Science and Politics* 34 (March 2001): 9–20.

139. Jerry Roberts, "What Dukakis Did Wrong," *San Francisco Chronicle*, November 10, 1988, p. A3.

140. Polsby, *Consequences of Party Reform*; Nelson W. Polsby and William Mayer, "Ideological Cohesion in the American Two-Party System," in Nelson W. Polsby and Raymond E. Wolfinger, eds., *On Parties: Essays Honoring Austin Ranney* (Berkeley: Institute of Governmental Studies Press, 1999), pp. 219–255.

141. Finley Peter Dunne, *Dissertations by Mr. Dooley* (New York: Harper & Brothers, 1906), p. 118.

142. Harry S Truman, *Memoirs: Year of Decisions* (Garden City, NY: Doubleday, 1955), pp. 19, 53.

143. Elizabeth Drew, *On the Edge: The Clinton Presidency* (New York: Simon and Schuster, 1994), pp. 227–229. Drew describes Gore as (up to then) "the most influential Vice President in history."

144. Ross K. Baker, "The Second Reagan Term," in Gerald M. Pomper, ed., *The Election of 1984: Reports and Interpretations* (Chatham, N.J.: Chatham House, 1985), p. 150.

145. Howard Reiter, *Selecting the President* (Philadelphia: University of Pennsylvania Press, 1985), pp. 119–120.

Chapter 4   The Nomination Process

1. Much of the historical discussion of the nomination process in this chapter is drawn from our own observations via the mass media, the personal observations of one of us who attended the Democratic National Conventions of 1960, 1968, 1972, and 1980 and the Republican National Conventions of 1964 and 1980, and from a classic set of basic texts on American parties and elections, including Moisei Ostrogorski, *Democracy and the Party System in the United States* (New York: Macmillan, 1910); Charles Edward Merriam and Harold Foote Gosnell, *The American Party System: An Introduction to the Study of Political Parties in the United States*, rev. ed. (New York: Macmillan, 1929); Peter H. Odegard and E. Allen Helms, *American Politics: A Study in Political Dynamics* (New York: Harper & Brothers, 1938); Pendleton Herring, *The Politics of Democracy: American Parties in Action*, rev. ed. (New York: W. W. Norton, 1965); E. E. Schattschneider, *Party Government* (New York: Farrar and Rinehart, 1942); D. D. McKean, *Party and Pressure Politics* (Boston: Houghton Mifflin, 1949); V. O. Key Jr., *Politics, Parties and Pressure Groups*, 5th ed. (New York: Crowell, 1964); Edward McChesney Sait and H. R. Penniman, *Sait's American Parties and Elections*, 4th ed. (New York: Appleton-Century-Crofts, 1948); Austin Ranney and Willmoore Kendall, *Democracy and the American Party System* (New York: Harcourt Brace, 1956); William Goodman, *The Two-Party System in the United States* (Princeton: Van Nostrand, 1960); and Gerald M. Pomper, *Nominating the President: The Politics of Convention Choice*, 2nd ed. (Evanston: Northwestern University Press, 1966). We also found quite useful a more specialized literature on nominations, including Paul T. David, Malcolm C. Moos, and Ralph M. Goldman, *Presidential Nominating Politics in 1952*, vols. 1–5 (Baltimore: Johns Hopkins University Press, 1954); Paul T. David, Ralph M. Goldman, and Richard C. Bain, *The Politics of National Party Conventions* (Washington, DC: Brookings Institution, 1960); and Richard C. Bain, *Convention Decisions and Voting Records* (Washington, DC: Brookings Institution, 1960). More recent texts on party organization and presidential nominations that a student might find useful include Samuel J. Eldersveld, *Political Parties in American Society* (New York: Basic Books, 1982); Joel L. Fleishman, ed., *The Future of American Political Parties* (Englewood Cliffs, NJ: Prentice Hall, 1982); Howard Reiter, *Selecting the President* (Philadelphia: University of Pennsylvania Press, 1985); William

J. Crotty and Gary C. Jacobson, *American Parties in Decline* (Boston: Little, Brown, 1980); Gerald M. Pomper, *Elections in America: Control and Influence in Democratic Politics*, rev. ed. (New York: Longman, 1980); Nelson W. Polsby, *Consequences of Party Reform* (New York: Oxford University Press, 1983); Everett Carll Ladd Jr., with Charles D. Hadley, *Transformations of the American Party System*, 2nd ed. (New York: Norton, 1978); Leon D. Epstein, *Political Parties in the American Mold* (Madison: University of Wisconsin Press, 1986); Austin Ranney, *Curing the Mischiefs of Faction: Party Reform in America* (Berkeley: University of California Press, 1975); and William G. Mayer, ed., *In Pursuit of the White House: How We Choose Our Presidential Nominees* (Chatham, NJ: Chatham House, 1996).

2. For each party's most recent delegate selection rules, see Democratic National Committee (Terence R. McAuliffe, chairman), "Call for the 2004 Democratic National Convention," available at http://www.democrats.org/pdfs/delegate_selection/convention.pdf; Republican National Committee (Ed Gillespie, chairman), "Call to the 2004 Republican National Convention," available at http://www .gop.com/Images/2004Call.pdf. After the 2000 election, the Democratic National Committee revised its rules in order to allow states other than Iowa and New Hampshire to select delegates beginning in early February rather than early March, thus matching the expanded delegate selection "window" already allowed by the Republicans. This change prompted additional front-loading of the primary season as several states moved up their primaries to take advantage of the new rules. See David S. Broder, "Election '04 Early Birds," *Washington Post*, November 28, 2001, p. A35. The Herman-Price Commission reforms adopted before the 2008 primary season authorize a second caucus in Nevada and a second primary in South Carolina prior to the opening of the "window" for other states. See Dan Balz, "Democratic Unit Votes to Add Early '08 Contests," *Washington Post*, December 11, 2005, p. A01.

3. Democrats have resisted "open" primaries in which any citizen can participate. The national Democratic Party has fought to prohibit Republicans from voting in Democratic presidential primaries. See Gary D. Wekkin, *Democrat versus Democrat* (Columbia: University of Missouri Press, 1984); see also *Tashjian v. Republican Party of Connecticut*, 107 S. 544 (1986). The rules of both national parties allow independents to vote in presidential primaries, but whether they can do so varies from state to state according to state law. Sometimes state officials attempt to manipulate these laws in order to help their favored nominees, as when Michigan Republicans opened their 2000 primary to independent voters with the expectation that they would help George W. Bush defeat Steve Forbes. This strategy ultimately backfired, as John McCain defeated Bush in Michigan partially on the strength of support from independents. See Bruce E. Cain and Megan Mullin, "Competing for Attention and Votes: The Role of State Parties in Setting Presidential Nomination Rules," in L. Sandy Maisel, ed., *The Parties Respond: Changes in American Parties and Campaigns* (Boulder, CO: Westview Press, 2002), pp. 99–120.

4. As the *New York Times* mused:

Now, a full year before the first 1984 delegate selection, the competition for attention among hopefuls is so intense that a new device has been introduced into national politics: the announcement of the announcement.

In mid-January, campaign planners for Senator Alan Cranston let it be known that the California Democrat would announce his candidacy February 2. The result: a small story, followed by a bigger one—more prominence than would have resulted otherwise. Planners for Senator Gary Hart observed this gambit and promptly let it be known that he would announce February 17. Planners for Walter F. Mondale said, not for attribution, that their man would do his thing on February 21; off the record, they said the event would be in St. Paul. Later they distributed a schedule confirming these rumors.

Representative Morris K. Udall handled his different problem differently. His staff let it be known that he would announce his presidential decision in a speech at the National Press Club. The day before, too late to affect attendance materially, a few reporters were told the Arizonan had reluctantly decided not to run after all.

Planners for Senator John Glenn, who is generally regarded as a little slower off the mark than the other Democratic competitors, have been willing to say only that they will not have an announcement about his announcement until March or April. Come to think of it, maybe that's a story. (Phil Gailey and Warren Weaver Jr., "The New Announcement," *New York Times*, February 14, 1983)

5. The Republican candidates in June 1987 were Vice President George H. W. Bush, Senator Robert Dole of Kansas, former Delaware Governor Pierre du Pont IV, the Reverend Pat Robertson, Representative Jack Kemp of New York, former Senator Paul Laxalt of Nevada, and former Secretary of State Alexander Haig. The Democrats were Massachusetts Governor Michael Dukakis, Senators Joseph Biden of Delaware, Paul Simon of Illinois, and Al Gore of Tennessee, the Reverend Jesse Jackson, former Arizona Governor Bruce Babbitt, and Representative Richard Gephardt of Missouri.

6. See Laura Stoker, "Judging Presidential Character: The Demise of Gary Hart," *Political Behavior* 15 (June 1993): 193–223.

7. See Rhodes Cook, "Buchanan to Reprise '92 Bid; Wilson Tests the Waters," *Congressional Quarterly Weekly Report*, March 18, 1995, p. 882.

8. Richard L. Berke, "Shorter Season Is Already Molding 2000 Race," *New York Times*, January 19, 1999, p. A12; "Quayle Hits the Campaign Trail," *San Francisco Chronicle*, January 23, 1999, p. A8; *The Hotline*, August 16, 1999, item 2.

The other Republicans running in March 1999 included former Vice President Dan Quayle, New Hampshire Senator Bob Smith, Arizona Senator John McCain, Representative John Kasich of Ohio, and Gary Bauer and Pat Buchanan, both of whom had worked in the Reagan White House.

9. Ronald Brownstein, "Getting an Early Start," *National Journal*, November 29, 1986, p. 2880.

10. Carroll J. Doherty, "Dole Takes a Political Risk in Crusade to Aid Bosnia," *Congressional Quarterly Weekly Report*, March 11, 1995, p. 761; see also Juliana Gruenwald, "Candidates' Voting Records Match Their Reputations," *Congressional Quarterly Weekly Report*, March 25, 1995, p. 882.

11. Citizens and politicians in these states seem to care deeply about their status as first in the nation and guard it jealously. Indeed, when Arizona began to consider challenging New Hampshire by scheduling an early primary for 1996, Senator Phil Gramm was widely criticized in New Hampshire for seeming to approve of that attempt; see "Rocky Start in Granite State Knocks Gramm Off Balance," *Washington Post*, February 26, 1995, p. A18. In the early spring of 2003, Michigan Democrats publicly threatened to schedule their 2004 caucus on the same day as the New Hampshire primary, potentially forcing candidates to choose between alienating New Hampshire voters and ignoring a large, union-dominated state necessary for victory in November. See John DiStaso, "NH Democrats May Ask Candidates to Boycott Michigan," *Union Leader* (Manchester, NH), March 26, 2003, p. B10. In the end, the Michigan Democrats dropped their challenge in exchange for the creation of a national party commission designed to review the traditional first-in-the-nation status of Iowa and New Hampshire for the 2008 primary season. See "Michigan Democrats Won't Vote Early," *New York Times*, April 27, 2003, sec. 1, p. 39. This commission, chaired by former Secretary of Labor Alexis Herman and Representative David Price of North Carolina, recommended in late 2005 that Iowa and New Hampshire retain the right to hold the first caucuses and first primary in the nation, respectively, but that one or two other states should be allowed to hold caucuses after Iowa but before the New Hampshire primary. The commission made these findings, in part, to address concerns that ethnic minorities and union members were not sufficiently represented in the Iowa and New Hampshire electorates, and therefore had too little influence on the Democratic nomination. See Adam Nagourney, "Democratic Panel Calls For More Early Contests in '08," *New York Times*, December 11, 2005, sec. 1, p. 51; and Dan Balz, "Balancing Act: Iowa, N.H. vs. Critics," *Washington Post*, December 28, 2005, p. A04.

Our discussion of Iowa and New Hampshire borrows freely from Nelson W. Polsby, "The Iowa Caucuses in a Front-Loaded System: A Few Historical Lessons," in Peverill Squire, ed., *The Iowa Caucuses and the Presidential Nominating Process* (Boulder, CO: Westview Press, 1989), pp. 149–162. See also Squire, *The Iowa Caucuses*; Gary R. Orren and Nelson W. Polsby, eds., *Media and Momentum: The New Hampshire Primary and Nomination Politics* (Chatham, NJ: Chatham House, 1987); "Special Report: Political Odd Couple," W. John Moore, "Rural Prospecting," and Burt Solomon, "Where America Is At," all *National Journal*, September 26, 1987, pp. 2394–2409; "When Iowa Becomes Brigadoon," *The Economist*, January 9, 1988, pp. 21–22; "Iowa," *Congressional Quarterly Weekly Report*, August 29, 1987, pp. 1994–1997; and "The Iowa Democratic Caucuses: How They Work," *New York Times*, February 7, 1988, p. 14.

12. On the Republican side in 1988, the numbers breathlessly reported on the networks on caucus night were the outcome of a straw poll ballot, conducted at the precinct caucuses, and phoned into the networks just like the real delegate divisions on the Democratic side. After the straw poll was conducted, Republican delegates to the next level up were selected in each precinct, without any necessary connection to the straw poll. As David Oman, cochairman of the Iowa Republican Party, described the process the week before:

> Essentially we have one very large straw poll taken in 2500 different locations simultaneously. . . . Those at the caucus will be given small cards and will mark on these cards their choice for president. The cards will be tallied. . . . Our straw poll is not tied to the process of choosing delegates. After the poll is taken and reported, the caucus will then pick its precinct committeeman and committeewoman, then pick the men and women who will go to the Republican county convention, and then discuss the platform. (*Presidential Campaign Hotline*, January 4, 1988, pp. 15–16.)

The county conventions met in March and picked delegates to district conventions, which met in June on the eve of the state convention. The district conventions selected three national convention delegates for each district and then the state convention selected the rest. Thus the straw poll might or might not predict the results of the delegate selection process accurately in any given year. In 1988, the preferences of the eventual delegates were sixteen for Dole, twelve for Bush, two each for Robertson and Kemp, and five uncommitted (*Congressional Quarterly*, August 6, 1988, p. 2161).

13. William C. Adams, "As New Hampshire Goes," in Orren and Polsby, eds., *Media and Momentum*, pp. 42–59, esp. p. 43.

14. Indeed, Henry E. Brady and Richard Johnston argue that the main educational effect of the entire primary process for voters is to inform them about candidate viability. See "What's the Primary Message? Horse Race or Issue Journalism," in Orren and Polsby, eds., *Media and Momentum*, pp. 127–186.

15. See Polsby, *Consequences of Party Reform*, for the full argument to this effect, and, for copious evidence, Byron E. Shafer, *Quiet Revolution: The Struggle for the Democratic Party and the Shaping of Post-Reform Politics* (New York: Russell Sage Foundation, 1983).

16. See R. W. Apple Jr., "Iowa's Weighty Caucuses: Significance by Accident," *New York Times*, January 25, 1988, p. A1.

17. As Muskie told Theodore H. White: "That previous week . . . I'd been down to Florida, then I flew to Idaho, then I flew to California, then I flew back to Washington to vote in the Senate, and I flew back to California, and then I flew into Manchester and I was hit with this [attack]. I'm tough physically, but no one could do that. . . ." White, *The Making of the President, 1972* (New York: Atheneum, 1973), pp. 81–82.

18. R. W. Apple Jr., "Carter Defeats Bayh by 2-1 in Iowa Vote," *New York Times*, January 20, 1976, p. A1.

19. "Ford's 1976 Campaign for the GOP Nomination," *1976 Congressional Quarterly Almanac* (Washington, DC: CQ Press, 1976), p. 900.

20. Elizabeth Drew writes of Carter: "Early successes and surprises were big elements in Carter's plan. . . . The basic idea was to show early that the southerner could do well in the North and could best Wallace in the South. . . . He visited a hundred and fourteen towns in Iowa, beginning in 1975 (and his family made countless other visits)." Drew, *American Journal: The Events of 1976* (New York: Random House, 1977), pp. 143–144, 466–467. See also Jules Witcover, *Marathon: The Pursuit of the Presidency, 1972–1976* (New York: Viking Press, 1977), p. 14.

21. See Witcover, *Marathon*, p. 14.

22. See Witcover, *Marathon*, pp. 202–205; Drew, *American Journal*, pp. 143–144, 466–467; and Martin Schram, *Running for President, 1976* (New York: Stein and Day, 1977), pp. 13–15.

23. Apple, "Carter Defeats Bayh." This was not the first time in 1976 that Apple had puffed Carter. Elizabeth Drew's diary of January 27, 1976 reported: "A story by R. W. Apple, Jr., in the *Times* last October saying that Carter was doing well in Iowa was itself a political event, prompting other newspaper stories that Carter was doing well in Iowa, and then more news magazine and television coverage for Carter than might otherwise have been his share." Drew, *American Journal*, p. 6.

24. Ibid., p. 16.

25. Nelson W. Polsby, "The Democratic Nomination," in Austin Ranney, ed., *The American Elections of 1980* (Washington, DC: American Enterprise Institute, 1981), pp. 37–60, at 47–48.

26. Ibid., p. 49.

27. Jack Germond and Jules Witcover, *Blue Smoke and Mirrors* (New York: Viking Press, 1981), p. 96.

28. David W. Moore, "The *Manchester Union Leader* in the New Hampshire Primary," in Orren and Polsby, eds., *Media and Momentum*, pp. 104–126, esp. pp. 116, 123.

29. Nelson W. Polsby, "The Democratic Nomination and the Evolution of the Party System," in Austin Ranney, ed., *The American Elections of 1984* (Durham, NC: Duke University Press, 1985), pp. 36–65. In the eight-day gap between Iowa and New Hampshire Gary Hart went from 10 percent in the public opinion polls to a 41 percent vote in the New Hampshire primary itself. See Peter Hart's comments in the *Presidential Campaign Hotline*, January 25, 1988, p. 19.

30. Howell Raines, "Hart Scores Upset with 41% in New Hampshire Primary," *New York Times*, February 29, 1984, p. A1.

31. Mickey Kaus with Mark Starr and Eleanor Clift, "Yes, We Have a Front Runner," *Newsweek*, July 20, 1987, p. 31; Richard L. Berke, "Iowa Eclipsing New Hampshire among Hopefuls," *New York Times*, September 6, 1987, sec. 1, p. 34; Thomas B. Edsall and David S. Broder, "Dukakis' New Hampshire Campaign Not Unraveled by Biden Videotape," *Washington Post*, October 3, 1987, p. A3; Mickey Kaus with Howard Fineman, John McCormick, Mark Starr, and Sue Hutchison, "Now, a Dukakis Fiasco," *Newsweek*, October 12, 1987, p. 40; Maralee Schwartz, "Dukakis Still a Top Fund-Raiser," *Washington Post*, November 8, 1987, p. A11; Gwen Ifill, "Bush and Dukakis Far Ahead in Poll," *Washington Post*, November 20, 1987, p. A8.

32. E. J. Dionne Jr., "Bush Overcomes Dole's Bid and Dukakis Is Easy Winner in New Hampshire Primaries," *New York Times*, February 17, 1988, p. A1.

33. See Polsby, "The Democratic Nomination and the Evolution of the Party System."

34. Monica Langley, "In Pre-New Hampshire Flurry, Images Prevail, and TV Coverage May be Pivotal to Candidates," *Wall Street Journal*, February 16, 1988, p. 64.

35. Charles T. Royer, ed., *Campaign for President: The Managers Look at '92* (Hollis, NH: Hollis Publishing, 1994), pp. 75–76. Several candidates considered attempting to score an easy coup by spending a little money in Iowa in order to finish second. The only candidate who actually did it, former Senator Paul Tsongas of Massachusetts, indeed finished second (with 4 percent of the vote), not counting the 12 percent of delegates who were uncommitted; the Tsongas campaign believed this took some pressure off of Tsongas in New Hampshire, where he had been identified as a regional candidate.

36. R. W. Apple Jr., "Democrats' Hopes Fade as Front-Runner Slips," *New York Times*, February 11, 1992, p. A22.

37. Robin Toner, "Bush Jarred in First Primary; Tsongas Wins Democratic Vote," *New York Times*, February 19, 1992, p. A1.

38. For the timetable of these events, see Royer, *Campaign for President*, pp. 305–309.

39. Ibid., p. 327.

40. Writing when Clinton was still neck-and-neck with Tsongas in New Hampshire opinion polls, R. W. Apple Jr. of the *New York Times* predicted that a Clinton loss would be "terribly damaging" (Apple, "Democrats' Hopes Fade"). By the time of the primary, Clinton had reduced media expectations to such an extent that his second-place showing was considered surprisingly strong.

41. *The Hotline*, February 13, 1996, items 3 and 9; *The Hotline*, February 14, 1996, item 4.

42. *The Hotline*, February 15, 1996, item 1.

43. *The Hotline*, February 21, 1996, items 1 and 4.

44. Alison Mitchell, "Concentrating on One State Was Key for McCain," *New York Times*, February 2, 2000, p. A17.

45. James Dao and Nicholas D. Kristof, "His Early Promise Vanished, Bradley Plans to Quit Today," *New York Times*, March 9, 2000, p. A1.

46. Adam Nagourney, "In the First Mile of a Marathon, Kerry Emerges as a Front-Runner," *New York Times*, February 26, 2003, p. A14.

47. See namely David S. Broder, "Dean Still Standing After Foes Take Shots," *Washington Post*, January 5, 2004, p. A06.

48. Adam Nagourney, "In Democratic Pack, the Race Is On For No. 3 and Maybe No. 4," *New York Times*, January 6, 2004, p. A18.

49. For an in-depth narrative of the events surrounding the 2004 Iowa caucuses, see Roger Simon, "Turning Point," *U.S. News and World Report*, July 19, 2004, pp. 34–75.

50. See Howard Kurtz, "Reporters Shift Gears on the Dean Bus," *Washington Post*, January 23, 2004, p. C01; and Kurtz, "Trailing in the Media Primary, Too," *Washington Post*, January 29, 2004, p. A01.

51. Rachel Smolkin, "Not Too Shabby," *American Journalism Review* 28 (April/May 2004): 40–45.

52. Sheryl Gay Stolberg, "Containing Themselves: Whoop, Oops and the State of the Political Slip,"*New York Times*, January 25, 2004, sec. 4, p. 1.

53. See Andres Martinez, "Will We Remember 2004 as the Year of the Dean Bubble?" *New York Times*, January 30, 2004, p. A24; and Alex Beam, "It's Game Over for Dean's Web Dreams," *Boston Globe*, February 10, 2004, p. E1.

54. Ceci Connolly, "Senator Enjoys Political Renewal," *Washington Post*, January 28, 2004, p. A13.

55. One mild exception to this rule occurred in the uncontested Iowa caucuses for Democrats in 1992. Far behind favorite son Senator Tom Harkin, Bill Clinton finished fourth behind "uncommitted," in second place, and Paul Tsongas, in third place. Since the national media had treated Iowa as an uncontested election, this did no harm to Clinton's campaign.

56. Richard M. Scammon and Alice V. McGillivray, *America at the Polls* (Washington, DC: Elections Research Center, Congressional Quarterly, 1988), p. 585.

57. Alice V. McGillivray, *Presidential Primaries and Caucuses, 1992* (Washington, DC: CQ Press, 1992), pp. 8–9.

58. Delegate counts vary between the parties, but to get a general idea, here are the electoral vote totals of states holding primaries or first-round caucuses in each month in 1992, 1996, 2000, and 2004 (see table 4.3 in the text):

TABLE 4.10 Electoral Vote Totals of Primary and Caucus States, by Month, 1992–2004

	Democrats			
Month	1992	1996	2000	2004
January	0	0	7	11
February	18	14	4	134
March	270	397	372	276
April	83	42	50	45
May	81	53	70	42
June	86	32	35	30

	Republicans			
Month	1992	1996	2000	2004
January	0	7	7	11
February	21	37	57	45
March	231	363	321	283
April	101	29	34	41
May	96	57	76	106
June	89	45	43	52

59. Rhodes Cook, "In '88 Contest, It's What's Up Front That Counts," *Congressional Quarterly Weekly Report*, August 23, 1986, pp. 1997–2002.

60. B. Drummond Ayres Jr., "War Between States For Nominating Glory," *New York Times*, February 7, 1999, p. A20; *The Hotline*, February 23, 1996, item 12.

61. Chris Cillizza and Zachary A. Goldfarb, "Democrats Tweak the Primary Calendar," *Washington Post*, July 23, 2006, p. A04.

62. Barbara Norrander, "Turnout in Super Tuesday Primaries: The Composition of the Electorate," paper prepared for delivery at the annual meeting of the American Political Science Association, August 31–September 3, 1989.

63. Bruce E. Cain, I. A. Lewis, and Douglas Rivers, "Strategy and Choice in the 1988 Presidential Primaries," *Electoral Studies* 8 (1988): 23–48.

64. B. Drummond Ayres Jr., "McCain Rethinks the Arizona Primary," *New York Times*, February 7, 1999, p. A20.

65. Cook, "In '88 Contest, It's What's Up Front That Counts," p. 1999.

66. Ibid., p. 2002.

67. Further discussion can be found in F. Christopher Arterton, *Media Politics: The News Strategies of Presidential Campaigns* (Lexington, MA: Lexington Books, 1984).

68. See Harry W. Ernst, *The Primary That Made a President: West Virginia* (New York: McGraw-Hill, 1962); and Theodore H. White, *The Making of the President, 1960* (New York: Atheneum, 1961).

69. See Theodore H. White, *The Making of the President, 1968* (New York: Atheneum, 1969), p. 89; Lewis Chester, Godfrey Hodgson, and Bruce Page, *An American Melodrama* (New York: Viking Press, 1969), pp. 79–99; Arthur Herzog, *McCarthy for President* (New York: Viking Press, 1969), p. 97; and Jack Newfield, *Robert Kennedy: A Memoir* (New York: Dutton, 1969), p. 218.

70. Royer, *Campaign for President*, pp. 79–80; Peter Goldman, Thomas M. DeFrank, Mark Miller, Andrew Murr, and Tom Mathews, *Quest for the Presidency, 1992* (College Station: Texas A&M University Press, 1994), pp. 132–135, 144–149.

71. See Tom Rosensteil, *Strange Bedfellows* (New York: Hyperion, 1993), p. 136.

72. Henry E. Brady and Michael G. Hagen, "The 'Horse-Race' or the Issues: What Do Voters Learn From Presidential Primaries?" paper presented at the Annual Meetings of the American Political Science Association, Washington, DC, August 1986. See also Brady and Johnston, "What's the Primary Message?" in Orren and Polsby, eds., *Media and Momentum*, pp. 127–186.

73. John G. Geer, "Voting in Presidential Primaries," paper presented at the annual meeting of the American Political Science Association, August 30–September 2, 1984, p. 6.

74. Poll results compiled by the Polling Report, available at http://www.pollingreport.com /wh04dem.htm.

75. Cited in Geer, "Voting in Presidential Primaries," p. 15.

76. Ibid., pp. 15–21.

77. Brady and Hagen, "The 'Horse-Race' or the Issues," pp. 38–39.

78. Larry M. Bartels, "Ideology and Momentum in Presidential Primaries," paper presented at the annual meeting of the American Political Science Association, Denver, CO, September 1982. See also Larry M. Bartels, *Presidential Parties and the Dynamics of Public Choice* (Princeton: Princeton University Press, 1988).

79. Lawrence S. Rothenberg and Richard A. Brody, "Participation in Presidential Primaries," *Western Political Quarterly* 41 (June 1988): 253–271.

80. See Austin Ranney, "Turnout and Representation in Presidential Primary Elections," *American Political Science Review* 66 (March 1972): 21–37, for the years 1948 to 1968. The same held true in 1976, when turnout averaged 28 percent in the primaries versus 54 percent in the general election. See Austin Ranney, *Participation in American Presidential Nominations, 1976* (Washington, DC: American Enterprise Institute, 1977), p. 20; and James Lengle, *Representation in Presidential Primaries: The Democratic Party in the Post Reform Era* (Westport, CT: Greenwood Press, 1981), p. 10. In 1980, the figures were 25 percent in primaries and 54 percent in the general election. Ranney, *American Elections of 1980*, pp. 353, 364. By 2000, turnout in primaries had dropped to 18 percent, while 51 percent of the voting-age population turned out in the general election. "Report: Turnout in Primaries 2nd Lowest in Past 40 Years," *Seattle Times*, September 1, 2000, p. A5 (citing a report by the Center for the Study of the American Electorate). Turnout in 2004 was high on the

Democratic side compared to previous years in states voting early in the process, such as New Hampshire, but dropped off considerably once Kerry became the presumptive nominee. Republican primary turnout was uniformly low in 2004, since President George W. Bush ran unopposed for renomination. See Anne E. Kornblut, "Democratic Turnout Seen So-So, Despite Party Assertions," *Boston Globe*, March 10, 2004, p. A3.

81. For an interesting argument along these lines, see Malcolm E. Jewell, "A Caveat on the Expanding Use of Presidential Primaries," *Policy Studies Journal* 2 (Summer 1974): 279–284.

82. James I. Lengle and Byron Shafer, "Primary Rules, Political Power, and Social Change," *American Political Science Review* 70 (March 1976): 25–40, at 35.

83. Thomas E. Mann, "Elected Officials and the Politics of Presidential Selection," in Ranney, *The American Elections of 1984*, pp. 100–128, at 103–105. See also David E. Price, *Bringing Back the Parties* (Washington, DC: CQ Press, 1984); Glenn, "Front-Loading the Race," p. 333; and Dennis W. Gleiber and James D. King, "Party Rules and Equitable Representation: The 1984 Democratic National Convention," *American Politics Quarterly* 15 (January 1987): 107–121.

84. Mann, "Elected Officials," p. 105–106. For evidence that caucuses, and not primaries, have yielded the "best" proportional representation results, see Stephen Ansolabehere and Gary King, "Measuring the Consequences of Delegate Selection Rules in Presidential Nominations," *Journal of Politics* 52 (May 1990): 609–621.

85. Mann, "Elected Officials," p. 119ff.

86. Elizabeth Drew, *Election Journal: Political Events of 1987–1988* (New York: Morrow, 1989), pp. 243–249.

87. Anthony L. Teasdale, "The Paradox of the Primaries," *Electoral Studies* 1 (1982): 43–63, at 43–44, 49.

88. See Brownstein, "Getting an Early Start," p. 2876ff.

89. See Ryan Lizza, "Kerry's Consigliere," *The Atlantic Monthly*, May 2004, pp. 32–34.

90. Federal Election Commission, "Both Major Parties to Receive Public Funding for 2004 Conventions," press release, June 30, 2003, available at http://www.fec.gov/press/20030630convention.html.

91. Michael Granberry, "San Diego Falls Short in Bid to Be GOP Host," *Los Angeles Times*, January 9, 1991, p. A3.

92. *National Journal Convention Special*, July 21, 1983, p. 38. San Francisco Mayor Dianne Feinstein, a Democrat, was elected on a nonpartisan ballot, as California law requires for local elections.

93. William Schneider, "Both Parties Embark on a Southern Strategy," *National Journal*, February 21, 1987, p. 436.

94. David Mark, "Convention Cities Ready Bids for '04," *Campaigns and Elections*, August 2002, p. 30.

95. This is the number that White (*The Making of the President, 1968*, p. 259) estimates the Democrats needed for their convention; Mark, "Convention Cities Ready Bids for '04," provides a comparable figure.

96. Richard Reeves, *Convention* (New York: Harcourt Brace Jovanovich, 1977), p. 32.

97. Democratic National Committee, "DNC Announces Dates for 2008 Democratic National Convention," press release, November 4, 2005, available at http://www.democrats.org/a/2005/11/dnc_announces_d.php; Republican National Committee, "RNC Announces 2008 Republican National Convention Dates," press release, April 6, 2006, available at http://www.gop.com/News/Read.aspx?ID=6225.

98. Material on the Kennedy organization in 1960 is drawn from Fred G. Burke, "Senator Kennedy's Convention Organization," in Paul Tillett, ed., *Inside Politics: The National Conventions, 1960* (Dobbs Ferry, NY: Oceana Publications, 1962), pp. 25–39.

99. Ibid., p. 39.

100. Recognizing the importance of communication at the Republican convention of 1860, a supporter of Abraham Lincoln carefully seated all of the solid Seward states close together and as far as possible from the states whose delegates were in some doubt about whom to support. Glyndon G. Van Deusen, *Thurlow Weed: Wizard of the Lobby* (Boston: Little, Brown, 1947), p. 253. Mayor Daley arranged for something similar at the Democratic National Convention in Chicago in 1968, but the level of protest about excessive security procedures and the lack of communication facilities reached such a pitch that whatever strategic advantages Daley might have hoped for dissolved in a flood of bad publicity.

101. See David, Moos, and Goldman, *Presidential Nominating Politics in 1952*, vol. 1; Robert Elson, "A Question for Democrats: If Not Truman, Who?" *Life*, March 24, 1952, pp. 118–133; Albert Votaw, "The Pros Put Adlai Over," *New Leader*, August 4, 1952, pp. 3–5; Douglass Cater, "How the Democrats Got Together," *The Reporter*, August 19, 1952, pp. 6–8; J. M. Arvey, as told to John Madigan, "The Reluctant Candidate: An Inside Story," *The Reporter*, November 24, 1953; and Walter Johnson, *How We Drafted Adlai Stevenson* (New York: Knopf, 1955).

102. F. Christopher Arterton, "Strategies and Tactics of Candidate Organizations," *Political Science Quarterly* 92 (Winter 1977): 663–671, at 664.

103. Jo Freeman, "The Political Culture of the Democratic and Republican Parties," *Political Science Quarterly* 101 (Fall 1986): 327–356, at 328. See also Byron Shafer, "Republicans and Democrats as Social Types: or, Notes toward an Ethnography of the Political Parties," *Journal of American Studies* 20 (1986): 341–354.

104. Freeman, "Political Culture," p. 329.

105. Ibid., p. 329.

106. Kirkpatrick, "Representation in the American National Conventions," p. 285.

107. Barbara G. Farah, "Delegate Polls: 1944 to 1984," *Public Opinion* 7 (August/September 1984): 43–45.

108. M. Kent Jennings, "Women in Party Politics," prepared for the Russell Sage Foundation Women in Twentieth-Century American Politics Project, Beverly Hills, CA, January 1987, pp. 11–12.

109. Jo Freeman, "Who You Know versus Who You Represent," in Mary Fainsod Katzenstein and Carol McClurg Mueller, eds., *The Women's Movements of The United States and Western Europe: Consciousness, Political Opportunity and Public Policy* (Philadelphia: Temple University Press, 1987), pp. 231–232.

110. Ibid., p. 242.

111. For extensive documentation, see Ladd, *Transformations of the American Party System*. See also Everett Carll Ladd Jr., and Charles D. Hadley, "Political Parties and Political Issues: Patterns in Differentiation Since the New Deal," Sage Professional Paper, American Politics Series, Beverly Hills, Calif., 1973, pp. 4–11; Herbert McClosky, Paul J. Hoffman, and Rosemary O'Hara, "Issue Conflict and Consensus among Party Leaders and Followers," *American Political Science Review* 54 (June 1960): 406–427; and Jeane Kirkpatrick, "Representation in the American National Conventions: The Case of 1972," *British Journal of Political Science* 5 (July 1975): 265–322, at 304.

112. John D. Huber and G. Bingham Powell, Jr., "Congruence Between Citizens and Policymakers in Two Visions of Liberal Democracy," *World Politics* (April 1994): 291–326; Torben Iversen, "Political Leadership and Representation in West European Democracies: A Test of Three Models of Voting," *American Journal of Political Science* 38 (February 1994): 45–74. An important early work is Maurice Duverger, *Political Parties: Their Organization and Activity in the Modern State* (London: Methuen, 1954).

113. Center for Political Studies, Institute for Social Research, "Convention Delegate Study: Report to Respondents," University of Michigan, Ann Arbor, 1985, p. 2.

114. Warren E. Miller, *Without Consent: Mass-Elite Linkages in Presidential Politics* (Lexington: University Press of Kentucky, 1988), chap. 2.

115. Nelson W. Polsby, *How Congress Evolves: Social Bases of Institutional Change* (New York: Oxford University Press, 2004).

116. See Polsby, "Democratic Nomination and Evolution of the Party System," p. 38; and Raymond E. Wolfinger, "Dealignment, Realignment, and Mandates in the 1984 Election," in Ranney, ed., *American Elections of 1984*, pp. 277–296, at 289. Also see Polsby, *How Congress Evolves*.

117. For the best analysis of the role of the modern convention, see Byron E. Shafer, *Bifurcated Politics* (Cambridge, MA: Harvard University Press, 1988); see also Polsby, *Consequences of Party Reform*, pp. 75–78.

118. The three big broadcast networks, in the days when they were the only sources of immediate coverage, featured "gavel-to-gavel" reporting, which meant that whenever the conventions were in session, the networks would switch from their normal programming to the convention. It did not mean that the networks necessarily broadcast whatever was happening at the podium, although they did spend plenty of time transmitting live speeches. In addition, the news teams supplied analysis, interviews with party

leaders and rank-and-file delegates, and other stories of interest. For the gradual end of the "gavel-to-gavel" standard, see Shafer, *Bifurcated Politics*, pp. 226–289. On cable television, CNN comes close to the old gavel-to-gavel coverage, while C-SPAN offers full coverage of the official proceedings, which the networks never did even in the days of gavel-to-gavel. C-SPAN, with its seemingly endless supply of airtime, also airs hours of viewer call-ins, interviews with party elites and rank-and-file delegates, and feature stories in which their cameras follow individual delegates from their hometowns to the convention floor, including in 1992 a trip to the laundromat with a delegate before she boarded a bus to the Democratic convention in New York City.

119. The focus on disunity during the coverage of the 1980 convention (see Joe Foote and Tony Rimmer, "The Ritual of Convention Coverage in 1980," in William C. Adams, ed., *Television Coverage of the 1980 Presidential Campaign* [Norwood, NJ: Ablex, 1983]) did not seem to affect the public, at least immediately. Carter's convention "bounce" was a historically large ten points (Shafer, *Bifurcated Politics*, p. 234).

120. These wrap-up shows may go "late," thereby extending the time on the air, especially if a speech shown live (typically, the presidential nominee's acceptance speech) runs long. On the other hand, in 1992 the second day of the Democratic convention coincided with baseball's All-Star Game. CBS chose baseball over politics and did not even have a wrap-up show from the convention that night. "Media Coverage: Take Me Out to the Ballgame," *The Hotline*, July 15, 1992. See also Rosenstiel, *Strange Bedfellows*, pp. 201–233; Edwin Diamond, "Scaling Back the TV Coverage," *National Journal Convention Preview*, June 16, 1992, p. 19.

121. Rosenstiel, *Strange Bedfellows*, p. 214.

122. The (temporary, as it turned out) withdrawal of Ross Perot from the race during the 1992 Democratic convention makes it very difficult to measure exactly how big the bounce attributable to convention advertising was. A typical result was the change in the *Newsweek*/Gallup poll. A preconvention poll taken on July 9–10 (the convention ran from July 13 through July 16) put Clinton in second place in a three-way race: Bush, 32 percent; Clinton, 31 percent; Perot, 28 percent. The *Newsweek*/Gallup poll taken the day after the convention gave Clinton a large lead in a two-way race, leading Bush 59 percent to 32 percent. The *Los Angeles Times* poll taken just after the convention reported 57 percent of those polled looked "favorably" on the Democratic nominee, compared to only 41 percent before the convention. According to Rosenstiel, *Strange Bedfellows*, most of the gain was early in the week, with Clinton moving into a clear lead "after only one night of the convention" (p. 212); a *New York Daily News*/*Hotline* tracking poll shows a growing gap as the convention went on. See *The Hotline*, July 13, 1992, and July 20, 1992. *Newsweek* only measured a three-point bounce for Bush after the Republican convention, although other polls indicated larger movement to the Bush ticket. See *The Hotline*, August 24, 1992. For bounces after conventions from 1964–1984, see Shafer, *Bifurcated Politics*, p. 234.

123. Evan Thomas and Peter Goldman, "Victory March: The Inside Story," *Newsweek Special Election Issue*, November 18, 1996, pp. 88–90, 97–98; Robert E. Denton Jr., "Five Pivotal Elements of the 2000 Presidential Campaign," in Robert E. Denton Jr. ed., *The 2000 Presidential Campaign: A Communication Perspective* (Westport, Conn.: Praeger, 2002), pp. 9–10.

124. Richard Morin and Dan Balz, "Bush Support Strong After Convention," *Washington Post*, September 10, 2004, p. A01.

125. Christopher Madison, "The Convention Hall and the TV Screen," *National Journal Convention Special*, July 23, 1988, p. 1950.

126. Rosenstiel, *Strange Bedfellows*, p. 224.

127. Unfortunately for the Republicans' efforts, losing candidate Pat Buchanan won the right to give a speech without prior vetting and promptly violated GOP plans to avoid some kinds of personal attacks on the Democratic nominee. Others who were not vetted included former President Ronald Reagan and the candidates. Christopher Madison, "Scripting a Scripted GOP Convention," *National Journal Convention Daily*, August 19, 1992, p. 10.

128. James Bennet, "Bush's New Vantage Point, From an Island of a Stage," *New York Times*, September 3, 2004, p. P3.

129. Jim VandeHei and John F. Harris, "Kerry: 'America Can Do Better,'" *Washington Post*, Friday, July 30, 2004, p. A01.

130. Rosenstiel, *Strange Bedfellows*, pp. 205–206. At the Democratic convention, Al Gore was told to pause fifteen minutes before beginning his vice-presidential acceptance address so that NBC's *Cheers*, the top-rated show in America at the time, could serve as the perfect lead-in to his speech.

131. In 1992, Republicans running for lower offices were dissatisfied with their allotment of time from the convention management; see Richard E. Cohen, "No Showcase for Rest of Ticket," *National Journal Convention Daily*, August 20, 1992, p. 34. Unlike the Democrats, who had one long session each day beginning in the evening, the Republicans divided into a prime-time session and a daytime session, thus (in the eyes of the daytime speakers) clearly signaling to reporters that only the prime-time session was newsworthy.

132. See Andrew Mollison, "Maestro of the Democrats," *New Leader*, June 27, 1988, pp. 3–4. On the other hand, the leader of a too-united party may need to create excitement, as George Bush apparently intended to do in 1988 by refusing to reveal his choice for vice president until the eve of the convention. James M. Perry and Ellen Hume, "Bush Aiming for Suspense as GOP Starts Convention," *Wall Street Journal*, August 15, 1988, p. 40. Lyndon Johnson attempted the same stunt in 1964.

133. Robert S. Boyd and Tom Fiedler, "Dukakis Hopes for Party Unity at Convention," *Philadelphia Inquirer*, July 18, 1988, p. 1A.

134. "Dukakis-Jackson Accord May Avert Floor Fight," *Los Angeles Times*, June 26, 1988, p. 36. See also E. J. Dionne Jr., "Harmonious Convention Closes With Jackson Hugging Nominee," *New York Times*, July 22, 1988, p. A9.

135. For the complete story, see Shafer, *Quiet Revolution*.

136. See Irving G. Williams, *The American Vice-Presidency: New Look* (New York: Doubleday, 1954); and Joel K. Goldstein, *The Modern American Vice Presidency* (Princeton: Princeton University Press, 1982).

137. Indeed, Lincoln filled his Cabinet with his strongest political rivals. See Doris Kearns Goodwin, *Team of Rivals: The Political Genius of Abraham Lincoln* (New York: Simon and Schuster, 2005).

138. David S. Broder and Bob Woodward, *The Man Who Would Be President: Dan Quayle* (New York: Simon and Schuster, 1992), pp. 13–30; and "Bush Takes Command But Quayle Draws Fire," *Congressional Quarterly Weekly Report*, August 20, 1988, pp. 2307–2309.

139. Thomas and Goldman, "Victory March," pp. 85–88.

140. Richard Brookhiser, *The Outside Story* (Garden City, NY: Doubleday, 1986), p. 155. In the event, Representative Ferraro's candidacy was mildly detrimental to the ticket. See Polsby, "Democratic Nomination and Evolution of the Party System," pp. 36–65.

141. Most of the 130-odd Goldwater delegates we interviewed at the 1964 Republican convention were prepared to sacrifice victory if victory meant becoming a "me-too" party or "going against principles" by adopting what they termed the "devious and corrupt" balanced tickets of the past.

142. Quoted in Ross K. Baker, "Outlook for the Reagan Administration," in Gerald M. Pomper, ed., *The Election of 1980* (Chatham, NJ: Chatham House, 1981), p. 167.

143. The year 2000 was a remarkable anomaly not only because the popular majority choice did not prevail, but also because the presidency was not determined by Congress as the Constitution provides, but by the Supreme Court. See Ronald Dworkin, ed., *A Badly Flawed Election: Debating* Bush v. Gore, *the Supreme Court, and American Democracy* (New York: New Press, 2002).

144. Rhodes Cook, "Dispute over Convention's Role: Brushing Aside Complaints, DNC Approves Rules for 1988," *Congressional Quarterly Weekly Report*, March 15, 1986, p. 627.

145. Mann, "Elected Officials."

Chapter 5   The Campaign

1. See Seymour M. Lipset, Paul F. Lazarsfeld, Allen H. Barton, and Juan Linz, "The Psychology of Voting: An Analysis of Political Behavior," in Gardner Lindzey, ed., *Handbook of Social Psychology* (Reading, MA: Addison-Wesley, 1954), pp. 1124–1175; Paul F. Lazarsfeld, Bernard Berelson, and Hazel Gaudet, *The People's Choice* (New York: Columbia University Press, 1948), pp. 87–93; Bernard R. Berelson, Paul F. Lazarsfeld, and William N. McPhee, *Voting* (Chicago: University of Chicago Press, 1954), pp. 16–17; and Richard A. Brody, "Change and Stability in Partisan Identification: A Note of Caution," paper delivered at the annual meeting of the American Political Science Association, Chicago, September 1974.

2. Nicholas von Hoffman, "Campaign Craziness: A Cracker-Barrel History," *New Republic*, November 5, 1984, pp. 17–19, at 17.

3. Patrick Anderson, *Electing Jimmy Carter: The Campaign of 1976* (Baton Rouge: Louisiana State University Press, 1994), p. 134.

4. Candidate visits during the 2004 campaign as tallied by Democracy in Action, George Washington University, http://www.gwu.edu/~action/2004/chrnfall.html.

5. See Darshan J. Goux and David A. Hopkins, "The Empirical Implications of Electoral College Reform," paper presented at the Annual Meetings of the Midwest Political Science Association, Chicago, Illinois, April 2006.

6. Dan Balz and Amy Goldstein, "Campaigns Cross Paths in Midwest," *Washington Post*, August 5, 2004, p. A01.

7. Jules Witcover, *Marathon: The Pursuit of the Presidency, 1972–1976* (New York: Viking, 1977), pp. 132–137.

8. Garry Abrams, "See How They Run: Why Do Candidates Dash Madly across the Map? Blame It on a Special Breed Called the Scheduler," *Los Angeles Times*, September 29, 1988, pt. 5, p. 1.

9. Ibid.

10. Ibid.

11. Alan J. Borsuk, "Kerry Rally in Madison Makes History—And Music," *Milwaukee Journal Sentinel*, October 29, 2004, p. A1.

12. "A Day in the Life of the Campaign," *Washington Post*, October 23, 1992, p. C1.

13. Jules Witcover, *The Resurrection of Richard Nixon* (New York: Putnam, 1970), pp. 237–239.

14. One study has found at least small effects from campaign visits; see Jeffrey M. Jones, "Does Bringing Out the Candidate Bring Out the Votes?" *American Politics Quarterly* 26 (October 1998): 395–419. Campaigns may allocate a variety of resources, including candidate visits and paid advertising, in a coordinated way, making it impossible for outside researchers or campaign managers to know which affected the voters.

15. Evan Thomas and Peter Goldman, "Victory March: The Inside Story," *Newsweek*, special election issue, November 18, 1996, p. 124.

16. Dom Bonafede, "Hey, Look Me Over," *National Journal*, November 21, 1987.

17. Ibid., p. 2967.

18. Peter Goldman, Thomas M. DeFrank, Mark Miller, Andrew Murr, and Thomas Mathews, *Quest for the Presidency, 1992* (College Station: Texas A&M University Press, 1994), p. 551.

19. Gwen Ifill, "Bus Trip Leaves Bandwagon Air for Time Being," *New York Times*, July 23, 1992, p. A1.

20. See Richard M. Nixon, *Six Crises* (New York: Doubleday, 1962), and especially Theodore H. White, *The Making of the President, 1960* (New York: Atheneum, 1961), for a discussion of two candidates' contrasting attitudes toward their "camp" of reporters. For the 1964 election, see Theodore H. White, *The Making of the President, 1964* (New York: Atheneum, 1965). For 1968, see Theodore H. White, *The Making of the President, 1968* (New York: Atheneum, 1969), p. 327ff. For 1972, see Timothy Crouse, *The Boys on the Bus* (New York: Random House, 1973). For 1976, see Witcover, *Marathon*. For 1980, see Jack W. Germond and Jules Witcover, *Blue Smoke and Mirrors* (New York: Viking, 1981), pp. 213–215, 260–264. On 1984, see Martin Schram, *The Great American Video Game: Presidential Politics in the Television Age* (New York: Morrow, 1987).

21. In 1984, Mondale's backers felt President Reagan was avoiding the issues in a campaign that stuck to broad, patriotic themes. The "great communicator," they argued, was exploiting the media with his carefully staged events. Many in the media agreed and did negative stories about the Reagan campaign's manipulative tactics. Negative coverage of this sort gave the Reagan camp grounds for complaints of their own concerning an anti-Republican "spin" to nightly newscasts. See Michael J. Robinson, "Where's the Beef? Media and Media Elites in 1984," in Austin Ranney, ed., *The American Elections of 1984* (Durham, NC: Duke University Press, 1985), pp. 166–202. Allegations of bias in the ABC newsroom tainted the 1992 campaign. They were fueled in part by the decision of anchor Peter Jennings to invite Clinton to respond to a speech President Bush gave after the Los Angeles riots. Jennings was called into the network's executive offices. ABC Vice President Richard Wald was concerned that Jennings was deliberately undermining President Bush.

Tom Rosenstiel reports: "This is wrong," he [Wald] yelled at Jennings. "This is a presidential occasion. A state of emergency, and the President has a right to go to the nation and speak to the people without making it a political occasion." Jennings disagreed, arguing that had Bush made the speech at the beginning of the crisis, then it would have been "presidential." Since he had waited a day after responding (Bush sent troops to Los Angeles the day before the speech), Jennings believed that the timing of Bush's comment was purely political. Although Wald disagreed, he did not order Jennings to change his plans, but the incident caused ABC's objectivity to be questioned throughout the rest of the campaign. Tom Rosenstiel, *Strange Bedfellows* (New York: Hyperion, 1993), p. 141.

22. Ibid., p. 139.

23. See Stephen Hess, *The Washington Reporters* (Washington, DC: Brookings Institution, 1981); S. Robert Lichter and Stanley Rothman, "Media and Business Elites," *Public Opinion* 4 (October/November 1981): 42–46, 59–60; and William Schneider and I. A. Lewis, "Views on the News," *Public Opinion* 8 (August/September 1985): 6–11, 58.

24. Howard Kurtz, "Out There, It's 10 Past Monica, America. Do You Know Where Matt Drudge Is?" *Washington Post*, March 28, 1999, p. F1; William Powers, "Punctured Franchise," *National Journal*, March 27, 1999, p. 843.

25. Jack Germond and Jules Witcover, *Whose Broad Stripes and Bright Stars?* (New York: Warner Books, 1989), p. 403.

26. Mandy Grunwald, "Free Media Scheduling," memorandum to Bill Clinton, April 27, 1992, reprinted in Goldman et al., *Quest for the Presidency, 1992*, p. 665.

27. Ibid., pp. 240–241. This is consistent with the public opinion polls—largely in support of Clinton—when his private life became more public during his impeachment crisis. See "Clinton's Popularity Up Despite His Plight," *CQ Weekly*, February 13, 1999, pp. 356–357.

28. Goldman et al., *Quest for the Presidency, 1992*, pp. 422–423.

29. Howard Kurtz, "Second Honeymoon with Press Didn't Last," *Washington Post*, October 4, 1992, p. A21.

30. Goldman et al., *Quest for the Presidency, 1992*, pp. 551–552.

31. Caryn James, "Where Politics and Comedy Intermingle, the Punch Lines Can Draw Blood," *New York Times*, November 4, 2000, p. B11.

32. Peter Johnson, "Worlds of Politics, Comedy Converge," *USA Today*, January 26, 2004, p. 1D.

33. Jim Puzzanghera, "Running for Office? Better Run from Colbert," *Los Angeles Times*, October 22, 2006, p. C1.

34. *Larry King Live*, CNN Transcript, "The New Media Politics," November 9, 1992.

35. Kirk Victor, "The Braintrusters," *National Journal*, February 13, 1988, pp. 394–395.

36. Ibid., p. 397.

37. Ibid.

38. Ibid.

39. Ibid., p. 393.

40. Ibid., p. 392.

41. Ibid., p. 393.

42. See, for example, the Gallup poll for June 25–28, 1982, in which 43 percent of a national sample said that the Democrats were the party best able to keep the country prosperous. Only 34 percent picked the Republicans. *The Gallup Report*, no. 204 (September 1982), p. 45. See also Angus Campbell, Philip E. Converse, Warren E. Miller, and Donald E. Stokes, *The American Voter* (New York: Wiley, 1960), pp. 44–59.

43. Transcript of presidential debates, *New York Times*, October 16, 1976. See also Campbell et al., *The American Voter*, pp. 44–59; and Angus Campbell, Gerald Gurin, and Warren E. Miller, *The Voter Decides* (Evanston, IL: Row, Peterson, 1954), pp. 44–45, esp. table 4-3.

44. John R. Petrocik, "Issue Ownership in Presidential Elections, with a 1980 Case Study," *American Journal of Political Science* 40 (August 1996): 825–850; Byron E. Shafer and William J. M. Claggett, *The Two Majorities: The Issue Context of Modern American Politics* (Baltimore: Johns Hopkins University Press, 1995).

45. James E. Campbell, "Why Bush Won the Presidential Election of 2004: Incumbency, Ideology, Terrorism, and Turnout," *Political Science Quarterly* 120 (Summer 2005): 219–242.

46. See Henry A. Plotkin, "Issues in the Campaign," in Gerald M. Pomper, ed., *The Election of 1984* (Chatham, NJ: Chatham House, 1985), pp. 48–52; Albert R. Hunt, "The Campaign and the Issues," in

Ranney, ed., *The American Elections of 1984*, pp. 129–165, at 142–144; William Schneider, "The November 6 Vote for President: What Did It Mean?" in Ranney, ed., *The American Elections of 1984*, pp. 203–244, at 239–242; Benjamin Ginsberg and Martin Shefter, "A Critical Realignment? The New Politics, the Reconstituted Right, and the Election of 1984," in Michael Nelson, ed., *The Elections of 1984* (Washington, DC: CQ Press, 1985), pp. 5–24; Morris P. Fiorina with Samuel J. Abrams and Jeremy Pope, *Culture War? The Myth of a Polarized America* (New York: Longman, 2004); and James Q. Wilson, "How Divided Are We?" *Commentary*, February 2006, pp. 15–21.

47. Richard Scammon and Ben Wattenberg, *The Real Majority* (New York: Coward-McCann, 1970), p. 39; see also pp. 37–43.

48. See Shafer and Claggett, *The Two Majorities.*

49. *The People, Press and Politics: A Times Mirror Study of the American Electorate*, conducted by the Gallup Organization (Los Angeles: Times Mirror Company, 1987).

50. Nelson W. Polsby and William G. Mayer, "Ideological Cohesion in the American Two-Party System," in Nelson W. Polsby and Raymond E. Wolfinger, eds., *On Parties: Essays Honoring Austin Ranney* (Berkeley, CA: Institute of Governmental Studies Press, 1999), pp. 219–254, at 232.

51. Larry M. Bartels, "What's the Matter with *What's the Matter with Kansas?*" *Quarterly Journal of Political Science* 1 (March 2006): 201–226.

52. See Jonathan H. Bernstein, "The Expanded Party in American Politics," Ph.D. dissertation, University of California, Berkeley, 1999.

53. See, for an early survey, Stanley Kelley Jr., *Professional Public Relations and Political Power* (Baltimore: Johns Hopkins University Press, 1956).

54. *Campaigns and Elections* 19 (March 1998), p. 4. Opposition research is the fastest-growing subfield in political consulting. For more information, see Ruth Shalit, "The Oppo Boom," *New Republic*, January 3, 1994, pp. 16–20.

55. Frank I. Luntz, *Candidates, Campaigns, and Consultants* (Oxford: Basil Blackwell, 1988), p. 52.

56. Ibid.

57. Ibid., p. 49.

58. Andrew Rosenthal, "Politicians Count on Computers," *New York Times*, May 9, 1988, p. D1.

59. Mark Petracca, "Political Consultants and Democratic Governance," *PS: Political Science and Politics* 22 (March 1989): 11–14, at 13.

60. Ibid.

61. Luntz, *Candidates, Campaigns, and Consultants*, p. 57.

62. James Moore and Wayne Slater, *Bush's Brain: How Karl Rove Made George W. Bush Presidential* (New York: John Wiley and Sons, 2003); Lou Dubose, Jan Reid, and Carl M. Cannon, *Boy Genius: Karl Rove, the Brains Behind the Remarkable Political Triumph of George W. Bush* (New York: Public Affairs, 2003).

63. Larry J. Sabato, *The Rise of Political Consultants: New Ways of Winning Elections* (New York: Basic Books, 1981), p. 13.

64. Luntz, *Candidates, Campaigns, and Consultants*, p. 51.

65. Sabato, *The Rise of Political Consultants*, p. 26.

66. Dick Kirschten and James A. Barnes, "Itching for Action," *National Journal*, June 4, 1988, p. 1478.

67. Luntz, *Candidates, Campaigns, and Consultants*, p. 72.

68. Ibid., p. 112.

69. Occasionally the roles are reversed and consultants find themselves more "dovish" than their employers. In the 1972 general election campaign, George McGovern ditched Charles Guggenheim, his media adviser, because the latter refused (on pragmatic grounds) to produce negatives. See Sabato, *The Rise of Political Consultants*, p. 121.

70. See Jonathan Bernstein, "The *New* New Presidential Elite," in William G. Mayer, ed., *In Pursuit of the White House 2000* (Chatham, NJ: Chatham House, 1999); Robin Kolodny and Angela Logan, "Political Consultants and the Extension of Party Goals," *PS: Political Science and Politics* 31 (June 1998): 155–159.

71. Luntz, *Candidates, Campaigns and Consultants*, p. 50.

72. Katharine Q. Seelye, "Dole Campaign Chief Relying on Determination, and Luck," *New York Times*, June 3, 1996, p. A1. For several such profiles, see Bernstein, "The *New* New Presidential Elite."

73. Sabato, *The Rise of Political Consultants*, p. 69.

74. Quoted in Scott C. Ratzan, "The Real Agenda Setters: Pollsters in the 1988 Presidential Campaign," *American Behavioral Scientist* 32 (March/April 1989): 451–463, at 451.

75. Quoted in Paul Simon, *Winners and Losers* (New York: Continuum, 1989), p. 165.

76. Sabato, *The Rise of Political Consultants*, p. 71.

77. Ibid., p. 21.

78. Gerald M. Goldhaber, "A Pollster's Sampler," *Public Opinion* (June/July 1984), p. 50.

79. Mark Levy, "Polling and the Presidential Election," in *Annals of the American Academy of Political and Social Science: Polling and the Democratic Consensus* (Beverly Hills, CA: Sage, 1984), p. 88; and Jerry Hagstrom and Robert Guskind, "Calling the Races," *National Journal*, July 30, 1988, p. 1974.

80. Hagstrom and Guskind, "Calling the Races," p. 1974.

81. Kathleen Hall Jamieson, *Packaging the Presidency: A History and Criticism of Presidential Campaign Advertising* (New York: Oxford University Press, 1984), p. 429.

In primaries, candidates can use polls to detect opportunities to surpass the media's expectations. Louis Harris analyzed 1960 polls in West Virginia and discovered that although conventional wisdom considered the primary a sure loss for Kennedy, JFK in fact had considerable support. Thus the Kennedy campaign targeted the state for a critical "upset" victory. In 1988, the Dukakis campaign used the same strategy in the Wisconsin primary against Jesse Jackson. In its preprimary polls, the press showed a tight race, but Dukakis pollster Tubby Harrison's numbers revealed a double-digit lead for Dukakis. According to Christine Black and Thomas Oliphant, "Dukakis' aides . . . privately reasoned that the bigger Jackson became in the press, the harder he would fall, and Dukakis would rise if Harrison's data were accurate." As it turned out, the Wisconsin results were as Harrison had foreseen: 48 percent for Dukakis, 28 percent for Jackson, and 17 percent for Gore. The surprisingly large margin—actually not a surprise for Dukakis—deflated Jackson's support, and Dukakis went on to win all subsequent primaries. See Sabato, *The Rise of Political Consultants*, pp. 69–70; Christine M. Black and Thomas Oliphant, *All by Myself: The Unmaking of a Presidential Campaign* (Chester, CT: Globe Pequot Press, 1989), p. 128.

82. See Tubby Harrison, Clifford Brown, and Lynda Powell, "Re: Target Voters and the Debate," memorandum, September 19, 1988; also, memorandum from Dukakis's pollsters, September 4, 1988. These memorandums are part of a set of unpublished internal campaign memos and other reports from Dukakis's pollsters to the candidate.

83. Goldman et al., *Quest for the Presidency, 1992*, p. 292.

84. See April memo from Fred Steeper to Bush reprinted in ibid., pp. 666–675.

85. Ibid, p. 531.

86. For one example of this phenomenon, see Carey Goldberg, "Political Battle of the Sexes Is Tougher Than Ever," *New York Times*, October 6, 1996, sec. 1, p. 1.

87. Richard Morin and Dan Balz, "'Security Mom' Bloc Proves Hard to Find," *Washington Post*, October 1, 2004, p. A05.

88. "Face Off: A Conversation with the Presidents' Pollsters Patrick Caddell and Richard Wirthlin," *Public Opinion* 3 (December/January 1981): 5.

89. "Pollsters on the Polls: An Interview with Vincent Breglio," *Public Opinion* 11 (January/February 1989): 4.

90. Germond and Witcover, *Whose Broad Stripes and Bright Stars?* p. 416.

91. Ibid.

92. Rosenstiel, *Strange Bedfellows*, pp. 279–280, and Goldman et al., *Quest for the Presidency*, 504–505.

93. Lyndsey Layton, "Cheney Hopes Aloha Stop Sways Hawaiians," *Washington Post*, November 2, 2004, p. A08.

94. Danny N. Bellenger, Kenneth L. Bernhardt, and Jac L. Goldstucker, *Qualitative Research in Marketing* (Chicago: American Marketing Association, 1976), p. 8.

95. Myril Axelrod, "10 Essentials for Good Qualitative Research," *Marketing News* 8 (March 14, 1975): 10.

96. Elizabeth Kolbert, "Test-Marketing a President," *New York Times Magazine*, August 30, 1992, p. 21.

97. William D. Wells, "Group Interviewing," in *Focus Group Interviews* (Chicago: American Marketing Association, 1979), p. 2.

98. Hagstrom and Guskind, "Calling the Races," p. 1974.

99. Peter Goldman and Tom Mathews, *The Quest for the Presidency, 1988* (New York: Simon and Schuster, 1989), p. 358.

100. David R. Runkel, ed., *Campaign for the President: The Managers Look at '88* (Dover, MA: Auburn House, 1989), p. 157.

101. Ibid.

102. "Pollsters on the Polls: An Interview with Irwin 'Tubby' Harrison," *Public Opinion* 11 (January/February 1989): 5.

103. Nicholas Mitropoulos and Nelson W. Polsby, "Retrospective Analysis of Campaign '88: Process and Politics," audiotape, Institute of Governmental Studies, University of California, Berkeley, 1989.

104. "Pollsters on the Polls," p. 51.

105. See April 27 memorandum from Stan Greenberg, James Carville, and Frank Greer to Bill Clinton on "The General Election Project," reprinted in Goldman et al., *Quest for the Presidency, 1992*, pp. 657–664.

106. Thomas and Goldman, *Victory March*, p. 45.

107. Hagstrom and Guskind, "Calling the Races," p. 1975.

108. Levy, "Polling and the Presidential Election," p. 91.

109. Goldman and Mathews, *The Quest for the Presidency, 1988*, p. 358.

110. Goldman et al., *Quest for the Presidency, 1992*, p. 257–258.

111. Ibid., pp. 563–564.

112. October 13, 1992 memorandum from Fred Steeper to George Bush on "Voter Reactions to the First Debate," reprinted in ibid., pp. 729–730.

113. Hagstrom and Guskind, "Calling the Races," p. 1974.

114. Goldman and Mathews, *The Quest for the Presidency, 1988*, p. 400.

115. Rosenstiel, *Strange Bedfellows*, pp. 327–331.

116. Ibid., p. 302.

117. Levy, "Polling and the Presidential Election," p. 86.

118. Ibid., p. 89.

119. Sabato, *The Rise of Political Consultants*, p. 112.

120. Jerry Hagstrom, "Peddling a President," *National Journal*, September 10, 1988, p. 2250.

121. Sabato, *The Rise of Political Consultants*, p. 113.

122. Hagstrom, "Peddling a President," p. 2250.

123. Longer ads are occasionally produced, especially for small, low-cost media markets, but primetime is dominated by ten- and thirty-second spots.

124. Luntz, *Candidates, Consultants, and Campaigns*, pp. 83–88.

125. Rosenstiel, *Strange Bedfellows*, pp. 285–288. For one of the newspaper critiques of the Bush ad, see Howard Kurtz, "30-Second Politics," *Washington Post*, September 24, 1992, p. A10.

126. David Chagall, *The New Kingmakers* (New York: Harcourt Brace Jovanovich, 1981), p. 218.

127. Sabato, *The Rise of Political Consultants*, p. 182.

128. National Cable and Telecommunications Association, "2005 Mid-Year Industry Overview," available at http://www.ncta.com/industry_overview/CableMid-YearOverview05FINAL.pdf, p. 23.

129. John Power, "Plug in to Cable TV," *Campaigns and Elections*, September/October 1987, pp. 54–57.

130. Luntz, *Candidates, Campaigns, and Consultants*, p. 210.

131. Rosenstiel, *Strange Bedfellows*, pp. 165–166, 174–175; Goldman et al., *Quest for the Presidency, 1992*, p. 665.

132. Rosenstiel, *Strange Bedfellows*, pp. 316–317.

133. Ibid., pp. 164–165.

134. Luntz, *Candidates, Campaigns, and Consultants*, p. 107.

135. Ibid., pp. 109–110.

136. Ibid., pp. 211–212.

137. Dan Koeppel, "A Race to the Finish Line: Election Fundraising Blends Old Standards with High-Tech Appeals," *Direct* (November 1992): 20.

138. Richard Armstrong, *The Next Hurrah: The Communications Revolution in American Politics* (New York: Beech Tree Books, 1988), p. 197.

139. Ibid., p. 198.

140. Goldman et al., *Quest for the Presidency, 1992*, pp. 209–210.

141. Occasionally, inducements of a less savory kind may be offered. For example, the Kennedy organization was alleged to have used bribes in the 1960 West Virginia primary. On the Republican side, in 1993, consultant Ed Rollins claimed, and later denied, that he had paid clergy in the community $500,000 to depress the African American vote during the New Jersey gubernatorial election. See Harry W. Ernst, *The Primary That Made a President: West Virginia, 1960* (New York: McGraw-Hill, 1962), p. 31; and Jerry Gray, "Whitman Denies Report by Aide That Campaign Paid Off Blacks," *New York Times*, November 11, 1993, p. A1.

142. There is another possibility: voters who turn out only by being dinned at by the media are likely to be less stable in their political orientations and will therefore vote less for the party and more for the candidate whose name or personality seems more familiar to them. See John R. Zaller, *The Nature and Origins of Mass Opinion* (New York: Cambridge University Press, 1992). This, in a year when an Eisenhower is on the ticket, might well mean that higher turnout produces Republican votes. The most thoroughly documented research on the question suggests that increasing turnout by relaxing registration rules would have little or no effect on the partisan distribution of the vote. See Steven J. Rosenstone and Raymond E. Wolfinger, "The Effect of Registration Laws on Voter Turnout," *American Political Science Review* 72 (March 1978): 22–48; and John R. Petrocik, "Voter Turnout and Electoral Preference: The Anomalous Reagan Elections," in Kay Lehman Schlozman, ed., *Elections in America* (Boston: Allen and Unwin, 1987), pp. 239–259. Petrocik argues that the 1980 election did not fit the general pattern. Low turnout, he claims, seriously hurt Jimmy Carter.

143. See Philip E. Converse, Angus Campbell, Warren E. Miller, and Donald E. Stokes, "Stability and Change in 1960: A Reinstating Election," *American Political Science Review* 55 (June 1961): 269–280, esp. p. 274. This is roughly what Stanley Greenberg, President Clinton's poll taker, calculated Clinton would have received in 1992 had Ross Perot not been a candidate. Stanley B. Greenberg, *Middle Class Dreams* (New York: Times Books, 1995), p. 13.

144. Marjorie Connelly, "How Americans Voted: A Political Portrait," *New York Times*, November 7, 2004, sec. 4, p. 4.

145. Raymond E. Wolfinger, "Dealignment, Realignment, and Mandates," in Ranney, ed., *The American Elections of 1984*, pp. 277–296.

146. There is a large scholarly literature attempting to determine the direction and extent of partisan bias in the electoral college. See James C. Garand and T. Wayne Parent, "Representation, Swing, and Bias in U.S. Presidential Elections, 1872–1988," *American Journal of Political Science* 35 (November 1991): 1011–1031; I. M. Destler, "The Myth of the Electoral Lock," *PS: Political Science and Politics* 29 (September 1996): 491–494; John E. Berthoud, "The Electoral Lock Thesis: The Weighting Bias Component," *PS: Political Science and Politics* 30 (June 1997): 189–193; and Bernard Grofman, Thomas L. Brunell, and Janet Campagna, "Distinguishing the Difference Between Swing Ratio and Bias: The U.S. Electoral College," *Electoral Studies* 16 (December 1997): 471–487.

147. See Campbell et al., *The American Voter*, pp. 537–538; and Herbert H. Hyman and Paul B. Sheatsley, "The Political Appeal of President Eisenhower," *Public Opinion Quarterly* 19 (Winter 1955–1956): 26–39.

148. In 1962 Raymond E. Wolfinger and his associates administered a questionnaire to 308 "students" at an anticommunism school conducted by Dr. Fred Schwarz's Christian Anti-Communism Crusade in Oakland, California. Among the findings of this study were that 278 of the 302 persons in this sample who voted in 1960 (or 92 percent of those who voted) had voted for Nixon and that 58 percent of those who answered the question chose Goldwater over Nixon for 1964. At about the same time, a nationwide Gallup poll showed Goldwater the choice of only 13 percent of Republicans. Raymond E. Wolfinger, Barbara Kaye Wolfinger, Kenneth Prewitt, and Sheilah Rosenhack, "America's Radical Right: Politics and Ideology," in

David E. Apter, ed., *Ideology and Discontent* (New York: Free Press, 1964), pp. 267–269. Analysis of various election returns and of a 1954 Gallup poll suggests that support for the late Senator Joseph McCarthy was importantly determined by party affiliation, with Republicans far exceeding Democrats or independents in the ranks of his supporters. See Nelson W. Polsby, "Towards an Explanation of McCarthyism," *Political Studies* 8 (October 1960): 250–271.

149. Louis Harris Survey News Releases, New York, July 13, 1964, and September 14, 1964. Some of the Harris survey findings on foreign affairs are shown here:

TABLE 5.6 Issue Differences between Voters and Goldwater, 1964

Issues	Voters Describe Goldwater Position		Voters Describe Own Position	
	July	*September*	*July*	*September*
Go to war over Cuba				
Percentage for	78	71	29	29
Percentage against	22	29	71	71
Use atomic bombs in Asia				
Percentage for	72	58	18	18
Percentage against	28	42	82	82
United Nations				
Percentage for	42	50	82	83
Percentage against	58	50	18	17

150. "Our Cheesy Democracy," *New Republic*, November 3, 1986, pp. 8–9.

151. Sabato, *The Rise of Political Consultants*, pp. 169–170. One writer claims that the height of negativity was reached in that year when Johnson's campaign, along with the daisy ad, included an "ad (never aired) that tied Goldwater to the Ku Klux Klan, a third that featured the eastern seaboard being sawed off and cast out to sea . . . , and a fourth that showed a little girl eating an ice cream cone laced with strontium 90 and cesium 137, the presumed result of Goldwater's commitment to nuclear testing." Armstrong, *The Next Hurrah*, p. 17.

152. Ibid., pp. 170–171.

153. Rich Galen, "Nail the Opposition," *Campaigns and Elections* (May/June 1988): 45. See also Rich Galen, "The Best Defense Is a Good Offense," *Campaigns and Elections* (October/November 1988): 29–34.

154. Sabato, *The Rise of Political Consultants*, p. 166.

155. Galen, "The Best Defense Is a Good Offense," p. 30.

156. Jamieson, *Packaging the Presidency*, p. 436.

157. Steven W. Colford, "Ailes: What He Wants Next: Bush Adman Aims Attack at Madison Ave.," *Advertising Age*, November 14, 1988, pp. 1, 67. Roger Ailes now runs the Fox News television network.

158. The Bush campaign tried to reap political rewards from the Swift Boat charges without being held responsible for their accuracy, or for illegal coordination with the independent ad campaign. Without directly agreeing with the claims made in the Swift Boat ads, Bush's ex-president father George H. W. Bush called them "rather compelling." See James Bennet, "Ex-President Bush Calls Charges of Swift Boat Group Compelling," *New York Times*, August 31, 2004, p. P5.

159. Lois Romano and Jim VandeHei, "Kerry Says Group Is a Front For Bush," *Washington Post*, August 20, 2004, p. A01.

160. "In elections at home, which Muskie contests vigorously and wins by handsome margins despite the state's strong Republican orientation, he rarely mentions his opponent's name, let alone attack him. He

dwells instead on his own positive (and pragmatic) approach to problems. . . . Throughout the campaign he waits hopefully for his opponent to strike, in desperation, some more or less low blow in response to which Muskie can become magnificently outraged. Then, voice trembling with indignation but still without mentioning the opponent's name, he chastises the opposition for stooping to such levels, and thus manages to introduce a little color into the campaign. Usually the opposition obliges him: 'I can always count on the Republicans doing something stupid,' he once said with satisfaction." David Nevin, *Muskie of Maine* (New York: Random House, 1972), p. 27.

161. Robert E. Sherwood, *Roosevelt and Hopkins* (New York: Harper, 1948), p. 821. The net effectiveness of underhanded tactics remains unknown. Dan Nimmo, *The Political Persuaders* (Englewood Cliffs, NJ: Prentice Hall, 1970), p. 50, argues that deviating from a vague sense of "fairness" that exists in the electorate may backfire. There is plenty of evidence on the other side as well. For a treasure trove of such material, see Kelley, *Professional Public Relations and Political Power*. See also Stephen Ansolabehere and Shanto Iyengar, *Going Negative: How Political Advertisements Shrink and Polarize the Electorate* (New York: Free Press, 1995).

162. Schram, *Running for President*, p. 369.

163. Ibid., pp. 362–363.

164. The best description of these events is found in Fred Emery, *Watergate: The Corruption of American Politics and the Fall of Richard Nixon* (New York: Times Books, 1994); see especially pp. 21–137. See also Stanley Kutler, ed., *Abuse of Power* (New York: The Free Press, 1997); Carl Bernstein and Bob Woodward, *All The President's Men* (New York: Simon and Schuster, 1974), pp. 112–162, 197, 199, 251–253, 285–286, 328; and Senate Select Committee on Presidential Campaign Activities, *The Senate Watergate Report* (Washington, DC: Government Printing Office, 1974).

165. Thomas and Goldman, "Victory March," p. 65.

166. For a study suggesting that negative advertising reduces voter turnout and lowers individuals' sense of political efficacy, see Stephen Ansolabehere, Shanto Iyengar, Adam Simon, and Nicholas Valentino, "Does Attack Advertising Demobilize the Electorate?" *American Political Science Review* 88 (December 1994): 829–838.

167. John G. Geer, *In Defense of Negativity: Attack Ads in Presidential Campaigns* (Chicago: University of Chicago Press, 2006).

168. Lloyd Grove, "When They Ask If Dukakis Has a Heart, They Mean It," *Washington Post Weekly Edition*, October 17–23, 1988, pp. 24–25.

169. Curt Suplee, "Bush's Candidacy Is Being Cooled Off by His Warmth Index," *Washington Post National Weekly Edition*, July 25–31, 1988, pp. 23–24.

170. Goldman et al., *Quest for the Presidency, 1992*, pp. 657–658.

171. See White, *The Making of the President, 1960*, pp. 269–275; White, *The Making of the President, 1964*, passim; and Crouse, *The Boys on the Bus*.

172. Thomas and Goldman, "Victory March," p. 63.

173. Department of Marketing, Miami University, Oxford Research Associates, *The Influence of Television on the Election of 1952* (Oxford, Ohio, 1954), pp. 151–160.

174. See White, *The Making of the President, 1960*, pp. 282–283; and Herbert A. Selz and Richard D. Yoakum, "Production Diary of the Debates," in Sidney Kraus, ed., *The Great Debates: Kennedy versus Nixon, 1960* (Bloomington: Indiana University Press, 1977), pp. 73–126.

175. Ibid.; see also Nixon, *Six Crises*, pp. 346–386.

176. Earl Mazo, *Richard Nixon* (New York: Harper, 1959), pp. 21–22, 362–369.

177. See Elihu Katz and Jacob J. Feldman, "The Debates in the Light of Research: A Survey of Surveys," in Kraus, ed., *The Great Debates*, pp. 173–223.

178. See Charles Mohr, "President Tells Polish-Americans He Regrets Remark on East Europe," *New York Times*, October 9, 1976; and R. W. Apple Jr., "Economy is Stressed by Dole and Mondale During Sharp Debate," *New York Times*, October 16, 1976.

179. See Hedrick Smith, "No Clear Winner Apparent; Scene is Simple and Stark," *New York Times*, October 29, 1980. After the election, Terence Smith of the *Times* wrote:

"The continual emphasis on Mr. Reagan's image as a hair-triggered proponent of American military intervention—the war and peace issue as it came to be called—may have been overdone, in the opinion of some Carter aides. In June, Mr. [Jody] Powell [Carter's press secretary] was telling reporters that Mr. Reagan was 'too benign' a figure to be painted as a warmonger, a la Barry Goldwater in 1964. 'It wouldn't be believable,' he said then.

"But beginning with his Middle Western swing the day after Labor Day, Mr. Carter stressed this point above all others, warning that the election was a choice between war and peace. He did so because of private polls taken by Mr. Caddell that showed this to be the public's greatest hidden fear about the Republican candidate. The President was hoist by his own hyperbole, in the view of some Carter aides, who feel the President grossly overstated Mr. Reagan's record and aroused the public's skepticism about his argument. In the end, they feel, Mr. Reagan's cool, collected, nonthreatening performance in the debate defused the issue." See "Carter Post-Mortem: Debate Hurt but Wasn't Only Cause for Defeat," *New York Times*, November 9, 1980.

180. Gerald M. Pomper, "The Presidential Election," in Pomper, ed., *The Election of 1984*, p. 76.

181. Richard Brookhiser, *The Outside Story* (Garden City, NY: Doubleday, 1986), p. 272.

182. Hunt, "The Campaign and the Issues," pp. 149–158.

183. Goldman et al., *Quest for the Presidency, 1992*, p. 559.

184. Ibid., pp. 563–564.

185. Ibid., p. 562.

186. Ibid., pp. 572–573.

187. Ibid., p. 577.

188. Thomas and Goldman, "Victory March," pp. 112–117.

189. Marjorie Randon Hershey, "The Campaign and the Media," in Gerald M. Pomper, ed., *The Election of 2000* (New York: Chatham House, 2001), pp. 60–63.

190. Richard L. Berke and Kevin Sack, "In Debate 2, Microscope Focuses on Gore," *New York Times*, October 11, 2000, p. A1.

191. Robert V. Friedenberg, "The 2000 Presidential Debates," in Robert E. Denton Jr., ed., *The 2000 Presidential Campaign: A Communication Perspective* (Westport, CT: Praeger, 2002), pp. 135–166.

192. Jodi Wilgoren and Richard W. Stevenson, "Day After Debate, Candidates Assess the Performances," *New York Times*, October 2, 2004, p. A10; Dan Balz, "Debate Leads to Shifts in Strategy," *Washington Post*, October 3, 2004, p. A01.

193. Richard Morin, "Singling Out Mary Cheney Was Wrong, Most Say," *Washington Post*, October 17, 2004, p. A05.

194. Dan Balz and Jim VandeHei, "A Deep Divide on Domestic Front," *Washington Post*, October 14, 2004, p. A01; Elisabeth Bumiller and David M. Halbfinger, "Bush and Kerry, Feeling Like Winners, Go to Las Vegas," *New York Times*, October 15, 2004, p. A21.

195. See Austin Ranney, ed., *The Past and Future of Presidential Debates* (Washington, DC: American Enterprise Institute, 1977).

196. Steve Gostel, "Argument Begins over Presidential Debates," *Oakland Tribune*, February 19, 1987. See also James A. Barnes, "Debating the Debates," *National Journal*, February 28, 1987, p. 527; and Newton Minow and Clifford M. Sloan, *For Great Debates: A New Plan for Future Presidential TV Debates* (New York: Priority Press, 1987).

197. Goldman et al., *Quest for the Presidency, 1992*, pp. 534–536, 554.

198. See Jules Abels, *Out of the Jaws of Victory* (New York: Holt, 1959).

199. Robert Alford, "The Role of Social Class in American Voting Behavior," *Western Political Quarterly* 16 (March 1963): 180–194; and Campbell et al., *The American Voter*, chap. 13.

200. White, *The Making of the President, 1960*, pp. 203–204.

201. Ibid., p. 315.

202. White, *The Making of the President, 1968*, p. 331.

203. David Shribman and James M. Perry, "Self-Inflicted Injury: Dukakis's Campaign Was Marred by a Series of Lost Opportunities," *Wall Street Journal*, November 8, 1988, p. 1.

204. "'Liberal' Tag Hurts Dukakis, Times Mirror Survey Finds," *Times Mirror News Interest Index*, September 22, 1988.

205. Ibid.

206. For extensive recital of these critiques, see Black and Oliphant, *All by Myself*.

207. Shribman and Perry, "Self-Inflicted Injury."

208. Karen M. Paget, "Afterthoughts on the Dukakis/Bentsen Campaign," *Public Affairs Report* 30 (January 1989): 1, 4.

209. John Jacobs, "Dukakis Admits Campaign 'Mistakes,'" *San Francisco Examiner*, October 14, 1989.

210. Michael J. Robinson, "Can Values Save George Bush?" *Public Opinion* 11 (July/August 1988): 11. This was a *Times Mirror* poll conducted by the Gallup organization.

211. John Dillon, "Mood of America: Shifting to Bush?" *Christian Science Monitor*, September 29, 1988, p. 1, reporting on a *Times Mirror* survey.

212. Ibid., p. 28.

213. Rosenstiel, *Strange Bedfellows*, p. 94.

214. Ibid., pp. 246–249.

215. Ibid., p. 283.

216. Thomas and Goldman, "Victory March," pp. 56–68, 80–90, 106–114.

217. Ibid., pp. 93–98, 120–125.

Chapter 6   Appraisals

1. See Commission on Presidential Nomination Timing and Scheduling Web site, http://www.democrats.org/page/s/nominating.

2. There are many examples of the party reform school of thought. See, for example, Woodrow Wilson, *Congressional Government* (Boston: Houghton Mifflin, 1889); Henry Jones Ford, *The Rise and Growth of American Politics* (New York: Macmillan, 1898); A. Lawrence Lowell, *Public Opinion and Popular Government* (New York: Longmans, Green, 1913); William MacDonald, *A New Constitution for a New America* (New York: B. W. Huebsch, 1921); William Y. Elliott, *The Need for Constitutional Reform* (New York: McGraw-Hill, 1935); E. E. Schattschneider, *Party Government* (New York: Farrar and Rinehart, 1940); Henry Hazlitt, *A New Constitution Now* (New York: McGraw-Hill, 1942); Thomas K. Finletter, *Can Representative Government Do the Job?* (New York: Reynal and Hitchcock, 1945); James M. Burns, *Congress on Trial* (New York: Harper, 1949); Committee on Political Parties, American Political Science Association, *Toward a More Responsible Two-Party System* (New York: APSA, 1950); Stephen K. Bailey, *The Condition of Our National Political Parties* (New York: Fund for the Republic, 1959); James MacGregor Burns, *The Deadlock of Democracy: Four-Party Politics in America* (Englewood Cliffs, NJ: Prentice Hall, 1963); Lloyd N. Cutler and C. Douglas Dillon, "Can We Improve on Our Constitutional System?" *Wall Street Journal*, February 15, 1983; and Lloyd N. Cutler, "To Form a Government," *Foreign Affairs* 59 (Fall 1980): 126–143. The work of the Committee on Political Parties, representing the collective judgment of a panel of distinguished political scientists in 1950, is the statement we refer to most often. In 1971 a member of the committee published a thoughtful reconsideration of its main ideas. See Evron M. Kirkpatrick, "Toward a More Responsible Two-Party System: Political Science, Policy Science, or Pseudo Science?" *American Political Science Review* 65 (December 1971): 965–990.

3. Committee on Political Parties, *Toward a More Responsible Two-Party System*, p. 1.

4. Ibid., p. 66.

5. Ibid., p. 15.

6. A sample of this literature might include Pendleton Herring, *The Politics of Democracy: American Parties in Action*, rev. ed. (New York: W. W. Norton, 1965); Herbert Agar, *The Price of Union* (Boston: Houghton Mifflin, 1950); Malcolm C. Moos, *Politics, Presidents and Coattails* (Baltimore: Johns Hopkins University Press, 1952); Austin Ranney and Willmoore Kendall, *Democracy and the American Party System* (New York: Harcourt, Brace, 1956); David B. Truman, *The Governmental Process* (New York: Knopf, 1953); John Fischer, "Unwritten Rules of American Politics," *Harper's*, November 1948, pp. 27–36; Peter Drucker, "A Key to American Politics: Calhoun's Pluralism," *Review of Politics* 10 (October 1948): 412–426; Ernest F. Griffith, *Congress: Its Contemporary Role* (New York: New York University Press, 1951); Murray Stedman and Herbert Sonthoff, "Party Responsibility: A Critical Inquiry," *Western Political Quarterly* 4 (September

1951): 454–486; Julius Turner, "Responsible Parties: A Dissent from the Floor," *American Political Science Review* 45 (March 1951): 143–152; William Goodman, "How Much Political Party Centralization Do We Want?" *Journal of Politics* 13 (November 1961): 536–561; and Austin Ranney, *The Doctrine of Responsible Party Government* (Urbana: University of Illinois Press, 1954).

7. Herring, *The Politics of Democracy*, p. 327.

8. Ibid., p. 420.

9. Committee on Political Parties, *Toward a More Responsible Two-Party System*, p. 19.

10. Bailey, *The Condition of Our National Political Parties*, p. 20.

11. Nelson W. Polsby and William G. Mayer, "Ideological Cohesion in the American Two-Party System," in Nelson W. Polsby and Raymond E. Wolfinger, eds., *On Parties: Essays Honoring Austin Ranney* (Berkeley: Institute of Governmental Studies Press, 1999), pp. 219–254.

12. See David B. Truman, "Federalism and the Party System," in Arthur W. MacMahon, ed., *Federalism: Mature and Emergent* (New York: Russell and Russell, 1962), pp. 115–136. This situation is deplored in Cutler and Dillon, "Can We Improve on Our Constitutional System?" One possible remedy, changing the terms of office of senators and members of Congress to coincide exactly with presidential elections, is analyzed in Nelson W. Polsby, "A Note on the President's Modest Proposal," in Polsby, *Political Promises* (New York: Oxford University Press, 1974), pp. 101–107.

13. In general, it is better met by Republicans than Democrats. See David R. Mayhew, *Party Loyalty among Congressmen* (Cambridge, MA: Harvard University Press, 1966).

14. Members of Congress with local strength not based on ideology are not at all uncommon. See, for instance, examples in Raymond A. Bauer, Ithiel de Sola Pool, and Lewis Anthony Dexter, *American Business and Public Policy* (New York: Atherton Press, 1963), chaps. 16, 18, and 19; Richard F. Fenno, *Home Style* (Boston: Little, Brown, 1978); and Bruce Cain, John Ferejohn, and Morris Fiorina, *The Personal Vote: Constituency Service and Electoral Independence* (Cambridge, MA: Harvard University Press, 1987).

15. Nelson W. Polsby, *How Congress Evolves: Social Bases of Institutional Change* (New York: Oxford University Press, 2004).

16. See Walter J. Stone, "On Party Switching among Presidential Activists: What Do We Know?" *American Journal of Political Science* 35 (August 1991): 598–607.

17. Nelson W. Polsby, *Consequences of Party Reform* (New York: Oxford University Press, 1983).

18. Polsby, *How Congress Evolves.*

19. The near removal in 1987 of Les Aspin as chairman of the House Armed Services Committee, however, was clearly based on policy differences, and so were several other threats to Democratic committee chairmen over the past decade. For a full account, see Polsby, *How Congress Evolves.*

20. Polsby, *Consequences of Party Reform*; Byron E. Shafer, *Quiet Revolution: The Struggle for the Democratic Party and the Shaping of Post-Reform Politics* (New York: Russell Sage Foundation, 1983).

21. For strong evidence on this point, see Samuel Stouffer, *Communism, Conformity and Civil Liberties* (Garden City, NY: Doubleday, 1955); and Julian L. Woodward and Elmo Roper, "Political Activity of American Citizens," *American Political Science Review* 44 (December 1950): 872–875. Two more recent studies have examined the voters' desire not to be interfered with by the government as well as the importance of their private lives to them as compared with national issues. See Paul M. Sniderman and Richard A. Brody, "Coping: The Ethic of Self-Reliance," *American Journal of Political Science* 21 (August 1977): 501–521; and Richard A. Brody and Paul M. Sniderman, "From Life Space to Polling Place: The Relevance of Personal Concerns for Voting Behavior," *British Journal of Political Science* 7 (July 1977): 337–360.

22. Evidence indicates that a sizable contingent of voters do make decisions based on this criterion. In general, perceptions of national conditions weigh more heavily than changes in voters' personal fortunes over the previous four years. See Donald R. Kinder and D. Roderick Kiewiet, "Sociotropic Politics: The American Case," *British Journal of Political Science* 11 (April 1981): 129–161; and Gregory Markus, "The Impact of Personal and National Economic Conditions on the Presidential Vote: A Pooled Cross-Sectional Analysis," *American Journal of Political Science* 32 (February 1988): 137–154. Some argue that this type of "retrospective voting" is not fully rational, since it often applies even to events such as natural disasters which incumbents clearly cannot control; see Christopher H. Achen and Larry M. Bartels, "Blind

Retrospection: Electoral Responses to Drought, Flu, and Shark Attacks," unpublished paper, Princeton University, 2004, available at http://weber.ucsd.edu/~jlbroz/PElunch/achen_bartels_blind.pdf.

23. See, for example, Jack Citrin, Herbert McClosky, J. Merrill Shanks, and Paul M. Sniderman, "Personal and Political Sources of Alienation," *British Journal of Political Science* 5 (January 1975): 1–31; and Arthur H. Miller, "Political Issues and Trust in Government: 1964–70," along with the "Comment" by Jack Citrin, both in *American Political Science Review* 68 (September 1974): 951–1001.

24. In systems like the United States, with its extremely frequent elections, this would require a lot of voting. See Anthony King, *Running Scared: Why America's Politicians Campaign Too Much and Govern Too Little* (New York: Martin Kessler, 1997).

25. Jürgen Habermas, *Legitimation Crisis* (Boston: Beacon Press, 1975).

26. An earlier statement of main themes in this section is Aaron B. Wildavsky's "On the Superiority of National Conventions," *Review of Politics* 24 (July 1962): 307–319.

27. Everett Carll Ladd, "Party Reform and the Public Interest," *Political Science Quarterly* 102 (Autumn 1987): 355–369. See, more generally, Gary R. Orren and Nelson W. Polsby, eds., *Media and Momentum: The New Hampshire Primary and Nomination Politics* (Chatham, NJ: Chatham House, 1987).

28. See V. O. Key Jr., *American State Politics* (New York: Knopf, 1956), chap. 6.

29. V. O. Key Jr., *Southern Politics in State and Nation* (New York: Knopf, 1949), namely, chap. 3 (Alabama) and chap. 9 (Arkansas).

30. Henry E. Brady and Richard Johnston, "What's the Primary Message? Horse Race or Issue Journalism," in Orren and Polsby, eds., *Media and Momentum*, pp. 127–186.

31. Key, *American State Politics*, p. 216.

32. Nelson W. Polsby, "Was Hart's Life Unfairly Probed?" *New York Times*, May 6, 1987.

33. See Austin Ranney, *The Federalization of Presidential Primaries* (Washington, DC: American Enterprise Institute, 1978), p. 507; see also Commission on Presidential Nomination and Party Structure (Morley Winograd, chairman), *Openness, Participation and Party Building: Reforms for a Stronger Democratic Party* (Washington, DC: The Commission, 1979), pp. 32–37.

34. A classic statement is Moisei Ostrogorski, *Democracy and the Party System in the United States* (New York: Macmillan, 1910), pp. 158–160. See also Elmo Roper, "What Price Conventions?" *Saturday Review*, September 3, 1960, p. 26.

35. The most famous account is still Ostrogorski, *Democracy and the Party System in the United States*, pp. 141–142.

36. See Herbert McClosky, Paul J. Hoffmann, and Rosemary O'Hara, "Issue Conflict and Consensus among Party Leaders and Followers," *American Political Science Review* 54 (June 1960): 406–427; Jeane Kirkpatrick, *The New Presidential Elite: Men and Women in National Politics* (New York: Russell Sage Foundation, 1976); and John S. Jackson III et al., "Political Party Leaders and the Mass Public: 1980–1984," paper presented at the annual meeting of the Midwest Political Science Association, Chicago, April 1987.

37. John Morris, "Negro Delegates Drop Plans to Walk Out as a Demonstration against Goldwater," *New York Times*, July 16, 1964.

38. Gerald M. Pomper, *Elections in America: Control and Influence in Democratic Politics*, rev. ed. (New York: Longman, 1980), pp. 185–187.

39. Alan D. Monroe, "American Party Platforms and Public Opinion," *American Journal of Political Science* 27 (February 1983): 27–42, at 38.

40. Ibid., pp. 27–42.

41. As we saw in 2000, the Supreme Court can short-circuit the Constitution by accepting a presidential candidate's invitation to intervene in the process (*Bush v. Gore*, 531 U.S. 98). An extensive literature emerged over this case and others relating to the Florida recount of 2000, including Howard Gillman, *The Votes That Counted: How the Court Decided the 2000 Election* (Chicago: University of Chicago Press, 2001); Cass R. Sunstein and Richard A. Epstein, eds., *The Vote: Bush, Gore and the Supreme Court* (Chicago: University of Chicago Press, 2001); and Ronald Dworkin, ed., *A Badly Flawed Election: Debating Bush v. Gore, the Supreme Court, and American Democracy* (New York: New Press, 2002). The court decision and much of the subsequent literature are reviewed in Richard L. Hasen, "A Critical Guide to *Bush v. Gore* Scholarship," *Annual Review of Political Science* 7 (June 2004): 297–314.

42. There are, of course, many other plans for "reform," involving almost all possible combinations of these three alternatives. For example, President Nixon at one point recommended that the 40 percent plurality plank that usually goes with the direct election proposal be applied instead to the present electoral college setup. See David S. Broder, "Mitchell Recommends Electoral Compromise," *Washington Post*, March 14, 1969. A second example is the "federal system plan" proposed by Senators Bob Dole and Tom Eagleton in 1970, which stated the following:

1. A candidate would be elected president by (a) winning a plurality of the national vote and (b) winning either pluralities in more than 50 percent of the states and D.C., or pluralities in states with 50 percent of the voters in the election.
2. If no candidate qualified, the election would go to an electoral college where the states would be represented as they are today, and candidates would automatically receive the electoral votes of the states they won.
3. In the unlikely event that no candidate received a majority of the electoral votes, the electoral votes of states that went for third-party candidates would be divided between the two leading national candidates in proportion to their share of the popular votes in those states. *Congressional Record*, March 5, 1970, S3026.

These plans had the following characteristics: (1) they were too complicated to solve any problems of public confusion or public perception that they are not "democratic"; and (2) they had no significant body of congressional support.

43. This argument roughly corresponds to one of the main approaches to calculating the strategic advantage of members of a coalition, pioneered by Irwin Mann and Lloyd Shapley. The argument proceeds as follows: "the Shapley value defines the power of actor A as the number of permutations (orderings) in which A occupies the pivotal position (that is, orderings in which A can cast the deciding vote) divided by the total number of possible permutations." See George Rabinowitz and Stuart Elaine MacDonald, "The Power of the States in U.S. Presidential Elections," *American Political Science Review* 80 (March 1986): 65-87, at 66. This approach shows the large states to be the winners. Their influence is more than proportional to their size. This model is often supplemented by an analysis that attempts to determine the influence of the average voter within each state. Along these lines, Lawrence Longley and James Dana Jr., conclude that residents of California (the most advantaged state) have more than twice the "relative voting power" of the inhabitants of Arkansas (the least advantaged state). See Longley and Dana, "New Empirical Estimates of the Biases of the Electoral College for the 1980s," *Western Political Quarterly* 37 (March 1984): 157-175.

Yet these calculations assume that all patterns of state voting are equally likely. This obviously is not a realistic assumption. Some states lean strongly toward one party. Building on this insight, Rabinowitz and MacDonald utilize the results of recent elections to identify likely pivotal states and make their own calculation of relative voting power. Once again, the large states are the winners. There are differences, however, from the results of the previous model. Most large states are even more influential, but the power of the states that lean strongly toward one party is diminished. Strongly Democratic Massachusetts is the biggest loser, dropping to a mere one-seventh of its influence as determined by the Shapley model.

Which model of state electoral power is more accurate? The second, which takes into account likely voting patterns, would appear more complete. Yet pivot patterns are imperfect guides to future behavior. With Jimmy Carter at the head of the ticket in 1980, Georgia was one of the most strongly Democratic states in the nation. In 1984, Walter Mondale lost Georgia by an even larger margin than the nation as a whole. Predicting future swing states from past behavior may lead to serious errors.

One might also question the emphasis on the importance of swing states. Is a state that provides a loyal and consistent base of support for one party necessarily unimportant? Is not a solid base as important to a winning coalition as more volatile swing states? In recent years, the Republicans have started presidential campaigns with a very strong position in the mountain states. Since the outcome in these states has not been in doubt, neither campaign expends much effort on them. Thus it could be said that one-party states are less important. On the other hand, a safe base is valuable. The Republicans start ahead and are able to focus their resources on other areas. Democrats would love to have such a safe base of their own (besides D.C.). In short, calculations of state influence depend heavily on the assumptions one begins with.

44. For example, Ed Gossett of Texas, original cosponsor of the district plan, asked: "Is it fair, is it honest, is it democratic, is it to the best interests of anyone in fact to place such a premium on a few thousand labor votes or Italian votes or Irish votes or Negro votes or Jewish votes or Polish votes, or Communist votes or big city machine votes, simply because they happen to be located in two or three industrial pivotal states? Can anything but evil come from placing such temptation and power in the hands of political parties and political bosses? Both said groups and said politicians are computed as a nation suffers." Cited in David Brook, "Proposed Electoral College Reforms and Urban Minorities," paper delivered at the annual meeting of the American Political Science Association, New York, August 1969, p. 6.

45. Eric R. A. N. Smith and Peverill Squire argue, following Shapley's logic, that the importance of states should be calculated according to the ease with which undecided voters can be influenced. While this method differs from ours, it also leads to the conclusion that southern states would gain in influence if the electoral college was abolished. See Eric R. A. N. Smith and Peverill Squire, "Direct Election of the President and Power of the States," *Western Political Quarterly* 40 (March 1987): 31-44.

46. In "The South Will Not Rise Again through Direct Election of the President, Polsby and Wildavsky Notwithstanding," *Journal of Politics* 31 (August 1969): 808-811, Professor Harvey Zeidenstein shows that the winner's margin of victory in eight large northern urban states, taken together, was greater than in the eleven states of the old Confederacy, taken together, in four of the six presidential elections between 1948 and 1968. From this he concludes that the influence of northern urban states, where the votes are, is likely to be very great under a system of direct elections. We agree, but we argue in the text that direct elections improve the strategic position of one-party states (including some southern states), as compared with the electoral college winner-take-all system. On this issue, Zeidenstein is silent.

47. On September 18, 1969, by a vote of 339 to 70, a direct-election plan with a 40 percent plurality runoff provision was passed by the U.S. House of Representatives. See *Congressional Record*, September 18, 1969, H8142-43; for the content of the bill, see *Congressional Record*, September 10, 1969, H7745-46. For more recent discussion of proposed reforms, see Committee on the Judiciary, U.S. Senate, *Hearings on the Electoral College and Direct Election*, 95th Cong. (Washington, DC, 1977). See also Robert W. Bennett, *Taming the Electoral College* (Stanford, CA: Stanford University Press, 2006).

48. In 1968, the figures were similar when George Wallace ran a strong third-party campaign in the race between Richard Nixon and Hubert Humphrey. As in 1992, a fourth candidate would have needed only 6 or 7 percent of the national total to keep either major-party candidate from having the required 40 percent (Nixon won with only 43 percent, although he had 56.2 percent of the electoral vote). The Michigan Survey Research Center finds that only 1.5 percent of the voters in 1968 felt that Senator Eugene McCarthy of Minnesota was the best man for president in the spring and still felt that way after the election. If all participants in the system had known that he was not going to be defeated and disappear but would be a serious candidate at least through the first election, it is at least possible to conjecture that he could have picked up an additional 4 or 5 percent. Philip E. Converse, Warren E. Miller, Jerrold G. Rusk, and Arthur C. Wolfe, "Continuity and Change in American Politics: Parties and Issues in the 1968 Election," *American Political Science Review* 63 (December 1969): 1083–1105, at 1092.

49. The article that deals most clearly with the electoral college in terms of its virtues of conciliation and broad coalition building is John Wildenthal, "Consensus after L.B.J.," *Southwest Review* 53 (Spring 1968): 113–130. Wildenthal argues, in part, "rather than complain about being deprived of a choice when both parties wage 'me too' campaigns, the American people should be thankful that the interests of a wide variety of Americans can be reconciled by both parties with similar programs."

50. One summary of this position was given by Representative Thomas Kleppe of North Dakota in the *Congressional Record*, February 3, 1969, H648. An interesting sidelight is his citation of Senator John F. Kennedy, who in 1956 had said, "After all, the states came into the Union as units. Electoral votes are not given out on the basis of voting numbers, but on the basis of population. The electoral votes belong to each state. The way the system works now is that we carry on a campaign in fifty states, and the electoral

votes of that state belong to that party which carries each state. If we are going to change that system, it seems to me it would strike a blow at states' rights in major proportions. It would probably end states' rights and make this country one great unit."

51. Roscoe Drummond, "Perils of the Electoral System," *Washington Post*, November 14, 1960. An argument in some ways parallel to our own is contained in Anthony Lewis, "The Case against Electoral Reform," *The Reporter*, December 8, 1960, pp. 31–33. See also Allan Sindler, "Presidential Election Methods and Urban-Ethnic Interests," *Law and Contemporary Problems* 27 (Spring 1962): 213–233.

52. Or, even worse, the Supreme Court, fearing "chaos," might step in and put its thumb on the scale, as in 2000. See Richard A. Posner, *Breaking the Deadlock: The 2000 Election, the Constitution, and the Courts* (Princeton: Princeton University Press, 2001); Richard A. Posner, "*Bush v. Gore* as Pragmatic Adjudication," in Dworkin, ed., *A Badly Flawed Election*, pp. 187–213.

53. See Estes Kefauver, "The Electoral College: Old Reforms Take a New Look," *Law and Contemporary Problems* 27 (Spring 1962): 197.

54. See Arthur Schlesinger Jr., "A One-for-All Electoral College," *Wall Street Journal*, August 19, 1988, p. 16; Arthur Schlesinger Jr., "How to Democratize American Democracy," in *A Badly Flawed Election*, ed. Dworkin, pp. 215–229.

55. Despite popular misconceptions, even the 1964 Republican platform, written by supporters of Barry Goldwater, contained explicit promises to preserve these programs.

56. See Kirk H. Porter and Donald Bruce Johnson, *National Party Platforms, 1840–1956* (Urbana: University of Illinois Press, 1956). There are immense differences in both party platforms between 1932 and 1952. Note, for example, the subheadings under domestic policy in the 1952 platforms dealing with a range of topics entirely missing in 1932. The 1952 Democratic platform includes subheadings on full employment, price supports, farm credit, crop insurance, rural electrification, the physically handicapped, migratory workers, river basin development, arid areas, wildlife, recreation, Social Security, unemployment insurance, public assistance, needs of our aging citizens, health, medical education, hospitals and health centers, costs of medical care, public housing, slum clearance, urban redevelopment, aid to education, school lunches, daycare facilities, specific steps under civil rights, and many other subjects completely absent in 1932. Most of these worthy causes were also supported in the 1952 Republican platform and were missing from the 1932 Republican platform. Nevertheless, there are differences between the parties in 1952 regarding use of the public lands, public housing, labor legislation, farm legislation, public power, aid to education, and much more. On education, for example, the 1952 Republican platform reads: "The tradition of popular education, tax-supported and free to all, is strong with our people. The responsibility for sustaining this system of popular education has always rested upon the local communities and the states. We subscribe fully to this principle." The corresponding Democratic plank reads in part: "Local, State, and Federal government have shared responsibility to contribute appropriately to the pressing needs of our education system. . . . We pledge immediate consideration for those school systems which need further legislation to provide Federal aid for new school construction, teachers' salaries and school maintenance and repair." Porter and Johnson, pp. 485, 504. See also Gerald M. Pomper, *Elections in America* (New York: Dodd, Mead, 1968), pp. 149–178.

57. David R. Mayhew argues in *Divided We Govern: Party Control, Lawmaking and Investigations* (New Haven, CT: Yale University Press, 1991) that sheer legislative productivity is not harmed by divided government, with its constraints on party responsibility.

Chapter 7　American Parties and Democracy

1. Morris P. Fiorina, with Samuel J. Abrams and Jeremy C. Pope, *Culture War? The Myth of a Polarized America* (New York: Longman, 2004); Herbert McClosky, Paul S. Hoffmann, and Rosemary O'Hara, "Issue Conflict and Consensus Among Party Leaders and Followers," *American Political Science Review* 54 (June 1960): 406–427.

2. This parallels in many respects an argument to be found in Robert A. Dahl, *A Preface to Democratic Theory* (Chicago: University of Chicago Press, 1956).

3. Angus Campbell, Philip E. Converse, Warren E. Miller, and Donald E. Stokes, *The American Voter* (New York: Wiley, 1960), pp. 525–527.

4. Richard A. Brody and Benjamin I. Page, "Policy Voting and the Electoral Process: The Vietnam War Issue," *American Political Science Review* 66 (September 1972): 979–995. See also William Schneider, "The November 4 Vote for President: What Did It Mean?" in Austin Ranney, ed., *The American Elections of 1980* (Washington, DC: American Enterprise Institute, 1981), pp. 212–262; and Nelson W. Polsby, "Party Realignment in the 1980 Election," *Yale Review* 72 (Autumn 1982): 43–54.

5. See Dahl, *A Preface to Democratic Theory*, pp. 124–131. The famous general statement from which this application is derived is Kenneth J. Arrow, *Social Choice and Individual Values*, 2nd ed. (New Haven: Yale University Press, 1963).

6. Raymond E. Wolfinger and Steven J. Rosenstone, *Who Votes?* (New Haven, CT: Yale University Press, 1980), p. 83.

7. See Nelson W. Polsby, *Consequences of Party Reform* (New York: Oxford University Press, 1983).

8. Ibid. See also the argument made by Marty Cohen, David Karol, Hans Noel, and John Zaller, *Beating Reform: The Resurgence of Parties in Presidential Nominations* (Chicago: University of Chicago Press, forthcoming.)

9. See Jack Dennis, "Trends in Public Support for the American Political Party System," *British Journal of Political Science* (April 1975): 187–230. A recent version of this argument is found in Fiorina, *Culture War?*

10. For the story on split-ticket voting and its effects, see Gary C. Jacobson, *The Electoral Origins of Divided Government* (Boulder, CO: Westview Press, 1990). See also Morris Fiorina, *Divided Government*, 2nd ed. (Boston: Allyn and Bacon, 1996).

11. See Richard J. Ellis, *Democratic Delusions: The Initiative Process in America* (Lawrence: The University Press of Kansas, 2002); David S. Broder, *Democracy Derailed: Initiative Campaigns and the Power of Money* (New York: Harcourt, 2000).

12. See Bruce E. Cain, Sara Ferejohn, Margarita Najar, and Mary Walther, "Constitutional Change: Is It Too Easy to Amend Our State Constitution?" in Bruce E. Cain and Roger G. Noll, eds., *Constitutional Reform in California: Making State Government More Effective and Responsive* (Berkeley, CA: Institute of Governmental Studies Press, 1995), pp. 265–290, esp. pp. 284–289.

INDEX

ABOUT THE AUTHORS

NELSON W. POLSBY was Heller Professor of Political Science and past Director of the Institute of Governmental Studies at the University of California, Berkeley, where he taught American politics for forty years. He was a former editor of the *American Political Science Review* and the *Annual Review of Political Science*, a Vice President of the Political Studies Association of the United Kingdom, and a former Brookings and Guggenheim Fellow. His other books include *Consequences of Party Reform* (1983), *New Federalist Papers* (with Alan Brinkley and Kathleen M. Sullivan, 1997), and *How Congress Evolves* (2004).

AARON WILDAVSKY was Class of 1940 Professor of Political Science and Public Policy at the University of California, Berkeley, and founding dean of Berkeley's Graduate (now Goldman) School of Public Policy.

DAVID A. HOPKINS is a Ph.D. candidate in the Department of Political Science at the University of California, Berkeley.